Interracial Communication:
Contexts, Communities, and Choices

Deborah A. Brunson

Linda L. Lampl

Felecia F. Jordan-Jackson

Kendall Hunt
publishing company

Book Team

Chairman and Chief Executive Officer Mark C. Falb
President and Chief Operating Officer Chad M. Chandlee
Vice President, Higher Education David L. Tart
Director of Publishing Partnerships Paul B. Carty
Editorial Manager Georgia Botsford
Senior Editor Angela Willenbring
Vice President, Operations Timothy J. Beitzel
Assistant Vice President, Production Services Christine E. O'Brien
Senior Production Editor Melissa King
Permissions Editor Renae Horstman
Cover Designer Janell Cannavo

Cover image © Shutterstock, Inc.

Kendall Hunt
publishing company

www.kendallhunt.com
Send all inquiries to:
4050 Westmark Drive
Dubuque, IA 52004-1840

Printed in the United States of America
10 9 8 7 6 5 4 3 2 1

Contents

Context I: Identity

Context II: Relationships and Families

Context III: Communities

Context IV: Academic Stories

Context V: Politics

About the Contributors

Blake Abbott is a doctoral candidate in the Department of Speech Communication at the University of Georgia, and Director of the university's Public Debate Series. He teaches undergraduate courses in public speaking, rhetorical criticism, and the intersections of rhetoric and privilege. He is currently working on his dissertation on the construction of economic citizenship in the wake of the 2008 economic crash and subsequent bailouts. His research expertise is on rhetoric, privilege, citizenship, identity, and hegemony.

Gordon Alley-Young (Ph.D., Southern Illinois University) is an Associate Professor of Speech Communication at Kingsborough Community College–City University of New York (CUNY). His research and publishing focus on the areas of intercultural communication, popular culture, and critical perspectives on identity and education. His publications include chapters in the recently edited books *Diversity and Mass Communication: Evidence of Impact* by Amber Narro and Alice Ferguson (Fountainhead Press, 2007), and *Mirror Images: Popular Culture and Education* (Peter Lang, 2008) by Zvi Bekerman, Nicholas Burbules, Henry Giroux, and Diana Silberman-Keller. He is also an author of several book reviews and journal articles, including the recent *Articulating Identity: Refining Postcolonial and Whiteness Perspectives on Race Within Communication Studies* (*Review of Communication*, 2008) and *Using 'The Lure of Gang Life' to Teach Interpersonal and Group Attraction* (*Communication Teacher*, 2009). He is a current book review co-editor for *American Communication Journal* and the President of CLASP: CUNY League of Active Speech Professors.

Cherie Avent is Assistant Director of Academic Enhancement Program of Athletics at UNC Greensboro (UNCG). She received a Master of Arts in Communication Studies from UNCG. Her research interests include identity, pedagogy, and conflict communication.

Theodore A. Avtgis (Ph.D., Kent State University) is an Associate Professor of Communication Studies at West Virginia University. He teaches courses in aggressive communication, organizational communication, and communication and personality. Among several awards, he was recognized as one of the Top Twelve Most Productive Scholars in the field of Communication Studies (between 1996-2001) and recognized as a member of the World Council on Hellenes Abroad, USA Region of American Academics. He was also named Centennial Scholar of Communication by the Eastern Communication Association. Dr. Avtgis has published articles in *Communication Education, Management Communication Quarterly, Communication Research Reports,* and the *Journal of Intercultural Communication,* among others. He serves on the editorial boards of *Argumentation and Advocacy, Communication Research Reports, Human Communication,* and *Journal of Intercultural Communication Research,* among others. He is co-author of four books, including *Arguments, Aggression, and Conflict: New Directions in Theory and Research* (2010). He is also co-founder of Medical Communication Specialists.

Sarah Blizzard is in her final year of the M.A. program in Communication Studies at the University of North Carolina Greensboro. Her current research is centered on conflicts of identity performance and cultural performativity.

Patricia Brown McDonald is an associate professor at Palm Beach State College, where she teaches literature and composition. She has developed an Afro-Caribbean course that is now offered at that institution, and her scholarly and teaching focus is the exploration of marginalized voices.

Sakile K. Camara (Ph.D., Ohio State University) is an Assistant Professor in the Department of Communication Studies at California State University, Northridge. Her research emphasizes the relationships among communication, power, and culture in a variety of contexts. Issues of uncertainty, and anxiety management in interpersonal interactions are also the foundation of her research interests.

Jonathan W. Camp (Ph.D., University of Memphis) is an Assistant Professor of Communication at Abilene Christian University, where he also serves as Director of the Master of Science in Organizational and Human Resource Development. He teaches organizational communication, health communication, and leadership. His research focuses on protecting human rights in international medical research, where his research has been published in *The Lancet: Oncology* and *Developing World Bioethics.*

Joseph A. Ciccarelli earned his B.A. from the School of Communication at Western Michigan University (WMU). An earlier version of this chapter was completed as an Independent Study with the second author and received a 2007 Research/ Creative Activity Award from WMU's Lewis Walker Institute for the Study of Race and Ethnic Relations.

Alan Copeland is a student at Abilene Christian University, double majoring in Exercise Science and Communication. He is involved with the student groups Essence of Ebony (which focuses on African American issues and ideas) and Fellowship of Christian Athletes.

Vanessa G. Cunningham-Engram received her B.A. in Communication and M.A. in English from the University of Louisville. She earned her J.D. from the Louis D. Brandeis School of Law at the University of Louisville, and was conferred the Ed.D. in leadership education by Spalding University. Her publications include an article titled "Experiences of black staff in university settings: A qualitative analysis" (with D'Silva and Cheatham), *Intercultural Communications Studies Journal* (2007). She has taught courses in cultural diversity, public speaking, business law, and ethics. Currently, she is an Associate Professor in the Department of Journalism and Mass Communication at North Carolina A&T State University in Greensboro, North Carolina, where she primarily teaches communication law and ethics. Her narrow research interest involves First Amendment issues affecting free speech, specifically the dissemination of obscenity and sexual content via technology and social media. She has given a number of presentations on this topic nationally.

Juan D'Brot (M.A., West Virginia University) is a Research and Evaluation Specialist at Edvantia, Inc., a non-profit educational research and development firm. Mr. D'Brot holds a bachelor's degree in communication studies and a master's degree in Communication Studies Theory and Research from West Virginia University. He is currently pursuing a Ph.D. in Industrial-Organizational Psychology. His research interests include organizational and performance psychology, organizational and interpersonal communication, program evaluation, and mixed-methods design. He currently lives in Charleston, West Virginia with his wife Alissa D'Brot.

Daniel Cochece Davis (Ph.D., University of Southern California) is an Assistant Professor in the Communication Department of Marist College. He teaches courses in intercultural communication, intracultural communication, advanced communication & culture, nonverbal communication, and small group communication. His research interests include culture shock, reentry shock, minority shock, and cultural competence.

Rubell S. Dingman was born and raised in Carson City, Nevada. A half Shoshone and Washoe Indian, Rubell was raised primarily by her mother. She was the first in her family to graduate from Carson High School in 2004. She attended the University of Idaho from August 2004 to December 2008. Rubell received a Bachelor of Arts degree in Journalism with a minor in American Indian Studies. In the Fall of 2007 Rubell began working with Rebecca Tallent on a series of articles dealing with Native American Press Freedoms. Rubell returned to the University of Idaho in the Fall of 2009 to pursue a second degree in Public Relations. She plans on attending law school in the Fall of 2010 and eventually going into the area of Tribal Law.

Jennifer Dodd is a student at Abilene Christian University, double majoring in Communication and Marketing. She currently works as an intern in the university enrollment office.

Christine Eith (Ph.D., University of Delaware) is an Assistant Professor in the Department of Sociology, Anthropology, and Criminal Justice at Towson University, with a current research focus on social justice and policing, including effective police leadership and aspects of quality service to the community. Her work has appeared in the books *Social Justice* and *Hurricane Katrina*, and the forthcoming *Minority Resiliency* and *The Legacy of Disaster*.

Kelli L. Fellows (Ph.D., University of Georgia) is an Assistant Professor at the University of North Carolina Wilmington. Her research focuses on social identity and its manifestations within health and interpersonal communication settings. Specifically, her research examines smoker identity, identity as a marketing strategy, and the role of identity in relational contexts. Her research has been published in journals such as *Health Communication*, the *Journal of Intercultural Communication Research*, and the *Southern Communication Journal*. She is a single-parent of two sons, Drury and Peyton.

Monica Flippin is a doctoral candidate in Communication with emphasis on media, rhetoric, and race, and works as a research assistant at the Research Institute for STEM Education (RISE) at the University of Oklahoma.

Cindy E. Foor is Associate Director/Research Associate at the Research Institute for STEM Education (RISE) at the University of Oklahoma. Cindy received her B.A. in Anthropology from the University of Oklahoma and M.A. in Cultural Anthropology from Western Michigan University. Research interests include ethnography of marginalized populations, cultural theory, issues of gender and underrepresented populations in STEM education, and the construction of women's cultural identities, with special focus on emerging nationalist projects.

Michele S. Foss-Snowden received her B.A. from Stanford University, her M.A. from the University of California, Davis, and her Ph.D. from the University of Florida. She is currently an Assistant Professor in the Department of Communication Studies at California State University, Sacramento. Her research interests include representations of race and mixed race in entertainment media, especially in the television genres of science fiction, situation comedy, soap opera, and reality-based programming.

James Graham is a student at Abilene Christian University, where he was President of Essence of Ebony, a student group which focuses on African American issues and ideas. He also works for The Alliance for Women and Children, a non-profit organization in Abilene, TX.

Rachel Alicia Griffin (Ph.D. in Human Communication Studies, University of Denver M.A. in Communication and B.S. in Communication and Sociology, Central Michigan University) As an Assistant Professor in the Department of Speech Communication at Southern Illinois University at Carbondale, her research interests span critical race theory, performance, black masculinity, and gendered violence. All of her current research projects speak strongly to notions of power, privilege, and voice, which she has presented at national conferences, social justice events, and diversity training sessions.

Erin Brining Hammond is a public speaking instructor at Faulkner State Community College and a Ph.D. candidate in the Speech Communication Department at the University of Southern Mississippi. Her research interests include diversity and communication, and political communication.

Tina M. Harris is a Professor in the Department of Speech Communication at the University of Georgia. She teaches undergraduate courses in the areas of interracial, intercultural, and interpersonal communication, and graduate courses in interracial communication and media, communication, and race. Harris, research expertise is on interracial communication, interracial dating, race relations, racial representations and the media, race and ethnic disparities in health, genetics and religious frameworks, and Christian identity and communication. Harris is a nationally renowned interracial communication scholar, and has co-authored the leading textbook *Interracial Communication: Theory to Practice (2008*; Sage Publications) with African American communication scholar Mark P. Orbe of Western Michigan University. This is the first textbook to be written on this topic since 1974.

Richie Neil Hao (Ph.D., Southern Illinois University, Carbondale) is an Assistant Professor in the Department of Human Communication Studies at the University of Denver. His research interests are at the intersections of intercultural, pedagogical and performance studies. He previously served as the Assistant Director of the Core Curriculum in the Department of Speech Communication at Southern Illinois University, Carbondale.

Sherick A. Hughes is an Assistant Professor of Minority and Urban Education in the Department of Curriculum and Instruction at the University of Maryland. In 2004, Dr. Hughes was awarded the Phi Delta Kappa Chapter Award for his dissertation on school desegregation, struggle, and hope. He earned an M.A. at Wake Forest University, and the M.P.A. and Ph.D. degrees from The University of North Carolina at Chapel Hill in Culture, Curriculum, and Change. His research interests are (a) urban teaching and teacher education; (b) marginalization and response bias; and (c) applied qualitative/mixed methods, critical theory, and pedagogy. Dr. Hughes' work has appeared in numerous refereed journals including the *Journal of Black Studies, Urban Review, International Journal of Inclusive Education, Educational Foundations*, and *Educational Studies*. His first of two books *Black Hands in the Biscuits Not in the Classrooms: Unveiling Hope in a Struggle for Brown's Promise* earned a 2007 Critics' Choice Award from the American Educational Studies Association. Both of Dr. Hughes' books are in circulation at over 130 universities worldwide.

Elizabeth H. Jeter is in her first year of the Ph.D. program at the University of South Florida. Her research focuses on forms of participant based qualitative methodologies and methods. She hopes to apply this work towards the study of sexual health.

Peter M. Kellett (Ph.D., Southern Illinois University) is Associate Professor and Head of Communication Studies at the University of North Carolina Greensboro. His work centers on the narrative analysis, understanding, and management of conflict communication.

Jacqueline L. Kelly is an undergraduate researcher and student at Marist College. Her course work and research focus on transethnic communication as expressed in both inter- and intra-cultural communication. She plans to pursue her graduate degree in cultural studies.

Kenneth A. Lachlan (Ph.D., Michigan State University) is an Associate Professor of Sociology and Director of the Communication Studies program at the University of Massachusetts Boston. His research interests include media violence and aggression, crisis communication, and quantitative research methods. Recent projects have examined violent content in video games, the role of disposition and motive in the moral appraisal of television violence, and the relative effectiveness of crisis messages that were aimed at those in the path of Hurricane Katrina. He has recently published in journals such as *Human Communication Research, Journal of Broadcasting & Electronic Media, Journal of Applied Communication Research, Journal of Emergency Management,* and the *American Journal of Public Health.*

Devorah Lieberman is Provost and Vice President for Academic Affairs at Wagner College. She assumed this position in January 2004, having been the Vice Provost and Special Assistant to the President at Portland State University in Portland, Oregon. Devorah received her Ph.D. in Intercultural Communication (1984) from the University of Florida and concurrently received her certification in Gerontology. As Provost and Vice President for Academic Affairs at Wagner College, Devorah oversees all academic, curricular, and student-related elements of the College. She sees her primary role as furthering the academic excellence that exists at Wagner. Coupled with this strong academic base, she believes that every student graduating from Wagner should have deepened their commitment to contributing to their local, national, and international communities around them in ways that enhance others' lives. Her academic grounding in intercultural communication keeps her deeply connected to diversity issues and internationalization on her campus and throughout higher education. Her work with civic education is closely tied to her commitment to educating the whole student while connecting theory to practice. She continues to focus her scholarly activities through research, publication, and presentation in the areas of diversity, intercultural communication, leadership, and institutional change.

Christy Teranishi Martinez argues, through her research, that identity development is tied to self-awareness and an understanding of how our identities develop over time and across contexts. She found that we weave our identities through a shared sense of goals, values, and expectations across the contexts of family, school, peers, work, and neighborhoods. Her teaching and research interests, in addition to support she received from family, friends and faculty mentors, led her along her educational and career path to earn her M.A. in Communications at San Diego State University, and her Ph.D. in Psychology at University of California, Santa Cruz. Her passion for teaching and research of identity and relationships continues as an Assistant Professor of Psychology at California State University, Channel Islands.

Tom Matyok (Ph.D., Nova Southeastern University) is Assistant Professor of Conflict Studies and Dispute Resolution at the University of North Carolina Greensboro. His research centers on oppression, modern-day slavery, and conflict worker education.

Michaele P. McCloud is a communication major at Abilene Christian University, where she serves as the Chaplain of the Sigma Theta Chi Social Club.

Taber Minner graduated with a B.S. in Communication from Abilene Christian University, where he was a member of the university's football team.

Eddah Mutua-Kombo is an Associate Professor of Communication Studies at St. Cloud State University. She teaches in the area of intercultural communication. Her research interests include peace communication initiatives in post-conflict societies, theory and practice of service-learning pedagogy in promoting interracial relations, and African communication education and research. Her work has been published in *Qualitative Inquiry* and *Africa Media Review.*

Scott A. Myers (Ph.D., Kent State University) is Professor of Communication at West Virginia University. He teaches courses in instructional communication, small group communication, and interpersonal communication. His research interests center primarily on the student-instructor relationship in the college classroom, with his research appearing in *Communication Education, Communication Research Reports,* and *Communication Quarterly.* He is a former Editor of *Communication Teacher,* a former Executive Director of the Central States Communication Association (CSCA), and currently serves as the Second Vice-President of CSCA.

Mark P. Orbe (Ph.D., Ohio University) is Professor of Communication & Diversity in the School of Communication at Western Michigan University where he holds a joint appointment in the Gender & Women's Studies Program.

Joshua Phillips (M.A., Central Michigan University). Via his academic and social justice endeavors, Josh's interests span white identity, gender violence, class oppression, and social resistance. Between his undergraduate and graduate work, Josh took a year off to volunteer in Camden, New Jersey working at homeless shelters and after-school programs, which heightened his commitment to raising social consciousness. When he returned to school to earn his M.A., he and two fellow activists created the group East Coast Walkers and successfully completed an 1,800 mile walk from Miami to Boston in the summer of 2008 to raise awareness about gender violence.

Christopher J. Porter (B.A., Marist College) is a recent graduate of Marist College. His course work and research focus on communication and culture, especially as expressed in sports communication contexts. He plans to pursue his graduate degree in communication studies.

Joshua Rogers is a master's student in the Gaylord College of Journalism and Mass Communication at the University of Oklahoma, studying strategic communication and new media. He is a graduate assistant for Gaylord College and Research Institute for STEM Education (RISE).

Nicole S. Rosini (B.A., Marist College) is a recent graduate of Marist College. Her course work and research focus on transethnic communication and cultural competence. She plans to return to London, if possible, for additional professional development in public relations.

David William Seitz is a Ph.D. candidate in the Department of Communication at the University of Pittsburgh, where he is currently a Mellon Predoctoral Fellow in the Humanities. His fields of interest include public memory, visual culture, and communication and culture.

Ruta Shah-Gordon is the Dean of Campus Life and Internationalization at Wagner College. She received her master's degree from Colgate University in 1996 in Psychology with her thesis being on Stereotype Threat: Effects on Students of Color. As the Dean of Campus Life and Internationalization, Ruta oversees residential education, co-curricular programs, and health and counseling services, as well as internationalization and diversity initiatives at Wagner College. She serves as the co-chair for both the Internationalization Action Council and the Diversity Action Council, and is responsible for furthering the strategic blueprints for the College around these areas. In her role at the College, she continues to bridge collaboration across students' academic and co-curricular experiences so that they have the opportunity to learn more about themselves as individuals in the context of being civically engaged and interculturally competent citizens of the world.

Sachiyo M. Shearman (Ph.D., Michigan State University) is an Assistant Professor of the School of Communication at East Carolina University. She teaches courses such as conflict and communication, communication research methods, and intercultural communication at both the undergraduate and graduate levels. Her research interests include intercultural communication, cross-cultural comparative studies, conflict communication, and negotiation. Specifically, she has conducted cross-cultural comparative studies in communication styles and preferences, and has examined the effect of individual differences such as dogmatism in interpersonal conflict interaction. She has published her research in journals such as *Human Communication Research, Communication Quarterly, Journal of Intercultural Communication Research, Language and Communication,* and *Asian Journal of Social Psychology.*

Earl Sheridan is a native of Wilmington, North Carolina. He received his B.A. degree in Political Science from Appalachian State University in 1975 and his Ph.D. degree in Political Science from the University of Tennessee at Knoxville in 1980. Since that time he has taught political science at the University of North Carolina at Wilmington. For eight years, from 1992–2000, he served as Chair of the Political Science Department. He is the author of several articles and papers on political ideology and race. Dr. Sheridan has been active in his community. From 1987 to 1996 he was President of the New Hanover County Branch of the NAACP. He also served on the 1898 Memorial Foundation, and is a member of the Commission of Afro-American History of the City of Wilmington. In 2005 he was elected to a term on the Wilmington City Council. He is married to his childhood friend and classmate Sandra.

Amber Smittick graduated with a B.S. in Psychology from Abilene Christian University. She is currently a Ph.D. student in Industrial-Organizational Psychology at Texas A&M University. She regularly volunteers for Big Brothers, Big Sisters.

Patric R. Spence (Ph.D., Wayne State University) is an Assistant Professor in the School of Communication at Western Michigan University. His research focuses on risk and crisis communication, examining audience perceptions of risk and emergency messages produced by emergency management, organizations, government, and news agencies, specifically, looking at how these messages motivate various publics to take action in light of perceived threats. Some of this research has recently been cited in the *National Consensus Statement on Integrating Racially and Ethnically Diverse Communities into Public Health Emergency Preparedness*, released by the Office of Minority Health in the U.S. Department of Health and Human Services. His recent work has been published in *Communication Research Reports, Journal of Modern Applied Statistical Methods, Journal of Applied Communication Research, the Journal of Black Studies, Journal of Health Care for the Poor and Underserved,* and *Sociological Spectrum.*

Rebecca J. Tallent (Ed.D., Oklahoma State University) joined the University of Idaho (UI) School of Journalism and Mass Media faculty in summer 2006 as a full-time, tenure-track professor. Becky is an award-winning journalist and public relations specialist with more than twelve years of experience as an energy, environmental, and financial journalist. She also has eighteen years of experience as a public relations specialist, primarily with state government agencies in science and medicine. In addition to her UI teaching, Becky was a 2007–2008 Diversity Leadership Fellowship with the Society of Professional Journalists (SPJ), served as the ombudsman for the Spokane *Spokesman-Review* in 2008, and is a member of the UI American Indian Studies Faculty. Becky is a member of both SPJ and the Native American Journalists Association (she is of Cherokee heritage), and she is the advisor to both student groups on campus. She earned both her Bachelor of Arts in Journalism and her Master of Education in Journalism from the University of Central Oklahoma. She earned her Doctor of Education in Classroom Teaching/Mass Communications from Oklahoma State University in 1995. As part of her continuing education, Becky attended the Poynter Institute for Media Studies in the summer of 2007 to learn more about teaching Diversity Across the Curriculum. Becky teaches media writing, news reporting, principles of public relations, public relations campaigns, media culture (philosophy) and cultural diversity and the media.

Bertha Boykin Todd has lived in Wilmington, North Carolina since 1952. With multiple degrees from both North Carolina Central University and East Carolina University, she was employed by New Hanover County Public Schools for 39 years, retiring as director of staff development in 1992. Her community work has garnered numerous honors including The Order of the Long Leaf Pine, the *Star News* Lifetime Achievement Award, and an honorary doctorate from the University of North Carolina Wilmington. She was married for 42 years to the late Edward M. Todd and is mother to Rita Todd Griffin, an elementary school teacher, and Brian Todd, a Delta Airlines captain.

Susan E. Walden (Ph.D., University of Oklahoma) is the founding Director of the Research Institute for STEM Education (RISE) at the University of Oklahoma, where she coordinates a multi-disciplinary research team using primarily qualitative methods to study how the complex milieu of factors such as faculty cultural competency, institutional policies, and academic cultures intersect with students' race, ethnicity, socio-economic background, and cultural capital to contribute to students' academic experiences in science, technology, engineering, and mathematics majors (STEM). Other research interests include K-12 STEM education and teacher professional development. With B.S., M.S., and Ph.D. degrees in Chemistry, she is also an Associate Research Professor in the College of Engineering and the founding Associate Director of the Sooner Engineering Education (SEED) Center.

Keith A. Weber (Ed.D., West Virginia University) is Associate Professor of Communication Studies at West Virginia University, where he also serves as Coordinator of the Communication Studies Graduate Program. His primary research focuses on the relevance of persuasion theory in applied contexts. Dr. Weber has received funding from the Department of Health Resources and Services Administration as well as the Environmental Protection Agency for his research on organ donation, drinking and driving, and community water treatment. Dr Weber has published his research in journals such as the *Journal of Applied Social Psychology, Journal of Applied Communication Research,* and *Communication Quarterly*.

Quintin S. Wilson graduated with a B.S. in Communication from Abilene Christian University, where he was a member of the university's football team.

Anna Wong Lowe recently received a doctorate from the University of Oklahoma in Communication with foci on race and culture. Her work examines the intersections of Asianness and whiteness among Asian/Americans living on the west coast and midwest. Research interests also include identity, qualitative methods, and intercultural communication.

About the Editors

Deborah A. Brunson

Deborah A. Brunson is an Associate Professor in the Department of Communication Studies at the University of North Carolina Wilmington (UNCW) where she teaches courses in communication theory, interracial communication, interpersonal communication, and diversity. In addition to her faculty appointment, Deborah has previously served as UNCW's Interim Director of Campus Diversity and Director of the Upperman African American Cultural Center. She is a co-editor of the volume *Letters from the Future: Linking Students and Teaching with the Diversity of Everyday Life* (Stylus Publishing, 2007). She has published articles in *The Journal of Leadership Studies*, *Communication Education*, and *Communication Teacher*. Her work also appears in the books *What We Still Don't Know About Teaching Race: How to Talk About It in the Classroom*; *Best Practices in University Teaching: Essays by Award-Winning Faculty at the University of North Carolina Wilmington*; *Communication and Collaboration in the Online Classroom*; and *Intrapersonal Communication Processes*.

Linda L. Lampl

Linda L. Lampl is President/CEO and co-founder of Lampl Herbert Consultants (LHC), a natural resource consulting firm based in Tallahassee, Florida. She consults in each of LHC's core service areas—business management, public policy, and the environment. She holds undergraduate and graduate degrees in cultural anthropology and a doctorate in communication research from Florida State University. Linda's experience in organizations includes work in strategic and business development, project management, assessment, leadership and community development, and capacity building. Her work appears in the co-authored chapter "Practical Strategies for Partnership: an Inside-Out View" in the volume *Partnering for Organizational Performance: Collaboration and Culture in the Global Workplace* (Rowman & Littlefield Publishers, Inc. 2008); she also served as co-editor of the volume *Letters from the Future: Linking Students and Teaching with the Diversity of Everyday Life* (Stylus Publishing, 2007).

Felecia F. Jordan-Jackson

Felecia F. Jordan-Jackson is an Associate Professor in the School of Communication at The Florida State University (FSU) in Tallahassee. She completed her M.A. and doctoral degrees in communication at West Virginia University (WVU) in Morgantown. Her teaching and research interests include interpersonal communication, interracial/intercultural communication, and issues related to sex/gender roles. Most recently, she has published research articles on verbal aggression, argumentativeness, and communicator styles as these variables relate to race and gender in interpersonal contexts. Her research outlets include *Human Communication Research, Communication Education,* and *Communication Quarterly.* She is a contributor to and co-editor of this volume. Felecia is married to Dale and has two daughters: Jordan and Angeleena.

Prologue

Interracial Communication: Contexts, Communities, and Choices fills a long-standing gap in the interracial communication conceptual and pedagogical literature. The publication of a trilogy of interracial communication books in the 1970s, titled *Transracial Communication* by Arthur L. Smith in 1973, *Interracial Communication* by Andrea L. Rich in 1974, and *Crossing Difference … Interracial Communication* by Jon A. Blubaugh and Dorthy L. Pennington in 1976 pioneered the formalization of interracial communication study within the communication discipline. Those books focused on race as an essentialized construct and identity marker in communication in the U.S. Moreover, interaction between Blacks and Whites was the predominant focus.

Now, some forty years later, the demography of the U.S. has been transformed by a major influx of ethnic and immigrant populations, necessitating a rethinking of the historic melting-pot metaphor for relations, along with the ongoing need to rectify historical and ongoing deficiencies in interracial communication. Communication scholars, teachers, and practitioners are now compelled to re-examine the existing paradigms and theories, as these observers witnessed racial identity being confounded by issues of ethnicity, culture, religion, and socioeconomic status. The educational, corporate, and social marketplaces demanded a comprehensive scope whose focus extended far beyond that of race. *Interracial Communication: Contexts, Communities, and Choices*, by Brunson, Lampl, and Jordan-Jackson is the long-awaited answer to that demand.

While this text embraces the conceptual changes and practices demanded by the global marketplace, readers will find that an underlying motif that runs throughout the book is that racial identity can still be problematic. What remains from the past is the competitive social and ritualized dance between an internal (self) identity and an external (other-imposed) identity, and the ways in which those identities become codes and signifiers that have dynamic, often undesirable, ramifications. The dance, which is often conflictual and ontologically hegemonic, is accompanied by discourse markers in which identities are embedded.

Interracial Communication: Contexts, Communities, and Choices describes and explores the communication contexts in which identity dances occur, and it presents both developmental and social theorists' perspectives on identity construction and perception. Contexts covered include the personal, interpersonal, social, educational, institutional, global, and the mass-mediated ones, including the context of interracial romantic relationships, a context that reframes the earlier group-based, social distance models and theories of interracial communication.

To complete its research-based, panoramic scope of interracial communication, this text's prescriptive creed for enhancing interracial communication is the need for readers and participants to develop a critical consciousness in interracial communication, one that will entail adaptations, expansions, and a reframing of current and historical pedagogy and practices.

Reading this book will underscore the need for the communication discipline to ascribe a dominant place to the study of interracial communication, replacing the current positions that range from those of invisibility to arbitrariness, to unevenness in the curriculum. The lingering problematic of race presents scholars, planners, and practitioners a prescient and clarion call to act proactively, rather than waiting for interracial communication crises to emerge. And yet, the call is not one of becoming problem-centered, but one of creating basic interracial communication consciousness, literacy, and proficiency. *Interracial Communication: Contexts, Communities, and Choices* by Brunson, Lampl, and Jordan-Jackson provides an essential tool for safely navigating the interracial communication terrain.

Dorthy L. Pennington
The University of Kansas

 # References

Blubaugh, J. A. & Pennington, D. L. (1976). *Crossing difference ... Interracial communication.* Columbus, OH: Charles E. Merrill Publishing Company.

Rich, A. L. (1974). *Interracial Communication.* New York: Harper and Row.

Smith, A. (1973). *Transracial Communication.* Englewood Cliffs, New Jersey: Prentice-Hall.

Acknowledgements

It is with great pleasure that we extend our gratitude to those who have helped us on the journey toward bringing *Interracial Communication: Contexts, Communities, and Choices* to fruition. First, we deeply appreciate the support provided by the Kendall Hunt team assigned to this project; they helped to bring our vision to light. We particularly acknowledge and thank Angela Willenbring, Senior Editor, whose expertise and professionalism were instrumental in navigating us through the publication process from conceptualization through production. Our sincere appreciation is also extended to Paul B. Carty, Director of Publishing Partnerships at Kendall Hunt who believed in and supported this project from its inception.

We thank each of our contributors to this volume. It was an honor working with old friends and getting to know new friends. Their work is first-rate and makes a valuable contribution to the body of knowledge on interracial communication. They represent a vibrant community of scholars who have significantly advanced the intellectual discourse within this vital segment of communication studies.

We would be remiss if we did not express our gratitude to those who put in many hours of background work, without which this volume would not have been possible. We wish to acknowledge the administrative support of the Lampl Herbert Consultants team: Vikteria Butler and Brooke Talgo; as well as staff in the University of North Carolina Wilmington (UNCW) Communication Studies Department: Roshni Desai and Brittany Deanes. Special thanks to Dr. Bruce McKinney, UNCW Communication Studies faculty for his helpful manuscript review, to Dr. Richard K. Olsen, Jr., Chair of the UNCW Department of Communication Studies for providing administrative support, and to Dr. Stephen McDowell, Director of The Florida State University (FSU) School of Communication for his help in providing scheduling and administrative support that aided in moving this project forward. We also appreciate the administrative support provided by Victoria Craven, Wilmington, North Carolina.

This venture would not have become a reality without God's love and grace. We thank and praise Him for supporting and guiding us throughout this process.

Finally and fondly, to our partners (Bernard L. Brunson, Thomas A. Herbert, and Dale L. Jackson), family, and friends: we love and thank you for the many hours of support, wise counsel, and patience you provided during the creation of this book. Quite simply, you are the best!

Introduction

Deborah A. Brunson, Linda L. Lampl, and Felecia F. Jordan-Jackson

We begin this introduction by challenging you to take a test: Over the next few days, monitor any news outlet (television, Internet news websites, blogs and tweets, radio, print magazines, newspapers) and count the number of stories you encounter that intersect with race. Before you embark on this challenge consider America's recent events. The United States made social and political history in November, 2008 with the election of Barack Obama, the nation's first African American president. This significant milestone prompted people of all races to wonder if we are now living in a fully "post-racial" nation. After you complete your content analysis of current news events it may become apparent to you that significant incidents and events connected with race continue to occur, despite many changes and reforms that guarantee civil rights for all citizens.

Whether the stories you find are positive or negative, we suggest that race relations remain an important and salient issue, particularly in such diverse societies as the United States. With all the benefits of such cultures there are inevitable drawbacks as well, with conflict being among the most prevalent. Often the conflict is fueled by real differences between people in their manner, custom, values, and beliefs. These differences may exist through culture, gender, age, ethnicity, sexual orientation, physical abilities, and also through race.

While the study of interracial communication is often subsumed under the intercultural communication frame, these areas of inquiry are also quite distinct. As we see them, both culture and race are similarly social constructions; the result of a collective consciousness that creates and directs the master narrative or story about a group (or groups) of people within a society. One may say that culture is a social construction that is generally based upon the folkways, practices, and traditions of a group, society, or nation (Hall, 1977, Lustig & Koester, 2006, Martin & Nakayama, 2010). As Stephen Pullum, professor of communication and Deborah's faculty colleague observed "Whenever someone asks me what culture is, I tell them that culture is a type of shared reality or way of looking at the world of a group of people who live in a particular geographic area. In other words, it's a collective mindset. While there are always individuals in a group who may not share the same reality, mindset, worldview, etc. this does not mean that a culture doesn't exist. In other words, not everyone who lives in a particular region has to share the same worldview in order for a culture to exist" (personal communication, September 25, 2009).

The term "race" as you will encounter it in this book, is also a social construction. We acknowledge that some physical or phenotypical features within human groups are commonly used to categorize people by that which has become known as "race." However, as you'll see in the sections that follow, definitions of interracial communication focus upon the nature of race as a social construction and the consequences such constructions have for individuals, groups, societies, and nations. We also maintain that the term "race" may encompass some aspects of culture but that its primary frame—its initial purpose and continuous function—is to classify people by outward physical characteristics which are often employed to determine status, power, relationships, and overall quality of life. As Montagu (1997) observed "We must constantly be on our guard against subscribing to a lexicon of unsound terms of which we elect ourselves the guardians, and make ourselves the prisoners of our own vocabularies" (p. 46).

In short, race is a difference that *can matter*—and historically the interpretations of physical differences known as "race" have had major implications in social life and on all levels. Race continues to confound relationships throughout society. Is it any wonder then that many individuals find it exceedingly difficult to initiate conversations about the topic? People are often presented with situations where race is a factor in determining relational, organizational, and societal outcomes, but they might not possess the intellectual grounding, emotional sensitivity, or behavioral skills to effectively respond. This reader is designed to address these concerns.

Interracial Communication: Contexts, Communities, and Choices offers opportunities for the reader to engage in thought, reflection, and dialogue around many of the issues that frame and inform interracial communication which necessarily affect the quality of these intergroup relationships. The 26 original essays in this edited volume explore a range of communication topics among, between, and across racial groups within a variety of contexts and communities. An underlying theme throughout these chapters is the continuing and varying influence interracial communication has upon the lives of everyday people. You will find this to be the case no matter the chapter's focus, the research methods used, or the context in which the communication takes place. Of equal importance to the book's construction is the notion of community. Although there is a specific section entitled "communities" each essay speaks to some element of this socializing process. Gudykunst (2004) observed that "a community is *not* a group of like-minded people; rather, it is a group of individuals with complementary natures who have differing minds" (p. 346). He proposed that building community with strangers (people in different group memberships such as race, gender, culture, disability, age, ethnicity, social class and other identities) is an essential process for developing positive intergroup relations. *Interracial Communication: Contexts, Communities, and Choices* closely mirrors this community-building theme through its diversity of topics, perspectives, and discussion questions. You'll also find a diversity of authors across these chapters—faculty, administrators, and students, consultants, and community members—who present their work by drawing from various research traditions, theoretical frameworks, research methodologies, and lived experiences. We see the authors' diversity as a major strength of this book; one that aptly represents the "community of otherness" Gudykunst expressed. We believe that the process involved in assembling this book has created a vibrant community: contributors whose work has resulted in an outstanding collection of essays that provide new frames through which to visualize communication within and across racial experiences.

Defining Interracial Communication

Definitions of interracial communication have often focused upon the communicative function of the interactants, the socio-political function of the interactants, or a combination of both. Jon A. Blubaugh and Dorthy L. Pennington (1976) (Dr. Pennington authored this book's prologue) identified and defined interracial communication as "… a special case of intercultural communication resulting from racial identification and different cultural influences that create barriers to interpersonal communication" (p. 19). They developed a "Cross-Difference Model" that identified factors each interactant must manage if interracial encounters are to be successful. These factors include racism, power, assumptions, language, nonverbal communication, and beliefs and values. Andrea Rich and Dennis Ogawa (1998) defined interracial communication as "communication between white and non-white in the U.S. and is characterized by strain and tension resulting from the dominant-submissive societal and interpersonal relationship historically imposed upon the non-white by the structure of white America" (p. 56).

Donald W. Klopf and James C. McCroskey (2007) noted that "Communication crossing so-called racial lines is interracial, race being defined as a group whose members share a certain set of inborn physical characteristics such as hair texture, skin color, and conspicuous physical features. Talk between African Americans and Anglo-Saxon Americans could be interracial" (p. 64). They also reiterated the arbitrary and biologically insignificant nature of race, emphasizing that its inherent power resides in social constructions by various groups and societies: "We have declared previously that at the genetic level, race does not exist. Studies of human DNA have found that individuals within any given 'racial' group have more generic variability than individuals between two such groups. … The U. S. Census Bureau, as we have noted, continues to divide Americans into distinct racial groups, making race an issue culturally and politically" (p. 64–65). Mark P. Orbe and Tina M. Harris (2008) who are both contributors to this volume, have defined interracial communication as "… the transactional process of message exchange between individuals in a situational context where racial difference is perceived as a salient factor by at least one person" (p. 6).

Drawing above from Orbe and Harris' reference to the primacy of transaction, and the acknowledgement of race by one interactant within the interracial communication environment, we offer the following definition: ***Interracial communication*** *is the transactional process of exchanging messages through verbal and nonverbal symbols between at least two individuals* *from different racial groups wherein race plays a significant role in the encoding, interpretation, and/or effects of the messages for one or both interactants.* As we view it, interracial communication exists in a multi-level, dynamic, and transactional environment. The environment is *multi-leveled* in that there are multiple roles involved, there are implicit and explicit rules of interaction, and as these roles (and rules) develop, power is negotiated between and among the interactants. It is *dynamic* because as one finds in all interpersonal settings, interracial relationships are constantly being altered and changed from moment to moment and over time. It is *transactional* in that interracial communication is a process where persons are simultaneously sending and receiving messages. In addition, as stated by Infante, Rancer, and Womack (1993) "the transactional nature of [interracial] communication means each communication situation is unique, to a degree" (pp 21–22) as each participant changes and adjusts their thoughts and behaviors with each encounter.

One of the factors that can make interracial communication difficult is that the individuals involved may or may not be aware that race is playing a role in the communication process. This may in part be due to the fact that interracial communication is framed by and enacted through the organizing social construct of "race" as it is identified and defined within a society and not exclusively or even necessarily within an individual. The strength or salience of interracial communication in a given situation is contingent upon several factors that include—but are not limited to—the relational history of the interactants, influence of racial identity, prejudice and stereotyping, power structures that influence personal and organizational outcomes (e.g. racism; discrimination), impact of current and/or previous socio-historical and socio-political frameworks, situational contexts, and pragmatic (e.g. rule-governed) considerations.

Organization of the Book

This collection is arranged in six divisions that we call contexts: Identity, Relationships and Families, Communities, Academic Stories, Politics, and Mass Media. Each chapter opens with an abstract followed by a list of key words, and concludes with discussion questions designed to further engage the reader with the issues and themes presented in the reading. Although the essays are clustered by context areas, we view the boundaries around them as porous and non-fixed. These loosely-formed boundaries exist because many of the chapters may just as plausibly be placed within one or more of the other contexts in the book. For instance, the first essay "Amidst the Color Line: Remembering Love at the End of Everyday" recounts the interplay of identity and different levels of conflict and engagement with the outside world between Rachel and Joshua, an interracial couple. This chapter may also offer insights if placed within the "relationships and families" context, or perhaps grouped with the essays under "communities." As you read the entries in each context, you may want to consider the multiple placements some of the essays could occupy across these various sections. As teachers, scholars, and students have come to understand and appreciate the multi-leveled, multidimensional nature of human communication, you will likewise see this complexity unfold throughout the book with its fluid contextual boundaries.

Context I: "Identity" contains essays that explore the development and presentation of the self based upon racial group membership and racial awareness. Framed around themes of a racialized self, the research and reflections in this section demonstrate how race may intersect with other identity frames. In the first chapter, Rachel Alicia Griffin and Joshua Phillips foreground the sometimes complex, delicate negotiations of personal and relational identity they encounter as an interracial couple in "Amidst the Color Line: Remembering Love at the End of Everyday". While author Patricia Brown McDonald's focus in chapter 2 is upon international intersections that explore the similarities and differences of racial experiences for Jamaicans and African Americans ("The Differences that Bind Us: an Informal Diasporan Conversation"), Michele S. Foss-Snowden asks readers in chapter 3 to consider the impact of a faulty racial coding system upon interracial communication scholarship and research agendas ("The Mis-Education of Race: Communication, Coding, and the Illogic of the Current Approach"). Next in this context is Sakile K. Camara's work which interrogates Black identity through wearing natural hair, and the manner in which African Americans express acceptance or resistance to physical expressions of self in "Conformed and Disrupted Black Bodies in Interracial Interactions: Deliberations on the Wearing of Natural Hair". Chapter 5, entitled "Grabbing from My Racial Tool Kit: Ethnic-Racial Socialization and African American, Asian American, Hispanic American, and Native American Students" written by Anna Wong Lowe, Monica Flippin, Joshua Rogers, Cindy E. Foor and Susan E. Walden invites readers to consider the impact of ethnic-racial socialization upon students of color, and the coping strategies these young people may employ in order to thrive and become successful within the university environment. In chapter 6, Christy Teranishi Martinez continues the theme of the previous essay, but with a particularized lens focused upon Latino/a experience ("The Role of Ethnic Identity, Ethnic Flexibility and Ethnic Peer Affiliations in First-Year Latino/a College Students' Perceptions of Future Opportunities").

Context II: "Families and Relationships" opens with a research report in chapter 7 by Juan M. D'Brot, Theodore A. Avtgis, Keith A. Weber, and Scott A. Myers in their chapter entitled: "The Development of a Typology for Interracial Relationships: An Extension of an Existing Model" that responds to the question: Can a model initially designed to explain black-white relationships be theoretically extended so that it applies to intimate dyads composed of other racial groups? Chapter 8, "Communication with Transethnically Adopted Individuals" by Daniel Cochece Davis, Jacqueline L. Kelly, Christopher J. Porter, and Nicole S. Rosini, explores several factors that influence the content and quality of communication with transethnically adopted children, particularly given the controversy that these forms of families have historically engendered. The authors explain the strength and resiliency these families display as they prepare their adoptive children to engage with their social worlds. This is accomplished by fostering strong bicultural socialization, ethnic identity, and communication coping skills. The two remaining chapters in this section focus upon interracial and intercultural romantic relationships and the influence of race, culture, and identity upon relational satisfaction. Sachiyo M. Shearman's essay "Is that Because She Is an Asian?: Attribution and Relational Satisfaction in Inter-Couples" (chapter 9) illustrates how the attribution process intersects with self-reported perceptions of relational satisfaction across a variety of interracial and intercultural intimate couples. She offers compelling insights regarding the influence of cultural attributions upon these individuals and their perceptions of why their relationships are working well, or why they are. In chapter 10 entitled, "If I'm White and you're Black, what does that make us?: Negotiating Racial Identity in Romantic Interracial Relationships") Kelli L. Fellows proposes that we pay closer attention to the influence of identity and identity development upon black-white romantic relationships. Through giving voice to candid, revealing interracial conversations with her students, Fellows' essay echoes the recurring patterns of relational satisfaction and relationship development introduced in chapters 7 and 9.

In *"Communities"* (*Context III*) four chapters offer helpful—and hopeful—models of productive interracial communication that are designed to ameliorate intergroup conflict and misunderstanding. Chapter 11, "Social Inequities and Communicating during Crisis" by Christine Eith, Patric R. Spence, and Kenneth A. Lachlan uses the backdrop of Hurricane Katrina to articulate the inherent dangers of crisis communication strategies that do not adequately consider needs of underserved populations throughout all stages of the emergency event. "Promoting Interracial Interactions through Service-Learning Pedagogy" (chapter 12) chronicles author Eddah Mutua-Kombo's work to infuse a critical pedagogy into her curriculum. This approach provided an intellectual base from which her college students were able to successfully engage in a community building service-learning project with high school students experiencing interracial and intercultural conflict. The next essay (chapter 13), entitled "1898: Reflections on a Southern Community's Racial History and Future" by Earl Sheridan and Bertha Boykin Todd is the story of Wilmington, North Carolina—a city that has begun to face its troubling racial history and to provide a space for healing and restoration between the community's Blacks and Whites through a variety of outreach, community-building programs. Chapter 14, "Confronting the Racial Double Bind at a Christian University: A Critical Ethnography" explores how incongruence between a community's stated goal of racial equality and healing can serve to mute the voices of some participants whose experiences belie the institution's diversity initiatives. Written by Professor Jonathan W. Camp and his students Amber Smittick, Alan Copeland, Jennifer Dodd, James Graham, Michaele P. McCloud, Taber Minner, and Quintin S. Wilson, these authors present their own and others' narratives of an academic institution's effort to heal racial divisions. They also relate how many of its members continue their struggle to make the ideal "real" through dialogue and engagement.

"Academic Stories" (*Context IV*), is comprised of five essays that situate race and racialized experiences within various educational settings. "Engaging a Campus in Effective

Intercultural and Interracial Communication Initiatives" (chapter 15) by Devorah Lieberman and Ruta Shah-Gordon reports on efforts taken by their institution (Wagner College) to intentionally develop a comprehensive, campus-wide initiative meant to foster more meaningful, effective intercultural and interracial relationships within the university community. The next academic story pivots the reader's view from a global perspective of campus-wide intercultural and interracial initiatives articulated by Lieberman and Shah-Gordon to the particularized, lived experience of "Lisa"—a female African American undergraduate college student—who experienced an act of racism (chapter 16). "Interracial Conflict and Campus Hate Speech: The Case for Dialogic Engagement in College Settings" by instructor Peter M. Kellett with student co-authors Tom Matyok, Sarah Blizzard, Cherie Avent, and Elizabeth H. Jeter employs an ethnographic frame to explicate what became a traumatic intergroup clash for Lisa in a campus residence hall. The essay provides space to understand how the use of the "N" word adversely impacted this student's educational experience. The chapter suggests strategies that institutions may implement as they respond to critical incidents of campus hate speech.

Chapter 17 chronicles a teacher's personal exploration of self and pedagogy as experienced within an education curriculum ("Considering Five Promising 'Interracial' Communication Practices in an Intercultural/Intergroup Education Course"). Framed by quantitative and qualitative data collected from his graduate students, Sherick A. Hughes offers the reader insights on five classroom communication techniques that may effectively intersect with learning outcomes within a course whose focus is race, culture, and intergroup relationships. "Reframing the Rhetoric of Race through Classroom Discourse" (chapter 18) presents a rhetorical analysis of narratives drawn from student journals in an undergraduate interracial communication course by focusing upon how these participants reflect upon the communication behaviors that they utilize to successfully address verbal acts of interracial hostility (racial microaggressions). Authors Tina M. Harris and Blake Abbott propose that these communication strategies may be applied beyond the classroom to ameliorate negative interracial interactions. Context V concludes with Richie Neil Hao's essay in chapter 19, which outlines how the struggle by international students to establish professional credentials in the United States is sometimes exacerbated by ideological challenges to their cultural and racial identity. "'America has a Dominant Language—Learn it': An Analysis of Whiteness in the Construction of International Teaching Assistant Identity in the *Daily Egyptian*" interrogates how this conflict is structured through the letters and commentary printed in a campus newspaper.

The intersection of race and the political process is the theme of *Context V (Politics)* and is explicated through two essays. Chapter 20 explores the impact of social media upon the 2008 Presidential race, with an analytical frame directed toward the campaign of then presidential candidate Barack Obama. "Change in the Oval Office: The Impact of Race on First-time African American Voters" by Vanessa G. Cunningham-Engram (chapter 20) queries the social media and digital technology uses of African American college students as they sought to gain access to information about this historic run for the White House. She also ascertains how political organizing of this population was activated through such digital tools as text messaging and Facebook. Chapter 21 offers an analysis of thematic patterns about race that have emerged among African American political speakers across 40 years of public discourse ("A Comparison of Major Democratic National Convention Speeches by High-Profile African American Political Leaders: How is Race Treated?"). Erin Brining Hammond's comparative work, which focused upon speakers Fannie Lou Hamer, Barbara Jordan, Jesse Jackson, Al Sharpton, David Alston, and Barack Obama suggests that the historical context and the orator's personal priorities significantly impact the manner in which raced is framed and articulated.

The final section, (*Context VI–Mass Media*) consists of five essays on race across various media channels. Each in its own manner invites the reader to consider the impact of race as media construction(s) upon the individuals, groups, communities, and countries who consume these mass-produced images and messages. In chapter 22 authors Joseph A. Ciccarelli and Mark P. Orbe suggest that the guiding vision of a corporate culture (Disney) can permeate the boundary of a "true story" the media corporation tells through film. The resulting process creates a collective memory of race and race relations that is distorted, inaccurate, and subsequently harmful to contemporary discussions about the significance of race within present-day society ("Based on a True Story" … But whose Story Is It and What's the Impact?: Critiquing the Disneyfication of Race Relations in *Glory Road*"). Chapter 23 asks us to consider inherent conflicts that may arise when a sovereign nation exists within another sovereign nation. This is the case for Native peoples living on tribal lands within the United States. As separate entities, American Indian nations have established laws that regulate all aspects of the nation's existence including media. In "Native Press Freedoms: Federal and Tribal Legal Issues Restricting Native Media" Rebecca J. Tallent and Rubell S. Dingman provide an overview of the legal history involving Native media regulation, how these laws affect who gets to report the news of Native American tribes, and the guidelines under which Native and non-Native journalists are required to operate in the Tribal arena. The next essay was written by Felecia F. Jordan-Jackson, one of this book's co-editors ("A Comparison of Perceptions of Verbal Aggression and Argumentativeness in Situation Comedies: Television in Black and White"). In chapter 24, she examines whether the perceptions of Whites and Blacks performing aggressive and argumentative statements in a mediated context (television) will be similarly or differentially identified by White and Black viewers. Her findings suggest that perceptions and reality are not necessarily the same when it comes to communication of Blacks and Whites even when the messages are created in the parasocial realm of television comedy.

"Cultural Identity in the Age of Ether: Black Entertainment Television and the Island of Guadeloupe" by David William Seitz (chapter 25) explores how a white-owned national programming outlet (Black Entertainment Television/BET) may wield unexpected influence upon the racial and cultural identity of young people through its distribution and consumption in a Caribbean nation. Seitz addresses this question via narratives of several adults and youths who expressed differing opinions about the impact of globalization through media. The final chapter in Context VI returns the reader to film, this time by interrogating portrayals of race, identity, and gender within the dynamics of student-teacher relationships. "She Has 50,000 Coaches: Re-envisioning Young Women of Color as Learners in Three Popular Films" by Gordon Alley-Young (chapter 26) frames the analysis through *Real Women Have Curves*, *Akeelah and the Bee*, and *Half Nelson*. Alley-Young asks the reader to critically reflect upon how young women of color are frequently portrayed in film through unflattering, stereotypical characterizations; to consider why film portrayals of white teachers solving the problems of inner city students and schools may be problematic; and to examine how these three films avoid being framed within these unproductive perspectives.

"Coda" to the Introduction

To borrow the musical term *Coda* (which means providing a conclusion to one section of a musical piece or exposition) we repeat a previous observation about the contents of this volume: *As you read the entries in each context, you may want to consider the multiple placements some of the essays could occupy across these various sections. As teachers, scholars, and students have come to understand and appreciate the multi-leveled, multidimensional nature of human communication, you will likewise see this complexity unfold throughout the book with its fluid contextual boundaries.* We hope that through this brief excursion across the opening pages of *Interracial Communication: Contexts, Communities, and Choices* you have a better sense of: a) the background of race as a salient factor in communication and b) the important ideas, questions, and perspectives offered by the contributing authors in this collection, and how their work has constructed an intriguing landscape filled with multi-leveled and multidimensional intellectual spaces and locales. We also hope as you engage these authors through consideration of their ideas within and across these intellectual spaces, the process will prompt your reflection upon the *choices that you have made and can potentially make* to improve interracial health and productivity—in every "context" of your life.

References

Blubaugh, J. A. & Pennington, D. L. (1976). *Crossing difference ... Interracial communication*. Columbus, OH: Charles E. Merrill Publishing Company.

Gudykunst, W. B. (2004) (4th ed.). *Bridging differences: Effective intergroup communication*. Thousand Oaks, CA: Sage.

Hall, E. T. (1977). *Beyond culture*. Garden City, NY: Anchor Books.

Infante, D. A., Rancer, A. S., & Womack, D. F. (1993) (2nd ed.). *Building communication theory*. Prospect Heights, IL: Waveland Press, Inc.

Klopf, D. W. & McCroskey, J. C. (2007). *Intercultural communication encounters*. Boston, MA: Pearson Education.

Lustig, M. W., & Koester, J. (2006) (5th ed.). *Intercultural competence: interpersonal communication across cultures*. Boston, MA: Allyn and Bacon.

Martin, J. N., & Nakayama, T. K. (2010) (5th ed.). *Intercultural communication in contexts*. Boston: McGraw-Hill.

Montagu, A. (1997) (6th ed.) *Man's most dangerous myth: the fallacy of race*. Walnut Creek, CA: AltaMira Press.

Orbe, M. P. & Harris, T. M. (2008) (2nd ed.) *Interracial communication: theory into practice*. Thousand Oaks, CA: Sage.

Rich, A. L. & Ogawa, D. M. (1998) (2nd ed.) "Intercultural and Interracial Communication: An Analytic Approach". In G. R. Weaver (Ed.), *Culture, communication, and conflict: Readings in intercultural relations* (pp. 54-59). Needham Heights, MA: Simon & Schuster.

Context I

Identity

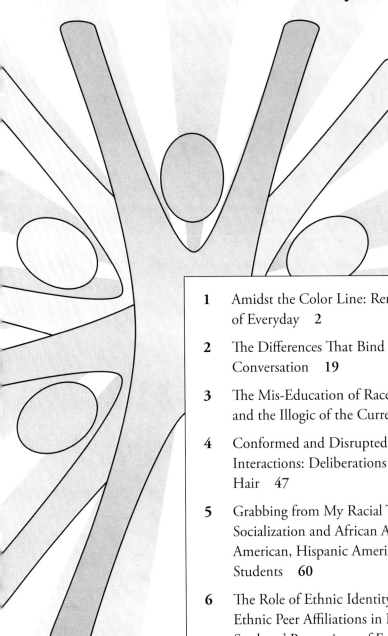

1

Amidst the Color Line: Remembering Love at the End of Everyday

Rachel Alicia Griffin and Joshua Phillips

Abstract

The purpose of this chapter is to reflect on our experiences as a black/white interracial romantic couple whose relationship is contextualized by historical, social, and political factors far beyond our control. Often we feel under suspicion for crossing racial lines, scrutinized for signs of love, and troubled by the remnants of history that seem to beckon for us to justify why we choose each other. Utilizing personal narrative in the hopes of raising consciousness about black/white romantic unions, we recover our voices at the intersections of ethnicity, gender, and sexual orientation. To do so, we process through the complexity of our relationship along three dimensions: (a) the politics of self-disclosure, (b) intersectionality in terms of the privileged and marginalized identities we hold, and (c) trust. Yet in the midst of the sociopolitical discourses that frame these three dimensions, what we find to be the most profound act of resistance at the end of everyday is the love that we share through and among our racial identities.

KEY TERMS: interracial relationships, history, ideology, personal narrative, self-disclosure, intersectionality, trust, love

Introduction

Sinful. Distrust. Threatening. Pathological. Erotic. Immoral. Unnatural. Not Right. Wrong. Disgraceful. Against God. Jungle Fever. Contamination. Culturally Taboo. Exotic. Improper. Hopeless. Impossible. Doomed.

As a black/white interracial couple, the list above reflects the prevailing lessons that we have learned about our love in accordance with the dominant ideologies of the United States. Oftentimes these lessons are bolstered by the assumption that we are not together (at restaurants the server almost always asks if we want separate checks), the anticipation of failure (raised eyebrows often reveal a "good luck" sentiment), and the concern for any children that we may have in the future (interestingly, people indicate that the children we don't have yet will likely be confused). Although we wholeheartedly believe that the negative socially constructed meanings imposed upon our relationship are a reflection of historical and contemporary racism rather than a reflection of our relationship (Thomas, Karis, & Wetchler, 2003), our survival as a couple depends on our ability to navigate and resist the dominant, racist constructions of our white male/biracial black female romantic relationship. Like other romantic couples, we must make an intentional effort to maintain a loving bond across our differences. However, the existence of socially constructed lines rigidly drawn between black and white communities requires more commitment to endure, since our relationship is not supported or nurtured by dominant culture. Thus, throughout history and extending into contemporary society, interracial relationships have been perceived as a cultural taboo that few welcome and that many seem to hope will deteriorate, disappear, or at least not appear in their own families and neighborhoods (Childs, 2005).

In this effort to share our experiences as an interracial couple, we must make clear that we, neither individually nor jointly, embrace a colorblind perspective (Bonilla-Silva, 2003) or any other perspective propagating that race does not matter. For us, race and racism *always* matter; we are not in love regardless of our racial identities, but rather we love each other as racialized beings. In order to uproot prejudicial attitudes and expose discriminatory behaviors, we believe that it is important to give voice to our racialized realities by speaking for ourselves rather than being spoken for (Alcoff, 1991). In doing so, we will address the violent histories shared among white males and black females (hooks, 1981), describe the historical stigmatization of white/black romantic relationships (Gaines & Brennan, 2001), and then explore our own relationship, which is often constructed in an objectifying and dehumanizing manner.

To achieve a cohesive discussion of the aforementioned topics, our chapter will move through four sections. The first section will provide a historical framework of black/white relationships, generating insight as to why contemporary interracial relationships are typically perceived as: (1) invalid, (2) pornographic, (3) an act of rebellion, and/or (4) a political position. Next, via personal narrative, we will share our experiences as an interracial couple as a means to raise social consciousness. Finally, we will end our chapter with closing comments rooted in the hope that, with time, insistence, and dialogue, more spaces will be created in which our love for each other as two people of African and European histories can be welcomed and celebrated.

Our Histories

The colonial history of Africans in the United States began with the onset of chattel slavery as a social institution in 1451 (Mustard, 2003) resulting in the roots of American society being implanted via the enslavement of Africans who were stolen, deceived, traded by, or sold to white Europeans. African men and women alike were forced to surrender their homelands, identities, labor, personal autonomy, and oftentimes their lives, to the overarching and demeaning power of white supremacy (Mustard, 2003; Steward, 1861). In this context, Blacks were dehumanized, denigrated, maimed, murdered, and regarded as subhuman by Whites. To ensure the social acceptance of this extreme cruelty, the enslavement of brown and black peoples required the social construction of dominant ideologies. According to Allen (2004), dominant ideologies "reflect experiences and perspectives of the ruling class, whose members construct and disseminate those ideologies that will most benefit them" (p. 32). Speaking directly to race and racism, Saint-Aubin (2002) describes racist dominant ideologies as "… a conscious effort to articulate, to justify, and to propagate a universal white supremacy based on the notion of an inherent black corporal, intellectual, and moral inferiority" (p. 255). Generally speaking, blackness was discursively situated as a social contaminant to the purity of the white race that coincided with stupidity, amorality, defect, pathology, danger, guilt, sin, dirtiness, ugliness, animalistic nature, disease, and deformity, while Whiteness was discursively positioned as being symbolic of cleanliness, innocence, peace, security, beauty, heaven, harmony, intelligence, moral purity, authority, and power (Baynton, 2001; Black, 1997; Fanon, 1967; Hecht, Jackson, Ribeau, 2003; Jackson, 2006; Staples, 1980).

In the context of racism, racial oppression manifested differently for black men and women. Black males were often regarded as dangerous, threatening, and hypersexual beings who necessitated white patriarchal control, with the utmost concern being to protect the pure virtue of white women (Brownmiller, 1975). By comparison, black females were often regarded as sexually impure women who were valuable only as caretakers, concubines, and breeders (Daileader, 2005; hooks, 1981). For white men and black women in particular, racist ideologies rooted in white supremacy created a master/slave relationship in which the physical and sexual domination of black women was used not only to dehumanize black women but also to emasculate black men. This mentality reflected the notion that in order to conquer a people and prove one's race superiority, one race must conquer the women of another race (Gordan, 1964). As such, open, loving, and consensual romantic relationships between black women and white men were invisible, if not impossible, in the context of U.S. American slavery.

When Blacks were legally freed from being the property of Whites in 1863[1], laws and social norms maintained the impossibility of white males and black females openly engaging in loving romantic relationships, to protect the purity of the White race (Weinbaum, 2007). Black women remained discursively positioned as concubines and erotic objects (Daileader, 2005; hooks, 1981) who were unworthy of genuine love, respect, and affection from white men. Simultaneously, white supremacist discourses campaigned for white males to uphold their moral obligation to preserve the purity of Whiteness by honoring only white women with their hand in marriage. Therefore, romantic and/or sexual relationships among black women and white men were not only illegal, but in the case that there was intimate contact it was assumed to be illegitimate, meaningless, and rooted in sexual exploitation. Likewise, any white man who sexually engaged with a black woman ran the risk of producing an impure child; a child who would not be accepted as White regardless of patriarchal lineage. Therefore, although it was an unspoken patriarchal norm (albeit highly visible given the number of biracial white/black children) for white men to have sex via force and/or consent with black women, interracial marriage was not socially acceptable, or even legal in most states. For example, "Maryland enacted the first antimiscegenation statute in 1661" followed by 37 additional states that criminalized interracial sex and marriage (Moran, 2001, p. 19).

To eliminate miscegenation laws, individuals and social organizations advocated for the decriminalization of interracial marriage. For example, abolitionists publicly approved the unions between Whites and Blacks in an effort to bring about reconciliation between the groups (Daileader, 2005). However, despite abolitionist support and the eventual legalization of interracial marriage via the 1967 Supreme Court case *Loving v. Commonwealth of Virginia*, the social taboos surrounding black and white romantic unions remain (Childs, 2005; Kennedy, 2003; Wallenstein, 2002; Yancey & Yancey, 2002). Although there are not laws preventing interracial marriage, sex, and/or contact in contemporary society; prejudicial attitudes, discriminatory actions, and racism remain customary. For example, interracial romantic relationships are often marked as invalid, pornographic, an act of rebellion for one or both parties, and/or rooted in one's desire (often the party of the non-dominant race) for social status and political power (Dyson, 2003; Gaines & Brennan, 2001; Kennedy, 2003; Sexton, 2001; Wallenstein, 2002). In addition, stemming from the negative perceptions and representations of interracial relationships is the racism that interracial couples encounter, including but not limited to the denial of goods and services, rudeness, intimidation, verbal and/or physical aggression, and even murder (Childs, 2005; Killian, 2003; Nealy, 2000; *The Washington Post*, 1986).

In contemporary society, dominant ideological norms function to keep interracial romantic relationships socially categorized as invalid. Not only are interracial relationships rarely perceived as loving and committed, but they are also subjected to scrutiny and public animosity combined with a lack of formal and informal support services (Childs, 2005; Killian, 2003). Because genuine affection in black/white relationships is viewed as invalid, any romantic or sexual contact that occurs between a white man and black woman in particular is often viewed as erotic, pornographic, and meaningless pleasure (Weinbaum, 2007; Sexton, 2001). Based upon the perceived lack of romantic involvement, interracial relationships are categorized as strictly fantasy, never real or long term.

In terms of rebellion, by participating in an interracial relationship and engaging in interracial sex, white males are often accorded an admired status as individuals rebelling against the system and conquering the exotic black woman. Thus any serious interest that a white male expresses toward a black woman may be deemed erotic: an adventurous endeavor to explore the sexual mysteriousness of black women (Wallenstein, 2002). The status of rebellion, however, is often quick to pass if a white male indicates that his feelings toward a black woman are genuine and rooted in the interest of a long-term relationship. Hence, the expectation still remains in contemporary society for white men to protect Whiteness as a form of property (Harris, 1995). Essentially, the prevailing attitude remains that no respectable white man would or should decrease his social standing by romantically engaging with and publicly committing to a black woman, especially in the context of available white women.

While interracial relationships are typically embraced in the interest of pornography, eroticism, and the admiration of adventure, once these interests subside voyeuristic fascination often becomes engulfed with fear, hostility, and condemnation (Daileader, 2005). As such, romantic relationships across racial identity groups are often shunned as immoral and unnatural (Sexton, 2001). The public disapproval of black/white interracial romantic unions elicits cultural pressure to persuade the individuals involved to dissolve their relationship for a number of different reasons (Harris & Kalbfleisch, 2004). White males often feel obligated to dissolve the relationship to maintain the purity of their race, while black females may feel obligated to protect and project the Afrocentric worldview by partnering with black males (Bair, 1999; Kennedy, 2003).

In sum, the violent history of racial interaction in U.S. American society and contemporary racial prejudice, have created a complex backdrop for white/black romantic relationships. Given the potency of black and white histories which are strife with exploitation, pain, and struggle; interracial relationships are therefore stigmatized as taboo. This stigmatization functions to discredit the relationship and the individuals involved, and beckons the desire and oftentimes need for additional defensive strategies (Goffman, 1963) to protect the relationship. More directly stated, for hundreds of years it was illegal for people who look like us to love each other while it was legalized, forcefully encouraged, and gainfully taught for people who look like us to gaze with suspicion across our racial differences. The lived experiences on both sides of the racial divide, rooted in the white desire to situate Whites as the best race (Harris, 1995; Jackson, 2006), birthed rigid categorizations and demeaning attributes to render interracial relationships seemingly impossible. Although a significant body of research addresses the history and cultural attitudes toward interracial relationships (Brownmiller, 1972; Day, 1972; Kennedy, 2003; Moran, 2001), very little research gives voice to those involved in interracial relationships.

Speaking to this gap in the literature, the next section consists of our personal narratives addressing our struggles as a black/white romantic couple. According to Ellis and Bochner (1992), "By making intricate details of one's life accessible to others in public discourse, personal narratives bridge the dominions of public and private life. Telling a personal story becomes a social process for making lived experience understanding and meaningful" (pp. 79–80). In addition, Corey (1998) contends that personal narratives can be utilized to disturb and contest the master narrative; as such we aim to disrupt dominant ideological constructions of our interracial relationship via what critical scholars have termed counter-hegemonic discourse, counter-stories, counter-speech, and/or resistant narratives (Delgado, 2000; Pollock, 1998; Pelias, 2005). Highlighting the power of narrative, Delgado (2000) says "stories can shatter complacency and challenge the status quo … they can show that what we believe is ridiculous, self-serving, or cruel" (p. 61). In doing so, of the utmost importance to recognize is that we do not aim to speak *for* all interracial couples but rather we are speaking *to* our own experiences (Alcoff, 1991) in the hopes that our voices may join in the larger conversation dedicated to revealing the much needed but often overlooked insights of interracial couples who are in healthy, loving, and enduring relationships.

Within and among our reflections, we contemplate our experiences in terms of self-disclosure, intersectionality (Crenshaw, 1995), and trust. A close reading of our narratives will illustrate the various ways in which we as an interracial couple strive for legitimacy and acceptance in a culture marred by racism. We coauthored this chapter over several shared moments–on the phone, on planes and trains, sitting on the couch–we wrote and rewrote different sections attempting to achieve perfection and yet we have come to understand that we will not be able to include or communicate everything that we want to say. However, we have worked diligently to embody the empowering nature of the written word to help readers understand and reflect upon our experiences.

Our Voices: The Story of Rachel and Joshua

Self-Disclosure

One of the major decisions that we are often faced with is the politics of self-disclosure. We regularly struggle with when to tell others that we are involved in an interracial relationship. Although we both struggle with when to disclose, how to disclose, and brace ourselves for what may come in response our decisions are bolstered by various reasons and often met with different reactions and consequences. For instance in U.S. American history, the traditional ideology of Whiteness has been one of forced choice for people who are biracial/Black and White like Rachel. In essence, you were either light enough to pass as White or you were Black, since the power of Whiteness is rooted in its ability to restrict access to privileges bestowed upon white skin (Harris, 1995); consequently, although Rachel identifies with both her white and black ethnic heritages, her Whiteness is disregarded by most.

Rachel: My body is always already political; born into the "color-line"[2] but I am often read as Black. Knowing the histories of my black and white heritages make me aware of the dominant assumption that I am "unsuitable" for Josh. What I find even more difficult to accept are the insinuations that it is "odd" or that I am "lucky" that a white man chose me. Sometimes it seems like I can feel the question "Why is he with a black girl?" Not that my being biracial should make a difference—I believe that people can love through and among any ethnic identities they hold—but it seems like the only thing a lot of folks consider is that my skin is brown and that in and of itself is enough reason for him and me not to be together.

By comparison, Joshua has access to racial privilege. Being White, society positions his racial identity as the unrecognized and unexplored racial norm by which all other racial groups should measure themselves (Sue, 2004; Tatum, 1997). Even though the privileges afforded to his identity are rooted in the exploitation, oppression, and genocide of non-Whites in an effort to gain power (Feagin, Vera, & Batur, 2001), these acts are often rendered invisible and victimless in today's culture because they took place generations ago. Given the ways that Whiteness has been positioned as superior by any means necessary, Joshua is rarely ever met with the idea that he isn't "good enough" for Rachel. In addition, because Joshua is an educated white male engaged in the movement to raise consciousness about racism, his choosing a black woman as a partner comes at the cost of often being perceived as a white male who actively seeks out relationships with women from marginalized racial communities to gain acceptance in those communities (Dyson, 2003).

Joshua: Deciding to tell people that I am dating a biracial black woman is, unfortunately, laced with political assumption and suspicion. What's more ridiculous is that the suspicion and judgment usually come from complete strangers and quasi-acquaintances. People assume that because I am dating a black woman it must somehow be directly tied to political and professional beliefs regarding some extreme sympathy for Black culture; some desire to identify "with the struggle." These assumptions are like labeling all heterosexual men as feminists because they date women.

Rachel: When I hear Josh talk about his struggles in disclosing, I think the decision about whom to tell and when to tell is more familiar to me since my mom is White and it seems that I have always had to explain and justify my relationship to Whiteness. However, I can relate to his naming "suspicion" as a way to describe how people can react; sharing that he is White has been met with a sense of hostility too. But is it different from the sometimes negative reactions that I get when people learn that I am biracial. My guess is that it is because I *choose* to be with Josh rather than having been *born* biracial.

Interestingly, we both feel as though we are marked negatively by our choices to be involved in an interracial relationship, but when it comes to disclosure, another difference in how we interpret its impact is on our perceived credibility as people dedicated to social justice.

Rachel: When identifying my partner as White, I often brace myself for the reaction. I think I anticipate the worst but hope for the best based on a myriad of past experiences. For me, I think the most difficult reactions to mindfully respond to are those that question my "authenticity" as a woman of color. If people already know that I am biracial, it can feel like a double whammy: (1) you're biracial and (2) you have a White partner. Usually, these reactions are followed by an explicit and/or implicit sense of disapproval. It is as though I cannot be dedicated to issues impacting people who look like me nor can I speak to my experiences as a woman of color because I am not Black *enough*. But since I expect these reactions and have experienced them firsthand too many times to count, I am pretty forthcoming about my partner being White.

In comparison to Rachel, Joshua tends to be less forthcoming about sharing Rachel's racial identity, which can be very complex and hurtful if his hesitance is perceived as shame or indifference. Although he imagines that some have perceived it that way, he explains his decisions below:

Joshua: In the classroom, I usually withhold disclosing my partner's gender or race unless it is directly inquired. I'm not going to actively withhold the information, but I'm not going to actively share it either. Because I do a lot of work surrounding the politics of Whiteness, disclosing the fact that Rachel is a biracial Black woman has its repercussions. All of a sudden, my positions on Whiteness are tainted with self-serving roots. No longer do White students or colleagues see the information I present about the historical and systemic injustices Whites forced onto non-Whites. Instead, all they see is an emotional White man screaming "racism" because his Black girlfriend thought some White person gave her a dirty look in the grocery store. Another difficult question is 'How do I deal with Whites when they say or do things that are overtly racist, without allowing my partner's race to enter the argument?' It's hard and I admit that it would be a lot easier talking to Whites about White privilege if my partner wasn't Black. If this were the case, Whites could never categorize my arguments as self-serving. I confront the ignorance, but it turns personal when most of the people I socialize with are close friends or colleagues. Someone in those close-knit circles is bound to know a few things about my personal life. I remember one time when five of us, all White, were hanging out. The new guy started making racist comments. Noticing the discomfort from others as they studied my emotions and waited for my cue, I kept silent waiting to see if someone would initiate. Finally, someone pulled him aside and told him that I had a Black girlfriend. It's amazing to know that the only reason cited for him to stop was my romantic relationship. No one said that racism was wrong or that racist jokes perpetuate hate, or that they personally didn't appreciate his racism. All they noted was the color of Rachel's skin.

Intersectionality

Although it is without question that our relationship bares the marks of racialized histories, we also work to be socially conscious about the privileges that we have access to as a couple as well. In essence, our identities as individuals involved in an interracial relationship operate at the political intersections of not only race and gender but also sexual orientation.[3] Inspired by Crenshaw's (1995) notion of intersectionality, it is important for us to speak to our experiences as an interracial *and* heterosexual couple in the context of our commitments to social justice. Thus as an interracial couple, we are relegated to the margins of society insofar as race is concerned, but as a heterosexual interracial couple we have access to privileges such as marriage and adoption that many of our same sex counterparts do not, which as a form of heterosexual privilege is equally as important to us as our racial marginalization.

Rachel: For me, our privilege as a heterosexual couple is an aspect of our relationship that I try to make visible for us and others. Two years ago, I was fortunate to participate in a course that brought the realities of heterosexism and homophobia closer to my heart. Since then, I have been working on remembering that Josh and I have a responsibility to use our heterosexual privilege. However, I have struggled to remain steady in my commitment to mask our heterosexuality on a consistent basis by using "partner" rather than "boyfriend" or "he." For example, when looking for apartments when we were getting ready to move to southern Illinois, I felt the need to make clear that we were an interracial couple (just to avoid any unpleasant "surprises" down the road since I have been told numerous times that I sound "White" on the phone). However, I also had the urge to lay claim to our heterosexuality as well. It was almost as if I wanted to acquire some sort of social approval from whomever we might rent from. To me, it was indicative of the seeming relief that heterosexual privilege can bring reflecting on how embedded homophobia is in my own consciousness—I think in my heart of hearts I was afraid that if I masked our sexual orientation that it would be even harder to find a place to live and I imagine that I was right; it would have been harder with more layers of prejudice and discrimination added on.

Joshua: In addition to being White and male, another obvious privilege is that I'm heterosexual; all of these privileges seem to collide at the intersections for me. Having been long-distance while I finished up my Master's in Michigan and Rachel finished up her Doctorate in Denver, I never had to face the added racial element of my relationship if I didn't want to. People never saw me in public with my Black partner because we weren't living in the same state. Furthermore, I'm a private person who rarely talks openly about my romantic life and few people even know about Rachel, let alone her race. Anytime people who are unaware of our relationship make racist remarks around me, it is always my *choice* to confront them. This is not to say I wouldn't confront people if I didn't have a romantic connection to a Black person, but to illustrate that White people have a *choice* in combating racism. If Whites want, we can take a day off and be silent with no penalty. Racism is not an issue we have to face on a daily basis unless we actively choose to face it. So it is very complex when I think about how to use our hetero-sexual privilege while I am also trying to work through my White male privilege too.

Rachel: I think we flip back and forth in terms of whether or not marriage is a socially conscious option for us. On the one hand, I can see how it could be an act of resistance, since we are stigmatized as an interracial couple, and yet I am continually humbled by Tim Miller's *Glory Box* performance where he compares getting married to eating in a White's-only restaurant. Since then I have chatted with several folks about the perspective that Miller raises and although I can't say that I agree with his comparison of marginalized realities, I cannot say that I disagree either, which, to me, sends a powerful message. For me the issue is participating in a social institution (marriage) that not everyone has access to. I try to think about it this way: how would I feel if interracial marriage was still illegal and same-race couples were getting married and could choose to celebrate and honor their love in that way when we couldn't?

For us, the marriage issue remains unresolved. We are not sure what we will decide to do, but we are committed to revisiting the topic when one or both of us feels the need. Marriage is complex and difficult at the intersections of privilege and marginalization; hence, we can see how strong and healthy interracial marriages resist the assumptions that interracial couples are destined for failure. Yet we also believe that unconsciously partici-pating in marriage as an oppressive social institution stands to fuel heterosexism and sub-sequently racism and sexism, which is a reality that makes us uncomfortable.

Trust

In addition to struggling with the politics of self-disclosure and intersectionality, we also require an exceptional amount of trust to support each other and protect our relationship from succumbing to the external pressures of dominant racial norms. In *White Like Me*, Tim Wise (2005) states, "The first thing a white person must do in order to effectively fight racism is to learn to listen, and more than that, to believe what people of color say about their lives" (p. 67). Both listening and believing across racial differences has played a crucial role in our effort to gain trust. When people of different racial backgrounds actively listen to and trust each other, they can begin to see how different experiences with privilege and/or oppression are a valid and legitimate means to understand the same situation in different ways (Feagin et al., 2001).

Rachel: Trust in our relationship is so important to me. As a woman of color and a critical intercultural scholar activist, my life and life's work[4] is deconstructing the complexities of power, privilege, and oppression. Quite often, I come home a mess, emotionally taxed, mentally depleted, and physically exhausted. I lean on Josh pretty heavily sometimes. I am sarcastic, I cry, I yell about the unfairness and sheer ignorance in the world and I need him. I need him to listen and validate my feelings even if he doesn't understand how my work hurts me as a woman of color.

Joshua: I have never and will never understand what emotions Rachel goes through on a daily basis. Sure, I hear the stories and hear the frustration in her voice, but I don't understand it. Usually in situations like these, the best thing for me to do is to just listen and let her know that I care. I can't fix it or even pretend like I know what's going on–because frankly, as a White male, I don't know. So my job is to trust that she knows her own experiences better than I do.

Rachel: The first moment when I consciously remember trusting him in the context of race and racism was when we were in Philadelphia. We had visited the archeological site where George Washington's presidential home was being unearthed. While listening to a live narrator tell the stories of Washington and his slaves to an audience of adults and children, my eyes filled with tears and I became absolutely furious. The narrator embodied the grand narrative of U.S. American history, depicting Washington as a hero, and (in my opinion) dehumanized the slaves who were forced to sacrifice their freedom, dignity, and family life. After listening to the narrative, we circled the blocks around the dig and I cried, complained, and yelled with tears running down my cheeks until I had run out of words. I was hurt; it hurt to listen to a person "informing" the public about history without sharing the pain and cruelty of slavery. Truth be told, it might be fair to say that Washington was "a man of his time" and some may feel that he was a good President, but it is also vital to recognize that as a slave master and President he facilitated the misery, suffering, and death of people who look like me, and that hurt.

Joshua: I remember this story vividly. This was probably the first moment in our relationship when I had no idea how to respond to her emotions. So, I listened. When appropriate, I would give small doses of validation and affirmation, but this didn't mean that I understood. Sure, I was mad at Whites for making slavery sound flowery and romanticized, but until this moment, I didn't know how Rachel felt about Blacks being subjected to such rhetoric. If anything, trust in our relationship is rooted in the idea that two people with two different identities experience things differently. Sure, we argue about issues concerning race sometimes, but in the end I trust that her perspective is valid for her and she trusts that my perspective is valid for me.

Author Wendell Berry (1989) writes, "A White man simply cannot learn all that he needs to know from other White men. That is because the White man's experience of this continent has so far been incomplete …" (p. 78). In this statement Berry is not suggesting that people of color have all the knowledge and therefore the experiences of race for Whites are void. Rather, he suggests that there are multiple ways to gain knowledge and that all groups' experiences are important in understanding and learning about current race relations. In the end, we have learned to trust each other because we have learned how to be open and to listen to each other's stories to better understand the multiple layers of racial experience. We do not pretend to be colorblind in these experiences, but instead we acknowledge our racial differences and embrace the realization that we have different ways of learning about and understanding the same experience.

Conclusion

"Love takes off masks that we fear we cannot live without and know we cannot live within."
—James Baldwin

Relationships like ours will always be impacted by the violent historical circumstances created by Whites at the severe expense of Blacks. However, as the United States becomes increasingly more populated by people of color and as social consciousness is raised with regard to race and racism, interracial relationships are likely to become more common; therefore, it is essential to create spaces and places where relationships like ours are welcomed, supported, and celebrated. For us, writing this chapter served as a meaningful way to do so; it was also cathartic to be able to recognize our histories and the relevance of race without being confined to oppressive ideologies about who we are and why we love each other. In many ways, our relationship is very similar to same-race relationships; we struggle like many other couples to balance the personal and professional realms of life, negotiate housework, and find enough time for each other, our friends, and our families. However, as asserted previously, our relationship is also contextualized by historical, social, and political forces far beyond our control. As such, in the context of contemporary racism, we work hard to seek peace and to remember our love at the end of everyday.

DISCUSSION QUESTIONS

1. Some feel that the existence of interracial couples indicates that the United States is colorblind, while others disagree. How do you feel?

2. How are interracial couples similar to and different from same-race couples? Are the politics of self-disclosure, intersectionality, and trust the key elements in both interracial and same race-couples?

3. How can people help create environments where interracial couples like Joshua and Rachel feel welcome?

4. Rachel and Joshua provide insight about themselves and their relationship through narrative comments. Which set of comments had the strongest impact upon you, and why?

---

[1] Legalized slavery "ended" (only three fourths of slaves were actually freed) with the Emancipation Proclamation in 1863 (Jackson, 2006).
[2] See Du Bois (1903/2003) for further discussion.
[3] Race, gender, and sexual orientation are the focus of our reflections here, but we also recognize that additional identities such as nationality, ability, class, religion, etc. play important roles at the intersections as well.
[4] See Kendall (2006) for further discussion.

References

Alcoff, L. (1991). The problem of speaking for others. *Cultural Critique, 20,* 5–32.

Allen, B. J. (2004). *Difference matters: Communicating social identity.* Long Grove, IL: Waveland Press Inc.

Bair, B. (1999). Remapping the black/white body: Sexuality, nationalism, and biracial antimiscegenation activism in 1920s Virginia. In M. Hodes (Ed.), *Sex, love, race: Crossing boundaries in North American history* (pp. 399–419). New York: New York University Press.

Baynton, D. C. (2001). Disability and the justification of inequality in American history. In P. Longmore & L. Umanski (Eds.), *The new disability history: American perspectives* (pp. 33–57). New York: New York University Press.

Berry, W. (1989). *The hidden wound.* New York: North Point Press.

Black, D. P. (1997). *Dismantling black manhood: Studies in African American history and culture.* New York: Garland Publishers.

Bonilla-Silva, E. (2003). *Racism without racists: Color-Blind racism and the persistence of racial inequality in the United States.* Maryland: Rowan & Littlefield Publisher, Inc.

Brownmiller, S. (1975). *Against our will: Men, women, and rape.* New York: Fawcett Columbine.

Childs, E. C. (2005). *Navigating interracial borders: Black-White couples and their social worlds.* New Brunswick, NJ: Rutgers University Press.

Corey, F. C. (1998). The personal: Against the master narrative. In S. J. Dailey (Ed.), *The future of performance studies* (pp. 249–253). Annandale: National Communication Association.

Crenshaw, K. W. (1995). Mapping the margins: Intersectionality, identity politics, and violence against women of color. In D. Danielson & K. Engle (Eds.), *After identity: A reader in law and culture* (pp. 332–354). New York: Routledge.

Daileader, C. R. (2005). *Racism, misogyny, and the Othello myth: Inter-racial couples from Shakespeare to Spike Lee.* Cambridge, MA: Cambridge University Press.

Day, B. (1972). *Sexual life between Blacks and Whites: The roots of racism.* New York: World Publishing.

Delgado, R. (2000). Story-telling for oppositionalists and others: A plea for narrative. In R. Delgado & J. Stefancic (Eds.), *Critical race theory: The cutting edge* (2nd Ed.) (pp. 60–70). Philadelphia, PA: Temple University Press.

Du Bois, W. E. B. (1903/2003). *The souls of Black folk.* New York: Fine Creative Media Inc.

Dyson, M. E. (2003). *Why I love black women.* New York: Basic Civitas Books.

Ellis, C., & Bochner, A. P. (1992). Telling and performing personal stories: The constraints of choice in abortion. In C. Ellis & M. J. Flaherty (Eds.). *Investigating subjectivity: Research on lived experience* (pp. 79–99). Newbury Park, CA: Sage Publications.

Fanon, F. (1967). *Black skin, White masks.* New York: Grove Press.

Feagin, J. R., Vera, H., & Batur, P. (2001). *White racism* (2nd ed.). New York: Routledge.

Gaines, Jr., S. O., & Brennan, K. A. (2001). Establishing and maintaining satisfaction in multicultural relationships. In J. Harvey & A. Wenzel (Eds.), *Close romantic relationships: Maintenance and enhancement* (pp. 237–253). Mahwah, NJ: Lawrence Erlbaum Associates.

Goffman, E. (1963). *Stigma: Notes on management of spoiled identity.* New York Simon & Schuster.

Gordan, A. I. (1964). *Intermarriage: Interfaith, interracial, interethnic.* Boston, MA: Beacon Press.

Harris, T. M., & Kalbfleisch, P. J. (2004). Interracial dating: The implication of race for initiating a romantic relationship. In R. L. Jackson II (Ed.), *African American communication & identities: Essential readings* (pp. 125–136). Thousand Oaks, CA: Sage.

Harris, C. (1995). Whiteness as property. In K. Crenshaw, N. Gotanda, G. Peller, & Thomas, K.(Eds.). *Critical race theory: The key writings that formed the movement* (pp. 276–291). New York: The New York Press.

Hecht, M. L., Collier, M. J., & Ribeau, S. A. (1993). *African American communication: Ethnic identity and cultural interpretation.* Newbury Park, CA: Sage.

hooks, b. (1981). *Ain't I a Woman: Black women and feminism.* Boston, MA: South End Press.

Jackson, R. L. (2006). *Scripting the black male body: Identity discourse, and racial politics in popular media.* New York: State University of New York Press.

Kendall, F. E. (2006). *Understanding White privilege: Creating pathways to authentic relationships across race.* New York: Taylor & Francis.

Kennedy, R. (2003). *Interracial intimacies: Sex, marriage, identity, and adoption.* New York: Pantheon Books.

Killian, K. D. (2003). Homogamy outlaws: Interracial couples' strategic responses to racism and partner differences. In V. Thomas, T. A. Karis, & J. L. Wetchler (Eds.). *Clinical issues with interracial couples: Theories and research* (pp. 3–31). New York: The Haworth Press.

Moran, R. F. (2005). *Interracial intimacy: The regulation of race and romance.* Chicago: The University of Chicago Press.

Morris, R. F. (2001). *Interracial intimacy: The regulation of race and romance.* Chicago: University of Chicago Press.

Mustard, D. B. (2003). *Racial justice in America: A reference handbook.* Santa Barbara, CA: ABC Clio.

Nealy, J. L. (2000 October 21). Hate crime trial // Roten: 'I just wasn't thinking'. *St. Petersburg Times.* Retrieved January 24, 2009 from http://0-www.lexisnexis.com.bianca.penlib.du.edu

Pelias, R. J. (2005). Performative writing as scholarship: My apology, an argument, an anecdote. *Cultural Studies/Critical Methodologies, 5*(4), 415–424.

Pollock, D. (1998). Performing writing. In P. Phelan & J. Lane (Eds.), *The ends of performance* (pp. 73–103). New York: New York University Press.

Sahlstein, E. M., & Baxter, L. A. (2001). Improvising commitment in close relationships: A relational dialectic perspective. In J. Harvey & A. Wenzel (Eds.), *Close romantic relationships: Maintenance and enhancement* (pp. 115–132). Mahwah, NJ: Lawrence Erlbaum Associates.

Saint-Aubin, A. F. (2002). A grammar of black masculinity: A body of science. *The Journal of Men's Studies, 10*(3), 247–270.

Sexton, J. (2001). There is no interracial sexual relationship: Race, love, sexuality in the multiracial movement. In S. Martinot & J. James (Eds.), *The problems of resistance: Studies in alternate political cultures* (pp. 135–154). Amherst, NY: Humanity Books.

Staples, R. (1980). *Black masculinity: The Black male's role in American society*. San Francisco, CA: The Black Scholar Press.

Steward, A. (1861). *Twenty two years a slave and forty years a freeman*. New York: Negro Universities Press.

Tatum, B. D. (2000). The complexity of identity: "Who am I?" In M. Adams, W. J. Blumenfield, R. Castaneda, H. W. Hackman, M. L. Peters, & X. Zuniga (Eds.), *Readings for diversity and social justice: An anthology on racism, Anti-Semitism, sexism, heterosexism, ableism, and classism* (pp. 9–14). New York: Routledge.

The Washington Post. (1986, February 15). Convicted killer found guilty in interracial couple's murder. *The Washington Post.* Retrieved January 23, 2009 from http://0-www.lexisnexis.com.bianca.penlib.du.edu

Thomas, V., Karis, T. A., & Wetchler, J. L. (Eds.). (2003). *Clinical issues with interracial relationships: Theories and research*. New York: The Haworth Press.

Wallenstein, P. (2002). *Tell the court I love my wife: Race, marriage, and law – an American history*. New York: Palgrave MacMillan.

Weinbaum, A. E. (2007). Interracial romance and black internationalism. In S. Gillman & A. E. Weinbaum (Eds.), *Next to the color line: Gender, sexuality, and W.E.B. DuBois* (pp. 96–123). Minneapolis: University of Minnesota Press.

Wise, T. (2005). *White like me: Reflection on race from a privileged son*. Brooklyn, NY: Soft Scull.

Yancey, G. A., & Yancey, S. W. (2002). (Eds.). *Just don't marry one: Interracial dating, marriage, and parenting*. Valley Forge, VA: Judson Press.

2

The Differences That Bind Us: An Informal Diasporan Conversation

Patricia Brown McDonald

Abstract

Black people worldwide share a common ancestral origin—Africa. In fact, Africa is now considered the birthplace of mankind. However, this paper addresses the peoples of the African diaspora, specifically those displaced by slavery and made to live and labor in the "New World" in a degrading and dehumanizing institution sanctioned by governments for over two hundred years. More specifically, this paper examines the relationship between African Americans and Caribbean peoples, particularly Jamaicans, who share much commonality through ancestry and historical development, but who through varying mutations of their commonalities have produced identities that have manifested in various ways. One such difference is how we see ourselves in relation to society, and conversely, how others see us.

KEY TERMS: New Africans, African American, foreign blacks, Caribbean, classism, racism

Introduction

More than 400 years since Africa was ravaged by "the peculiar institution of slavery," its echoes still reverberate among her denizens who were kidnapped and scattered halfway across the world to become beasts of burden, all the while propelling the offending powers to First World status (Bennett, 1988). Notwithstanding the horrors inflicted upon the men, women, and children who were violently uprooted from their African homelands, and the concomitant psychological tsunami attendant with such a separation, New Africans, that is, those transplanted during this violent period, suffered not only a physical separation from the Mother country but a psychological separation from each other as well.[1]

In the hundreds of years that ensued and the struggles embarked upon, Africans sold in the various slave-holding nations would eventually construct identities reflecting the particular country in which they were sold and deposited. Over time, those delivered to Jamaica became Jamaicans, those in Trinidad became Trinidadians, those in Guyana became Guyanese, and so on. However, those Africans sold in America not only came to acquire the appellation "American" but always had a defining color or origination descriptive actively attached to identification, such as "Negro," "Colored," "Black," and most recently "African American." Black people in the United States of America are color-coded at their every turn. For example, every application/identification I have come across in the U. S. requires an ethnicity or origination descriptor; even purchasing groceries at a supermarket as recently as 1989 required race recognition on personal checks. This is not so in Jamaica. No one is required to identify one's race on any document generated within the society—not on birth, death, or marriage certificates, driver's licenses, school records, and so on. For example, one would only be required to provide the following information on a marriage certificate: 1) "When Married," 2) "Name and Surname," 3) "Condition" (whether single, divorced, or widowed), 4) "Calling" (profession), 5) "Age," 6) "Parish and Residence at the time of Marriage," and 7) "Father's Name and Surname."

In spite of the fact that Caribbean countries have had their fair share of migration to the region from places like the Middle East, Asia, and Europe, there is no need to identify people according to their "origin." Everyone is considered first and foremost a citizen of the Caribbean country to which he or she was born—race or ethnicity is secondary. In Jamaica, for example, the national motto bears this out: "Out of Many, One People." Dr. Martin Luther King himself commented in *A Knock at Midnight* on the overwhelming sense of the Jamaican identity he felt exuding from the Jamaican people while he visited that country at the request of the Jamaican government:

> ... over and over again I was impressed by one thing. Here you have people from many national backgrounds; Chinese, Indians, so-called Negroes, and people from many, many nations. Do you know they all live there and they have a motto in Jamaica, "Out of many people, one people" (Carson & Holloran, 1998, p. 91).

An African American friend of mine once expressed to me that he is reminded every day of his life that he is a black man, and to be reminded that you are Black in the United States of America has not historically been a positive attribute. He explained that after purchasing two expensive pairs of shoes at an upscale mall with his credit card, he returned home to find a message awaiting him on his answering machine asking for verification of the purchases of the said shoes by the card's owner. For him, the unstated assumption was that a black man could not afford such expensive shoes; ergo the card must have been stolen. There may have been several explanations for this security check, but considering the historical circumstances of race in America, to conclude that this was a racist act was not unreasonable on his part. For him, even the simple act of buying good quality shoes exposed him to racism. A Jamaican, new to the soils of the U.S., would not have arrived at such a conclusion because prejudice of this nature is not familiar territory. I am not inferring that racism does not exist in Jamaica; it does. Every country that experienced slavery remains tied to the aftershocks of race, color, and socio-economic divisions; in Jamaica, however, classism takes precedence. The poor are constantly reminded of their impoverished state and the attendant disenfranchisement that accompanies that poverty in the Jamaican society, but there is not a constant reminder of one's race at every turn. The difference is worth noting because poverty is not a fixed variable; difficult as it may be, one may be able to negotiate one's way up the economic ladder. Race, on the other hand, is fixed.

As a newcomer to the U.S. in the late 1980s, I did not easily recognize racist behavior. The overt forms of prejudice I could discern, but it was the more subtle forms that had often eluded me. One of my earliest memories of being oblivious to racism occurred at a large southern university in 1987, which I attended on scholarship from Jamaica to study for a master's degree in communications studies. I was at the campus bookstore where I found myself during the first days of the semester diligently searching for required class texts, as did other students. However, for reasons unknown to me at the time, many white students approached me asking where they could find their books. Unfamiliar as I was with this new text of racism, I instinctively responded and helped whom I thought were simply needy students locate their books. Twenty-two years later, if this were to happen, I would have reacted differently, but at the time it never occurred to me that I was targeted as hired help because I am Black.

Although I am very dark complexioned, having lived in Jamaica for the first 27 years of my life in a privileged middle class, I enjoyed the advantages of an essentially class-stratified society. I remember one such instance when the boon of belonging to the middle class was abundantly clear. Jamaicans are required to obtain visas for travel to America, and to get an American visa was better than winning the lottery. Prior to the 1980s, however, folk stood in line overnight to be at the front of the queue when the Embassy doors opened. The lines would begin forming at approximately 8:00 p.m. the day before and would wind and curl around the building before pouring into the street. Vendors sold their produce and self-appointed linesmen kept your "space" in line for a fee while you attended to other business. There was entertainment, too, of course. It was carnivalesque—an experience somewhat akin to going to an incredible early morning Thanksgiving Sale at a Best Buy store. The festive atmosphere was interrupted, however, by two uniformed policemen who, in the name of keeping law and order, perused the crowd, callously plucking anyone from the line who "didn't look like they came for a visa" but were there instead selling spaces in the queue. Predictably, the unfortunate persons who were denied the opportunity of applying for visas were those who looked poor, and no amount of evidence or protestation could save them from being transported to an overnight lockup.

While teaching an African American literature class at a south Florida college, an African American student marveled to me that he was pleasantly surprised while on a trip to Haiti, where the people of Haiti saw him as an American, a Yankee; his race, though obvious, was not primary. This idea of representing one's nationality first, and race second, is reminiscent of African American soldiers who fought in Europe during World War II returning to the United States with a new sense of identity (*A History of the Civil Rights Movement*, 1992). Just like my student, these soldiers were received as American, not African American. Interestingly, the reverse was the case when Jamaican volunteers went to Britain to fight in the same war. In one story my father told me, he said he enlisted in the British army at a young age to escape a smothering mother and a rural life in Jamaica during the 1940s. For my father, his sojourn to Britain, a country with a predominantly white population and a history steeped in slavery, opened his eyes to a type of prejudice and racism that he had never before encountered. The British saw his color and reacted to that first and foremost. For the first time in his life my father was seen as a black man and little else. During the 1960s, a period of intense civil rights unrest in America, my father again left his homeland of Jamaica to study in New York, in the U.S. At that time, he and my mother had planned for him to be a harbinger of sorts. After he had finished studying and settled into a job, the family was to join him in the land of opportunity, the U.S.A. It never happened. A recipient of American racism, my father quickly aborted those plans and returned to Jamaica after graduating, never again harboring thoughts of migration. He was determined that his family, especially his children, not be exposed to such a toxic society. He said he wanted his children to be firmly rooted in who they are, which meant not being constantly discriminated against because of the color of their skin.

Like my father, the famous actor Sidney Poitier outlines a similar but potentially more deadly story that took place in pre-Civil Rights America. After leaving Cat Island, Bahamas, to live with his brother and sister-in-law at age fifteen, he too recounts the racial psychological shift to which he had to adjust. He says, "New to me was the way the society was structured; you had segregation in Miami—very intense" (Glass & Lee, 1999).

Poitier recounts being a delivery boy delivering a package to a white lady at her front door. He said, "She opened it and said what are you doing here? I said, I came to deliver this package to you, ma'am, and she said go around to the back door. I said but you're here, and here's the package, and she said get around to the back door, and the door slammed in my face … I didn't know what was going on" (Glass & Lee). Poitier goes on to recount that that evening, upon returning home, he found all lights out and the house deathly quiet. When he rang the doorbell, he said he was snatched into the house and told that the KKK had come looking for him. After that incident, Poitier, penniless, left the South and headed north to New York where he says he found "safety" in the large African American population there. Sidney Poitier went on to become the first black man to receive an Oscar for Best Actor in 1963. Looking back, he concludes that he owed much of his success to his upbringing in the Bahamas during his formative years. He says, "I went to America with much of myself already congealed. I came from a culture in the Bahamas where we were 90 percent of the population, which allowed me to go to America with a sense of myself. Pride and entitlement I carried with me. I had brought it with me from Cat Island" (Glass & Lee).

There is a difference in how African Americans and Caribbean folk view the landscape—our lenses are naturally colored by our frames of reference. It is with us as it is with all people: Our collective and individual histories define us. Because of the differences in historical development, black people from the Caribbean tend to view their race collectively to a greater extent and individually to a lesser extent. Although they are well aware of their race, they are not exposed to the daily excretion of subliminal and not so subliminal messages underscoring this point, as is the case with African Americans in America. For instance, in Jamaica, to refer to someone being Black is a reference to the hue of one's skin color; that is, whether the person is dark or light complected. It is the dark skinned/light skinned parallel in the United States. As Sidney Poitier pointed out, in the Bahamas where 90 percent of the population is Black, as it is with most of the Caribbean, race is a given. To refer to someone in the U.S. as Black, however, primarily refers to one's race, with the subtext of hue primarily existing within the African American community. It is here—the way in which we internalize our race—that the seeds of psychological separation between Blacks in the diaspora begin to take shape, just like the dividing fertilized egg that produces more than one organism. As our African selves metamorphosed into new identities, our similar but divergent experiences molded our sensibilities. While the African root in all of us is intact, it is buried. We, of the African Diaspora, the New African, became the above-ground trunk, branches and leaves, all blooming differently. Our peculiar post-slavery histories bear this out.

Brief Historical Overview of African American and Caribbean Peoples

Slavery in the United States of America began approximately in 1619 when the first Africans landed in Virginia. Their state of serfdom held firm until the Civil War was fought, resulting in the Emancipation Proclamation of 1863, which laid the foundation for freeing all slaves. Although legally speaking, slaves were now free, a series of formal and informal laws particularly in the South impeded any progress toward realizing that freedom for approximately another one hundred years. At the time of their "freedom," the African American population operated as a much marginalized minority within a hostile white majority. As a result, African Americans were literally powerless in all respects: political, economic, and social. This in itself presented significant obstructions to self-actualization on an individual and collective level for some time. For Southerners, during the years after the Emancipation Proclamation was signed and the period known as Reconstruction followed, Blacks endured terrorism of a nature that was heretofore unprecedented, and which was carried out with a vehemence that made it even worse than slavery itself. No longer having the need to preserve their property, Ida B. Wells-Barnett says, "with freedom, a new system of intimidation came into vogue; the Negro was not only whipped and scourged; he was killed" (Gates & McKay, 2004, p. 677).

Although the 13th Amendment to the Constitution abolished slavery in 1863, the Black Codes, Jim Crow, and the Klu Klux Klan reinstated it in similar fashion (Elwood & Kulish, 1990). The 14th Amendment, guaranteeing citizenship rights was superseded at every turn, culminating in the landmark case of *Plessy v. Ferguson* of 1896, which virtually negated any gains made by the passage of the Amendment (Elwood & Kulish, 1990). Likewise, enactments thwarting the 15th Amendment (extending voting rights to black males) flourished (Elwood & Kulish). Consequently, while free on paper, ex-slaves were far from being free in practice. The struggle for equal rights to actualize their freedom persisted another 100 years, which manifested in the Civil Rights Movement of the 1960s, spearheaded by renowned leaders Dr. Martin Luther King and Malcolm X.

Conversely, the black slave population in the English speaking Caribbean, colonies of Britain, was emancipated in 1834, approximately 30 years before their sisters and brothers in the United States. The "recovery" period that most parallels the Reconstruction period of the United States was the Apprenticeship System. While the slaves in some Caribbean territories were "full free," such as Antigua and Bermuda, the slaves in Jamaica, and other territories, "became apprenticed to their former masters, the field-labourers [sic], or predials[sic], for six years (up to the 1st August 1840), and the non-predials[sic] for four years (up to 1ˢᵗ August 1838), after which time they were to be completely free" (Black pp. 99–100). Although the apprenticeship system undoubtedly held the ex-slaves in a servile condition, there were no existent comparable oppressive laws to those in the Southern U.S. In fact, the apprenticeship system prematurely ended two years early in Jamaica, in 1838, because it was not working. The British government frowned upon the practice of having ex-slaves imprisoned in "workhouses" and coerced to work for the former masters under intolerable conditions (Black, 1973, p. 103). Historian Clinton Black (1973) states, "The discipline of the workhouses was hard and it was usual for prisoners to be worked in chains. The dark cell, solitary confinement, flogging, starvation, the treadmill—these were punishments the apprentice might have to suffer even for small offenses" (p. 103). Furthermore, the ex-slaves believed that they were completely free and, not accepting this extended state of serfdom, did not cooperate with the new system by striking often. Blacks in Jamaica, and the Caribbean in general, although subjected to colonial rule long after emancipation, experienced a level of "freedom" much sooner than did Blacks in the United States of America, when one takes into account the later emancipation date and the ensuing 100 years of institutionalized oppression approximating three generations in the U.S.

Language and Culture

In addition to brutal oppression during and after slavery, African Americans function as a minority in America. To be a minority in the United States essentially refers to population ratios; however, much more is at stake in the definition. It means that one's language and culture are subsumed. Black culture flourishes in black communities but very little outside of it. W. E. B. Dubois points to the psychological struggle of being a minority in a majority culture. Dubois defined it as a state of "double consciousness":

> Dubois developed the concept of double consciousness to show the juxtaposition between a dominant mainstream (White) and outsider (Black) perspective of the world. Dubois' concept of double consciousness refers to the perception held by outsiders (e.g., people of color) that their everyday life is often void of value in the eyes of the dominant mainstream majority (e.g., white society). DuBois' double consciousness also connotes the notion of a dual black identity that is simultaneously African and American, where both aspects of the dualistic identity are valuable. (Beckman, 2004)

An article tracking the growth of minorities in America, "On hold: Asian, Hispanic growth in U.S." (2009), reports the population pie as follows: Blacks, 12.2 percent;

Asians, 4.4 percent, and Hispanics, 15 percent. Even at little more than 12 percent of the U.S. population, the number of Blacks in the U.S. was bolstered by immigration from the Caribbean and Africa. In an article entitled, "'What Then Is the African American?' African and Afro-Caribbean Identities in Black America," Violet Showers Johnson (2008) states, "The 2000 Census revealed that the non-Hispanic Afro-Caribbean population grew almost 67 per percent in one decade" (p. 81). She also adds, "More than Afro-Caribbeans, it was Africans who most exemplified the explosion of the foreign black population at the close of the twentieth and the beginning of the twenty-first centuries. From 1980 to 1989, 134,000 black Africans were admitted into the United States" (p. 82).

In Jamaica, Blacks comprise more than 90 percent of the population and are therefore the majority (Agency 2002). As descendants of Africans, our Africanness surrounds us at every step: we eat, sleep and breathe it. One would be hard-pressed to avoid it. In "The Rhythm of the Caribbean: Connecting Oral History and Literacy," Glasceta Honeyghan (2000) speaks about growing up in Jamaica. She remembers it as a rhythmic experience during which she was constantly surrounded by the rhythm of the village, the rhythm of death, the rhythm at home, the rhythm in church, and the rhythm in school. Even though Caribbean culture is a composite of African and European cultures that have produced a distinctly Caribbean persona, it is the African that dominates. Folklorist and poet Louise Bennett (1995) explains in the local language of Patwa what she identifies as the "real Jamaica language." In an audio rendition, transcribed here, she says, "*When de Asian culture and de European culture buck up pon de African culture in de Caribbean people, we stir dem up an' blend dem to wi flavor. Wi shake dem up an' move dem to our beat, we wheel an' tun dem, an' wi rock dem an' wi soun' dem, an' wi tempa dem, and lawks, di riddim sweet.*" She further explains that the Jamaican language is derived from the English, Portugese and Spanish languages, but "*de basic ting dat we derive from is African. Plenty of de African words dem inna fi wi language whey dem sey a corruption a good, good African wud. Good, good African wud dat come from a nice African language named chwi. Yeah, man, it spell T-w-i but it pronounce chwi*" (Bennett). St. Lucian literature Nobel laureate Derek Walcott (1996) also ascribes to the notion of a "blended" Caribbean consciousness. In "The Muse of History," he concludes that, not because of but in spite of, our terrible history, "What seemed to be surrender was redemption. What seemed the loss of tradition was its renewal. What seemed the death of faith was its rebirth" (Walcott p. 358).

In a 2008 video interview entitled *Jamaica … Some Reflections*, former civil rights activist and former U.S. congressman and mayor of Atlanta, Georgia, Andrew Young;

musician and actor Harry Belanfonte; and South African musician Hugh Masakela gave their impressions on being in Jamaica. Andrew Young comments on the indelible impact a visit to Jamaica in the 1960s had on him: "I was born in the South, and the Caribbean was the first place I had ever been where black people were running anything. It was a thrill to go to Jamaica and see black policemen. We didn't have black policemen in Atlanta then." He also says that Martin Luther King used to go regularly to Jamaica, and wrote most of his books there. Harry Belanfonte, who was born in Harlem to Jamaican parents, recalls migrating to Jamaica with his family when he was only one year old. Belanfonte makes the following comment:

> I always felt that the destiny of Jamaica was inextricably linked to Black America and vice versa, and that fact alone kept me connected. Jamaica's independence [1962] was extremely important to me. In New York City, my mother was a very strong Garveyite. … when I came to Jamaica in that youthful period of my life, Bustamante [then Prime Minister] was very busy giving the British a very difficult time in the rule of the island, and so I was always around an environment that rebelled against its oppression, and that alone gave me linkage. Now, when you talk about the culture and the music and the art, that was so indelible to my experience and became so central to my own cultural expression that there was just no question that I was a Jamaica man and would wind up being that for the rest of my life (Jamaica … Some Reflections, 2008).

Lastly, renowned South African musician Hugh Masakela says while performing in Jamaica, he felt "a sort of spiritual, ancestral ambience" in the environment. He says he could feel the past; he could feel the "Africanness," and that "Jamaica is one of those countries where the African spirit lives forever very intensely (Jamaica … Some Reflections). Caribbean culture, however, is not without its critics. For example, Trinidadian literature Nobel laureate V. S. Naipaul describes Caribbean culture as mere mimicry. W. Pritchard (2009) points out that Naipaul "admitted to the French that *The Mimic Men* was 'an important book for the cultural emptiness in colonial people'" (p. 436).

No matter where Blacks come from, however, be it the Caribbean or Africa, when they get to America they become a minority and must operate within that limiting parameter. No longer do they enjoy the benefits of being the majority culture acting as signifier (the act of defining). They are now the signified (the non-act of being defined). The relationship between signifier and signified is an important one because as Elizabeth

Grosz (1990) states, "the signifier and the signified are ... two hierarchical structured networks in which the signifier always has primacy over the signified" (p. 96).

Friction in the Diaspora

It is obvious that the various slave-holding nations responded in different ways to a free black population; consequently, assimilation progressed in different ways, over different time periods, with different struggles. Although we all came off the same proverbial slave ship, it is this "difference" that has sometimes kept us apart with antagonistic dialogue between what has been defined as African American Blacks and "foreign blacks." It is natural, however, to expect friction among people, no matter who they are and from where they come. Among African Americans, there is the metaphorical house negro and the field negro (Green, 2000); there is a rift between light-skinned Blacks and dark-skinned Blacks (Layng, 2006, pp. 56–58; Breland, 1998, pp. 294–312) there is estrangement between upwardly mobile Blacks and those low on the economic scale (Allen, 1995, pp. 569–592; Cole, & Oman, 2003, p. 785), and there are attitudinal differences between Northern Blacks and Southern Blacks (Tolnay, 1998, pp. 487–514; Tolnay, Vesselinov, & Crowder, 1999, pp. 666–686). Additionally, there is also the cultural barrier between American Blacks and foreign Blacks.

Violet Showers Johnson (2008) eloquently addresses the idea of difference when she speaks of President Barack Obama and the questioning of his African American birthright because he was born to a black Kenyan father and a white American mother. Further, an article published in the *South Florida Sun Sentinel* blares the headlines, "Meaning of 'African-American' Debated: Foreign-born Blacks raise thorny query" in which Rachel Swarns (2006) states the following:

> The prickly question is increasingly being raised as the growing number of foreign-born b[B]lacks in this country inspires a quiet debate over who can claim the term 'African American,' which has rapidly replaced 'b[B]lack' in much of the nation's political and cultural discourse.

Swarns continues saying, "Many argued that the term 'African-American' should refer to the descendants of slaves brought to the United States centuries ago, not to newcomers who have not inherited the legacy of bondage, segregation, and legal discrimination". This assertion, however, that foreign Blacks did not suffer bondage, segregation, and legal discrimination, is inaccurate. To read the 1831 autobiography of Bermudan Mary Prince in *The History of Mary Prince, A West Indian Slave: Related by Herself* is to read the biography of Sojourner Truth, Frederick Douglass, and countless others who suffered greatly at the hands of cruel slave-masters and an unjust system. The stories are the same—our stories begin to diverge, however, when we examine our post-slavery development, as earlier discussed. Paradoxically, if Keyes questions the now President Obama's claims to being African American, Keyes, and others of his ilk, would also have to question the "African Americanness" of Malcolm X, who was born to an African American father and Grenadian mother (Deleon, 1994).

The friction between African Americans and foreign Blacks is exacerbated, however, because of the meeting ground: a racist United States of America. Whites, the economic and political trustees in America, are more accepting of foreign Blacks than they are of their black citizens. One reason Whites may be more "comfortable" with foreign Blacks may be as Johnson (2008) reports in "What then Is the African American?" that "the complicated face of race is lost on many of the post-1965 arrivals who see a post-racial America. Jamaican American scholar Patrick Grant observes that when it comes to race and racism, black immigrants have come to America 'with their eyes wide shut'" (p. 87). However, one should also keep in mind that Caribbean folk have been actively involved in America's pre-1965 struggles to gain racial equality. It was Jamaican born Marcus Garvey who formed the Universal Negro Improvement Association (UNIA) in the 1920s rousing thousands of African Americans to believe in repatriation to Africa and economic independence from white society (Bennett Jr, pp. 328–329). Later, it was Trinidian born Stokely Carmichael (later known as Kwame Toure), another of America's notorious civil rights figures, who "popularized" the Black Power Movement of the 1960s (Hunter).

In her article, Johnson brings up the point that "Convinced of their ability to tap into the social and cultural capital that they bring, black immigrants have relished their ability to 'make it' in America, the 'land of unlimited opportunities'" (p. 87). She also points to the Jamaican poet of the Harlem Renaissance, Claude McKay, and other black immigrants in general who she says, "related how they were treated favorably once they established their foreignness, mainly through their accents and language" (p. 86). There has been payoff, too, for these immigrants. In an article from *The New York Times* entitled "Black incomes surpass [W]hites in Queens," the author points to "the growth of two-parent families and the successes of immigrants from the West Indies" (Roberts). Another article from *The New York Times* reiterates this imbalance between American and foreign Blacks: "Top Colleges Take More Blacks, but Which Ones?" points to the fact that America's Ivy League schools disproportionately admit, "West Indian and African immigrants or their children, or to a lesser extent, children of biracial couples"

(Rimer and Arenson, 2004). Compounding the friction existing between American Blacks and their foreign counterparts are those black immigrants, ignorant of the legacy of slavery and racism in The United States, who blame American Blacks for their position in the American society.

Conclusion

Research abounds concerning migration patterns and assimilation of Caribbean and African peoples in developed countries such as the United States of America and England. A cursory search of academic journals produced a plethora of hits: "The Secret of West Indian Success" by Suzanne Model (2008), "The Mental Health of Black Caribbean Immigrants: Results from the National Survey of American Life" by David R. Williams et al. (2007), "Collecting on their investments, one woman at a time: Economic partnerships among Caribbean immigrant women in the United States" by Dianne M. Stewart (2007), *The Occupational Attainment of Caribbean Immigrants in the United States, Canada, and England* by Toussaint-Comeau, M. (2003), and the list goes on. However, there seems to be a paucity of information regarding African American settlement in developing countries of the Caribbean and Africa. A search provided practically no success in unearthing any research on this matter. In fact, my research on African American migration to the abovementioned territories proved circular, producing the same information as did my search involving Caribbean migration. Although migration from the developed to developing countries is far less than the reverse, it would be interesting to see what impact African Americans who migrate to these developing territories have made in their adopted homelands.

It is my belief that those individuals who voluntarily take the bold step to leave the familiarity of their birth country to settle in foreign lands are uncharacteristically motivated individuals. The psychology of these individuals would also be a fascinating area of research. Writer Colin Channer (2008), himself a Jamaican, speaks to the migratory history of the Jamaican people. He says, "Migration is one of the central themes of Jamaican existence. To be Jamaican means to move—to Panama in the 1920s, to Cuba in the 1930s, to New York in the 1940s, to London and other parts of England in the 1950s, to Canada in the 1960s, to New York and Miami and Hartford, Conn., from the 1970s until now." With the exception of Liberia in the 1800s (Guyutt, 2009, pp. 986–1011), the first large scale African American movement outside the borders of America occurred during World War II when large numbers of African American soldiers were dispatched to Europe. It was a movement that helped to stoke the Civil Rights fire by awakening in the soldiers the possibilities of a less racialized society. Additionally, one needs to take into account the intense societal pressure to succeed that Caribbean immigrants experience when they immigrate, legally or illegally, to the United States. In his very popular song "Deportee/Things Change" *(Germain, Kelly, Myrie, & Charles, 2001, track 7)*, from the album entitled *Ultimate Collection: Buju Banton*, Jamaican dancehall singer Buju Banton derides the illegal immigrant who is deported from the U.S. back to Jamaica with nothing more than with what he had left. Sidney Poitier sums it up best when he explains why it took him eight years before he returned to his homeland of the Bahamas. He says the reason is simple: "In the Bahamas, when you leave for America, you are leaving for a place where the streets are paved in gold. It is expected that you would gather up gold and send it home to help the family in their survival. It seemed to me if you have nothing to put in the envelope, what do you say is your excuse?" (Glass & Lee, 1999). Caribbean peoples who migrate to America are driven because there is a nagging societal conscience demanding success. Anything less is not only failure on a personal level but on a public one as well.

Regardless of how we of the African diaspora have come to see ourselves today, we need to remember our singular past: how we got here. We need to remember this past to understand the divisive forces to which we are still subjected today—we are still trading our sense of brotherhood and sisterhood for the metaphoric tobacco, guns, and liquor of yesteryear when we try to advance at the expense of the other. Knowledge is, indeed, power, and if we put our histories in the proper perspective, we will be better equipped as a people to grapple the fragmenting forces that continue to divide us. No matter what we may think or how we may feel, we must remember who we are and from where we came to fully appreciate the fact that our differences really do bind us.

DISCUSSION QUESTIONS

1. Which of the following perspectives do you think is of greater significance in the formation of one's sense of self: the way in which one views one's self in relation to society, or the way in which one is viewed by society? Explain your answer.

2. Patricia Brown McDonald, the author of the "The Differences That Bind Us," says that in spite of the differences among peoples of the African diaspora, their common ancestral heritage should act as a unifying force to overpower those differences. Do you agree? Why or why not?

y(s) do you think African Americans and Caribbean peoples have
nfluenced each other?

rences do you perceive, if any, between the impact of institutionalized
socialized racism upon the development of a people? Explain your

---

[1] My coinage of the term "New African," is akin to "The New Negro" of the Harlem Renaissance and is here
meant to convey a similar psychological modification/reinvention of self.

# References

A History of the Civil Rights Movement. 1992. Black Americans of achievement. (Video). Wynnewood: Schlessinger Media.

Agency, C. (2002, January). CIA: The World Factbook 2000: Jamaica. CIA World Fact Book, Retrieved September 12, 2009, from History Reference Center database.

Allen, W. (1995, December). African American family life in societal context: crisis and hope. *Sociological Forum, 10*(4), 569–592. Retrieved June 15, 2009, from Academic Search Complete database.

Beckman, J. (2004). Double consciousness. Affirmative action. *The African American Experience,* (1) A-1. Retrieved April 10, 2009 from http://aae.greenwood.com/doc.aspx?i=0&fileID=GR3023& chapterID=GR3023-2177&path=/encyclopedias/greenwood/

Bennett Jr, L. (1988). *Before the Mayflower: A history of black America.* New York: Johnson Publishing Company, Inc.

Bennett, L. (Speaker). (1995). Jamaica language. *Yes m'dear.* (Audio CD). Kingston, Jamaica: Sonic Sounds.

Black, C. (1973). A new history of Jamaica. London: Collins.

Breland, A. (1998, October). A model for differential perceptions of competence based on skin tone among African Americans. *Journal of Multicultural Counseling & Development, 26*(4), 294–312. Retrieved August 10, 2009, from Academic Search Complete database.

Carson, C & P. Holloran, eds. (1998). The American dream. *A knock at midnight: Inspiration from the great sermons of Reverend Martin Luther King, Jr.* New York: IPM/Warner. pp. 91–92.

Channer, C. (2008, August 9). "Cool runnings" are heating up. *The Wall Street Journal.* Retrieved August 12, 2008, from http://online.wsj.com/article_email?SB121823832648825809-lMyQj ...

Cole, E., & Oman, S. (2003, December). Race, class and the dilemmas of upward mobility for African Americans. *Journal of Social Issues, 59*(4), 785. Retrieved May 9, 2009.

Deleon, D., ed. (1994). Malcolm X (El-Hajj Malik El-Shabazz) (Malcolm Little) 1925–1965. Leaders from the 1960s, A biographical sourcebook of American activism. *The African American Experience.* Retrieved 2 March 2009 from http://aae.greenwood.com/doc.aspx?fileID=DCDP& chapterID=DCDP-2&path=/chunkbook//

Elwood, W. (Producer/Director), & Kulish, M. (Director). (1990). *The road to Brown.* [Motion picture]. United States: California Newsreel.

Gates Jr., H. L. & McKay, N. Y. (Eds.). (2004). "Ida B. Wells Barnett." *The Norton Anthology of African American Literature.* New York: Norton. 675–686.

Germain, D., Kelly, D., Myrie, M., and Charles Von Wayne. (1993). Deportees (Things Change). [Recorded by Buju Banton]. On *Ultimate collection: Buju Banton* [CD]. California: Universal Music Enterprises. (2001).

Glass, P. (Writer), & Lee, G. (Director). (1999). Sidney Poitier: One bright light [Television series episode]. In Lacy, S. (Executive Producer), American masters. New York: Thirteen/WNET.

Green, J. (2000, January). A life of slavery. We came to North America: The Africans. Retrieved September 10, 2009, from History Reference Center database.

Grosz, E. (1990). *Jacques Lacan. A Feminist Introduction.* Routledge: New York.

Guyutt, N. (2009, March). The outskirts of our happiness: Race and the lure of colonization in the early republic. *Journal of American History, 95*(4), 986–1011. Retrieved September 12, 2009, from History Reference Center database.

Honeyghan, G. (2000, May). The rhythm of the Caribbean: Connecting oral history and literacy. *Language Arts, 77*(5), 406–413.

Hunter, E. (2006, January). Stokely Carmichael. Retrieved September 11, 2009, from History Reference Center database.

Jamaica … Some Reflections. (2008). Retrieved March 9, 2009, from http://www.youtube.com/watch?v=y7kmTGhkB-w.

Johnson, V. (2008). "What, then, is the African American?" African and Afro-Caribbean identities in Black America. *Journal of American Ethnic History, 28*(1), 77–103.

Layng, A. (2006, March). Color counts. *USA Today Magazine*, pp. 56–58. Retrieved February 23, 2009, from Academic Search Complete database.

Model, S. (2008, November). The secret of West Indian success. *Society, 45*(6), 544–548. Retrieved September 10, 2009, from Academic Search Complete database.

On hold: Asian, Hispanic growth in the U. S. (2009, May 13). MSNBC.com. Retrieved May 13, 2009, from http://www.msnbc.com/id/30732546/print/1displaymode/1098

Pritchard, W. (2009). Naipaul unveiled. *Hudson Review, 61*(4), 431–440.

Rimer, S., and K. Arenson. (2004, June 24). Top colleges take more blacks, but which ones? *The New York Times*, p. 24A

Roberts, S. (2006, October 1). Black incomes surpass whites in Queens. *The New York Times*. Retrieved October 6, 2006, from http://www.nytimes.com/2006/10/01/nyregion/01census.html?_r=1&ex=1160366400&en=8facf724d6a80add&ei=5070&emc=eta1.

Stewart, D. (2007, January). Collecting on their investments, one woman at a time: Economic partnerships among Caribbean immigrant women in the United States. *International Journal of African Renaissance Studies, 2*(1), 35–57. Retrieved September 11, 2009.

Swarns, R. (2006). Meaning of "African-American" debated. South Florida Sun-Sentinel. Retrieved March 13, 2010 from http://iw.newsbank.com/iw-search/we/InfoWeb.

Tolnay, S. (1998, December). Educational selection in the migration of Southern Blacks, 1880–1990. *Social Forces, 77*(2), 487–514. Retrieved January 18, 2009, from Academic Search Complete database.

Tolnay, S., Vesselinov, E., & Crowder, K. (1999, December). The collective impact of Southern migrants on the economic well-being of Northern-born black males, 1970. *Social Science*

Quarterly (University of Texas Press), *80*(4), 666–686. Retrieved September 10, 2009, from Academic Search Complete database.

Toussaint-Comeau, M. (2003, Spring). The occupational attainment of Caribbean immigrants in the United States, Canada, and England. *Journal of American Ethnic History, 22*(3), 98. Retrieved September 11, 2009, from Academic Search Complete database.

Walcott, D. (1996). The muse of history. In A. Donnell & S. L. Welch (Eds.), *The Routledge Reader in Caribbean Literature* (pp. 354–358). New York: Routledge.

Williams, D., Haile, R., Neighbors, H., González, H., Baser, R., & Jackson, J. (2007, January). The mental health of Black Caribbean immigrants: results from the national survey of American life. *American Journal of Public Health, 97*(1), 52–59. Retrieved September 11, 2009.

3

The Mis-Education of Race: Communication, Coding, and the Illogic of the Current Approach

Michele S. Foss-Snowden

Abstract

In 1993, *Time* magazine created a digital cover model, a composite of the world's ethnicities (Gaines, 1993). They called her "The New Face of America," implying that growing minority populations have blended with the primarily European "face" of the United States, resulting in a browning of the average resident. It would be impossible to accurately determine the model's ethnic background just by looking at her, but the impossibility did not stop many who gazed at the magazine's cover from assigning a race to the woman who did not exist. Assigning race to a subject in a study or experiment is referred to as racial coding. This essay proposes a number of changes to the current model of racial coding, working from the perspective that in certain education arenas, race has shaken off its widely agreed upon designation as *social* construct and has regressed into being a *biological* construct, which was a reality of the overtly biased past. A better understanding of the nature of race and mixed race, racial identity, and interracial communication within the frame of communication education allows the next generation of race-based research to move closer to some form of modern social truth.

KEY TERMS: mixed race, multiracial, Other, racial coding, race-based research

Introduction

Many rhetorical and philosophical battles about race have been waged and won. Scholars no longer need to argue that race is at least partially a social construction (instead of a solely biological one). The United States Federal Government, when creating definitions of race for the 2000 Census, created categories that "generally reflect a social definition of race recognized in this country. They do not conform to any biological, anthropological, or genetic criteria" (U.S. Census, 2001). No researcher worth the weight of her literature review contests the notion that, although the phenotypical, or physical traits associated with race might be passed from parent to child, the full meaning or reality of race cannot be found beneath the lens of a microscope. Academics (scholars and college teachers) seem to have reached consensus across their varied disciplines: the study of race and ethnicity is a humanistic endeavor, or a social scientific pursuit at best. The academic community has been vocal about its agreement. The notion of race as a social construction has crossed academic borders and reached the mainstream. Mark P. Orbe (2008), a scholar of interracial communication, says that during his college years he became a member of a predominantly African American fraternity, yet he does not mention needing to provide proof of African American blood or any amount of genetic material from an African ancestor before he was granted membership. According to Harvard professor Stephan Thernstrom, a white parent can have a black child but the reverse, a black parent with a white child, is impossible (2000). A popular understanding of race as a biological construct should bring out the skeptic or the critic in any audience, yet these statements meet little (if any) resistance. To scholars and the general public alike, the idea of race as a biological construct is dying (Provine, 1973). Or is it?

In 1993, *Time* magazine created a digital cover model, a composite of the world's ethnicities (Gaines, 1993). They called her "The New Face of America," implying that growing minority populations have blended with the primarily European "face" of the United States, resulting in a browning of the average resident. Though managing editor Jim Gaines, in the introduction to the special issue, warned readers that the "beguiling if mysterious" cover model existed only metaphysically (Hammonds, 1997, p. 113), many who looked at the invented model thought she looked real enough. Her appearance resembled millions of real women of Latin, African, Southern European, Native American, or mixed ethnic ancestry. It would be impossible to accurately determine the model's ethnic background without the cover story or just by looking at her. Yet, the discussion about *Time*'s "New Eve" continued as if, like New Eve, actual humans could be broken down into percentage points, like a hybrid plant or a cooking recipe. Critics of New Eve's creation argued that "to most Americans, race is embodied and, even with racial mixing, the existence of primary races is as obvious as the existence of primary colors in the Crayola crayon palette" (Hammonds, 1997, p. 118). So, while the popular press gave itself a pat on the back for a multicultural job well done, those in the academy shrugged their shoulders and went back to the work of dismantling more than a century's worth of racial ignorance.

The academy has made and is continuing to make progress on this front, but the academic community is also experiencing collective selective amnesia about the death of race as a biological construct, especially as a construct that can be quantified or observed. Scholars of all levels, in all disciplines, continue to conduct studies about race based on the idea that one can determine or assign the race of an individual in a glance. When a glance is not enough, we seem unbothered by relying on the racial default position: "Other." In one moment, we will argue that there are significant differences between a person who identifies as an African living in the United States and a person who identifies as an African American. We will argue that giving both of these people the label of "Black" tells only part of the story. With the very next breath, we will conduct our studies using traditional methods of coding for race. This duplicity is illogical, and it damages our credibility as a critical community.

This essay proposes two important changes to the current model of racial coding, working from the perspective that visual assignment of race will always produce either inaccuracy and errors, or an increase in the use of the term "Other" as a catch-all category at best (or a surrender to hegemony at worst). The first change involves adjusting the level of importance placed on accurate or "correct" racial labels; the second and more difficult change would require communication researchers interested in race to agree to early retirement for a category often referred to as ("Other") that, in this author's opinion, has worn out its welcome. In order to understand the need for these changes, this chapter must begin by discussing race-based research in general and then racial research specific to the field of communication. The argument will then focus on the problem of accuracy and the lack of logic in the current approach before arriving at the suggested changes.

Racial Research

While the current approach to race-based research has its flaws, the great tragedy would be a solution calling for the elimination of all such research. Halting all research on race until we can figure out how to do it the "right way" cannot be the answer. The social benefits that come from educated people asking and answering the right questions about race are many. Race sits at the head of the table when we all sit down to discuss why we can't just get along. Most (if not all) modern research about race comes from a desire for the same goal: cracking the race code and figuring it all out in order to have an improved society. However, our current path is forked, and the time has come for us to reevaluate our strategy to attain this goal. According to Omi and Winant (1994), race-based research has the responsibility to challenge what came before it when the old theories no longer explain the changing nature of race in the present. Our current and future research on race must reflect a progressive understanding about mixed race, identity development, and appearance, or we run the risk of sliding back into the kind of research that supported our nation's least proud moments.

The focus here is on race research and communication, but a similar racial "mis-education" is taking place across the academy. In medicine or human biology, certain diseases or disorders are linked with one race over another. For example, according to the National Marrow Donor Program (NMDP), race and ethnicity are very important in matching a bone marrow donor to a patient, and donors of color, including "mixed heritage" donors, are especially needed (National Marrow Donation Program, 2008). Should a hard science application, like medicine, be based on a socially constructed scientific designation such as race? What if a student with very fair skin and blue eyes, raised by adopted European American parents, noted her European American ancestry on her bone marrow donor information sheet? She might not have known that her birth parents were both fair skinned, like our donor, but they identified as African American. Several researchers (e.g. Nei & Roychoudhury, 1993; Andreasen, 2000) recognize that there is considerable genetic diversity within racial categories, just as there is between them, making lighter skin completely possible within the African American population. The well-intentioned NMDP request for mixed heritage donors would miss our student donor. If race is scientifically inadequate as a genetic variable (Hunt & Megyesi, 2008) why continue to use it, and why continue to apply the results of studies that use it to a population that does not and cannot mirror the distinct categories used in the creation of the study?

The social sciences and humanities face their own challenges. Anthropologists and psychologists endure a love/hate relationship with race (it explains everything and nothing, all at the same time) while legal scholars and those who study criminal and political science have the added burden of enforcing the inequality. Perhaps illogical race research in communication is the most alarming because of its connection to other fields. It is because of communication that we learn about race research in many other fields, either through traditional reports and presentations, or through fictional re-creations of the material in scripted and performed programming. Thus, changing the approach to research (and coding, specifically) for race in communication might blaze a trail for other disciplines to follow.

Racial Research and Communication

In teaching communication research methods, especially in mass communication (including advertising, journalism, film or television studies), students who are interested in race often provide or create coding sheets that use standard indications similar to those used by the U.S. Government (www.census.gov): black (or African American), white (or Caucasian), Asian or Pacific Islander, Hispanic/Latino, and so on. Professors and students use similar tools in their research, but no one prioritizes the consideration of how we come to assign an individual to each of these racial categories.

Perhaps a researcher wants to examine characterizations of mixed race in Spike Lee films, and perhaps this researcher has a hypothesis that characters of mixed race are marginalized in the story. So, the researcher views a given film, searching for those characters of mixed race. If the researcher observes a character in the film with deep brown skin, she might code this person as monoracial (or representative of only one racial/ethnic group). Then, the character speaks a line, in Spanish. Should the researcher now code this character as mixed race (looking one way and sounding another)? Does the researcher need to create a new category for characters representing countries where the majority of the population is multiethnic (such as many Caribbean, Central, and South American countries)? Does the researcher keep this character in the monoracial category and decide to avoid coding for language? Should the researcher examine the script for clues about the character's ethnicity left by the writer or hope that the director spoke to the matter in an interview? Of course, our researcher might wish to avoid the inevitable bias that would come with knowing the filmmaker's intent. Each decision this researcher could make would only lead to another question; we start to see how deep this rabbit hole goes.

If we use actor Halle Berry as an example, we would face little debate for coding her as Black (much ado was made in 2002 about her being the first African American female to win an Academy Award in a leading role). As a person, she seems to identify as African American, but she has always been very open about the fact that her mother is European American (Dagbovie, 2007). Do we or should we concern ourselves with the way the actor (not the character) identifies, especially when it might represent our one chance at accuracy? What if this actor's self-identification is false or incomplete, due to political, economic, or personal reasons, or perhaps to a lack of knowledge? When it comes to race, do public figures give up any expectation of a separation of fiction (character) and fact (actor)? Or, are we polluting our results by incorporating information from outside of a given narrative? In other words, as researchers, should we not focus on the artistic and deliberate creation of the character within the narrative, instead of the identification of the actor?

If, for the sake of accuracy, we agree to consider the ethnic background of the actor as a determining factor, especially since our natural curiosity for race and fascination with mixed race will likely cause us to seek out this information anyway, what do we make of the nameless model or extra in a commercial or an establishing shot? What do we do with non-famous individuals appearing in reality-based, news, or sports communication outlets? Race appears outside of fame-defined borders, and as such, studies about race in these non-celebrity locations need the most adjustment; these studies lose the one method (regardless of the *quality* of the method) of gaining accuracy in racial assignment. In the vast majority of research locations, the racial background search is either impossible or far too cumbersome to be realistic for our agendas.

One possible solution to the "coding for race" problem could be to place multiple coders at work on the project, but this answer is a result of oversimplification (Glascock, 2003). Five coders working on a project satisfy most critics, but a scholar could train and employ hundreds of coders and reach compelling reliability statistics, and the only thing that scholar would have proved is that we in the United States have been taught that we can identify someone's race just by looking at that person. This incomplete racial education has been very effective, and when questions arise, we have been encouraged to accept "Other" as a default category. Unfortunately, "Other" is not and has never been an acceptable label for the ethnically ambiguous. Creating a category to hold the unidentifiable or undesirable establishes an unnatural separation between dominant and subordinate (Spickard, 1992). Accepting the Other category "makes it easier for the dominators to ignore the individual humanity of their victims" (Spickard, 1992, p. 19). In a hegemonic twist, researchers that accept Othering are actually damaging the exact communities they are likely trying to elevate and advance.

It is interesting to note that scholars will use elaborate multiple point scales to assess characteristics such as attractiveness or body type (Mastro & Stern, 2003), but will offer no such complexity in their description of racial coding. When descriptions of the racial coding process are offered, all indicators suffer from the same problem. For example, in an examination of race and portrayals of crime in television network news, Dixon, Azocar and Casas (2003) offered the following description: "The following apparent race indicators were used to assess the race of perpetrators and victims: 1) shown on videotape, 2) mug shot shown, 3) artist's sketch shown, 4) photo shown, and 5) race is stated"

(p. 507). The authors also used variables (such as surname) to infer racial category when no apparent indicators were available (Dixon, Azocar, & Casas, 2003). Researchers who use these "apparent" race indicators fail to recognize the impossibility of accuracy inherent in such indicators (Harrison, 2006). When I look at you and attempt to assign your race, whether I am looking at you face-to-face, you on videotape, a photograph of you, or an artist's sketch of you, I am relying on stereotype and nineteenth-century racial logic. I am following every line of the one-drop rule (if I see even the slightest suggestion of what I have decided are racial indicators, such as hair type, skin color, or facial features, I will decide that the presence of even a drop of the race that curled your hair or shaped your eyes or darkened your skin will be enough to earn your membership in that racial group). And, the Other option is still present. As offensive as it should be, it remains, frequent, unquestioned, and overused.

Nakashima argues that "multiracial/multiethnic people navigate a racial existence where, in some instances, they identify themselves and their ethnicity to others—and in other instances, people classify them with no real interest in how they identify themselves" (2001, p. 115). A similar situation appears in research about racial existence: because multiracial people exist, visual coding for race can only be incomplete at best, and wholly inaccurate at worst.

Inaccuracy, Illogic, and the Current Approach

The current approach to communication research on race operates under the assumption that race can be observed, which is a scientific and biological notion. Today's racial coding follows one of two paths: A) mixed race is a myth or a non-factor, or B) mixed race is the Other. To follow the first path is to deny what cannot be denied. As long as there have been people, there have been multiracial people. The unique experiences of people who could belong to more than one race/culture/ethnicity cannot be ignored, which means that ANY research on race that improperly handles mixed race falls short. One might suggest that a simple inclusion of a mixed race category could alleviate if not fix the problems on this first path. A researcher could use contextual clues (remembering to stay within the confines of the narrative) to determine the necessity of a mixed race category. Unfortunately, this solution does nothing to address the problem of inaccuracy. It is more inclusive than the current approach, but inclusivity without accuracy surely lacks the appeal it would need in order to be successful as a common research practice.

To follow the second path is, as stated above, adding another hegemonic brick to the barrier between the dominant group and other co-cultural groups in society.

In order to maintain the status quo, the dominant group in society needs to convince the subordinate groups of the validity of the racial hierarchy, which needs little additional description due to the very effective mis-education (Woodson, 1933) of race in the United States. The creation of a new group, the Other, solidifies the hierarchy as the co-cultural groups mistakenly feel elevated and relatively dominant over the racial/cultural groups who are arguably too low on the hierarchy to merit an actual recognized label. The Other rests on the rung lower than the lowest on the racial ladder. The non-Other receives an artificial promotion. Surely, modern scholars who choose to study race seek the counter-hegemonic; ANY research that perpetuates the Other also falls short.

A Change is Gonna Come

It is quite possible that most of the problem on the first path is caused by the scientific need for accuracy. In the kinds of research described here, accuracy is an impossible goal to reach. In order to conduct communication research with a focus on visual identification of race and racial representation, we must discard our (quantitative) need for accurate results. It is not reasonable to assume any level of accuracy. So, if we cannot offer accuracy, do we automatically invalidate this kind of research? Do changes to the current model mean that, since accuracy is no longer possible, research about race is no longer needed? Is denying accuracy equal to embracing the "melting pot" metaphor (we are all blended together)? The answer may lie in changing how we feel about the need for accuracy. Perhaps we can approach all racial research (especially or at least in communication) with a caveat: we cannot offer accuracy (which damages a quantitative study much more so than a qualitative one), but we can offer one researcher's assumption or perception. Should a researcher still decide to include a mixed race category, this caveat would keep the results honest and socially just.

The problem with research that follows the second path is not as easy to fix. Eliminating the Other from racial research would require a paradigm shift for the ages. Other-ing racial groups pre-dates research about mixed race, but the mixed race community has surely worn the Other label. Recent movements in national understanding of race and mixed-race (for example, the election of our first mixed race President of the United States) suggest that this second solution might not be as out of reach as we thought. Perhaps race researchers will soon agree to see what they previously ignored, to include what they previously excluded, and to advance the body of knowledge in a way that benefits us all.

DISCUSSION QUESTIONS

1. According to Foss-Snowden, the way researchers classify race is erroneous because it is illogical. What are her reasons for this claim? Do you agree or disagree?

2. Can you identify examples in advertising where racial diversity is featured more often today than in the past? Examples in film and television programming? Is the race of models/actors in these programs usually easy to determine? How important is that knowledge to you, as a viewer?

3. The author offers two alternative changes to the current system for visual race coding in the section "A Change is Gonna Come." In your opinion what groups might support her suggestions? Which groups might resist them? Are there potential negative consequences for adopting the proposed changes?

4. Foss-Snowden argues that the second solution to improving research on race in communication—eliminating the "Other" racial category—is the more difficult to accomplish. Why does the author suggest this is so? Do you agree or disagree?

References

Andreasen, R. O. (2000). Race: Biological Reality or Social Construct? *Philosophy of Science, 67* (Supplement): 653–666.

Dagbovie, S. (2007). Star-Light, Star-Bright, Star Damn Near White: Mixed Race Superstars. *Journal of Popular Culture, 40*(2): 217–237.

Davis, F. J. (1996). *Who is Black? One Nation's Definition.* University Park, PA: The Pennsylvania State University Press.

Dixon, T., Azocar, C. L., & Casas, M. (2003). The Portrayal of Race and Crime on Television Network News. *Journal of Broadcasting & Electronic Media, 47*(4): 498–523.

Gaines, J (Ed.). (1993, November 18). The New Face of America: How Immigrants Are Shaping the World's First Multicultural Society (cover). *Time, 142*(21).

Glascock, J. (2003). Gender, Race, and Aggression in Newer TV Networks' Primetime Programming. *Communication Quarterly, 51*(1): 90–100.

Hammonds, E. (1997). New Technologies of Race. In J. Terry & M. Calvert (Eds.), *Processed Lives: Gender and Technology in Everyday Life.* [pp.?] London and New York: Routledge.

Harrison, K. (2006). Fast and Sweet: Nutritional Attributes of Television Food Advertisements With and Without Black Characters. *The Howard Journal of Communications, 17*: 249–264.

Hunt, L. M., and Megyesi, M. S. (2008, June 1). Genes, race and research ethics: Who's minding the store? *Journal of Medical Ethics, 34*(6): 495–500.

Mastro, D. E., & Stern, S. R. (2003). Representations of Race in Television Commercials: A Content Analysis of Prime-Time Advertising. *Journal of Broadcasting & Electronic Media, 47*(4): 638–647.

Nakashima, D. (2001). A Rose by Any Other Name: Names, Multiracial/Multiethnic People, and the Politics of Identity. In T. Williams-León & C. Nakashima (Eds.), *The Sum of Our Parts: Mixed Heritage Asian Americans.* Philadelphia: Temple University Press.

National Marrow Donor Program. (2008). FAQs about joining the registry [On-line]. Retrieved March 20, 2009, from http://www.marrow.org/HELP/Join_the_Donor_Registry/FAQs_about_Joining_the_Registry/index.html#race.

Nei, M., Roychoudhury, A. K. (1993). Evolutionary Relaionships of Human Populations on a Global Scale. *Molecular Biology and Evolution, 10*(5): 927–943.

Omi, M., & Winant, H. (1994). *Racial Formation in the United States.* London and New York: Routledge.

Orbe, M. P., & Harris, T. M. (2008). *Interracial Communication: Theory into Practice.* Los Angeles, Sage Publications.

Provine, W. B. (1973). Geneticists and the biology of race crossing. *Science, 182*: 790–796.

Spickard, P. (1992). The Illogic of American Racial Categories. In M. P. P. Root (Ed.), *Racially Mixed People in America*. Newbury Park, CA: Sage Publications.

Thernstrom, S. (2000). New Life for the "One Drop" Rule [On-line]. Retrieved March 29, 2009, from http://www.tysknews.com/Depts/Constitution_Issues/one_drop_rule.htm.

United States Census Bureau. (2001). Questions and Answers for Census 2000 Data on Race [On-line]. Retrieved September 17, 2009, from http://www.census.gov/Press-Release/www/2001/raceqandas.html.

Woodson, C. G. (1933). *The Mis-education of the Negro*. Washington, D.C.: Associated Publishers.

4

Conformed and Disrupted Black Bodies in Intraracial Interactions: Deliberations on the Wearing of Natural Hair

Sakile K. Camara

Abstract

Hair, like skin color, is a social marker that distinguishes Blacks from others and has essentially functioned as a way to position some in the racial group outside the sanctified realm of beauty and acceptance that has existed since slavery. This chapter explores the ways in which African Americans experience and think about wearing natural hair. Two critical questions are explored: (1) What impact does the choice to wear natural hair have upon the individual and upon the individual's intraracial relationship with members of her/his racial group? and (2) How are these preferences for a conformed (straightened hair) or disrupted (natural hair) physical appearance articulated through intraracial interactions? The following narratives on natural hair resonate from myriad centers of intraracially defined, and self-positioned, black bodies.

KEY TERMS: natural hair, intraracial interaction, black body politics

Introduction

Hair, like skin color, is a social marker that distinguishes Blacks from others and has essentially functioned as a way to position some outside the sanctified realm of beauty and acceptance since slavery. Thus, natural hair, like black skin is devalued (Mercer, 1987; Shane, 1996). Natural hair, as spoken in the black community, is the same as "nappy hair," but technically denotes the non-use of chemical agents to straighten or change the biological texture of the hair—as a specification of rupture or a principle for challenging mainstream images of beauty. Natural hair for Blacks, especially black women, is therefore conflicting. It functions as a symbol of liberation and freedom as well as social and political marginalization (hooks, 1992; Magubane, 2007)—it is a personal and public matter, which concerns the intersection of race, gender and culture. In an interview April 13, 2007 on National Public Radio (NPR), Rosario Schuler, owner of Oh My Nappy Hair Salon, suggests that the word "nappy hair" is not an offensive expression except when used as an adjective to a negative. However, when I was growing up, calling someone "nappy headed" was insulting and grounds for fighting.

In 2007, radio personality Don Imus experienced how offensive the term could be when he was temporarily fired after referencing the Rutgers' women's basketball team as "nappy-headed hos" after they lost the NCAA championship game. His comment stirred up controversy that was particularly problematic for the black community. The first, and most obvious reason for the controversy as suggested by Schuler (2007) in her interview on NPR is that Imus, a privileged white male used "nappy hair" as an adjective to a negative. Imus's comment separated the black players from the white players on the team. This divisiveness symbolized, when prescribed by outsiders publicly, that Blacks have not moved from their subject positioning. The comment represents the dilemma that Blacks historically and presently face in fitting into the social culture of everyday life (Ferguson, 2007). Whether we want to believe it or not, black hair perpetuates the domination of subordinated racial and gendered groups (Caldwell, 1997), and is what Gaskin calls a cesspool of racial politics that has historical and long-term consequences for the black body (1996). Blacks who wear natural "nappy" hair (i.e., afros, locks, twist, and other hairstyles without the use of chemical agents) are conceptually and visually impaired in mainstream society, which means they become disrupted black bodies. A disrupted black body refers to the things (i.e., hair, skin color, shape of nose and body) that distinguish black people from other people, resulting in heightened identification or self-denigration (Morrison, 1981) and resulting from social, economic, and political seclusion. When compared to the white ideal of beauty, natural hair exists in an uneasy coexistence (Ashe, 1995) and is yet another reminder that long flowing hair represents a conformed black body—a body manipulated through the use of hair straightening agents, skin-lightening cremes, and plastic surgery in order to be socially acceptable to the majority. This kind of change is partially related to deflecting one's own racial identification, yet emphasizes how social and cultural ideas of beauty are further transmitted through the body beyond skin color.

Second, the Imus comment was a put-down of Black women and was deeply offensive to those like Renee Ferguson, a 2007 Nieman Fellow and investigative reporter for

WMAQ TV, NBC-5 in Chicago, Illinois, who had emotionally liberated herself from being judged by what was occurring on the outside of her head rather than what was going on inside her head (2007). In early American history, black skin and coarse hair marked slaves as unintelligent and unattractive (Morrow, 1973). If a slave could pass as White, the kink of the hair was the true test of blackness; therefore, runaway slaves, who could pass for White, cut their hair to liberate themselves from bondage (Byrd & Tharps, 2001). Byrd and Tharps (2001) and Walker (2007), articulate that many Blacks embraced their natural hair during the "Black Power" and "Black is Beautiful" era in the late 1960s and 1970s. This time period not only demonstrated freedom, but a black consciousness and identity untainted by majority views. Griffin (1996) and Lee (1996) contend that African American literature also theorizes about the black body through literary work (*Annie Allen, Is your hair still political*, and *Zami*), neo-slave narratives (*Beloved* and *Dessa Rose*), poetry, narratives and film (*For colored girls who considered suicide, Nappy edges, Tenderheaded*, and *School Daze*), and folklore (*Sula, The bluest eye, Song of Solomon, Tar baby, Passing*) as a means of raising consciousness. Imus' comments were a big deal because they transcend aesthetic issues to suggest that black hair represents self-struggles socially, politically, and historically (Banks, 2000; Shukra, 1995; Simkins, 1990).

Lastly, Imus placed the phrase "nappy head," a private context for Blacks, in the streets for public review; he exposed the deep connection that Blacks have with the residual effects of racial superiority, which is materialized through the dialectics or tensions of good hair versus bad hair. Many scholars locate the origin of the good hair/bad hair argument in the days of and following slavery (Byrd & Tharp, 2001; Little, 1996; Morrow, 1973). Byrd and Tharp (2001) note that there was a "skin-shade, hair-texture hierarchy developed within the social structure of the slave community" (p. 19) reinforced by slave masters who divided slave labor (house slaves vs. field slaves) on the basis of skin tone and hair texture. Additionally, house slaves could be sold for five times more than a field slave. As a result, Blacks have battled this ideology for decades within their own community and this is the subtext that surrounds Imus's comments.

The purpose of this study is to understand a unique, but not-so-unique experience related to personal philosophies of natural hair in intraracial interactions. Intraracial interactions refer to ongoing dialogues within a specific racial community on specific topics that are multi-layered and complicated. This means the topic under discussion isn't an easy task, but it is surrounded by an abundance of factors that cannot be easily unveiled or understood. What makes this study not-so-unique is that Blacks are not the only people with natural hair, nor do they have a particular epistemology or learning patterns of experiences related to natural hair (Weitz, 2004). What is unique and perhaps more appealing is the role being played out by members who belong to the same community (intraracial interactions). The center of the discussion is on how Blacks uniquely impose a white standard of beauty on other Blacks, which is missing from discussions on natural hair.

These findings are an attempt to become conscious of how intraracial experiences play a role in understanding the ways that individuals describe the wearing of natural hair. They reveal that black men and women who wear natural hair are often confronted with estrangement from, and mandates by, primary association groups such as family, friends, and peers to accept a body aesthetic. This body aesthetic is dissonant to their own bodies, thereby conforming to an unattainable body. Data were drawn from videotaped interviews and focus group discussions collected in 1997, and these collected interviews will serve as data for investigating the disruption of black bodies in intraracial communication interactions. In particular, I was seeking to examine the following research questions: How do African Americans describe their experiences of wearing natural hair? What does natural hair signify? Given the exploratory nature of this line of research, an inductive methodological approach–like that which is inherent to phenomenology–was enacted. These methods assume a first-person point-of-view of how a person relates to the lived world that she or he inhabits (Lanigan, 1988) and follow a three-step process (Nelson, 1989).

First, data were collected from interviews with forty African Americans (thirty females and ten males) in fourteen personal interviews and two focus group discussions. Participants for this study were drawn from a large Midwestern community through nonprobability sampling methods. Recruitment was conducted by strategically placing fliers about the study on local college campuses, majority black communities, through word-of-mouth, and a local, black audience radio station. After receiving permission to solicit participants from business owners, a set number of individuals were interviewed and two focus groups were conducted. Fourteen separate individual interviews were conducted and two focus groups were formed, with a total of twenty-six participants. All interviews were video recorded face-to-face and transcribed later for analysis. All interviews were led by the author, who asked general questions concerning what they thought about the wearing of natural hair, and their personal experiences with natural hair. A questionnaire was used to gather demographic information including age, race, and education level. Participant ages ranged between 18 and 52, with a mean age of twenty-six. All individuals self-identified as African American with 78 percent (n = 27) reporting they had a college education, and 22 percent (n = 13) with no college experience. The second step involved a reduction of descriptions of lived experience into essential themes. The third stage centered on producing an interpretation of themes.

Thematic Insights: Understanding Conformed and Disrupted Black Bodies

Descriptions of intraracial encounters provided substantial insight to the realities of black body politics—how black bodies are portrayed, represented, socially constructed, and constituted at the institutional level (i.e., media) that manifest itself at the micro-level—interactions with others. The crux of this analysis focuses on how participants perceive natural hair and how that perception is disrupted through experiences of wearing natural hair. In particular, I explicate three essential themes with their sub-themes: (1) Hair style versus hair statement, including the sub-themes "personal choice," "cultural affirmation," and "signs of resistance"; (2) Natural hair in captivity, which includes sub-themes "ascribed passé and African identities," and "attributes of social class"; and (3) The disposability of black bodies, including the sub-themes undesirable and unfeminine.

Hair Style versus Hair Statement

One theme that emerged from this phenomenological inquiry focused on natural hair as just a hair style and the significance of natural hair as (1) personal choice, (2) cultural affirmation, (3) signs of resistance. From the perspective of participants, natural hair transcended the problems Blacks face in defining a black identity, to affirming a sense of ethnic pride, authenticity, independence, and personal choice. One black male, for instance, stated:

> When I think of natural hair I think of freedom and pride. Black people in general spend an inordinate amount of money on hair care products and it seems natural; it seems correct. They have a sense of who they are and where they come from and that makes me feel good.

Another black male described what natural hair signified for him. He states "It makes me think that they [natural hair wearers] are confident. That they are natural and more beautiful." In other interviews, such as one involving a young black female with natural hair, more points of cultural affirmation are discussed:

> I also think that it is a pride thing because I know that generally it [natural hair] is going against the images you see portrayed in the media. You can go to any magazine rack and when you flip through you don't see too much of that. You see processed hair. You see blondes and things like that.

An older black male echoes a similar statement when he suggests that the natural black body is a sign of resistance. He states, "Oh, I love it. I love it. I think it brings more independence, and strong willedness. They are not caught up in the system. [They are] going back to the Afro thing."

Although the natural black body was not interpreted as opposing straightened hair, discussion about the meaning of it went on. One female with natural hair regards the choice of wearing natural hair or straightened hair as creative and individualistic:

> I think it's great that they [straightened hair wearers] want to have their own style. I think it looks fine. If that's what they want to do, that's fine. It is individuality. I would want anyone to have the freedom of having their own creative style whether it's natural or unnatural. What that says to me is do you understand who you are? Are you doing that because you don't want to be Black, or are you doing that because that's just your style? Do you tell people that that is a weave in your hair or are you trying to fake it some how?

A female with straightened hair focuses on making her hair easier to comb, "I can't deal with the thickness of my hair and this [straightened/permed hair] is more manageable. I don't think that the natural hair style would fit me."

These examples highlight several key factors about how natural hair is perceived. First, most respondents suggested that the natural black body is about connecting to "blackness" or to a community of worldwide oppressed and stigmatized bodies. Anything that disrupts the standard is ridiculed and must be strong to survive it. In other words, natural hair is a developed sense of self-confidence, power, and consciousness. Second, natural hair is a sign of resistance—trying to exist within the dominant system and to maintain a cultural and unique self. Respondents noted that the natural black body is in a system that says you must conform to a particular beauty standard, and retaining your natural structure is therefore necessary for acceptance or success. This is apparent in the response "natural hair goes against the existing system." Third, wearing either the natural hair style or straightened hair is individually motivated rather than socially motivated. In other words, it's a matter of choice in how individuals wear their hair. Accordingly, participants related hair to the style of dress that "changes with the wind." Individuals were seemingly in touch with diverse spheres of the black community, and perceived either style as a factor of personal difference. Not surprisingly, the pride and beauty discussed in the aforementioned narratives are not apparent in the experiences of natural hair wearers in the next thematic insight.

Natural Hair in Captivity

Although the natural body is liberating to the wearer in one sense, it is confining in another. Accordingly, individuals who wore natural hair often faced strong reactions because their hair was misperceived as passing for some other cultural group or lacking class status. This section explicates different sub-themes including (1) ascribed *passé* and African identities, and (2) attributes of class based on or nurtured in internalized prejudice. For instance, several women and men related stories of ascribed *passé* recalling how others had mistakenly assigned them to a certain racial-ethnic group because of the texture of their hair (e.g., "You got some Indian in your family?", "You Puerto Rican or something"). A black female recounted this experience when she straightened her hair:

> A brotha walked up to me one day and said, 'How did you get hair like that. Black people don't have hair like that.' I said, 'Excuse me? I was born with hair like this.' That was when I thought about wearing my hair natural. I had more questions when I had relaxed hair. Those were the most hurtful things I've heard. I'm either not supposed to have hair like this or something is in my hair.

The notion of good hair appeared to be rooted in biology and ethnicity outside of a black cultural identity. The implication is that the kink is vital to one's blackness. Anything outside of that must come from another cultural group or some mixture thereof. This dynamic was also marked in the experience of a female who had an encounter with family members who accused her of trying to be too African:

> It was for a holiday, Christmas. I went over to my cousin's house and they were like, 'You are taking this African stuff way too far. You are not African. You are American. You can be African American or even Black American, but you're taking that African stuff way too far.' They were making a correlation with natural hair, or short natural hair, with Africans.

The majority of examples where this theme was seen involved black women who faced being redefined by standards of beauty that are unattainable without reconstructing the self. Their descriptions of being labeled were by individuals who did not approve of their natural hair choice. In some cases it was a stranger, and in other cases it came from friends and family. Interestingly, some of the instances reflected being boxed into a category. For instance, one woman with natural hair stated:

> It's funny how black people will say African like it's not a good thing. Like you're trying to be too Black; whatever that is. I think that once you start to

grow locks, there are these groupies on the other side that like to box you into a category that may not apply to you like being Rastafarian, an Israelite, even African-centered because I don't think that everybody with locks is African-centered or conscious or righteous or all those other things that kind of come along with natural hair.

Two natural hair wearers, for example, described their experiences as relating to social class (e.g., having a good job and being well educated). In one instance, a female was told by her mother and grandmother after disclosing a desire to braid her hair "you can't do this. You've been to college and you have an education, you have a job." The other woman was interviewing an elderly woman for her book. At one point in the conversation, the elder leaned over to make a statement about the interviewer's research assistant, who wore locked hair, "she so smart, why don't she do something with her hair?"

As so indicated in these passages, the stigma of hair is related to passing as others, too African-centered, and status. Labels not only pathologized black features, but demoralized others as unattractive, uneducated and inferior. "Good hair," as the politics of black identity, assumes certain privileges and benefits that kinky hair cannot afford you. With status, one can do better with one's hair. Straight hair decodes to financial viability. In short, this theme focused on how natural hair punishes those who step outside of social norms, indicating that hair is a means to an economic end, but is not truly about freedom.

The Disposability of Black Bodies

The interviews featured a number of instances whereby individuals were disparaged because of their natural hair, and devalued and labeled as lacking beauty by others. The hair policing resulted in disposing of the black body with sub-themes related to gender and sexuality. This theme was most evident within the descriptions provided by three women with natural hair. In each of the narratives, individuals reported that there were clear thoughts about being less feminine or lesbian. For example, one female described a situation with a friend:

> Women are supposed to have long hair. It doesn't matter if it's permed or not, but they are supposed to have long hair. With me cutting my hair, I am not feminine anymore.

This statement is indicative of the theme of disposable black bodies, in that the body is no longer an object to be desired. As this story suggests, the respondent has somehow de-emphasized her feminine persona by cutting her hair short. Another example was described by a female who cut her hair and went home to visit her mother. She stated:

> I walked into the door and my mother standing toward the stairs took off my hat. She looked at me and said, "You had such gorgeous hair." And she turned around and walked away and she did not speak to me the whole weekend. The thing that I don't think she realized was that I still have gorgeous hair.

A similar dynamic of disposable black bodies was apparent in narratives regarding sexuality. In several instances, people who cut their hair reported being perceived as lesbian. The following example from a natural hair woman nicely captures this type of experience with her grandmother when the word "dyke" was used to demonstrate the disposability of her body by associating it with being lesbian:

> It seems like either you're trying to be Afrocentric or you're trying to be a lesbian. It's always something. There is never a middle ground. When I got my hair cut, I came home, and my grandmother was like "you look like a dyke." And there was so much venom in the way she said that. You know, I was really hurt, but it's always perceived as one or the other, not an extension of who you are, where you are right now. There is always something outside of you motivating you, or it can be internally you. It could be something practical like I got tired of getting up an hour before a class to beat the girls to the shower so I could curl my hair and looking like Penny on *Good Times* (black cast sitcom that aired in 1974) with burns on my forehead and the back of my ears and stuff because I didn't take care of my hair.

Respondent experiences also contained descriptions of prejudicial commentary from other Blacks. Similarly, a black gay male states his experience with continually being defined and not accepted by friends due to his locked hair style:

> Black gay male culture is very Eurocentric. They were like, "why are you doing that to yourself?" For me it was alienating. They were still my friends, but when they would come to my house they would tell me how much they hated my hair and how ugly it was and how they wished I would stop trying to be something I wasn't. It was the hardest thing because I really didn't have support from my friends, and my family thought I was trying to be African or something.

Here femininity still tends to rest solidly on a white beauty aesthetic. The natural beauty of Blacks is not held in high regards unless it mirrors that of whiteness or is associated with something other than just black. The implication is that the black body is estranged from its naturalness and is intraracially devalued. Manyani (1977) agrees and further notes that individuals are alienated from their bodies, and that when the body is emotionally mutilated, it is incomplete and marred. Negative self-evaluation arises from this mutilation and creates a conflict between the ego and the body. This ruptured self manifests itself in the body to distinguish good hair and bad hair.

Furthermore, these unattainable aesthetics create problems in relating to the natural black body because the body to be experienced intimately is feminine and White. The Eurocentric ideal beauty is most adored and sought after. Having short, nappy, unstraightened hair is not desirable. As one gay male in the focus group echoes "Even in black gay male culture, drag queens long to impersonate white women." The shared narratives suggest there are popular perceptions surrounding the natural black body whether gay or straight; interracial or intraracial.

Conclusion

Examining the ways in which individuals experience wearing natural hair is instrumental to the ambiguity associated with the use of the phrase "nappy headed." Although a disrupted black body is most commonly understood from institutionalized roles, arrangements, and meanings (Mercer, 1987), it can and does function as cultural affirmation and versatility (Jeter & Crittendon, 1994). In the context of the narratives, natural hair intraracial experiences addressed the ideals of attractiveness as evidence of a not-so-distant past grounded in oppression. Accordingly, descriptions of interactions with same group members often times denigrated black bodies as lacking femininity and desirability. The maintenance of intraracial hierarchies and the expression of natural hair, most often focused on ideas of one's identity expressed through making hair statements through their hair styles. However, hair described as captivating and disposing of black bodies was the reconstruction of mainstream constructions of beauty in intraracial interactions where individuals' black bodies were devalued by individuals in the same cultural group. In the final analysis of it all, the controversy surrounding Imus's "nappy headed ho's" comment was clear reminder of how the black community maintains age-old hierarchies between themselves about hair textures and standards of beauty. His comment was an opportunity to deal with the hurtfulness. The rejection of natural hair at the intraracial level of analysis where communication is happening among African Americans, points to processes by which individuals shape their social and community climate. The intraracial interactions beg for theorizing natural black hair as an important identity of black people (Spellers, 2002) and promoting intraracial harmony.

This study is significant in that it provides insight into how members of the same group celebrate, define, adopt, and redefine natural hair identities socially and politically (Shukra, 1995). Many individuals described the stigma of their hair in interpersonal interactions with others who were the same as them. One contribution of the study is that these narratives are reflective of the importance of hair in the black community. Second, this topic is an important effort in the development of a critical approach to intraracial communication–one in which hierarchical maintenance structures are acknowledged and studied. Third, this study uses these men and women's experiences to seek knowledge related to the power dynamics that occur both at the interpersonal level and the social level with respect to traditional signifiers of superiority (i.e., race, sex, sexuality, and ability). Having discussed these issues in relation to black hair/black body politics lends itself to commentary directed toward creating a space for nappy hair to be conceptualized as beautiful hair. One respondent says it best as she describes her natural hair epiphany while using a product to straighten her hair: "One day I was perming my hair. I had this take home perm set from the beauty supply store that came with hair grease and gloves. When I put the gloves on my hands to apply the perm, it finally hit me that anything I need gloves to apply should not be used on my head."

DISCUSSION QUESTIONS

1. Camara discusses the impact of hair choices upon intraracial communication among African Americans. Which of her six sub-themes do you think most challenges these conversations?

2. Based upon the narratives in this chapter and your own experiences, can hair be used as a political statement? Why or why not?

3. Why do you think Camara included the Don Imus controversy in this chapter? What issue/s does the controversy raise about race and gender in our society?

4. What is the difference between a conformed black body and a disrupted black body?

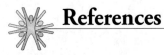

References

Ashe, B. D. 1995. Why don't he like my hair?: Constructing African American standards of beauty in Toni Morrison's *Son of Solomon* and Zora Neal Hurston's *Their eyes were watching God*. *African American Review, 29,* 579–592.

Banks, I. 2000. *Hair matters: Beauty, power, and black women's consciousness*. New York, NY: New York University Press.

Byrd, A., & Tharps. 2001. *Hair Story: Untangling the roots of black hair in America*. New York, NY: St. Martin's Press.

Caldwell, P. M. 1997. A hair piece: Perspectives on the intersection of race and gender. In Adriene Wing (ed.), *Critical race feminism: A reader*, 297–305.

Ferguson, R. 2007. A dilemma for black women in broadcast journalism. Nieman Reports, Vol. 61 Issue 2, 80–81.

Gaskin, B. 1996. The symbolic role of hair. *Chronicle of Higher Education, 43,* October 4, p. B76.

Griffin, F. J. 1996. Textual healing: Claiming black women's bodies, the erotic and resistance in contemporary novels of slavery. *Callaloo, 19,* 519–536.

hooks, b. 1992. *Black looks: Race and representation*. Boston, MA: South End Press.

Jeter, T., & Crittendon, D. 1994. Black hair: A crown of glory and versatility. Crisis 101, 2.

Lanigan, R. L. 1979. The phenomenology of human communication. *Philosophy Today, 23,* 3–15.

Lee, V. 1996. *Granny midwives and black women writers: Double-dutched readings*. New York, NY: Routledge.

Little, B. 1996. *Good hair*. New York, NY: Simon and Schuster.

Magubane, Z. (April 12, 2007). Why 'nappy' is offensive. The Boston Globe.

Manyani, N. C. 1977. *Alienation and the body in a racist society: Study of a society that invented Soweto*. New York, NY: NOK Publishers.

Mercer, K. 1987. Black hair/style politics. In Ken Gelder and Sarah Thornton (eds.), *Subculture reader*, pp. 42–435. New York: Routledge.

Morrison, T. 1981. *Tar baby*. New York: Alfred A. Knof, Inc.

Morrow, W. L. 1973. *400 years without a comb: The untold story*. San Diego, CA: California Curl.

Nelson, J. 1989. Phenomenology as feminist methodology: Explicating interviews. In K. Carter & C. Spitzack (Eds.), *Doing research on women's communication: Perspectives on theory and methods* (pp. 221–241). Norwood, NJ: Ablex.

Schuler, R. 2007, April 13. *On NPR (producer) Day to Day*. New York: National Public Radio.

Shane, W. 1996. Slave hair and African American culture in the eighteenth and nineteenth centuries. *Journal of Southern History, 61*, 45–76.

Shukra, K. 1995. Reconstruction of a black political identity: From black power to black perspectives. *Youth and Policy, 49*, 5–19.

Simkins, A. A. 1990. Function and symbol in hair and headgear among African American women. In Barbara Starke, Lillian Holloman and Barbara Nordquist (eds.), *African American dress and adornment: A cultural perspective*, 166–171. Dubuque, Iowa: Kendall/Hunt.

Spellers, R. E. 2002. Happy to be nappy! Embracing an Afrocentric aesthetic for beauty. In Judith N. Martin, Thomas K. Nakayama and Lisa A. Flores (eds.), *Readings in Intercultural communication: Experiences and contexts*, 52–59. Boston: McGraw Hill.

Walker, S. 2007. *Style and status: Selling beauty to African American women, 1920–1975*. Lexington, KY: University Press of Kentucky.

Weitz, R. 2004. *Repunzel's daughters: What women's hair tells us about women's lives*. New York: Farrar, Straus and Giroux.

5

Grabbing from My Racial Tool Kit: Ethnic-Racial Socialization and African American, Asian American, Hispanic American, and Native American Students

Anna Wong Lowe, Monica Flippin, Joshua Rogers, Cindy E. Foor, and Susan E. Walden

Abstract

Ethnic-racial socialization refers to the ways people are equipped to negotiate within a racially and ethnically based society. As part of a larger project (NSF 0431642), this study analyzes forty ethnographic interviews of African American, Asian American, Hispanic American, and Native American undergraduate students enrolled in the College of Engineering at a large, predominantly White, Midwestern university. Through this analysis, we demonstrate how the student participants' general ethnic-racial socialization contributes to their perceptions of interracial communication and informs their responses to racial events that involve discrimination and racial isolation. We characterize the presence of particular attitudes, beliefs, and behaviors as a racial tool kit. A racial tool kit consists of individual skills and resources that help students frame and respond to racial and ethnic experiences. Results indicate that some of the participants have difficulty recognizing and acknowledging discriminatory experiences, and are differentially equipped to effectively handle and communicate racial issues. We also found that the four racial-ethnic groups have similarities and differences in their descriptions of discrimination experiences, their reactions to these experiences, and their ethnic-racial socialization. These results further demonstrate that ethnic-racial socialization is an ongoing process that is continuously developed and influenced by participants' interactions with peers, family members, classmates, instructors, and strangers.

KEY TERMS: ethnic-racial socialization, contestation, discrimination, racial tool kit

Introduction

A racial tool kit equips people to navigate through a racially and ethnically based society. This tool kit consists of individual skills and resources built on attitudes, beliefs, and behaviors learned through ethnic-racial socialization. Since certain facets of ethnic-racial socialization buffer perceptions of discrimination experiences, support self-esteem for African American youth (Harris-Britt et al., 2007; Neblett et al., 2006) and provide "racism stress management" (Stevenson et al., 1997), this socializing process contributes to building a racial tool kit. Ethnic-racial socialization has also been linked to racial identity and acculturative stress in African American college students (Thompson et al., 2000).

Original research on ethnic-racial socialization concentrated on how African American parents and familial guardians prepared their children to navigate in a society with negative stereotypes toward Blacks (Hill, 1999; Coard & Sellers, 2005). Later ethnic-racial socialization researchers broadened their focus to understand how other racial and ethnic groups prepared their young for a race-based society (Hughes, 2003). Though families were often credited as the primary context for ethnic-racial socialization, some research examined the role of peers during older adolescent and young adult years in understanding race (Coard & Sellers, 2005).

While these studies formed a strong foundation, the field lacked a qualitative comparison of ethnic-racial socialization and discrimination relationships across different racial-ethnic groups. Furthermore, prior research had not engaged how college-age students actively addressed day-to-day racial interactions, in which students drew from their "tool kit" of racial resources (Coard & Sellers, 2005; Hughes et al., 2006; & Stevenson et al., 2002). In this work, we examined interracial communication—experienced as racial isolation and discrimination—by university students across four racial-ethnic groups: African American, Asian American, Hispanic American, and Native American. We analyzed the 40 participants' reflections and sense-making of these incidents and their reactions through an ethnic-racial socialization framework.

We used the Hughes et al. (2006) description of ethnic-racial socialization primarily because their work synthesized prior research into a single framework and provided potential application across diverse racial-ethnic groups. Five categories of ethnic-racial socialization were presented in Hughes et al. (2006). *Cultural socialization* indicated items, beliefs, and practices learned about race and ethnicity such as ethnic holidays, food, and language, as well as history of the racial-ethnic group. *Preparation for bias* referred to messages that aided in the awareness of racial inequalities and stereotypes, and the ability to cope with these inequities. *Promotion of mistrust* referenced "practices that emphasize the need for wariness and distrust in interracial interactions" (Hughes et al., 2006, p. 757).

(The key difference between *preparation for bias* and *promotion of mistrust* was that *promotion of mistrust* messages did not impart strategies to deal with negative racial-ethnic interactions.) *Egalitarianism* referred to ways in which people were socialized to believe in racial equality, or that racial group membership did not affect educational, social, and/or economic success. *Egalitarianism* included the ideals of a color-blind society and the idea that individual qualities such as hard work and intelligence overrode societal stereotypes. Lastly, *silence about race*, indicated race was not discussed between primary caregivers and children. Avoiding issues of race, whether done intentionally or unintentionally, was viewed as a communicative message in itself. In the following sections, we present the methodology used to explore these issues and our findings.

Methods

The primary source of data was 90-minute semi-structured interviews of African American, Asian American, Hispanic American, and Native American students in their sophomore, junior, and senior years in engineering majors at a large, predominately white, midwestern university. Age of participants ranged from 19 to 39. Each participant completed a preliminary questionnaire regarding demographic information, an engineering attitudes survey, and a 1-2 hour intensive interview. In several cases, second and third interviews were completed a year apart to provide longitudinal perspectives and to track the progress of participants still attending the university as engineering majors. Each interview was transcribed, coded for analysis, and then assessed using an iterative-inductive analytic approach (O'Reilly, 2005). Through the iterative-inductive process, we identified, elaborated, and refined insights from and for the interpretation of participants' interviews. From the insights, we drew meaning from participant experiences and narrated their important stories.

To date, 159 students participated in this study with 227 interviews conducted. Since this analysis was part of a much larger, ongoing study (NSF 0431642), we focused on a sample of these students to conduct an analysis of racial discrimination experiences, strategies for dealing with discrimination, and ethnic-racial socialization. For this chapter, forty participants were chosen for analysis (ten participants from each racial-ethnic group). The participants chosen were representative of all the study's participants who reported racial isolation and discrimination experiences. They were also intentionally selected based on factors such as gender, community of origin, and immigration generation. For example, among the project's Asian American and Hispanic American participants were students who immigrated to the U.S., as well as children and grandchildren of immigrants. Because students who were born outside the U.S. may have a dual ethnic-racial socialization experience, only students who were born in the U.S. were included in this analysis.

We coded the responses specifically for racial discrimination and isolation experiences. We defined *discrimination* as inequitable treatment or contestation based on phenotype (physical characteristics) or societal perceptions of national origin, ethnicity, or race. Each racial-ethnic group encountered different forms of discrimination; yet, they shared the common experience of facing discrimination. We defined *racial isolation* as being the only one—or one of a handful—of a racial or ethnic group in a setting. For instance, in the historically white male dominated field of engineering, it was not uncommon for an African American female to be the only African American female in a classroom.

After coding for racial discrimination and isolation experiences, we examined how the participants dealt with racial incidents. The reactions to racial discrimination and isolation were not mutually exclusive. Participants could utilize one or more tools in response to any given racial-ethnic event. Tools used by the participants were labeled as:

- *Acceptance*—recognition of the incidents as part of daily life for a person of color;
- *Anger*—a response in which the participant was upset, frustrated, and/or emotionally distraught over the incident;
- *Dismissal of incident as unimportant*—minimizing the experience or regarding the experience as an isolated incident;
- *Teaching moment*—when participants used the opportunity of racial discrimination to educate others on more accurate perceptions of race and ethnicity;
- *Confrontation*—speaking up about the incident within the context and moment of the discrimination;
- *Rationalization*—statements that the incident occurred only because of lack of knowledge or degree of naiveté of the offending individual;
- *Code-shifting*—behavior in which an individual foregrounds or backgrounds a particular racial or ethnic identity within a particular context in order to diffuse racial isolation and/or discrimination. For example, while at home with family and extended kin, native language, customs and cultural restrictions may be practiced. When at school or the workplace, however, the individual may use the dominant culture's language, customs and cultural restrictions.

Finally, the participants' interviews were reviewed to ascertain the source(s) of ethnic-racial socialization, and how that socialization contributed to producing the tools they used when responding to racial discrimination and isolation. The analysis was guided by the majority of Hughes et al. (2006) categories of ethnic-racial socialization: *cultural socialization*, *preparation for bias*, *promotion of mistrust*, and *egalitarianism*; however, we allowed the participants' responses and descriptions to drive the analysis. Since each racial-ethnic group had its own expression of ethnic-racial socialization, we did not assume that these categories were universal for all groups. We did not code for *silence about race* since students were not specifically asked about ethnic-racial socialization; thus, we could not assume that these conversations were part of their families' lives based on the absence of this narrative in their interviews.

Through the analysis, explained in the next section, we demonstrate how the student participants' general ethnic-racial socialization contributes to their perceptions of inter-racial communication and informs their responses to those racial events. The discussion section offers across-group comparisons of the socialization patterns, perceptions, and selected responses to racial-ethnic events through racial tool kit strategies selected by group members.

Results

We present here the experiences of discrimination, reactions to discrimination through tool kit strategies, and ethnic-racial socialization for each racial-ethnic group in our study: African American, Asian American, Hispanic American, and Native American. These experiences are more fully captured through excerpted quotations from the interview transcripts. Pseudonyms are used to protect anonymity. In these quotations, < > indicates a substitution of a term to preserve the anonymity of the participants, whereas [ ] references a contextual phrase we added for clarification. Within the group's analysis, we note the most common racial discrimination experiences, the prominent strategies or "tools" utilized during and after these experiences, and lastly, where and from whom, if available, the participants learned these strategies.

African American

The ten African American participants include five women and five men. All are born in the United States and none are children of immigrants.

Discrimination Experiences of African American Participants

Most of the participants relate to some form of discrimination. The experiences occur in campus residential halls, during course related activities, and in the surrounding community. In particular, these participants acknowledge the difference between traditional and modern discrimination. Traditional discrimination is more blatant, where hatred and negative stereotypes are clearly presented to the participant or, as one participant says, "nasty." Modern discrimination, similar to modern racism, is subtler, embedded in the ways people act toward Blacks and often a result of incorrect information and stereotypes. In these instances, people sometimes do not even know they are discriminating. Sean explains his thoughts about the differences between traditional and modern discrimination in this excerpt:

> Now-a-days it's [discrimination is] not going to be something so grievous … It's still those little things … For example, there's one time that the team [class project] leader … has the key for our laboratory room. He didn't show up and I went downstairs to ask one of the people to let me into the room … They were like, "Well, no, you got to talk to the professor and get permission [to get into the laboratory]." And I was like, "Okay, never mind." So I called my team leader and he was like "That's weird. They let me in there the other day because I left my key." … I don't know if it was just an attitude. Maybe they know him and they've never seen me before. I can't say.

In this example, Sean needs access to a laboratory room for a class project and is unable to gain access because the person who has the key is not at the meeting. He is denied access even though previously the team leader is able to gain access. The discrimination is subtle—it is the assumption that he does not have permission to enter a laboratory.

Betty, in this example, refers to her discrimination experiences as unfair treatment toward students of color as compared to her white peers. In this way, discrimination is:

> not something you can talk about because it's not something you can document or say "This is what happens." … Many of [engineering students of color] have complained that we would go to a professors' office to ask for help and they would kind of rush through it or … make you feel inadequate when you go … patronizing. … It seems like they were kinder to our Whiter counterparts most of the time, maybe because they can relate to them better. But to us they were like just, "Whatever."

Betty discusses a difference in the professor's reaction to students during office hours. According to Betty, the professor provides better help to white students than to students of color. This unequal treatment is another form of modern discrimination.

Tool Kit of African American Participants

African American participants' primary strategy for deflecting discriminatory experiences is *acceptance* with statements such as, "You don't always want to be the difficult person and so you just kind of let it go and try to graduate" or "I don't like it, but I realize that it is just how things are … There is nothing I can do to change them." Some who *accept* the event also reach out to racial peers and family members. Margaret states, "I just ate it up and told my mom." The family and racial peers become a support for the participants—aiding them to emotionally and mentally manage their experiences and to *rationalize* and *accept*. In the previous examples, Sean and Betty utilize *rationalization*. Sean notes that his perception of discrimination could be "just an attitude. Maybe they know him and they've never seen me before." One participant, Roswell, uses a *teaching moment* with a hall-mate in the residence hall:

> When I got here my freshman year [laughs] there was this … White girl on my [dormitory] floor … She swore up and down that the reason why that Black people are more athletic is because they have extra muscles in their legs [laughs]. And it is humorous, but that's not true! [laughs] … But she came from a completely all White high school … They taught her that in science … I sat her down and explained it to her … I didn't get mad, actually I started laughing … and was like, … "One, that's not true and two, don't go around saying that stuff because a lot of people may not be as understanding. I'm trying to be patient right here right now with you … We're all the same, just like you." … That's not going to get me as mad, if someone makes a mistake out of ignorance as long as they want to listen and correct that mistake by talking to them.

Since Roswell acknowledges his hall-mate is referring to a stereotype based on ignorance and poor education during high school, he is able to enlighten her about the misinformation.

Ethnic-Racial Socialization of African American Participants

Half of the African American participants directly comment on how parents, a family member, or professor provide some ethnic-racial socialization. Most participants refer to some *cultural socialization*, which the participants describe as cultural traditions, storytelling, participation in religious activities, and taking African/African American studies courses. For these students, the primary source of *cultural socialization* is from African/African American studies courses and ethnic organizations, not from parents. From their parents and family members, participants receive messages containing combined elements of *promotion of mistrust* and *preparation for bias*. For this reason, *preparation for bias* and *promotion of mistrust* are collapsed into one category. The messages received include warnings of potential racism, strategies for dealing with these issues such as passive *acceptance*, and generational storytelling of past racial experiences. For instance, James refers to warnings of discrimination and unfair stereotypes toward Blacks: "My uncle tells me it'll come … and once you get into the real world it'll come," whereas Betty explains receiving some *preparation for bias* from a white professor:

> I remember talking to one of my professors about it last semester because I was complaining about the teamwork: it's not working and it's driving me crazy … This has been one of the first years that I feel that you really had to fight for getting respect or equality within people of your own age … I didn't expect to get a racial barrier as strong as it's been this year. So it's been kind of weird and he was saying that obviously it's something that you are going to continue to encounter forever as a minority, and he's White … He was just like, "I think … that it's good to go through now because when you go into work it's something you're going to encounter probably every day and you're just going to have to learn how to make people work around it without being difficult, but make sure you stand up for yourself." Which is why he gave us the idea of operational rules and I think he talked to some of the professors to actually suggest making rules a part of the guidelines for teamwork because this year they actually mentioned it. Last year they never said anything about it.

Betty's professor warns her that the racial conflict with her teammates is common for students of color, and she should prepare for this in the future work force. He acknowledges that racial discrimination exists. To reduce the potential conflict, the professor suggests the teams create "operational rules" for group assignments.

Roswell has learned about *preparation for bias* from his parents. His father advises him to use the emotions of the inequities to drive him to accomplish his goals.

> [M]y parents warned me before I came like, "You've got to get used to it. The system changes the rules to benefit them, so you just do it." My dad is always like … "Don't get mad and irate. You just stay quiet and do your thing, do what you do … You can get pissed off, but allow it to drive you more instead of allowing it to stop you from achieving what you want, so change the rules if they want."

The participants do not address specifically attitudes of *egalitarianism*. Though many refer to using hard work to get ahead, they have not accepted the belief that equal efforts will reap them equal rewards.

Asian American

Of the ten Asian American participants, seven self-report as Vietnamese, two Chinese, one Filipino, and one Asian Indian. The five male and five female participants are born in the United States to immigrant parents from their respective countries.

Discrimination Experiences of Asian American Participants

Overall the Asian American participants express varied experiences with racial isolation and discrimination. The Asian American participants report teasing based on their linguistic heritage or racially specific last names, and incorrect labeling of their Asian ethnicity such as being confused for Vietnamese when Chinese. One participant gives an example: "I was talking … in Vietnamese and somebody walked by and said … like mocking things like 'ching chang.'" A few express shame in their Asian identity at a younger age due to childhood taunting and teasing. Participants also report racial discrimination experiences based on the model minority stereotype. The model minority stereotype is the belief that all Asian Americans are successful in society despite racial oppression (Lee, 1996). This stereotype infers all Asian Americans are overachievers, especially in academics. Specifically, Asian Americans are stereotyped to be hard-working, intelligent, and uncomplaining (Lee, 1996). For instance, as reported by one participant, a professor announced he would be stricter on all the Asian students because Asian students studied more.

Tool Kit of Asian American Participants

In response to those racial experiences, participants mostly *dismiss incidents as unimportant* and/or *rationalize* the perpetuator's actions. Mark, one of the Chinese participants, provides an example of *rationalization* of actions:

> I think maybe it was <at a local shopping chain> so there's going to be a lot of people from outside school … [I]t might have been a couple of kids from high school. They're obviously still … immature and they still don't know everything … They said something behind my back … and I just totally ignored them. But I heard them. I don't think it's a big deal to me … [M]aybe because when I'm here [in college] there's so little of it. When I'm back at home, there's a lot of it in <southeastern state> … It's because … of … the kids or there's a lot of people that are older there. They haven't even graduated high school either so … they're just not as educated. I don't know why that is either.

Mark briefly describes this incident, and *rationalizes* the racist behavior. He particularly highlights that the perpetuators were of high school age or elderly who were, in his opinion, uneducated. Mark's reaction to this incident is representative of most of the other participants.

A couple of participants respond with *anger* toward racial inequities and behaviors. Lee, a Vietnamese American, recounts his feelings toward Whites after an incident with his older brother at a local restaurant:

> Like my brother, he dated a White girl, and … we walk into <a restaurant> …
> They hold hands like couples hold hands but it was just like White people were

like "Oh." ... Like this one girl ... she was in college because she was wearing <local university logo> stuff and she was ... eyeballing the whole time ... like mad-dogging us ... I feel that I've got to become better than them, better than White people; show White people what I'm made of ... I don't hate all Whites ... But it's just like ... I have good friends who are White ... I'm not too entirely racist, but I feel versus White people, see I said versus, like I kind of feel like it's a competition ... like I have to become better than them.

Lee uses the *anger* from these racial interactions with Whites as motivation to succeed.

Ethnic-Racial Socialization of Asian American Participants

Most of the participants do not specifically address how they learned to deal with racial discrimination or isolation. Instead, the majority of the Asian American participants comment on *cultural socialization*, specifically their ability or inability to communicate in their ethnic language, their understanding of cultural rituals and behaviors, and their co-ethnic friends and social activities. Since all of the Asian American participants are children of immigrants to the United States, parental socialization is more aligned with a goal of preserving cultural identity rather than with preparing children for a potentially difficult adjustment into a race-based society. Those participants with difficult and conflicted relationships with their parental figures express limited to no *cultural socialization* prior to attending college. A few of the participants learn additional *cultural socialization* by joining and actively participating in racially specific social groups and clubs, such as an Asian technical society or a fraternity with a predominant Asian membership.

Preparation for bias and *promotion of mistrust* are also combined in the analysis of Asian American participants. *Preparation for bias* messages do not enter the ethnic-racial socialization of these participants until they reach the university and become involved with race-specific student organizations, or attend cultural events to learn more about the history of Asians and Asian Americans in the United States.

We postulate that the ethnic-racial socialization of the Asian American participants is mostly *cultural* and not *preparation for bias*. This could be because these students are children of immigrants. If they were third generation or greater, their experiences may be either more *egalitarianism* (a sign of assimilation with mainstream White dominant culture) or *preparation for bias* (in recognition of the history of Asian Americans in the U.S.).

The majority of the participants, however, believe in *egalitarianism*, which they identify as "hard work achieves success." They express the belief that hard work provides a pathway that supersedes race. These participants do not engage in discussions of race with their friends, indicating that it is not worthy of conversation since race does not make a big difference in their daily lives.

Oscar, a Filipino American, responds to a discriminatory incident by educating his Asian American fraternity brothers about race. In this next excerpt, Oscar recounts how many of his Asian American friends have little understanding of race and racism in their lives.

> I was pretty surprised a lot of [my Asian American fraternity brothers] had never experienced racism or anything like that … We were in <a restaurant> … There was a big group of … high schoolers or country boys but they blatantly squinted their eyes going, "Ching, chang, chong, there's the Chinese brothers," and laughing … [My Asian American fraternity brothers] didn't realize it. He didn't know what was going on. He asked what was going on and I said, "Dude, they're making fun of us." He was like, "Why?" … I said, "Because we're Asian."

Oscar becomes a resource for other Asian Americans helping them be more aware of the attitudes surrounding them, socializing his racial peers with messages of *preparation for bias* and *promotion of mistrust*. Oscar is the only Asian American participant to report utilizing a behavioral strategy of educating people as a response to a discriminating act. In his previous excerpt, he helps his Asian American fraternity brothers recognize racist acts. In this next excerpt, his parents encourage him to attend a symposium on Filipino history. This *cultural socialization* experience gives him the tools to respond to a racial incident with a *teaching moment*.

> A lot of times I get angry. I've never been in a fight or anything but pretty close … [M]ost of the time I just snap back with something smart, some remark … [O]ne time one guy told me to go back to my country. He said, "Get off American soil" … It happened to be … after a time I went to some Filipino … symposium thing … [with] my parents … I found out that the first Asians were actually Filipino slaves who escaped Spanish trading ships in Louisiana … They're like … [some] predominantly Filipino cities or towns in Louisiana. But none of them can trace back their families in the Philippines since they came to Louisiana … I found out that Filipinos … c[a]me to Florida [before] pilgrims came to America … I told that dude, "Hey dude, why don't you go back to Europe? We've been here longer than you." And he said, "Nu uh" and I go, "Yeah." I told him, "You heard of those Spanish people in Florida? The Filipinos escaped there before you guys even decided to … come across the Atlantic," and that dude was like, "Oh."

Hispanic American

Of the ten Hispanic American participants, six report familial heritage from Mexico, one from Cuba, one from El Salvador, one from Columbia and Portugal, and one from Mexico and Puerto Rico. The sample includes six women and four men. Unlike the Asian American participants, not all Hispanic American participants' parents are immigrants to the U.S. The participants range from second generation in which participants were born in the U.S., to immigrant parents, to fourth generation where participants, their parents, and grandparents were born in the U.S.

Discrimination Experiences of Hispanic American Participants

Discrimination experiences for Hispanic Americans include facing questions of their racial-ethnic identity and status as legal residents and experiencing teasing based on stereotypes of Mexicans. Many of the participants are teased by other Latino/as for their lack of fluency in Spanish. Pablo, a Mexican American, offers an example of challenges to legal status by his girlfriend's father based on a popular stereotype that Pablo's family must be illegal immigrants, even though he and his family are U.S. citizens.

> That was just like an example of when I was in high school … [My girlfriend's father] called my house one time saying he was immigration, saying something about me leaving his daughter alone. It was stupid … He was trying to scare my parents, my mom.

Many participants recall teasing or name-calling from friends and others as the form of discrimination they have experienced either at the university or sometime in their past. Alva, a Mexican/Puerto Rican, offers an example of teasing based on Mexican stereotypes. She participates in the racial joking even though she recognizes it as inappropriate.

> The only thing is just between friends making fun of the stereotypes of the [Mexican] people who come over. And … it's just so natural that we just don't think about it. We just mess with each other saying, "Oh, if you're from Mexico you know how to run and jump a fence," and things like that—just stupid stereotypes that we shouldn't be making fun of, but we do.

Tool Kit of Hispanic American Participants

Common strategies for racial isolation and discrimination among the Hispanic American participants are, in order of frequency: *dismissal of incident as unimportant, acceptance*, and *anger*. A few respond with *confrontation*. The participants do not express any *teaching moments* or *rationalization*. Elaine, a Mexican American, explains how Whites and Mexicans assume she speaks Spanish and they are upset when they realize she does not.

Eventually the challenge to her language ability causes a self-reflection of her cultural identity. Even though she provides a cursory *confrontational* response to the challenge of her language ability, she later indicates a belief that she needs to learn Spanish to provide this linguistic *cultural socialization* to her future children.

> Everybody automatically thinks you speak Spanish automatically … It's a lot of White folks, but boy it's even worse by the Mexicans … [T]hey automatically walk up to you and, "blah, blah, blah, blah, blah." and it's just like, "Yeah. No habla espanol." I'm like, "Habla English?" And they're like, "No." And I'm like … I don't know anything. I don't know how to help you … I tell them, my friends, that I don't speak Spanish, and they're like, "What? But you're Mexican!" "Yes I understand this. What's your point? Just because I'm a Mexican doesn't mean I have to speak Spanish."
>
> …
>
> [I'm learning Spanish for] two reasons: one, you need a foreign language to graduate in most colleges and you need it in the Engineering College; and two, it's not spoken in my family and it's kind of a part of our heritage … I want to bring it back in so when I have kids … I can try to bring it in to influence them to learn it. Try to get back to our … roots. We're Americanized. There's no way we're going to get back to the true Hispanic Mexican roots—little things here and there.

Jasper, a Mexican American, has experienced discrimination with a sales clerk at a local shop in town. He has mixed reactions to the incident. Though *angry*, he realizes *confrontation* would not have been right for him at that moment. He chooses to *accept* the incident instead of escalating the situation. He also seeks support from someone he believes has an understanding of daily racism.

> Yeah I mean obviously it's going to make me angry but at the same time I just don't want to deal with people's ignorance. It's just not worth it to me … I could've sat there and taken it and waited for that person to be done and then try to talk some sense but it probably would have been pointless at that point. I would have been too angry and it just would have been a bad situation … I took it with a grain of salt and blew it off … That's all I could do … I discussed it with my current roommate who is a Black girl … She obviously knows a little bit about racism as well, but I mean, in <our state> you really don't see it too much.

Ethnic-Racial Socialization of Hispanic American Participants

Cultural socialization for the Hispanic American group includes language proficiency, much like the Asian American group. Half of the participants are fluent in Spanish, none in Portuguese. In addition to language, *cultural socialization* includes observing Hispanic celebrations and holidays such as the Day of the Dead, Posadas, or Quinceañera; participating in extended family gatherings to engage in cultural traditions; attending Mass for support of cultural values; and embracing "ethnic pride"—the belief their ethnicity and culture brings them strength. All participants have some form of *cultural socialization* prior to college. The majority of the participants have learned about cultural practices from extended family gatherings, while a few observed Hispanic celebrations and holidays. Elise provides one example of *cultural socialization*:

> [First] Communion's huge … [and] is a really important thing like they say it's for the rest of our lives … That's a big deal and you get little gifts for our first Communion. I had a Quinceañera and my other sisters, they're going to have Quinceañeras. My sister, she just turned fifteen, and she had one. It was awesome! It was huge just like a wedding … all out ceremony, church reception … with a big … tower cake … I had a great time. I had a white gown and everything. We definitely love being Mexican, but we love being Americans. We're not exactly like biased or prejudiced in any sense. We just take everything for what it's worth.

Though the majority of the participants attended Mass as a child with their family, they do not practice their religion or attend Mass while in college. Many of the participants disclose ethnic pride. They believe that their ethnic pride, developed from a strong sense of family and connection with their racial-ethnic community, makes them more resilient to discrimination. For instance, after a racial-ethnic comment, John retorts, "I'm proud to be Spanish … Yep, it's better than you!"

Numerous participants report behaviors in the *egalitarianism* category, which include meritocracy and *denial* of blatant racial-ethnic discrimination. Alva provides an example:

> Like you normally see racial groups hanging out together, but once you get into your major courses, there is so few people that it just doesn't matter. You just start talking to everyone and anyone, just to make connections and to get help and whatever … I pretty much have the same 60–70 people in every class in just about every class, so it is hard to get help outside of the class. After awhile, it is just like we are all together and it doesn't really matter.

For Alva and many others, the meritocracy of the major transcends; the challenge of engineering is the great equalizer.

Although the participants do not report *preparation for bias* or *promotion of mistrust* messages in their ethnic-racial socialization prior to college, they indicate developing *mistrust* from challenges to their Hispanic identity from interactions with more linguistically identified Hispanics in college. Because of this, many stop attending Hispanic-student events due to the prominence of Spanish-speaking students at these events.

Native American

Seven of the Native American participants are male and three female. Nine of the ten participants are biracial, and four students self-identify as Caucasian. The participants report varying ties and origins to Cherokee, Chickasaw, Choctaw, and Creek tribes. None is born or raised on a reservation; and none of the participants or their parents speaks a tribal language, though a few participants' grandparents still do. Three participants are from out-of-state, an important distinction discussed below.

Discrimination Experiences of Native American Participants

Most Native American discrimination experiences can be characterized as contestations to Native American identity and status claims. While all participants legally claim Native American status, they possess a wide range of blood quantum (one-half to $1/516^{th}$), and knowledge of and experience with Native American culture and socialization. Contestations to identity and status arise from more traditional Native Americans questioning whether students are "Native enough" from majority and other minority students' resentment of resources that accrue to Native American status, and finally from teasing by white friends because the participants exhibit white phenotype. Will offers an example of contestation by more traditional Native Americans during a Native American event.

> Because I am not 100 percent Indian, sometimes some of the Native Americans will look at you differently and … treat you differently. It really sort of bothers me because I respect my heritage and I really enjoy learning about it. I feel like a lot of times full-blooded Native Americans will pretty much disrespect me by putting that look on their face like, "You have no idea [about being Indian], you don't know, you are not part of this" … You can feel that … a lot of times … [T]he Native American Scholars had to serve food at the pow-wow/Stomp Dance. There are [full-blooded] people who will just look at you … eye to eye and just look at you with the worst looks on the face of the Earth.

Because she is not easily recognized as a Native American, Sarah experiences resentment for her financial assistance but escapes discrimination from peers.

> I just think that there are other people that are mad that I get financial assistance and they don't … I don't think people look at me and they are like, "Oh, she's Native American." So I don't think I've experienced a lot of that [discrimination] because they don't really … they can't … they don't really see me as a minority.

Tool Kit of Native American Participants

Responses to racial isolation and discrimination experiences are informed by the context in which the student is raised, a student's prior experience with identity contestation, and the degree to which the student identifies as Native American. The primary tool used by Native American students growing up in-state is *code-shifting*. Bane, who grew up in a rural small town in the heart of Indian country, understands the benefits of choosing an identity to communicate based on context.

Interviewer:	How do you identify yourself?
Bane:	Depends on if I was just talking to somebody [at the university], I would say I'm White because I'm 1 and 500th American Indian.
Interviewer:	Now when you were in high school, you said … you were **identified** as White because of your blood amount … How did **you** identify yourself?
Bane:	I'd probably say Native American, just because everyone else was … the town that I'm from <in-state>. If you're not Native American … you're White. But there are not many people that are just White … I'd say 90 percent of the people there are Native American …
Interviewer:	So what changed from high school coming into <college>?
Bane:	There's mostly I feel White people up here now.
Interviewer:	So if you were to walk into a classroom and there was a Native person, would you feel comfortable going up to that person?
Bane:	Yeah … I've been around it all my life.

Even though *code-shifting* is the primary tool for in-state students, some participants *dismiss incidents as unimportant*. Only one participant chooses to *confront* peers and *attempt to educate them* at the same time.

The in-state students are experienced with *code-shifting* because they were raised in a context where biracial and full-blooded Indians live side by side along with the majority culture. The opposite is true for the three out-of-state students who have no context for identity contestation. These students are ill-prepared for contestations from more traditional Indians and white peers and their tool kit development becomes on-the-job training at college.

Ethnic-Racial Socialization of Native American Participants

For the few students with exposure to their Native American culture prior to college, *cultural socialization* results from observing or participating in pow-wows or stomp dances as children, hearing their grandparent(s) speak their tribal language(s), or listening to family and tribal stories. The participants with no exposure to tribal culture prior to college find *cultural socialization* thrust upon them when volunteering at American Indian Student Association (AISA) sponsored events. Often, these events are the first time they observed Native American traditions. Two students have enrolled in tribal language or Native American history classes in an attempt to become more familiar with their tribal history and culture.

Where present, *preparation for bias* and *promotion of mistrust* are not expressly the result of parental teaching. Karina, an in-state student, recounts *preparation for bias* from a cousin who had experienced intra-group bias when he attended a meeting of a university chapter of American Indian Student Association (AISA). He warns her that she would not be comfortable in AISA and instead, should look for a community in AISES (American Indian Science and Engineering Society).

> I've heard of AISA … I heard that I probably wouldn't fit in … from someone that is more Indian than I am … My cousin went to one of the meetings and he said he didn't feel comfortable … because my cousin has blonde hair.

For most in-state students, *preparation for bias,* manifesting in the strategy *code-shifting*, results from living in a local society where identity negotiation is as familiar as breathing. Out-of-state students do not claim Native American status prior to college and do not have the same local context for socialization; so, they cannot draw upon the *code-shifting* tool for managing contestations. The university prompts their ethnic-racial socialization by exposing them to contestation in connection with scholarship requirements and racial-ethnic student organizations. The lack of *preparation* is evident in the following excerpt:

> [I]n <my hometown>, there wasn't much opportunity to learn about the Cherokee or to interact with the Cherokee … Another difficulty is the <Native American scholarship program> … All of the people in there are out-of-staters so they generally do not have a lot [of]connection with their tribe. And

unfortunately a good number of them are about as White as I am … Sometimes I'm lumped in the same boat as those … who are just there for the money, just because of my skin color … As you can see I'm White, and there's been people who are like, "Oh I'm more Native American than you, I'm from <in-state>." … When I was a freshman I made the mistake of telling a few friends or people my bloodline and there are people who think that that's the only measure of a Native American … It's hard dealing with being a White Native American. Unfortunately people still see color and skin as what makes you who you are and that's something that I think I'll probably be struggling with until I die.

Close to half of the participants offer examples of *egalitarianism*, beliefs associated with meritocracy and an individual mindset of succeeding against all odds. Because many of the participants identify as White, this result is not surprising. Exposure to and adoption of mainstream values are part of their ethnic-racial socialization process. Tucker, a Cherokee, when asked if the college provides adequate help for Native American students says:

I don't necessarily believe they treat certain races differently. I think they all have the same chances everybody else has. That's probably just because I'm White [look White]. I haven't had to deal with certain things other races have, but to be honest there isn't anything you need to do differently to serve races. I think they should all be treated the same … If you have it in you, you can overcome just about anything.

The majority of students do not talk about race with family or friends. Only one student, Will, finds a group of friends with whom he can discuss racial issues. Though his current response to teasing is to *accept* and *rationalize*, Will finds a community of peers where he can discuss racial issues and further develop a tool kit.

Interviewer:	Do you ever discuss race and ethnicity among your friends?
Will:	Oh yeah, all the time … We just talk about stuff. My friends think it is funny that I consider myself Native American. They are like, "You are still White, aren't you?" I am like, "Yeah, I know that but it is still a lot of my heritage." I have really gained a lot of respect for my heritage since I've come here … We talk a lot. We joke a lot. But race does take a forefront in communications.

Discussion

The four racial-ethnic groups have similarities and differences in their descriptions of discrimination experiences, their reactions to these experiences, and their ethnic-racial socialization. African American participants are more cognizant of racial-ethnic discrimination experiences than the other groups. They frame their experiences directly as discrimination, and offer differentiations between blatant and subtle discrimination. The Asian American and Hispanic American participants are more likely to frame their experiences as "teasing" rather than racial discrimination and isolation. Hispanic Americans and Native Americans report discrimination by members of their racial-ethnic group or lateral discrimination. Passive methods of coping such as *dismissal of incident as unimportant*, *rationalization*, and *acceptance* are tools utilized by all groups. African Americans primarily use *acceptance* and seek support from family members and peers. Asian Americans and Hispanic Americans are more likely than the other groups to employ the tool of *dismissal of incidents as unimportant*. While African Americans and Asian Americans utilize *rationalization*, Hispanic Americans do not have messages that fit this strategy. Although some Native Americans use *dismissal of incidents as unimportant*, this group's participants primarily employ the *code-shifting* tool to cope with lateral-discrimination experiences.

Asian American and Hispanic American participants discuss *cultural socialization* from parental figures more than the other groups. The majority of the Asian American and Hispanic American participants have some knowledge of cultural practices, language, and events. African American participants are more likely to take ethnic studies courses offered by the university than any other group as a form of *cultural socialization*. Compared to other groups, Native Americans report little Native American *cultural socialization*; however, in-state Native American participants report more than out-of-state participants.

Unlike the other groups, African Americans report *preparation for bias* and *promotion of mistrust* socialization from family members. Only two of the Asian American participants give accounts of *preparation for bias* and *promotion of mistrust*, which they learned from educational settings rather than from family members. Native American students do not convey direct *preparation for bias* or *promotion of mistrust* from their parents. The absence of this type of socialization contributes to difficulties responding to identity contestation. Asian American, Hispanic American, and Native American participants present messages of *egalitarianism*, unlike the African American participants.

The out-of-state Native Americans, the African American students enrolled in ethnic studies courses, and the case of the Asian American participant *preparing* his racial-ethnic peers *for bias* show that participants continue to be ethnically and racially socialized during college. A few of the Asian American participants find connections with racial-ethnic peers in student organizations. The responses show joining student organizations helps in *preparation for bias* and *cultural socialization*.

Ethnic-racial socialization occurs throughout our lifetimes, not only from family members during a person's formative years. This study shows ethnic-racial socialization is called upon and continues through college. On most college campuses, students encounter interracial situations in their everyday life experiences in dormitories, classrooms, student organizations, and the surrounding community. Because of these expanded opportunities for interracial communication and discriminatory experiences, students need items in their tool kit for coping. For some individuals, college is the first time they are aware of a racial tool kit or encounter the need to develop one. There is no "easy" way to talk about race, but it is important to educate all students about the different discourses associated with racial and ethnic diversity in this country. There are positive and healthy ways to promote interracial communication experiences.

DISCUSSION QUESTIONS

1. How would you define a racial tool kit? What do you think is necessary for an effective racial tool kit?

2. Give an example of preparation for bias. Compare and contrast that with an example of cultural socialization.

3. How are Native American participants similar to and different from other participants in their reactions to discrimination and ethnic-racial socialization?

4. What are some traditions that aid in your cultural identity?

References

Coard, S. I., & Sellers, R. M. (2005). African American families as a context for racial socialization. In V. C. McLoyd, N. E. Hill, & K. A. Dodge (Eds.), *African American family life: Ecological and cultural diversity* (pp. 264–284). New York: Guilford Press.

Harris-Britt, A., Valrie, C. R., Kurtz-Costes, B., & Rowley, S. J. (2007). Perceived racial discrimination and self-esteem in African American youth: Racial socialization as a protective factor. *Journal of Research on Adolescence, 17*(4), 669–682.

Hill, S. A. (1999). *African American children: Socialization and development in families*. Thousand Oaks, CA: Sage

Hughes, D. (2003). Correlates of African American and Latino parents' messages to children about ethnicity and race: A comparative study of racial socialization. *American Journal of Community Psychology, 31*(1/2), 15–33.

Hughes, D., Rodriguez, J., Smith, E. P., Johnson, D. J., Stevenson, H. C., & Spicer, P. (2006). Parents' ethnic-racial socialization practices: A review of research and directions for future study. *Developmental Psychology, 42*(5), 747–770.

Lee, S. J. (1996). *Unraveling the "model minority" stereotype: Listening to Asian American youth*. New York: Teachers College Press.

Neblett, E. W., Philip, C. L., Cogburn, C. D., & Sellers, R. M. (2006). African American adolescents' discrimination experiences and academic achievement: Racial socialization as a cultural compensatory and protective factor. *Journal of Black Psychology, 32*(2), 199–218.

O'Reilly, K. (2005). *Ethnographic methods*. New York: Routledge.

Stevenson, H. C., Cameron, R., Herrero-Taylor, T., & Davis, G. Y. (2002). Development of the teenager experience of racial socialization scale: Correlates of race-related socialization frequency from the perspective of Black youth. *Journal of Black Psychology, 28*(2), 84–106.

Stevenson, H. C., Reed, K., Bodison, P., & Bishop, A. (1997). Racism stress management: Racial socialization beliefs and the experience of depression and anger in African American youth. *Youth & Society, 29*(2), 197–222.

Thompson, C. P., Anderson, L. P., & Bakeman, R. A. (2000). Effects of racial socialization and racial identity on acculturative stress in African American college students. *Cultural Diversity and Ethnic Minority Psychology, 6*(2), 196–210.

Acknowledgement

This work was made possible through the work of principal investigators, research assistants, local and national advisory boards at the Research Institute for STEM Education (RISE) at the University of Oklahoma. For a complete list of contributors, visit http://www.ou.edu/RISE. This material is based upon work supported by the National Science Foundation's Directorate of Undergraduate Education's STEM Talent Expansion Program Grant No. DUE-0431642. Any opinions, findings and conclusions or recommendations expressed in this material are those of the authors and do not necessarily reflect the views of the National Science Foundation.

6

The Role of Ethnic Identity, Ethnic Flexibility and Ethnic Peer Affiliations in First-Year Latino/a College Students' Perceptions of Future Opportunities

Christy Teranishi Martinez

Abstract

Ethnic identity is a salient aspect of identity for many Latino/a adolescents, particularly as they make the transition from primarily Latino high schools and neighborhoods to colleges and universities where they are underrepresented. Research based on developmental identity theories has focused on how youth develop a strong, positive, and coherent sense of ethnic identity over time by examining their *strength of ethnic identity*, their sense of belonging and affirmation, exploration and commitment, and ethnic behaviors (Phinney, 1992). Research based on social identity theory has focused on how or why ethnic identity might vary across social contexts, such as by examining ethnic minority college students' *ethnic flexibility* and their use of different ethnic labels across social contexts (Stephan, 1992; Teranishi, 1998). This study utilizes qualitative and quantitative methods of inquiry to examine the roles of ethnic identity, ethnic flexibility, and ethnic peer affiliations in predicting first-year Latino/a college students' perceptions of their future opportunities. Results indicated that strength and flexibility of ethnic identity predicted perceived challenges to future opportunities, while peer affiliations did not play a role. Latino/a college students reported that their Latino/a peers caused them difficulties in attaining their future goals. Ethnic flexibility was related to greater perceived resources to future opportunities. Findings underscore how Latino/a college students' ethnic identity and ethnic peer affiliations across home and school contexts play an important role in their higher educational attainment.

KEY TERMS: Latino/a college students, ethnic identity, ethnic flexibility, perceptions of future opportunities

Introduction

The central question adolescents often ask themselves, especially when confronted with deciding what to do after high school is "Who am I?" In the transition from high school to college, Latino/a youths may encounter challenges due to conflicting goals, values, and expectations across their family, school, peer, neighborhood, and community contexts. For example, an 18-year old Latina girl who wants to go to college to become a doctor encounters conflict with her mother, who wants her to get married so her husband can provide for her. She confronts traditional cultural expectations that to be an adult means to be a wife and a mother, while she desires an American dream of obtaining her college degree to open up her career opportunities. She negotiates these conflicting goals and tells her mother that she has received a minority scholarship to go to college so that she does not need a man to support her.

The Multiple Worlds Model helps to understand how adolescents negotiate different goals, values, and expectations across family, peer, and school worlds. Phelen, Davidson, and Yu (1991) found that youths must navigate psychosocial, sociocultural, socioeconomic, gender, and linguistic borders in order to make transitions across their multiple worlds. Through qualitative open-ended interviews, observations of students, and teacher ratings, Phelan and her colleagues found four patterns to describe how diverse ethnic minority high school students negotiated the borders across their family, school and peer worlds. The first group, those who experienced smooth transitions across their worlds, had worlds that were similar: Their own goals, values, and expectations were congruent with those of their parents, friends, and teachers. The second group experienced different worlds due to differences in culture, ethnicity, socioeconomic status, or language; however, crossing borders between their worlds was manageable, such as by negotiating between mainstream values at school and traditional cultural values when at home and with their same-ethnic peers. A third group had very different worlds and experienced difficulty making transitions across borders, while the fourth group had extremely distinct worlds, and border crossing was impenetrable. Cooper and her colleagues built upon the Multiple Worlds Model to examine how Latino, African American, Japanese American, Japanese, and European junior high, high school, and college students' academic competence is related to various resources and challenges across their multiple worlds (Cooper, Gjerde, Teranishi, & Onishi, 1994; Cooper, Jackson, Azmitia, Lopez, & Dunbar, 1995; Cooper, Labissière, & Teranishi, 1997). These studies illustrate the different developmental pathways adolescents may take; however, they do not examine the complexity of the role ethnicity plays as adolescents negotiate their identity across cultural contexts.

Ethnic Identity Development

Ethnicity is a salient aspect of identity for many Latino/a youths, particularly as they make the transition from primarily Latino/a high schools and neighborhoods to colleges and universities where they are underrepresented. Developmental psychologists define ethnic identity as a "sense of belonging to an ethnic group and the part of one's thinking, perceptions, feelings and behavior that is due to ethnic group membership" (Rotheram & Phinney, 1987, p. 13); it is the process that adolescents and adults utilize to explore and make decisions about the role of ethnicity in their lives (Erikson, 1968; Phinney, 1992). Based on interviews with Asian American, Black, Latino/a, and European American junior and senior high school students, Phinney (1989) identified three stages of ethnic identity development. Fifty percent of the students were at an initial *unexamined* stage, showing a lack of exploration and little or no interest in the role of ethnicity in their lives. Twenty-five percent of the students were at the stage of *exploration*, demonstrating an active interest in understanding what it meant to be a member of their ethnic group. And 25 percent of the students were at the third and final stage of *ethnic identity achievement*, showing commitment and a deeper understanding and appreciation of their ethnic identity. Longitudinal research with Asian American, Black, and Hispanic youth shows a significant progression from lower to higher stages of ethnic identity development between the ages of 16 and 19 years old (Phinney & Chavira, 1992).

Ethnic Flexibility

Ethnic flexibility is operationalized as the number of important ethnic labels that students use to identify themselves across the contexts of their family, school, peers, neighborhood, and community contexts. Social identity theorists define ethnic identity as an aspect of a person's social identity which is "part of an individual's self-concept which derives from his[/her] knowledge of his[/her] membership in a social group(s) together with the value and emotional significance attached to that membership" (Tajfel, 1981, p. 255). Ethnic identity becomes a social identity when it is an important aspect of a person's self-concept or is emotionally significant. However, it is important to examine the distinctions and overlap between ethnic identities and social identities. On the one hand, a person's ethnic identity might be a separate category of group membership among various social identities. For example, a person might say "I am Latina, I am a woman, I am a graduate student, and I am poor," describing ethnic identity as one aspect among multiple social identities. Some studies examine the importance of one's ethnic identity in relation to other social identities (e.g., student, friend, co-worker) to see how central ethnicity is to her/his identity and self-concept (Ethier & Deaux, 1994). On the other hand, a person's ethnic identity might be intertwined with other social identities. For example, a person might describe their nationality as, "I am a U.S. citizen, I am an American of Mexican descent, I am Mexican American, and I am American."

For some adolescents, a single ethnic label may not accurately describe their ethnic identity, because they feel a sense of belonging to more than one ethnic/cultural group. For example, Latino/a adolescents may feel part of both ethnic minority and ethnic dominant groups and identify themselves as Mexican in one context and American in another (Phinney & Devich-Navarro, 1997). Latinos may also feel a part of a larger ethnic group, and identify themselves using pan-ethnic identities, such as Hispanic or Latino (Oboler, 1995). Often recent immigrants identify themselves by their nationality (e.g., Salvadoreños, Gualtemaltecos), and many U.S.-born college students identify themselves as Chicano/a (Padilla, 1995), although this also depends on the geographic location of the group. For example, Latinos in some parts of Texas or in New Mexico do not see themselves as Chicano/a, and many identify themselves as Hispanic (Buriel, 1987). Thus, use of different ethnic labels may vary across different contexts.

Relationship Between Ethnic Identity and Ethnic Flexibility

On one hand, using a large number of ethnic labels might suggest having an unexamined ethnic identity or a lack of clarity of the meaning of one's ethnic identity. Phinney (1993) found that Latino/a students in 9th and 10th grades in California tended to describe their ethnic identity in concrete, dualistic terms. For example, some ninth grade students "considered themselves Mexican because they spoke Spanish, ate tacos, celebrated Mexican holidays, and liked soccer; they saw themselves American because they spoke English, ate hamburgers, celebrated 4th of July, and enjoyed baseball" (Phinney, 1993, p. 53). On the other hand, individuals who use multiple ethnic labels to identify themselves might think about their ethnic identity in a more abstract, differentiated, and integrated way. One Mexican American adolescent described the meaning of her ethnic identity as, "I am a new race, bilingual, which is a mixture of the two countries. I am the new generation … a different race which knows about both cultures, Mexican and American" (Phinney, 1993, p. 55). Phinney suggests that adolescents move from concrete, dualistic thinking about multiple group identities, through a period of increasing awareness of conflict, to a more abstract, differentiated, and integrated sense of ethnic identity. Buriel (1987) reported that individuals of Mexican-descent might use one or more ethnic labels to describe their ethnic identity, including Mexican, Mexicana/o, Mexican American, and Chicana/o. He argued that from an outsider's perspective the use of different ethnic labels might suggest identity confusion or uncertainty of the meaning of one's ethnic identity, but from an insider"s perspective the use of multiple ethnic labels may represent "situation-specific identities" that enable them to maintain ethnic pride and a positive self-concept when confronted with discrimination and prejudice.

Ethnic Identity and Ethnic Peer Affiliations

Latino/a adolescents who do not have a strong ethnic identity may be ambivalent about the ethnicity of their peer affiliations (Phinney, 1990; 1992; 1993). Developmental studies indicate that as students develop a strong sense of their ethnic identity, they also develop more positive attitudes and relations with peers of their own ethnic group (Phinney, 1993; Phinney & Chavira, 1992). Phinney, Ferguson, and Tate (1997) found that those with a strong ethnic identity had more positive attitudes towards their own group, which in turn predicted more positive attitudes towards other ethnic groups. Hamm (1994) found that 84 percent of the Latino high school students reported having at least one cross-ethnic friend, and a significant proportion indicated having many cross-ethnic peer affiliations. Although some students felt closer to their own ethnic peers, this did not interfere with developing positive relationships with cross-ethnic peers. In a study of diverse high school students in California, Yu, Soukamneuth, and Lazarin (1999) found that students who had a strong ethnic identity and more cross-ethnic peer affiliations developed a more positive understanding and appreciation of both their own ethnic background and others' cultures. These findings suggest those with a strong sense of ethnic identity would have both Latino/a and cross-ethnic peer affiliations.

Ethier and Deaux (1994) argue that one way first-year Latino/a college students maintain a stable ethnic identity as they make the transition from home to college is by developing new relational support for their ethnic identity. In a study conducted at two Ivy League universities, they found that while first-year Latino/a college students' ethnic identity was initially supported by their family, stability of their ethnic identity was maintained through their Latino/a peers in college. Gurin, Hurtado, and Peng (1994) found that Latinos with more flexible ethnic identities (defined as more numerous and differentiated social identities) had more affiliations with White, African American, Asian, and American Indian friends, coworkers, and neighbors, and had fewer affiliations with those of their own ethnic group. Conversely, Latinos/as who had less flexible ethnic identities had more affiliations with members of their own ethnic group and fewer cross-ethnic affiliations. These findings suggest that those with higher ethnic flexibility would have fewer Latino/a and more cross-ethnic peer affiliations.

Ethnic Identity, Ethnic Peer Affiliations and Perceptions of Future Opportunities

Some students may perceive challenges to future opportunities due to the racial and economic inequalities and oppression their group has faced. They also may observe the day-to-day hardships and challenges their parents and grandparents have confronted. Matute-Bianchi (1991) found that some California Latino/a high school students felt that, no matter how hard they work, they would encounter a job ceiling and few opportunities for upward mobility. However, peers may also be a source of conflict and pressure in the school setting (Fordham & Ogbu, 1986; Ogbu, 1987, 1991). In Matute-Bianchi's (1991) study, some Latino/a students reported feeling that school success was equal to "acting White" and they would be betraying their Latino/a peers, so they developed an oppositional identity, rejecting the American educational system. In contrast, other Latino/a students indicated that their ethnic identity and involvement in Latino/a peer groups and organizations helped foster their ethnic pride, academic achievement, and positive perceptions of their future goals (Matute-Bianchi, 1991). Research suggests that high-achieving minority high school students were able to accommodate the rules and standards of the American educational system while maintaining a positive sense of ethnic identity and their ethnic peers (Gibson, 1988; Matute-Bianchi, 1986, 1991).

Other research suggests that having a strong sense of ethnic identity and Latino/a peers in college help buffer first-year Latino/a college students' perceived discrimination. Academically oriented peer groups and university outreach programs enabled African American and Latino/a middle school, high school, and college students to develop positive academic identities while preserving their ethnic and cultural identities (Cooper et al., 1995; Mehan, Hubbard, & Villanueva, 1994). Yu, Soukamneuth, and Lazarin (1999) found that ethnically diverse high school students who had a strong ethnic identity and cross-ethnic peers anticipated fewer challenges and positive intergroup relations across family, school, and peer contexts. Similarly, Hamm (1994) found that although a majority of ethnic minority high school students perceived greater challenges due to their ethnic identity in attaining educational goals, having positive cross-ethnic peer affiliations enhanced their ability to deal with stereotypes and discrimination. These studies suggest that having both Latino/a and cross-ethnic peers would be related to perceptions of fewer challenges and greater resources to their educational and career goals.

Building upon both developmental and social identity theories, the present study examines the role of ethnic identity, ethnic flexibility, and ethnic peer affiliations in first-year Latino/a college students' perceptions of future opportunities. It is predicted that, for first-year Latino/a college students, having a strong, flexible ethnic identity and having both Latino/a and cross-ethnic peer affiliations would be related to perceiving fewer challenges and greater resources in attaining their future educational and career opportunities.

Method

Participants

Participants were 87 first-year college students (49 females, 38 males) of Latin American heritage, attending a public university in California of approximately 11,500 students. The ethnic composition of the student body was predominantly European American (44%) and Asian American (31%), and 14 percent were Latino/a. Participants' mean age was 18-years-old (*SD* = .85, Range = 18 to 24). Seventy-four percent of the participants described themselves as Mexican (*N* = 64); 10 percent were mixed-heritage (*N* = 9); 6 percent were Salvadoreño (*N* = 5); 2 percent were Colombian (*N* = 2); 2 percent were Peruvian (*N* = 2) and the remaining participants were Guatemalan, Cuban, Puerto Rican, Ecuadorian, and Bolivian. Seventy percent of the students were U.S.-born (*N* = 61), and 30 percent were born in Latin America (*N* = 26). For 70 percent of the students, both parents were born in Latin America (*N* = 61); 14 percent had one parent who was born in the U.S. (*N* = 12); and 13 percent had both parents who were born in the U.S. (*N* = 11). Three students did not report their parents' birthplace.

On average, students reported that their parents' highest level of education was some high school and that they worked in semi-skilled occupations. Approximately 22 percent had one or two years of college, while 13 percent had a four-year college degree or higher. In addition, about 13 percent of the parents were clerical or sales workers, while approximately 20 percent of the parents were higher executives, business managers, and administrative personnel. About two-thirds of the students were immigrant or second-generation children of immigrants, and approximately 45 percent of the students grew up in primarily Latino/a neighborhoods and attended high schools with a primarily Latino/a student body, indicating they were comparable to the larger Latino/a college student population at the university.

Measures

Strength of Ethnic Identity. Phinney's (1992) 14-item Multigroup Ethnic Identity Measure (MEIM) was used to assess strength of ethnic identity. The MEIM includes three subscales: 1) *sense of belonging* (5 items; e.g., " I have a strong sense of belonging to my own ethnic group"); 2) *ethnic identity achievement* (7 items; e.g., "I have a clear sense of my ethnic background and what it means for me"); and 3) *ethnic behaviors* (2 items; e.g., "I am active in organizations or social groups that include mostly members of my own ethnic group"). Respondents rated items on a four-point scale from 1 "Strongly Disagree" to 4 "Strongly Agree." Strength of ethnic identity was calculated by summing across the 14 items and obtaining the mean. Cronbach's alpha reliability of this measure is .89.

Ethnic Flexibility. This measure was developed to examine the number of ethnic labels students used to identify themselves across contexts. Participants were provided a list of ethnic labels based on pilot study findings and Latino ethnic identity literature (Bernal & Knight, 1993; Matute-Bianchi, 1991; Oboler, 1995), consisting of Latino/a, Chicano/a, Mexican, Mexicano/a, Mexican American, Hispanic, American, and Other. They were given the opportunity to list any other ethnic identities that were important to them. Students were then asked to circle the ethnic label(s) they used to describe the ethnic group(s) they felt most closely affiliated with across the contexts of their family, school, closest friends, neighborhood, and ethnic community (e.g., church, ethnic group organization, etc.). Next, students were asked to rate the importance of their ethnic identity in each of the five contexts, on a four-point scale ranging from "Not Important" to "Very Important." Ethnic flexibility was assessed by summing the number of important ethnic identities students reported across the five contexts rated "Quite" to "Very" Important. Higher scores indicated higher ethnic flexibility. This measure was similar to Stephan's (1992) in that it assessed the number of ethnic identities students reported across contexts, but it differed in that it (1) provided students with a list of ethnic labels derived from the Latino/a identity literature in addition to allowing for open-ended responses; (2) assessed the importance of ethnic identity in each context; and (3) derived a score of ethnic flexibility.

Ethnic Peer Affiliations. Students' ethnic peer affiliations were assessed using a measure adapted from Gurin et al. (1994). Students were asked to rate the number of male and female Chicano/Latino, White/Anglo, African American, and Asian American friends on a five-point scale ranging from "None" to "All." Latino/a peer affiliations were calculated by summing students' ratings of male and female Chicano/Latino peer affiliations, and obtaining the mean. Because there were high intercorrelations among the items assessing White/Anglo, African American, and Asian American peer affiliations, and a factor analysis produced one factor, a composite score was developed to represent cross-ethnic peer affiliations, summing all of the items and obtaining the mean.

Perceptions of Future Opportunities. assessed students' perceptions of challenges and perceptions of resources in attaining their educational and career goals. First, students were asked their highest educational and career goals. Over 85 percent of the participants reported their highest educational goal was to obtain a post-graduate degree (e.g., J.D., M.D., Ph.D.), and the most frequently mentioned career goals were doctor (18%), business executive (15%), school teacher (10%), and psychologist (8%). Students were then asked to rate the extent to which they perceived their ethnicity caused them difficulties in attaining their educational and career goals. The measure was rated on a four-point scale ranging from 1 "Causes No Difficulties at all" to 4 "Causes Many Difficulties."

A composite score was developed for *perceptions of challenges* by summing the scores for the two items assessing perceived difficulties in attaining educational and career goals and obtaining the mean. Cronbach's alpha reliability of this two-item scale was .84. Next, students were asked to rate the extent to which they perceived their ethnicity was helpful in attaining their future educational and career goals on a four-point scale ranging from 1 "Not Helpful At All" to 4 "Very Helpful." A composite score was also developed for *perceptions of resources* by summing the scores for the two items assessing perceptions of resources in attaining educational and career goals and obtaining the mean. Cronbach's alpha reliability of this two-item scale was .78.

Focus Group Interviews

A phenomenological approach was used to inductively examine participants' meanings of their ethnicity and perceptions of challenges. After the survey was conducted and analyzed, a follow-up focus group interview was conducted among a subgroup of eight participants selected based on gender, ethnicity (self-report of parents' ethnic descent), strength of ethnic identity, and ethnic flexibility. All focus group participants were first-year Latino/a college students of Mexican descent. Students were asked to describe the ethnic labels they used to identify themselves across the contexts of their family, school, peers, neighborhood, and ethnic community, and whether they perceived their ethnic identity was stable and unchanging or flexible and changing across contexts. They were also asked the extent to which they perceived challenges and resources due to their ethnic identity in attaining their educational and career goals. Videotapes were transcribed (Pseudonyms are used to ensure the anonymity and confidentiality of the participants in this study). Qualitative data were coded and analyzed using a phenomenological approach. Students' narratives provide helpful perspectives to understand the meanings of their ethnicity. The rich details illustrate their feelings and thoughts about their perceived challenges due to their ethnicity.

Quantitative Analyses

Survey data were analyzed using the Statistical Package for the Social Sciences (SPSS) version 17.0. Descriptive statistics (means, standard deviations and ranges) and Pearson's correlational analyses were conducted with all key variables. Stepwise multiple hierarchical regression analyses were conducted to test the primary hypotheses.

Results

Means, standard deviations, ranges, and bivariate correlations of all key variables are presented in Table 1. On average, students scored moderately high on strength of ethnic identity ($M = 3.23$, $SD = .57$). On average, students reported low ethnic flexibility, reporting a single ethnic label to signify their ethnic identity across contexts ($M = 1.31$, $SD = .84$); however 57 percent of the students used two or three ethnic labels to identify themselves across contexts. Table 2 shows the various ethnic labels that students reported using across the contexts of family, school, peers, neighborhood, and community contexts.

TABLE 1. Descriptive Statistics and Intercorrelations of all Key Variables

Variable	Mean	SD	1	2	3	4	5
1 Strength of Ethnic Identity	3.23	.57	—				
2 Ethnic Flexibility	1.31	.84	.22*	—			
3 Latino Peer Affiliations	3.50	1.04	.42**	.28**	—		
4 Cross-Ethnic Peer Affil.	2.16	.58	−.02	−.02	−.22*	—	
5 Perceptions of Challenges	2.21	.87	.21*	.34***	.25*	.03	—
6 Perceptions of Resources	2.41	.93	.08	.24*	.18	.08	−.01

Note: $N = 87$. *$p < .05$. **$p < 01$. ***$p < .001$.

TABLE 2. Frequencies of Ethnic Identities Used Across Family, School, Peer, Neighborhood, and Community Contexts

Ethnic Labels	Family		School		Peers		Neighborhood		Community	
	N	%	N	%	N	%	N	%	N	%
Latino/a	9	10	18	21	11	13	8	9	19	22
Chicano/a	11	13	21	24	13	15	6	7	9	10
Mexicano/a	16	18	3	3	5	6	8	9	7	8
Mexican	18	21	9	10	10	12	19	22	11	13
Mexican American	13	15	11	13	11	13	12	14	14	16
Hispanic	1	1	2	2	2	2	1	1	2	2
American	7	8	15	17	16	10	16	18	3	3
Other	12	14	8	9	18	21	14	16	11	13
N/A or Missing	0	0	0	0	1	1	3	3	11	13

Note: $N = 87$.

The majority of participants reported having many Latino/a peers (M = 3.50, SD = 1.04), but few cross-ethnic peers (M = 2.16, SD = .58). Approximately 60 percent of the students reported that most to all of their peers were Latino/a. One student reported having no close friends and was eliminated from this analysis. Strength and flexibility of ethnic identity was positively correlated with Latino/a peer affiliations ($r(86)$ = .42, $p < .01$ and $r(86)$ = .28, $p < .01$ respectively), but neither was related to cross-ethnic peer affiliations. On average, students reported that their ethnicity caused them some difficulties (M = 2.21, SD = .87) and was somewhat helpful (M = 2.41, SD = .93) in attaining their educational and career goals.

Multiple hierarchical regression analyses were conducted to examine the extent to which perceptions of future opportunities were predicted by strength of ethnic identity, ethnic flexibility, and Latino/a and cross-ethnic peer affiliations. All variables were first transformed to standardized z-scores. A multiple hierarchical regression analysis was performed to examine strength and flexibility of ethnic identity, and Latino/a and cross-ethnic peer affiliations as predictors of students' perceptions of challenges (see Table 3). Strength of ethnic identity was entered at Step 1 (β = .21, $p < .05$). At Step 2, ethnic flexibility significantly contributed to the model (β = .31, $p < .005$). At Step 3, neither Latino/a (β = .15, $n.s.$) nor cross-ethnic peer affiliations (β = .08, $n.s.$) significantly contributed to the model. The final model was significant ($F_{overall}(4, 85)$ = 3.76, $p < .01$), indicating students who had strong, flexible ethnic identities perceived greater challenges to their future educational and career goals, while ethnic peers did not play a role.

TABLE 3. Stepwise Hierarchical Multiple Regression for Factors Predicting Perceived Challenges

Model		R	R²	AdjR²	β	FΔ	df	p(FΔ)
Step 1	Strength Ethnic Identity	.21	.05	.03	.21	3.95	1, 84	.05
Step 2	Ethnic Flexibility	.37	.14	.12	.31	8.97	1, 83	.004
Step 3	Ethnic Peer Affiliations	.40	.16	.12		.88	1, 81	.42
	Latino/a Peers				.15			
	Cross-Ethnic Peers				08			

Note: $F_{overall}(4, 85)$ = 3.76, $p < .01$.

A second hierarchical regression analysis was performed to examine factors predicting perceptions of resources to future goals. The final overall model was insignificant ($F_{overall}(4, 85) = 1.83$, $p < .10$). Only ethnic flexibility was related to students' perceived resources; students who had more flexible ethnic identities across contexts perceived greater resources to future opportunities.

Discussion

The 18-year old Latina girl described in the beginning of this chapter experienced conflict between her mother's traditional cultural expectations that she get married and be supported by a man, and her own goals and aspirations of pursuing a higher education and becoming a doctor. From the Multiple Worlds perspective, she has different worlds but manages border-crossing by confronting her mother and letting her know that she received a minority scholarship to help her attain her educational goals. From an identity development perspective, we can also examine how minority youths negotiate their ethnic identity across cultural contexts.

One focus group participant, an 18-year old second-generation Latina, *Mirella (pseudonym)*, scored high on Phinney's MEIM (3.60), and used four different ethnic labels across contexts. She identified herself as Mexicana in her family, American at school, Mexican American with her friends and in her neighborhood, and Latina at church. Although Mirella identified herself using different ethnic labels across contexts, she demonstrates having a differentiated and integrated sense of ethnic identity:

> "Even though I feel like I'm different under different situations, I think I'm generally just both [*Mexican and American*]. What I guess is different is I guess how I communicate, but I'm always the same person and I always consider myself the same person."

From a social identity theoretical perspective, Latino/a students may express their ethnic identity using different ethnic labels across different contexts as a means of self-categorization, but this does not necessarily mean they lack a strong sense of ethnic identity. This supports Buriel's (1987) finding that some Latinos/as use multiple ethnic labels to represent situation-specific identities, helping them maintain ethnic pride and a positive self-concept.

From a developmental perspective, high ethnic flexibility might reflect identity diffusion or lack of a clear sense of ethnic identity (Phinney & Rosenthal, 1992). However, on average, the first-year Latino/a college students in this study reported having a strong sense of ethnic identity and low ethnic flexibility, suggesting that many of these students have a strong, stable, and coherent sense of ethnic identity across contexts. Data provide evidence in support of Erikson's (1968) and Phinney's (1992) developmental identity theories.

Both strength of ethnic identity and ethnic flexibility were related to first-year Latino/a college students' perceived challenges to their future opportunities. Latino/a students in this sample resemble the Mexican-descent students in Matute-Bianchi's (1991) study who had a strong ethnic identity and perceived greater challenges to their future goals. Although participants in the present study were academically successful students who gained admissions into a university, they grew up in predominantly Latino/a neighborhoods, attended primarily Latino/a high schools, and primarily associated with Latino/a friends. This might have contributed to greater perceived challenges as they entered their first year in a predominantly White and Asian university. This supports Ethier and Deaux's (1994) findings, suggesting that as first-year Latino/a college students undergo both a developmental and contextual transition moving away from home to college, an increase in salience or awareness of their ethnic identity might contribute to greater perceived challenges.

Strength of ethnic identity and ethnic flexibility were also related to more Latino/a peer affiliations. These findings are congruent with Phinney and colleagues' research that strength of ethnic identity was related to more positive attitudes and relations with members of one's own ethnic group (Phinney, 1992; Phinney et al., 1997). One possible explanation for why strength and flexibility of ethnic identity were related to Latino/a peer affiliations is that while adolescents' exploration and awareness of their ethnic identity often begins in the family, it continues to be important in the context of their peers (Ethier & Deaux, 1994; Phinney & Rotheram, 1987; Phinney et al., 1997). Grotevant and Cooper (1998) found continuity between family and peer relations, suggesting that Latino/a youths with strong family cultural ties might also develop strong ties to their ethnic peers. Findings also extend Ethier and Deaux's (1994) research that showed that first-year Latino/a college students who had a strong sense of ethnic identity linked to a strong family cultural background became more involved in Latino/a peer groups and organizations in college.

Contrary to predictions, students' ethnic peer affiliations were not related to their perceptions of future opportunities. One possible reason is that 45 percent of the sample grew up in Latino/a neighborhoods and attended primarily Latino/a high schools, and 60 percent reported the majority of their friends were Latino/a. Participants in this study resemble a subgroup of California high school students in Yu et al.'s (1999) study who had a strong sense of ethnic identity and friendships with members of their own ethnic group. Hurtado, Dey, and Trevino (1994) found that ethnic minority students attending primarily White/Anglo universities participated in their own ethnic peer groups and organizations as a form of cultural support in order to buffer perceived racism and discrimination.

Although quantitative analysis did not reveal a significant relationship, qualitative focus group interviews revealed that some students described those within their own ethnic group as a source of challenge and conflict. Some participants stated that their Latino/a peers pressured them not to be "white-washed," "a sell-out" or assimilated while striving to attain their future goals. One Latina focus group participant, *Cris*, was raised in Japan from second to tenth grade while her father was in military service. She described her ethnic identity as "American" in the contexts of her family, neighborhood, and community, and "Japanese" in the contexts of school and friends. Cris indicated that her ethnic identity would be very helpful in attaining her educational and career goals, but it also caused her challenges due to pressure from peers and those within her ethnic group. She said, *"I will be able to fit in with my colleagues since most doctors in America are White … However, Mexicans will think I'm a traitor for not being close to my own ethnicity."* This example highlights the complexity of challenges Latino/a college students encounter associated with their ethnic identity, and provides evidence in support of Stephan's (1992) research that indicated that some people identify themselves to a group to which they were not biologically related but to which they had cultural exposure.

Students reported challenges from other external forces such as being an under-represented minority in their college, majors, and careers they wished to pursue. Some students described perceptions of racism and discrimination at school and in their community. Cooper and colleagues (1995) suggested that Latino/a students perceived challenges due to both discrimination and the pressure to succeed, and that support and proactive coping contribute to their self-confidence in attaining their future goals. The present study extends these findings, indicating that first-year Latino/a college students' strength and flexibility of ethnic identity were associated with perceptions of both challenges and resources to future goals. This is further illustrated by the following quotes from focus group participants:

Participant A   "People feel as though being 'Mexican' means I somehow lack knowledge of the American society, even though I was born and raised here. [But] it opens the door because I am bilingual, and based on stereotypes and other ideologies, it's rare for a Mexican American woman to be out in the professional world."

Participant B   "Being Mexican will provide me with benefits to improve my education and also with the motivation from people who relate to me. But, there is always the issue of discrimination and prejudice. I may be looked down upon for being Mexican."

Participant C   "Culture, ethnic pride, and awareness of my people push me to achieve my higher educational goals ... but racism, discrimination, and inequality are extremely prevalent in this society. I want to speak up as a representative of my ethnic group."

Suggestions for Future Research

Because this study is based on correlational analyses, the direction of the relationship between strength and flexibility of ethnic identity is unclear. Does higher ethnic flexibility contribute to a stronger, more positive understanding of one's ethnic identity? Or does having a stronger ethnic identity contribute to higher ethnic flexibility across contexts? Further research is necessary to achieve a better understanding of the relationship between developmental and contextual processes of ethnic identity. Also, it is unclear whether students developed a stronger sense of ethnic identity and used different ethnic labels across contexts as a conscious effort or a strategy in response to perceived challenges. Alternatively, having a stronger sense of ethnic identity and higher ethnic flexibility may have contributed to heightened perceptions of challenges, perhaps due to their ability to "pass" in and out of different social contexts. Since the directionality of the relationship between these variables is unclear, future research is needed to better understand the causal nature of their relationship.

This study utilized both quantitative and qualitative analyses, which enhanced my understanding of the complexity of first-year Latino/a college students' identity, peers, perceptions, and experiences. Further research is necessary to achieve a better understanding of the process by which adolescents develop a differentiated and integrated sense of ethnic identity, linking both qualitative interviews with quantitative survey methods. Longitudinal research is also needed, extending upon Ethier and Deaux's (1994) work to examine the extent to which first-year Latino college students' strength and flexibility of ethnic identity change over time and across contexts.

Gándara (1993) found that academically successful Latino high school students had two different peer groups—one at home and a different one at school. She found that by the time these students graduated from high school, they were able to move easily between their high-achieving Anglo friends and friends who would never leave the barrios or go to college. Further research is needed to examine the complexity of first-year Latino/a college students' ethnic peer networks across home and school contexts, and the role different peer groups play in helping students attain their various goals for the future, which may include close friendships, romantic relationships, and educational and career goals. For example, future research could build on the Multiple

Worlds Model to examine how first-year college students' network of relationships assist them in developing positive ethnic and academic identities in their transition from home to college. Findings underscore how Latino/a college students' ethnic identity and peers across home and school contexts play an important role in their higher educational attainment.

The present study provides continual support for identity development theory. By the time Latino/a adolescents have entered their first year of college, they have developed a strong, positive ethnic identity. Interestingly, strength and flexibility of ethnic identity were related to perceptions of both challenges and resources to future opportunities. On one hand, those who have a strong, flexible ethnic identity may "pass" in and out of different cultural contexts exposing them to more blatant racism and discrimination. On the other hand, they are also able to see how their ethnicity may help them—with both tangible resources such as grants and scholarships, and indirect resources such as support and guidance from mentors and role models—to be able to attain their future goals. There is evidence that shows those who have a more differentiated and integrated sense of ethnic identity have a higher tolerance for conflict and ambiguity of having multiple group identities, and an ability to proactively cope with stereotypes and discrimination (Phinney, 1993). The present study opens new questions about how ethnic and cultural identities are negotiated across family, school, peer, neighborhood and community contexts to enhance the educational and career opportunities of ethnic minority youths.

DISCUSSION QUESTIONS

1. What strategies might individuals use to negotiate their ethnic/cultural identity across cultural contexts?

2. How did the home communities in which these Latino/a students grew up influence their identity and ethnic peer affiliations?

3. What types of challenges and resources did the Latino/a college students encounter in attaining their educational and career goals? In what ways did the qualitative and quantitative analyses reveal different results?

4. Do you see the issues of ethnic identity, ethnic flexibility, and ethnic peer affiliations addressed in other chapters of this book? How are these questions of identity and belonging resolved? (See Also: Chapter 26, "'She has 50,000 Coaches': Re-envisioning Young Women of Color as Learners in Three Popular Films").

References

Bernal, M. E., & Knight, G. P. (Eds.). (1993). *Ethnic identity: Formation and transmission among Hispanics and other minorities.* Albany, NY: SUNY.

Buriel, R. (1987). Ethnic labeling and identity among Mexican Americans. In J. S. Phinney & M. J. Rotheram (Eds.), *Children's ethnic socialization* (pp. 134–152). Newbury Park, CA: Sage.

Cooper, C. R., Gjerde, P. F., Teranishi, C., & Onishi, M. (1994, April). *Antecedents of competence in early and late adolescence: An ecocultural analysis of Japanese, Japanese American, and European American adolescents.* Paper presented at the meeting of the Western Psychological Association, Kona, HI.

Cooper, C. R., Jackson, J.F., Azmitia, M., Lopez, E., & Dunbar, N. (1995). Bridging students' multiple worlds: African American and Latino youth in academic outreach programs. In R.F. Macias & R. G. Ramos (Eds.), *Changing schools for changing students: An anthology of research on language minorities* (pp. 211–234). Santa Barbara, CA: University of California Linguistic Minority Research Institute.

Cooper, C. R., Labissière, Y., & Teranishi, C. (1997). *Strategies for linking qualitative and quantitative analyses of childhood: Lessons from studies of ethnicity and identity.* Final Report to the John D. and Catherine T. MacArthur Foundation Research Network on Successful Pathways Through Childhood.

Erikson, E. H. (1968). *Identity: Youth and crisis.* NY: Norton.

Ethier, K. A., & Deaux, K. (1994). Negotiating social identity when contexts change: Maintaining identification and responding to threat. *Journal of Personality and Social Psychology, 67,* 243–251.

Fordham, S., & Ogbu, J. U. (1986). Black students' school success: Coping with the burden of "acting White." *The Urban Review, 18,* 176–206.

Gándara, P. (1993). *Choosing higher education: The educational mobility of Chicano students.* Berkeley, CA: California Policy Seminar.

Gibson, M. A. (1988). *Accommodation without assimilation: Sikh immigrants in an American high school.* Ithaca, NY: Cornell University Press.

Grotevant, H. D., & Cooper, C. R. (1998). Individuality and connectedness in adolescent development: Review and prospects for research on identity, relationships, and context. In E. E. A. Skoe & A. L. von der Lippe (Eds.), *Personality development in adolescence: A cross-national and life span perspective* (pp. 3–37). New York, NY: Routledge.

Gurin, P., Hurtado, A., & Peng, T. (1994). Group contacts and ethnicity in the social identities of Mexicanos and Chicanos. *Personality and Social Psychology Bulletin, 20,* 521–532.

Hamm, J. V. (1994). Negotiating the maze: Adolescents' cross-ethnic peer relations in ethnically diverse schools. In L. H. Meyer, H. S. Paria, M. Grence-Silneger, I. S. Schwartz, & B. Ham (Eds.), *Making friends* (pp. 243–261). Baltimore, MD: Brookes-Cole.

Hurtado, S., Dey, E. L., & Treviño, J. (1994, April). *Exclusion or self-segregation? Interaction across racial/ethnic groups on college campuses.* Paper presented at the annual meeting of the American Educational Research Association, New Orleans, LA.

Matute-Bianchi, M. E. (1986). Ethnic identities and patterns of school success and failure among Mexican-descent and Japanese American students in a California high school: An ethnographic analysis. *American Journal of Education, 95,* 233–255.

Matute-Bianchi, M. E. (1991). Situational ethnicity and patterns of school performance among immigrant and non-immigrant Mexican-descent students. In M. A. Gibson & J. U. Ogbu (Eds.), *Minority status and schooling: A comparative study of immigrant and involuntary minorities* (pp. 205–248). NY: Garland Press.

Mehan, H., Hubbard, L., & Villanueva, I. (1994). Forming academic identities: Accommodation without assimilation among involuntary minorities. *Anthropology and Education Quarterly, 25,* 91–117.

Oboler, S. (1995). *Ethnic labels, Latino lives: Identity and the politics of (re)presentation in the United States.* Minneapolis, MN: University of Minnesota Press.

Ogbu, J. U. (1987). Variability in minority responses to schooling: Non-immigrants versus immigrants. In G. Spindler & L. Spindler (Eds.), *Interpretative ethnography of education: At home and abroad* (pp. 255–280). Hillsdale, NJ: Erlbaum.

Ogbu, J. U. (1991). Minority coping responses and school experience. *The Journal of Psychohistory, 18,* 433–456.

Padilla, A. M. (Ed.). (1995). *Hispanic psychology: Critical issues in theory and research.* Thousand Oaks, CA: Sage.

Phelan, P., Davidson, A. L., & Yu, H. C. (1991). Students' multiple worlds: Negotiating the boundaries of family, peer, and school cultures. *Anthropology and Education Quarterly, 22,* 224–250.

Phinney, J. S. (1989). Stages of ethnic identity development in minority group adolescents. *Journal of Early Adolescence, 9,* 34–49.

Phinney, J. S. (1992). The multigroup ethnic identity measure: A new scale for use with diverse groups. *Journal of Adolescent Research, 7,* 156–176.

Phinney, J. S. (1993). Multiple group identities: Differentiation, conflict, and integration. In J. Kroger (Ed.), *Discussions on ego identity* (pp. 1–11). Hillsdale, NJ: Erlbaum.

Phinney, J. S., & Chavira, V. (1992). Ethnic identity and self-esteem: an exploratory longitudinal study. *Journal of Adolescence, 15,* 271–281.

Phinney, J. S., & Devich-Navarro, M. (1997). Variations in bicultural identification among African American and Mexican American adolescents. *Journal of Research on Adolescence, 7,* 3–32.

Phinney, J. S., Ferguson, D. L., & Tate, J. D. (1997). Intergroup attitudes among ethnic minority adolescents: A causal model. *Child Development, 68*, 955–969.

Phinney, J. S., & Rosenthal, D. A. (1992). Ethnic identity in adolescence: Process, context, and outcome. In G. R. Adams, T. P. Gullota, & R. Montemayor (Eds.), *Adolescent identity formation* (pp. 145–172). Newbury Park, CA: Sage.

Phinney, J. S., & Rotheram, M. J. (Eds.) (1987). *Children's ethnic socialization.* Newbury Park, CA: Sage.

Rotheram, M. J., & Phinney, J. S., (1987). Introduction: Definitions and perspectives in the study of children's ethnic socialization. In J. S. Phinney & M. J. Rotheram (Eds.), *Children's ethnic socialization* (pp. 10–28). Newbury Park, CA: Sage.

Stephan, C. W. (1992). Mixed-heritage individuals: Ethnic identity and trait characteristics. In M. P. Root (Ed.), *Racially mixed people in America*, (pp. 50–63). Newbury Park, CA: Sage.

Tajfel, H. (1981). *Human groups and social categories: Studies in social psychology.* Cambridge, MA: Cambridge University Press.

Teranishi, C. (1998, April). *Ethnic identity and adaptive strategies among first-year Chicano/Latino students.* Paper presented at the annual Western Psychological Association Conference, Albuquerque, New Mexico.

Yu, H. C., Soukamneuth, S., & Lazarin, M. (1999, April). *Navigating the ethnic and racial borders of multiple peer worlds.* Oakland, CA: Social Policy Research Associates.

Context II

Interracial Relationships and Families

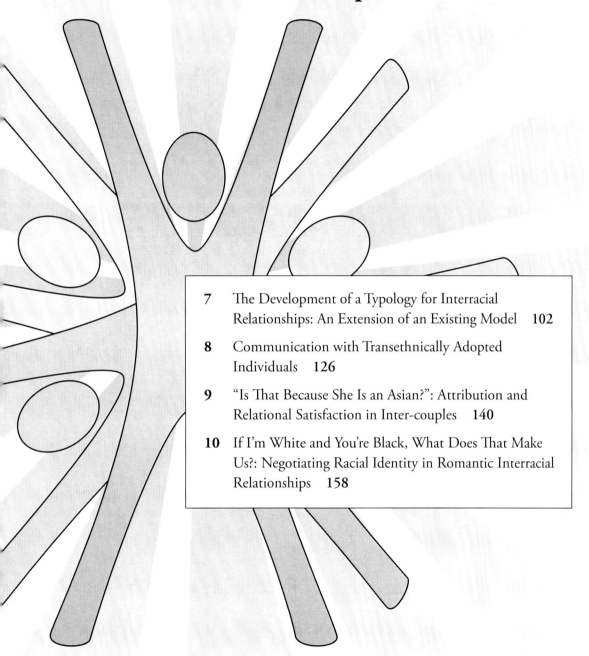

7

The Development of a Typology for Interracial Relationships: An Extension of an Existing Model

Juan M. D'Brot, Theodore A. Avtgis, Keith A. Weber, and Scott A. Meyers

Abstract

The significant number of non-White people in the United States, coupled with an increase in non-White immigration, adds to an increased probability of people participating in interracial relationships. With such a high percentage of the United States population being non-White, an inclusive typology examining the development and functioning of interracial relationships should be created. The purpose of this study was to determine if the Foeman and Nance (1999) model of interracial relationship development between Black and White couples could be adapted into a generalizable, interracial relationship typology, and if there would be distinct differences in the affective, cognitive, and behavioral dimensions of each stage. Long-table analysis of four focus group interviews confirmed differences among the four stages of the Foeman and Nance model (racial awareness; coping with social definitions of race; identity emergence; maintenance). Further examination of focus group transcripts revealed some differences among the affective, cognitive, and behavioral dimensions of each stage, with fewer differences emerging between the affective and cognitive dimensions across stages. Implications for the study of interracial relationship development are discussed.

KEY TERMS: Foeman and Nance model of interracial development, interracial conflict, interracial relationship typology, dimensions (affective, cognitive, and behavioral), relational maintenance

Introduction

The number of interracial marriages has dramatically increased in the United States since the abolition of laws prohibiting such unions. The large-scale immigration in recent decades, especially from Latin America and Asian countries, has contributed to the increase in the population of mixed race couples in the United States (Results of the 1996 Race and Ethnic Targeted Test, 2001). According to the U.S. Census Bureau (1998), only 21.2 percent of the interracial marriages in the United States were between Black and White individuals. Of all interracial marriages, 24.6 percent were American Indian and White couples, 18.1 percent were Asian and Pacific Islander couples, and 35.9 percent were other race (i.e., Hispanic and any other race not identified as Black, White, Asian and Pacific Islander, American Indian, Eskimo, or Aleut) and White couples (U.S. Census Bureau). These numbers, however, may not provide an accurate illustration of all interracial relationships. That is, couples not containing a White partner and non-married couples are not part of these statistics. The significant number of non-White people in the United States, coupled with an increase in non-White immigration, adds to an increased probability of people participating in interracial relationships.

Much of the research on communication patterns focuses on Caucasian-American college sophomores within the U.S (see DeWine & Daniels, 1992) with little or no research on patterns between non-White populations. As of the 2000 U.S. Census, 24.9 percent of the U.S. population identified themselves as non-White and 12.5 percent identified themselves as Hispanic or Latino (U.S. Census Bureau, 2000) (Retrieved from U.S. Census Bureau. Profile of General Demographic Characteristics: 2000: http://censtats .census.gov/data/US/01000.pdf on Oct. 7, 2009). It is expected that these numbers will have increased by the 2010 U.S. Census. With such a high percentage of the United States population being non-White, an inclusive typology examining the development and functioning of interracial relationships should be created.

Scholars have studied relational aspects, such as willingness to date interracially and characteristics of those who have dated interracially (DeWine & Daniels; Kaplan, 2002). Kaplan examined the motivations and willingness of White college students to date interracially. He found that external factors (i.e., physical attractiveness, approval, personality) were the main determinants of dating interracially. Although White men's involvement in interracial relationships was determined by external factors, White men generally preferred other White partners to all other minorities. Yancey (2002) found several characteristics prevalent in White people that determined participation in interracial relationships. These exhibitors included being male, Catholic, younger, politically liberal, attending an interracial school, and living in an integrated community. It is important to note that these characteristics were not a profile but independent factors, which increased participation in interracial relationships. The interracial couple may face differences in uncertainty stemming from individual differences, societal pressures, status differentials, and cultural origins that may not be experienced by same-race couples (Hall, 1976; Kaplan, 2002; Yancey, 2002). Thus, research should focus on the influence of these unique features on relational development specific to interracial couples.

Because individual cultures are different from one another, people with backgrounds rooted in different cultures may experience unique challenges in interactions, especially during relational development. Not only do relational guidelines differ between cultures, but status differentials between races and cultures could further complicate interactions (Hofstede, 1984). There may be socially inherent differences between races in terms of status that could play a role in how couples communicate. For example, people from more masculine cultures "expect men to be assertive, ambitious, and competitive … [and] expect women to serve and to care for the nonmaterial quality of life, for children and for the weak" (Hofstede, 1984, p. 390). Additionally, differences between cultures (e.g., power distance or uncertainty avoidance) can lead to inconsistencies in the amount of information each member of an interracial relationship either discloses or desires to receive (Hofstede). Not only could status differentials affect how couples interact with each other, but also status differentials could impact how couples interact with others. Because of the assumption that there are inherent differences associated with racial status (i.e., majority/minority) (Kaplan, 2002), individuals in interracial relationships may experience more strain and ostracism than their intraracial counterparts. These majority/minority differences may stem from powerlessness and lack of self-affirmation resulting from historical group or culture power differences (Hall, 1976).

The Foeman and Nance (1999) examination of groups through the lens of Harding's (1991) Standpoint Theory further support this explanation. Interracial relationships may be different from same-race relationships because of the strain or ostracism that people in interracial relationships may experience as a result of group membership and cultural differences (Hall, 1976; Hofstede, 1984; Houston & Wood, 1996; Kaplan, 2002; Yancey, 2002). However, even when examining interracial relationships, researchers have primarily examined Black and White couple interactions (Baldwin, Day, & Hecht, 2000; Martin, Hecht, & Larkey, 1994; Mills, Daly, Longmore, & Kilbride, 1995; Watts & Henriksen, 1998; Yancey & Yancey, 1998). For example, Harris and Kalbfleisch (2000) found that society and family were the primary deterrents of people becoming involved with interracial partners. However, people who became involved in interracial relationships enacted social distancing strategies more than individuals in same-race relationships, whereas same-race couples used more social approach strategies. The research on interracial relationships, other than Black and White couples, is not necessarily representative of the relational activity of other non-White couples (see Yancey, 2002).

Stages of Interracial Relationship Development

Foeman and Nance (1999) developed a model of interracial relationship development specific to Black and White interracial couples. To develop this model of relational development, the researchers conceptualized the strategies of successful interracial relationships and suggested four stages of interracial relational development stemming from previous theoretical and empirical investigations. The stages identified were:

(a) racial awareness,

(b) coping with social definitions of race,

(c) identity emergence, and

(d) maintenance.

Because these stages were developed specific to Black and White couples (see Foeman & Nance, 2002), these stages may be present in other interracial relationships, given the stressors on interracial relationships discussed earlier. Although differences within interracial couples involving members of various races probably exist unique from same-race couples, the stages involving the development of Black/White interracial relationships may be relevant to the development of any interracial relationship. That is, the differences experienced during the development of Black/White interracial relationships are likely mirrored during the development of any interracial couple.

Racial Awareness

According to Foeman and Nance (1999), an interracial couple's first stage of racial awareness is both an interpersonal and cultural experience marked by awareness of attraction toward the other individual and sensitization of the racial place of the other individual. Becoming sensitive to another's racial place involves understanding each other's group membership, becoming aware of their social roles in relation to their group, and developing a common perspective in the role race plays in relationships (Foeman & Nance, 1999). They also noted how same-group couples differ from Black and White couples in learning patterns and recognizing intentions. This is attributed to the fact that same-group couples belong to a homogenous group and are familiar with that group's norms.

The same dissimilarity in regards to group membership has been observed in other non-White groups (e.g., Hispanic, Asian, Eskimo, etc.) (Hofstede, 1984). The members of interracial couples should become aware of four perspectives: the individual's own point of view, his/her partner's, his/her collective racial group's, and his/her partner's racial group (Foeman & Nance, 1999). Couples in this stage may also recognize how race plays a role influencing the development of the relationship. During racial awareness, the members of an interracial couple acknowledge his/her attraction toward a member of a differing racial group and how that attraction will be scrutinized socially. The volatility of such attraction may not be limited to that of White and Black couples, but could be present among any couple of differing races.

Racial awareness is also created through people sensitizing themselves to their partner's racial place and status in society. Foeman and Nance discussed how cultural privileges differed between White and Black partners during everyday interactions, and how both members of the relationship "develop sensitivity to a sometimes uncomfortable alternative perspective" (Foeman & Nance, 1999, p. 550). An individual may take interest in their partner's culture or language, or purposefully immerse themselves in their partner's circle of friends. Foeman and Nance argue that the development of racial sensitivity is an important prerequisite for the development of a racial consciousness necessary to sustain interracial relationships.

Coping with Social Definitions of Race

According to Foeman and Nance (1999), once interracial couples have established racial awareness, the couple begins to cope with social definitions of race. The authors argue that in order to understand how couples cope with social definitions of race, it is important to first understand the construct of race. According to the Definitions of Race (2001), there are many definitions and origins of race. Merriam-Webster's Collegiate Dictionary (2004) alone presents eight different definitions of race, which range from the social to the biological. Because of the diverse ways in which race can be defined, the authors of this study propose a parsimonious definition of race: a class or kind of people unified by geographical, cultural, and ethnic origin.

During the second, or coping stage, the couple develops proactive and reactive strategies to handle a society that does not embrace interracial relationships, which may cause an interracial couple to insulate themselves from potentially damaging or harmful situations and settings. In addition to insulation, the couple also becomes competent in negotiating destructive situations that may be unavoidable. As an interracial couple becomes proficient "in the process of insulation and negotiation, they begin to work together to establish sets of characteristic responses to a variety of situations" (Foeman & Nance, 1999, p. 552). That is, an interracial couple is expected to develop a repertoire of behaviors that can be easily engaged and are designed to avoid or defend from potentially harmful situations. For example, an interracial couple may join a support group or circumvent a racial issue by linking it to a bigoted source. Foeman and Nance also noted interracial couples learn how to avoid racially charged issues or language in public settings, which may be damaging to the relationship. The coping stage provides a channel through which the couple strengthens relational bonds by working through challenges faced by the couple. A couple will or will not survive based on how they develop their own definitions of interracial couples and race (Foeman & Nance, 1999).

Interracial relationships as a whole could face societal pressures different from the societal pressures faced by same-race relationships. Similar to Black and White interracial relationships, other non-White individuals in interracial relationships also develop coping strategies to minimize the societal harm to which they may be exposed. However, how this is accomplished has yet to be empirically explored.

Identity Emergence

The Foeman and Nance (1999) third stage, identity emergence, is a process by which the members of an interracial couple redefine themselves by managing images of each other and their relationship. When interracial couples enter the identity emergence stage, they continue to develop and enact behaviors that are helpful for the survival of the relationship. The behaviors present during identity emergence typically arise from coping with social definitions of race. Interracial couples are able to redefine and label their experience in a way that challenges previously held norms (e.g., intraracial marriage, same-race children, similar family size, etc.), as well as taboos of society (e.g., interracial couples, interracial children, differing family traditions, differing religions, etc.). Because of the increasingly multicultural nature of the United States, Foeman and Nance speculate that interracial families may become more accepted in society. Until acceptance is the norm, identity emergence is an important part of sustaining an interracial relationship. With the increase in non-White U.S. residents and the number of interracial children climbing so quickly (Results of the 1996 Race and Ethnic Targeted Test), people may want to maintain their racial identity when entering an interracial relationship. Through the maintenance of racial identity, individuals in interracial relationships may identify the inclusion of a differing race in their lives as a source of strength and positivity (Foeman & Nance, 1999), rather than as a point of contention.

In order to maintain racial identity, one must constantly engage in identification with his/her racial culture or the racial culture of their partner. For instance, a couple may experience an increase in solidarity stemming from defending their relationship to outsiders, or begin to incorporate traditions from each others' backgrounds that become norms within their own relationship; however, it is not uncommon for one to engage in disassociation with his/her racial culture. According to Hall (1976), identification can function "as an individual dynamism that is more or less unique of a particular person; and as a manifestation, and probably one of the chief manifestations of culture" (p. 204). The construct of disassociation is a vehicle that an individual can utilize to persist with actions involved with identification, but to a different culture "… so that self-respect can also be maintained" (Hall, 1976, p. 206). By disassociating the self from actions that could harm feelings of belonging, the person enacting disassociation behaviors believes he/she is in fact identifying with his/her own culture, despite the other's awareness of disassociation (Hall). In order for people in interracial relationships to view their interactions with each other as beneficial (e.g., supporting cultural awareness, diversity, openness to new experience, collective experience dealing with race, etc.), each should identify with his/her own race while being aware of his/her partner's race identification.

Maintenance

The fourth stage of the Foeman and Nance (1999) model is maintenance. This stage is marked by an emergence of a couple's effective strategies and perspectives. Through the process of maintenance, interracial couples are able to revisit previous stages in response to any given need that arises. Although Foeman and Nance (2002) noted that maintenance may result in revisiting different stages when raising interracial children, the concept of maintenance is present in every type of relationship (e.g., married, non-married, romantic, non-romantic, interracial, same-race). Over the past two decades, researchers have studied relational maintenance in a variety of contexts and relationships, including marital relationships, dating relationships, cross-sex non-romantic relationships, and same-sex relationships (Dainton, Zelley, & Langan, 2003; Dindia & Baxter, 1987; Haas & Stafford, 1998; Hess, 2003; Stafford & Canary, 1991; Messman, Canary, & Hause, 2000; Vogl-Bauer, 2003).

Early examinations of relational maintenance behaviors of minority relationships occurred in the Haas and Stafford (1998) study of gay and lesbian romantic relationships. The researchers examined the validity of commonly held assumptions of differences that exist between same-sex and opposite-sex romantic relationships. Using the Dainton and Stafford (1993) typology, Haas and Stafford determined that same-sex partners used the same relational maintenance behaviors as opposite-sex partners. Same-sex partners, however, used two additional strategies: they participated in gay/lesbian support environments, and/or viewed their relationships as similar to or the same as heterosexual relationships.

Researchers have examined various types of relationships, but most of the participants in studies have been White college students or people in those college students' social networks. Within these social networks, it follows that most participated in same-race, majority group relationships. The Haas and Stafford (1998) study of gay and lesbian relationships was among the first to examine a minority group. Although the couple, compared to societal norms of sexuality, is considered a minority, an examination of the members within the couple highlights the similarity they have to one another (in their sexual orientation). This type of couple may parallel a same-race relationship in that the members of the couple can provide support for one another and be sensitive of each other's social place (e.g., their group membership, their social roles, and the role of sexuality in their relationship). In interracial relationships, couples may need to be continually cognizant of, and effectively manage, the concerns that emerged throughout the previous stages. A couple in the maintenance stage, however, may have discovered the most effective ways to defend their relationship: become more effective at considering the other's perspective and/or come to terms with the notion that outsiders may not be accepting of interracial relationships. An examination of the thoughts, feelings, and behaviors during the maintenance stage of interracial relationship development could shed light on the differences between partners in their group membership, social roles, cultural origins, and the role of race in the relationship.

Extension of Interracial Relationship Model

The Foeman and Nance (1999) model of Black/White interracial relationship development provides an excellent theoretical backdrop for examining the dynamism of other interracial relationships. The model appears to be a sound approach to examining and understanding the stages of interracial relationship development, but the model is purely conceptual. Research should focus on operationalizing the stages of this model to determine whether differences actually exist among each stage of interracial relationship development. Researchers have often utilized the tripartite of human action (i.e., cognition, affect, and behavior) to examine various relationships (e.g., Avtgis, West, & Anderson, 1998; Bagozzi, 1982; Lutz, 1977). According to Huitt (2006), *cognition* is the act or process of knowing through which knowledge is gained from perception or ideas. *Affect* is a feeling or emotion as distinguished from cognition, thought, or action (Huitt, 1999). While many definitions of *behavior* exist, with five found in Merriam-Webster's Collegiate Dictionary (2004) alone, the authors propose defining *behavior* as an individual's manner of action, reaction, or pattern of response to a given circumstance or stimulus. By determining the specific cognitive, affective, and behavioral processes that people enact in interracial relationships, researchers can more fully understand the development of such relationships.

Additionally, Foeman and Nance (1999) presented this model based on differences between Black and White interracial relationships. The differences between Black and White relationships may mirror the differences between members of interracial couples from other races. These differences may stem from the cultural origins of each race. Although there may be unique differences among various types of interracial relationships, the tensions that arise from those differences as stated in the Foeman and Nance model may be similar across interracial relationships. Because of the possible differences between interracial and same-race relationships in a myriad of factors including individual differences, group memberships, status differentials, and cultural origins, variations in relationship development may occur. When these characteristics are combined with the stressors (e.g., societal pressures, racism, and stereotypes) unique to interracial couples, the relational developmental process could be fundamentally different from that of same-race couples. The end-result may be that the cognitive, affective, and behavioral characteristics in interracial relationships manifest themselves differently from those in same-race relationships. As such, the following research questions are forwarded:

RQ1: Can the Foeman and Nance (1999) model of interracial relationship development be adapted into a generalizable interracial relationship development typology?

RQ2: Will there be a distinct difference in the affective, cognitive, and behavioral dimensions experienced in each stage of the Foeman and Nance (1999) model?

Method

This study employed a focus group methodology because it provides "a way to better understand how people feel or think about an issue ..." (Krueger & Casey, 2000, p. 4). This type of methodology provides an environment conducive to the generation of multiple perspectives and unique information regarding the stages of interracial relationship development. Focus groups also provide a forum for discussing personal experiences relevant to those in interracial relationships. Previous research using this method has provided a typology of relational maintenance behaviors through inductive analysis (see, for example, Canary, Stafford, Hause, & Wallace, 1993).

Through the process of induction, focus group interviews provide researchers with an opportunity to understand the specific thoughts, feelings, and behaviors of a cohort, and to generalize those findings to a given population. For example, Avtgis et al. (1998) conducted focus groups to inductively determine the feelings, thoughts, and behaviors present in Knapp's (1978) stages of coming together and coming apart. The results of Avtgis et al.'s study indicated that the focus group methodology was effective in explicating the thoughts, feelings, and behaviors associated with relational typologies.

Participants and Procedures

Participants were recruited from a large Mid-Atlantic university. The criteria for inclusion consisted of people presently or previously involved in an interracial romantic relationship, who were offered extra credit towards their final grade to participate in focus groups. Students who did not wish to participate or who did not fit the participant criteria were offered alternative opportunities to receive research credit (e.g. research paper or survey completion).

A single-category design (i.e., a design that examines differences among groups exhibiting the same characteristics) was used for four focus groups. Focus group participants were between the ages of 18 and 26, and relationships ranged from two months to five years. All terminated relationships that were referenced occurred within the last two years. Please note that the first race listed in each pair refers to the participating member. Additionally, all participants were individuals who represented a current or previous relationship. That is, in no case did both members of a couple participate in a focus group. The first focus group consisted of four women and six men, which included members of six current White-Black relationships, a former White-Black relationship, two current Black-White relationships, two current White-Hispanic relationships, a current Hispanic-White relationship, and …, a current White-Asian relationship. The second focus group consisted of four women and one man, and included members of three current White-Black relationships and two current White-Hispanic relationships. The third focus group consisted of three women and two men, and included members of three current White-Black relationships and two current White-Hispanic relationships. The fourth focus group consisted of five women, and included members of three current White-Black relationships, a current White-Hispanic relationship, and a former White-Indian relationship.

Students who agreed to participate in the focus groups were invited to sit in an empty classroom while the moderator offered refreshments and snacks. Prior to beginning the questioning route, participants were asked to sign a consent form. Participants were then given two handouts, one outlining Foeman and Nance's four stages and the other containing the focus group questions. All groups followed the same questioning route, which consisted of 15 questions identifying the thoughts, feelings, and behaviors during different relationship development stages. The focus groups lasted approximately two hours. Each focus group was audio-taped and transcribed by the first author. At conclusion, the participants were thanked and dismissed.

Analysis of Data

The participants' audio-taped responses were transcribed and analyzed. All responses were divided into individual units and sorted by the question it answered (e.g., the behaviors exhibited during racial awareness or the feelings experienced during identity emergence). After initial sorting, the responses were further divided based on whether they were characteristic of affect, cognition, or behavior. The descriptive summaries were then compared among groups to note similarities and differences.

Comments were given different levels of importance based on the frequency (i.e., the more often a topic was mentioned, the more important), specificity (i.e., the greater the specificity to which a topic was discussed, the more important), emotion (i.e., passion or enthusiasm attached to comment as evidenced by vocal inflection or speed of speech as interpreted by the audio recording and subsequent transcription), and extensiveness (i.e., how many different people mention something about the comment of another participant) of the comment. Through this, continually reoccurring themes were identified.

Results

The first research question asked whether the Foeman and Nance (1999) model of interracial relationship development could be adapted into a generalizable interracial relationship development typology. Long-table analysis of focus group transcripts revealed four themes for the stage of racial awareness, five themes for the stage of coping with social definitions of race, four themes for the stage of identity emergence, and three themes for the stage of maintenance (see Table One). These themes are not mutually exclusive, and all of the themes emerged in each of the four focus groups.

TABLE 1. Typology of Interracial Relationship Development

Strategy	Example
Racial Awareness	
Perspective Taking	"I tried to see where he was coming from, what kind of stuff that he had to deal with that I didn't."
	"I learned how to act with her family and she learned how to act with mine."
Social Networks	"I hung out with his friends more, even though they did things that I wasn't interested in."
	"We made an effort to include each other in almost everything we did with our own families."
Interest in Partner's Differences	"I was excited to be dating someone who was so different than me."
	"I was attracted to the whole exotic thing."
Attributing Transgressions Partner's Differences	"I made concessions about his behavior, maybe that's his culture."
	"I just figured he had a different way of thinking, you know, a different perspective."

(Continued)

TABLE 1. Typology of Interracial Relationship Development (*Continued*)

Strategy	Example
Coping with Social Definitions of Race	
Ignoring	"I try not to pay attention to what other people say."
	"If someone makes a racial comment, we would just walk away."
Adapting Behavior	"We would try to downplay the differences if we were with people who weren't approving or situations that either one of us weren't comfortable in."
	"We stopped the whole PDA thing when we were around the elderly or people who we thought would try and make us feel uncomfortable about our relationship."
Avoidance	"My family has a problem with it, so we don't go anywhere near them."
	"We didn't feel safe at the bar, it was just the two of us and like six of them who were bothering us, so we left."
Retaliation	"If someone's going to stare at me, then I'm going to stare right back."
	"I confronted this woman who just turned her head all the way around and said, 'That's disgusting.'"
Protection	"I had to defend my boyfriend to my grandmother when she said I shouldn't be dating that dark skinned boy."
	"When my family would speak in a different language so she couldn't understand, I would make them stop and explain what they were saying."
Identity Emergence	
Togetherness	"We started doing more things alone, trying to avoid other people, 'cause you never know who can cause you problems.'"
	"We had to defend and justify our relationship together and that made us a lot stronger for it in the end, faster than in any of my other relationships."
Talk	"We talked more in our relationship than I ever had in a same-race relationship. There was just so much more to learn about each other and his culture."
	"We tried to share interests, so I would tell him what interested me that I thought he never did, and he told me what he liked that he thought I had never done."

(*Continued*)

TABLE 1. Typology of Interracial Relationship Development (*Continued*)

Strategy	Example
Involvement	"I tried new foods, tried to learn her language, and experienced new traditions."
	"We both tried new things that we did that the other had never done before."
Social Support	"We tried to surround ourselves with people who didn't have a problem with it, being interracial I mean."
	"I got a lot closer with his friends 'cause they were a lot more accepting of our relationship than my friends."
Maintenance	
Efficiency of Selection	"It got easier as our relationship went on. We knew what worked for us and what didn't in terms of dealing with other people."
	"We learned that we couldn't just ignore everyone all the time, so we just don't visit my family anymore. It becomes avoidance now instead."
Awareness of Differences	"We don't attack each other because we know that we come from different families and backgrounds. We realize now how our differences affect our decisions and how we react to certain people, situations, or things."
	"We listen to each other more now. I know he has a different perspective than I do and vice versa."
Awareness of the Demographic Nature of Differences	"I feel like its outside elements that makes an interracial relationship what it is. If it were just about the relationship itself, there would be no interracial term, it's a society thing."
	"There are some internal differences, but the difference between skin color is the same difference between eye color and height. If I dated someone who was four feet tall, I'd probably deal with the same problems that if I dated a Hispanic girl."

Racial Awareness

The four themes that emerged during the stage of racial awareness were *perspective-taking, social networks, interest in partner's differences*, and *attributing transgressions to partner's differences*. For the purposes of this study, a transgression is defined as the violation of a relational contract. The *perspective-taking* theme refers to an individual's attempt to understand the partner's perspective and racial place in society. Participants indicated that they tried to act appropriately when in the presence of the other partner's group. A representative response was "He's a lot more aware of cops than I am. He doesn't speed and is always looking around."

The *social networks* theme involves expressing interest by using different social networks. Participants spent more time with their partner's friends and family than they would have otherwise done if the partner were of the same race. Participants also indicated that regardless of the activities, they would interact with their partner's friends to appear interested in and accepting of them. A representative response was "I stopped hanging out with my friends as much and started hanging out with all of his Asian friends."

The *interest in partner's differences* theme refers to the showing of interest in activities, customs, or differences apparent in a partner (e.g., hair texture, skin color, customs). Participants noted that they were attracted to someone who looked or sounded different. This attraction included showing excitement and eagerness when around the partner. A representative response was "I was attracted to the whole exotic thing."

The *attributing transgressions to partner's differences* theme was marked by giving more leeway to a partner after committing a misbehavior. Participants specified that they were less apt to reprimand, chastise, or inform their partner after the transgression took place than if they were of the same race. The lack of action was attributed to differences in culture or upbringing. A representative response was "You look past things that you normally wouldn't if it had been someone else."

Coping with Social Definitions of Race

The five themes that emerged during the stage of coping with social definitions of race were *ignoring, adapting behavior, avoidance, retaliation,* and *protection.* The *ignoring* theme refers to people not addressing or recognizing negative comments, behaviors, or actions. Participants indicated that when confronted with a racially charged comment or situation, they would not acknowledge the issue or would change the subject. A representative response was "If someone said something to me or him about my race, one of us would just change the subject."

The *adapting behavior* theme involves behaving differently depending on the circumstances and environment of the interaction. Participants explained that they would behave in a more subtle manner in order to downplay any obvious differences. Subtle behavior could include changing word choice or speech style, dressing differently, or eliminating public displays of affection. A representative response was "I told my boyfriend that he had to wear khakis and a shirt that hit above his knees if he was going to come over for Christmas dinner. I didn't want my parents getting on us for me dating a 'gangsta.'"

The *avoidance* theme concerns behaviors used to avoid situations that could be perceived as negative. Participants identified behaviors such as not spending time with specific family members or friends and removing themselves from an uncomfortable or dangerous situation. An uncomfortable or dangerous situation may be a circumstance where race is such a volatile issue that the tension may cause discomfort for the members of the couple or escalate to violence. A representative response was "We have to plan our vacations differently. We have to think about where we're going to be and what kind of people we are going to see."

The *retaliation* theme involves directly dealing with a negative event or circumstance. Participants reported that when another person behaves in a way that is perceived as negative, one member of the couple reacts directly to the instigator similarly or in a way that describes his/her feelings towards the behavior. For instance, if someone were to stare for too a long a period of time, someone may say, "What are you looking at?"

The *protection* theme concerns the actions taken to defend a partner, depending on the circumstance or situation. Participants identified confronting a person who they perceived to be attacking their partner. Protecting the partner included warning someone who had made a harmful comment or justifying the relationship to a critical outgroup member. A representative response was "When my friends made a racist joke, I would call them out on it and tell them that that's not cool."

Identity Emergence

The four themes that emerged during identity emergence were *togetherness, talk, involvement,* and *social support*. The *togetherness* theme refers to the increased amount of time the couple spends alone and the behaviors enacted by the couple that establishes a sense of unity. Participants noted that they avoided other people who they thought could create a negative situation, as well as reacted to situations similarly and in unison. A representative response was "We have an opportunity to learn more about each other because we are forced to see how we both react to the same situation. That makes us not only stronger, but it gives us a common enemy."

The *talk* theme involves the conversations that specifically concern learning more about the other person. The partners used the new information and experiences to better identify with the other person. Participants acknowledged that more conversations took place because there was more to learn about the other person (e.g., culture, traditions, customs, perspectives, etc.). Additionally, they noted that they would disclose information explaining interests, experiences, and viewpoints to which their partner had not been exposed. A representative response was "We talked so much more than in any of my same-race relationships. We always talked about so many more things because I had never done a lot of the things he had done and he had never done a lot of the things that I have done."

The *involvement* theme refers to the new experiences that both partners experienced with each other. Participants indicated that they set out to try new experiences with which their partner was familiar with and vice versa. These experiences included, but are not limited to, trying new foods, visiting new places, interacting with people differently, and experiencing new holidays.

The *social support* theme is marked by the couple placing themselves in environments conducive to the health of their relationship. Participants identified that one of the most important things necessary for their own well-being and the well-being of their relationship was that of support from their family and friends. If family and friends were not supportive, people stopped associating with family and friends. In addition, participants would actively seek out other people who did approve of interracial relationships. A representative response was "I got a lot closer with his friends because they were a lot more accepting of our relationship than my friends."

Maintenance

The three themes that emerged during the maintenance phase were *efficiency of selection, awareness of differences,* and *awareness of the demographic nature of differences.* The *efficiency of selection* theme was marked by an understanding of the strategies and behaviors deemed most effective and appropriate for the couple. Participants tended to revisit previous stages in the Foeman and Nance (1999) model and used those strategies that worked best for them. A representative response was "We avoided people or places we thought could be a problem. If we don't have to deal with it, then it doesn't become a fight or worry for us." Most participants identified avoidance, ignoring, and social support as the easiest and most effective strategies to use.

The *awareness of differences* theme is marked by an increase in understanding each partner's differences, strengths, and weaknesses. Participants indicated that they were slower to react negatively to a partner's transgressions than they would have earlier in the relationship. That is, the participant exhibited an increased threshold for negative affect when dealing with their partner's transgressions. This was attributed to the fact that they were already cognizant of their partner's typical reactions and perceptions. Participants also indicated that they approached potentially problematic or racially charged situations with more trepidation because of an awareness of how their partner could or would react. A representative response was "We don't fight as much as before because we are more aware of where our differences are and what we don't see eye-to-eye on. Now, we just avoid the topic or accept that there are differences."

The *awareness of the demographic nature of differences* theme focuses on the realization that many of the differences present within a relationship are not due to race but a myriad of individual differences. Participants noted they did not think of themselves as involved interracially until someone outside of the relationship forced that upon them or a drastic difference presented itself (e.g., language, the way someone's hair grows, getting a sun burn). Most participants identified the term *interracial relationship* as a product of society. Participants also noted that the differences between people of different skin color mirrored that of the differences between height, weight, eye color, or hair color. A representative response was, "I don't think race is a big deal to us who are in one [interracial relationship]. If it was, I wouldn't be dating someone who is 'different' than me. I think race isn't a big deal, but religion, geography, or socioeconomic status, that's more of a big deal."

The second research question asked if there would be differences among the affective, cognitive, and behavioral dimensions experienced in each stage. Long-table analysis of focus group transcripts revealed some important distinctions. Although the behavioral dimension differed across stages, the affective and cognitive dimensions exhibited few differences across stages. The affective dimension exhibited little variability across each stage of interracial relationship development. Affective responses included, but were not limited to, excitement, discomfort, indifference, feeling out of place, apprehension, hurt, and anger. A pervasive theme that emerged was that of anger or indifference when dealing with people who have a problem with interracial relationships. Further, participants exhibited feelings of discomfort, nervousness, and frustration when having to enact behaviors through all stages of interracial relationship development. Interestingly, participants noted a simultaneous sense of happiness, excitement, and pride in being able to share the experience with their partner, learning new things about their partner, and being generally unaware of racial differences. That is, the participants believed that the only reason race became a salient issue within their relationship was because people outside the relationship raised concerns regarding race. It should also be noted that couples in the maintenance stage attributed less negative affect stemming from the people within the relationship. People believed that the negative affect they experienced was a result of dealing with people outside the relationship who did not approve of interracial relationships.

The cognitive dimension also exhibited little variability across the stages of interracial relationship development. A few pervasive themes emerged in all focus groups and across most of the relational development stages. That is, participants often noted they did not think race was an issue during relationship development or across the life of the relationship.

The interracial nature of the relationship became salient when the couple was forced to deal with a person or situation that did not approve of the interracial nature of the relationship. Participants also identified several benefits to being in an interracial relationship. Participants attributed the benefits of interracial relationships to culture, religion, family background, and geographical location instead of race. In addition, participants believed they bonded as a couple faster and more efficiently than in their same-race relationships because they were forced to deal with racially charged situations. This sentiment was exhibited by people who felt they put more emotional and behavioral effort into the relationship because of increased stress. The behavioral items which emerged matched the themes answering the first research question.

Discussion

The purpose of this study was to determine whether the Foeman and Nance (1999) model of interracial relationship development could be adapted into a generalizable typology and if there would be distinct differences in the affective, cognitive, and behavioral dimensions of each stage. The first research question concerned the adaptability of the model into a typology. The evidence of this study supports the adaptation of the model into a typology of interracial relationship development. People in interracial relationships engage in various behaviors during the development of their interracial relationship that transcend the "type" of interracial relationship.

The findings of the present study provided initial support for the Foeman and Nance (1999) model of Black/White interracial relationship development. The results also suggest that this model may be applicable beyond that of Black/White interracial relationships. Participants made it evident that an Asian/White interracial couple faced the same social situations that a Hispanic/Black or Black/White interracial couple would face. Thus, Foeman and Nance model is generalizable to other minority/majority relationships.

In terms of investigating differences among affective, cognitive, and behavioral dimensions within and across each stage of interracial relationship development, interestingly, only the behavioral dimension differed across stages. The affective and cognitive dimensions demonstrated little variability across stages. The only difference was during discussions of the maintenance stage; participants reported less negative emotions toward each other because of a heightened awareness of ingroup/outgroup differentiation than was reported in other stages. That is, couples attributed the emotions attached to the enactment of behavioral strategies to a reaction toward people outside the relationship forcing issues regarding racial differences. Couples did not believe the emotions attached to the behavioral strategies enacted stemmed from individual differences.

The findings pertaining to the behavioral dimension were not surprising given that people may be expected to behave differently during distinct stages of relational development. One would not enact the same behaviors when learning about his/her partner as he/she would when having to deal with a potentially harmful situation involving race once the interracial relationship has moved past the initial stage(s). The findings pertaining to the affective and cognitive dimensions are noteworthy. More specifically, although the two dimensions are distinct from each other, the same themes appeared across all stages. This finding may be attributed to the association of a feeling or thought to a particular behavior and not to the developmental stage of the relationship. Although the feelings and thoughts someone may experience in an interracial relationship may change over time, they may experience similar thoughts and feelings when enacting the behaviors indicative of each stage of interracial relationship development. An individual who is forced to see differences not previously considered and an individual who has to either avoid, ignore, or retaliate in racially charged situations may not behave similarly, but perhaps exhibit the same thoughts and feelings. Participants repeatedly differentiated between people who would consider being in an interracial relationship and those who would not (i.e., people outside of the relationship or hypothetical individuals whom the participants used as comparisons to themselves during conversations). Those individuals who entertain the idea of being in an interracial relationship reported not thinking race was an issue and only contend with racially related situations when brought up by others (e.g., family members and friends).

Another issue is whether the proposed typology is truly unique to interracial relationships. According to Foeman and Nance (1999), couples in the stage of racial awareness should become aware of how race plays a role in the development of the relationship, how the attraction to someone different may be scrutinized socially, and how a member of the couple should become aware of his/her partner's role in society regarding race. The behaviors that emerged during this stage were perspective taking, using social networks, becoming interested in partner differences, and attributing transgressions to partner's differences.

Perspective taking behavior may appear to be a more salient issue for people in interracial relationships, but repeatedly, participants felt that perspective taking was a part of every relationship. Certain issues were more relevant when dealing with race (e.g., awareness of police presence, discrimination, racism) but the majority of the responses were indicative of learning and empathizing towards the other relational partner. The use of social networks was a behavior that people used to become closer to the other partner's friends. Periodically, people noted that this behavior was not limited to interracial couples but rather a tactic used to show interest in the other person and to establish common ties. The interest in partner differences emerged as a product of increased individual differences. Attributing transgressions to a partner's differences was perhaps the behavior most affected by race during this stage. Continually, many of the participants mentioned that various relational transgressions were grounded in racial differences between participants. Thus, social desirability, or the tendency to behave in a way we believe is socially acceptable and desirable, would prompt them to either stay in the relationship or overlook certain transgressions because of the interracial nature of the relationship. A person who leaves their partner because of an action that may be attributed to race (e.g., being boisterous in public, making a sexist remark, different table manners, etc.) may be viewed with negativity in society.

The behaviors enacted during the stage of coping with social definitions of race appeared to be situation-specific and salient to interracial relationships. Although the examples presented by all participants pertained to race (e.g., negative comments, looks, positively and negatively valenced questions, positively and negatively valenced behaviors), the thoughts and feelings surrounding those behaviors may be experienced by anyone dealing with the same situations stemming from a different issue. An individual who is in a romantic relationship with someone from a different religion, socioeconomic background, or location may easily experience a negatively perceived situation stemming from any of these characteristics. Thus, that individual may enact different behaviors but go through the same stage of coping with social definitions of religion, socioeconomic status, or geography when under social scrutiny as would someone in an interracial relationship.

The stage of identity emergence may not be limited to interracial relationships. It could be argued that the more differences that exist between members of the couple, the more behaviors regarding identity emergence would be enacted; therefore, relationships with members who believe themselves to be different with regard to other characteristics (e.g., height, weight, dress, language) would exhibit the same behaviors as those people who believed themselves to be different in interracial relationships, thus minimizing the impact of race as a latent factor, and reframing it as just another individual difference.

In the maintenance phase, all participants noted they developed a repertoire of strategies and behaviors that worked most efficiently, effectively, and appropriately for themselves and their partner. Although it seems logical to believe any couple type should enact the most efficient behaviors, the efficiency of the selection of behaviors emerged as a distinct strategy in the stage of maintenance. The awareness of differences emerged as a product of people understanding the limitations and boundaries of their partner and their relationship. People also expressed listening and empathizing more. Participants disclosed that this behavior was not based on race, but rather on a concern for the other person and the well-being of the relationship. Realization of the source of interracial differences was marked by the interracial couples realizing that although outgroup members perceived the relationship as different because of race, couple members saw race as another individual difference. Most participants emphasized they were not concerned about race unless someone outside the relationship raised the issue of race.

Interracial couples may be the couple type that contends with the most socially stigmatized individual difference; however, it is because of individual differences that the proposed typology of interracial relationship development may not be limited to interracial relationships. The individual behaviors within each stage may be unique to interracial relationships, but the stages of relationship development may be applicable to other relationships. Although the interracial nature of a relationship and the presence of different skin colors could be the most obvious difference to someone outside the relationship, other differences may exist. Two White individuals living on opposite ends of the country may have more differences to contend with than a Hispanic and an Asian individual who grew up in the same city. Any two individuals who are vastly different from each other (e.g., dress, language, style, height, social networks, religion) may confront the same issues that present themselves in interracial relationship development. It may be possible that race is another demographic variable that contributes to the overall amount of effort that couple members put into the relationship for the relationship to continue.

Confounding this further is the sex or gender composition of the couple. For example, can we assume that interracial dynamics are influenced by whether or not the male is black and the female is white as opposed to whether the female is black and the male white? In the end, perhaps researchers should focus as much research on the differences that exist within interracial couples as they do researching the differences that exist between interracial couples.

DISCUSSION QUESTIONS

1. The Foeman and Nance model of interracial development consists of four stages. What are they? Have you experienced these stages in your relationships, whether they are same-race or mixed-race?

2. Which statements in Table 1 have you heard from others? What was your response to the person(s) making the statement? Which of these statements have you made, and how did others respond?

3. Why do you think the authors used a focus group format to gather their data? What are the advantages and disadvantages to applying this method?

4. The authors end their chapter by observing "It may be possible that race is another demographic variable that may contribute to the overall amount of effort that couple members put into the relationship for the relationship to continue." Why do they suggest this possibility?

References

Avtgis, T. A., West, D. V., & Anderson, T. L. (1998). Relationship stages: An inductive analysis identifying cognitive, affective, and behavior dimensions of Knapp's Relational Stages Model. *Communication Research Reports, 15*, 280–287.

Bagozzi, P. R. (1982). A field investigation of causal relations among cognitions, affect, intentions, and behavior. *Journal of Marketing Research, 19*, 562–583.

Baldwin, J. R., Day, L. E., & Hecht, M. L. (2000). The structure(s) of racial attitudes among White college students. *International Journal of Intercultural Relations, 24*, 553–577.

Canary, D. J., Stafford, L., Hause, K. S., & Wallace, L. A. (1993). An inductive analysis of relational maintenance strategies: Comparisons among lovers, relatives, friends and others. *Communication Research Reports, 10*, 5–14.

Center for the study of White American culture: A multiracial organization website (2001). *Definitions of Race*. Retrieved January 12, 2006, from http://www.euroamerican.org/library/definitions race.asp.

Dainton, M., & Stafford, L. (1993). Routine maintenance behaviors: A comparison of relationship type, partner similarity and sex differences. *Journal of Social and Personal Relationships, 10*, 255–271.

Dainton, M., Zelley, E., & Langan, E. (2003). Maintaining friendships throughout the lifespan. In D. J. Canary & M. Dainton (Eds.), *Maintaining relationships through communication: Relational, contextual, and cultural variations* (pp. 79–102). Mahwah, NJ: Erlbaum.

DeWine, S., & Daniels, T. (1992). Beyond the snapshot: Setting a research agenda in organizational communication. *Communication Yearbook, 16*, 331–346.

Dindia, K., & Baxter, L. A. (1987). Strategies for maintaining and repairing marital relationships. *Journal of Social and Personal Relationships, 4*, 143–158.

Foeman, A. K., & Nance, T. (1999). From miscegenation to multiculturalism: Perceptions and stages of interracial relationship development. *Journal of Black Studies, 29*, 540–557.

Foeman, A. K., & Nance, T. (2002). Building new cultures, reframing old images: Success strategies of interracial couples. *The Howard Journal of Communications, 13*, 237–249.

Haas, S. M., & Stafford, L. (1998). An initial examination of maintenance behaviors in gay and lesbian relationships. *Journal of Social and Personal Relationships, 15*, 846–855.

Hall, E. T. (1976). *Beyond culture*. Garden City, NY: Doubleday.

Harding, S. (1991). *Whose science whose knowledge? Thinking from women's lives.* Ithaca, NY: Cornell University Press.

Harris, T. M., & Kalbfleisch, P. J. (2000). Interracial dating: The implications of race for initiating a romantic relationship. *The Howard Journal of Communications, 11*, 49–64.

Hess, J. A. (2003). Maintaining undesired relationships. In D. J. Canary & M. Dainton (Eds.), *Maintaining relationships through communication: Relational, contextual, and cultural variations* (pp. 103–124). Mahwah, NJ: Erlbaum.

Hofstede, G. (1984). The cultural relativity of the quality of life concept. *Academy of Management Review, 9*, 389–398.

Houston, M., & Wood, J. T. (1996). Difficult dialogues, expanded horizons: Communicating across race and class. In J. T. Wood (Eds.), *Gendered relationships* (pp. 39–56). Mountain View, CA: Mayfield.

Huitt, W. (1999). The affective system. *Educational Psychology Interactive.* Valdosta, GA: Valdosta State University. Retrieved May 8, 2006, from http://chiron.valdosta.edu/whuitt/col/affsys/affsys.html.

Huitt, W. (2006). The cognitive system. *Educational Psychology Interactive.* Valdosta, GA: Valdosta State University. Retrieved May 8, 2006, from http://chiron.valdosta.edu/whuitt/col/cogsys/cogsys.html.

Kaplan, A. M. (2002). Factors predicting Whites' involvement in interracial relationships. *Dissertation Abstracts International, 65*, 12B.

Knapp, M. L. (1978). *Social intercourse: From greeting to goodbye.* Needham Heights, MA: Allyn & Bacon.

Krueger, R. A., & Casey, M. A. (2000). *Focus groups: A practical guide for applied research* (3rd ed.). Thousand Oaks, CA: Sage.

Lutz, R. J. (1977). An experimental investigation of causal relations among cognitions, affect, and behavioral intention. *Journal of Consumer Research, 3*, 197–208.

Martin, J. N., Hecht, M. L., & Larkey, L. K. (1994). Conversational improvement strategies for inter-ethnic communication: African American and European American perspectives. *Communication Monographs, 61*, 236–255.

Merriam-Webster's Collegiate Dictionary, (2004). Retrieved January 12, 2006, from Merriam Webster Collegiate Web site: http://www.merriam-webstercollegiate.com.

Messman, S. J., Canary, D. J., & Hause, K. S. (2000). Motives to remain platonic, equity, and the use of maintenance strategies in opposite-sex friendships. *Journal of Social and Personal Relationships, 17*, 67–94.

Mills, J. K., Daly, J., Longmore, A., & Kilbride, G. (1995). A note on family acceptance involving interracial friendships and romantic relationships. *The Journal of Psychology, 129*, 349–351.

Stafford, L. & Canary, D. J. (1991). Maintenance strategies and romantic relationship type gender and relational characteristics. *Journal of Social and Personal Relationships, 8*, 217–242.

United States Census Bureau (1998). *Race of Wife by Race of Husband.* Retrieved November 17, 2005, from http://www.census.gov/population/socdemo/race/interractab1.txt.

United States Census Bureau (2001). *Results of the 1996 Race and Ethnic Targeted Test*. Retrieved November 17, 2005, from http://www.census.gov/population/www/documentation/twps0018/section-1.html.

Vogl-Bauer, S. (2003). Maintaining family relationships. In D. J. Canary & M. Dainton (Eds.), *Maintaining relationships through communication: Relational, contextual, and cultural variations* (pp. 31–49). Mahwah, NJ: Erlbaum.

Watts, R. E., & Henriksen, R. C., Jr. (1998). The interracial couple questionnaire. *The Journal of Individual Psychology, 54*, 368–374.

Yancey, G., & Yancey, S. (1998). Interracial dating: Evidence from personal advertisements. *Journal of Family Issues, 19*, 334–348.

Yancey, G. (2002). Who interracially dates: An examination of the characteristics of those who have interracially dated. *Journal of Comparative Family Studies, 33*, 179–190.

8

Communication with Transethnically Adopted Individuals

Daniel Cochece Davis, Jacqueline L. Kelly, Christopher J. Porter, and Nicole S. Rosini

Abstract

This chapter focuses on interactions involving transethnic adoptees' interpersonal relationships. It follows up on decades of existing academic research on transethnic adoptions by synthesizing this literature with basic communicative concepts and theories. It also provides an overview of transethnic adoptions in the United States, background information on ethnic identity, and intertwines interracial/intercultural communication concepts, showing similarity across key lines. The history of transethnic adoption in American society has been met with great controversy, yet such adoptions are increasing. Though transethnic adoption could cause confusion in the adoptee's overall stability, if families and communities teach cultural competence, adoptees will be able to create unique identities and more readily cope with discrimination. In this sense, adoptees may actually possess superior communication skills from those in monocultural/racial situations.

KEY TERMS: adoption, culture, ethnicity, interracial communication, race, transethnic

Introduction

During the 1960s the United States civil rights movement created increased interest in the academic literature surrounding "transracial adoption." Transracial adoption is the term used when a child of one race is adopted by parents of another race (Silverman, 1993). Since that time, several studies on psychological and social impacts of transracial adoptions explored a variety of perspectives. Yet, while much of academia provides significant insight into how being raised by parents of a different race affects adoptees, issues regarding the parenting of a child from a different ethnicity, involving *both* cultural and racial backgrounds of both the parents and the child, were less common. Even less common within the majority of extant information was any examination of the communicative aspects involved in such a system.

The purpose of the present chapter, then, is to gain a better understanding of the communicative dimensions of interracial/interethnic communication pertaining to transethnic adoptees, their identity development, and the communicative aspects of their socialization and ethnic selection processes. As such, this chapter seeks to understand and synthesize existing psychological and sociological literature with fundamental communicative concepts.

The increase in numbers of transethnically adopted individuals in the United States causes a heightened need for cultural awareness, as well as a need for understanding identity formation issues within multiethnic households. Increasing national cultural competence aids in facilitating effective communication with adoptees of any ethnicity, as well as interracial communication in general. Therefore, it is necessary to understand culture, communication, and ethnic disclosure in interpersonal communication on theoretical levels before integrating previous research with such fundamental concepts as acculturation, initiation of relationships, and levels of tolerance.

Ethnic Identity

Those opposing transethnic adoption maintain that it negatively impacts an adopted child's sense of racial and cultural identity, causing damage to the individual's overall stability (Moos & Mwaba, 2007). Racial and cultural identities are the two components comprising a person's *ethnic* identity (Hammond, Goodman, Greer, Hall & Taylor, 1975). Although research shows most adoptees experience some degree of difficulty in creating their own ethnic identities, it has also been shown that child-rearing that stresses cultural competence positively impacts these children and aids them in forming ethnic identities that are healthy, strong, and stable (Friedlander, Larney, Skau, Hotaling, Cutting & Schwam, 2000; Ishizawa, Kenney, Kubo & Stevens, 2006; Mohanty & Newhill, 2006; Vonk, 2001).

Race, in addition to being one of the key elements of ethnic identity, is "a category of persons believed, by themselves or by others, to have shared a common ancestry" (Goode, 1984, p. 547). It refers to the physical attributes of a person, such as body proportions, color of the eyes and skin, texture and straightness or curliness of hair, and jaw and nasal structure. The categorization of a person into a certain race, as such, is based purely on physiological fact (Landis, 1958). Contrary to early thinking, race has nothing to do with the health, personality, values, or beliefs of an individual. A majority of those characteristics are determined by culture, thereby delineating "race" from "culture" and "ethnicity." In reality, however, the concepts are often related to varying, and often significant, degrees. Interestingly enough, studies show that those who identify themselves under racial terms are doing so as a result of categories constituted by legal and historical preconditions influencing their behavior (Gaganakis, 2006). Gaganakis (2006) argues that, in this respect, race affects subjectivity in forming self identity.

Culture is generally used to make reference to behavior patterns, including beliefs, values, and ideas that are the shared possessions of individuals using symbolic communication (Culture, 2001). Culture can also involve artifacts or products handed down in a physical sense, but the significance resides in relationships of human behavior via the form of a symbol (Lindesmith, Strauss, & Denzin, 1977). In many respects, culture is the embodiment of an agreed upon set of public symbols coming together to communicate a certain worldview (Lie, 2003). Cultural identification has an inherent impact on the groups and categories people associate with. Social Identity Theory holds that the categories individuals place themselves into define who they are as a person (Hogg & Terry, 2001). Affiliation with these categories greatly impacts a developing a sense of self, and ultimately influences a person's outlook and reality (Hogg & Terry, 2001). Furthermore, cultures can provide individuals with a set of common understandings and answers to ethical issues (Vander Zanden, 1970). The process by which individuals learn culture, which is known as socialization, is facilitated by an individual's family, school, and community (Thomas & Tessler, 2007). In order to fully understand culture, it is essential to comprehend that, unlike race, culture is completely learned. That is, it is not innate within an individual, and has the ability to change over time.

The term "ethnic identification" is used to "refer to viewing oneself as a member of a national or regional group" (Friedlander, et al., 2000, p. 196). Each region or country has its own culture, but these areas are also comprised of individuals from different backgrounds. This overlapping of culture, race, and ethnicity, in association with identity of one's country, causes serious issues in the *creation* of ethnic identity, especially in transethnically adopted children.

There are many cultural factors contributing to an individual's unique transethnic identity. Culture serves as a mirror of social reality and has the power to unite people provided the person is willing to transcend previously held beliefs to cross social, national, and historical divides (Griswold, 2004). These "cultural spheres" give a unique dimension to communication (Berry & Epstein, 1999). The spheres shape perceptions and beliefs of the individuals and can lead to mutual social differentiation. Jandt (2001) describes these differentiations as acculturation, assimilation, and integration. Acculturation, also known as cultural adaptation, "refers to an individual learning and adopting norms and values of a new host culture" (Jandt, 2001, p. 356). Contrary to previous research concerning acculturation, recent studies show that individuals are able to maintain their birth culture even after being in contact with the mainstream societal group (Matsudaira, 2006, p. 471). Assimilation results from giving up one's cultural identity and moving into full participation in the new culture. True integration is the medium in which a person maintains important parts of their original culture, as well as adopting parts of the new culture (Jandt, 2001). Ethnic identities form due to subjective experiences of acculturation, and refer to having explored the meaning of one's ethnicity in a positive light (Schwartz, Zamboanga, Rodriguez & Wang, 2007). This includes the concept of cultural relativism. "Cultural relativity" assumes that any event or happening must be considered under a distinct framework in order to hold meaning or value (Villareal, 2007, p. 231). This concept ties into cultural receptivity and cultural complexity. Cultural receptivity is a term developed by two social workers in their study to measure parents' openness toward activities promoting their child's cultural development (Coakley & Orme, 2006). Cultural complexity delves even deeper into cultural relativism, dealing with differences such as the gender relations, language, food, commodities, and so forth(Mohammadi, 1997).

History of Transethnic Adoptions

Transracial adoption can be theoretically defined as "the joining of racially different parents and children together in adoptive families" (Silverman, 1993, p. 104). "Transethnic adoption" extends this concept by referring to any ethnicity adopting children from another ethnicity. Jennings (2006) indicates that Caucasian families in the United States represent the majority of foster parents (i.e., parents raising a child who is not their own by birth), who adopt children of different ethnicities. Because of the potential cultural and racial differences between the foster parent and child, transracial/ethnic adoptions would be seen as the most *noticeable* of all forms of adoption (Lee, 2003). As a result, these differences have created great political and social controversy surrounding transethnic adoptions, and numerous changes have been made to the systems by which these minority children are taken in by foster parents (Lee, 2003).

In the United States, expectations of ethnic homogeneity led to anti-miscegenation laws that made domestic transethnic adoption illegal in many states until they were struck down by the Supreme Court in 1967 (Fisher, 2003; Ishizawa et al., 2006). Elsewhere, one of the first cases of domestic transethnic adoption can be traced back to 1960 during the Civil Rights era, when a group called the Open Door Society (ODS) was formed in Canada to find homes for black foster children (Simon & Altstein, 2000). Black leaders and media saw great importance in finding black homes for these individuals, but the initiative ultimately failed because of lack of interest from members of the black community (Simon & Altstein, 2000). Because of this, the ODS instead turned to white families, which set the stage for the first group of transethnic adoptees in the United States (Simon & Altstein, 2000). Transethnic adoption was quickly met with opposition from minority communities such as the National Association of Black Social Workers (NABSW) and a variety of Native American tribes. These groups viewed transethnic adoption as a form of cultural genocide because they believed children would not have the proper skills necessary to deal with stereotyping and discrimination in racist societies (Lee, 2003). For decades to come, this ideology held by minority communities, combined with systematic changes in adoption processes that gave preference to same race adoptions, caused Black-White adoptions to decrease from 2,754 in 1971 to 1,400 in 1987 (Bachrach, Adams, Sambrano & London, 1990). In its entirety, however, social acceptance of transethnic adoptions has seen large increases from the 1970s to present day (Miall & March, 2005).

Although the problems with domestic adoptees are credible enough to warrant concern, these adoptees also have already been part of the culture of the United States since birth. In that respect, there is less confusion as to the *cultural* identity of the individual. Conversely, international child adoptees have little concept or exposure to their places of birth (Friedlander, et al., 2000). In the 1960s and 1970s, older, infertile white couples took advantage of international adoption, as opposed to domestic adoption, because it was more feasible and less controversial (Lee, 2003). International transethnic adoptions have been traditionally viewed as a product of numerous political and social influences, including war, poverty, dearth in social welfare, and social upheaval (Lee, 2003). For example, the United States saw an increase in the number of Asian children from abroad following World War II, the conflict in Korea, and the Vietnam War (Fisher, 2003). In 1992, China legalized international adoptions as a result of an unmanageable number of abandoned infant girls living in orphanages (Thomas & Tessler, 2007).

Even though international adoption is historically less controversial than its domestic counterpart, many individuals feel as though international adoptees are more prone to behavioral and medical problems than domestic adoptees (Lee, 2003). There have also been concerns about unfair practices in baby selling, kidnapping, and forced labor overseas. As a result, a large number of countries have been banned by the United States in adoption practices. Many third world activists also see international adoption as a form of colonialism and cultural imperialism, commodifying children to be bought and sold (Tessler, Gamache & Liu, 1999). To combat these problems, international rules and laws were established in order to standardize international adoption and ensure fair practice on both ends (Lee, 2003).

From 1991 to 2003, the number of international adoptees in the United States nearly doubled (Mohanty & Newhill, 2006). Americans currently adopt children from over 100 nations throughout the world, with a large majority of these children coming from China, Russia, South Korea, Guatemala, Ukraine, and Romania (Ishizawa et al., 2006). Currently, 85 percent of all transracial or transethnic children in the U.S. are adopted from another country (Lee, 2003), and by 2000, the U.S. had over 200,000 foreign-born children living with foster parents (Ishizawa et al., 2006). Also, 61 percent of all United States foster parents travel to their child's birth country before adopting the child in order to help facilitate the process and gain a better understanding of the child's birth culture (Hellerstedt, Madsen, Gunnar, Grotevant, Lee & Johnson, 2008). Despite these numbers, intercountry adoption is still seen as a last resort. The 1993 Hague Convention on Protection of Children and Co-operation in Respect of Intercountry Adoption stresses the importance of ensuring that children who are adoptees remain in their own country and with their own family. Many other countries around the world also hold this sentiment, asserting the importance of "personal, familial, communal, and national identities" (Ishizawa et al., 2006, p. 1210). Despite this, when adoption does occur, certain Euro-American nations hold that when an adoptee moves into a new country, s/he is considered a *clean slate*. This means that if the adoptee is completely removed from her or his country of birth, s/he is assumed to become fully part of the new culture as if s/he had never even lived anywhere else (Yngvesson, 2007).

Identity Formation in Transethnic Adoptees

Transethnically adopted children become aware of their adoption at an early stage, often because of visible physical differences existing between themselves and their adopted families (Friedlander et al., 2000). Many adoptees can describe the transition occurring from being simply a child in a family to an outsider in an Anglo society. From that point forward, the child begins to construct her or his ethnic identity. Immediately, individuals begin to feel alienated from those around them (Mohanty & Newhill, 2006). The consciousness of standing out amongst her or his peers plays a significant role in the development of ethnic identity, because although race and culture are fundamentals of ethnic identity, the *age* of the adoptees plays a significant role in shaping personality (Meinhof & Galasinski, 2005).

Outside pressure to conform to stereotypes associated with a single ethnicity puts pressure on adoptees to conform in society. This pressure is encouraged by a society's tendency to label people or objects as a means of preliminary understanding. These labels are first created by a society; consequently, the individual is expected to behave based on this *society (forced to choose) → home (themselves)*

label (Hammond, Goodman, Greer, Hall & Taylor, 1975; Vander Zanden, 1970). This causes individuals to feel pressure to choose a certain ethnicity (Friedlander et al., 2000). Since ethnicity can be twofold or more, transethnic adoptees become torn in their choice between race and culture. However, studies indicate that, although children feel the need to choose an ethnic identity because of pressure from society, at home they are comfortable in expressing their own individuality (Vidal de Haymes & Simon, 2003).

learning birth culture 2

Transethnic adoptees feel a strong sense of security in regard to their overall self-identity at home because a majority of transethnic parents are practicing *bicultural socialization*. Bicultural socialization is the way in which individuals learn the culture of two ethnic groups: in these cases the ethnic group of birth origin and the ethnic group of current residency (Thomas & Tessler, 2007). Bicultural socialization has historically been the reflection and bulk responsibility of the parents, but through increasingly connected and technologically informed societies, entire communities can now play a role in this process (Thomas & Tessler, 2007).

In Western cultures, it is often taught that all parents are supposed to love their children equally. Despite the negative stigma associated with adoption, this also holds true for an adopted parent and their adoptee (Wegar, 2000). Though it may be difficult raising children of different ethnic origins, research indicates a positive resultant effect on the well-being of the adoptee and the tolerance level of the family and community. Transethnic adoption blurs racial boundaries for those in the family and people who are intimately related to these adoptees (Ishizawa et al., 2006).

physically different same mind

In raising a transethnic adoptee, it is important for parents to help with the creation of a healthy ethnic identity. Children develop most healthily when parents recognize their physiological differences, but stress their psychological similarities (Benson, Sharma & Roehlkepartain, 1994). Many foster parents consider it important for children to be knowledgeable and prideful about their birth heritage: "Ethnic self-identity and pride are related to the family's attitude and the child's exposure to the birth culture" (Friedlander et al., 2000, p. 189). Since children aren't initially from the same birth culture as their parents, it becomes the parents' responsibility to become culturally competent and help the adoptees remain connected to their country of origin (Thomas & Tessler, 2007). The amount of exposure a child has to her/his birth ethnicity is directly correlated with the amount of self-esteem a transethnic adoptee possesses. The self-esteem of the adoptee is also shown to be positively influenced when parents are culturally competent (Mohanty & Newhill, 2006). Vonk (2001) describes parental cultural competence in three parts: a) racial awareness (sensitivity to racism and discrimination), b) multiracial planning (providing opportunities for the child to learn about her/his culture of origin), and c) social survival skills (ability of parents to prepare the children to deal with racism).

parents play role in child's cultural development

While it is the parent's responsibility to prepare the child for the discrimination s/he will face as an ethnic minority, some suggest that adoptees living in culturally diverse areas are more comfortable with their appearance and experience less discrimination than adoptees living in predominantly white neighborhoods (Feigelman, 2000). Conversely, a poor self-concept can develop as a result of not socializing with people who are of the same race or ethnicity (Moos & Mwaba, 2007). Exposure to different ethnicities beyond their own allows more space for adoptees to explore all aspects of their ethnicity (e.g., from both the birth country and country of residence), because "the formation of a healthy biracial [ethnical] identity is compromised by society's stigmatization of the minority group" (Friedlander et al., 2000, p. 189). Additionally, culturally diverse neighborhoods are often more accepting of minorities; therefore, some parents feel strong convictions that moving into an ethnically diverse neighborhood is in the best interest of the child (Vidal de Haymes & Simon, 2003).

Despite the cultural competence of the parents and community tolerance surrounding a transethnic adoptee, individuals create their own healthy or unhealthy ethnic identity. Previously discussed techniques only aid in creating optimal environments for adoptees to make this decision. Over a third of adopted children recall problems with their peers calling them names and teasing them because of their racial background, lacking consideration for the type of community in which they were raised (Mohanty & Newhill, 2006). Thus, regardless of the neighborhood, the survival skills taught by culturally competent parents are *vital* to an adoptee's healthy development. Ethnic identity is a critical development issue because children's self-identity as adolescents often shapes who they become as adults (Mohanty & Newhill, 2006).

Transethnic Adoptee Communication

Expression of oneself during communication seeks to obtain two vital results: the reception and understanding of a message (Meadow, 2006). *reception understanding* This requires not just composing words, but also providing receivers with comprehensible messages.

As a whole, dissimilarities between individuals hinder the development of accurate understandings of persons and messages from both sides. Thus, when adding ethnicity to a variation of the Shannon-Weaver Model of Communication (Shannon & Weaver, 1949), ethnic differences could serve as "noise" in this situation, reducing the overall "fidelity" of a message's transfer from source to destination. Yet, differences can sometimes function as conversation starters in the initiation of friendships (Sias, Drzewiecka, Meares, Bent, Konomi, Ortega & White, 2008). Additionally, negotiating shared objectives aids interracial and intercultural communication (Bennett & Salonen, 2007). Yet, levels of tolerance differ by individual and become apparent in situations of interaction between those of different ethnicities (Leigh, 1998). Transethnic adoptee messages are interpreted either positively or negatively depending on the receptiveness of their peers.

Conflicting values amongst cultures and ethnicities create social distance: "In many cultures of the world, there is a strong hierarchy or sense of status, in which certain members or groups exert great influence and control over others" (Littlejohn, 2002, p. 161). According to McQuillen (2003), psychological distance created between communicators of different ethnicities will result in a loss of fidelity. Many variables, including race, ethnicity, and culture, are definitive elements in whether the distance between two individuals can be bridged (Leigh, 1998). These factors are influential in the communicator's mental categorization, which can distinguish people based on ethnic differences. This judgment, often impeding communication, is called a *stereotype*.

Stereotypes are commonly used to refer to negative or positive judgments made about individuals based on observable or believed group membership (Jandt, 2001). Organizing the social world into categories or groups is a cognitive process defined as *social categorization*. Stereotypes provide the content for these social categories. Researchers commonly call a socially shared stereotype a *cultural stereotype* (Hewstone & Giles, 1986). Since individuals of the same ethnicity have comparable cultural tendencies, it is likely that their cognitive categorizations are also similar (Aronoff & Baskin, 1980). As such, when a person communicates with someone of their own ethnicity, each can expect a higher level of communicative ease than when communicating with someone completely foreign to their culture and race. This difference of ease can be quantified as a higher or lower amount of energy being expended, and so, *ceteris paribus*, interracial/interethnic/intercultural communication can be typified as higher energy communication than intraracial/intraethnic/intracultural communication.

Discussion

The academic literature surrounding transethnic adoption contains studies conducted from psychological and sociological perspectives. Building on these, the present chapter approaches transethnic adoption from a communicative standpoint, setting a foundation for future researchers. Individuals seeking similarity, highly predictable behaviors, and confirmed expectations, are likely to also possess minimal tolerance for social difference. *Tolerance* is developed via encounters with difference and the unexpected: the more complex one's expectations, the greater the tolerance for difference within the given area. In relation to transethnic adoption, a well developed, diversified identity is one in which both the birth culture and adoptive culture are each recognized and expressed.

Watzlawick, Beavin, and Jackson's (1967) five axioms regarding communicating even if one is not trying to communicate also explain that whether or not individuals are aware of it, they are subconsciously affecting others perceptions. The adoptees may or may not know how their self-expression increases awareness and tolerance of transethnic adoption, yet some individuals may see transethnic adoption as a vehicle for breaking down ethnic barriers.

One major factor in transethnic adoptees' negotiated identity is that the child understands s/he is adopted and of a different ethnicity much earlier than children of the same ethnicity as their parents; the child also often feels pressured to choose between ethnicities. This may include disclosure of their status as an adoptee, identifying them as a transethnic adoptee. How parents of such an adoptee communicate information regarding the child's birth ethnicity, and how they communicate with the child in preparing the child for peer communication and communication with other community members for the possible, if not anticipated, discrimination and ethnic challenges, all contribute to the transethnic adoptee's identity formation and ethnic health. Issues of ethnic tolerance, appreciation, and celebration all relate to the interpersonal communication one engages in and/or receives regarding ethnicity. For that matter, questions remain regarding how much of a transethnic adoptee's identity is tied to their *chosen* ethnicity and how this plays a role in their communication with peers and community members. As already discussed, many parents of a transethnic adoptee consciously select diverse communities as residences, due to the higher perceived levels of ethnic identity support and tolerance these communities may provide.

In sum, the history of transethnic adoption in American society has been met with great controversy. Since the 1960s, many minority communities have opposed the idea of transethnic adoption as a form of cultural genocide. Nonetheless, the numbers of transethnically adopted individuals over the last 40 years have seen steady increases. From a psychological and social standpoint, researchers believe that transethnic adoptions could cause confusion in the adoptee's overall stability. The ethnic identity crisis is due to difficulties balancing the difference between one's own race and the culture in which they are raised. However, if families and communities teach cultural and communicative competence, adoptees can create unique identities and more readily cope with discrimination. As a result, transethnic adoptees may actually possess superior communication skills, due to additional opportunities for social negotiation, ethnic explanation and consideration, and the higher levels of cultural awareness they are forced to address at earlier ages than those in monocultural/racial situations.

DISCUSSION QUESTIONS

1. How was domestic transethnic adoption in the U.S. initially received by minority communities? Do you think attitudes have changed about this form of adoption?

2. What are some of the political, cultural, and legal issues surrounding international transethnic adoption? Can you recall any recent, high-profile cases concerning this form of adoption that have appeared in the media?

3. How is the identity formation of transethnic adoptees affected by their family membership? How does *bicultural socialization* impact the adoptee's identity development?

4. What are some of the interracial communication challenges a transethnic adoptee might experience in her/his lifetime? When would these occur (e.g., childhood, adolescence, adulthood, etc.)?

# References

Aronoff, C. E., & Baskin, O. W. (1980). *Interpersonal communication in organizations.* Santa Monica, CA: Goodyear Publishing Company.

Bachrach, C. A., Adams, P. F., Sambrano, S., & London, K. A. (1990). Adoption in the 1980s. *Advanced Data from Vital and Health Statistics of the National Center for Health Statistics, 181.*

Bennett, J. M., & Salonen, R. (2007, March/April). Intercultural communication and the new American campus. *Change*, pp. 46–50.

Benson, P. L., Sharma, A. R., & Roehlkepartain, E. C. (1994). *Growing up adopted: A portrait of adolescents and their families.* Minneapolis, MN: Search Institute.

Berry, E., & Epstein, M. N. (1999). *Transcultural experiments.* New York: St. Martin's Press.

Coakley, T. M., & Orme, J. G. (2006). A psychometric evaluation of the cultural receptivity in fostering scale. *Research on Social Work Practices, 16,* 520–533.

Culture. *Encyclopedia of Sociology.* (2001). (2nd ed., Vol. 1, pp. 562–572). New York: Macmillan Reference.

Feigelman, W. (2000). Adjustments of transracially and inracially adopted young adults. *Child and Adolescent Social Work Journal, 17,* 165–183.

Fisher, A. (2003). Still not quite as good as having your own? Towards a sociology of adoption. *Annual Review of Sociology, 29,* 335–361.

Friedlander, M. L., Larney, L. C., Skau, M., Hotaling, M. Cutting, M. L., & Schwam, M. (2000). Bicultural identification: Experiences of internationally adopted children and their parents. *Journal of Counseling Psychology, 47,* 187–198.

Gaganakis, M. (2006). Identity construction in adolescent girls: The context dependency of racial and gendered perceptions. *Gender and Education, 18,* 361–379.

Goode, E. (1984). *Sociology.* Englewood Cliffs, NJ: Prentice Hall.

Griswold, W. (2004). *Cultures and societies in a changing world* (2nd ed.). Thousand Oaks, CA: Sage Publications.

Hammond, P. E., Goodman, L. W., Greer, S., Hall, R. H., & Taylor, M. C. (1975). *The structure of human society.* Lexington, MA: D.C. Health and Company.

Hellerstedt, W. L., Madsen, N. J., Gunnar, M. R., Grotevant, H. D., Lee, R. M., & Johnson D. E. (2008). The international adoption project: Population-based surveillance of Minnesota parents who adopted children internationally. *Maternal & Child Health Journal, 12,* 162–171.

Hewstone, M., & Giles, H. (1986). *Intergroup communication.* London: Edward Arnold.

Hogg, M. A., & Terry, D. J. (2001). *Social identity processes in organizational contexts.* Philadelphia: Psychology Press.

Ishizawa, H., Kenney, C. T., Kubo, K., & Stevens, G. (2006). Constructing interracial families through intercountry adoption. *Social Science Quarterly, 87,* 1207–1224.

Jandt, F. E. (2001). *Intercultural communication: An introduction* (3rd ed.). Thousand Oaks, CA: Sage Publications.

Jennings, P. K. (2006). The trouble with the Multiethnic Placement Act: An empirical look at transracial adoption. *Sociological Perspectives, 49,* 559–581.

Landis, P. H. (1958). *Introductory sociology.* New York: The Ronald Press Company.

Lee, R. M. (2003). The transracial adoption paradox: History, research, and counseling implications of cultural socialization. *The Counseling Psychologist, 31,* 711–744.

Leigh, J. W. (1998). *Communicating for cultural competence.* Needham Heights, MA: Allyn & Bacon.

Lie, R. (2003). *Spaces of intercultural communication.* Cresskill, NJ: Hampton Press.

Lindesmith, A. R., Strauss, A. L., & Denzin, N. K. (1977). *Social psychology* (5th ed.). New York: Holt, Rinehart and Winston.

Littlejohn, S. W. (2002). *Theories of human communication* (7th ed.). Belmont, CA: Wadsworth Group.

Matsudaira, T. (2006). Measures of psychological acculturation. *Transcultural Psychiatry, 43,* 462–486.

McQuillen, J. S. (2003). The influence of technology on the initiation of interpersonal relationships. *Education, 123,* 616–624.

Meadow, C. (2006). *Messages, meaning, and symbols: The communication of information.* Lanham, MD: Scarecrow Press.

Meinhof, U. H., & Galasinski, D. (2005). *The language of belonging.* Basingstoke, NH: Palgrave MacMillan.

Miall, C., & March, K. (2005). Open adoption as a family forum: Community assessments and social support. *Journal of Family Issues, 26,* 380–409.

Mohammadi, A. (1997). *International communication & globalization.* Thousand Oaks, CA: Sage Publications.

Mohanty, J., & Newhill, C. (2006). Adjustment of international adoptees: Implications for practice and a future research agenda. *Children and Youth Services Review, 28,* 384–395.

Moos, A., & Mwaba, K. (2007). Beliefs and attitudes about transracial adoption among a sample of South African students. *Social Behavior and Personality, 35,* 1115–1120.

Schwartz, S. J., Zamboanga, B. L., Rodriguez, L., & Wang, S. C. (2007). The structure of cultural identity in an ethnically diverse sample of emerging adults. *Basic and Applied Social Psychology, 29,* 159–173.

Shannon, C., & Weaver, W. (1949). *The mathematical theory of communication.* Urbana, IL: University of Illinois Press.

Sias, P., Drzewiecka, J. A., Meares, M., Bent, R., Konomi, Y., Ortega, M., & White, C. (2008). Intercultural friendship development. *Communication Reports, 21,* 1–13.

Silverman, A. R. (1993). Outcomes of transracial adoption. *The Future of Children, 3*(1), 104–118.

Simon, R. J., & Altstein, H. (2000). *Adoption across borders: Serving the children in transracial and intercountry adoptions*. Lanhan, MD: Rowman & Littlefield.

Tessler, R., Gamache, G., & Liu, L. (1999). *West meets East: Americans adopt Chinese children*. Westport, CT: Bergin & Garvey.

Thomas, K. A., & Tessler, R. C. (2007). Bicultural socialization among adoptive families: Where there is a will, there is a way. *Journal of Family Issues, 10*(10), 1–16.

Vander Zanden, J. W. (1970). *Sociology: A systematic approach*. New York: The Ronald Press Company.

Vidal de Haymes, M., & Simon, S. (2003). Transracial adoption: Families identify issues and needed support services. *Child Welfare, 82*, 251–272.

Villareal, C. (2007). Cultural relativity: My world, your world, our world. *Et Cetera: A Review of General Semantics, 64*, 230–234.

Vonk, M. F. (2001). Cultural competence for transracial adoptive parents. *Social Work, 46*, 246–255.

Watzlawick, P., Beavin, J., & Jackson, D. (1967). *Pragmatics of human communication: A study of interactional patterns, pathologies, and paradoxes*. New York: Norton.

Wegar, K. (2000). Adoption, family ideology, and social stigma: Bias in community attitudes, adoption research, and practice. *Family Relations, 49*, 363–370.

Yngvesson, B. (2007). Refiguring kinship in the space of adoption. *Anthropological Quarterly, 80*, 561–579.

9

Is that Because She Is an Asian?: Attribution and Relational Satisfaction in Inter-Couples

Sachiyo M. Shearman

Abstract

This chapter considers the history of 'inter-relations' and the challenges that inter-couples may face in the United States. The author discusses studies that examine the different types of attributions we make within relationships in general and how such attributions impact relational satisfaction. The author pairs this information with the findings from an online survey of undergraduate students who have dated or are currently dating interracially to provide insight on the association between attribution and relational quality and the perceived challenges and benefits within such relationships.

KEY TERMS: inter-relations and inter-couples (interracial or intercultural relationships), attribution, types of attributions

Introduction

We are "sense-making" social animals, as we often feel the need to make sense of our own and other's behaviors in our daily lives. This sense-making process is called "attribution". Various scholars have examined the process and types of attribution in different contexts (Heider, 1958; Kelley, 1973; Weiner, 1974). Several types of attributions have been identified and, while some can be damaging, others can be constructive to the relationship (Fincham & Bradbury, 1992; Roloff & Miller, 2006). We try to understand the behaviors of others based on factors including personality, mood, appearance, socio-economic status, social role, and so forth. Oftentimes, our understanding of the others' behavior is not necessarily explicitly stated. Rather, it is implied in phrases such as "Oh, that is how he is all of the time" or "Wow, it seems like she is in a bad mood today." In an interracial or intercultural relational context, do we "make sense" of others' behaviors based on his or her cultural background? For instance, if your classmate was being quiet in a group conversation, you might think, "Is she quiet because she is bored, tired, or not interested in this?" If the classmate happens to be an Asian, you might think, "Is she being quiet because she is an Asian"? It is one thing to think about the reasons for a behavior, but it is another to be certain about it. Without explicitly communicating with the other person about the reasons for a behavior, it is likely that our attribution regarding the behavior is inaccurate. At least, it is often safe not to jump to a conclusion, as it may not be true or definite.

Although some researchers report that interracial couples are not very different from intra-racial or mono-racial couples (e.g., Rosenblatt, Karis, & Powel, 1995), there are persistent claims that interracial couples face unique difficulties as they navigate their relationship (Chen, 2002; Henderson, 2000; Killian, 2000). Chen (2002) reported that many intercultural couples face difficulties in dealing with parents, extended family members, relatives, friends, and their communities. Interracial couples often have to negotiate with others in their social networks, as the social climate against interracial couples has been negative, or at least not normative in society (Killian, 2000). In addition, interracial couples have to negotiate with each other regarding their perspectives and expectations that might not seem normative to one another. Gaines and Brennan (2001) pointed out that an interracial couple's conflicts might entail unique challenges because an individual's belief system is likely to be influenced by respective cultural groups and may not be shared by the other person. In fact, according to the National Center for Health Statistics, the divorce rate for inter-ethnic couples is higher than for same-ethnicity couples in the United States (Bramlett & Mosher, 2002).

There is no question that all romantic relationships require commitment to working through individual differences and idiosyncrasies and possible difficulties in the course of their relationship. Given the above literature review, individuals in intercultural romantic relationships may experience hardships in maintaining a harmonious relationship because of racial or cultural differences as well as individual differences. It can be said that an intercultural romantic relationship is the integrative context where individuals are committed to work through their differences to maintain a constructive relationship even with the possible challenges they face (Williams & Anderson, 1998). It is therefore worthwhile to examine various aspects of communication behaviors of intercultural couples. In this chapter, I review the history of inter-relations in the United States and the challenges that inter-couples face. Then I revisit some studies that have examined different types of attributions we make in the relational context and their impact to relational quality. The findings of an online survey conducted among those who have dated or are currently dating interracially are shared. Specifically, this survey examined what these participants reported as to the challenges and benefits of being in an interracial relationship and different types of attribution that they would make in a given relational situation. In addition, the association between attribution and relational quality of an intercultural relationship among the participants in this study are discussed.

Inter-what? Couples

Before starting the discussion of romantic interracial relations, I want to clarify the terms "race" and "interracial relation". Race is a now-discredited scientific concept that attempted to link biological differences–including skin color and other physical characteristics–to differences between human groups. Race has been studied extensively; it has been some time since scholars asserted biological evidence accounted for behavior (American Anthropological Association, 1998). Today the concept of race is recognized as a social construct albeit a social construct that allows attribution based on differences in physical appearances; thus, the concept of "race" that we refer to is simply a social construct or socially constructed meanings that are attributed to the differences in our physical appearances (American Anthropological Association, 1998; Smedley, 1993, 2007).

Yet the concept of race as an acceptable scientific concept remains in some quarters and is still misused to explain social inequality among peoples. Due to the way it has been used historically in the United States, race has a persistent impact on daily life in this country. Race influences how we interpret our experiences, how we identify or define ourselves and others, and how we interact with each other (Omi & Winant, 1994). Consequently, race remains an important construct in communication studies and useful in delimiting our interpersonal experiences.

Researchers who have studied the issue of inter-group relations have used the terms "interracial" to refer to relations between individuals of different racial background; therefore, this term is used in this chapter. Oftentimes when we think of interracial relations, we typically think of a relationship between individuals of different races, most likely Blacks and Whites but not those who are mixed or bi-racial, those in the other minority groups, or those who are from other countries. Various other terms exist to refer to certain kinds of "inter-relations" such as inter-ethnic, inter-national, inter-generational, inter-faith, or inter-religious relations. Therefore, terms such as "inter-relation" or "mixed marriage" can be used to be inclusive. These terms avoid defining how "inter" or "mixed" the relationship is according to race, faith, ethnicity, or nation (e.g., Heller & Levy, 1992). Also, the term "inter-cultural relationship" or "intercultural couples" can be more encompassing, in that they refer to the differences in the shared values, beliefs, or customs of the specific cultural groups to which each individual belongs. For this reason, I use terms such as "inter-relations," "inter-couples," or "intercultural couples" rather than interracial couples. When referring to studies by other authors (e.g., Rosenblatt et al., 1995; Williams & Andersen, 1998), however, I use the term interracial couples. Regardless of the terms used, the emphasis is placed on the romantic relationships of couples composed of individuals of different racial or ethnic backgrounds.

Intermarriages in the U.S.

In this country's not-so-distant past, a personal choice such as finding a partner for dating or marriage was subject to societal bias and structural racism. The societal endorsement for endogamy, or the practice of marrying a member of one's own social group, was so strong that exceptions to endogamy were illegal. As early as the mid-1600s, legislation banning Black and White interracial marriage was established. Anti-miscegenation laws that prohibited marriage, cohabitation, and sex between races (specifically between Whites and non-Whites) were in place in 30 states (Lovingday. org, 2009). After World War II, several states repealed the anti-miscegenation laws. Only after the landmark case of *Loving v. Virginia* in 1967 did anti-miscegenation laws become unconstitutional across the country.[1] This ruling allowed people to choose a partner freely, without consideration of racial backgrounds. In 2000, Alabama removed its anti-miscegenation law and officially became the last state in the U.S. to do so (Hartill, 2001).

In the last several decades, the number of interracial marriages has been steadily on the rise. According to the Census Bureau's American Community Survey in 2005, there are about 1.32 million interracial marriages, making up roughly 3 percent of all marriages in the United States (U.S. Census Bureau, 2005). Although that is still a small fraction of the overall population, the percentage of cross-cultural marriages is growing. *The Washington Post*, the Kaiser Family Foundation, and Harvard University (2001) conducted a large survey and reported that Americans in general are more accepting of persons with different backgrounds in their family than they used to be. Although American families in general are more accepting of interracial marriages to their household, this same survey reported that interracial couples (White-Black, White-Asian, and White-Hispanic couples) experience various difficulties within their families.

Challenges and Bias toward Inter-relations

Due to the historical background discussed above, it may seem logical for researchers to examine the qualities of interracial relations. In fact, many scholars seem to assume that interracial relationships can be examined in comparison with mono-racial relationships, in that they are different from mono-racial relationships and possibly suffer a poorer relational quality (e.g., Kalmijin, 1993; Shibazaki & Brennan, 1998; Yancey & Yancey, 1998). Some scholars hypothesized that an interracial relationship can be examined with economic, educational, and social class indicators. For example, scholars examined economic reasons that motivated people to engage in an interracial relationship. They reported that economics motivated the lower-class members to marry higher-class members, forming interracial marriages as a way to move up socioeconomically (e.g., Kalmijin, 1993; Yancey & Yancey, 1998). Other scholars examined the relational quality of interracial couples in comparison to mono-racial couples, predicting inferior relational quality among interracial couples (e.g., Shibazaki & Brennan, 1998).

Although many scholars assumed heightened difficulties for interracial couples due to racial, ethnic, or cultural differences (e.g., Gaines & Ickes, 1997; Henderson, 2000), various researchers reported that interracial couples are not very different from intra-racial (or mono-racial) couples in quality (e.g., Rosenblatt et al., 1995; Troy, Lewis-Smith, & Laurenceau, 2006). Troy, Lewis-Smith, and Laurenceau (2006) reported that, among the couples they surveyed, there was no significant difference between interracial couples and mono-racial couples. In fact, interracial partners reported no differences in conflict patterns, and reported higher relationship satisfaction than mono-racial couples. This study implies that, if managed well, interracial couples can strengthen the bond between them and have a more satisfied relationship than mono-racial couples regardless of the difficulties they may face.

Nevertheless, the fact that interracial couples often do face unique and difficult challenges cannot be ignored. According to the National Center for Health Statistics, there is a higher divorce rate for inter-ethnic couples than same-ethnicity couples (Bramlett & Mosher, 2002). Various scholars have reported and examined unique challenges that the intercultural couples face as they navigate their relationships (e.g., Chen, 2002; Gaines & Ickes, 1997; Henderson, 2000; Killian, 2000). Those involved in interracial relationships not only deal with who they are as an individual regarding their own racial or cultural identity, but also with their relational identity as a mixed couple. Additionally, as they navigate their relationship, they need to figure out ways to define themselves while dealing with each other's different racial or cultural networks and backgrounds. Others in their social network, as the social climate toward interracial couples has been negative or at least not normative in our society (Henderson, 2000; Killian, 2000).

Chen (2002) reported that intercultural couples face difficulties in dealing with parents, extended family members, relatives, friends, and community. Interracial couples often face more family oppositions than mono-cultural couples (Mills, Daly, Longmore, & Kilbride, 1995). Even when family members accept their relationship, the couple may face unwarranted prejudice by their own network, commu-nity, or society (McNamara, Tempenis, & Walton, 1999). In fact, scholars have noted that Black and White couples are often reminded of their *interracial status* by the negative stares, racially and sexually stereotypical comments and sometime blatant discrimination (e.g., Killian, 2000; Thompson & Collier, 2006; Williams & Andersen, 1998).

Like mono-cultural couples, intercultural couples have to negotiate their individual perspectives and expectations that might not be normative to each other. In addition to these kinds of challenges that any other couples face, intercultural couples may face added difficulties due to the differences in their use and preferences for language, accents, and/ or conflict styles. According to Ting-Toomey and Chung (2005) the intercultural couples may bear greater potential for conflict and cultural clash than mono-cultural couples. Gaines and Brennan (2001) pointed out that intercultural couples' conflict might have unique challenges, because the individuals' belief systems are likely to be influenced by their respective cultural groups, which may not be shared with each other.

Interracial romantic relationships can be important, as these individuals must work through differences regardless of obstacles constructed by the society. It is valuable for us to further understand how individuals in an interracial relationship can integrate their differences and prosper together even with societal adversity. Williams and Andersen (1998) pointed out that "what has long been missing in interracial union research is a focus on the constructive communication, affirmation, and intimate bonds that are established within interracial romantic relationship" (p. 181).

Attribution in Relationship

In our daily lives, we tend to try to "make sense" of our environment or people around us. Heider (1958) used the word 'naïve scientists' to refer to this tendency that we all have. Many of us cannot help but to make some kinds of interpretations about why people act the way they do (Heider, 1958; Kelley, 1976). For instance, imagine that your significant other arrived late explaining simply that s/he was trying to look good for you. There is no indication of remorse. You may think to yourself, "Well, s/he seems to be happy to see me," and you may even think his or her reason for being late is kind of cute. On the other hand, if you are a type of person who values punctuality over almost any-thing else, you may think s/he does not care about you enough. These are all examples of the "sense-making" we do in our daily lives based on our observation of a simple behavior such as being late. You may attribute the reason for behaviors to one's personality, mood, charm, lack of love, and so on.

What kind of attributions would you be making in an intercultural relationship? In an intercultural relational context, would you make sense of the other's behavior based on his or her cultural background? If a Brazilian friend of yours came to a meeting late, would you assume that "Oh, he is late because he is from Brazil and they are just so laid back?" Or, if an Asian student was being quiet in a conversation, would you attribute this behavior to the person being bored, tired, or to the fact that s/he is an Asian? This sense-making process can be unspoken, but implied. In an intimate relationship, it is more likely that these attributions will be expressed and discussed. The kind of attribution one is making and how or whether it is expressed may strongly impact the relationship. Here, I would like to review different types of attributions and their impacts on a relationship.

Basic and Other Types of Attributions

Various types of causal attributions have been studied and there are three basic dimensions of attribution that has been most extensively examined: *locus* (internal vs. external), *stability* (stable vs. unstable), and *globality* (global vs. specific) (e.g., Fincham, Bradbury, & Scott, 1990; Sillars, 1980). An attribution can be internal or external. In other words, the causes for a behavior would be associated with one's personality or who he or she is (internal factors), or alternately, the causes would be associated with situational or environmental (external) factors. Let's use a simple criticism expressed by a partner as an example. Rachel and Shoji have been dating for months. One evening, Shoji criticizes Rachel for how she spends her time. What would be a reason or causal attribution for him to do that?

Rachel may say it is because that is who he is: he is just an openly critical person (internal cause) or she could say he is not like that usually, so he must be having a bad day today (external cause). A second dimension for attribution is stability, or the use of stable or unstable causes. When Shoji criticized Rachel, she could think that he has said things like this ever since she has met him (stable cause) or she may think to herself that he is acting like this because he is stressed about an upcoming exam that is important to him (unstable cause). A third dimension of attributions concerns how global or specific an attribution is. The more globally you see the cause, the more likely you will think it applies to many other behaviors of the other person. For instance, when Shoji criticizes Rachel, she may think that he is like that all the time, no matter what the issue or which person is involved, as he is critical of professors, classmates, and politicians alike (global cause). Or she may be able to say that he is not a critical person in other contexts, rather he is being critical in this instance because he is being honest and opening up to me (specific).

Other types of attributions were also found to be useful in examining our cognitive processes in close relationships (Fincham & Bradbury, 1992). They include intentionality (intentional vs. unintentional) and responsibility/blame (responsible vs. not responsible). Intentionality refers to the degree to which a behavior is perceived as intentional or not intentional. Responsibility refers to the degree to which a behavior or an event is perceived as something the other is responsible for. Rachel might perceive Shoji's behavior as something that he has done intentionally and he is responsible for. Alternately, she could think he did something that was unintentional, so he is not responsible and should not be blamed for what he did.

Behavior can be understood based on the role that one takes (e.g., boyfriend, student, etc.), or the behavior based on the culture that one may ascribe to. Shoji might be critical of Rachel because he may perceive that it is his role as a partner (role attribution) to be open and motivate her to do things. Or, Shoji can be critical of Rachel because of his cultural background, where being "critical" means "caring" for the other (cultural attribution). If so, Shoji's comment toward Rachel could be understood not as a criticism but as caring advice, as he cares so much about her that he was trying to help her.

Positivity, Negativity, and Errors in Attributions

When you encounter a behavior that is unexpected or unfamiliar, or when a behavior is unwelcome, you would very likely attempt to make sense of it. Roloff and Miller (2006) claim that people are more likely to make attributions about negative behaviors or uncooperative behaviors than positive or cooperative behaviors observed in an interpersonal conflict settings. Attributions by their nature entail biases and mistakes, which are called *actor-observer bias* or *fundamental attribution error* (Kelley, 1973). There is a tendency for us to make rather harsh, unfair, and destructive attributions for other's behaviors, while making more fair and constructive attributions to our own behaviors. In general, we are more likely to make positive attributions (e.g., external, not stable, and specific) about our own behaviors and use negative attributions (e.g., internal, stable, and global) for the other's behavior (Bradbury & Fincham, 1990; Cropley & Reid, 2008; Sillars, Roberts, Leonard, & Dun, 2000; Vangelisti, 1994). This is found to be especially true when unhappy couples have a conflict (Sillars, et al., 2000).

Relational Satisfaction

Several scholars have examined how attribution, or this cognitive causal reasoning process, is associated with perceived quality of the relationship. When happy couples and unhappy couples are compared, some researchers have found differences in how they make attributions about each other's behaviors (e.g., Bradbury & Fincham, 1990; Cropley & Reid, 2008; Fincham, Harold, & Gano-Phillips, 2000). General findings indicate that those who are in satisfying relationships tend to make attributions that are positive to the relationship and that attributions related to negative behaviors such as criticizing are linked with causes that are external, unstable, and specific. In contrast, those who are in a distressed relationship make attributions that are negative to the relationship, such as the internal, stable, and global causal attributions (Bradbury & Fincham, 1990; Vangelisti, 1994).

In other words, if you are in an unhappy relationship and you observe your partner's negative behavior, you are likely to think "Oh that is because of who he is (internal), he is not likely to change (stable), and that he is like that all of the time (global)." In contrast, if you are in a positive relationship, you may think, "Oh that is because he is having a bad day (external factor), he is just under a lot of stress (unstable), and he is not going to be like this all the time (specific)." The opposite can be true, however, when a positive behavior is observed in a relationship. For instance, one day Shoji tried to surprise Rachel with a flower as a random gift. Rachel can interpret this as positive behavior because Shoji is just a lovable and caring guy, or negatively in that he may have something to hide from her. You can imagine how these attributions can impact our relationships!

Scholars have also found that making negative attribution not only relates to lowered relational satisfaction or quality but also correlates with destructive conflict communication. Specifically, when we attribute negative behaviors to internal, stable, and global causes, we are more likely to respond using negative and distributive conflict (Sillars, 1980; Davey, Fincham, Beach, & Brody, 2001). Scholars also report that a judgment of responsibility (or believing that your partner is responsible for the action) is also associated with the intention to blame your partner in a conflict (Fincham & Bradbury, 1987). This can create a vicious cycle and aggravate a couple's conflict communication, hence affecting ideas about the overall quality of the relationship.

Listening to the Voices of Intercultural Couples

To examine the experiences of intercultural couples, attributions made among intercultural couples, and its association with the relational satisfaction, an online survey targeting individuals involved in an intercultural relationship was conducted. This study looked at ways inter-couples make attributions about behaviors and reported their overall relational satisfaction. In addition, their narratives about the challenges and benefits of interracial relations are shared in the voices of the participants.

Participants

Participants were recruited through the University's e-mail newsletters distributed among college students in a state university in the Southeastern United States. The criteria for participation were set for those who are undergraduate students and are currently in an interracial relationship or have dated interracially within the past five years. As an incentive to participate in the survey, they were informed that five out of all who participated would have a chance to win a $20 gift card from a retail store.

Seventy-seven participants (11 males and 66 females) responded to the online survey questionnaire. The survey included several demographic questions, including relationship history, age, education, and racial/ethnic backgrounds of participant and partner. The average age of the participants was 24 years old with a range of 18 to 53. Twelve participants (15.6%) are married, and 47 (61%) are currently in an intercultural dating, while the remaining 10 (23.4%) reported about a previous interracial dating experience. The average length of the dating period was 2.9 years, with individual dating relationships ranging from 2 months to 7 years. The average length of intercultural marriage was 1.5 years with individual marriages ranging from ten months to 23 years.

Survey

Participants were asked to indicate what attribution they would make in response to a certain relationship-related scenarios. Further, they identified perceived challenges and benefits associated with an intercultural relationship. Relational Attribution Measures by Fincham and Bradbury (1992) were included in the survey. Participants were asked to think of a confrontation in their own relationship (i.e., your partner criticizes something you say) and then were asked to rate several statements that measure different types of attributions that they are likely to make. Types of attributions measured include causal attributions (local, stability, and globality) and responsibility-blame attributions (intent and responsibility/blame). Two other external attributions (role and culture) were also measured. Norton's (1983) Marriage Quality Index measures were revised to read "relationship" instead of the word "marriage" to be applicable of the dating relationship. Evaluative statements such as "I believe our relationship is strong" and "My relationship with my partner makes me happy" were included in the survey.

Survey Findings on Attribution and Relationship Quality

The descriptive statistics on relational quality measures and relational attribution measures are displayed in Table 1. The distribution was negatively skewed with the mean on the high end of the relational quality measure (M = 3.92, SD = 0.91). This indicates that the majority of intercultural couples self-reported high relational quality. More normal distributions were observed for seven types of relational attribution measures. Internal attribution (attributing to the individuals' personality) had the highest mean among other attribution types, indicating that these individuals are more likely to make an internal or external causal attribution than other types of attribution. Cultural attribution was not higher than other types of attributions, while role and blame attributions received lower mean scores.

TABLE 1. Descriptive Statistics on Relational Quality Measure and Relational Attribution Measures

		Sample Size	Mean	Std. Dev
	Relation Quality Measure	77	3.92	.906
	Internal	77	3.25	1.07
	Stability	77	2.81	1.11
Relational	**Globality**	77	2.74	1.22
Attribution	**Intention**	77	2.88	1.20
Measure	**Blame/Responsibility**	77	2.53	1.06
	Role	77	2.42	1.10
	Culture	77	2.91	1.38

Associations among relational quality and types of attributions were examined. Correlation analysis indicated that certain types of attributions are significantly negatively related with the relational quality measure. Specifically, higher scores on the relational quality measure were significantly negatively associated with the attribution to a stable cause, $r = -.28$, $p < 0.05$, with the attribution to a global cause, $r = -.48$, $p < 0.001$, and with blame or responsibility $r = -.271$, $p < 0.05$. These results are consistent with the literature discussed at Relational Satisfaction that reported negative attribution-making is associated with the reduced relational quality. None of the other types of attributions, including internal, intention, role, and the cultural attribution, were significantly correlated with the relational quality score.

The associations between cultural attribution and other types of attributions were examined. Interestingly, there were some significant positive correlations between cultural attribution and globality, $r = .25$, $p < 0.05$; intention, $r = .32$, $p < 0.01$; blame, $r = .28$, $p < 0.05$; and role, $r = .47$, $p < 0.001$. This indicates that making a cultural attribution about a behavior can co-occur with other types of causal perceptions, including globality, intention, blame and role attributions. For example, the cause of a partner's behavior may be understood as global, intentional, responsible, and possibly due to the partner's social and cultural role in a given situation. Those who are involved in an intercultural relationship may use a cultural attribution and it might be coupled with other types of attributions (such as globality, intentionality, blame, and role).

Voices of the Inter-Couples

Participants were also asked to report what they believe are the challenges and benefits of being in an intercultural relationship. Most of the participants (88%) volunteered their answers for these two open-ended questions. Out of 77 participants, 37 (48%) reported various challenges, 27 (35%) reported benefits of being in an intercultural relationship, and the rest provided no comments or other feedback.

Voices on challenges

Participants listed various challenges including: family (family opposition, lack of acceptance, lack of trust, or skepticism toward the health of relationship), friends (lack of acceptance, opposition, or judgments from friends), societal prejudice (stares from others, negative or unwelcomed comment from others, or police stopping them for no reason), language barrier (communication difficulties), and differences in beliefs, values, and morals (differences in behavioral norms).

The majority of their reports can be grouped into two main themes: familial or societal pressure, and negotiation within the relationship. Participants mentioned they have to deal with lack of support, disapproval, or judgments from their social networks, including their families, friends, and other people. One participant stated that "obviously not everyone in your family or friends approves of our relationship and you cannot get let [sic] that interfere with your feeling." Another participant reported "Sometimes I believe the way people that you don't know view you just from seeing us together is very tough. People sometimes don't understand what we have in common because appearance and background are so different."

Respondents also mentioned other kinds of challenges related to managing their differences in beliefs, values, and behavioral norms. A few participants reported that a language barrier was an issue, as it impeded their communication, adding that "even though he spoke five languages … sometimes he did not think in English." One participant commented on the "different beliefs and other differences that seems irreconcilable at times" as a challenge. Another participant stated, "When you are raised differently, you learn to put more value on different things and view things differently. For the things that you value, your partner might not see as important."

Voices on benefits

Participants also listed various benefits of being in an intercultural relationship. They stated that they could expand their knowledge about new perspectives, new cultures, and new outlooks on life. It can be exciting and even entertaining to learn something that is new to them. They also noted that they feel they have a stronger bond with their partner because of the challenges that they face. Overall, two main themes appeared in their comments: personal growth from the relationship and stronger bond between partners.

Many participants mentioned that inter-relationships can be amazing learning experiences which expand their perspective or outlook on life. For example, a participant stated that "it's exciting and entertaining to learn something new–I am exposed to things that I may not have otherwise been exposed to." One participant reported the benefits saying that "we are able to learn more from each other and become stronger, more patient, and open minded through our learning experiences and tolerances." She also added that being in this relationship, combined with their education, had made them "very open to other ways of doing things, other viewpoints and worldviews, and reduced the knee-jerk 'different = bad' reaction that people often have when they encounter anything new or strange." Another participant provided an insightful comment about being reflective about one's own values and behavioral norms, noting that nothing can be taken for granted:

> "… you cannot take anything for granted. You cannot automatically assume that your partner has the same idea as you about anything, whether it's how to wash the dishes or how to raise children."

Roughly 12 percent of participants chose not to report about either challenges or benefits. There were three sub-groups among these participants. The *first group* of participants was those who left no comments or simply reported that there were no major difficulties due to cultural differences. One stated "I have not found there to be any substantial difficulties in my relationships with my partner due to our cultural differences." The *second group* of participants claimed that the challenges and benefits are *no different* from other relationships. As one telling quotation stated: "I see the benefits and challenges as being the same as those of any romantic relationships because there are always differences in such relationships." This participant emphasized that interracial relationships are no different from any other, as individual differences at varying degrees exist in all other romantic relationships. The *third group* emphasized interpersonal qualities, admitting that there are some challenges but these challenges are based on personal characteristics and not on race, culture, or ethnicity. One stated that "we don't have many challenges that deal with our races; it's mainly to do with our egos."

At varying degrees, it can be said that these participants are practicing cultural- or color-blindness, where individuals intentionally (or unintentionally) attempt to ignore racial or cultural differences. It can be said that these participants emphasize individuality over cultural factors, which Williams and Andersen (1998) termed as "trans-framing or de-socialization of racial construction," where they relate to each other on an interpersonal level while minimizing or ignoring the societal level stereotypes or racial categorizations (p. 183). After all, many intercultural couples may emphasize more personal characteristics than racial, ethnic, or cultural factors. Although these diverging factors might be more salient to outsiders, for those who are involved in an intercultural relationship, they are only one of many interpersonal attributes on which relational partners may attend.

Conclusion

In this chapter, the author revisited the history of 'inter-relations' in the United States and the challenges that intercultural romantic couples may face. Different types of attributions, including the cultural attribution, were defined and discussed, along with their association with relational quality. Results of an online survey of those who have dated or who are currently dating interracially were reported. The survey findings indicated that those who are involved in an intercultural relationship use cultural attributions in addition to other types of attributions (such as globality, intentionality, blame, and role). The cultural attribution was associated with other types of causal perceptions including globality, intention, blame and role attributions, yet the cultural attribution was not significantly associated with the overall relational quality.

Consistent with previous studies of intra-couples (Fincham et al., 1990; Sillars et al., 2000; Vangelisti, 1994), the negative attribution-making (attributing to internal, stable, and global cause for a confrontation) was negatively associated with relational quality among the survey participants involved in inter-relations. Some participants evidenced cultural or color-blindness or trans-framing in their rhetoric, as they reported no challenges or benefits and emphasized the individual differences rather than racial or cultural factors, claiming that inter-relation is not any different from other types of romantic relationships. The majority of participants reported both challenges (i.e., familial or societal pressure and negotiation within the relationship) and benefits (i.e., personal growth and stronger relational bond) as a result of being in an interracial relationship. It is extremely valuable to understand the benefits of these relationships, as the 'difficulties' of inter-relations seem to be overemphasized by both laypeople and researchers. It can be said that a romantic inter-relationship is an ultimate integrative context where individuals of diverging backgrounds are determined to triumph over the various challenges. Therefore, further examinations of inter-relationships offer a unique perspective from which to view and learn about unique cultural and relational dynamics.

DISCUSSION QUESTIONS

1. What does it mean to say that race is a social construct? What do you think of the use of such terms as "interracial couples" or "intercultural couples"?

2. What is an attribution? What are the different types of attributions that we make in an interracial relational context? What types of attributions might be constructive or destructive to romantic intercultural relationships?

3. Do you think it is more difficult to maintain an interracial relationship than a mono-racial relationship? What motivates us to view "inter-couples" as different from mono-couples?

4. What did participants in the survey say were the benefits and the challenges of an interracial relationship? Can you think of other challenges and benefits that were not identified and discussed by these participants?

---

[1] The anniversary of this case, June 12, has marked as "Loving Day" and celebrated by many in the U.S. and around the world, since the "Loving Day Project" had been created by Ken Tanabe and other volunteers to "fight racial prejudice through education and to build multicultural community", according to the website, Lovingday.org.

References

American Anthropological Association. (1998). *American Anthropological Association Statement on "Race."* Retrieved on January 25, 2009 from http://www.understandingrace.org/about/statement.html.

Bramlett, M. D., & Mosher, W. D. (2002). *Cohabitation, marriage, divorce, and remarriage in the United States (Vol. 23).* Hyattsville, MD: National Center for Health Statistics.

Brudbury, T. N., & Fincham, F. D. (1990). Attributions in marriage: Review and critique. *Psychological Bulletin, 107*, 3–33.

Chen, L. (2002). Communication in intercultural relationships. In Gudukunst, W. B., & B. Mody (Eds.), *Handbook of International and Intercultural Communication* (pp. 241–257). Thousand Oaks, CA: Sage.

Cropley, C. J., & Reid, S. A. (2008). A latent variable analysis of couple closeness, attributions, and relational satisfaction. *The Family Journal, 16(4)*, 364–374.

Davey, A., Fincham, F. D., Beach, S. R. H., & Brody, G. H. (2001). Attributions in marriage: Examining the entailment model in dyadic variable. *Journal of Family Psychology, 15*, 721–734.

Fincham, F. D. & Bradbury, T. N. (1992). Assessing Attributions in Marriage: The Relationship Attribution Measure. *Journal of Personality and Social Psychology, 62(3)*, 457–468.

Fincham, F. D., Harold, G. T., & Gano-Phillips, S. (2000). The longitudinal association between attributions and marital satisfaction: Direction of effects and role of efficacy expectations. *Journal of Family Psychology, 14*, 267–285.

Fincham, F. D., Bradbury, T. N., & Scott, C. K. (1990). Cognition in marriage. In F. D. Fincham and T. N. Bradbury (Eds.), *The psychology of marriage: Basic issues and applications* (pp. 118–149). New York: Guilford.

Gaines, S. O. & Ickes, W. (1997). Perspectives on interracial relationships. In S. Duck (Ed.), *Handbook of Personal Relationships: Theory, Research, and Interventions* (pp. 197–285). Chichester: Wiley.

Gaines, S. O. & Brennan, K. A. (2001). Establishing and maintaining satisfaction in multicultural relationships. In J. Harvey & A. Wenzel (Eds.), *Close romantic relationship. Maintenance and Enhancement* (pp. 237–253). Mahwah, NJ: Lawrence Erlbaum Associates.

Hartill, L. (2001). A brief history of interracial marriage. *Christian Science Monitor*, 93, 15.

Heller, M. & Levy, L. (1992). Mixed marriages: life on the linguistic frontier. *Multilingua, 11*, 11–43.

Henderson, D. A. (2000). Racial/Ethnic Intermarried couples and marital interaction: Marital issues and problem solving. *Sociological Focus*, 33(4), 421–440.

Hider, F. (1958). *The psychology of interpersonal relationships.* New York: Wiley.

Kalmijn, M. (1993). Trends in black/white intermarriages. *Social Forces, 72*, 119–146.

Kelley, H. H. (1973). The processes of causal attribution. *American Psychologist, 28*, 107–128.

Kelley, H. H. (1967). Attribution theory in social psychology. In D. Levine (Ed.), *Nebraska symposium on motivation* (Vol. 15, pp. 192–238). Lincoln: University of Nebraska Press.

Killian, K. D. (2000). Dominant and marginalized discourses in interracial couples' narratives: Implications for family therapists. *Family Process, 41(4)*, 603–620.

LovingDay. (2009). *Where were interracial couples illegal?* Retrieved on January 25th, 2009 from http://lovingday.org/map.htm.

McNamara, R. P., Tempenis, M., & Walton, B. (1999). *Crossing the line: Interracial couples in the South*. Westport, CT: Greenwood.

Mills, J., Daly, J., Longmore, A., & Kilbride, G. (1995). A note on family acceptance involving interracial friendships and romantic relationships. *Journal of Psychology, 129*, 349–352.

Norton, R. (1983). Measuring marital quality: A critical look at the dependent variable. *Journal of Marriage and the Family, 42*, 63–69.

Omi, M., & Winant, H. (1994). Racial Formation in the U.S.: From the 1960s to the 1990s. New York: Routledge.

Roloff, M. E., & Miller, C. W. (2006). Social cognition approaches to understanding conflict and communication. In J. G. Oetzel & S. Ting-Toomey (Eds.), *The SAGE handbook of conflict communication* (pp. 97–128). Thousand Oaks, CA: Sage.

Sillars, A. L. (1980). The sequential and distributional structure of conflict interactions as a function of attributions concerning the locus of responsibility and stability of conflicts. In D. Nimmo (Ed.), *Communication Yearbook 4* (pp. 217–235). New Brunswick, NJ: Transaction.

Sillars, A., Roberts, L. J., Leonard, K. E., & Dun, T. (2000). Cognition during marital conflict: The relationship of thought and talk. *Journal of Social and Personal Relationships, 17*, 479–502.

Shibaseki, K. & Brennon, K. A. (1998). When birds of different feathers flock together: A preliminary comparison of intra-ethnic and inter-ethnic dating relationships. *Journal of Social and Personal Relationships, 15(2)*, 248–256.

Smedley, A. (1993). *Race in North America: Origin and Evolution of a Worldview*. Boulder, CO: Westview Press.

Smedley, A. (2007). *Race in North America: Origin and Evolution of a Worldview*. (Third Edition). Boulder, CO: Westview Press.

Ting-Toomey, S., & Chung, L. (2005). Understanding Intercultural Communication. Los Angeles, CA: Roxbury.

Troy, A. B., Lewis-Smith, J., & Laurenceau, J. P. (2006). Interracial and intraracial romantic relationships: The search for differences in satisfaction, conflict, and attachment style. *Journal of Social and Personal Relationships, 23(1)*, 65–80.

Rosenblatt, P. C., Karis, T. A., & Powel, R. D. (1995). *Multiracial couples: Black and white voices*. Thousand Oaks, CA: Sage.

Thompson, J. & Collier, M. J. (2006). Toward contingent understandings of intersecting identifications among selected U.S. interracial couples: Integrating interpretive and critical views. *Communication Quarterly, 54(4)*, 487–506.

U.S. Census Bureau (2005). *2005 American Community Survey*. Retrieved on March 14, 2007 from http://factfinder.census.gov/servlet/STTable?_bm=y&-geo_id=01000US&-qr_name=ACS_2005_EST_G00_S1201&-ds_name=ACS_2005_EST_G00_

Vangelisti, A. L. (1994). Messages that hurt. In W. R. Cupach and B. H. Spitzberg (Eds.), *The dark side of interpersonal communication* (pp. 53–82). Hillsdale, NH: Erlbaum.

Washington Post, the Kaiser Family Foundation, and Harvard University (2001). *Race and Ethnicity 2001: Attitudes, Perceptions, and Experience*. Retrieved on March 17, 2007 from http://www.kff.org/kaiserpolls/3143-index.cfm.

Weiner, B. (1974). *Achievement motivation and attribution theory*. Morristown, NJ: General Learning Press.

Williams, S., & Andersen, P. A. (1998). Toward an expanded view of interracial romantic relationships. In V. Duncan (Ed.), *Toward achieving maat*. Dubuque, IA: Kendall-Hunt.

Yancey, G. & Yancey, S. (1998). Interracial Dating: Evidence from Personal Advertisements. *Journal of Family Issues, 19(3)*, 334–348.

10

If I'm White and you're Black, what does that make us?: Negotiating Racial Identity in Romantic Interracial Relationships

Kelli L. Fellows

Abstract

Individuals enter romantic relationships with implicit romantic relational construct expectations. Intertwined within these expectations is an individual's notion of self or identity. Within the current chapter it is argued that relational development models are problematic because of their inattention to the identity construct. This lack of integration, it is suggested, is particularly problematic for the study of interracial romantic relationships because Black individuals are influenced differently by their racial identity from Whites by the notion of Whiteness. The chapter begins with an interpersonal communication class discussion that provides the framework in which to explore the role of identity, racial identity, and Whiteness. Social identity theory (SIT) and optimal distinctiveness theory ground the recommendation of incorporating the identity construct in romantic relational development models and research (both among intra- and interracial partners). Finally, identity negotiation within interracial dating contexts is explored, and directions for future research are discussed.

KEY TERMS: interracial dating, interracial relationships, optimal distinctiveness theory, racial identity, romantic relationships, social identity theory, Whiteness

Introduction

Relationships are established for a variety of reasons, and evolve through self-disclosure of both partners. Each individual brings specific expectations (whether acknowledged or not) into a relationship. These expectations may develop through observations of relational behavior within his or her social networks (i.e., how do others that I know begin and sustain their relationships?), through mass media portrayals, or via the individual's prior experience. The culminating expectations are intertwined within each individual's conception of him or herself–one's *identity*. The recognition of one's identity may be more prominent for some individuals than others. Specifically, prior research suggests racial identity is more pronounced for black individuals than the notion of Whiteness is for white individuals.

The following chapter begins with an interpersonal communication classroom discussion about romantic relationships in which students evidenced their implicit relational expectations that were consistent with their identity. As the discussion progressed, the students' pre-existing implicit boundaries that encompassed romantic relationships were challenged by manipulating specific presumed variables including sexuality, age, and race. This classroom discussion provides a frame in which to examine models of relational development, implicit romantic relational construct expectations, and the roles of racial identity and Whiteness within the confines of interracial romantic relationships.

Interpersonal Communication Classroom Discussion

Teaching interpersonal communication always provides an opportunity for rich discussion of relationships. That semester was no different. I was teaching at a university in North Carolina on the shores of the Atlantic Ocean. My interpersonal communication class had progressed approximately halfway through the curriculum, and students had established an open rapport among one another. The class of 40 students was predominantly White with four Black students and one Asian student. I began our discussion that day about romantic relationships by having the students define the parameters that constituted a friendship versus a romantic relationship. Traditionally, the literature has distinguished between these relationships by the presence or absence of sexual relations (Armstrong, 1985; Bisson & Levine, 2009; Brehm, Miller, Perlman, & Campbell, 2002; Verdeber, Verderber, & Berryman-Fink, 2007; Werker, 1997). Romantic relationships are characterized as those of individuals who engage in physical contact consistent with sexual interest (although sexual intercourse is not a necessity). I questioned the students about the different types of romantic relationships. And while the existence of other relationships blur these lines (e.g., friends with benefits; see Bisson & Levine, 2009; Hughes, Morrison, & Asada, 2005), I decided to focus on the traditional distinction for clarity. The discussion evolved in a fruitful, yet predictable, direction.

In order to have the students challenge their presumptions, I began with a generic story about a heterosexual couple who had been seeing each other romantically for a couple of months. I asked the students to provide me with specifications regarding what such a relational definition meant. Students began articulating various notions including hanging out, going to dinner or the movie together, and not engaging in kissing or other physical relations with other individuals. Their comments indicated a common understanding of the boundaries across the students in the class. In order to discern underlying assumptions the students had about the hypothetical couple, I altered the age difference between the partners. "Would it be different if the man were 10 or 15 years older than the woman? What if she was 21? What if the woman was 10 to 15 years older and the man was 21?" I asked. Immediately the room was charged with opposition–clearly there were established rules of propriety in the romantic relationship criteria that had not emerged in the initial guidelines articulated by the students. Female students were alarmed at the thought of an older woman dating a man close to their age, with comments including "Why does she want to act like she is 21 again? And "Doesn't she feel trashy having to chase young boys?" Consideration of a man "their dad's age" dating someone their age was not pleasing either. One student observed, "That is just creepy–those old men are creepers!" Male students on the other hand were quite intrigued by "cougars" and offered personal stories of being pursued by, and being romantically involved with older women. As for older men, they praised their virility and referred to them as "silver foxes" and "players" that they aspired to be when they were the same age.

After several personal disclosures from students, I began to wonder if the students' presumptions regarding the hypothetical couple also included that they were of the same race. In order to explore this area, I manipulated the scenario again. "What if the woman was White and the man was Black? What if the man was White and the woman was Black?" I asked. The room fell silent. I looked around the room and observed the blatant discomfort with the topic. I repeated the questions in order to elicit a response to open the dialogue again. Finally, a white female student said, "That is just asking for trouble." Then a black male replied, "It is a difficult situation–no doubt." The silence fell again and fidgeting became rampant. Presuming that the discussion was not going to progress, I broke the class up into groups with one minority student in each. I instructed the groups to discuss my questions regarding interracial relationships and to brainstorm reasons why such relationships might be problematic. Immediately the discussions erupted, and the groups began speaking louder and louder.

After approximately 15 minutes, I had a representative from each group write the discussion results on the board at the front of the classroom. Once completed, we reviewed the data to identify common themes. Quickly we noticed the trends–social scrutiny, deviance, lack of acceptance, tension, and relational strain. I probed the groups and asked if these themes emerged from personal experience (i.e., a group member had been in an interracial romantic relationship), observations of a friend's experience (i.e., a close friend dated interracially and experienced the problems cited), or from mass media portrayals

like row questions/ discussions started.

(i.e., how television and/or movies portrayed these relational types). Of the class of 40 students, four students (two black males, one black female, and one white female) had previously been in an interracial relationship. I asked these students to expand on their experiences for the class so that we may have a better understanding of how the common themes manifested across their interracial relational experiences.

Social scrutiny was evidenced among friends, co-workers, and strangers according to the stories. From "disapproving looks" to "friends just dropping out of sight," the students each shared common negative experiences. One observation that was interesting was the perception that they were being deviant because they were in an interracial relationship. *Neg. exp.* As one black student explained it, "I thought she was beautiful and enjoyed hanging out with her. But all the looks we got made me feel like I was doing something wrong–ya' know–like I was breaking a rule or something." The students suggested that a general lack of acceptance was experienced at all relational levels within their life. "I remember telling my mom and dad that I was dating someone–it was awkward because I knew that I had to tell them he was Black and I wasn't sure how they would react," noted one white female *scrutiny* student. "Well that's better than my ex-girlfriends' folks–they banned us from seeing each other because I was Black," added one black male student. Another black male student said that his mother was blatantly opposed to his interracial relationship. He said, "She said there's no way you are gonna date no white girl–no way!"

The interracial daters further explained that their external experiences led to feelings of tension both for them as individuals and as relational partners. One white female student said, "I was so frustrated with the situation–not with my boyfriend–but with all of the other people around us." And the other students agreed that the tension became *It should* overwhelming. The black female student said, "the tension pushed our relationship so *be personality* hard that we finally broke up." When asked if he or she would date interracially again, *not race.* the students said that they were unsure. "It's just so hard—I'm just not sure it's worth it," said one black male student.

I considered what the students had offered in support of the themes presented, and then asked the rest of the class if they had any comments to add to our discussion. One white female student raised her hand and asked, "Am I supposed to feel bad because I don't want to date interracially? I mean, it isn't because the guys are Black–it's because I am not attracted to them." I noticed other White students nodding their heads in agreement. I asked why she would feel bad, to which she replied "because I am White and I don't like black guys in that way–ya' know what I mean? I am just not attracted to them–it isn't because I think black guys are better or worse than white guys, I just don't like them in that way." Another white female student added, "I just don't want all of the drama–relationships are hard enough as it is."

Class Discussion Implications

The classroom discussion provides a nice example of how individuals have romantic relationship expectations that are implicitly understood. When these expectations were overtly challenged via manipulating variables (e.g., age difference, gender roles, race), students were left searching for a cogent explanation that left them in a comfortable space to exist. While dialogue was comfortable among some variable manipulation (i.e., age difference, gender roles), consideration of interracial relationships was stifled. Once the class was broken into small groups, discussion became engaged and the students were more forthright with their thoughts and observations. Based on the data presented above, there are experiences (anticipated and/or experienced) associated with romantic relationships in general, and interracial relationships specifically, that do not appear to be accounted for in traditional relational development models. Within the current chapter it is argued that identity in general, and racial identity and Whiteness specifically, are key constructs that should be considered in romantic relationship development and dissolution. This argument is grounded in the theoretical framework of social identity theory and optimal distinctiveness theory, while drawing correlations back to the student discussion presented at the beginning of this chapter. The following sections mark the start of our journey as it explores relational development theories.

Romantic Relational Development

Within the literature, numerous theories and models have been developed that provide propositions designed to form a framework of understanding of how relationships evolve (e.g., social exchange theory, social penetration theory, ten-stage model, dialectical tension process model, etc.). What is not addressed in these theories and models is the role of identity in general, the notion of race specifically, and the associated implications that may influence the relational development and/or dissolution processes.

Physical attraction is a prominent factor in relationship initiation (Duck, 1988). Individuals observe beauty in a variety of contexts (e.g., interpersonal encounters, mass media, etc.). Based on Duck's model, relationships evolve through self-disclosure and general interaction. Knapp and Vangelisti (2005) suggest that relationships move through ten specific stages during their development and dissolution. During the initial stages, individuals evolve from initial casual interaction to increased breadth and depth of disclosure. Subsequent stages are characterized by recognition as a couple by the individuals in the relationship and by the public. The latter five stages of the model represent the dissolution of the relationship. During the differentiating stage, relational partners move their focus away from themselves as a couple and focus on their individual identities.

In contrast with the early stages of relational development, subsequent dissolution stages are characterized by less self-disclosure and identification as a couple.

Knapp and Vangelisti's stage model has been criticized for a few reasons. First, stage models imply that all relationships develop and deteriorate in a linear, orderly process. Additionally, it does not allow the provision of partners being individuals who may not perceive the relationship at the same stage as the other relational partner. Finally, the model does not account for the tensions that exist in any relationship and how those tensions influence the development and/or decline.

Baxter's dialectical tensions (1990) suggest that relationships are constantly in developmental flux as partners evaluate and redefine their relational needs. Dialectical tensions reflect intrapersonal struggles that exist in three realms: (1) autonomy and connection; (2) novelty and predictability; and (3) openness and closedness. The autonomy/connection dialectic reflects an individual's desire to be his or her own person while wanting to be relationally close with his or her relational partner. Individuals crave stability and predictability in relationships. However, as the second dialectical tension suggests, there is also a desire for newness and spontaneity. The final tension reflects the desire to engage in self-disclosure while retaining a private side.

Across these models of relational development, commonalities emerge. Relational initiation is characterized by uncertainty as individuals begin to get to know one another, and may be followed by the use of self-disclosure to enhance relationship depth and reduce ambiguity. If the relationship continues to progress positively, the partners may decide to become exclusively involved. This decision is demonstrated, in part, via naming (e.g., best friends, boyfriend/girlfriend, etc.), using inclusive terms such as *we* or *us* in conversations with friends and/or family, and introducing the partner to important relational others (e.g., friends, family, colleagues). Intra- and interpersonal facets intertwine as the partners negotiate the meaning of being themselves while being in a relationship. However, these models do not provide specific attention to the individual partner's identities (and related expectations) that are present and how those identities intersect.

As demonstrated by the earlier class scenario, there are underlying expectations that exist about romantic couples. These expectations are often facilitated by social and cultural guidelines that may include that the couple be heterosexual, of comparable age, of similar physical attractiveness, and the same race. In order to understand these expectations, the overarching premise of identity must be considered.

Consideration of the Identity Construct

The notion of identity is a socially constructed phenomenon (Lloyd & Lucas, 1998) with a variety of definitions (e.g., Snow and Anderson, 1987; Breakwell, 1983;

Collier, 2001; Stryker, 1987; Tajfel & Turner, 1979; Ting-Toomey, 1993). These definitions provide a conception of identity that ranges from the engagement of self (Ting-Toomey, 1993) to an evolving array of intrapersonal processes that predict behavior (Breakwell, 1983). While the specific linguistic identification may vary, three tenets are consistently used to describe the identity construct.

Tenets of Identity

The three tenets of identity, according to Deaux (1996) are: cognition, affect, and behavior. Cognition suggests that individuals cognitively place themselves (i.e., associated) or other individuals (i.e., ascribed) into specific groups. Through this process of categorization, sensemaking of the individuals' environment occurs. In tandem, specific beliefs (either stereotypical or self-generated meanings) are continually created. Affect depicts the emotional draw and/or bond generated through group association (Deaux, 1996) that may be experienced at varying levels within the individual. This tenet complements cognition by explaining the connection of the individual with a group that traverses beyond basic categorization.

The final tenet of identity is behavior. Associated behavior of a given identity plays a dual role for individuals. Behavior provides external demonstration of an identity to others, as well as provides an internal affirmation of the identity's value to the individual. Categorization (a component of the cognition tenet) suggests identities may have a social component. Behavior unites the categorization tenet because identity-related behavior may be enacted alone or in group situations. These interactions reinforce the identity preference.

When considered together as the unified construct of identity, one reaches a platform for understanding the intertwined relationship of group membership. As human beings, association with a given group is an innate drive that provides both a sense of belonging and a script of behavioral parameters in which to demonstrate that membership. Social identity theory (SIT) (Tajfel & Turner, 1979) suggests that individuals align themselves with specific groups. This alignment leads to the discernment of ingroups versus outgroups, and ethnocentrism is reinforced (Fellows & Rubin, 2006).

Individuals may have multiple social identities; in turn, identity conflict may arise (Melville, Darlington, Whitlock, & Mulligan, 2005). Brewer's (1991) Optimal Distinctiveness Theory (ODT) addresses this tension by suggesting that, while individuals want to be part of the group, they also value their role as a separate individual (Fellows & Rubin, 2006). In order to find balance, individuals may create a new unique identity that resolves the identity tension (Brewer, 1999). Minority groups, in particular, appear to have stronger social identity ties and are more likely to manage identity tensions (van Hiel & Mervielde, 2002).

When examining the scenario of the interracial couple posited in the relational development exercise, the notion of identity provides an interesting facet to explore. As couples engage in a romantic relationship, each person brings a host of social identities with him or her. The individuals must navigate the intrapersonal identity tensions as well as co-construct a new, unique relational identity. This process may be particularly challenging for individuals in interracial relationships. First, the individuals are likely operating outside of the expected behavior afforded to their given social identities. Further, the racial minority member has an identity that the non-racial minority partner may not readily perceive about himself or herself. In order to flesh out the identity challenges that each partner brings to the relationship, an understanding of racial identity and Whiteness will be explored.

Racial Identity

Race is itself a socially constructed phenomenon commonly associated with phenotypical attributes (e.g., skin color), not one based on genetic fact (Crewe & Fernando, 2006; Hochschild & Weaver, 2007; Luke & Carrington, 2000). Categorization according to race is powerful. It influences daily interactions, behavior, and identity construction and maintenance (Darity, Jr., Mason, & Stewart, 2005; Fellows & Rubin, 2006; Rockquemore & Arend, 2003). Phenotypical characteristics make the notion of racial identity (both associated and ascribed) plausible (Luke & Carrington, 2000). Theoretically, individuals who are Caucasian have an identity with other individuals of the same descent. This position makes precisely defining racial identity challenging. Definitions of racial identity (see Helms, 1990; Phinney & Kohatsu, 1997; Neblett, Jr., Smalls, Ford, Nguyen, & Sellers, 2009) focus on an individual's perception of heritage in common with a specific racial group (Worrell & Gardner-Kitt, 2006). Implicit to these definitions and subsequent measures developed, is the notion that racial identity relates best to minorities (Frankeberg, 1993; hooks, 1992; Martin, Krizek, Nakayama, & Bradford, 1996; Miller & Fellows, 2007; Sleeter, 1995). Specifically, Blacks tend to have a more prominent racial identity in comparison with other minorities (Yancey, 2009). This finding is critical when examining interracial dating, particularly between Blacks and Whites (Wang & Kao, 2007).

In stark contrast, the notion of a racial identity among Caucasians (i.e., Whiteness) is ambivalent and/or absent. Whites have (and perform) a variety of social identities but have a relatively limited recognition of race as an identity (Frankenberg, 1993; hooks, 1992; Martin, Krizek, Nakayama, & Bradford, 1996; Miller & Fellows, 2007; Sleeter, 1995). This ambivalence is a result of their position in the majority. They do not discern other Whites as an in-group. Whereas racial identities are salient components in sense-making among minorities, the notion of Whiteness remains elusive (Charmaraman & Grossman, 2008; Grossman & Charmaraman, 2009; French, Seidman, Allen and Aber, 2000). Several plausible explanations may provide insight into this phenomenon. For minorities, strong adherence to a racial identity may be a defense mechanism generated in response to negative historical events such as racial oppression (Helms & Cook, 1999). In light of this history, Whites may be hesitant to acknowledge and/or openly embrace Whiteness as an identity because they are afraid of negative perceptions, such as being deemed racist, by others (Frankenberg, 1993; Grossman & Charmaraman, 2009). Another consideration is that White identity does not have the pronounced system of cultural beliefs and practices as ethnic identities possess (Phinney, 1990).

When the poles of racial identity/Whiteness awareness and performance are considered in the interracial romantic relational context, the differences among the relational partners are further exacerbated. For example, the dating partners enter the relationship realizing that they are operating outside of traditional social identity ingroup expectations. And while race (as evidenced by phenotypical attributes), per se, may not be an issue for the relational partners, Whiteness may become salient. The influence of Whiteness is not known at the onset of an interracial relationship, but prior research suggests the difference in race (as evidenced by phenotypical attributes) is not discussed among the partners as the problems are imposed on them by social ingroups and outgroups (Foeman & Nance, 2002; 1999; Luke & Carrington, 2000; Wang & Kao, 2007; Wang, Kao, & Joyner, 2006).

Again, consider the classroom discussion presented at the beginning of the chapter and the students' reactions to the notion of interracial dating. The common themes that emerged from the discussions revolved around external assertions imposed on and/or about the couple. This theme is consistent with the propositions of both social identity theory and ODT. These individuals may be operating outside of ingroup expectations by crossing the race boundaries but choose to pursue the relationship anyway. This pursuit correlates with ODT's assertion that individuals want to retain their social identities while individuating themselves. In some areas, interracial relationships may not be the norm. Thus, the occurrence of interracial relationships demonstrates relational development across group boundaries, and suggests that, for some individuals, race may not serve as the primary determinant in pursuing a romantic partner (Wang, Kao, & Joyner, 2006).

Implications for Identity Negotiation Within Interracial Dating Relationships

From the moment of physical attraction to someone of a different race, a sense of risk-taking may be aroused. Further, public disclosure of such an attraction is threatening when interpreted within the context of the complexities of race relations in the U.S. (Foeman & Nance, 1999; 2002). Individuals may initiate existing stereotypes as a means of sense-making regarding the implications of a specific partner. Clearly, such an attraction may be readily explained, but the decision to initiate a romantic relationship with an individual of a different race posits the person to be operating outside the boundaries of social expectations. This operation outside societal norms is grounded in social and historical contexts within the U.S. in tandem with associated myths that shroud inter-racial relationships (Aldridge, 1978; Foeman & Nance, 1999; George & Yancey, 2004; Harris & Kalbfleisch, 2000; Root, 2001). As a result, social stressors may be experienced and the interracial dating partners' subsequent communicative behavior may be altered. Recognition of their relationship as engaging in risky behavior is demonstrated in an array of interpersonal communicative behaviors, such as hesitance to or complete avoidance of introducing friends or family to the relational partner, reduced public displays of affection (Vaquera & Kao, 2005), or not naming the relationship (i.e., not referring to the person as a boyfriend/girlfriend). These behaviors reflect awareness among the relational partners–an awareness of race.

There is a paucity of research on how race awareness manifests on the intrapersonal and interpersonal levels of the dating partners. This research gap is problematic because there are so few accounts of the thoughts, discussions, or consideration of race among interracial daters. Future research in this area would provide a clearer understanding of the actual role of race–be it racial identity, Whiteness, or the negotiation of common ground. It would be interesting to explore how race is handled from the acknowledgement (verbally) of the racial differences as a spontaneous topical choice, if it is in response to specific negative events, or if anticipation of future events lead to the discussion. It may be presumed that individuals who engage in interracial relationships are not at issue with operating outside the prescribed societal boundaries, but we do not have a clear understanding of how they progress developmentally with their partner. It may be that race is not perceived as a topic worthy of discussion because it is not considered problematic by the individuals in the relationship. On the other hand, individuals whose Whiteness or racial identity becomes salient may have intrapersonal conflicts regarding generalized racial disparities (minorities versus the majority). If these conflicts arise, what influence do they have on the dating partners on an intrapersonal and/or interpersonal level?

Points to Consider

When we turn our focus back to the classroom discussion presented at the beginning of the chapter, we are left with numerous unanswered questions. Some of these questions include: made the discussion of interracial dating intimidating to the point that no one in the class would respond; if race was an issue, was it responsive to previous experiences (either friendship or romantic relationships)?; With respect to those who had not been involved in an interracial dating relationship, was it because of a lack of opportunitiy (i.e., limited dating partners) or because it was not deemed appropriate (i.e., condoned by friends and/or family)?; For individuals who commented on their prior interracial dating experiences, were their conversations regarding race organic, or imposed on them by others (either members of ingroups or outgroups)?

Exploring the notion of identity in general is difficult because it must consider the tenets of cognition, affect, and behavior. This consideration is challenged by the selection of appropriate methodologies that will illuminate identity constructs and their subsequent influence on the relationship in general and the relational partners specifically. Both qualitative and quantitative methodologies offer positive features and drawbacks that must be weighed. One limitation of the work explored in this chapter is that the constructs of racial identity research and Whiteness do not appear to include each of the tenets of identity or examine how they operate together. Another limitation is demonstrated that engenders future research is demonstrated in the students' discussion presented at the beginning of the chapter. That is, the role of identity was not apparent to them until the discussion was guided to question their implicit expectations. These are among the challenges that engender future research on this topic.

Concluding Thoughts

The current chapter began with a recounting of a classroom discussion where interpersonal communication students explored implicit expectations of romantic relationships. The subsequent expectations were challenged according to age difference, gender roles, and race. The emergent discussion demonstrated facets of relational development that were not readily identifiable. In this chapter it is argued that this gap was the notion and role of identity. It was also suggested that identity (in general and racial identity and Whiteness specifically) plays a particular role in interracial relationships. In reflecting on previous research and on the information presented in this chapter, we are poised to chart the future course of interracial relationship research.

DISCUSSION QUESTIONS

1. When individuals of differing races engage in a romantic relationship, they are aware of their phenotypical attribute differences. Based on this knowledge, is it

plausible that race (and differences) should be discussed between the couple? If so, at what point in the relationship is this discussion appropriate and/or necessary?

2. The students in Fellows' class engage in fruitful dialogue on interracial romantic relationships after they are organized into small discussion groups. How did this arrangement facilitate the dialoguing process? Are there other approaches that could also encourage active classroom participation on this topic?

3. What level of discussion should occur regarding race between an interracial couple? How does this discourse differ from self-disclosure in an intraracial couple?

4. What messages have you received from society (family, friends, mass media) about interracial romantic relationships? How have these messages influenced your thoughts and opinions concerning these intimate relationships?

References

Aldridge, D. (1978). Interracial marriages: Empirical and theoretical consideration. *Journal of Black Studies, 8*, 355–368.

Armstrong, R. L. (1985). Friendship. *Journal of Value Inquiry, 19*, 211–216.

Baxter, L. A. (1990). Dialectical contradictions in relationship development. *Journal of Social and Personal Relationships, 7*, 69–88.

Bisson, M. A., and Levine, T. R. (2009). Negotiating a friends with benefits relationship. *Archives of Sexual Behavior, 28*(1), 66–73.

Breakwell, G. M. (1986). *Coping with threatened identities*. London and New York: Methuen.

Brehm, S., Miller, R., Perlman, D., & Campbell, S. (2002). *Intimate relationships*. New York: McGraw-Hill.

Brewer, M. B. (1991). The social self: On being the same and different at the same time. *Personality and Social Psychology Bulletin, 17*, 475–482.

Brewer, M. B. (1999). Multiple identities and identity transition: Implications for Hong Kong. *International Journal of Intercultural Relations, 23*, 187–197.

Collier, P. (2001). A differentiated model of role identity acquisition. *Symbolic Interaction, 24*, 217–235.

Crewel, E., and Fernando, P. The elephant in the room: Racism in representations, relationships and rituals. *Progress in Development Studies, 6*(1), 40–54.

Darity, J., W. A., Mason, P. L., and Stewart, J. B. (2006). The economics of identity: The origin and persistence of racial identity norms. *Journal of Economic Behavior & Organization, 60*, 283–305.

Deaux, K. (1996). Social identification. In E. T. Higgins and A. W. Kruglanski (Eds.), *Social psychology: Handbook of basic principles* (pp. 777–798). *New York, NY: The Guildford* Press.

Duck, S. (1988). *Human relationships* (3rd ed.). Thousand Oaks, Calif.: Sage.

Fellows, K. L., and Rubin, D. L. (2006). Identities for sale: How the tobacco industry construed Asians, Asian Americans, and Pacific Islanders. *Journal of Intercultural Communication Research, 35*(3), 265–292.

Foeman, A. K., & Nance, T. (1999). From miscegenation to multiculturalism: Perceptions and stages of interracial relationship development. *Journal of Black Studies, 29*, 540–557.

Foeman, A. K., & Nance, T. (2002). Building new cultures, reframing old images: Success strategies of interracial couples. *The Howard Journal of Communication, 13*, 237–249.

Frankenberg, R. (1993). *White women, race matters*. Minneapolis: University of Minnesota Press.

French, S. E., Seidman, E., Allen, L., Aber, J. L. (2006). The development of ethnic identity during adolescence. *Developmental Psychology, 42*(1), pp. 1–10.

George, D., and Yancey, G. (2004). Taking stock of America's attitudes on cultural diversity: An analysis of public deliberation on multiculturalism, assimilation and interm\arriage. *Journal of Comparative Family Studies, 35*, 2–19.

Grossman, J. M., and Charmaraman, L. (2009). Race, context, and privilege: White adolescents' explanations of racial-ethnic centrality. *Journal of Youth Adolescence, 38*, 149–152.

Harris, T. M., & Kalbfleisch, P. J. (2000). Interracial dating: The implications of race for initiating a romantic relationship. *The Howard Journal of Communication, 11*, 49–64.

Helms, J. E. (1990). Introduction: Review of racial identity terminology. In J. E. Helms (Ed.). *Black and white racial identity: Theory, research, and practice* (pp. 3–8). NY: Greenwood Press.

Hochschild, J. L, and Weaver, V. (2007). The skin color paradox and the American racial order. *Social Forces, 86*(2), 643–670.

hooks, b. (1992). *Black looks: Race and representation*. Boston: South End Press.

Hughes, M., Morrison, K., and Asada, K. J. K. (2005). What's love got to do with it? Exploring the impact of maintenance rules, love attitudes and network support on friends with benefits relationships. *Western Journal of Communication, 69*, 49–66.

Knapp, M. L., and Vangelisti, A. L. (2005). *Interpersonal communication and human relationships* (5th ed.). Boston: Allyn & Bacon.

Lloyd, B. and Lucas, K. (1998). *Smoking in Adolescence: Images and Identities*. NY: Routledge.

Luke, C. and Carrington, V. (2000). Race matters. *Journal of Intercultural Studies, 21*(1), 5–24.

Martin, J. N., Krizek, R. L., Nakayama, T., and Bradford, L. (1996). Exploring Whiteness: A study of self labels for White Americans. *Communication Quarterly, 44*, 125–144.

Miller, A. N., and Fellows, K. L. (2007). Negotiating White Racial Identity in Multicultural Courses: A Model. In L. M. Cooks and J. S. Simpson (Eds.) *Whiteness, Pedagogy, Performance* (pp. 49–66). NY: Lexington Books.

Miville, M. L., Darlington, P., Whitlock, B., and Mulligan, T. Integrating identities: The relationships of racial, gender, and ego identities among White college students. *Journal of College Student Development, 46*(2), 157–175.

Neblett, Jr., E. W., Smalls, C. P., Ford, K. R., Nguyen, H. X., & Sellers, R. M. (2009). Racial socialization and racial identity: African American parents' messages about race as precursors to identity. *Journal of Youth Adolescence, 38*, 189–203.

Phinney, J. S. (1990) Ethnic identity in adolescents and adults: A review of research. *Psychological Bulletin*, 108, 499–514.

Phinney, J. S., & Kohatsu, E. L. (1997) Ethnic and racial identity development and mental health. In J. Schulenberg & J. Maggs (Eds.), *Health risks and development transitions during adolescence* (pp. 420–443).

Rockquemore, K. A., & Arend, P. (2003). Opting for White: Choice, fluidity and racial identity construction in post civil-rights America. *Race & Society, 5*, 49–64.

Root, M. P. P. (2001). *Love's revolution: Interracial marriage*. Philadelphia: Temple University Press.

Sleeter, C. E. (1995). An analysis of the critiques of multicultural education. In J. A. Bankds and C. A. M. Banks (Eds.). *Handbook of research on multicultural education* (pp. 81–96). New York: Simon & Schuster Macmillan.

Stryker, S. (1987). Identity theory: Developments and extensions. In K. Yardley (Ed.), *Self and identity: Psychosocial perspectives* (pp. 89–103). Oxford, UK: Wiley.

Tajfel, H., and Turner, J. C. (1979). An integrative theory of intergroup conflict. In W. G. Austin & S. Worschel (Eds.), *Psychology of intergroup relations* (pp. 33–47). Pacific Grove, CA: Brooks/Cole.

Ting-Toomey, S. (1993). Communicative resourcefulness: An identity negotiation perspective In R. L. Wiseman & J. Koester (Eds.), *International and intercultural communication annual* (Vol. XVII, pp. 72–111). Newbury Park, CA: Sage.

Van Hiel, A. and Mervielde, I. (2002). Social Identification Among Political Party Voters and Members: An Empirical Test of Optimal Distinctiveness Theory. *The Journal of Social Psychology, 142*(2), 202–209.

Vaquera, E., and Kao, G. (2005). Private and public displays of affection among interracial and intra-racial adolescent couples. *Social Science Quarterly, 86*(2), 484–508.

Verderber, R. F., Verderber, K. S., and Berryman-Fink, C. (2007). *Communicate!* Boston, MASS: Wadsworth Publishing.

Wang, H., and Kao, G. (2007). Does higher socioeconomic status increase contact between minorities and whites? An examination of interracial romantic relationships among adolescents. *Social Science Quarterly, 88*(1), 146–164.

Wang, H., Kao, G., and Joyner, K. (2006). Stability of interracial and intraracial romantic relationships among adolescents. *Social Science Research, 35*, 435–453.

Worrell, F. C., and Gardner-Kitt, D. L. (2006). The relationship between racial and ethnic identity in black adolescents: The cross racial identity scale and the multigroup ethnic identity measure. *Identity: An International Journal of Theory and Research, 6*(4), 293–315.

Werking, K. (1997). *We're just good friends: Women and men in nonromantic relationships.* New York: Guilford Press.

Yancey, G. (2009). Crossracial differences in the racial preferences of potential dating partners: A test of the alienation of African Americans and social dominance orientation. *The Sociological Quarterly, 50*, 121–143.

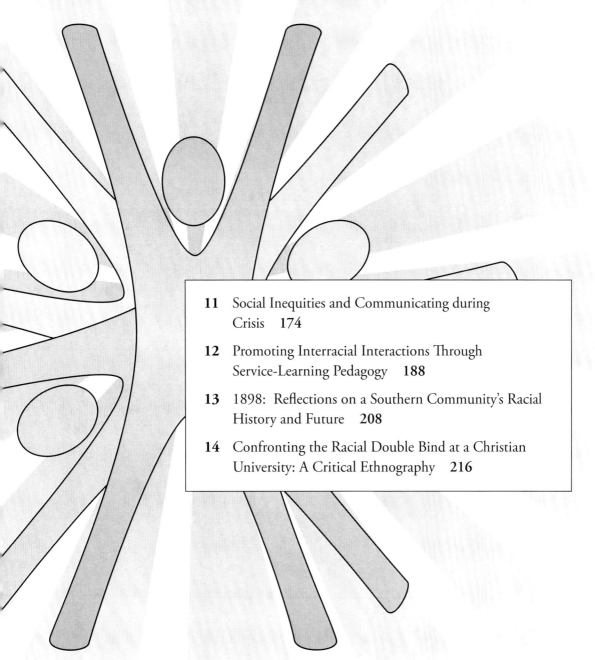

Context III

Communities

11

Social Inequities and Communicating During Crisis

Christine Eith, Patric R. Spence, and Kenneth A. Lachlan

Abstract

Research in communication science, sociology, and social psychology has provided evidence of inequality in the nature of information that is available to underserved populations. This chapter addresses the importance of understanding the mechanism of communication within diverse and underserved communities in the context of crises and other extreme events, and the value this knowledge has on successful post-disaster recovery. The chapter focuses on lessons learned through the experiences of New Orleans' Ninth Ward during Hurricane Katrina and its aftermath. It outlines and identifies the value of considering cross-cultural communication as part of emergency planning rather than relying on a uniform method to transmit emergency messages for preparations and mitigation. The chapter ends with a discussion of how those in positions of institutional power can work to better communicate with different ethnic groups to build and maintain relationships before a disaster emerges, through particular strategies and best practices.

KEY TERMS: crisis communication, knowledge gap, underclass, mental models, communication networks, Hurricane Katrina, microinequalities, microinequities

Introduction

Vulnerability is partially the product of social inequalities, that is, the social factors that influence or shape the susceptibility of particular groups to harm, and impede their ability to respond (Wilson, 1987). For some individuals, in particular racial minorities, compounded social inequalities have increased their vulnerability in everyday life. This intersection between social inequalities and increased vulnerability is particularly evident in urban settings where minorities reside in higher concentration areas with lower housing quality. Past research supports the contention that racial minorities are typically hit hardest during natural disasters and other cataclysmic events (Baker, 2001; Bolin & Bolton, 1986; Dash, Peacock, & Morrow, 1997; Peacock & Girard, 1997; Williams & Olaniran, 2002). However, this vulnerability is not unique to disaster preparation; it exists after the disaster is over and continues as recovery begins. During recovery, information is an important tool to minimize harm and move the affected communities to a sense of normalcy. This chapter examines the differing experiences of high-risk populations during post-disaster recovery, namely their access to vital emergency management information through media and emergency management personnel.

After Hurricane Katrina made landfall on August 29, 2005, the world became aware of the vulnerability of the poor who were living in New Orleans. The individuals who populated this community were predominately African American and were already facing daily difficulties. According to the 2000 U.S. Census, 28 percent of the population of New Orleans was living in poverty prior to the natural disaster, which is approximately one out of every four people. Further, 54 percent of poor households in New Orleans did not own their own means of transportation; the proportion rises to 65 percent for poor, elderly households. The situation was even graver for African American households. One in three African American households in New Orleans was without means of transportation; three of every five African American households without transportation were poor. These statistics show the vulnerability of the population that existed prior to the disaster, and fueled the despair and eventual anger that bubbled to the surface during the post-Katrina recovery when communication was at a premium, yet not effectively distributed.

History of Miscommunication

With America polarized on the issue of race and ethnicity, all affected groups experience fear and distrust; the breakdown in effective communication across these racial-ethnic lines is evident and contributes to increased doubt and perceptions of injustice. The miscommunication across racial and ethnic groups may also be explained through the unique social construction of race and ethnicity in American society. Race is more than simply the color of someone's skin (*race*) or a shared set of cultural customs and or language (*ethnicity*); rather, it is a label that is affixed to a population usually by a politically or culturally dominant group. Given America's unique history with colonialism and the Native American population, it can be argued that our country has a long history of socially constructing race and ethnicity. For instance, W.E.B DuBois (1903; 1935) argued the role of African Americans in early American history at a time when white scholars ignored the contributions of black people in historical accounts. Those who have been in positions of social, religious, and especially economic power have historically been Caucasian; thus, this population has been the one to socially construct race and ethnicity as well as render the policy decisions that often protect their own interests while being perceived as unjust to the other non-majority populations. What is therefore continually recreated is a hierarchy based on the intersection of social class and non-majority status.

An argument can be made that over the past 50 years these majority-focused policy decisions have benefited those in positions of power, while intensifying the social problems of those not in power. In particular, those with limited power are in socially disadvantaged inner-city neighborhoods, leading many racial and ethnic minorities to rely on their own resiliency to succeed in sustaining as well as improving their life (Anderson, 1990; Wilson, 1987).

Unfortunately, these urban areas are rarely thought to be resilient. While many residents of these disadvantaged urban neighborhoods have historically experienced higher levels of joblessness, female-headed households, serious crime, and teenage pregnancy, the neighborhoods were often found to have a sense of community, collective efficacy, and evident norms against criminal or deviant behavior (Anderson, 1990; Wilson, 1987). Although the norms against criminal behavior may exist, these neighborhoods still contain some of the highest concentration of crime in major metropolitan statistical areas. In part this participation in crime as well as opportunities that are tied to the underground economy, may actually be a sign of the community's resilience. Finding economic opportunities where no legitimate opportunity exists and creating an informal network of communication within the neighborhood can become a primary alternative to the traditional economic outlets.[1]

During the civil unrest of the 1960's when the burden of an inferior socially constructed racial status became palpable, the cumulative effects of social isolation on the basis of race as well as the structure of inequality began to produce social change in these socially disadvantaged neighborhoods. Although the literature from the 1960s is at best controversial, what can be deduced is this decade marked a period of change for socially disadvantaged inner-city residents many of whom were African American and ethnic minorities, leaving many vulnerable to further isolation and becoming marginalized in the overall social structure.

The underclass, to use a term from Wilson (1987), has been isolated from the labor-force, has experience with crime and the underground economy, and is acutely aware of the pains of poverty. Wilson argues that this is a reality not captured by the classification of "lower class." The depressed communities in which these individuals live have been abandoned by the flight of the working- and middle-classes, have undoubtedly been forgotten by the public policy makers, and remain in structural disrepair without the economic and social capital needed to improve their surroundings, thus improving their chance at resiliency in the face of a disastrous event. It is not until a natural disaster occurs, garnering international media coverage, that the plight of the underclass reaches the attention of those in positions of power–those said to be working for their welfare–and leaves onlookers asking "why did this happen?"

Such an internationally televised catastrophe occurred in 2005 with Hurricane Katrina when millions of viewers watched the recovery efforts, in disbelief that an event of this magnitude could happen in the United States. The public response was charged by the memories of devastation felt when a tsunami hit Phuket, Thailand in 2004. Many were questioning if those in power did everything possible to evacuate the areas of New Orleans where the impact was most severe, as well as why anyone would choose to stay in their home to ride out a major storm. What was never addressed in the public media forum was how could someone with little to no resources afford to evacuate in the face of impending danger–assuming that the severity of the situation was in fact effectively communicated to these individuals prior to the event.

Understanding Intercultural Communication and Knowledge Gaps

In the days during the aftermath of Hurricane Katrina, the country as well as the rest of the world saw the images of individuals begging to be rescued and waiting for someone to bring aid. During the long wait for aid, distrust and disdain for the government and first responders grew more fervent. Reporters and the media outlets descended upon this urban center, namely the inner-city areas which were most severely hit. The world saw the struggles of a community that largely remained invisible to the majority, except for the media images depicting the residents of these inner-city areas as criminal and dangerous (Garfield, 2007; Tierney, Bevc, & Kuligowski, 2006). These images led many viewers to address their own cognitive dissonance and recognize that the framework under which they understand race and ethnicity was subject to perception error.

A key element in effective intercultural communication is recognizing that perception error can occur and may come about based on an individual's previous experiences. An individual's previous experience will often dictate his/her current perception of reality; this is otherwise known as a *"mental model"* (Johnson-Laird, 1983). These models serve as a filter of past experience through which all current experience is interpreted. Mental models influence our communication; they affect every piece of information we process on a daily basis (Eckert, 2005). For instance, many individuals in the Gulf region have survived many hurricanes and may have believed that Katrina was going to be no different from those that preceded it. Mental models, however, influence our visual perceptions as well as what information we take in and choose to process, and are often the mechanism by which prejudice and bias take shape and get passed on from person to person and generation to generation. During coverage of the disaster, there were instances in which images of African American males carrying packages were presented to audiences with captions suggesting looting or other criminal activity, while similar photos of white males were accompanied by captions suggesting survival and heroism (see Rodríguez, Trainor, & Quarantelli 2006). The perception that an African American running from a store with a package represents theft, while a white male engaged in the same activity constitutes survival, suggests that mental models have impacted perception and the way a situation is defined.

It is clear from U. S. Census statistics that the vulnerable population in New Orleans had a very low probability of evacuating the area under their own means, yet there was a dearth of communication directed at the most vulnerable population at a time when information was critical. This may suggest an issue with emergency preparedness: There is no "one-size fits all" model to communicate vital emergency information to an entire population. Although emergency preparedness is vital, one overlooked component is the need for focus on intercultural communication, with particular attention on focused messaging that is aimed at the most vulnerable populations.

Perception error is a common outcome of mental models. Because an individual uses past experience to interpret current information, there is often a "top down" bias where existing knowledge limits or even prevents the individual from receiving new information. There is also a desire to seek out information that affirms an individual's current beliefs; this leads to a "confirmation bias" or selection effect (Eckert, 2005). These perception errors can lead to tension when communicating across races and/or other cultures, causing a breakdown in effective communication.

In the wake of Hurricane Katrina many were left asking why the individuals in the Ninth Ward did not evacuate, as that is what they would have done. There were questions about why one of the world's greatest superpowers was not able to quickly and effectively design a disaster management plan and rescue effort to aid its citizens. An event the magnitude of Hurricane Katrina challenged the thinking of most Americans and brought to light some of the microinequities, or subtle injustices, present in the country. We argue that the lack of attention to or understanding of the struggles experienced by underserved minority and poor populations—such as those individuals in the Ninth Ward, for example—suggests a lack of situational understanding by some individuals with economic resources and social capital, who believe that remaining in the path of a natural disaster is a choice. These various entities appeared to assume that individuals would choose to place themselves in harm's way when other options are viable and available. Further, we suggest that this line of thinking leads to tension in interracial and intercultural communication, even unwittingly placing the blame on the victim of a natural disaster.

In the instance of Hurricane Katrina, these issues illustrate that the perception of equal access to services and economic position–which would normally allow individuals' self-efficacy–instead demonstrate these microinequities that can have catastrophic outcomes for vulnerable populations. Given these factors we suggest that there is a general lack of awareness or recognition of social inequalities between vulnerable and non-vulnerable populations. As previous literature suggests, social inequities are at the core of much of the tension shaping the framework for interracial and intercultural communication (Bailey, 2000; Rudman, Ashmore, and Melvin, 2001). In addition to the core tensions of social inequities, individuals will experience communication, conflicts, and tensions differently based on characteristics such as gender, age, social position, and intragroup differences within the community.

Research in communication science and social psychology has provided evidence of inequality in the nature of information that is available to underserved populations. Consistent with the thinking behind microinequalities and the impact of these subtle injustices on the underserved, previous research indicates differences in the availability of crisis information across different social strata (Lachlan et al., 2007). The inevitable outcome of microinequality in terms of subpopulations who have not received timely or adequate information concerning an impending crisis or disaster is that there may be differences in terms of motivation to respond and awareness of remedial behaviors that can reduce the potential harms presented by the event.

The relationship between socioeconomic status and access to timely and effective crisis messages is best explained theoretically by a phenomenon known as the *Knowledge gap* process. "Knowledge gap" is a term typically used in communication and psychology research to refer to differences in access to information across different socioeconomic strata. It implies that the less affluent have less access to information which renders them less able to make reasoned and informed decisions (Lachlan et al., 2007; Tichenor, Donohue, & Olien, 1970). The original studies in this area demonstrated stark socioeconomic differences in public affairs knowledge (Tichenor, Donohue, & Olien, 1970). In these groundbreaking studies, secondary analyses of American Institute of Public Opinion data indicated that those of higher socioeconomic standing, over time, accumulated more knowledge concerning the link between smoking and cancer, the NASA lunar program, and new developments in satellite technology. Tichenor and colleagues (1970) further explicated these processes, offering evidence of differences of knowledge about a newspaper strike between communities that did or did not receive a great deal of media exposure to news of the strike. In this instance, the Knowledge gap was more pronounced when accounting for coverage, suggesting that those of higher status may have greater access to information about public events. Since the original research, dozens of studies have provided further evidence that that there are socioeconomic differences in exposure to vital information (Viswaneth & Finnegan, 1996). These studies have been primarily concerned with identifying mediators, such as level of concern (Lovrich & Pierce, 1984), training in public affairs (Griffin, 1990), motivation (Ettima & Kline, 1977), and personal interest (Bailey, 1971).

More recently, research in this area has turned its attention specifically to fewer Knowledge gap processes that are related to public health. Kahlor, Dunwoody, & Griffin (2004) examined socioeconomic differences in obtaining information about a parasitic water supply and the ramifications of ingesting this parasite. Results indicated that those of higher status were more likely to have access to this information and to comprehend it. High status respondents also indicated more background knowledge concerning the source of the contamination.

At least one study has explicitly investigated Knowledge gap processes during Hurricane Katrina. Lachlan, Spence, & Eith (2007) surveyed over 700 Katrina evacuees at relief centers across the country. Their data suggest that lower socioeconomic status evacuees indicated a greater desire to seek information, and suggest that this may be indicative of both perceptions of vulnerability and the unavailability of adequate information. Further, lower socioeconomic status evacuees reported less comprehension of evacuation messages and expressed less satisfaction with the messages that they did receive. The study further argues that members of underserved populations may experience greater social isolation. As a result, emergency responders should not only target these vulnerable and underserved groups but should also prioritize them. These underserved groups may have fewer or more specialized social networks; therefore the dissemination of emergency information may be passed through interpersonal channels as opposed to traditional state-recognized systems.

Building and Maintaining Relationships: Some Best Practices

Those in positions of institutional power can work to better communicate with different ethnic groups to build and maintain relationships before a disaster emerges by helping such communities prepare for action before a disaster or other extreme events occur. One such approach is taking steps to eliminate the Knowledge gap. This can be accomplished through effective message design and placement.

Previous studies suggest that African Americans are more likely than others to indicate a distrust of institutions of government to protect the public health and safety (Burby & Strong, 1997; Freimuth et al., 2001; Gamble, 1997). Moreover, past research has supported the position that racial and ethnic minorities are less likely to accept a risk or warning message as credible without confirmation of the message from others (specifically interpersonal networks), thus causing a delay in response time (Fothergill, Maestas, & Darlington, 1999; Lindell & Perry 2004). In the wake of the Anthrax attacks, studies revealed distrust of government messages by racial minority groups. These results are troubling when adherence to government directives may be essential to issues of health and safety (Braveman, et al., 2004; Quinn, Thomas, & McAllister, 2005). If the credibility of a risk message is dependent upon interpersonal networks, then those in institutional power need to facilitate the building and bolstering of these networks. In this section, four Best Practices that have emerged from previous disasters and disaster literature are outlined concerning how to build relationships and communication with specific targeted publics—(see the Journal of *Applied Communication Research* 34 (3) and *Public Affairs in Health* (http://www.cdc.gov/about/pah), the electronic Journal of the Centers for Disease Control and Prevention.)

Best Practice Number One: *Establish a working relationship with existing community opinion leaders and change agents*

Such collaborative relationships allow institutional powers to coordinate their messages and activities. Developing a pre-crisis network is an effective way of coordinating and collaborating with other credible sources in specific populations and improving reach. Coordinating messages with opinion leaders will enhance the probability of a consistent message and may reduce the confusion that occurs during a crisis event.

Involved with this Best Practice is the idea of building social capital (Putnam, 1995; 2000). The level of community development is often measured by economic and social indicators; in particular, indicators of physical, human, and most importantly social capital (Schellong, 2007). Social capital is often defined as an individual's social network, often formed by shared norms and values, which provides resources such as social support, and leads to collective action (Coleman, 1990; Wall, Ferazzi, & Schryer, 1998). As indicated by Coleman (1988), a significant element of social capital is an effective channel of communication. Although social capital is seen as an asset within a community, it can also be exclusionary. Those who are on the fringes of social life within a community, specifically those living in lower socioeconomic conditions and minority communities, are often the most vulnerable and least likely to acquire needed messages. Increasing social capital through using opinion leaders and change agents can facilitate the creation of opportunities for community participation in local community organizations such as local government, community readiness organizations, or neighborhood watch programs. This kind of participation promotes the strong social networks necessary for the emergence of a viable communication network.

In the area of disaster preparations, social capital can be a key to limiting the harm, severity, and duration of a crisis. The underclass is at a disadvantage in terms of crisis preparedness because they are more likely to have lower incomes and be unemployed (Gladwin & Peacock, 1997). They may live in more vulnerable areas and are less likely to have access to transportation. The variability in crisis preparedness across ethnicity and socioeconomic status has been demonstrated in previous research (Spence et al., 2007; 2008). With the absence of physical capital, social capital may be an alternative means of survival.

Therefore, working with opinion leaders to help dissemination information from institutional powers can increase the information potential of a community (Coleman, 1990). Working with opinion leaders involves both formal and informal partnerships. Through these relationships information about evacuations, shelters, food and medicine can be distributed. In the case of Hurricane Katrina, about 49 percent of the evacuees in Houston, Texas shelters indicated that in the days before the hurricane hit, they had heard the order to evacuate and that the order included detailed instructions. Of those that stayed, about three in 10 stated that they had heard an evacuation order but that it had not provided instructions (Brodie et al., 2006, Spence et al., 2007; 2008). In one study 34 percent of respondents indicated they didn't leave because of lack of transportation. This is one such area where institutional powers can use opinion leaders to disseminate pre-crisis information. Providing accurate information on how to find safety or evacuate is a first step.

Although institutional powers may work with and seek the aid of specific opinion leaders, this effort also involves an informal partnership with the public (Seeger, 2006). Moreover, having relationships with community opinion leaders can bolster the effectiveness of the messages and help minimize rumors or misinformation. Public suspicions of scientific experts and government as noted are already high and in some communities are increasing for a variety of reasons, including access to more sources of conflicting information, a reduction in the use of scientific reasoning in decision-making, and political infighting (Peters, Covello, & McCallum, 1997; Seeger et al., 2003, Renyolds, 2006). If messages from community opinion leaders are congruent with those of institutional leadership, more protective action may be taken.

Phrasing questions such as "Is your home mitigated" or "Do you have a personal emergency plan" often are not effective to all audiences. Current websites such as ready. gov give broad messages that are not specifically targeted to any audience. Moreover, many in disadvantaged areas may not have access to such sites. Therefore institutional authorities need to work with representatives not only to place messages, but also to use similar others and build networks to deliver those messages, and ensure that the messages are clear to the target audience.

Best Practice Number Two: Carefully select the messenger

Alongside of the distrust toward institutional power is the concept of similarity and social trust. Similarity between individuals is one influence of social trust. Social trust is the willingness to rely on individuals or institutions that have the responsibility for making decisions, as well as taking or suggesting actions related to the management of the environment or issues of public health and safety. However, minorities may have less similar others or individuals to turn to for information. In the area of information seeking, research has demonstrated individuals are more likely to direct their search for information toward those who possess similar attributes (Ibarra, 1993; 1995), and it can be reasonably assumed racial minorities will have fewer similar others to target for information and fewer media outlets perceived as similar. Because of this, it is less likely that such messages from institutional powers will be accepted, or trusted. Therefore, examine the media figures that are reporting agents for institutions. These agents should reflect the diversity of the audience. This does not mean hiring multiple spokespersons; as with the previous Best Practice, it involves working with diverse populations and ensuring that they are represented during the reporting and information dissemination process.

Best Practice Number Three: Carefully select the placement of messages

Even if similar others are used to build trust, if the message is not received it is not effective. A study on information acquisition about mercury levels in fish in urban New Jersey found that ethnic differences emerged in the sources of information, in their knowledge about fishing advisories, and in their knowledge of the correct advisories. The study suggested that in general, Whites took advantage of written sources of information a higher percentage of times than did Blacks, and more than Hispanics. An ethnic difference also emerged in perception of the presence of advisory signs near the fishing and crabbing locations. Results suggest that the techniques authorities used to inform the public, which included newspaper advertisements, brochures, flyers, and public meetings about fishing and crabbing which warned of the dangers from consuming contaminated fish, were not effective to ethnic populations (Burger et al., 1999). Knowing the information-seeking habits of the target population will allow messages to be placed in media with the most reach, and granting the most exposure.

Best Practice Number Four: Communicate with Compassion

A final Best Practice is communicating with compassion, concern, and empathy, particularly toward underserved communities that are already distrustful of institutional authority. As noted by Reynolds (2006) empathy, caring, competence, commitment, and compassion all contribute to trust. The more that members of an underserved community know about efforts to share accurate information openly, the more they may trust the institution as the source (Peters et al., 1997). Therefore, whether it is the institution or the designated opinion leader communicating with target populations, these principles should be maintained. Persons respond positively to messages that acknowledge their concerns and demonstrate compassion towards the situation. If the public perceives an expression of genuine concern and empathy, faith in the actions being undertaken can be built.

Conclusion

The effectiveness of traditional approaches to communicating in disasters is largely narrow and problematic for specific segments of the population. Because of these shortfalls, institutional authorities need to reexamine how they communicate. This involves a restructuring of how messages are designed, where they are placed, and the characteristics of delivery. It requires building relationships before disaster strikes, and maintaining those relationships throughout the crisis lifecycle. Models and plans for pre-crisis and crisis communication and actions need to move toward a more focused approach. Planning is a community concern, and planning will not be effective unless the entire community is involved.

DISCUSSION QUESTIONS

1. How can mental models impede effective communication from institutional authorities during a crisis?

2. What are some of the concerns associated with the response of underserved populations to messages from government officials? What are some potential solutions to these problems?

3. How may "microinequities" influence the effectiveness of disaster communication?

4. What are Knowledge gaps? Why do they happen? What can emergency managers and crisis communication practitioners do to prevent them from happening?

---

[1] The underground economy is not solely populated by criminal syndicates; it also encompasses any income generating activities that are conducted beyond the purview of the government and results in revenue that goes untaxed.

References

Anderson, E. (1990). *Streetwise: Race, Class, and change in an urban community*. Chicago: University of Chicago Press.

Bailey, B. (2000). Communicative behavior and conflict between African-American customers and Korean immigrant retailers in Los Angeles. *Discourse & Society, 11*, 86–108.

Bailey, G. A. (1971). The public, the media, and the knowledge gap. *Journal of Environmental Education, 2*, 3–8.

Baker, G. (2001). Race and reputation: Restoring image beyond the crisis. In R. L. Heath & G. Vasquez (Eds.), *Handbook of Public Relations* (pp. 513–520). Thousand Oaks, CA: Sage.

Bolin, R. C., & Bolton, P. (1986). *Race, Religion, and ethnicity in disaster recovery*. Boulder: University of Colorado Press.

Braveman, P., Egerter, S., Cubbin, C., & Marchi, K. (2004). An approach to studying social disparities in health and health care. *American Journal of Public Health, 94*, 2139–2148.

Brodie, M., Weltzien, E., Altman, D., Blendon, R. J., & Benson, J. M. (2006). Experiences of hurricane Katrina evacuees in Houston shelters: Implications for future planning. *American Journal of Public Health, 96*, 1401–1408.

Burby, R., & Strong, D. (1997). Coping with chemicals: Blacks, Whites, planners, and industrial pollution. *Journal of American Planning Association, 63*, 469–480.

Burger, K., Pflugh, K. K., Lurig, L., Von Hagen, L. A., Von Hagen, S. (1999). Fishing in urban New Jersey: Ethnicity affects information sources, perception and compliance. *Risk analysis, 19*, 217–229.

Coleman, J. (1990). *Foundations of Social Theory*. Cambridge, MA: Belknap Press.

Coleman, J. S. (1988). Social capital in the creation of human capital. *American Journal of Sociology, 94* (supplement), 95–120.

Dash, N., Peacock, W. G., & Morrow, B. H. (1997). And the poor get poorer: A neglected black community. In W. G. Peacock, B. H. Morrow, & H. Gladwin (Eds.), *Hurricane Andrew: Ethnicity, Gender and Sociology of Disasters* (pp. 206–225). London: Routledge.

DuBois, W. E. B. (1903) *The souls of black folk*. New York: Oxford University Press Classics.

DuBois, W. E. B. (1935) *Black reconstructionists in America 1860–1880*. New York: Simon and Schuster.

Eckert, S. (2005). *Intercultural Communication*. Cengage Publishing.

Ettema, J. S. & Kline, F. G. (1977). Deficits, differences and ceilings: Contingent conditions for understanding the knowledge gap. *Communication Research, 4*, 179–202.

Fothergill, A., Maestas, E. G., & Darlington, J. D. (1999). Race, ethnicity and disasters in the United States: A review of the literature. *Disasters, 23*, 156–173.

Freimuth, V. S., Quinn, S. C., Thomas, S. B., Cole, G., Zook, E., Duncan, T. (2001). African Americans' views on research and the Tuskegee Syphilis study. *Social Science and Medicine, 52,* 797–808.

Gamble, V. N. (1997). Under the shadow of Tuskegee: African Americans and health care. *American Journal of Public Health, 87,* 1773–1778.

Garfield, G. (2007). Hurricane Katrina: The making of unworthy disaster victims. *Journal of African American Studies, 10,* 55–74.

Gladwin, H., & Peacock, W. G. (1997). Warning and evacuation: A night for hard houses. In W. G. Peacock, B. H. Morrow, & H. Gladwin (Eds.), *Hurricane Andrew: Ethnicity, gender and sociology of disasters* (pp. 52–74). London: Routledge.

Griffin, R. J. (1990). Energy in the eighties: Education, communication, and the knowledge gap. *Journalism Quarterly, 67,* 554–566.

Ibarra, H. (1993). Network centrality, power, and innovation involvement: Determinants of technical and administrative roles. *Academy of Management Journal, 36,* 471–501.

Ibarra, H. (1995). Race, opportunity, and diversity of social circles in managerial networks. *Academy of Management Journal, 38,* 673–703.

Johnson-Laird, P. N. (1983). Mental Models: Toward a Cognitive Science of Language, *Inference and Consciousness*. Harvard University Press.

Kahlor, L. A., Dunwoody, S., & Griffin, R. J. (2004). Accounting for the complexity of causal explanations in the wake of an environmental risk. *Science Communication, 26,* 5–30.

Lachlan, K. A., Spence, P. R., & Eith, C. A. (2007). Access to mediated emergency messages: Differences in crisis knowledge across age, race, and socioeconomic status. In R. Swan and K. Bates (Eds.) *Through the eyes of Katrina: Social justice in the United States* (pp. 203–220). Durham, NC: Carolina Academic Press.

Lindell, M. K., & Perry, R. W. (2004). *Communicating environmental risk in multiethnic communities.* Thousand Oaks, CA: Sage.

Lovrich, N. P., & Pierce, J. C. (1984). Knowledge gap phenomenon: Effects of situation specific and trans-situational factors. *Communication Research, 11,* 415–434.

Peacock, W. G., & Girard, G. (1997). Ethnic and racial inequalities in hurricane damage and insurance settlements. In W. G. Peacock, B. H. Morrow, & H. Gladwin (Eds.), *Hurricane Andrew: Ethnicity, Gender and Sociology of Disasters* (pp. 171–190). London: Routledge.

Peters, R. G., Covello, V. T., & McCallum, D. B. (1997). The determinants of trust and credibility in environmental risk communication: An empirical study. *Risk Analysis, 17*(1), 43/54.

Putnam, R. (1995). Bowling alone: America's declining social capital. *Journal of Democracy, 6,* 65–78.

Putnam, R. (2000). *Bowling alone: The collapse and revival of American community.* New York: Simon and Schuster.

Quinn, S. C., Thomas, T., & McAllister, C. (2005). Postal workers' perspectives on communication during the anthrax attack. *Biosecurity and Bioterrorism, 3,* 207–215.

Reynolds, B. (2006). Response to best practices. *Journal of Applied Communication Research, 34,* 249–252.

Rodríguez, H., Trainor, J., & Quarantelli, E. L. (2006). *The ANNALS of the American Academy of Political and Social Science, 604*, 82–101.

Rudman, L. A., Ashmore, R. D., & Gary. M. L. (2001). 'Unlearning' automatic biases: The malleability of implicit prejudice and stereotypes. *Journal of Personality and Social Psychology, 81*, 856–868.

Schellong, A. (2007). Increasing social capital for disaster response through social networking services (SNS) in Japanese local governments. National Center for Digital Government Working Paper No. 07-005.

Seeger, M. W. (2006). Best practices in crisis communication: An expert panel process. *Journal of Applied Communication Research, 34*, 229–331.

Seeger, M. W., Sellnow, T. L., & Ulmer, R. R. (2003). *Communication and organizational crisis.* Westport, CT: Quorum Press.

Spence, P. R., Lachlan, K. A., & Burke, J. M. (2008). Crisis preparation, media use, and information seeking: Patterns across Katrina evacuees and lessons learned for crisis communication. *Journal of Emergency Management, 6*(2).

Spence, P. R., Lachlan, K. A., & Griffen, D. (2007). Crisis communication, race and natural disasters. *Journal of Black Studies, 37*, 539–554.

Tichenor, P. J., Donohue, G. A., & Olien, C. N. (1970). Mass media flow and differential growth in knowledge. *Public Opinion Quarterly, 34*, 159–170.

Tierney, K., Bevc, C., & Kuligowski, E. (2006). Metaphors matter: Disaster myths, media frames, and their consequences in hurricane Katrina. *The ANNALS of the American Academy of Political and Social Science, 604*, 57–81.

Viswaneth, K. & Finnegan J. R., Jr. (1996). The knowledge gap hypothesis: Twenty-five years later. *Communication Yearbook, 19*, 187–227.

Wall, E., Ferazzi, G., & Schryer, F. (1998). Getting the goods on social capital. *Rural Sociology, 63*, 300–322.

Williams, D. E., & Olaniran, B. A. (2002). Crisis communication in racial issues. *Journal of Applied Communication Research, 30*, 293–313.

Wilson, W. J. (1987). *The Truly Disadvantaged: The Inner City, the Underclass, and Public Policy.* Chicago: University of Chicago Press.

12

Promoting Interracial Interactions Through Service-Learning Pedagogy

Eddah Mutua-Kombo

Abstract

In this essay the author travels through an experience that impels connecting community problems to service-learning pedagogy in order to foster meaningful race relations. It draws from theoretical work on critical pedagogy, critical service-learning pedagogy, intergroup contact theory, and interracial friendships. These theories provide strategies that coalesce to promote race relations, and support an integrated theory and practice that give students an orientation to addressing social problems. This assumption is explored through a service-learning project that allowed culturally and racially diverse students to respond to a community problem expressed by East African refugees residing in a midwest U.S. community. The students partnered to engage in dialogue to chart ways to improve interracial interactions in two local public high schools.

KEY TERMS: service-learning pedagogy, race relations, intercultural/interracial interactions, knowledge, refugees

Introduction

"How *can you help us? We want our children to go to school to get an education, not to* fight".

As I thought about how to respond, Amina[1] retorted *"you know you can do something, tell us how."* "I *am not sure what I can do right away but I will* think *about it and let you know,"* I responded with some hesitation.

This conversation occurred during an informal visit with my female friends who are refugees from the Sudan and Somalia, and now living in a predominantly white community in the upper mid-western region of the United States. The focus of this essay is a discussion about the context in which I was asked for help, and how my response to this interaction led to a decision to use service-learning pedagogy as a tool to address racial relations in the now "shared" community. The essay is framed around the questions: 1) How is service-learning (or more generally a community–based project) itself an intercultural/interracial concept and interaction? 2) How does it heighten community issues and at the same time offer means to resolve issues identified? 3) How does it create a learning environment that engages students to develop knowledge that is community-based and geared towards raising critical consciousness about community issues?

My thesis begins with the questions posed by the women mentioned earlier. In my view, they are culturally and racially marked questions and as such my response should serve to explicate ways to address racial issues in the community. In this essay, I seek to make an argument for a pedagogy that addresses community issues by utilizing diverse community members as collective producers of knowledge. The knowledge that is generated through this pedagogy focuses on offering mutual insights to understanding ideologies of race and cultural differences for purposes of promoting race relations and community-building. First, I theorize the cultural context of the stated problem, and then build on it to argue for a pedagogy that engages students to generate and apply knowledge that empowers them to address racial issues in their community. Second, I draw from theoretical perspectives that explain ways to engage racially and culturally diverse people, as theorized by Orbe & Harris (2000) and Allport (1958). The argument developed shows that the integration of these perspectives with critical pedagogy and service-learning pedagogy can present a theoretical formation relevant to promoting race interactions.

The Setting

It was summer of 2006 when my help was sought by East African refugee women to keep their children (high school students) focused on school and not school yard and cafeteria fights. The prolonged conversations about the challenges facing the refugee children and the entire community often took place when I visited Atatia at her rented townhouse located in a residential area predominantly resided by refugees from Somalia and the Sudan. This particular visit when my help was sought was not unusual. I had been visiting with Atatia and her neighbors since I accepted a professorial job in a local state university in 2005. I was particularly close to Atatia because I had known her longer than the other women. My visits to her house were frequent because my son and Atatia's two sons love to play soccer with other African kids in the neighborhood. Additionally, the Boys and Girls Club is down the street from this residential area, where the refugee children get the opportunity to interact with other culturally and racially diverse students.

'How can you help us? We want our children to go to school to get an education, not to fight.'

The question posed by Amina and the accompanying statement allows one to see the embedded racial and cultural nuances evident in her words. The racial makeup of the community where the women live explains the basis of their concerns. The rapid change in the racial composition of the community was the issue about which the local refugees and white community felt most concern. For the women, it was the reality of living in a racialized community where—in addition to racial identity—their cultural, national and religious identities were unwelcome.

It all began when Somali immigrants fleeing civil war in Somalia started settling in the region in early 2000. The 5,000 Somali refugees who live in this community account for about seven percent of the community's 68,000 residents. It is estimated that the local school district has an enrollment of about 9,000 students: 79 percent White, non-Hispanic, 12 percent Black, non-Hispanic, four percent Asian, four percent Hispanic, and one percent American Indian (The St. Cloud Independent School District web site: www.isd742.com). The evident demographic changes in this community that was culturally homogeneous until about a decade ago is what evoked interracial conflicts between Somali and European American high school students. The causes of violent racial and prejudiced acts were the stark religious and cultural differences between the students. At the same time, lack of knowledge about each other further isolated the students. Overall, the seemingly disruption of what the local residents were "used to" became a matter of concern to all who shared the community.[2]

Even though the issues facing this midwest community are not new to most communities in the United States, they took a new dimension in the context of the refugee women's cultural backgrounds. The manner in which the problem was enacted and resolution sought reflects aspects of African communication patterns that the women still maintain in their new (American) cultural environment. As noted earlier, the women and I would talk about challenges of cultural adaptation in informal settings. In Africa, communication is almost entirely through the interpersonal mode carried out in dyads, small groups (e.g. family members, neighbors, and friends) and large groups such as village meetings or the marketplace (Moemeka, 1996). These settings not only provide forums for discussing community affairs but they also induce communal participation in finding solutions to community problems.

Contextualizing *'we need your help'*

The context in which my help was sought deserves a brief explanation in order to justify my involvement in the solution to the identified community problem and the decision to use service-learning pedagogy to promote meaningful interracial interactions in the community. Amina's request for help was culturally enacted. Taking note of how she used the pronoun 'we' reveals cultural values, attitudes and expectations informed by the philosophical foundation of African culture. Additionally, it is reflective of the basic principles of African culture that underscore interactions among community members and how community problems are handled. Moemeka (1996) observed that "community as unit takes precedence over its members. The desires, wants, and needs of the individual members of the community are not, as it might seem, subjugated to those of the community; rather they are merged with community needs in a holistic attempt aimed at ensuring effective prioritization" (p. 202). African cultural values that define self-concept, relational orientations, status, respect, and community belongingness in part explain why the women chose to seek my help.

My status in the community as a teacher is mostly understood through interpretive lenses of the African cultural values that also define how I am expected to respond to these cultural expectations. The cultural expectations placed on a teacher reveal that it is difficult to demarcate their role inside and outside the classroom. Generally, a teacher is revered in the African culture as a community leader, wise person, responsible, and at the service of the community[3]. Teachers are perceived as custodians of knowledge, and as such are expected to play a greater role in socializing members of society. Specifically, a teacher is entrusted by society to "sharpen" the minds of the youth, socialize, and give them guidance as they grow to become responsible members of society. Similarly, the teacher is expected to offer solutions to societal problems because they have or rather are assumed to have the "knowledge" to do so. The knowledge they possess is perceived to be communal, and intended to serve the interests of the community. The teacher serves the community in both formal and informal educational settings.

'You know you can do something, tell us how?'

As noted at the beginning of this essay, my response to Amina was not forthright. I should explain why I was hesitant to respond, yet the women were forthright with what they wanted me to do. It is important to mention that I was aware of the cultural meaning assigned to their request, despite the fact that an immediate response was not given. My hesitation to respond directly about what I could do was tempered by an unspoken response that lingered in my mind at the time:

> I do not have the answer to what you are asking me to do right now. I wish you could know that this place is not like back home where teachers have a lot of power to make things happen. In addition, you just don't know how racism complicates things. And, I am also new around here just like you.

My hesitancy to respond directly to the women is explained in part by my position as an insider-outsider in the two worlds I inhabit as an African and 'Americanized African' in the United States. On one hand, I am an insider to the African way of life and on the other hand, I am both an insider and outsider to the American way of life. As an insider, I understand my obligations as an intercultural communication professor and a member of different communities where I have lived during my nine-year stay in the United States. I understand the need to engage in efforts geared at promoting interracial and intercultural relations between diverse cultures. Specifically, I recognize the need to productively use my academic training and personal intercultural experiences to build bridges across cultures.

This being the case, there are moments however when I feel like an outsider to the American society. One of those moments as mentioned earlier, was my inability to respond immediately to the women. This is a fact that sometimes slows down my efforts to fully fulfill expected community obligations. For example, I am well aware of the challenge of unlearning prejudiced and racist attitudes and behaviors that characterize this new place that has become our "home." I was not born and raised in the United States and it is painful to fathom what it means to be born, raised, live, and die in a racialized society. I can barely handle the "heat" in the fourteen years I have voluntarily lived outside of my country of birth, Kenya. It's hard for me to fathom what it is like for those whose choice to live in the United States, a racialized society, was not ever really their choice. Rather, the "choice" was involuntary; this is the case for many African Americans whose ancestors were brought here. And, this involuntary choice now falls upon refugees from war-torn countries.

The varied experiences among diverse groups of people in the community informed how I was going to respond to Amina's question. I decided to use my classroom and the community to collectively seek solutions to the identified community need. It was not possible to singly act on the problem because it was not only a personal issue but also one that was rooted in the fabric of the society and therefore required a response that was community-centered in effort and interests. The community, including high school and university students, local high schools and university administrators, community leaders and parents needed to collaborate in generating what Christine Cress (2006) calls responsive knowledge to address identified community needs.

Laura Finley's (2004) work on transforming violence candidly identifies the classroom as the place to start the transformation. She observes that "if we wish to transform our world into a more peaceful place, including all that the notion of positive peace entails, it seems as though one logical place to start is the classroom" (Finley, 2004, p. 2). My vision to seek a community-based response to Amina's question was realized once I made the decision to use my classroom and my positionality as a professor (in addition to being a community member) as the catalyst for change. It is then that service-learning pedagogy became the apparent choice to facilitate the process of generating knowledge pertaining to how to address voiced community concerns. The choice for this pedagogical practice is justified by the recognition that "improving our communities now and in the future is dependent upon providing the leadership to give students the knowledge, skills, and experiences that are less self-referenced and more community referenced" (Astin & Astin, 2000, cited in Cress, 2006, p. 5).

Defining Service-Learning

The operational definition of service-learning is informed by the work of Eyler & Giles (1999), who define it as a form of experiential education where learning occurs through a cycle of action and reflection as students work with others to achieve real objectives for the community, and deeper understanding and skills for themselves. According to Cress (2006), the goal of service-learning is to develop civically minded students who possess analytical problem-solving abilities and self-identity as community change agents as a direct consequence of their community-based learning experience.

In communication studies, the value of service-learning cannot be underestimated. The National Communication Association (NCA) has taken a leading role in bringing to the forefront the critical link between service-learning, student learning, development of civic responsibility and contribution of diversity to a strong democracy.[4] In the last decade, NCA has "embarked on a comprehensive effort to create a more engaged communication discipline: fostering research and teaching addressing the most pressing public problems at the dawn of the 21st century" (NCA). This commitment is based on the premise that "service-learning is an effective method for enhancing student learning and civic responsibility." In their book, *Service-Learning in Communication Studies: a Handbook,* Isaacson, Dorries & Brown (2001) assert that service-learning is an educational opportunity that allows students to promote more effective service to their communities through communication skills acquired in the classroom. Furthermore, "serving the community enriches students' understanding of how communication principles operate in the real world and offers opportunity to compare perspectives of common experiences" (p. i).

Service-Learning Pedagogy in Promoting Race Relations: Theoretical Foundations

This section responds to the question: How does service-learning pedagogy enhance learners' understanding of the methods they may use to promote race relations in American communities? Fundamentally, I am advancing the case for service-learning as a means to produce community-based knowledge to address community issues such as race tensions among racially and culturally diverse high school students. The decision to use service-learning pedagogy was purposely done to address an historical and political problem. Such a response gives the process of seeking a solution to the problem at hand a political character. This character is exemplified in theoretical approaches used to produce a pedagogical and ideological formation that defines what is to be done, how, and for what purpose. In turn, this approach helps students define their understanding as well as analyze and act on the problem identified. In this regard, service-learning is able to induce action that produces knowledge that is responsive to the problem.

Theoretical foundation that brings service-learning to the forefront in addressing racial problems draws its meaning from the field of critical pedagogy and from theoretical perspectives that explain ways to connect and develop meaningful relationships among diverse racial groups. Daigre's (2000) work on critical service-learning pedagogy cites Biesta (1998), who argues that "critical pedagogies are in one way or another committed to the imperative of transforming the larger social order in the interest of justice, equality, democracy, and human freedom" (p. 499). Similarly, Giroux (1998) observes that this practice allows for opportunities to address social problems where students understand what it means to exercise rights and responsibilities as critical citizens actively engaged in forms of social learning that expand human capacities for compassion, empathy, and solidarity (Giroux, cited in Torres, 1998). Overall, it would seem that critical pedagogy presents the process of learning as one that involves the participation of both the student and teacher and acknowledges their diverse lived experiences in the production of new knowledge (See Denzin, 2006; Freire, 2001; Giroux, 1998).

Both critical theory and service-learning have been rigorously theorized and contested. For example, Bruce Herzberg (cited in Daigre, 2000) expresses doubts that questions about social justice issues are raised by service-learning/community service. On the other hand, critical pedagogy is faulted for lacking examples of concrete practice (Cuban and Hayes, 1997 cited in Daigre, 2000). Notwithstanding the contention, Daigre's (2000) research on the intersection of service-learning and critical pedagogy reveals that "some grounding in critical pedagogy can provide students with an ideological framework that encourages their analysis of social problems to move individual or personal explanations to more systemic criteria" (p. 2).

The Service-Learning Project

The service-learning project developed was intended to mirror Eric Daigre's perspective. It was designed to engage university and high school students in a problem-solving approach that would empower them to generate knowledge from their shared experiences, and utilize that knowledge to promote healthy race relations amongst themselves and others. The project also offered space to move from the micro level (individual/personal) to consider ramifications of these interracial challenges on a macro level (systemic criteria) as expressed by Eric Daigre. For example, the experiences of the Somali and Sudanese refugee students allowed participating students (notably American students) to gain a greater understanding of how issues of conflict and war, national insecurity, forced migration, poor governance, and global economic inequalities impact those in the U.S and elsewhere in the world. In all, the students were able to see the value of joining hands to denounce all forms of injustices and inequalities in the world in general and in their immediate communities in particular.

Service-learning combines theoretical perspectives that explain ways to connect and improve relations among racially diverse groups. The basis of Allport's (1958) contact theory and the Orbe and Harris, (2000) work on interracial friendships inform interracial relational phenomenon. The premise of contact theory is only contact that leads people to do things together is likely to result in changed attitudes (Hansell, 2000). On the other hand, Orbe and Harris (2000) see the function of interracial interactions as the ability to challenge interactants to reflect internally on stereotypical beliefs about racially different others with whom they have had little or no contact. This phenomenon is conceptualized in a view of contact theory that is based on the premise that prejudice may be reduced by increased interactions—under optimal conditions—with racially diverse groups in the pursuit of common goals.

The decision to incorporate service-learning pedagogy into my teaching and scholarship was apt in two important ways. First, service-learning brings together perspectives that validate theories that provide a better understanding of how interactions between people of diverse racial memberships can foster positive race relations. Additionally, its application generates and brings together knowledge that allows students as community members and change agents to learn to respond to community-based problems.

I redesigned one of my intercultural communication courses—*Problems in Intercultural Communication*—to incorporate service-learning pedagogy. The intent was to allow university and high school students to develop a consciousness about community problems and how to manage them by participating in organized learning activities. Service-learning sessions were organized to allow university students the opportunity to combine knowledge acquired in the classroom and knowledge emerging from their interactions with high school students, in order to chart new approaches for addressing race relations in the local high schools. A partnership between my university and the local school district resulted in a project modeled on the NCA's "*Communicating Common Ground*" (National Communication Association). The project became the platform where racially and culturally diverse students could dialogue about issues that kept them apart as well as what could bring them together. Since Spring 2007, the project's focus remains on improving racial and intercultural understanding between diverse students in our local high schools. The project has made it possible for 115 young people to gain relevant knowledge and skills about (1) creating a climate of acceptance; (2) knowing how to constructively respond to cultural differences; and (3) incorporating the thinking of students as well as staff and professors in this endeavor so they become engaged citizens who can lead the local community in becoming an accepting racially and culturally diverse community.[5]

Service-learning pedagogy allowed dialogue to occur among the students in ways envisioned by Ellis and Moaz (2006). They propose that

> Dialogue is a search for deep differences and shared concerns. It asks participants to inquire genuinely about the other person and [to] avoid premature judgment, debate, and questions designed to expose flaws (p. 232).

The university students were to use knowledge they gained from the course content and combine it with knowledge generated through service-learning dialogue sessions to analyze, make meaning of racial tension in the community, and address the problem through application of the knowledge and skills learned. Knowledge acquisition was made possible through prolonged (semester long) interactions between my students, high school students, educators and invited community leaders participating in the project as guest speakers and/or observers. Among the fifty-five participating high school students, 90 percent were minority students and 10 percent Caucasian. Members of my class were 70 percent Caucasian and 30 percent minority students. The eleven (11) professionals who served as guest speakers included one African American, two Hispanics, one Asian American, and seven Caucasians all drawn from diverse professional backgrounds. They were employees of local city government, non-profit organizations and the state university.

In the spirit of learning to serve and serving to learn, students enriched their experiences as participants in community issues through well-planned and coordinated group dialogue sessions. Six sessions were structured to generate knowledge about the following topics: (1) Building community; (2) Recognizing problems in interracial/intercultural settings and crafting a new narrative; (3) Intercultural communication skills & non-violent communication principles; (4) Becoming an ally; (5) Bridging differences & managing intercultural conflicts effectively; and (6) Feeling part of my community and another community. Through dialogue they were able to express themselves, share experiences, and acknowledge similarities and differences among them. Together they engaged in meaningful exchanges that allowed them to chart new paths toward peaceful co-existence in their communities.

Promoting Positive Interracial Interactions through Service-Learning Pedagogy

The viability of service-learning pedagogy in promoting race relations is evident in how the pedagogy became an avenue for students to interact, dialogue, and discover avenues to acquire interracial understanding. The ability to act for desired change was informed by knowledge created during service-learning group dialogue sessions. The students documented what they learned together–with and from each other—in the form of journal entries, reflection writing assignments, and a feedback survey administered at the end of the 2007 and 2008 Spring semesters. Excerpts from students' responses are highlighted in the following pages to demonstrate the ways that service-learning pedagogy promotes interracial interactions. The excerpts from students' writing assignments contain demographic data while those without this background information were extracted from anonymous feedback surveys. The themes emerging from students' responses were used to explain two foundations through which service-learning promotes race relations: service-learning opens avenues to create knowledge relevant to promoting racial relations; and service-learning involves generating and applying community-based knowledge that responds to identified community needs.

1) *Service-learning opens avenues to create knowledge relevant to promoting racial relations.*

In the effort to integrate theory and practice, service-learning allows students to learn more about themselves and the community in which they live and serve. Students learn about differences, how to voice what they learn from and with each other, plan to act on what they learn, and begin to see themselves in new roles as leaders and people willing to make a difference in their communities. Responses about the benefits of service-learning pedagogy indicated that students' interactions generated a better understanding of racial tensions in the community and ways to improve the situation. They genuinely inquired about each other and by so doing, identified their personal cultural differences and similarities. At the same time, they learned to voice their shared concerns and seek common goals about improving racial relations in the community. The numerous benefits credited to service-learning pedagogy are illustrated by students' responses highlighted in the following excerpts.

High school students' responses to a question about what they had learned about communicating with people from different racial and cultural backgrounds revealed the following:

> All people struggle with different issues. I learned how to talk to people from different cultures and also that there are people in the world who care. (Somali female student)

> I think it is really good to communicate with different people so that you can learn more. … how to open my mind to different people and things. (Caucasian female student)

> I learned that if some people do not understand my culture then it is my job to make fellow students and teachers understand so that they will know where I am from. (Somali female student)

> Misunderstandings happen a lot. We need to be more accepting, open minded … jumping into conclusions is also a big problem. (Caucasian female student)

While these responses about what students learned may not be new to many of us and the students themselves, their significance lies in the context of the students' participation in the project. Their participation in activities that actualize the realization to do things differently reveals the positive outcome of being in direct contact with groups of people from diverse backgrounds. Moreover, for a portion of the university students who participated, the actual practical application of theories enhanced academic learning through experiential understanding of the objectives set for the project and the course. The experiential knowledge gained was expressed in the following excerpts:

> Hands-on experience and application of concepts learned in class was made possible in a meaningful way.

> I was able to give face to interracial conflicts in a way I would have never known had I not interacted with the high school kids especially those who experienced these conflicts on a daily basis.

> It made intercultural conflicts and racial tensions that affect others more personal.

> It helped me to see a different perspective on things.

The manifestation of a service-learning project is evident in the way that these students became critical learners. Barnett (1997) characterizes students engaged in this type of meaning-making reflection as "critically connected beings" (as cited in Cress, 2006 para. 15). University students' responses to a question asking them to state some of the memorable moments of the experience revealed what they had observed and/or became aware of during their interactions. It was apparent that they were aware of what was happening in their surroundings, and paying attention to dynamics of the interactions created by this form of learning.

Watching the high school kids talk openly. The honesty of the students was amazing.

Guest speakers such as the Chief of Police, the local Major and the professors showed efforts needed to improve racial relations in the community.

The words used by students during the last session: "blessed," "honored," "diversity," "community," and "amazingly hopeful" were insightful to my learning.

Discussing prejudices and discrimination that have been thrust upon us was empowering.

When a high school student came up and told me she was really happy that we took the time to meet with them and that she waits for Wednesdays to meet us.

Observing the high school kids grow throughout the semester. I observed change in attitude among the students—that was huge for me.

These responses resonate with Halpern's (1996) observation that students become mindful of their interdependence with the community members when service-learning allows them to be more consciously aware of their actions and thought processes in the midst of application (Halpern, 1996 cited by Cress).

2) *Service-learning involves generating and applying community-based knowledge that responds to identified community needs.*

Students' involvement in the service-learning positioned them to generate and apply knowledge to the community issue at hand. The knowledge acquired from the course material and the service learning sessions allowed participants a greater understanding of their role in addressing an identified community need. Their first-hand experience of getting to hear each others' story generated community-based knowledge that empowered them to collectively act for the betterment of the community. Here, community-based knowledge refers to knowledge generated by the students from being in contact with each other while sharing and connecting their diverse experiences. The outcome is the critical awareness of the issues at hand and how to respond to them. This community-based knowledge registers students' critical consciousness of their role as citizens, and empowers them to enact positive change that benefits the community at large. What initially seemed unattainable is now realized once the link between learning to serve and serving to learn is brought into focus. This is an important feature of social learning that allows students to demystify the image of institutions of higher learning as "ivory towers." This awareness affirms what the students have learned by taking the concepts and ideas introduced in their university classroom to the community (local high schools) and bringing community-based knowledge back with them to their academic setting.

High school students identified knowledge and skills acquired to improve race interactions in their schools as experiential knowledge gained by participating in the project. Notably, the responses reveal individual awareness developed from a collective effort with others about ways to respond to racial and cultural differences.

> The session on intercultural conflict skills helped me to understand why people get into conflicts and also how to transform the conflicts.

> I now know communication skills and styles are needed to effectively talk about differences. It helps you understand those who are different from me.

> I learned to listen to what others have gone through. It helps to be more accepting of others and want to educate others so that they can be more accepting also.

> I will try to respect other people.

Generally, the responses heighten the understanding of communication skills needed to promote race relations among the students. Similarly, university students identified three components of meaningful communication across racial groups as indicated in sample excerpts below:

(a) *Knowledge and motivation to learn about the other*

> I always thought that the experiences I go through as an Ethiopian on this campus could never be understood by anybody and so I kept my feelings to myself. But after all the service-learning sessions, I came to understand that if we all are given a chance to be heard, then our differences and experiences can help us to promote intercultural/interracial relations in our schools. I also learned to appreciate and acknowledge our differences. We may all come from different backgrounds but if we sit down and get to know one another, using culturally sensitive communication skills then we are able to see more similarities than differences (Ethiopian female student).

> A recurring theme during the service-learning sessions was knowledge. It really was important to me to see the high school students value knowledge in ways that it can do for them particularly in intercultural conflict situations (Caucasian female student).

I now know that it takes a willingness to participate along with an understanding of the 'other' in order to bridge knowledge gaps that result into conflicts (Caucasian male student).

(b) *Patience and willingness to embrace differences*

Communication is effective when you understand diverse cultural values and act appropriately. This occurs because of the willingness to adapt to differences. This was proven to me on the last day of the project. One of the African students in my group said how she appreciated me and another Caucasian group member for being in the group with them. We both provided a different perspective of our experiences. At the same time we were willing to hear and understand where they are coming from. This made me feel good as a person, to know that I am progressing and making a difference in society. (Caucasian male student).

(c) *Compassion and determination*

I could relate to some of the issues, which is why I shared my high school experiences and what made me a successful person. My ESL teacher Mrs. Olson (not her real name) became my guidance and mother-like figure to help me get through the issues I faced. My parents were not around. I lived with my aunt, who did not understand the problems experienced at school or the school system all together. Mrs. Olson understood everything and helped me better manage my situation by simply being there for me as a guide. She was compassionate and determined to help me. This is why I am in college today (Somali female student).

The responses are indicative of the fact that students worked together to create shared meaning between and among them. The course content and service-learning project helped to develop students' awareness about community issues and their role in addressing them. They were able to examine the issues from different perspectives and also reflect on their "shared" experiences. As a professor, I observed students' positive interactions and affirmed from their writings that the course content and service-learning sessions had served to support academic, civic and personal growth. I would also say that the service-learning praxis ignited students' consciousness to focus on ways to transform their circumstances. The learning process allowed students to reflect in ways that Huber-Warring (2006) affirms. She construes reflection as

substantial rethinking–guided, intended, informed–the kind of thinking that requires one to revisit deep wells of memory and personal experiences in order to extract a clearer picture of personal meaning intended and the extrapolated meaning that readers (read learners) can subsequently take and apply to their own lives, circumstances and work with curriculum and instruction (p. 41).

An example to illustrate this 'substantial rethinking' is evident in the following excerpts by two university students' responses to how their views about intercultural/interracial conflicts had changed over the course of the semester:

> Throughout the semester, I learned (and also witnessed) that problems in intercultural and interracial communication can actually be an opportunity to bring people closer if those involved are willing to learn from one another. We talked together and learned to appreciate each other's efforts towards making a difference in our communities (Caucasian female student).

> I have changed from believing that I do not have a place in intercultural communication. Today, I understand that I play a valuable role in bridging communication between cultures and racial groups (Caucasian male student).

In view of these responses, perhaps a question one may ask is how this kind of students' learning was enhanced by the knowledge they created and applied from this experience? Weiley (2008) observed that active learning strengthens meaning. The meaning generated from students, learning activities allowed for the development of guiding principles for effective interactions with those different from them. These principles were delineated in high school students' responses about how they would apply knowledge learned from participating in the program in their personal life and at their schools. The words frequently recurring in the responses were: "treat others …," "understand," "not to….," "open-minded."

> I will treat other people with more respect.
>
> I will tell people not to treat others different because they are from a different race.
>
> I will try to understand where the other person is coming from.
>
> Getting to know more people; asking where they are from and what is their story. Hopefully, try to help other people understand how not to be judgmental and get to know new people also.
>
> Not to say stuff that will hurt other people's feelings. I will be nice to people.
>
> I will maintain an open mind to people of all cultures. I will make a conscious effort not to stereotype other people.

I will get to know others and not just assume you know them by their religion.

I will stay open-minded.

I will think about what to say before saying it and be open about what other people are about.

Undoubtedly, these responses indicate significant milestones that become achievable when we do not ignore or totalize the experiences of others. Perhaps I would have found it easier to regard the question posed by Amina as not unusual; and by so doing unknowingly deny the students who participated in this project the opportunity to become the change we want to see in the world. As Orbe and Harris (2000) note, it is not until we examine ourselves and our relationships with others that we will begin to bridge the racial divide that continues to plague our interpersonal networks and society at large.

Lessons Learned

The issues that led to the initiation of this project are not new to American communities. Racism has inhibited, and continues to inhibit, meaningful interactions among diverse racial groups in America. Nevertheless, what is significant in engaging students in this type of learning is the transformation that occurs following their reflection upon themselves and community needs. Students came together to learn with and from each other. These interactions charted ways to improve race relations in our community. Students took responsibility to address the issue at hand. At no given time did students think they had no role to play in transforming their schools. The project gave them a sense of responsibility that connects personal, community and national obligations.

In this essay, I explained how service-learning pedagogy works to improve race relations by coalescing theoretical approaches and engaging students and community members. It creates learning sites where all involved parties learn to become learners and change agents. These interdependent roles work to minimize hierarchies and give a sense of responsibility that favors collective actions. Participants learn to respond to identified community needs collectively rather than seeing them as acts of a single player or a given group of people (e.g. people of color). Additionally, service-learning offers an opportunity for those students who may never know what it means to be racially discriminated against to learn about the reality from the experiences of their peers and to take action to transform it.

As I reflect on my observation of students' growth and development from participating in the project, some lessons about the benefits of learning and acting together emerge.

The project offered students a forum to share their experiences with the intent to create a community that recognizes and respects differences among its people. The learning experience motivated students to become proactive rather than reactive. In the three years of the project's existence, the proactive aspect of learning was evident in students' conversations that sought to create a new narrative about promoting racial relations in their community. Some questions that students raised at the start of the project were "Are we here because we do not get along?" and "Why should I be the one doing this when those who do the bad things do not bother to come to the program?" However, as the project developed I heard students' conversations evolve, where they would ask questions and offer solutions to minimize racial tensions in their schools. In their small group discussions, the dialogue focused on "What can we do together to get along?" and "This is what we can do." Learning and acting together for change became the focus of the students; embracing words and actions that seek and cherish acceptance, inclusion and belongingness.

My writing of this essay is from a vantage point of teacher-scholar whose teaching and scholarship is shaped by, and intersects with, every other dimension of my life as a mother, black/African woman, and a leader in my community. It is also the case that my spiritual, moral, and cultural convictions inform my desire to challenge different forms of injustice. Would I say that this essay is all about popularizing the practice of service-learning and exaggerating its value? No. The essay seeks to show how giving a thought and paying attention to one person's dilemma can offer others a chance to learn about things they would have otherwise never known. It is my hope that fellow educators will heed my call to perform ourselves in the classroom and the community. This performance involves combining the personal knowledge we possess as educators with theoretical knowledge we have acquired over the years, and continue to acquire, in order to challenge personal and systemic challenges of racism through education.

My personal experience coordinating this project brings texture to our understanding of the benefits of taking the classroom to the community and bringing the community to the classroom. This approach to learning allowed my students to explore issues of under-represented groups in our community. I do recognize that service-learning pedagogy is not a panacea to racial tension in America. Nonetheless, its transformative nature to learning cannot be underscored enough. As Angela Leonard (2004) notes, service-learning pedagogy inspires hope, promotes social justice, advocates agents of change, commitment to building community, and cultivating a universal recognition and respect.

DISCUSSION QUESTIONS

1. In your view, do you think that Amina's concern/question about the school conflict is justified or does the response reflect her not being born and raised in the United States (e.g. her immigrant status)? Give reasons for your answer.

2. You may be familiar with racially-motivated fights in high schools or communities. If so, would the conflict resolution strategies featured in this chapter be reasonable and workable in situations that you have observed?

3. How does service-learning pedagogy promote interracial interactions?

4. If you think service-learning does not work well, or it works only to a certain extent, what pedagogical practices would you recommend that communication professors use to promote interracial/intercultural communication?

---

[1] Names of actual women mentioned in this essay have been changed to assure confidentiality.

[2] The problems in the local schools began before I was a resident in the community. I got there when much of the violent acts had minimized. I relied on Somali students' anecdotal evidence of students who had experienced the violence first hand, and a prominent Somali elder with whom I had prolonged interactions and the mothers of these students. I also interviewed a European American mom who told me what her daughter used to tell her about the violence. My goal in getting involved in the 'problem' was to ensure that the gains achieved were sustained and that students had opportunity to acquire knowledge and life skills to build a community that is welcoming to all.

[3] Among African people, the notion of a teacher in the formal sense in which we all know is a product of colonialism and introduction of Christianity in Africa. Before coming into contact with missionaries and European colonizers, Africans practiced informal education. This is where respected community members and families were expected to be "teachers" in the community. The responsibility of socializing the young ones was placed in the hands of the community. This is true of the adage: it takes a village to raise a child. As Africans began to obtain education those who trained as teachers attained the status of a leader in society as governed by (in the words of Andrew Moemeka 1996) the sanctity of authority in traditional Africa societies. Moemeka says that the community expects of the leader no less than what the status and honor bestowed on him demand.

[4] Details on service-learning in communication studies can be found at the National Communication Association (NCA) website http://www.natcom.org/nca/Template2.asp?bid=268

[5] The 115 young people participating in the project include sixty (60) students enrolled in my class during Spring semester in 2007, 2008 and 55 high school students.

References

Allport, G. (1958). The nature of prejudice. Garden City. NY: Doubleday.

Biesta, G. J. J. (1998). Say you want a revolution: suggestions for the impossible future of critical pedagogy. *Educational Theory 48*(4): 499–510.

Cress, C. (2006). Defining a service-learning pedagogy of access and success. Campus Compact. Retrieved 12/12/08 http://www.compact.org/20th/read/defining_a_service-learning_pedagogy

Daigre, E. (2000). Toward a critical service-learning pedagogy: a Freirean Approach to civic literacy. *Academic Exchange Quarterly*. Retrieved 12/13/2008. http://findarticles.com/p/articles/mi_hb3325/is_4_4/ai_n28806168

Denzin, N. (2006). Politics and Ethics of Performance Pedagogy: Toward a Pedagogy of Hope. In D. Soyini Madison and Judith Hamera. (ed.) (pp. 325–338). *The Sage Handbook of Performance Studies*. NY: Sage Publication.

Ellis, D. and Maoz, Ifat. (2006). Dialogue and cultural communication codes between Israeli Jews and Palestinians. In Larry A. Samovar, Richard E. Porter & Edwin R. McDaniel (ed.). *Intercultural communication-a reader*. (pp.231–237). 11th edition. Belmont, CA: Thomson Wadsworth.

Elyer, J. and Dwight, G. (1999). Where's the learning in service–learning? San Franscsco: Jossey-Bass.

Hansell, L. Putting contact theory inot practice: using the paterners program to develop intercultural competence. Electronic Magazine of Multicultural Education. Fall 2000. Vol.2. No. 2. http://www.eastern.edu/publicatios/emme

Huber-Warring, T. (2006). Developing critical self-reflection in teachers: understanding our own culture in international contexts. *International Journal of Curriculum and Instruction, 6*(1), 41–61.

Freire, P. *Pedagogy of the oppressed*. (2001). (30th anniversary ed., M.B. Ramos, translation). New:York: Continuum.(Original work published 1971).

Finley, Laura (2004). The current state of teaching for peace in higher education. *The Online Journal of Peace and Conflict Resolution*. Issue 6.1/Fall 2004. Retrieved 5/29/07.

Herzberg, B. (1997). Community service and critical teaching. In L. Adler-Kassner, R. Cooks, & A. Watters.(ed.). *Writing the community: Concepts and models for service learning in composition* 57–69. Washington, D.C.: American Association for Higher Education.

Leonard, A. (2004). Service learning as a transgressive pedagogy: a must for today's generation. *CrossCurrents*, Summer 2004, Vol. 54, No 2. Retrieved December, 12, 2008. http://www.crosscurrents.org/Leonard0204.htm

Moemeka, A. (1996). Interpersonal communication in Communalistic societies in Africa. In W. Gudykunst, S. Ting-Toomey, and N Tsukada, N. (ed.). *Personal Communication Across Cultures*. (pp.197–216). Thousand Oaks, CA: Sage.

National Communication Association. Communicating Common Ground Division Retrieved from http://www.natcom.org/nca/Template2.asp?bid=268)

Orbe, M. & Harris, T. (2000). Interracial communication: theory into practice. Belmont, CA: Wadsworth/Thomson Learning.

Torres, Carlos Alberto (1998). *Education, Power, and Personal Biography: dialogues with critical educators.* New York: Routledge.

Weiley, K.C. (2008). Seeking solidarity through global and indigenous service-learning. In Tonya Huber-Warring (ed.), *Growing a soul for social change: building the knowledge base for social justice.* (pp. 295–344). Charlotte, NC: Information Age publishing, Inc.

Service-Learning Course Design Workbook. Michigan Journal of Community Service Learning, 2001. A publication of The Edward Ginsberg Center for Community Service and Learning at the University of Michigan.

13

1898: Reflections on a Southern Community's Racial History and Future

Earl Sheridan and Bertha Boykin Todd

Abstract

The racial violence that occurred on November 10, 1898 in Wilmington, North Carolina is a painful chapter in the city's history. Known as the only *coup d'état* to take place on American soil, it had far-ranging effects by retarding the growth of black political and economic progress in Wilmington for several generations and ushering in an age of disfranchisement across North Carolina. In this essay, two African American members of the current Wilmington community reflect upon their knowledge of this event and recount their involvement in promoting city-wide racial healing and reconciliation.

KEY TERMS: Wilmington Coup and Violence of 1898, White Declaration of Independence, 1898 Foundation, People's Declaration of Interdependence

A Wilmington Native Confronts 1898

Earl Sheridan:

On November 10, 1898 a group of Whites, including citizens from some of the most prominent families in the area, took over the city government of Wilmington, North Carolina in what has been called the only *coup d'état* to take place on American soil. Additionally, a mob of Whites burned down the offices of the black-owned newspaper, killed several black citizens, and expelled other Blacks and sympathetic Whites from a city in which Blacks had held considerable political and economic power. The event was part of an orchestrated effort on the part of the North Carolina Democratic Party under the leadership of figures like future governor Charles B. Aycock, Furnifold Simmons, and *Raleigh News and Observer* editor Josephus Daniels to wrest political control from a biracial coalition of Republicans and Populists that had governed the state since the last election. This event was like many other acts of anti-Black violence that took place across the South around the turn of the century. It had far-ranging effects, retarding the growth of black political and economic progress in Wilmington for several generations, and ushering in an age of disfranchisement across North Carolina (Luebke, 1990). One hundred and ten years later, I am an African American city council member in that city and a member of a biracial group of citizens who helped to plan a commemorative event and memorial to the victims of the Wilmington Coup and Violence of 1898. Truly, our city has made quite a journey from its racist past to its more tolerant present, a journey that is far from complete but nevertheless a substantial one. Following is a brief discussion of my role in this journey.

As a child growing up in Wilmington I knew nothing about the Wilmington Coup and Violence of 1898. We did not read of it in school, not even when I took North Carolina History in the 7th grade. All we heard about Governor Charles B. Aycock was that he was the "education governor." We did not know, as scholar Paul Leubke has written, that he could also have been dubbed the "segregation governor" and that he only pushed education for Whites to help him disenfranchise Blacks. I did hear the elderly lady down the street, Mrs. Bell, talk in hushed, vague terms of a time when Whites killed Blacks and threw their bodies in the Cape Fear River, but I did not know what that meant. So 1898 was not something that the black or white community talked about openly in Wilmington, but its presence was always there under the surface. Its memory could be subtly invoked by Whites to frighten Blacks into acquiescence. Dr. Hubert Eaton, who led the battle for school integration 70 years after 1898, wrote later that it still had a chilling effect on the black community. According to Eaton (1984), "The terrorism applied by Wilmington [W]hites...frightened the colored community into pitiful docility … Those older citizens who remembered the race riot of 1898 also feared for their safety, as did many younger members of the colored community who had heard the tales of the riot from their parents and grandparents" (p. 43).

As an adolescent in the 1960s and early 1970s, I witnessed a tumultuous racial environment in Wilmington. Despite the lingering memory of 1898, there were Blacks, especially young Blacks, who engaged in sit-ins and marches to break down the barriers of Jim Crow. Although I was too young to take part in the sit-ins, I do remember taking part in one march in which we strode to the steps of the city hall and sang freedom songs and demanded our equal rights as American citizens. In 1968 a riot occurred after the assassination of Dr. Martin Luther King, Jr. However, the worst situation took place in 1971 when tension over the integration of schools led to a riot in which two people were killed and ten people arrested and placed on trial for supposedly conspiring to fire bomb a grocery store. This was the infamous Wilmington Ten case, which gained international attention as a miscarriage of justice and a violation of human rights. Eventually the ten people were pardoned; however, the case further exacerbated Wilmington's racial climate. Still, 1898 was not openly discussed though its impact still hung over Wilmington like malodorous smog.

I was in college at Appalachian State University before I read anything detailed on the 1898 riot. A fellow student had done a master's thesis on the event. Considering what I have learned since about the riot, it was a rather conservative retelling of the event, but it did give me a better glimpse of this incident that had so affected my home town. In the 1980s there was a bit more discussion of 1898, some of it surrounding a book written by historian H. Leon Prather, Sr. (1984) entitled *We Have Taken a City*. The daily newspaper ran some feature stories on 1898. Still, it was a sore subject, partially because some of the descendants of the substantial men who had carried out the coup were still prominent members of the community.

However, as the one hundredth anniversary approached, events occurred that brought 1898 back out into the open. First, UNCW English professor Philip Gerard published a novel based on the Wilmington Riot of 1898 called *Cape Fear Rising* in 1994. It was not the first novel based on the 1898 riot; Charles Chestnut 1969 had written a novel based on the Wilmington Coup and Violence in 1901 called *The Marrow of Tradition*. Gerard's book and the publicity surrounding it in the local media once again focused attention on 1898. Secondly, furtive plans were being made to commemorate the 1898 riot. Two separate groups were discussing plans for a commemoration. I was a member of an informal group of university professors. The other group was composed of various community members, who met under the name of the Wilmington Alliance for Community Transformation or ACT. Eventually these two groups merged and formed the 1898 Foundation, Inc. As articulated by this group, the purpose of the commemoration effort was to "tell the story"–recover the history of 1898, which had been largely repressed; "heal the wounds"–bring about community healing and racial reconciliation through public events; and "honor the memory"–come up with a physical monument to the victims of 1898. The group chose to sidestep the controversial issue of reparations, saying that reparations should be something pursued by the descendants of the victims, not by the commemoration effort. The commemoration effort could help those seeking reparations indirectly by shedding light on the actual events of 1898, but reparations would be outside the purview of the group.

The group faced many obstacles. There were people in Wilmington, many of them quite prominent, who did not want a commemoration. Wilmington had had a troubled racial history and many people were concerned that dredging up these painful events might aggravate old wounds and even cause violence. Others thought the effort did not go far enough. They felt the group should have pursued reparations. Still others did not like the composition of the group. They felt the group was too middle-class and did not have enough "grassroots" participation.

Despite this, the 1898 Foundation was successful in many ways–putting together a series of commemoration events over a two year period including a biracial economic development group, a theatrical play, a radio play, and a school essay contest. There was also a series of dialogue groups in which Whites and Blacks discussed their differences. At the beginning of 1998 there was an event attended by several political leaders to start off the year of commemoration, and President Bill Clinton sent a letter. Independently of the 1898 Foundation, the University of North Carolina Wilmington held a symposium on the subject. The keynote speaker was historian John Hope Franklin. On November 10, the anniversary of the coup a massive program was held at Thalian Hall, the site where Whites had met one hundred years earlier to pass the White Declaration of Independence declaring that, "we will no longer be ruled and we will never again be ruled by men of African origin" (Bellamy & Cantwell, 2008, p.42). That night the assembled throng passed the People's Declaration of Interdependence saying, "we will no longer be ruled and will never be ruled again by the racist prejudices of the past …" (Bellamy & Cantwell, p. 43). The crowning achievement of the commemoration effort was the erection of the 1898 Memorial which was dedicated in November of 2008. It stands in close proximity to the area where much of the worst fighting took place and near the entrance to the historic downtown area of the city. The funds to build the memorial were raised from private sources, with descendants of both victims and initiators of the coup being among the contributors.

The 1898 Commemoration is a testament to the change that has come to America and to the ability of a small group of dedicated people to prod a cautious community into a cathartic event that improves that community. Wilmington, like America, still has racial problems but it is not the same place it was in 1898, thanks to the willingness of a community to look at the unflattering aspects of its past and talk about them, reflect on them, argue about them, memorialize them, and work toward a better future.

1898: Acknowledging the Past–Moving Forward Together

Bertha Boykin Todd:

A snatch of a conversation was all I remembered about the Wilmington violence of 1898. Sitting in front of the fireplace in our rural Sampson County, North Carolina home, my stepfather told my mother what he had heard. Someone from Wilmington told him that the Cape Fear River "ran red with blood" in 1898. As a child of eight or nine neither the town nor the words registered with me. The next time I would hear them would be in 1952 when I first arrived in Wilmington as an employee of the New Hanover County Board of Education.

I was immediately struck by the strained interactions between Blacks and Whites. A suspiciousness marked their exchanges. In whispered tones native Blacks spoke with pride about relatives and friends who held elected and appointed offices in 1898. Some had first-hand recollection of the incident 54 years earlier. They would talk about how Blacks hid in the cemetery, were drowned or killed and thrown in the Cape Fear River. Some talked of white families protecting them. This hushed history never went beyond closed circles in 1952. I listened, but still did not understand the full impact of the 1898 violence.

That is, not until 1996. Dr. Bolton Anthony and Attorney William "Bill" Fewell were organizing a special 1898 special interest group and sought my input on correspondence and program planning. When Bill Fewell returned to his Pennsylvania law practice in 1997, I agreed to serve as co-chair of the newly chartered 1898 Centennial Foundation. When Bolton Anthony became its executive director, Dr. James Megivern served as my co-chair.

The 1898 Foundation and its subcommittees were purposefully led by a black and a white co-chair. Through numerous community speaking engagements we began the daunting task of telling the story, healing the wound, honoring the memory, and restoring the hope. Committees were formed to find appropriate ways to accomplish our missions. The mission of the Education Committee was "to tell the story." The committee provided books, hosted public lectures, produced a documentary, and sponsored essay contests in schools and in the greater community. The Education Committee also wrote the People's Declaration of Interdependence in response to the White Declaration of Independence written in 1898. Hundreds of area citizens signed the new document on the 100th anniversary of the *coup d'etat*.

The Reconciliation Committee's mission was "to heal the wound." Wilmington was designated as one of 55 host cities for the National Days of Dialogue on Race Relations. The Reconciliation Committee set a goal of recruiting and training 100 facilitators to produce 50 racially balanced teams for Study Circles, a nationally recognized interracial dialogue project. The program was customized by adding a session on "Dealing with 1898." The committee recruited about 400 people for Study Circles, a program that was later adopted by the YWCA of the Lower Cape Fear.

The mission of "restoring the hope" fell to the Economic Development Committee, which formed Partners for Economic Inclusion. With a goal of improving the economic prospects of the black community, the Partners for Economic Inclusion formed to identify obstacles that impeded inclusive business practices and to employ corrective actions that would establish the region as a competitive and ethnically diversified economy for the 21st century. The group sponsored several annual conferences before eventually reforming as the Black Chamber Council of the Greater Wilmington Chamber of Commerce.

To "honor the memory" the Memorial Committee began planning for an appropriate monument. Co-chair Laura W. Padgett and I began meeting with the North Carolina Department of Transportation about a triangular plot of land at Wilmington's North Third and Davis streets. An international solicitation for a fitting memorial attracted 66 artists. Three finalists were selected by a panel of local art historians and artists. Models from the three finalists were displayed, and the artists made presentations at Cape Fear Museum in November 2000. The Odeleye Group's model was the overwhelming favorite among the seven-member 1898 panel who voted on it, and among the general public ballots collected at the New Hanover County Public Library where the models were displayed. The State of North Carolina constructed and landscaped the proposed park, until it was deeded to the City of Wilmington. The City of Wilmington agreed to maintain the site and monument in perpetuity. The 1898 Foundation dedicated the park on November 8, 2008, the 110th anniversary of the 1898 violence. The commemorative book *Moving Forward Together* (2008), edited by journalists Rhonda Bellamy and Si Cantwell was released on November 8, 2008 to coincide with the park dedication.

As I spoke to people about our efforts the question would inevitably arise: "Why is the foundation bringing up something that occurred one hundred years ago?" to which I would offer that the events of November 1898 inflicted a serious wound on the public psyche. Our goal was to lance the wound so it could heal properly. I often quoted George Santayana's line from his 1905 book *The Life of Reason*, "Those who cannot remember the past are condemned to repeat it" (p. 284). The work required a great deal of sensitivity, given its controversial nature. I wrote the Foundation Philosophy as I prepared to appear before New Hanover County Commissioners to request seed money and county representation on the 1898 Centennial Foundation.

> "No one living in Wilmington today was a participant in the events of 1898. Consequently, none among us bears any personal responsibility for what happened. But all among us–no matter our race or history, whether we have arrived here only recently or come from families that have called Wilmington home for generations–all among us are responsible for 1998. On each of us falls the personal responsibility to make our community one where economic justice and racial harmony flourish. Surely this is a challenge we are willing to accept."

It's been more than 70 years since I first heard my mother and stepfather talking about the 1898 violence. It's been more than 50 years since I was reminded of that fateful event by those who remembered it firsthand. It's been more than 10 years since our community accepted the challenge of opening their hearts and minds to this painful history–not to point blame, but to take responsibility for ensuring that we are not doomed to repeat a history we do not want to remember.

Editors' Note: *For additional information about the 1898 violence and contemporary efforts to promote positive interracial relations through commemorating this event, access these Internet resources:*

1898 Foundation website located on Randall Library webpage, University of North Carolina Wilmington. http://library.uncw.edu/web/collections/1898 Foundation/

1898 Memorial Park Dedication (city of Wilmington) http://www.wilmingtonnc. gov/Home/TodaysHighlights/tabid/324/ItemID/279/View/Details/Default. aspx

Final Report of the Wilmington Race Riot Commission (North Carolina Office of Archives and History) http://www.history.ncdcr.gov/1898-wrrc/

DISCUSSION QUESTIONS

1. What political and social forces involving race contributed to the violent events of 1898 in Wilmington, North Carolina? Why is 1898 known today as a *coup d'etat?*

2. Sheridan and Todd describe the importance of the 1898 Foundation. What were the key functions of this organization?

3. Compare and contrast how Sheridan and Todd discuss the ways in which they learned about 1898. From what sources did they receive their information? What were their impressions of the event and its impact upon Wilmington?

4. Are you aware of instances involving community-wide racial violence elsewhere that are not openly discussed? How did you learn about these events? Have there been any efforts to promote racial healing and reconciliation in these communities? Why or why not?

 # References

Bellamy, R. and Cantwell, S. (Eds.). 2008. *Moving forward together: a community remembers 1898.* Wilmington, NC.: The 1898 Memorial Foundation.

Chestnut, C. W. (1969). *The marrow of tradition.* Ann Arbor, MI: University of Michigan Press.

Eaton, H. 1984. *Every man should try.* Wilmington, NC: Bonaparte Press.

Prather Sr., H. L. (1984). *We have taken a city: Wilmington racial massacre and coup of 1898.* Rutherford, NJ: Fairleigh Dickinson University Press.

Santayana, G. (1905). *Life of reason, reason in common sense.* NY: Scribner's.

Luebke, P. 1990. *Tar heel politics, myths and realities.* Chapel Hill, NC: University of North Carolina Press.

14

Confronting the Racial Double Bind at a Christian University: A Critical Ethnography

Jonathan W. Camp, Amber Smittick, Alan Copeland, Jennifer Dodd,
James Graham, Michaele P. McCloud, Taber Minner, and Quintin S. Wilson

Abstract

Through an analysis of observational field notes and 22 semi-structured interviews with students and faculty, we explored how authentic interracial community is hindered by the implicit denial of systemic White privilege. We argue that the common tendency among White students to view racism through an individualist lens and to advance the myth of a "color-blind society" frames the race conversation in such a way that puts minority students and faculty in a "racial double bind," often leading to silence. We argue that improved communication can be enacted through affective and cognitive restructuration of discussions about race in the classroom.

KEY TERMS: double bind, racialization, White privilege, structuration, Christian university, critical ethnography

"I feel like racial reconciliation is for racist people. Why would you have to reconcile if you're not racist?" —Interview with a White female student at Abilene Christian University, Fall, 2008

Difficult Conversations

At Abilene Christian University (ACU) in Abilene, Texas, conversations about race are difficult. This is especially true in the classroom as illustrated in a conversation that gave birth to this chapter. Early in the fall semester of 2008, I (JWC, first author) was leading my Organizational Communication class through the material on organizational culture, when I decided to have the class form small groups to discuss the organizational culture of our university. After the break-out session, I invited members of each small group to summarize their discussion while I wrote key themes on the board. One of the groups, which was composed of three African American students and one Nigerian student—all male—mentioned several themes that were similar to what the other groups discussed. I thought they were wrapping up when one student from this group said, somewhat apologetically, "We didn't know if we should bring this up–and we don't want to be seen as playing the race card or anything–but we talked about how race can be a touchy issue on this campus."

The tension created by this statement was palpable. As I became conscious of my sudden anxiety—an elevated heartbeat, beads of perspiration on my forehead, a sudden urge to clear my throat—I noticed signs of uneasiness among the students in the room—looking down, smiling nervously, shifting in their seats. This was the only group to mention race, and I could have simply written "race" on the board and continued. Yet, as one who believes that we should not necessarily avoid discomfort in the classroom, I altered my plan for the discussion. I was gripped not by *what* the student said, but by *how* he said it: apologetically, with some discomfort. And I was gripped by the effect this utterance had on the discourse of this particular class, where the majority, including me as the instructor, was white. In this discussion of our university's organizational culture, I could not suppress the pedagogical impulse to linger on this student's utterance, asking the class: *Why did this student sound apprehensive in making this statement? Why are several of us feeling anxiety right now? What is it about our organizational culture that made this student feel like he had to say, 'I don't want to play the race card or anything?' Do we feel free to talk openly about race on campus? What aspects of our university culture pose barriers to open discussion about race? Most importantly, what must happen to overcome these barriers?* After I dismissed the class, a racially diverse group of seven students stayed to explore these questions, allowing me the rare opportunity to gain deeper insight into how these students experience communication about race at our university.

After follow-up conversations with these students, we agreed to explore these questions through a critical ethnographic study of the experience of the racial double bind at our university. By "double bind," we mean a rhetorically constructed situation in which a person is caught between diametrically opposing social forces, creating an inescapable "no-win" situation that can threaten her or his emotional or psychological well-being and impede effective interpersonal communication (Bateson, 1999; Watzlawick, Beavin & Jackson, 1967). As an example of a *racial* double bind, an African American co-author (AS) conveys in her field notes how she felt uncomfortable with a white professor when the topic of the 2008 Presidential election came up:

> After Obama won, a professor said to me, "I bet you're excited about the results [of the election]." I honestly did not know how to respond to this comment.

I know that he did not mean it in any derogatory or offensive way, but I felt as if it was an assumption that he made purely because of the color of my skin. I wanted to respond in a way that confronted him on his misinformed statement, but I hated to be seen as disrespectful to a person in authority or as playing the race card and making a big deal out of nothing.

Caught between the double bind of resisting being racially stereotyped as an Obama supporter on one hand, and being respectful to a professor on the other, the student reported psychological discomfort by the professor's stated assumption, because it placed her in what she perceived to be a no-win situation—a double bind.

We seek not only to describe similar experiences of the double bind along with the type of discourse that creates and sustains it, but also to give voice to minority organizational members, including students and faculty, who often feel marginalized by the silencing effects of the double bind. Therefore, we are practicing critical ethnography; our goal is overtly political and not just descriptive (Charmaz, 2008; Thomas, 1993). Though we believe our approach and insights are suggestive of how to improve communication in other social contexts, our main focus is improving conversations about race at ACU by bringing both transparency and critical thinking to bear on such conversations. Given our particular focus, we now turn to a brief description of our study context.

ACU–On the "Cutting Edge" of Racial Reconciliation

Abilene Christian University is located in central Texas and had a Fall, 2008 enrollment of about 4800 students. ACU was founded in 1906 by members of Churches of Christ, a religious group that traces its origins to the American Restoration Movement of the early 19th century. As a unity movement that traditionally emphasized a rationalistic approach to Christian Scripture (Hughes, 1996) from the beginning, Churches of Christ were remarkably active in establishing other colleges and universities besides ACU throughout the nation, among which are Pepperdine University (California), Harding University (Arkansas), Lipscomb University (Tennessee), and Oklahoma Christian University. As is the case with many southern colleges and universities, racial integration came relatively late to ACU which admitted its first African American student in 1965 (The JBHE Foundation, 2001). In the Fall of 1999, in an invited speech during a celebration of the 50th anniversary of Southwestern Christian College (a historically African American college affiliated with Churches of Christ) ACU President Royce Money said, "We are here today to confess the sins of racism and discrimination and to issue a formal apology to all of you and to ask for your forgiveness" (ACU Apology, 2000). Even before this landmark apology, ACU's administration had grown in its overt dedication to promote diversity on campus and in affiliated churches. For example, in the 1990s the university established an office of multicultural enrichment and initiated a program to fund the doctoral education for minority faculty members. Although the demographic profile of the university has yet to reflect the diversity of society at large, enrollments among minority students have risen from 19 percent in 2000 to 23 percent in 2008, and minority faculty hires have risen from 2 percent in 1996 to 8 percent in 2008. The "One in Christ" conference, an annual event on ACU's campus that attracts church leaders from across the nation, has strengthened relationships between predominately African American and predominately white congregations. Referring to such progress an African American faculty member who was a participant in this study noted that ACU was on the "cutting edge" of racial reconciliation among Christian colleges and universities, and churches.

Despite significant progress toward promoting racial diversity at ACU race remains a difficult topic of conversation, just as churches across America continue to struggle with unity across racial lines (Emerson & Smith, 2000). Although we can celebrate the historical decline of Jim Crow-style racism in American Christianity, racial division persists while the social forces shaping the division have become more covert. No longer is it common to hear the Bible used to justify slavery as was the case in an earlier era when many white Americans and Europeans believed that Africans were inferior descendents of the biblical character Ham, the cursed son of Noah and slave to his brothers (Basaninyenzi, 2006; Johnson, 2004). In fact, according to a phone survey conducted by sociologists Emerson and Smith (2000) most white evangelical (i.e., "born again") Christians in the U.S. identify themselves as non-racist and express the desire for racial reconciliation. The problem, they argue, is that most white evangelicals though well-intentioned fail to see the more subtle forms of systemic White privilege, and that in their attempts to speak and act to end racial division "they likely do more to perpetuate the racial divide than they do to tear it down" (p. ix). Likewise, we argue that the shape of the discourse especially as manifested in such utterances as "I am not a racist," "playing the race card," and "you're acting too white," often undermines attempts to promote racial reconciliation. Furthermore, we argue that the implicit denial of systemic White privilege in the discourse about race at ACU creates the conditions for the racial double bind among minority students and faculty, complicating authentic conversations about race, often resulting in uneasy silence (Brown et al., 2003; Kinefuchi & Orbe, 2008).

Our study was bound by two events on ACU's campus that elicited conversations about race. First was the discovery of a noose in the office of the student association president in September, 2008. The incident drew media attention and provoked strong condemnations by the administration as well as by students in the campus newspaper,

The Optimist. The second event, which occurred near the end of our study was the presidential election of Barack Obama. Because conversations about race emerged more than usual from these events we were provided an ideal opportunity to explore how as a university we talk about race.

Methods

To explore the experience of the racial double bind at ACU, the eight members of the research team conducted participant observation and semi-structured individual interviews with 22 participants. Consistent with the reflexive nature of ethnographic research, it is important to describe not only the research participants, but the research team as well. The research team consisted of a 35-year-old white male professor and seven students: four male and three female in a section of an Organizational Communication course. The student researchers ranged in age from 21 to 25. Three of the student researchers identify themselves as African American, two as bi-racial, and three as white. At the beginning of the study, the research team met to discuss initial impressions and personal experiences with conversations about race, noting how we experience these conversations differently based on how we identify ourselves racially. After reading an article on race and Standpoint Theory (Kinefuchi & Orbe, 2008) we discussed how our racial positionality might shape both our observations and interviews. Such reflexivity allowed us to critically reflect on our diverse lived experience as "a specific cultural site that offers social commentary and cultural critique" (Alexander, 2008, p. 91). Observations from the research team, therefore, served as data that were analyzed alongside the responses of the interviewees.

Because of the size and diversity of our research team, as well as the fact that the study time-frame was limited to the duration of a semester-length course, we reasoned that convenience sampling techniques would be the best method for the selection of participants for this exploratory study. Each student researcher selected between two and four fellow students from among their personal acquaintances, totaling 19 student participants, and the professor selected three African American faculty members with whom he had conversed about race prior to this study. Of the 22 participants, 15 were African American and seven were white, including 12 females and nine males. We each interviewed our self-selected participants using the same interview guide, asking the following questions: 1) What did you think about the university's response to the "noose incident?" 2) What does racial reconciliation mean to you? 3) Do you think that ACU has achieved racial reconciliation? Why or why not? 4) Do you feel comfortable talking about race at ACU? Explain. When interviewing participants of color, we asked additional questions: 5) When you are in class or other ACU settings, do you ever keep from expressing your concerns about how you or someone else is treated? 6) Do you ever feel like it's hard to be yourself at ACU? 7) If you could change anything about

ACU, what would it be? Only the three faculty interviews conducted by the professor were recorded and transcribed. Time limitations and equipment shortages prevented the students from recording and transcribing their interviews. Instead, each student researcher took careful notes during their interviews, and then individually wrote a term paper that incorporated their interview notes and observational field notes with personal reflections. These papers, along with the three faculty interview transcriptions, served as the data set. As a result, some of the quotes in this study come from the reflections of the student researchers, and not all from the interview subjects. Finally, using a Grounded Theory approach to data analysis (Glaser & Strauss, 1967), the first and second authors read the seven papers and three transcripts and inductively developed a coding scheme to be systematically applied to the data.

Results

Our critical reflections on observational field notes and analysis of the interviews suggest the possibility that at ACU authentic interracial communication can be inadvertently sabotaged by implicit denials of systemic White privilege, or explicit statements such as "I am not a racist." This theme may create a tendency among Whites to minimize the need for critical discourse on race, and could perpetuate the conditions for the racial double bind experienced by minority students and faculty. The double bind constantly demands that minority students and faculty weigh the cost of being perceived as either "playing the race card" or, being perceived as "acting too White" when they hold back their opinions about racism. Either way, the shape of the discourse can create a burden for minority students and faculty that is rarely experienced by their white counterparts. The result of this rhetorical gridlock is often silence, broken only by events such as the aforementioned "noose incident." These events trigger conversations about race that often conform to the same discursive patterns as before. Although the desire to improve race relations is often expressed on the part of students and faculty, the communication practices engaged when the topic of race is discussed can undermine this desire.

As stated before our goal as critical ethnographers is to move beyond description of the racial double bind and suggest how to confront it productively. But first we present the diverse voices from our study, including the reflections of co-authors, which shed important light on the apparent denials of systemic White privilege and the resultant racial double bind.

Denials of White Privilege

Although the actual phrase "White privilege" only occurred in one interview, we identified three general ways in which participants in our study implicitly expressed a denial of systemic White privilege. They are *"I Am Not a Racist": The Individualist*

Perception of Racism; A "Color-Blind" Society?; and Minimizing the Need for Discussions about Race.

"I Am Not a Racist": The Individualist Perception of Racism

When prompted to answer the question, "What does racial reconciliation mean to you?" many of the white participants expressed that neither they nor the university is racist. Many of them strongly denounced racism, but framed the problem of racism at the level of the individual, rather than on the systemic level. For example, one white student said, "I feel like racial reconciliation is for racist people. Why would you have to reconcile if you're not racist?" This student perceived racism as an individual problem and because she perceived that she did not struggle with this problem, she was able to excuse herself from actions related to racial reconciliation at ACU. In another instance, a white student athlete said he noticed "a dramatic change over the course of his life in the unity of Blacks and Whites at ACU." As an example, he referred to the recent locker room banter following the election of Barack Obama:

> The guys on the team have a close enough relationship that they often tease one another about "black power" and racial jokes. But we really have a strong foundation as a team, and we are able to overcome our differences and bond together around our common interest, which is football.

We suggest that this student is able to minimize the effects of racial joking because of his confidence in the "unity" shared by all on the team; a unity that he thinks is devoid of what he would consider racism. This attitude reflects an individualist perception of racism that overlooks the structural effects of continued locker room jokes at the expense of another group. We also suggest that not all of the individuals in the locker room viewed the "racial jokes" in the same way. To illustrate, we offer this African American's perspective of the same locker room banter occurring after Obama's election:

> It's amazing what people can say and do when they have a hard time accepting the facts. For example, I received forwarded text messages saying …, "George Washington was on the one dollar bill, Abraham Lincoln was on the five dollar bill, Obama will be on the food stamp." "Hunters get your traps; there's a coon in the White house." "All white people report to the fields at 6 a.m. for orientation tomorrow morning." People were even saying racist things in their Facebook status and posting blogs about how all white people should wear black to mourn the death of our country. Players in the football locker room were showing their true colors by saying things I never thought any of them would say or think.

We found that minority students consistently expressed frustration with the prevailing attitude among Whites that racism is a moral failure of individuals manifested in blatant acts of hatred, rather than as subtle patterns of interactions that privilege one group over another.

A "Color-Blind" Society?

One white student said, "I think we should look past the color of someone's skin and just be friends." Several white students maintained their ability to do just that. Each of the seven white students in our sample expressed in some form what we coded as the "color-blind society," which we define as the belief that current disparities are no longer due to differences in skin color, but to differences in culture and values. One white participant emphasized that our societal problems are due to cultural differences and that race has nothing to do with it. The danger of this belief according to Brown et al., (2003) is that it bolsters the notion that racial stereotyping is a thing of the past, and that the only factors holding back African Americans politically and economically are their own cultural problems. Furthermore, this view contradicts the experiences of non-Whites whose racial location routinely surfaces in social interactions with Whites (Simpson, Causey, & Williams, 2007). As we narrated above, the white professor's assumption that the African American student was happy that Obama won the presidential election illustrates how the "color-blind approach to race" ignores the reality encountered by many people of color–that race is indeed the first thing noticed by Whites and it is used to form stereotypes. The color-blind myth can therefore easily generate cynicism and undermine critical discussion about race and privilege.

Minimizing the Need for Discussions about Race

Our analysis suggests that the individuation of racism and the belief in a color-blind society contributes to the tendency for Whites to minimize the need for deeper discussions about race. Dismissive phrases were deployed to describe racial problems at our university. For example, one white student said that racial issues are mostly due to what he called "a big misunderstanding." He and other white participants expressed the belief that ACU does not have a race problem so much as a problem with cultural differences. Another white student stated, "I don't feel like I really talk about race, because I don't have many African American friends and it's not a very pertinent issue. If someone is going to be your friend, then why does it matter?"

As it might be expected at a Christian university, several participants made references to God and to the Bible when talking about the need to be united on campus despite racial differences. A faculty member pointed out that this emphasis on faith sometimes complicates the discussion about race at our university: "I think here the culture and the message is not about race; it's about Christianity. … And I think it complicates it a little bit. I think you have people who are trying to do the right thing." We suggest that the conversation about race is both enhanced and complicated by religious language. For instance, in denouncing racism one student said, "We just need to hold up the Word of God." Another student said, "We should see people as God sees them." While such statements can inspire serious efforts in our community to foster racial reconciliation, they can also gloss over the social forces that sustain White privilege while bolstering a self-righteous sense of moral progress that minimizes the need for more intellectual and honest conversations about race.

Caught in the Racial Double-Bind

It is our contention that the prevailing denial of systemic White privilege within the campus community can perpetuate an experience of the racial double bind among minority students and faculty. Most of the participants in this study, including the three faculty members identified themselves as African American. Their perspectives shed important light on what it is like to experience the racial double bind.

Student Perspectives

Minority students noted that the pressure to abide by certain rules was especially strong when speaking of certain topics, namely the noose incident and the presidential election. They expressed the need to "be respectful," "avoid certain topics," and to behave as if "it's no big deal." One student researcher who identifies himself as bi-racial commented on the atmosphere after the noose incident:

> For the most part I think everybody tried to act like it was not a big deal and move on; nobody as far as I could tell wanted to focus on it and make it an issue that got 'stretched out of proportion.' That's why my black friends and I talked among ourselves for a couple of days but then for the most part dropped it; I don't even remember us talking to our white friends about it.

This same student reflected on his experience of white teammates on the football team who made racial jokes after the election of Obama, saying that his response "was not to call them on it but to chuckle and move on like it was no big deal in hopes to not cause problems or create issues."

Part of the experience of the racial double bind is the pressure that some minority students feel against being perceived as "acting too white" or as being a "sell-out." As the second author (AS) reflects on her experience in her field notes,

> I personally experience racial tension and the double bind being a part of a social club [similar to a sorority at secular universities] at ACU. Social clubs are

primarily composed of white students and I feel the tension from other black students because I am a part of [a social club] and sometimes looked as a sell-out to my race. I am often labeled as an 'oreo,' black on the outside and white on the inside, because of who I hang out with, how I talk, and how I act.

In another example, an African American student researcher reflected on his decision to come to ACU to play football, and the pressures associated with staying away from any controversy surrounding race:

It was the fall of 2004 when I arrived at ACU to play for the Wildcats … I was dedicated to playing football. … If there was racism here at the college, I wouldn't be caught near it or in it because I didn't want anything jeopardizing my chances to play the love of my life. It's also a Christian school, so therefore they expect more out of you about how you represent yourself as a person. So it was important to me to not have any incident experiencing racism here because I didn't want to be just another statistic here at the school, so I knew that I would have to stay on top and just take care of business.

This comment indicates the perception of a very high risk associated with entering into serious discourse about race: so much so, that this student felt inclined to avoid these conversations altogether. Unfortunately, the sentiment expressed above was repeated among other students and faculty.

Faculty Perspectives

The comments expressed by one of ACU's African American faculty members shed important light on the social cost of entering into race dialogue at ACU, and explains how the socially constructed double bind ultimately leads to silence:

Students [of color] know where it is safe to talk about these issues and where it is not safe, and they discern between the two. They say things in one environment that they won't say in another. They too are concerned about their academic career. And that's the advantage that our white brothers and sisters have when it comes to White privilege. Because White privilege puts our white brothers and sisters in a position of power to where the discussion can be framed in such a way, that you almost in a sense program the thinking in the minds of minority groups to believe that it is inappropriate to even bring up the race issue. Who came with the idea of "playing the race card," you know? Where did that originate? It certainly did not originate from people of color. That phrase itself originated in the privileged community. And so, if you hear that enough, as a person of color, you begin to think within your own mind, *am I really playing the race card? will I be perceived as playing the race card?* And what are the penalties that are attached to playing the race card, if you are perceived as playing the race card. … And when you begin to unpack that and explore the penalties then you can see why people would prefer to remain silent, as opposed to being perceived as one who is "playing the race card."

This faculty member continued by noting how his attempts to talk seriously about race puts him at risk of being considered "the race man" who is perceived as "carrying feelings of animosity or rage." He noted that students of color often prefer to be silent rather than take the risk of speaking openly. It is apparent that faculty and students at ACU share similar perspectives on this issue.

Another faculty member reflected on the negative evaluations she has received from students who note that "she talks too much about race":

> I feel fine about it. That's what I do. I'm basically a Black Studies scholar. … But I find a couple of things disturbing about the reaction to the discourse. … For example, I've taught several courses and the students' perception is that I talk too much about race. But if you look at the syllabus … then you'll see that race may have only been the topic for two weeks, out of a fifteen-week semester. But to me, the presence of my black body in the classroom, mentally, is a marker for the students in terms of what they're hearing. So it's like, when I'm talking about race …, that's all they remember.

This participant shared that a white professor who taught the very same syllabus did not receive student complaints of an over-emphasis on race, which confirmed to her the notion that her "black body in the classroom" creates a threatening situation for white students. Because she was "sick of these evaluations," she has "toned it down," changing her approach to the integration of African diasporic literature in the classroom. Despite the prevailing notion of "color-blindness," it is disturbing to see how the inability of students to see beyond skin color has affected decisions about teaching.

Equally disturbing are the comments of a third faculty member who feels like she can't fully express her African heritage through dress:

> Do I seem like it's hard for me to be myself? [Laughs]. I mean, I don't wear the clothes I used to wear. Like I usually have my hair wrapped and that kind of thing but now it's different. I don't do the head wraps. …, 'cause I don't want to scare people. People out here are a little closed-minded. I just kind of. … Students here are scared of … I mean, when I first got here I wore my hair

wrapped and I had people who couldn't talk to me because they were looking at my head, trying to figure out, *she's a professor at ACU which means she's got to be a Christian, so what is this thing on her head?*

We suggest that students' educational enrichment is hindered when existing communication patterns at the university prevent freedom of self-expression on the part of the faculty.

Study Implications

Studies on university campuses across America have found that interracial communication is complicated by the different ways that students situate themselves racially (Cooks, 2003; Giroux, 2003; Harris, 2003; Hendrix, Jackson & Warren, 2003; Kinefuchi & Orbe, 2008; Simpson, Causey & Williams, 2007). In particular, Simpson et al., (2007) note the difficult position minority students find themselves in when white students express that "racism is over" (p. 42). Our research, conducted on the campus of a racially diverse, private Christian university expands upon these studies by examining the structure of the racial double bind, the conditions that create it, and ways to overcome it. Through collaborative, in-depth research into the perceptions of race at ACU we argue that authentic interracial communication is impeded by a structure of interaction that sustains a perceived double-bind among African American students and faculty. At the base of this inequitable structure are the prevailing denials of systemic White privilege and a tendency among Whites to view racism at the individual level; what Kinefuchi & Orbe (2008) call a "toxic individuation of racial antagonism (i.e., racism is no more than the acts of racist individuals)" (p. 85). Holding the structure together are at least three explicit utterances often heard in our interviews: Among Whites, "I am not a racist," and, among African Americans, "I don't want to play the race card" and "you're acting too White." The first utterance reveals a denial of systemic White privilege as well as a naïve and overly-individualistic conception of what racism really is. The second and third utterances represent the two opposing social forces that place African Americans in the inescapable double bind. These utterances further complicate authentic discourse and lead to silence. We must break that silence and create a communication space between these problematic utterances. We conclude this chapter by attempting to do just that.

Restructuring Race Discourse in the Classroom

In the university, the classroom is the place to begin to change the way we talk about race. By thinking critically about inequities along racial lines, we may begin to question individualistic conceptions of racism and see how it becomes institutionalized through patterns of interaction. Giddens' (1984) structuration theory is especially helpful because it explains how our patterns of interaction create structures that in turn constrain our communication. Unfortunately we often continue to enact the same structures because we engage in the same interaction patterns. Yet, we have the power to change those structures through changes in our interaction patterns. Essentially we are bound by the structure, but have the power to change the structure. We suggest the these patterns may be improved through *diffusing classroom anxiety*, and *adopting the term "racialization" to promote critical thinking*.

Diffusing Classroom Anxiety

To change the patterns of interaction in the classroom so that the classroom becomes a safe space to talk openly about race, we must first recognize that conversations about race can generate feelings of fear or cause defensive reactions (Kinefuchi & Orbe, 2008; Simpson et al., 2007). Instructors can help diffuse some of these feelings by their own transparency. Simpson et al., (2007) suggest that instructors "model how self-reflection can lead to a more complex understanding of one's own racial identity, of others' perspectives, and of race itself" (p. 47). I (JWC) tried to model such transparency in my conversations with the students on the research team. I spoke plainly about the fear I sometimes feel when talking about race with minority students; I fear that I might say something that is interpreted the wrong way, or that makes a minority student feel uncomfortable. I also explained that my feelings of fear could raise the anxiety level of the classroom experience. After I disclosed this feeling to the group, a bi-racial co-author (AC) said with a big smile, "Yeah, Dr. Camp, I've noticed that whenever you talk about race, your voice shakes and your face turns a little bit red." This humorous interchange diffused much of the anxiety in the group and allowed other members of the research team to speak more freely about their own feelings regarding the topic of our study. These patterns of interaction thus subverted the prevailing structure hindered by fear and built a new and more humane structure.

Adopting the Term "Racialization" to Promote Critical Thinking

We also suggest that classroom conversations about race can be more productive by introducing the concept of "racialization," or the process by which we form racial identities through social interaction (Emerson & Smith, 2000; Omi & Winant, 1994). Because this term is likely new to most students it will be less likely to trigger the automatic associations and defense responses as may the words "racist" or "racism," and instead will allow instructors to guide students to think critically about race as a socially constructed system that continues to have effects long after the civil rights period (Orbe & Harris, 2008; Young & Braziel, 2006). Accordingly, Emerson and

Smith (2000) contend that a "racialized society is one in which intermarriage rates are low, residential separation and socioeconomic inequality are the norm, and our definitions of personal identity and our choices of intimate associations reveal racial distinctiveness … *a society wherein race matters profoundly for differences in life experiences, life opportunities, and social relationships*" (p. 7). Such reframing allows us to see how the practices that lead to racial division are increasingly covert, although still embedded within "the normal, everyday operation of institutions," and that "people need not intend their actions to contribute to racial division and inequality for their actions to do so" (p. 9). The problem with the term "racism," they contend, is that many Whites in the U.S. use a Jim Crow-standard of racism as their reference for judging what constitutes racism today. When using this definition, it is natural to conclude that racism has ended. However, by adopting a racialization perspective we begin to see how some of the least overtly prejudiced can still perpetuate processes of racialization (Emerson & Smith, 2000).

By adopting a framework of racialization, instructors can guide students to question the myth of a color-blind society and acknowledge how our racial positionality affects what students see and hear surrounding the issue of race. For example, alluding to an aforementioned phrase uttered by an African American faculty member in an interview, instructors could ask students, "How does the presence of my 'black body' [or my 'white body,' or my 'Latino body,' etc.] in the classroom affect what you are hearing when we talk about race? How does the presence of racial diversity in this classroom shape how we talk about race?" When asking questions of this nature it will be critical for instructors to maintain a non-anxious presence, yet be ready to intervene if students feel marginalized or threatened by excessively belligerent responses.

Such restructuring of our conversations about race in the classroom can lead students to "an intellectual (re)awakening" (Harris, 2003, p. 313) leading to new ways of thinking and talking about race. One such intellectual awakening occurred with one of the white co-authors (JD) in the process of conducting this study, as she records in her field notes:

> … As a student, when I am constantly bombarded with an issue that I cannot identify with, I turn a deaf ear. Honestly, I was among those who did not understand the true issues still evident on campus until I began asking questions. I now see that ACU still struggles to a certain extent with racism, segregation, and discrimination based on differences.

To engage students in such affective and cognitive restructurings, faculty must identify the particular ways in which racialization occurs in their respective disciplines, even when issues of race are typically considered to be outside the domain of a particular discipline, and to make necessary modifications to the curriculum to address issues of race and diversity (Simpson et al., 2007). Without such restructurings, the uneasy silence that characterizes interracial interactions will persist.

Limitations and Conclusion

This study was limited in that we did not explore the perceptions of Latino and Asian American students and faculty even though they make up a sizeable portion of our university. Making a point of including "majority" faculty members as participants in the study would have given this study an added dimension. Our small sample size and method warrants additional, more methodologically rigorous qualitative studies combined with larger-scale, quantitative measures to test and refine our initial findings.

In their monumental study of the current state of race relations in U.S. evangelical Christianity, Emerson and Smith (2000) conclude that evangelical religious organizations, as structured today are not likely to make a difference in a racialized society; in fact, as we have seen they often legitimize historical divides despite members' desires to break down racial barriers. The tendencies to hold an individualist view of racism and to advocate the myth of a "color-blind society" are especially strong in mainstream U.S. churches. It is no wonder then, to see the same tendency among students who are socialized by these faith communities and who arrive on Christian colleges and universities. The ACU Board of Trustees approved an ambitious 21st Century Vision (2007) for how the university will form students. We argue that this document provides the language that must be invoked to lead our efforts to improve interracial communication. Accordingly, students are to be "critical thinkers, creative problem-solvers, global citizens and volunteers." Moreover, we read that by 2020

> ACU will emerge as a thought leader among those interested in Christianity and culture. Our faculty will engage in research and scholarly activities that not only promote their expertise, but also serve as a resource to mainstream Christian communities. Students, faculty, and staff will do more than talk about community and global issues—they will be strongly encouraged to tackle them head-on, with passion.

This vision points to the revolutionary impulses within Christianity to establish a contrast community, free to confront the dehumanizing forces that divide people. Such a vision will cultivate citizens, professionals, community leaders and church leaders who are equipped to engage in interracial dialogue based on a Christian notion of radical hospitality (Pohl, 1999) combined with a sophisticated understanding of racialization and a reflexive understanding of how our socially constructed racial identities impart meaning to knowledge and experience. This formation will require a campus community that is structured to reflect the ideal it seeks for its students. We hope this study contributes to that end.

DISCUSSION QUESTIONS

1. Have you ever experienced a racial "double bind" as described in this chapter? Besides racial double binds, what other double binds exist, and how have you experienced them?

2. Do you believe we live in a "color-blind society" or is this a myth? How might your own racial positionality affect how you approach this issue?

3. What do you think people mean when they say, "You're acting too White?" Is this a legitimate categorization? Explain your answer.

4. Do classroom discussions about race make you feel anxious or defensive? Why or why not? How can classroom instructors create a safe and productive setting for conversations about race?

References

Abilene Christian University 21st Century Vision. (2007). Retrieved 5, January, 2009 from http://www.acu.edu/aboutacu/vision.html.

ACU apology marks gain in race relations. (2000, February 22). *Abilene Reporter-News*. Retrieved 24 November, 2008, from http://www.acu.edu/events/news/000222-editorial.html.

Alexander, B. K. (2008). Performance ethnography: The reenacting and inciting of culture. In Denzin, N. & Lincoln, Y. S. *Strategies of qualitative inquiry* (pp. 75–118). Thousand Oaks, CA: Sage.

Basaninyenzi, G. (2006). "Dark-faced Europeans": The Nineteenth-Century colonial traveloque and the invention of the Hima race. In Young, J. & Braziel, J. E. *Race and the foundations of knowledge* (pp. 114–126). Chicago: University of Illinois Press.

Bateson, G. (1999). *Steps to an ecology of mind: Collected essays in anthropology, psychiatry, evolution, and epistemology*. Chicago: University of Chicago Press.

Brown, M. K., Carnoy, M., Currie, E., Duster, T., Oppenheimer, D. B., Shultz, M. M., et al. (2003). *Whitewashing race: The myth of a color-blind society*. Berkeley, CA: University of California Press.

Charmaz, K. (2008). Grounded theory in the 21st Century: Applications for advancing social justice studies. In Denzin, N. K. & Lincoln, Y. S. *Strategies of qualitative inquiry* (pp. 203–242). Thousand Oaks, CA: Sage.

Cooks, L. (2003). Pedagogy, performance, and positionality: Teaching about whiteness in interracial communication. *Communication Education, 52*(3–4), 245–257.

Emerson, M. O., & Smith, C. (2000). *Divided by faith: Evangelical religion and the problem of race in America*. New York: Oxford University Press.

Giddens, A. (1984). *The constitution of society. Outline of the theory of structuration*. Cambridge: Polity.

Giroux, H. A. (2003). Spectacles of race and pedagogies of denial: Anti-black racist pedagogy under the reign of neoliberalism. *Communication Education, 52*(3–4), 191–211.

Glaser, B. G., & Strauss, A. L. (1967). *The discovery of grounded theory: Strategies for qualitative research*. New York: Aldine.

Harris, T. (2003). Impacting student perceptions of and attitudes toward race in the interracial communication course. *Communication Education, 52*(3–4), 311–317.

Hendrix, K. G., Jackson II, R. L., Warren, J. R. (2003). Shifting academic landscapes: Exploring co-identities, identity negotiation, and critical progressive pedagogy. *Communication Education, 52*(3–4), 177–190.

Hughes, R. T. (1996). *Reviving the ancient faith: The story of the Churches of Christ in America.* Grand Rapids, MI: Eerdmans.

The JBHE Foundation. (2001). The nation's best Bible college gets low grades on racial diversity. *The Journal of Blacks in Higher Education, 31*, 43–45.

Johnson, S. A. (2004). The myth of Ham in Nineteenth-Century American Christianity: Race, heathens, and the people of God. New York: Palgrave MacMillan.

Kinefuchi, E., & Orbe, M. P. (2008). Situating oneself in a racialized world: Understanding student reactions to *Crash* through standpoint theory and context-positionality frames. *Journal of International and Intercultural Communication, 1*(1), 70–90

Omi, M., & Winant, H. (1994). *Racial formation in the United States: From the 1960s to the 1990s* (2nd ed.). New York: Routledge.

Orbe, M. P., & Harris, T. M. (2008). *Interracial communication: Theory into practice* (2nd ed.). Thousand Oaks, CA: Sage.

Pohl, C. D. (1999). *Making room: Recovering hospitality as a Christian tradition.* Grand Rapids: Eerdmans.

Simpson, J. S., Causey, A., & Williams, L. (2007). "I would want you to understand it": Students' perspectives on addressing race in classroom. *Journal of Intercultural Communication Research, 36*, 33–50.

Thomas, J. (1993). *Doing critical ethnography.* Thousand Oaks, Sage.

Watzlawick, P., Beavin, J. H., & Jackson, D. D. (1967). *Pragmatics of human communication: A study of interactional patterns, pathologies, and paradoxes.* New York: W. W. Norton & Company.

Young, J., & Braziel, J. E. (2006). *Race and the foundations of knowledge.* Chicago: University of Illinois Press.

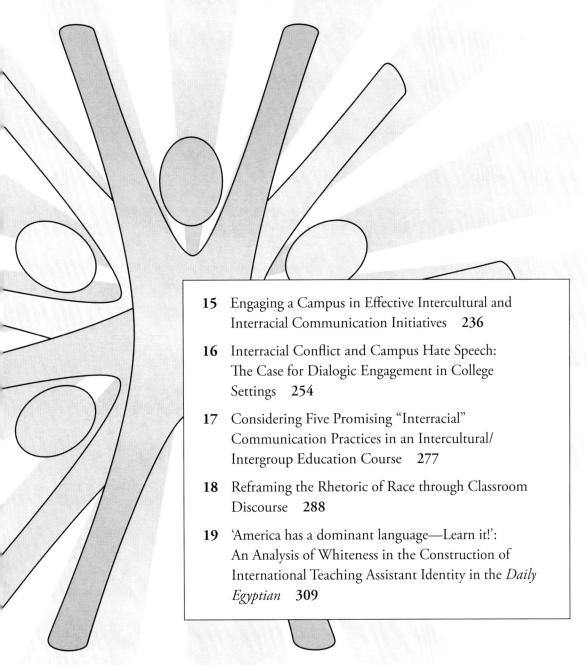

Context IV

Academic Stories

15

Engaging a Campus in Effective Intercultural and Interracial Communication Initiatives

Devorah Lieberman and Ruta Shah-Gordon

Abstract

Higher education literature asserts that college campuses fostering an inclusive climate and bringing interracial and intercultural communication into the co-curriculum and the academic curriculum will graduate students with an enhanced appreciation of diversity and practical skills for success in professional and personal environments. This chapter identifies strategies designed and implemented by several colleges and universities that intentionally focused on campus-wide awareness and improvement of interracial and intercultural communication. These institutions created campus cultures that attract, support, and retain racially and culturally diverse students, faculty, and staff. Strategic concepts are presented within the context that triggered one institution's awareness of its need to address intercultural and interracial communication deeply and systematically. The challenges and roadblocks faced by the college are reported with strategies for overcoming issues. The authors describe outcomes, positive and negative, anticipated and unexpected, to provide ideas that can be generalized across institutions of higher education, irrespective of the size, the structure, or the mission.

KEY TERMS: intercultural communication, the inclusive campus, Diversity Action Council, diversity audit, diversity curriculum, diversity blueprint

The authors wish to express our appreciation for John Ross's (RossWrites) valuable assistance with the completion of this document.

Diversity and Interracial Communication: The National Conversation

Institutions of higher education loudly lament the lack of, and proclaim the need for increased and improved, intercultural and interracial communication within the classroom and throughout the campus. Although the desire to achieve these outcomes may be either explicitly or implicitly articulated, the ability to reliably produce them is inconsistent across most campuses [www.diversityweb.org/diversity_innovations/institutional_leadership]. In addition, efforts to address this issue are often spearheaded by a particular group within the faculty, the student body, or the staff, or even constituencies external to the immediate campus community. Leaders for these initiatives may be characterized as having "one-item agendas," leaving many across these groups feeling marginalized, resentful, or left behind. Without campus-wide depth, breadth, assessment, and continual reframing of the intention of the activities supporting interracial and intercultural communication, positive outcomes are often inconsistent across an entire campus. Unless the majority of campus constituencies embrace and support efforts toward enhanced and improved interracial communication, the initiatives may be short-lived or relegated to the province of only one "special interest group" [www.diversityweb.org/diversity_innovations/institutional_leadership].

Higher education literature asserts that campuses that foster an inclusive climate and bring interracial and intercultural communication into the co-curriculum and the academic curriculum will graduate students who have an enhanced appreciation of diversity, and additional skills for success in their professional and personal environments [www.diversityweb.org/diversity_innovations/institutional_leadership].

Based on the assumption that interracial and intercultural communication needs to be clearly articulated for the campus and intentionally embedded throughout the curriculum and the co-curriculum, this chapter identifies strategies designed and implemented by several colleges and universities that have strategically focused on campus-wide awareness and improvement of interracial and intercultural communication. These institutions have intentionally created campus cultures that attract, support, and retain racially and culturally diverse students, faculty, and staff. A particular event triggered one institution's awareness that it needed to more deeply and strategically address issues of intercultural and interracial communication. Additionally, the chapter reports the challenges and roadblocks the college faced, and its strategies for overcoming them. We describe outcomes, positive and negative, anticipated and unexpected. Our goal, as authors, is to provide useful ideas that can be generalized across institutions of higher education, irrespective of the size, the structure, or the mission.

Interracial and Intercultural Communication Initiative at Wagner College

When Wagner, a small liberal arts college in New York City with an enrollment of approximately 1900 undergraduate students and 350 graduated students, interviewed Devorah Lieberman for the position of Provost and Vice President for Academic Affairs, she asserted that diversifying the faculty and the student body at the College would be one of her first priorities. Within two weeks of taking office, she was approached by two faculty and two administrators who suggested that in order to increase diversity at the College, a four-year education at no expense should be available to all African American students regardless of their academic ability or financial need. From that conversation, it was apparent to her that there were many more conversations and variables that needed to occur across the campus in order to thoughtfully, strategically, and effectively increase and retain a diverse, inclusive, and successful student population.

This process of educating began in that meeting. The definitions of diversity and underrepresented populations were discussed, as well as the importance of creating a positive and inclusive campus climate that attracted and retained individuals from all underrepresented populations; the importance of setting and maintaining particular academic standards; the tuition structure in relation to an institutional budget, and some of the national data about diversity and higher education. By the close of this meeting, it was apparent that a campus that is well-intentioned in areas of creating a diverse community must take into account many more variables than good intentions in order to be successful at this initiative. Those attending the meeting agreed that the following list of variables offered a good departure point:

- Identifying and assessing the need for enhanced interracial communication at the College (in other words, doing a diversity audit);

- Developing a campus wide strategic plan for improved interracial and intercultural communication;

- Generating a pervasive institutional commitment to enhance interracial and intercultural communication;

- Embedding topics of interracial communication into classroom content and curricula;

- Creating and embedding effective interracial communication skills into co-curricular activities;

- Providing interracial communication training for the campus community (administrators, faculty, staff, students);

- Creating safe spaces on campus for interracial communication discourse;
- Sustaining the commitment through monitoring interracial communication to identify emerging issues and strategies for addressing them.

To explore these issues, Devorah Lieberman appointed the first Diversity Action Council, which began meeting in the Fall of 2005, co-chaired by the Dean of Campus Life as well as a well-respected faculty member. The Provost intended to create a council that felt empowered and strove to represent the greater good for all, in its goals to achieve the above variables. They were not to be perceived as an arm of the administration, but rather an independent council that would seek support from administration, faculty, staff, and students. The charge the Provost gave the Diversity Action Council contained five outcomes:

- Identify ways to strengthen relationships with diverse communities outside Wagner College;
- Suggest activities throughout the campus, curricular and co-curricular, that further address issues of diversity;
- Recognize and honor exemplary actions of individuals that contribute to a supportive campus climate;
- Suggest additional approaches to recruitment and retention of faculty, staff, and students from underrepresented populations;
- Bring to the appropriate faculty standing committees suggested changes that fall within the faculty and/or the Faculty Handbook domain.

The Diversity Action Council set out to facilitate focus groups with various constituents throughout the campus community to answer this question: *What would Wagner College need to do to create a campus climate that attracted and retained diverse faculty, staff, and students?* Meeting twice monthly during the 2005–2006 academic year, the Diversity Action Council completed a diversity audit through facilitated conversations with faculty, administrators, staff, and students about diversity requirements and related elements within the general education curriculum. Among topics explored were: the Admissions and Enrollment Office's outreach to underrepresented populations; demographic data about diverse faculty, staff and students; previous and reported college incidents that included race, gender, or culture as a significant and/or intervening variable; and general perceptions of the campus culture and inclusivity. The Diversity Action Council also invited a national diversity consultant and scholar to assist in gathering further data from campus-based focus groups.

Reviewing and analyzing these data, the Diversity Action Council created a campus-wide diversity blueprint. The blueprint, containing specific goals, timelines, and responsible parties, was presented to the faculty senate, to the academic department chairs, to the student senate, and to the board of trustees. The Provost committed to supporting the Diversity Action Council's campus blueprint as much as possible within budgetary constraints. (For a copy of the most updated and current blueprint, see: http://www.wagner.edu/departments/centerforinterculturaladvancement/diversityactioncouncil).

Generalizing Campus Specific Interracial Communication Activities and Positive Outcomes

In her article "Political Correctness: The Truth about Diversity and Tolerance in Higher Education" for *Diversity Web*, Debra Humphreys (n.d.) reported that the new scholarship around diversity has "opened the curriculum to perspectives and intellectual traditions that had been ignored in the past." Humphreys wrote: "This new scholarship has been accompanied by a newly invigorated commitment to classroom teaching designed to provide students with skills they will need in today's diverse and increasingly interconnected global society." In support of this assertion, existing courses at Wagner College, such as Intergroup Relations, Interracial Communication, Conflict and Community or, the most recently implemented, Intercultural Awareness Workshops incorporate students' lessons in intercultural communication, conflict resolution, and collaborative problem-solving. (See Appendix A for additional reading on training).

During the fall of 2007, the Wagner College Diversity Action Council brought a national diversity consultant to campus to review its blueprint and to assess the campus culture. She recommended that Wagner undertake a series of open meetings and facilitated group sessions to determine the extent to which the blueprint was affecting behaviors on campus. To our chagrin, we discovered that, despite a year's work with students, staff, faculty, and administrators, many did not know enough about the council or its initiatives. We learned that there was more need for training around interracial/intercultural communication. In the spring of 2008, the consultant returned to campus to develop this approach. Working with her, the Diversity Action Council designed a framework for a two-day *train-the-trainer* workshop (totaling 15 hours) to be presented to several campus constituencies. In final form, the interracial and intercultural portfolio of workshops range from three to seven hours depending upon the attendants. The trainers' workshop is currently seven hours; while the faculty and staff workshop is four hours; and the student workshop is three hours. (See Appendix B for Wagner College five-year diversity data).

Interracial and Intercultural Awareness Workshops

The trainers' workshop is presented two or three times per year and is facilitated by faculty and staff who helped with the development and participated in the first 15-hour workshop. The basic curriculum includes common language for students and staff/faculty as well as challenges that they may encounter while working with a group. These new trainers are paired with experienced "mentor trainers" who facilitate these workshops. What follows is a basic description of the workshops.

In the student workshop, participants collectively establish common language around diversity. Each student then completes a personal shield that identifies the culture and race to which they belong. The next workshop component is the theory-practice element that includes providing time to identify how the English language shapes perceptions, creates stereotypes, and influences behavior. This activity is grounded in the understanding of adjectives, word usage, and word choice. For example, using word choices such as smart/stupid; ugly/beautiful, cruel/kind, lazy/industrious, open-minded/closed-minded, embodies and furthers stereotypes that often lead to incendiary interracial and intercultural miscommunication.

In order to bring these theories to realistic practice, students participate in an exercise named "Describe, Own, and Encourage." This activity was first developed by Devorah Lieberman (Voegele & Lieberman, 2005) and implemented into the higher education intercultural communication courses she was teaching. First, they learn about the importance of "describing" an incident with specific behaviors, rather than relying on traditional adjectives; then they learn to "own" and communicate their feelings; and finally they learn strategies to "encourage" and continue open communication. The students describe their reluctance and unease in wanting to participate; but once they do, they find all aspects of the workshop to be translatable to daily life and they report that the three hours passed much more quickly than they anticipated (see Wagner website for a copy of the Interracial Intercultural Awareness Workshop). For staff and faculty, we added a portion that assesses their knowledge of diversity initiatives or activities at the college. Additionally, faculty/staff complete an analysis of Strengths, Weaknesses, Opportunities, and Challenges. This provides further information and assists the Diversity Action Council in strengthening the overall communication around diversity issues on campus and within their offices/departments. Workshop evaluations and participant feedback positively reported on the systematic approach to addressing interracial and intercultural communication as well as appreciation of a common language and communication strategies to employ.

Understanding the Larger Campus Culture

Each workshop participant is introduced to the Diversity Action Council blueprint. This helps them understand how the blueprint is related to and complements other initiatives underway at Wagner College. Strong interracial/intercultural communication is a key aspect for a community that respects each other. At the close of each workshop, each participant writes a letter to him/herself which addresses new awareness and strategies gained in the workshop and how they are going to incorporate these into their daily lives. These letters are collected and put aside for three months. They are then returned to the participants for their review. The elapsed time has given the participant 12 weeks to incorporate these skills into multiple situations. The Residential Education Staff then follows up to facilitate these conversations by reviewing the letters and their commitments.

The Intercultural Awareness Workshops have become an integral part of the conversation around improved intercultural and interracial communication on campus. All incoming freshman are expected to complete this workshop during freshman orientation. During the first two years of workshops, over 900 students and 75 faculty/staff have taken part in workshops. Participants report that the reason these activities have been successful on our campus is because the workshop climate has been interactive and non-threatening, and it provides not only theory, but skills to interact with people who are different from themselves in race, culture, gender, and so forth.

Our goal over the next two years is to have every Wagner faculty member, staff member, and student complete this initial workshop. We anticipate that this will result in a cultural shift where everyone has some skills to be a part of the solution rather than the problem. We believe these workshops are the basic inoculation to be followed by "boosters" that include additional programs that further embed interracial and intercultural communication into the fabric of the college. (See Appendix C for Wagner College five-year intercultural/interracial communication activities).

The Reality: Dealing with Bias and Hate Crimes

Despite the intensive training, Wagner is not immune to hate crimes. In a spring 2009 student election, posters of an African American candidate were defaced. The campus was unsure of the motivation behind these acts. Our initial response was surprise and anger that an incident such as this could occur after the intensive efforts by so many to create a positive and inclusive campus climate. Immediately, the college collaborated with the New York State Police Department's Hate Crimes Task Force to investigate the incident and to identify the perpetrator. They labeled this as a "bias crime."

But of greater importance is how the campus community reacted to the incident. The immediate response by so many was remarkable. No one was passive. Students held speak-outs, had a sit-in, assisted in the development of a half-day workshop: "Be the Change: Hate is Not Acceptable." Students showed their support through "No Room Here for Hate," a campaign that promoted serious dialogue with administrators, faculty, and fellow peers about being a minority on a predominantly white campus. Faculty passed a motion of "no tolerance for bias." The administration wrote letters and emails to faculty, students, parents, and alumni, condemning the incident. "Civility" buttons were worn by all across the campus. **No one was a bystander. The Wagner community came together as one voice**. We believe that the immediate efforts by all to take action against this bias crime are directly related to the ongoing, systematic, and consistent efforts to create a campus climate that welcomes, respects, and includes diversity of race and culture.

Fostering Interracial and Intercultural Communication Is a Shared Responsibility

The Diversity Action Council fills the lead role in infusing awareness and understanding and mitigating negative interracial and intercultural communication issues on campus. The process begins with new student orientation. Before any incoming freshman or transfer student arrives on the Wagner campus for fall orientation, she or he is assigned a book to read with an interracial focus. During fall orientation faculty and staff lead students in seminar discussions of issues identified in the book, and often require them to write short essays. Titles have included: _Honky, Finding Mañana, Secret Daughter, Me to We_, and, Obama's _Dreams from my Father_.

Academic departments are also part of the process and the solution. Each fall the Department of Theatre and Speech develops a "Diversity Night" which presents issues of interracial communication through dance, plays, musicals, and revues. Some performances are held in our primary theatre–Main Stage–while others utilize Stage One, an intimate studio theatre on campus. Every incoming freshman student is required to participate in the "Diversity Night" with their freshman learning community.

Wagner also commissioned choreographer Danny Buraczeski to perform "Ezekiel's Wheel," which was performed along with a number of works by student, faculty, and another guest artist's choreography. Additionally, the same department brings these types of shows into residence halls. Designed to promote audience engagement, Neil LaBute's _Bash_ and Israel Horowitz's _The Indian Wants the Bronx_ were chosen because these provocative scripts encouraged students to have dialogue with "characters" in the play after the performance.

Interracial/Intercultural Communication beyond the Campus

Wagner is located on Staten Island, the most culturally diverse of the five boroughs of New York City, itself one of the world's most multicultural metropolitan areas. To achieve students' needs for practical interracial/intercultural experiences linked to their academic and career plans, and to serve pressing needs for assistance in community organizations, Wagner conceived Civic Innovations in 2006 (funded by the Corporation for National and Community Service). Civic Innovations embodies an intensive system of academic course and community organization collaborations that support the college's commitment to civic engagement to address the needs of disadvantaged youth and adults on Staten Island.

This program adds strategic and intentional depth to the integration of curricular offerings, experiential learning, and community engagement. The initial plan was to engage six academic departments over three years, at a rate of two new agencies and academic departments per year, so that faculty would become more attuned to the needs of community-based not-for-profit agencies. We called these "Community-Connected Departments." Each department partnered with a single agency (a "Department Connected Agency"). Together they co-designed courses to meet student learning outcomes and concurrently meet the agency's needs to deliver service to the disadvantaged. The courses are developed with community youth-serving organizations and involve 1200 Wagner College students in related student learning activities. The academic, social, and leadership needs of 8,000 disadvantaged youth are addressed by college students, who serve as role models, mentors, and tutors.

Building on this project, Wagner is developing a more concerted effort in the community by focusing on one neighborhood: the Port Richmond Partnership. With this new endeavor, Wagner will refine its current Intercultural Awareness Workshops to create opportunities for dialogue and training for not only its campus but also for the larger neighborhood of Port Richmond, arguably the most diverse community on Staten Island. Survey data from students participating in Civic Innovations' courses indicate significant increases in awareness of racial differences, comfort level in interacting with racially different populations, and, most importantly, abilities at perspective-taking, empathy, and interracial communication.

Identifying Other Campuses' Initiatives for Enhancing Interracial and Intercultural Communication

The New American Colleges and Universities (NAC&U), a consortium of 23 institutions, includes schools with the following common elements: (1) private institutions;

(2) fewer than 5,000 students; (3) support liberal arts and professional/graduate programs; (4) an interdisciplinary focus; (5) civic engagement as part of their institutional mission. Because these institutions attract and serve students and faculty who seek these five elements (all or a portion of), the authors of this chapter selected two model programs as examples.

University of Redlands: Difficult Diversity Discussion Series

At the University of Redlands (Redlands, California) the Campus Diversity and Inclusion Team actively participates with Academic Affairs and engages faculty in dialogue in ways to bring these issues into the classroom. These discussions are termed: Difficult Diversity Discussions. From its first year, these discussions developed into a themed series of events that are now eagerly anticipated by the faculty. In fact, many faculty wait to see what is being presented before finalizing their syllabi. Faculty provide ideas about an annual theme, around which a year's worth of programming is devised. These are facilitated by the Office of Campus Diversity and Inclusion.

In an effort to begin dialogue on these issues on their campus, the University of Redlands began a series of conversations with individuals across campus in an attempt to develop a sustainable model for dialogue. Particular thought was given to ways that partnerships could be developed with faculty across a variety of disciplines. At the core of this collaboration was the following premise: Why is it that so many conversations stop just at the point that discussions seem most interesting? What prevents people from voicing their opinions on a wide variety of subjects? When the area under discussion concentrates on certain topics, among them race/ethnicity, sexual orientation, gender, disability, the terrain suddenly seems very shaky and maintaining silence becomes the easiest option. They began with using the campus community to create a set of guidelines for these discussions. While the program relied heavily on faculty members leading discussions the first year, the themed component helped to strengthen the commitment of the faculty to incorporate the speakers into their syllabi.

This initiative has allowed University of Redlands to support the long-term strategic goal of the institution, "A Redlands education goes beyond training to embrace a reflective understanding of our world; it proceeds from information to insight, from knowledge to meaning" (University of Redlands, n. d.).

Ithaca College: Center for the Study of Culture, Race, and Ethnicity

The primary mission of the Center for the Study of Culture, Race, and Ethnicity at New York's Ithaca College is to prepare students to live in a multiracial and polycultural world by understanding how race and ethnicity shape an individual's identity and life chances. To this end, the center offers courses that engage with the experiences of

ALANA people (African Americans, Latino/a Americans, Asian Americans, and Native Americans) who are generally marginalized, under-represented, or misrepresented in the U.S. as well as in the curriculum.

The center was founded in 1999; its mission also includes hosting a year-long discussion series on a different topic each year so as to promote a meaningful dialogue on themes that may not be well covered in the college-wide curriculum. The center has four faculty lines and is governed by a permanent steering committee and several advisory committees composed of faculty and administrators drawn from across the campus.

The center offers two minors, one in African Diaspora Studies and the other in Latino/a Studies. The aim of these minors is to help students live ethically and knowledgeably in a multi-racial, multi-ethnic, and poly-cultural world, by studying the experiences of groups that have traditionally been marginalized, underrepresented, or misrepresented in our society as well as in the curriculum. By exploring the relationship between Self/Other (whether conceived in terms of race or of the interconnections between the United States and the rest of the world), students will be better able to understand their own identities and location in the world.

A Glass Half Full

As stated at the beginning of the chapter, the desire to achieve increased and improved intercultural and interracial communication may be explicitly articulated or merely implied. These goals may be embedded in the campus mission statement, in tactical objectives, or demonstrated in organized activities. However, without campus-wide depth, breadth, assessment, and continual reframing of the intention of the activities supporting interracial and intercultural communication goals, positive outcomes are often inconsistent across an entire campus.

Without a blueprint, transparency, and involvement from multiple constituencies, success will be slow coming. However, explicit institutional commitment, appropriate funding, an activist champion at the highest levels of administration who sees opportunity in issues, and consistent perseverance over time to engage all members of the campus community in enhancing their intercultural and interracial understanding and behaviors will result in steady improvement of the campus climate and will facilitate recruitment and retention of students, faculty, and staff of diverse backgrounds. It is our belief that alumni who graduate from such campus communities will positively influence their colleagues and neighbors, and thus accelerate the reshaping of our society.

DISCUSSION QUESTIONS

1. Why are university campuses interested in creating a campus climate that attracts and retains a diverse student body?

2. What are various elements of a campus climate that are considered welcoming, inclusive, and supportive of all students, regardless of ethnicity, socio-economic background, gender, or geographic background?

3. How is interracial communication different from or similar to intercultural communication?

4. If a campus creates a "Diversity Blueprint," what are the ways that everyone on campus can have a voice in its creation and its implementation?

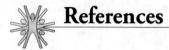

References

Humphreys, D. (n. d.). *Political Correctness: The Truth About Diversity and Tolerance in Higher Education*. Retrieved from http://www.diversityweb.org/research_and_trends/political_legal_issues/politics_campus_diversity/pc_briefing.cfm.

University of Redlands. (n. d.). *Mission*. Retrieved from http://www.redlands.edu/x100.asp.

Voegele, J. D. & Lieberman, D. A. (2005). Failure with the best of intentions: When things go wrong. In M. Cress, P. Collier & V. Reitenauer (Eds.), *A Student Guidebook for Service-Learning Across the Disciplines* (99–111). Sterling, VA: Stylus Press.

✳ Appendix A

Further reading texts that support campus trainings for interracial communication include, but are not limited to:

Bowen, W. G. (5 February 2007). *Lecture I: In Pursuit of Excellence* [PDF document]. Retrieved from Andrew W. Mellon Foundation Web site: http://www.mellon.org/news_publications/announcements-1/details/pursuitofexcellence.pdf.

Bowen, W. G., Kurzweil, M. A., Tobin, E. M., & Pichler, S. C. (2005). *Equity and Excellence in American Higher Education*. Charlottesville: University of Virginia Press.

Chang, M. J. & Astin, A. W. (n. d.). *Who Benefits from Racial Diversity in Higher Education?* Retrieved from http://www.diversityweb.org/Digest/W97/research.html.

Humphreys, D. (1997). General Education and American Commitments. A National Report on Diversity Courses and Requirements. Washington, D. C.: Association of American Colleges and Universities.

Tompkins, R. (n. d.). *SVRC Briefing Paper: Hate Crimes on the College Campus* [Word document]. Retrieved from http://www.arsafeschools.com/Files/Hate%20CrimesBP.doc.

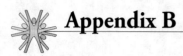

Appendix B

Wagner College Five-Year Diversity Data

Wagner College	2003	2008
Percentage of students of color	12	13.8
Percentage of entering freshman students of color	12.8	17.6
Percentage of students of color graduating	11.5	15
Number of HR grievances based on race, gender, or culture	0	0
Number of student behavior incidences reportedly based on race, culture, or gender	No data available	3

Appendix C

Wagner College—Five Year Intercultural/Interracial Communication Activities

GOAL	2003	2008	Continued Activities Plus—2009
Establish a Diversity Action Council	Non-existent	Made up of faculty, students, administrators, and staff. Co-chaired by a faculty member and administrator	Incorporate more student voices
Create Diversity Action Council Campus wide Blueprint	Non-existent	Extensive and posted on website at http://www.wagner.edu/departments/internationalization/diversityactioncouncil	Revise and Expand
Include Diversity in Campus Mission statement	Addressed in Mission Statement	Addressed in Mission Statement	Continue
Address Diversity in campus strategic plan	No strategic plan	Addressed in campus wide strategic plan	Continue and Deepen
Intentionally embed "diversity" into Curriculum	Diversity Night in First Year Program	"Diversity Night" in First-Year Program (Theatre Program)	Continue
	General Education Requirements	Domestic Diversity Requirement	Continue
		International Perspectives Requirement	Continue
		Diversity Competencies in General Education Outcomes	Embed and assess intercultural communication requirements into many courses

(*Continues*)

Wagner College—Five Year Intercultural/Interracial Communication Activities (*Continued*)

GOAL	2003	2008	Continued Activities Plus—2009
Intentionally embed "diversity" into Co-curricular Activities	Academic and Cultural Enrichment Series (A.C.E.)	A.C.E. Series Monthly Social Justice Luncheons Difficult Dialogues: Interracial, Intercultural, International (Annual Series)	Continue Continue Addressed in co-curricular core competencies
Intentionally embed "diversity" into faculty hiring process	Random	Diversity Hiring Resource Team established. Boilerplate for advertisements created	Continue
Create and provide Intercultural and Interracial communication development training for faculty, staff and students	None	National Intercultural Communication Consultant assessed campus culture and climate Intercultural Consultant designed train the trainer intercultural communication workshop • 25 facilitators trained to facilitate workshops • Additional 50 faculty/staff participated in workshops • 750 incoming freshman participated in workshops • 150 upperclass students participated in the workshops • Training assessed and modified	Completed Completed Expand and continue trainings Require all incoming freshman to participate Embed into First Year Program Learning Communities

(*Continues*)

Wagner College—Five Year Intercultural/Interracial Communication Activities (*Continued*)

GOAL	2003	2008	Continued Activities Plus—2009
Provide Intercultural and interracial mentoring program for faculty	None	Mentoring program for all new faculty	Deepen mentoring program for new faculty
Consistently communicate to campus diversity activities and accomplishments	No intentional process	Diversity Action Council Newsletter	Continue
		Diversity Action Council report to faculty senate	Continue
		Embedded in the Provost's annual goals	Continue
		Posted on the DAC website	Continue
Increase faculty scholarly activities and accomplishments that addresses diversity	No intentional process	Increased number of articles published that address issues of diversity	Continue to increase; offer small grants to facilitate scholarly activities
Increase number of student experiential learning activities that include diverse community populations	No intentional process	Intentional learning community sites	Foster relationship with particular Staten Island community; Port Richmond
		Alternative spring break experiences	Continue
		Civic Innovations	Strengthen

16

Interracial Conflict and Campus Hate Speech: The Case for Dialogic Engagement in College Settings

Peter M. Kellett, Tom Matyok, Sarah Blizzard, Cherie Avent, and Elizabeth H. Jeter

Abstract

This paper provides a co-cultural analysis of an interracial conflict that profoundly shaped the first year college experience of an African American woman–Lisa. The story centers on the use of the "N" word in a racially charged dorm neighbor conflict. The personal narrative provides rich insight into the way that hate speech affects her college experience and how race comes to organize differences and create divisions. Strategies for campus preparedness and response to interracial conflicts suffused with hate speech are developed.

KEY TERMS: hate speech, "N" word conflict, college campus, dialogue

Introduction

"Hate speech is seldom an invitation to politely chat. It is more like a breathtaking punch to the stomach, a quick stiff jab to the nose, or a forcible slap in the face. Hate speech pummels, ambushes, cuts, insults, and silences" —(Cortese, 2006).

Despite the widely held goal on many increasingly diverse college campuses to move toward inclusivity, acts of hate speech that have a racial and ethnic focus quite often remain underreported by victims and therefore under-heard by administrators and others—particularly in terms of their vivid nature as captured by Cortese above. In fact, because of increasing diversity on many campuses, and the complexity of how to prepare for and respond to hate speech, the challenges of addressing and transforming acts of hate are becoming more complex. Schmitt (2000) estimates that as many as 25 percent of students are subject to ethnoviolence and that a third of these students are attacked more than once. The Southern Poverty Law Center notes that every day a hate crime occurs on

American university and college campuses and that every minute a bigoted slur or epithet targets a student somewhere.

These statistics push us to take Kirk-Whillock and Slayden's assertion to heart that, rather than being the rare act of a few extreme people, hate is more prevalent in the everyday subtle negotiations of daily modern (campus) life than we might believe (Kirk-Whillock & Slayden, 1996). Victims—particularly minorities–often feel that there is nowhere to go with their experiences of hate speech or–as traumatic as it may be–that they should simply handle it as part of being successful in the white/middle-class environment of predominantly white institutions. After all, as Cortese points out above, hate speech does not invite response or discussion, let alone reporting. Administrators, often well-meaning, rarely understand the communicative dynamics by which acts of hate speech occur on their campuses, the existential impact of hate acts, and the reasons why such acts often remain underreported. What often results is an experiential and organizational communication *gap* that needs to be more fully understood, addressed, and recast as an organizational dialogic opportunity.

This chapter engages the reader with a deep and extensive case in the form of a personal narrative of a conflict experience that illustrates the issues associated with understanding how to be prepared for, and respond to, hate speech. We draw on co-cultural communication theory in order to develop theoretically grounded guidelines for more effectively understanding and engaging with conflicts that have a racial hate speech component on college campuses (Camara & Orbe, 2008; Groscurth & Orbe, 2006; Hopson & Orbe, 2007; Orbe, 2004; Orbe & Groscurth, 2004; Urban & Orbe, 2007).

In this chapter we are not arguing that all interracial conflict has to be suffused with or based on hate. Lisa's (a pseudonym) story could quite easily have remained on the level of a dispute about noise and considerateness as dorm neighbors. However, we will show that in this particular conflict the interracial component was *always present* in driving the conflict and in fueling it, so that the incident escalated into racial hate speech. We argue that Lisa's conflict with some of her white dorm neighbors was always about race at a deep structural level. As such, this instance of interracial conflict provides a window into prejudicial attitudes and related communicative practices that framed these dorm neighbors' relationships with Lisa and how conflict brings these attitudes and practices to the surface. Simply, the interracial conflict provides a communicative vehicle for expressing dimensions of hate that pre-dated the dorm dispute. We maintain that the racial dimension of the conflict created negative energy that resulted in the situation escalating and spiraling far beyond what we might expect from people disagreeing over noise and inconsiderate behavior. The more the conflict progresses, the more about race it becomes. We therefore see in this story a dynamic interplay of hate speech and interracial conflict.

The Context of Conflict and Hate in Dorm Life

When first-year college students arrive on a college campus to move into their residence hall or dorms, they are not simply entering a new environment where they will eat and sleep and study. They are joining a communal space with others that will be a cornerstone of their lived-experience for the academic year and, in some ways, far beyond. They are often full of hopes, dreams, and perhaps a few fears that are centered on the magnitude of what lies ahead for them, and the stakes involved in being "successful" students (Hardigg, 1995). Added to this, for minorities, there are often concerns with the challenges of being successful in a more or less unfamiliar world that may not be tuned to listening to their experiences. The first year of college is often a transformative time in terms of identity formation and development of independence and adulthood. It may also be the first time that many traditional college-age students experience the challenge of living with, and around, others who are often quite different from them. Lifestyle habits such as levels of tolerance for noise, as well as deeper differences of core values and beliefs, family background, sexual orientation, religion and race/ethnicity, and class often provide the basis of valuable learning as well as division and even difficult conflicts and hateful acts (Heckert, Mueller, & Roberts, 1999; Ogletree, Turner, & Vieira, 2005). These challenges may be compounded by decreasing levels of preparedness to adapt and negotiate differences by students who are increasingly from smaller families with larger living spaces (Dunnewind, 2005).

The communal space of dorm life is co-constructed through communication among its members. As such, students will undoubtedly bring with them their family experiences and related cultural identities, including ways of experiencing, interpreting, valuing, and judging the world around them. Thus, the communal life space of a dorm is imbued with the students' prior experiences and identities. Those deeper, identity grounded layers of meaning imply that conflicts occurring in and around dorm life are often more complex for students than it might seem on the surface. Herein lies the focus and purpose of this chapter in explicating Lisa's experience and its implications. We will see through the story below that the communal space of dorm life can become conflicted around racial differences, and see how hate speech, hateful thoughts, and actions occur as a result of student(s) bringing a prejudice into their dorm life-space where they find an opportunity to express it. We will ask what the dynamics of such a conflict can teach us about students' ways of managing difficult conflicts with hate speech and their experience of institutional support in the aftermath of the experience. Finally, we are interested in drawing out lessons about how campus officials and administrators can better understand and help manage conflicts based on this co-cultural understanding of a race-based dorm conflict.

To address these questions, this study provides a deep reading of a personal narrative experience of hate speech that is centered on the use of the "N" word. This *interpretive* reading is grounded in co-cultural theory. The analysis provides practical implications for campus preparedness and response to a variety of hate-based conflicts that might also be constructively grounded in co-cultural theory.

Co-Cultural Theory, Hate Speech, and a Personal Conflict Narrative

Drawing on *personal narrative theory and methodology* we collected a specific case of conflict in the form of a student's personal narrative as well as the interview-based perspective of an administrator (see Kellett, 2007). We are discussing one personal story–just one person's experience of the conflict–as well as one administrator's more general approach to conflicts of this type. First, as a collected story and an interview-based account, we are, as Kellett points out, distanced from direct observation (p. 4). At the same time, we assume that narratives can provide excellent interpretive "data" because they directly and richly represent how people engage in and make sense of conflicted experiences. Second, a "good" story can provide a window into (i) the way that people behave as they co-create oppositional or conflicted interaction such that we understand the dynamics of what happened in the conflict; (ii) the deeper issues and meanings of the division between them, for example, as racist hate; (iii) the underlying cultural and relational context and patterns in and through which the conflict has meaning, for example, as part of a broader struggle for people to navigate racial inequality or use race as a way of expressing other less concrete divisions such as in/out group membership; and (iv) the purpose or meaning of the conflict, for example, as a way of expressing how deeply people dislike or hate each other and defining their relationship as such (pp. 5–8). We would also hope that the analysis might lead to broader, thought-provoking implications—another marker of a good narrative (Kellett & Dalton, 2001, p. 88–90).

Coupled with the narrative approach is the application of co-cultural theory as a way of explicating the conflict dimensions captured in and behind the story (Camara & Orbe, 2008; Groscurth & Orbe, 2006; Hopson & Orbe, 2007; Orbe, 2004; Orbe & Groscurth, 2004; Urban & Orbe, 2007). We use a co-cultural approach because it enables us to examine the close dynamics of the conflict in terms of speech/behavior, the stance she (Lisa) and her neighbors make communicatively, reactions to speech/behavior chosen (assertive, accommodative, etc.), sense-making and adaptive processes, and psychological impacts. Most importantly, perhaps, is that co-cultural theory enables us to explicate the meaning of communicative dynamics as an expression of the relationship between a member of a more powerful group (the white dorm neighbor) and the person with more marginalized social (cultural outsider) and local status (the African-American neighbor and narrator). Particularly useful are the categories provided by Camara & Orbe (2008) which include examples of communicative practices created by the intersection of dimensions such as non-assertive/assertive, assimilation/accommodation, and separation. More specifically, we use these categories to examine the internal dynamics of the conflict that move between relative peace, hate, leaving, and effects and the external dynamics such as race, family, and institutional contexts or layers.

The third part of the framework for this study has to do with hate speech and the role of the "N" word as hate speech (Asim, 2007; Cortese, 2006), which is the focal point of this conflict and the narrator's experience of it. Specifically, we push the application of co-cultural theory past the explication of marginal and less powerful groups of students to examine the conflict dynamics that surround and emanate from a moment of hate speech when the "N" word is used in a dorm context. This enables us to understand the intensity and meaning of the conflict and develop implications for campus preparedness and responses to such speech acts.

We tie these concepts together into a phenomenological analysis of a personal narrative shared with us by a student to focus on explication and understanding of lived-experiences of phenomena. Specifically we ground our *phenomenological description, reduction, and interpretation* (See Kellett, 2007) of a narrative account of a conflict in co-cultural theory. We do this in order to understand how the "N" word is used to structure the dynamics and meaning of the conflict captured in the following personal narrative (*description*), to understand the essential thematic structure of the conflict as a co-cultural event (*reduction*), and to explore the possibilities for rethinking how we approach campus hate speech based on this understanding (*interpretation*).

A Personal Narrative "My UNCX Freshman Experience"

By Lisa

(Note that her name and all other identifying characteristics have been changed to protect the identity of those involved.)

"The year 2004, also known as "Senior Year," I had done my college applications early so by February I had already received my acceptance letter from UNCX and was more than anxious about finally getting to college. I thought the high school drama would be gone, the people more mature, and most importantly I'd get to be away from home. Luckily my best friend Rachel had been accepted, and we decided to room together.

Move-in day approached. I had already packed everything the night before and was ready for my little one-hour drive. I had been assigned to a freshman high-rise dorm with the tiniest rooms I have ever seen!! I remember thinking this looks nothing like dorms on t.v., but still I was excited. While moving in, there were even students assisting the new freshmen in carrying up their luggage. I even remember this one guy carrying my fridge up the stairs because the elevator line was out the door. I couldn't help but think WOW. People here are so friendly and kind!!

I had met a few girls on my hall, introduced myself and felt as though I was getting the hang of college. A few weeks passes [sic], the girls on my hall began to get a little rowdy. Times when I would try to study, I'd be disrupted by loud noise. And it definitely didn't help that my room was directly across from the bathroom. And though we had "quiet hours" and an RA down the hall, I never reported anybody, never complained; I knew that I wasn't at home anymore. I was sharing my quarters and that I had to be considerate of not just myself but others. I just wish they'd have the same respect.

The noisy days and nights continued. There were girls who preferred to scream across the hallway holding conversations, girls who liked to shower and sing at 4 or 5 in the morning, girls who enjoyed returning to the hall drunk and ridiculously loud at all times of night, and those who'd rather talk on their cell phones in the hallways for all to hear. I even had a neighbor who would get pretty vocal when her boyfriend showed up, if you know what I mean ... And NEVER did I complain ...

The issue arose when Rachel and I had two of our friends from high school come to visit. They attended NCA&M, so we were all excited about being so close, and shared our new stories of what had been going on these past few weeks. Before I even mentioned the disrespectful hall-mates my friends witnessed the noise themselves. They asked me if it was always that loud, and before I could answer Rachel gave a quick "Hell yea!" We ended up watching some t.v., "Fresh Prince" to be exact. It's the episode that Tisha Campbell is starring in and her and Will get locked in the attic during an earthquake. I remember the episode because to this day whenever I see it I think of what was to come. The drama stemmed from laughter, yes laughter. Will was singing some comedic song and we all laughed ... granted it might have been loud, but can't a girl laugh? Well, apparently not. No more than 5 minutes later my next-door neighbor came banging, not knocking … but banging at the door. Informing us that her roommate was sick, she asked if we could keep it down in a not so polite way. And let me remind you that I had said nothing to those other loud girls who weren't even being loud in the privacy of their own room but disrupting the entire floor. Yet, and still, I apologized and told the girl we'd try our best not to disturb them again. Once again I was trying to keep away from the conflict, something that I had already had my share of in life. After I closed the door, immediately my roomie and I just looked at each other, knowing exactly what the other was thinking. "Are you serious," I said, "All that damn noise I put up with and I can't even laugh. My roommate agreed and we dismissed the confrontation, but in my mind I noted that the next time she got loud I'd be sure to point it out to her as well.

The NEXT evening my boyfriend, Rachel, and I were hanging out in my room. I was on my computer playing music that we hadn't heard in a long time, and we all were just reminiscing about past events during middle school and high school. Football games, old hook ups … typical "remember when's". Then there was AGAIN a bang on the door. I looked at Rachel; Rachel looked at me … both of us knowing from the type of so-called knock who was at the other side of the door. My boyfriend even questioned who was knocking like that. I took a deep breath and opened the door. Immediately I hear, "Yesterday I asked you to keep it down, I guess today I gotta tell you … SHUT UP!" these were her exact words. To this day I remember them, Rachel remembers them, and even my boyfriend remembers how rude this girl was. Without even thinking I just went back at her and let her know that number one I wasn't her child and number two she better watch how she talks to me and, as loud as she is, she better not even knock on my door again. I proceeded to close the door in her face. The rest of the night the confrontation bothered me. I didn't like that I let her get me so upset, and I really didn't like the way she came at me … I felt disrespected. I replayed the door scene over and over and over, wondering if I was in the wrong. Rachel and I had even called our mothers, updating them on this rude neighbor. They had already been hearing all the stories about the loud noise and just urged us not to get into any more arguments and to keep it moving. I remember my mother reminding me what I was there for, and agreeing.

I didn't go to an RA (Resident Assistant) because I assumed we were all adults, and that since it was quite clear we weren't going to get along we wouldn't communicate. No more fake smiles upon passing, no hello's, none of it was necessary. That's how I was raised to deal with things, on my own. Not to enlist anyone else's help especially with something that seemed so "minor" … so we didn't get along, she wasn't the first person I had it out with and I was sure she wouldn't be the last.

That night Rachel and I were in our beds, still awake but attempting to go to sleep, when we heard something at the door. It sounded as if someone was writing on our dry erase board. We had other friends on the hall and in the building that'd leave us little messages, so we thought nothing of it.

The next morning I got up, grabbed my shower caddy, took a shower and on my way back into my room read my dry erase board … "N … r"–that's what they wrote. I remember reading the word probably a hundred times, standing out in that hallway. I woke Rachel up and told her to come and look at what they wrote. We stood in disbelief. Not only had some mysterious person wrote that disrespectful and ignorant word on MY dry erase board but in permanent marker, which was I guess to make sure I never forgot it.

Immediately I called my mother, tears in my eyes. Of all the things for someone to say in retaliation for whatever argument we had, that's what she wanted to say? I called my mother and could barely deliver the story without crying … crying from just hurt and anger. And when I finally could speak my first reaction was to go bang on my neighbor's door just as she had done to me and just let the old me come out, I wanted to beat her @#$. There's no other way to describe it than that. My Mother calmed me down, told me not to stoop to their immature level and reminded me that there would be people in this world that I would run into who were completely ignorant and she was one of them. She told me not to prove her right, not to get ignorant with her but to thrive. And though I agreed in the back of my mind I was thinking, "You aren't living on a floor with a bunch of white girls, who think calling you a "n … r" is funny." Immediately I began to generalize, if that's how she felt well then, hey, they must all think that way. I withdrew myself … not just from hall activities, but class discussions, campus activities … I honestly felt attacked. As if I was not welcome nor wanted on this campus.

But, technically I couldn't identify who wrote it, although I am quite sure it was my neighbor and I never confronted anybody. I didn't go to an RA; I just held the anger in. I felt like telling someone in authority would do nothing but heighten the conflict, and honestly I just wanted to be done with it.

It changed my outlook of everyone on that hall. Of UNCX as a university and, I'm embarrassed to say, of white people. Even though I had attended a diverse high school in Durham, and had never had any other problems with white people, I generalized. I stereotyped, assuming that secretly most if not all only saw me as that.

I got a new dry erase board and a couple of weeks later woke to find that someone had sprayed my board with some type of liquid that stripped it of its erasability; I'm not sure what and on top of that kept stealing our dry erase pen!! These girls were childish and I had had enough. I didn't come to college to be provoked. I explained that to my mother and that I wasn't sure if I could deal with these girls anymore. My mother told me that those girls were just trying to get a reaction out of me and not to give them the benefit. But, at this point, mommie's inspirationals just weren't doing it. Instead around November I decided that UNCX wasn't for me and transferred back at home to a college in Durham, NC. I had let that girl run me off a campus that months ago you could not have told me any wrong about.

I stayed there until the fall of 2006 when I decided to return to UNCX. Over time I realized she was just one of the thousands of students on this campus and that I let one person completely change not only my outlook on college but on white people as a whole; I was just being as ignorant as she was. I came back to UNCX and I've enjoyed all my time thus far. The professors are great, the campus is beautiful and, most importantly, the student body is diverse—something that became important to me. The only thing I regret is allowing that girl to ruin my college experience. She took away my freshman year … memories and experiences I will never be able to get back. I still have the dry erase board, I'm not exactly sure why. Every now and then when I'm cleaning my closet I'll find it and just look at it."

A Co-Cultural Understanding

We begin the process of analysis with a phenomenological description of the dynamics and processes in this event (phenomenon) *as an interracial conflict.* This will enable our co-cultural analysis by reducing the story to its conflicted structure of key moments, moves/counter-moves and so on, and allow us to pose discussion questions for the reader to engage with the story. These questions form the basis of our subsequent analysis and the discussion of what might be more effective organizational dialogue about such hate speech. We are particularly interested in how the communicative practices change as a result of this hate speech and related events. By analyzing (describing, reducing, and interpreting) these changes we can see how hate speech affects the co-cultural reality of their dorm relationships.

Description: The Phenomenon as Interracial Conflict (with Descriptive Questions)

In the following section we provide a careful co-culturally grounded description of the narrative structure, story dynamics, and personal experience of the phenomenon Lisa calls "… My UNCX Freshman Experience." We are interested in arriving at an understanding of the phenomenon as a conflict that has a rich contextual reality and nuance for Lisa who lived it *as her lived-experience of racially motivated hate speech*. In addition we include questions intended to help the reader engage with the phenomenon and build the understanding that will form the basis of the reduction and interpretation steps that follow.

Co-Cultural Practices Pre-Hate Speech

Lisa is excited about moving away to college and rooming with her (African American friend) Rachel.

Q: *How is the move to a predominantly white campus away from home significant to her sense of evolving identity—why is it exciting? Why does she cling to familiarity in the form of her friend from back home? How does her subsequent experience of hate speech impact that excitement, her identity, and relationships to others?*

Her initial impression of college: A friendly, welcoming, and kind environment.

Q: *How aware is the organization that this does not necessarily remain consistent as an enduring experience for many freshmen, and particularly for minorities?*

Noise starts to become a divisive issue between neighbors.

Q: *Where is the support and expertise to help them handle this commonplace and manageable conflict? Do the neighbors turn to available resources?*

Lisa does not complain but does start to notice a double standard or gap in being respectful and considerate.

Q: *How much is this double standard based on normal levels of immaturity and how much is it based on race?*

She has friends over and has loud laughter in the room—neighbor bangs on door and demands quiet (consideration).

Q: *Why does the (White) neighbor assume she can demand respect that Lisa cannot? Why does Lisa not have the same working assumptions about everyday dorm life?*

Lisa apologizes and agrees to curb noise but the considerateness gap becomes more obvious.

Q: *Why does she comply with the neighbor's demand even though it is obviously unfair?*

Lisa empowers herself by promising to call her neighbor on her behavior if needed later.

Q: *Is this an effective empowerment strategy? What might be effective ways of empowering herself in this conflict?*

Next incident neighbor demands quiet and orders her to "SHUT UP!"

Q: *Why are "demanding" and "ordering" used as tactics that the neighbor assumes she can enforce?*

There is a confrontation where Lisa counter-demands that she not talk down to her.

Q: *Is this counter-demand effective? Is "talking down to" connected to their interracial relationship?*

She experiences this as disrespect and it preys on her mind, causing hurtful stress.

Q: *What can students do to ensure that the respect gap and double standards don't end up as stressful disrespect? How does the conflict begin to dismiss her as a human with rights in the situation?*

Voice of family (particularly mother) urges them to stay out of confrontation and be stoic.

Q: *Why does her family urge placation and avoidance as a strategy, and how is this connected to race?*

Non-verbal expression of estrangement and division on the dorm floor.

Q: *Where is the mediation/counseling service to these students? Why do they not choose to seek help?*

To summarize in co-cultural terms, Lisa entered an environment where she was a cultural outsider (Urban & Orbe, 2007). She assimilates by convincing herself that she is in an environment where the obvious differences do not appear to connect to dominance and subordination or insider/outsider—a clue to the fact that her preferred outcome is to be accepted and treated equally—to fit in. A conflict ensues that for Lisa highlights an inequality or double standard, and this begins to attack her sense of being an insider. Her neighbors' demands and orders—which are confrontational ways of forcing accommodation—further erode her sense of well-being. She feels disrespected and "othered" (made to feel an outsider). The neighbors begin to force an aggressive separation with her around race. At the same time her family urges her to keep a positive face to attempt to repair her status to insider—classic non-assertive assimilation. She helps maintain the emerging barrier with her neighbors. The separation is expressed in various ways and may have served as a precursor to hate.

Moment of Hate Speech

"N … r" written on Lisa's dry erase board anonymously during the night.

Q: Why does a conflict seemingly about noise end up with a dehumanizing act of hate speech? Was this issue under the surface all along or did it emerge as a way for the neighbor to express her power and to escalate the conflict? What impact did the perpetrators intend?

Co-Cultural Practices Post-Hate Speech

Disbelief that the disagreement could go in this racial direction.

Q: What is the connection of the conflict over noise to race and racial hate? Did the neighbor fully understand what impact the speech act might have?

Lisa wanted to confront whom she suspected did it, but mother urges her not to go to that level of ignorance but choose to thrive.

Q: Why is reporting and engaging the conflict assumed to be in opposition to "thriving"?

Lisa began to assume that all on the floor thought of her as a "n … r".

Q: What sense-making processes occur after hate speech, and what impact does hate speech have on her?

Lisa felt attacked, withdrew, held the anger in, and did not report it. She assumed reporting it would do nothing but make it worse.

Q: Why was it assumed that nothing would happen, or it would be worse if she spoke up about her experience?

Lisa began stereotyping white people as similar to her hateful neighbor.

Q: Is this a typical psychological/communication effect of hate speech? How does this act of hate create further act of micro-aggression?

Antagonism continued and Lisa left for an HBCU.

Q: What was the purpose of the continued antagonism (micro-aggression)? Did anyone feel responsible for dehumanizing a fellow student to the point of stopping it or doing something constructive during this period of antagonism?

Lisa came back to a more diverse campus—kept the erase board as a reminder of the memory.

Q: Did she come back because the campus became more diverse or was this a fortunate coincidence? What memories of similar incidents are held privately and collectively, and how could these—as well as discussion of the importance of memory in conflict–provide valuable insights to administrators and dorm residents?

Lisa harbors regret and a sense of loss at allowing the neighbor to ruin her experience, and she positions herself as moving forward/learning from the experience.

Q: Lisa stories the event as a learning experience that entails lingering negatives, but how might her neighbor story that same event at the same moment in time? What, if anything, does she remember?

To summarize in co-cultural terms, Lisa is shocked by the hate. She struggles with the desire to assert her cultural identity and push her neighbors to understand and adapt to who she is but stops short. The family voice once again favors accommodation. She continues to separate—alternating between assertive (stereotyping others, acting strong and fighting back) and non-assertive forms of separation (avoiding and maintaining barriers). The aggressive actions of her neighbors that tell her she is not wanted, does not belong, and is hated, continue. The psychological effects of her struggle and inability to report the event as well as demand accommodation for her as a full cultural member of the dorm haunt her and leave much of the conflict unresolved.

Next we argue that there is an intimate relationship between this experience as a conflict and the co-cultural dynamics we just explicated. Building on Folger, Poole, and Stutman's definition of conflict (2005) we assume the following main essential features for an experience to be defined as conflict communication (Kellett, 2007). *First*, there should be conflicted interaction in the form of communication between people. Clearly this conflict escalates and manifests in both volatile as well as mutedly micro-aggressive communication between these neighbors. *Second*, there should be a specific dispute or difference that has become oppositional. In this case, the conflict seemed to begin over noise and the theme of consideration where both parties see the other as the cause of the problem. *Third*, linked to this, is the presence of characterizations of self and other in conflicted terms. Both appear to see themselves as victims of the actions of the other. We do not have the neighbor's account of this conflict, but our guess is that she might see herself as reasonable and Lisa as the antagonist. *Fourth*, the interaction and resulting characterizations should manifest and be manifestations of underlying patterns and/or themes. Specifically in this case, there is a clear conflicted pattern to their relationship in which a difference emerges; the difference is interpreted and managed as an attack. The attack in the form of door-banging, demands, accusations, shouting, and so on leads to escalation and estrangement. This leads to an eruption in the form of hate speech, followed by hurt and continued antagonism. These are all patterns indicative of a conflict. *Finally*, there ought to be a deeper meaning to the conflict. We argue that this deeper meaning is racial division that suffuses, fuels, and eventually takes over/replaces the meaning of the conflict over noise and consideration.

From the above descriptive analysis, this phenomenon engages the main definitive characteristics of a conflict. Further, it is a conflict where race plays an important and interesting role–both structurally to the meaning of the experience *as a conflict*, and in the particularities of this *as her personal conflict experience*. Specifically, this conflict might well have occurred in a non-racially charged environment. Yet it seems to us that the intensity, energy, the patterns of representation of the motives and actions of the other, escalation patterns, outcome, and long-term aftermath of the conflict requires the addition divisive layer of meaning such as race to fuel and give form to the division that began seemingly over noise. Race is, therefore, an essential feature to the form, content, and experience of this as a conflict that begins over noise and ends as hate. Grounded in this description, we move on to provide a closer thematic examination (reduction) of the conflict phenomenon as racially charged hate speech.

Reduction: A Co-Cultural Approach to the N Word, Hate Speech, and Interracial Campus Conflict

One way to read the story behind/underneath this story has to do with explicating the intricate dynamics of how race, hate speech, conflict, and communication intersect thematically in the conflict being analyzed. In particular we explore how Lisa's experience and communicative practices are linked co-culturally to hate. Reduction involves uncovering the essential themes that constitute this as a hate speech-based (student) campus conflict.

Cortese (2006) offers a valuable place to start the reduction phase of this analysis by providing a clear and concise set of four characteristics for defining hate speech. First, there is intent through hate speech to *denigrate,* to put down someone and hurt them based on some characteristic of who they are. Words are used as projectiles—thrown to hurt others (Von Franz, 1997). We see that in Lisa's experience the use of the N word was intended to slap her, to attack her and to do violence to her (Coates & Wade, 2007), and to tell her that she does not belong in the predominantly white dorm. As such the act symbolically "drags [her] to the lowest rung of the social ladder" (Haupt, 2005, p. 26)— not something she expected given her pace in college and the welcome she received. Ironically, perhaps we could argue that the perpetrator drags herself to that low social rung in putting Lisa down in this way. We note above how she reacts in co-cultural terms to the dehumanizing and denigrating actions and how the seeds of this hate exist before the act of hate speech.

Second, hate speech attempts to *silence* the recipient by negating them as people with a voice, or by implication of further threat. In Lisa's story she naturally feels completely disrespected, denied, and humiliated by the hate speech she encounters. It reminds her of how she might be viewed by others, by everyone and, as such, is designed to do psychological damage to her and create existential stress for her. Is this how everyone sees me? Should I just leave if I don't belong? These are deep questions that the hate speech suggests she ask—each one designed, in Ma's terms, to destroy a little bit of her spirit (2005). Similarly, hate speech may be done in ways that eliminates the possibility of response–such as through anonymous forms. The anonymous and cowardly act of writing the N word and running away in the night clearly negates the possibility of a response unless Lisa escalates the conflict to a further level of confrontation or a formal process complaint. Yet she is outnumbered and does not know how the system might react to her experience. "N … r" is partly a taunt directed at showing her the perils of responding. Her co-cultural response is to act silenced–ultimately to "avoid" by leaving—what Orbe would call non-assertive separation (Camara & Orbe, 2008).

Third, hate is usually connected to the production of *additional micro-aggressions and unequal treatment of the person(s) hated*—further destroying civility and soul. Note how, for example, the anonymous antagonism continues after the event–almost like a game. Those acts also reproduce the same inequality implied in how the neighbor treated her as a "noisy neighbor" versus how she might have treated a white person in a similar dispute. This *othering* of Lisa appears to strategically attack her identity, and leads to additional acts designed to undermine her well-being and sense of security in being able to think of herself as a full and valued member of the campus community (Hicks, 2001). We have seen how, after the hate speech, the demeaning actions of the other girls continues to occur, further affecting Lisa's stance/response patterns that continue to establish a co-cultural relationship of inequality.

Fourth, hate speech ultimately *speaks of the messenger as much as the target* in terms of their assumptions about themselves, their expression of self interests in the conflict, their racial/ethnic identity in relation to the target, and the social/cultural context that supports such hate. In the act of writing the N word and the communicative performance that surrounds it (verbal and non-verbal expressions), the white perpetrators are asserting dominance both in their majority status in this situation and more broadly in culture. They are quite clearly showing Lisa that her behavior will be judged differently—as a sign of ignorance–which, ironically, is the very quality they are projecting from themselves onto her. They are also quite clearly showing that age old institutionalized forms of hate, based on racial inequality, can still be invoked and expressed—*reproduced* in Van Dijk's terms (1995)–in ways that show her she is not fully accepted and that her own behavior is used actually to justify that lack of acceptance. In short, she gets blamed for her own hateful treatment as a final co-cultural expression of dominance and subordination, or cultural insider and outsider. Cleverly perhaps, if unwittingly, they are showing her that she is her own worst enemy for bringing this on herself—to whit: *If she wasn't such a n ... r we wouldn't have had to call her one.*

We move on to interpret these findings as meaningful opportunities for preparing for and responding to campus hate speech.

Interpretation: Campus Preparedness and Response to Hate Based Conflict as Dialogic Opportunity

> *"Nothing's going to change. You can't make prejudiced people understand."*
> —(Anonymous freshman student)

> *"To really eliminate hate speech, we must nip it in the bud. Prevention is more effective and less costly than treatment."*   —(Cortese, 2006, p. xvi)

Phenomenological interpretation involves placing the phenomenon back into lived reality. For us this means exploring communicative possibilities brought to the surface by our description and reduction of the phenomenon. Specifically, we move here to a broader understanding of the campus context of how racially charged hate speech is understood and how it might be approached dialogically based on our understanding of it as a lived phenomenon. As such, perhaps there is more hope than the freshman above assumes—more hope for the prevention that Cortese calls for.

Looking at current practices, it is interesting that some campuses have begun to put in place processes as well as cultural changes that improve preparedness and responses to hate speech by foregrounding the importance of speech communication and its relationship to racial and ethnic attitudes (as well as other differences), behavior, and resulting problems. An example of this would be adopting a speech code that makes explicit the expectations of how to speak, why hate speech is unacceptable, and what happens if the code is violated. Some argue that this walks on, or even crosses, the "free speech" line in that it could be construed as limiting free speech unnecessarily (Cortese, 2006). Perhaps it also casts the problem within a discipline and punishment discourse in limiting ways. Many campuses have added diversity sensitivity training to the curriculum especially in freshman classes and university orientations. It is a challenge to make sure such training generalizes out to everyday thoughts, speech, and actions. Still other campuses and systems have found it challenging to find the resources to staff such courses and experiences. Sometimes diversity and related topics are implemented as part of dorm programs, but these may not be mandatory and may be attended sparsely unless the people are interested in the topic to begin with. Finally, a common strategy has been to create learning communities as part of the freshman experience so that intimacy and understanding across and beyond racial and ethnic differences are encouraged culturally. These are all important ways to help change cultures and related behaviors proactively. The key question for us is: How much do these programs successfully create change through real understanding of the phenomenon—the lived experience–of hate speech? Perhaps they do to some extent but, in response to the freshman quoted above, and based on the lessons from Lisa's story, we would like to propose that the challenge of understanding is a dialogic opportunity upon which we can expand.

In a similar vein, administrators are often frustrated at the lack of productive talk and reporting of critical incidents to them. In this case they respond by pointing to procedures and services the university has in place to deal with such problems. According to an Assistant Dean of Students at Lisa's campus we interviewed for this study, the above situation would ideally have been handled in the following way:

1) Student realizes that this is an important and serious situation, which needs to be handled immediately.

2) Student tells a Community Advisor (a person who is an advice resource for dorm residents), who will then tell someone in Student Affairs

   (a) Seek counseling through the Health Center

   (b) Seek support from the Office of Multicultural Affairs

   (c) Potentially get moved to another residence hall

3) Contact campus police to investigate

4) Charge students in violation and provide appropriate sanctions

5) Community Advisor provides a program on the hall to educate students on hate speech/crime

6) Provide counseling and academic support for victim though Student Affairs.

It was also pointed out to us at the time of this interview that there are mediation services, as well as interests in assisting students through offices of multicultural and student affairs. This assistant dean also expressed frustration that hate speech is not reported when it occurs, and that he, as an administrator, would love to know how to do more, and what to do. Clearly, hate speech is cast as a problem-solution/violation-sanction scenario, in which proper procedures should be followed, and authorities alerted. The procedures outlined also focus on individual responses to and responsibilities for the event and how it is handled. We would argue that hate speech and people's responses to it, are better understood from within the complex co-cultural interrelationships that help explain the origins and experiences with hate speech. As such the problem-solution, violation-sanction approach is overly simplistic. Is hate speech best viewed as a problem with a solution in the form of ways of handling the problem, or a violation with appropriate disciplinary/punishment formulated bureaucratic organizational responses, or even as a form of hurt to an individual that requires certain forms of "help" for that individual?

If we take the quote by Cortese at the opening of this chapter to heart, and Lisa's experience of being dehumanized by hate speech, is it realistic to assume victims would appreciate or even use procedures as part of their response when they already feel denied as people? One dangerously simplistic question behind this perspective has to do with why students such as Lisa don't simply follow the process and procedures provided for them—get help, resolution, and move on. An equally dangerously simplistic conclusion might be that either it does not occur very much, or the victims don't care enough to follow through with the clear procedures (see statistics in the introduction). A mindset of "are we doing enough to *help*" might be less useful than one of "are we doing enough to *understand*"? Communicative gaps can widen when hate speech is approached from within a cultural framework that does not promote genuine understanding of hate speech as it is experienced *by people*. We move on to develop a clearer understanding of how these communicative gaps can be addressed by members of campus communities.

Lessons from Lisa's Story and Broader Dialogic Strategies

Drawing on the lessons gleaned from our phenomenological analysis of Lisa's story, and building on the above concerns having to do with centering preparedness and responses on a more co-cultural understanding of hate speech, we develop the following set of guidelines for approaching (interpreting) hate speech as a dialogic opportunity. More specifically these guidelines are meant to be a resource for (1) thoughtful examination of current campus practices, (2) people developing and designing programs to address hate speech, as well as (3) ideas to be mindful of when trying to understand and know how to react to hate speech as an administrator, faculty member, or fellow student.

First, *understand the co-cultural preconditions for hate so that a deeper contextual understanding of factors that contribute to—and set the stage for hate speech might be understood.* This might enable campus personnel to address the co-cultural assumptions and patterns that diverse people bring with them to campus, and understand more fully how these assumptions and patterns interconnect to form preconditions. In Lisa's story, for example, there are quite different assumptions of access to assertiveness, aggressiveness (confronting, demanding) and patterns of blaming (Sillars, 1980) that are divided by race as well as simultaneously by perceptions of being in the dominant (insider) or minority (outsider) culture. There are quite different assumptions about what it takes to be regarded as a member. There are also issues associated with how race is allowed to transform the energy and meaning of a conflict. All of these issues are clustered around how inequality and background culture intersect with communicative practices.

Second, *develop an understanding of the actual events called hate speech and the dynamics around such events so that hate speech itself is understood co-culturally.* Hate speech should be understood as a complex and situated phenomenon rather than as a problem in search of a solution, an individual rogue act in need of discipline/punishment, or simply as a hurt in need of help (for example, counseling). It is important to be mindful of how hate is experienced as denigration as a dehumanizing blow that has an existential shock for the victim. Hate silences, and it is also connected to a myriad of other micro-aggressions as well as subtle and not-so-subtle co-cultural dynamics that occur in and around the event. It is important to understand how—as in Lisa's story—this shock has an enormously important effect on communication, thoughts, and actions. The person reacts, responds, makes sense, and tries to recover face, and seeks advice from others and simultaneously try to figure out what this act means on several levels personally, ethnically, organizationally. It is also crucial to understand the selves in the context of their lives that perform acts of hate speech. It is in the interconnections of self and other that the choice to use hate speech gets made. Real and useful understanding on campuses might best begin with a genuine invitation to share and learn from these experiences and understand their patterns and co-cultural interconnections.

Third, *to understand and change patterns of low reporting, it is crucial to understand the impact, aftermath, and repercussion issues associated with experiencing hate speech.* Lisa's story and the subsequent administrator's perspective show us an intricate web of actions, thoughts, struggles and communications that form the aftermath of how she, her family, the perpetrators and the institution respond to the hate speech. Lisa's story and others that mirror her experience provide rich and valuable insight into interracial conflict especially in terms of why people (a) respond and react the way they do (aggressive, assertive, accommodating conflict style): (b) why they make certain choices for example in leaving the situation–a nonassertive conflict style, as opposed to the victim taking an assertive accommodation stance—reporting the incident and demanding fairness, equality, and so on. Taken together, these guidelines affirm the value of a co-cultural approach to the lived phenomenon of hate speech as exemplified by Lisa's story and the administrator's perspective.

Conclusion

If we agree with Jensen that "our responsibility is not to silence hate speech but to answer it" (1993, p. 11) then we have done much in this chapter to work on exploring how we answer hate speech particularly racially charged hate speech in a campus setting. We have shown that, rather than approaching hate speech solely through hurt/help, problem/solution, or discipline/punish discourses where counseling, programs, and reporting procedures with relevant penalties for perpetrators stand in place of real talk about the experience of hate speech, we should approach this first and foremost as a *communicative phenomenon*. As such, co-cultural theory enables us to unpack the layers of communicative practices within a framework of cultural inequality so that the communicative dynamics of how people construct and respond to hate become explicit. Our hope is that such understanding can help us to prepare and respond to hate speech and its communicative and psychological impacts from a place of understanding.

DISCUSSION QUESTIONS

1. How are hate speech incidents reported and handled on your campus?

2. How did the co-cultural analysis of Lisa's experience change how you see hate speech and its role in interracial conflict?

3. What other forms of hate speech that might occur on your campus besides that directed at interracial relationships are important to understand using this co-cultural framework?

4. How are interracial conflicts and hate speech interconnected?

References

Asim, J. (2007). *The N word: Who can say it and who shouldn't.* Boston, MA: Houghton Mifflin.

Camara, S. K., & Orbe, M. P. (2008). Analyzing strategic responses to discriminatory acts: A co-cultural communicative investigation. *Paper presented at the annual convention of the National Communication Association, San Diego, CA: November, 2008.*

Coates, L., & Wade, A. (2007). Language and Violence: Analysis of four discursive operations. *Journal of Family Violence 2*, 511–522.

Cortese, A. (2006). *Opposing hate speech.* Westport: CT: Praeger.

Dunnwind, S. (2005). Dormitory détente: Roommate conflicts are a growing part of the college experience. *The Seattle Times, Nov 7.* [p?]

Folger, J. P., Poole, M. S., & Stutman, R. K. (2005). Working through conflict: Strategies for relationships, groups, and organizations. New York: Longman.

Groscurth, C. R., & Orbe, M. P. (2006). The oppositional nature of civil rights discourse: Co-cultural communicative practices that speak truth to power. *Atlantic Journal of Communication, 14, 3*: 123–140.

Hardigg, V. (1995). Living with a stranger: Thrown together, roommates can become the best of friends—or enemies. *U.S. News and World Report, 119, 12.* p. 90.

Haupt, C. (2005, Fall). Regulating hate speech–damned if you do and damned if you don't: Lessons learned from comparing the German and U.S. approaches. *Boston University International Law Journal* (23 B.U. Int'l L.J. 299). Retrieved from InfoTrac Expanded Academic Index.

Hechert, T. M., Mueler, M. A., & Roberts, L. L. (1999). Personality similarity and conflict among female college roommates. *Journal of College Student Development, 40, 1*: 79–81.

Hicks, T. (2001). Another look at identity-based conflict: The roots of conflict in the psychology of consciousness. *Negotiation Journal, January*: 35–45.

Hopson, M. C., & Orbe, M. P. (2007). Playing the game: Recalling dialectical tensions for black men in oppressive organizational structures. *The Howard Journal of Communication, 18*: 69–86.

Jensen, M. (1993). Developing ways to confront hateful speech. *The Speech Communication Teacher, 8*: 1–3.

Kellett, P. M. (2007). *Conflict dialogue: Working with layers of meaning for productive relationships.* Thousand Oaks, CA: Sage.

Kellett, P. M., & Dalton, D. G. (2001). *Managing conflict in a negotiated world: A narrative approach to achieving dialogue and change.* Thousand Oaks, CA: Sage.

Kirk-Whillock, & Slayden, (1995). *Hate Speech.* Thousand Oaks, CA: Sage.

Ma, A. (1995). Campus hate speech codes: Affirmative action in the allocation of speech rights. *California Law Review*, 693–732.

Ogletree, S. M., Turner, M. G., & Vieira, A. College living: Issues related to housecleaning attitudes. *College Student Journal, 39, 4*: 729–733.

Orbe, M. P. (2004). Negotiating multiple identities within multiple frames: An analysis of first-generation college students. *Communication Education, 53, 2*: 131–149.

Orbe, M. P., & Groscurth, C. R. (2004). A co-cultural theoretical analysis of communicating on campus and at home: Exploring the negotiation strategies of first generation college (FGC) students. *Qualitative research Reports in Communication, V*: 41–47.

Parekh, B. (2006). Hate speech: Is there a case for banning? *Public Policy Research*, 213–223.

Schmitt, R. (2000). Radical philosophy: Philosophers combating racism conference. *American Philosophical Association Newsletter, 99*(2) (Spring). The Southern Poverty law Center (2000).

Sillars, A. L. (1980). Attributions and communication in roommate conflicts. *Communication Monographs, 47, 3*: 180–201.

Urban, E., & Orbe, M. P. (2007). "The syndrome of the boiled frog:" Exploring international students on US campuses as co-cultural group members. *Journal of Intercultural Communication Research 36, 2*: 117–138.

Van Dijk, T. (1995). Elite discourse and the reproduction of racism. In Rita Kirk Whillock and David Slayden (Eds). *Hate speech*. (1–27) Thousand Oaks, CA: Sage.

Von Franz, M. (1997). *Archetypal dimension of the psyche*. Boston: Shambhala.

17

Considering Five Promising "Interracial" Communication Practices in an Intercultural/ Intergroup Education Course

Sherick A. Hughes

Abstract

This chapter pivots the center of oppression to race (although not in an effort to weigh race against gender and class). Race-based data were drawn from two sections (Fall 2004 and Fall 2005) of a graduate level intercultural/intergroup education course taught a large urban university in the Midwest. From these data emerged five promising "interracial"[1] communication practices that qualitatively and quantitatively improved the teaching and learning environment of the course. I candidly detail the five strategies as both painstaking and illuminating. In the end, I also consider how the five practices helped me connect better to my students, while addressing the challenges that awaited them in my class each week at the often uncomfortable and disjointed intersection of "old-self" racialized identities and "new-self" knowledge.

KEY TERMS: interracial communication, intercultural/intergroup education, reflexivity, privilege, triangulation, Pedagogy of Hope, course evaluations

Introduction

A critical mass of respected peer-reviewed research of the new millennium suggests that my biased responses can negatively influence student performance and aptitude (e.g., Blanchett 2006; Bloom 2001; Darity et al., 2001; Gordon 2005; Skiba et al., 2000). Although my students and I inherit a host of privileges and problems, the race, class, and gender nexus comprises a *matrix of domination* (Hill-Collins 1990),– i.e., the matrix–that is insidious, and yet difficult to resist in my courses. For four academic years before coming to the University of Maryland, College Park I taught a graduate course titled *intercultural/intergroup education*, as one of few Black male faculty members at predominantly white institutions of higher education. These courses discussed issues of power, privilege, and diversity in teaching and learning. I found that race became particularly poignant when the course was comprised of an "interracial" group of graduate students. Through critically mindful communication, I came to understand my students and me not deterministically, as different races, but as influenced and informed differently by a U.S. history of race, racialization, and racism.

Blanchett (2006) contends that we must continue intellectual dialogues about how White privilege and racism create and maintain inequity and oppression at six levels (e.g., the individual, institutional, educational, research, policy, and practice levels) "to develop appropriate strategies and interventions to eradicate these practices." She argues unequivocally for the necessity of graduate education courses in this effort, "above all, assisting [students] in deconstructing issues of White privilege and racism should decrease the likelihood that these issues will negatively influence teachers' decisions" (p. 27). Blanchett's (2006) work alludes to the necessity of the continuous development of promising communication strategies for teaching about race in "racially" isolated and "interracial" learning environments. This chapter attempts to pivot the center of oppression to race (although not in an effort to weigh race against gender and class) to discuss five key promising "interracial" communication practices. These promising practices were initiated by me (Hughes, 2008), and then they evolved into co-generated and co-applied practices with my former Intercultural/Intergroup Education students.

STRATEGY ONE: Modeling Reflexivity

The first strategy was difficult, as it required my students and me to locate and focus upon meaningful, personalized central questions, and to engage productive diverse groups that challenge us to see and resist the matrix through those questions, all the while trying "not to separate [our] personal and professional philosophies" (Milner, 2003, p. 205). Throughout the sixteen-week-long courses, I tried to support diverse group-work by creating in-class and out-of-class opportunities to engage "interracial" communication. Communication practices like "critically engaged dialogue" (Milner 2003, p. 201), and "intergroup dialogue" (Gurin and Nagda, 2006) were particularly useful. However, I also found a need for "intragroup or offstage conversation" (Taliaferro-Baszile 2005, p. 85), which also can be described as finding in-class time and space to balance intragroup and intergroup socialization (Tatum, 1997). I searched for verbal and nonverbal cues in a text and in students' initial responses to it students in order to co-suggest a need to separate to discuss certain issues of race. Students seemed to like this practice as it worked to decrease vulnerability and increase participation prior to discussing the issue with the entire "interracial" class. These intergroup and intragroup communication approaches essentially operated in tandem to create homogenous (to meet and discuss an issue in nearby, but separate classrooms) and heterogeneous groups based on self-identified experiences of the matrix of race, class, and gender. Third, dropping the editorial "we" of our public transcript (Scott, 1990) was a challenge because my students and I were used to enlisting unsolicited representation to articulate any given point we are trying to make. Another problem for us involved the reality of being critically conscious while considering how we might be complicit in problems of "interracial" communication.

STRATEGY TWO: Personalizing Privilege and Penalty

Hill-Collins (1990) alludes to the point that systems of oppression like racism present "few pure victims or oppressors" because an "individual derives varying amounts of penalty and privilege from the multiple systems of oppression in which everyone lives" (p. 230). For example, from her Black feminist standpoint, "white women are penalized by their gender, but privileged by their race" and "depending on the context, an individual may be an oppressor, a member of an oppressed group, or simultaneously oppressor and oppressed" (Hill-Collins 1990, p. 224). Cleveland (2006) builds upon Hill-Collins' work by having his students "unpack" or identify a range of privileges on their own. I adapted Cleveland's work in my courses and enlisted my students to do the same. In the predominantly white graduate courses, it became extremely important to discuss white privilege last and toward the end of the semester after building trust within the "interracial" class. After the first couple of semesters that I taught these courses, a clear pattern for the most educable order of privilege discussions emerged. My students and I learned most by first discussing the privileges that penalized us the least before progressing to those privileges that penalize us most including: (a) ability privilege, (b) heterosexual privilege, (c) class privilege, (d) male privilege, and (e) White privilege. Similar to Cleveland (2006), I found three primary reasons for the promise that emerged from this communication practice: (a) it avoids "shame or blame"; (b) it identifies everyone as privileged and penalized in one way or another and, as a result, some more than others; and (c) it informs/reminds us that as a result of our privileges, we are all capable of oppressing others.

STRATEGY THREE: Leveling Experience

Hill-Collins (1990) describes oppression including race as being experienced on at least three levels: "personal biography; group or community level of the cultural context created by race, class, and gender; and the systemic level of social institutions" (pp. 226–227); also see Bullough and Pinnegar (2001). The group or community level of the cultural context is particularly important to reconsider as it seems to be a major social site for reproducing racially biased responses (Swim and Stangor, 1998). The connections of the systemic level of social institutions to ourselves is examined by my students and me through discussions of critical literature reviews, chiefly from academic books and peer-reviewed journal articles. These discussions were enhanced when our communication reflected multiple levels of our lived experiences, which allowed us to further:

1) Cross-check a range of theoretical perspectives informing and challenging preconceived notions regarding oppression

2) Engage a dialogic and dialectic approach between speaker and listener

3) Induce self-critique of social positioning

4) Discard the editorial "We" and replace it with the first person "I" by:

   (a) finding the "I" and "me" that distinguishes "I" and "me" from "others"

   (b) checking the distance separating the "I's" represented in my *public vs. private transcripts* (Scott, 1990)

   (c) confronting the things that "I" would prefer not to see in "me"

5) Consider and engage a sincere search and critique of connections of race, class, gender etc. to one's own history of teaching and learning experiences

STRATEGY FOUR: Triangulating

Triangulation of sources of evidence involves gaining evidence from at least three sources addressing the same issue. Moreover, as Bullough and Pinnegar (2001) suggest, a triangulation of "themes should be evident and identifiable across the conversation represented or the narrative represented" (p. 20). Preferably, at least one of those three sources shouldn't share ethnicity, class, or gender classification with the author. Because narratives are flawed with subjectivity, evidence from narrative triangulation eventually charged me to learn to be less concerned about whether students were lying dialogues, but more tuned in to "gaps and inconsistencies and associations" (Luttrell, 2000, p. 14). Dialogic/dialectic communication (Gurin and Nagda, 2006) can expose the type of gaps, inconsistencies, and associations that are tantamount to productive triangulation of narratives.

Similarly, member-checking involves asking for the critique and permission of outside participants whose stories are shared as part of your story. Triangulation can also be added to member-checking to challenge an author to compare/contrast her or his interpretations and analyses against at least two additional sources comprising both congruent and dissonant voices. By triangulating narratives from our fallible, but educable "selves," most of us began to acquiesce to the ever-humbling, yet exciting and hopeful episodes of authentic, promising "interracial" communication.

STRATEGY FIVE: Balancing Struggle and Hope

In *Pedagogy of Hope*, Freire (1996) challenges teachers and students to reconsider hope and struggle as reciprocal actions that are integral for sustainability and prosperity, in this case, for sustainable and prosperous "interracial" communication.

> The idea that hope alone will transform the world … is an excellent route to hopelessness, pessimism, and fatalism. [T]he attempt to do without hope, in the struggle to improve the world, as if that struggle could be reduced to calculated acts alone, or a purely scientific approach, is a frivolous illusion. … Without a minimum of hope, we cannot so much as start the struggle. But without the struggle, hope … dissipates, loses its bearing, and turns into hopelessness. One of the tasks of the serious progressive educator, through a serious, correct, political analysis, is to unveil opportunities for hope, no matter what the obstacles may be (Freire 1996, pp. 8–10).

Much of the way teaching and learning is considered today can be traced back to Paulo Freire (1970; 1996). In his 1993 speech transcribed by Wink (2005) in Southern California on teaching and learning, Freire stressed that "There is no possibility for teaching without learning. … as well as there is no possibility for learning without teaching" (p. 85). Freire's *Pedagogy of the Oppressed* (1970) and *Pedagogy of Hope* (1996) describe hope and struggle as necessary concomitant forces ultimately working for a critical pedagogy, where students are adequately educated to both read and transcend social oppression—hopefully without reproducing it. In arguing that hope is a fundamental human need, Friere (1996) warns us against teaching and learning that separates hope from action.

Like Freire, I worked with my "interracial" classrooms to co-construct teaching and learning opportunities to further the process of unveiling opportunities for educational hope. When I considered Wink's (1995) transcription alongside my previous background in Freirean-style teaching and learning (Hughes, 2005), I began understanding and applying curriculum and instruction to co-create *a critical art and social science of teaching and learning*—(a) of *sculpting* promising units and lessons for all students in attempts to prepare them for survival, thriving, and social responsibility as they graduate from one stage of education in life to the next, (b) of *scaffolding* to *paint* a heightened portrait for all students in attempts to help them reach their highest potential, and (c) of conscientious *performance* with a collage of content knowledge-based, inquiry-based, promising practice-based, and emotion-evoking instruction methods in attempts to engage an education that instills a critical temper.

Freire's work from 1970 and 1996 essentially helped me move beyond understanding a one-dimensional frame of teaching to understand the complexities of our "interracial" educational settings as multi-dimensional spaces of teaching and learning; privilege and oppression; power and problems (Freire, 1970). This critical temper seemed to afford our class some hopeful strategies to recognize and alleviate oppression of self and others while balancing life with the thoughts and actions that breathe hope. In other words, we co-constructed a classroom environment where it became expected that struggle and hope would operate in some very complex ways together to inform us. It then became imperative for us to answer the call daily to balance "interracial" communication of critique with "interracial" communication of possibility.

Tangible Fruits of Promising Communication Practices?

In addition to the information below in Chart 1, which came from analyses of Scantron sheets, students are also given a blank sheet of paper and invited to write supplementary anonymous comments regarding the course. My experience with students in the graduate intergroup/intercultural education who write comments on the end-of-course evaluations tend to reflect the few students who either (a) have a major gripe, or (b) find the course to be positively life-changing. In the Fall of 2004 when I taught the course, only four students responded to this opportunity; two with promising remarks and two with the pertinent discouraging remarks noted below. In the Fall of 2005 when I taught the course, only one student responded, and that student shared quite encouraging remarks.

Fall 2004 Pertinent Discouraging Remarks

Student C

Unclear expectations for assignments

Student D

In future classes perhaps being more specific when describing the interior of the paper would ease a little tension. Also, not having a chip on your shoulder like Blum and Tatum do will allow you to enjoy life's pleasures and not think everyone's out to get you just because you are not … [gasp] White.

Fall 2005 Encouraging Remarks
Student E

Wow! What a class?! I especially enjoyed the layout of this course with the opportunity to collaborate with facilitated discussion in our groups. Don't know if I could teach a course like this, how Dr. ___stays fueled, it's got to be pretty incredible. The instructor was well-versed in content area and research. Inspired me to seek outside class literature for my own inquiry. Every educator should have to take this course and more like this one. The topic of race and education cannot fully be explored and digested in one semester course. Best wishes to you Dr. ___ and Keep the Faith.

CHART 1 Highest Mean Changes from University Course Evaluations: Teaching Intercultural/Intergroup Education before vs. after Promising Practices

Statements from University Course Evaluation Form	Pre-"Five Promising Practices" Fall 2004 4-Point Likert Scale (Mean)	Post-"Five Promising Practices" Fall 2005 4-Point Likert Scale (Mean)	t-test sig.
Instructor made topic interesting	2.8	3.4	p <. 01
Writing assignments consistent with course goals	2.6	3.4	p <. 01
Instructor explained concepts, principles, and related course content clearly	2.6	3.25	p <. 01
Course required me to use information and ideas presented rather than simply recognizing or recalling them	3.2	3.8	p <. 01
Examinations covered the knowledge gained and concepts learned in the course	2.4	3.5	p <. 01
Instructor promoted meaningful learning by providing relevant examples relating new ideas to familiar concepts	3	3.6	p <. 01
I would recommend this instructor to other students	2.6	3.3	p <. 01

Concluding Thoughts: "Interracial" Communication Challenges and Possibilities

One substantiated challenge of my approach to "interracial" communication was articulated well by scholars of Communication Studies, Education, and African American Studies. It was a fear stemming from the concern that teaching students to be equitably critical of various forms of privilege will move more white students to feel "let off the hook" for White privilege at worst; or it will diminish the insidious penalty of White privilege in their eyes, at best. Yet, there was decreasing evidence of this phenomenon in my courses. In fact, even my most challenging white students in "interracial" graduate courses appeared to become more obligated to at least consider how they may have come to benefit from privileges while simultaneously having been disenfranchised by penalties. The five promising "interracial" communication strategies above can be both painstaking and illuminating. In the end, the five strategies highlighted above helped my students and me to address the challenges that awaited us at the often uncomfortable and disjointed intersection of "interracial" communication and course content.

DISCUSSION QUESTIONS

1. Discuss the importance of reflexivity during "interracial" communication.

2. How are privilege and penalty related to "interracial" communication? What does the author mean by "leveling experience?"

3. Discuss the relationship(s) between hope and struggle.

4. Why does the author always choose to place the terms "race," "racial," and "interracial" within quotations? (see endnote)

---

[1] Similar to Dr. Fred Riggs of the University of Hawaii, I portray the terms "race," "racial," and "interracial" within quotation marks for two key reasons: (1) To remind us that the words are suspect as deterministic descriptors of human groups, and rather indicative of social group identity, knowledge, and hierarchy, and (2) to remind us that the terms are part of an international dialogue or conversation (like the quotation marks noted around the responses of characters).

References

Blanchett, W. (2006). Disproportionate representation of African American students in special education: Acknowledging the role of White privilege and racism. *Educational Researcher, 35*, 24–28.

Bloom, L. (2001). I'm poor, I'm single, I'm a mom and deserve respect: Advocating schools as and with mothers in poverty. *Educational Studies, 32*, 300–316.

Bullough, R., & Pinnegar, S. (2001). Guidelines for quality in autobiographical forms of self-study research. *Educational Researcher, 30*, 13–31.

Cleveland, D. (2005). Creating productive space: Approaching diversity and social justice from a privilege perspective in teacher education. In S. A. Hughes (Ed.), What we still don't know about teaching Race: How to talk about it in the classroom (pp. 53–73). Lewistown, NY: Mellen Press.

Dalton, M. M. (2003). Media studies and emancipatory praxis: An autoethnographic essay on critical pedagogy. *Journal of Film and Video, 55*, 88–97.

Darity, W., Castellino, D. & Tyson, K. (2001). *Report on Increasing Opportunity to Learn via Access to Rigorous Courses and Programs: One Strategy for Closing the Achievement Gap for At-risk and Ethnic Minority Students* North Carolina Department of Public Instruction, Raleigh, NC.

Freire, P. (1970) *Pedagogy of the Oppressed.* New York: Continuum.

Freire, P. (1996) *Pedagogy of Hope.* New York: Continuum.

Gordon, J. (2005). Inadvertent complicity: Colorblindness in teacher education. *Educational Studies, 38*, 135–152.

Gurin, P., & Nagda, B. A. (2006). Getting to the what, how, and why of diversity on campus. *Educational Researcher, 35*, 20–24.

Hill-Collins, P. (1990). *Black Feminist Thought: Knowledge, Consciousness, and the Politics of Empowerment.* London: HarperCollins.

Hughes, S. (2005). What we still don't know about teaching Race: How to talk about it in the classroom. Lewistown, NY: Mellen Press.

Hughes, S. (2008). Toward good enough methods for autoethnography: Learning to resist the matrix with another promising red pill. *Educational Studies, 43(2)*, 125–143.

Luttrell, W. (2000). Good enough methods for ethnographic research. *Harvard Educational Review 70*, 499–523.

McIntosh, P. (1989, July-August). White privilege: Unpacking the invisible knapsack. *Peace and Freedom*, 8–10.

Milner, H. R. (2003). Reflection, racial competence, and critical pedagogy: How do we prepare preservice teachers to pose tough questions? *Race, Ethnicity, and Education, 6(2)*, 193–208.

Scott, J. C. (1990). *Domination and the arts of resistance: Hidden transcripts*. New Haven, CT: Yale University Press.

Skiba, R. J., Robert, S. M., Abra, C. N., & Peterson, R. (2000). *The color of discipline: Sources of racial and gender disproportionality in school punishment (Report #SRS1)* Indiana Education Policy Center, Bloomington, IN.

Solórzano, D., & Bernal, D. (2001). Examining transformational resistance through a critical race and LatCrit theory framework: Chicana and chicano students in an urban context. *Urban Education 36*, 308–342.

Swim, J. K., & Stangor, C. (Eds.). (1998). *Prejudice: The target's perspective*. San Diego, CA: Academic Press.

Tatum, B. D. (1997) *Why are all the black kids sitting together in the cafeteria? and other conversations about race*. New York: Basic Books.

Taliaferro-Baszile, D. (2005). Pedagogy "Born of Struggle: From the notebook of a black professor." In S. A. Hughes (Ed.), What we still don't know about teaching Race: How to talk about it in the classroom (pp. 75–94). Lewistown, NY: Mellen Press.

Wink, J. (2005). (3rd Ed.). *Critical pedagogy: Notes from the real world*. New York: Pearson.

18

Reframing the Rhetoric of Race through Classroom Discourse

Tina M. Harris and Blake Abbott

Abstract

Using critical race theory as the theoretical framework, we use the rhetorical tool of cluster analysis to examine the self-reflection journals from students enrolled in an Interracial Communication (IRC) course. The goal of this chapter is to illustrate how students in this course are able to identify racial microaggressions, or racially-charged verbal messages, that serve as barriers to effective or positive interracial communication. Students use the journals to reflect on race-related experiences they have during the semester, and to think critically about the communication strategies they believe most effectively assist them in their individual efforts to combat racism within their interpersonal networks. Their ability to address the microaggressions (either successfully–or not) is linked to the repeated exposure to issues of race (i.e., racism, discrimination, prejudice, the power of language) during their time in the IRC course. These findings have implications for students and the choices they make in interracial situations. We anticipate their responses will serve as models of positive interracial communication behaviors that can be used by society at large. By challenging readers to adopt and enact these behaviors within and outside of the college classroom, this study has significant potential for facilitating positive race relations on an individual, and eventually institutional, level, one relationship at a time.

KEY TERMS: interracial communication, microaggression, proverbial other, race and pedagogy, racial microaggression, rhetoric of race, white privilege

Introduction

At the end of every spring semester, I, Tina M. Harris, engage in deep self-reflection about how my two classes evolved. I have taught Interracial Communication (IRC) and

African American Relational Communication at the undergraduate level for the last eight years. I have used a similar template for each course, and hesitate to change, although teaching the course this way leaves me mentally, physically, and emotionally exhausted by semester's end. Each semester as I contemplate whether to change my strategy, I usually reach the same conclusion: "If it ain't broke, then don't fix it." Some revisions of different aspects of the course are warranted, such as film choice or focus of written narratives, while other activities appear to be the thread that holds the class together. These are the mechanics of IRC that are often contemplated; however, it is the intellectual lubricant of self-reflection that remains fairly constant semester after semester. Such assignments as reaction papers, role-playing activities, journal submissions, and attending cultural events create opportunities for students to engage in self-reflection about their privilege and race as a social construct that continues to shape our lived experiences. Because many of them have never had to deal with the issue of race, these moments of self-reflection challenge them to think about their journey toward awareness, and to give strong and careful consideration to how they will use this information, experiential knowledge, and skill acquisition outside of the college classroom.

I often tell my students that although it is not a required or measurable dimension of the IRC course, it is my sincere hope and wish that by the end of the semester they will become ambassadors for positive race relations wherever their life journey will take them after graduation. Deep in my heart, however, I pray that a seed has been planted that will eventually grow to stop the vicious cycle of racism, one relationship at a time. The classroom and the process of self-reflection are the fertile soil in which the seed nests, and the circumstances that place students in the position of deciding whether or not they will join in the fight, per se, are the opportunities I believe present opportunities for growth. Specifically, through reading their journal entries, I am, in a sense, witness to the deep thought that occurs as they begin to grapple with the "revelation" that racism is a matter of societal power that further marginalizes and oppresses those already at a disadvantage. This newfound knowledge is a hard pill to swallow when they are introduced to the reality that, because race was borne out of a systemic and institutional effort to discriminate against non-whites, those oppressed cannot be racist as they do not have the power to withhold the benefits of the privileged (Orbe & Harris, 2008). Given that this is one of many perspectives on race, it is imperative and essential that those who possess societal power become active agents of change as we collectively work toward a world where our differences are celebrated and appreciated, not just tolerated or "put up with." It is the purpose of this essay to highlight the experiences students have had with the interracial course. By using excepts from student journal submissions for the class from the last five years, this essay will provide readers an opportunity to gain in-depth understanding of communication phenomena such as rhetoric and race, interracial communication, and microaggression, and how they each have individual and collective roles in dismantling racism through the college classroom.

Critical Race Theory and the IRC Course

For the reasons stated earlier, and many others, I believe that the IRC course and other communication courses can be sites for initiating efforts aimed at impacting race relations through rhetoric and discourse. These problematic rhetorical encounters can be described as incidents of discourse between and/or from interactants that perpetuate both the racial divide and the oppressive forces that fuel the cycle of racism as we know it. Sadly, many of us have participated in or stood idly by as these egregious acts took place, either perplexed about what to do or too frustrated to do anything. In so doing, we only become a part of the very problem we are committed to solving. If we are to turn the tides on this ever-present wave of progression, it is our hope that the pedagogy we bring to our classrooms engages both student and teacher in processes that aim to break the cycle. More pointedly, by moving theory into practice, we can use our real-world experiences as sites for advancing efforts that achieve the goal of dismantling racism and ultimately facilitate racial healing. Thus, in this critical essay we attempt to engage this movement through use of "evidence" from a cursory thematic analysis of student narratives on their real encounters with racism that occurred outside of the IRC classroom. We hope that other students will also learn how the knowledge gained in their own classrooms has practical application in the real world.

The theoretical lens that best embodies this epistemological understanding of the intersection of race, privilege, and societal power is critical race theory (CRT). As Dixson and Rousseau (2005, p. 70) describe it, there are six themes that capture the essence of critical race theory (see also Gilbron, 2006):

1) Recognizes that racism is endemic to American life;

2) Expresses skepticism toward dominant legal claims of neutrality, objectivity, colorblindness, and meritocracy;

3) Challenges ahistoricism and issues on a contextual/historical analysis of the law;

4) Insists on recognition of the experiential knowledge of people of color and our communities of origin in analyzing law and society;

5) Is interdisciplinary;

6) Works toward the end of eliminating racial oppression as part of the broad goal of ending all forms of oppression.

Essentially, CRT argues that racism is assuredly a part of our lived experiences in the U.S., more so for some than others; and it is not until we shift our conceptualizations of race from notions of neutrality to subjectivism that our scholarship can facilitate societal change.

Historically, the goal of CRT is "to address the immediate needs of those who are oppressed" (Orbe & Harris, 2008 p. 114) which involves the use of narrative voice (Delgado & Stefancic, 2005; see Delgado 1995, 2005). According to Delgado and Stefancic, this is critical to CRT in that "[t]he voice exposes, tells and retells, signals resistance and caring, and reiterates the most fearsome power–the power of commitment to change" (p. 80). CRT is a theoretical framework that aims to articulate for the privileged the realities of racism by removing the blinders and giving voice to the experiences of the marginalized (e.g., people of color), thereby providing a context for understanding the systemic forms of oppression borne out of a legal system that has purportedly fought for equality and justice for all. As our U.S. history tells us, this has not been the case. Rather, the laws designed to protect the less powerful have essentially been used to turn the tides against the very people who need the protection the most. Thus, CRT scholars purposed in their work to challenge institutional racism by giving intellectual space to marginalized voices that affirmed their assumptions.

As I reflect on my classroom experiences, I recognize that my pedagogy is clearly informed by CRT and critical pedagogy. It is my aim that the IRC course facilitates social change via myriad assignments that generally lead to varying degrees of change in how students conceptualize the social construction of race. (Because I am the sole instructor teaching this course, the goals for this course remain consistent and within my purview.) Students are also presented with the opportunity to identify communication behaviors that can be used to potentially inform interpersonal interactions they might have where racial transgressions or manifestations of racial prejudices manifest themselves.

Gilborn (2006) states that, "Frustration with the silence on racism prompted CRT scholars to foreground race and to challenge not only the foci of existing analyses, but also methods and forms of argumentation that were considered legitimate" (p. 19). This initiative to rouse the racial consciousness of a country with a history of racism paved the way for "a new wave of radical scholars" to engage in intellectual inquiry that continues to draw our attention to the marginalized and the oppressed. Such is the case with communication scholars who have "drawn [from] this emerging theoretical approach to inform their research on race, ethnicity, and communication" (Orbe & Harris, 2008, p. 113). What is more important regarding CRT is its usefulness in revealing the ways in which discourses that appear neutral or void of race actually function to implicitly reinforce existing racial/ethnic dynamics (Hasian & Delgado, 1998).

In terms of interracial communication, this emerging body of work contributes to a more complex understanding of how race affects our everyday communication. Because it is through the act of communication that these voices are heard, we consider it imperative that communication scholars use our scholarship and pedagogy to explore the rhetorics of race. Doing so would only function to further solidify the marriage between "scholarship and social justice" espoused by CRT (Tate, 1997, p. 235). While CRT has successfully brought our attention to its commitment to radical critique of the law (which is normatively deconstructionist) and its commitment to radical emancipation by the law (which is normatively reconstructionist)" (Delgado & Stefancic, 2005, p. 79), the interpersonal interactions in which these racial transgressions (i.e., racism, discrimination, racial slurs) occur should be a site for further interrogation or exploration.

Critical Race Theory as Critical Race Pedagogy

Recognizing that other areas of scholarship could benefit from the application of this theory, scholars across disciplines have begun to integrate CRT into critical pedagogy. As Dixson and Rousseau (2005) note, this integrative process essentially uses CRT as "fuel for social transformation" by exposing racism in education. Lynn et al. (2006) state that critical analysis in education would necessarily focus on "curriculum, instruction, assessment, school funding, and desegregation, as exemplars of the relationship that can exist between CRT and education, schools and the larger society" (p. 21). Their argument is bolstered by the suggestion that explicit efforts must be made to include in our discourse about racial and social injustices the "unwitting" and "thoughtless" acts that contribute to their very existence (Lynn, 1999). Such a transition would direct our attention away from *intent* and toward "the *outcomes* of actions and processes" (Lynn, 2004, p. 21). Within an educational context, CRT offers a challenge to educational students more generally, and to the sociology of education in particular, to cease the empty citation of "race" as just another point of departure on a list of exclusions to be mentioned and then bracketed away. CRT insists that, "racism be placed at the centre of analyses and that scholarly work be engaged in the process of rejecting and deconstructing the current patterns of exclusion and oppression" (Lynn 2004, p. 27).

In keeping with CRT, critical race pedagogy (CRP) centers its attention on race and racism as they occur within the urban classroom, and also include class and gender in the discussion (Lynn, 2004). Thus, the focus is on "the ways in which race and racism shape what happens in the classroom" and "focuses on teachers [as they] help students develop not only a racial consciousness but become full participants in the struggle to end racism on multiple fronts" (Lynn 2004, p. 22). Lynn et al. also note that the classroom—as a site for understanding—brings students to an awareness of inequalities that occur there, as well as the larger social world.

In a critique of CRT and critical pedagogy, Parker and Stovall (2004) share that students enrolled in their course were engaged with the theory and its social implications as they were responding to a racial incident where six black students received a two-year expulsion because of a melee at a football game in 1999 in Decatur, IL. They [the students] recognized the incident as racially motivated and were inspired to engage with the community to bring about social justice for these students who, in their eyes and many others, were receiving a harsh judgment because of their racial identity. From this experience and their commitment to the intermarriage between CRT and CP, Parker and Stovall (2004) call for educators to assume the role of agents who are "working for social change and equity in schools and communities" (p. 168).

The works of the aforementioned scholars are instrumental in articulating for many the larger and broader implications CRT and CP have for countless communities; however, the missing link is a critical understanding of the role communication or discourse plays in contributing to the rhetoric that ultimately perpetuates the racist ideologies in question. As previously noted, a tenet of CRT scholarship is that awareness and change occur through the narrative voice of the oppressed. In this essay, we espouse this belief and aim to advance CRT and CP by recognizing communication as one of several means by which these experiences are shared. While we acknowledge and believe wholeheartedly that marginalized experiences do indeed illuminate the reality of racism, we also believe that healthy discourse about race and its implications in larger society must involve an understanding and critique of the power language has in our interpersonal interactions. *Thus we ask the question, "How do private discourses among the privileged, or those with (un)acknowledged societal power, contribute to the cycle of racism?"* More specifically, we challenge people to engage in critical thinking about (a) the discourses that occur in the *absence* of the 'Other' and (b) the responses they have when rhetorics of race in daily discourse only function to preserve and widen the racial divide.

To answer these and other questions relative to the rhetorics of race, the following cluster analysis was conducted. Using CRT and CRP as our theoretical framework, we contribute to this very important body of research by proposing that we include the privileged in our discourse about breaking the cycle of racism. Rather than perpetuate the notion of a colorblind ideology, we aim to explore the significance of "narratives of privilege" and how they aid in identifying both effective and ineffective communicative responses to discourses that ultimately only contribute to ineffective interracial communication. It is our belief that a critical analysis of narratives created and written by white students about racial encounters, and their responses to them, can be useful in demonstrating to others (e.g., students, scholars) that communication is an important component in our understandings of the intersection of race, power, and social injustice.

Student Journaling as a Self-Reflective Experience

Critical components of the IRC course that I offer are the journal entries students are required to submit throughout the semester in partial fulfillment for course credit. For many of the students who enroll in this course, this is their first in-depth exposure to the issue of race. They are engaging in a variety of activities and experiences designed to promote increased knowledge and understanding of social location as it relates to race; thus, I believe it is essential that the course assignments create opportunities for self-reflection. The assignments include exams, journal entries, cultural events, critical essays on film, and a diversity-training workshop. While the assignments individually and collectively function to enlighten students to the realities of racism or an affirmation of their experiences with societal oppression, the journals are of particular importance, given the cognitive engagement expected from the students as they reflect on their observations of what I term "racial encounters" occurring within or outside of the interracial classroom.

The instructions for this assignment require students to identify naturally occurring events in their daily lives that involve the issue of race in some way. Although they most likely identify encounters in which they are directly involved, they are also encouraged to be observant of their surroundings or the behaviors of others in a concerted effort to understand the real-life implications of our societal preoccupation with race. These racial encounters are quite similar to what Solorzano, Cieja, and Yasso (2000) refer to as "*microaggressions*," which are "subtle insults (verbal, nonverbal, and/or visual) directed toward people of color, often automatically or unconsciously" (p. 60). It is our contention that the vicious cycle of racism continues to thrive due to the failure of individuals (be it purposeful or not) to actively engage in the process of identifying and directly addressing the perpetrators who commit these insensitive acts that ultimately function to demean, insult, or belittle microcultures, or members of minority groups. The consequences of such societal infractions are plenteous; however, it is our hope that through their learning experiences in the IRC classroom, students are equipped with the skills and knowledge essential to (a) identifying racial microaggressions as they occur in their public and private spheres and (b) developing individualized strategies eradicating racism on an individual interpersonal level.

Deconstructing the Process: A Cluster Analysis

As noted by Sonya Foss (1996) and Carol Berthold (1976), the critic is in search of patterns that exist within an artifact and provide a framework for understanding the rhetor's worldview. Cluster analysis is a methodology that allows one to gain knowledge of a rhetor's interpretation or understanding of an artifact. This qualitative approach involves a four-step process, which includes "(1) formulating a research question and selecting an artifact; (2) selecting a unit of analysis; (3) analyzing the artifact; and (4) writing the critical essay" (Foss, 1989, p. 65). Foss also points out that "the critic may create a method from a concept or concepts related to the artifact and the question. The question may be a theoretical construct from communication or another field" (1989, p. 18).

The rhetor for this analysis is the student, and it is their own responses to their observations of race-specific encounters (i.e., journal entries) that are the artifact of interest. The journal assignment in the IRC course specifically outlines an expectation that students follow a four-step process when recording each entry: (1) identify a racial encounter; (2) describe the scenario and behaviors engaged in to address or resolve the matter; (3) offer a critique of the effectiveness or ineffectiveness of those behaviors; and (4) discuss communication strategies they believe should have been used by them or a third party involved in the encounter (i.e., What would you do differently? Would you do the same thing? Why or why not?). The assignments are evaluated on the student's ability to clearly articulate and describe the racial encounter and the extent to which they engage in self-reflection. More pointedly, the students are challenged with the task of giving careful and critical thought to their daily experiences and how racial microaggressions, or racial infractions on an individual level, play a critical role in silencing opportunities for eradicating the social system of racism and social justice.

For the purpose of this exploratory study, a random sample of 38 journal entries written by white undergraduate students was selected as the unit of analysis. These entries were chosen from a larger sample of approximately 900 journal entries collected from White, Black, Asian, Jewish, Hispanic, and biracial students enrolled in the class between 2004 and 2007. Because this is a predominately white institution (PWI), we have limited our attention to a convenience sample of white students. The primary criterion used to determine appropriate units of analysis was that the student must have clearly identified an encounter that, from her/his perspective, warranted a possible opportunity for a resolution of some sort. A second criterion called for narratives that captured a clear assessment by the student of her/his handling of the encounter. This typically involved critical thought about the experience and their involvement in it. In order to provide an additional perspective, I invited my co-author, a white male doctoral student, to assist with the analysis of the data.

The Four-Step Process: Identifying and Working through Microaggressions

An initial analysis of the journal entries suggests that students who successfully complete this assignment are engaging in a four-step process.

1) **"Identify the microaggression,"** which involves contextualizing the encounter for their reader to ensure clarity regarding how the encounter evolved.

2) **"Identify three cues"** that precede a vital and important part of the process: (a) *relational*; (b) *contextual*; and (c) *emotional*.

Relational cues refer to the relationship that exists between the student and other rhetors involved in the encounter. The relational intimacy between the two interactants was noted as directly influencing how the student responded to the microaggression. *Contextual cues* refer to the physical environment within which the microaggression occurred. For example, if the encounter occurred in a very public setting, the student might be more pensive about how to handle the matter than if they were in the privacy of their home. The third cue, *emotional*, involves those instances where the microaggression elicits an emotional response from the student. As we will describe later, this involves encounters where an emotion such as anger, frustration, or sadness overcame the student and was more salient in her/his decision-making process than other cues. It must be noted that enactment of these cues varied across students, and in some instances multiple cues were employed.

3) **"Reaction"** involves a description of her/his reaction to and employment of communication strategies to deal with (or not to deal with) the racial microaggression of focus.

4) **"Outcome"** relates to the consequences of the reaction and the student's assessment of how effective or ineffective her/his choice was in dealing with racism.

This four-step process is a recurring theme in the artifacts and is illustrative of a self-reflective experience with which these students engaged in varying degrees.

Careful analysis of the journal entries revealed eight different types of microaggressions identified by students as problematic communicative behaviors relative to discourse about race. Each racial microaggression occurred outside of the classroom and elicited a response or reaction that warranted a journal entry, according to the student. Because this data set is part of a larger project, we will limit our discussion to an overview of the general themes that emerged from the analysis. We are also limiting our focus to a critique of the self-reflective process rather than the content of the journal entries. While the content directly informed our analysis and general conclusions about this class assignment, the themes will be used to construct our argument that multicultural classrooms are essential to understanding the larger discourse of rhetorics of race occurring in real world contexts. More importantly, we argue that the approaches used by the students to address racial microaggressions also function as models for behaviors that can be used in everyday discourse.

The following analysis will offer exemplars of communication behaviors that have occurred in real world contexts and function to problematize and/or facilitate opportunities for discourse about race. Identifying these racial microaggressions will also function as a site used by rhetors (students) for recognizing cues that inform the decision to use or not to use certain communication strategies initiated as a means for combating racism within a variety of interpersonal contexts. As we present the microaggressions, we discuss the cues that appear to inform the reaction or response students have to the racial transgression, which will also be addressed in the following sections.

Identifying a Racial Microaggression

1-8

The eight racial microaggressions that emerged from the data are as follows: (1) *racial slur*; (2) *racial labeling*; (3) *racial joke*; (4) *stereotype perpetuation*; (5) *covert racism*; (6) *ethnic humor*; (7) *self-incrimination*; and (8) *overt racism; [note]*. Racial microaggressions in the form of a racial slur, racial label, racial joke, or stereotype perpetuation were negative discourse about a racial/ethnic group that clearly framed the group in a very negative light. Derogatory terms as "the n-word," China Lady, and "Mex-e-can" were used by individuals who were identified as being a part of the students' interpersonal network. This included conversations with parents, roommates, a friend's boyfriend, a grandmother, and teammates in a bicycle club. These blatant instances of inappropriate and offensive language often elicited a response from students that reflected their level of comfort in dealing with the racial transgression. Students also appeared to give critical thought to one or more cues (e.g., relational, contextual, or emotional) to determine what strategy, if any, would be used to "deal with" the infraction.

Responses to Racial Microaggressions

1-9

There were nine reactions which clustered around the racial microaggressions noted above and include the following: (1) *avoidant*–purposeful (active) efforts to avoid confronting the behavior which may include avoiding future interactions with the offender or perceived opportunities for confrontation; (2) *casual consciousness*–pointed efforts to apply classroom knowledge and informally educate others about race without invoking guilt, shame, or blame; (3) *aggressive confrontation*–deliberate effort to address the racist behavior of an offender regardless of the consequences; (4) *active confrontation*–deliberate effort to address racist behavior of an offender but with careful caution; (5) *helpless bystander*–perception of an inability to significantly impact the racist and inappropriate behaviors of others; (6) *self-preservation*–the decision to not engage in confrontational behaviors that risk one's face; (7) *self-censure*–the choice to self-monitor for fear of being offensive; (8) *mediation*–an individual's assumed role as mediator (between the offender and the offended party) in an effort to resolve racial tensions while recognizing the offensive nature of the racial microaggression; and (9) *concerted self-reflection*–a purposeful engagement in self-reflection on the topic of race and how to best understand its significance in real world contexts after being an outsider to or observer of a race-centered experience that warrants no direct response.

Avoidant

For at least eight instances where a *racial slur* was used, rhetors considered their relationship with the offender in order to determine whether or not they should confront the person and their behavior. Two such instances involved the use of an avoidant strategy where the relationships were power-laden. The first situation involved a group of offenders (white Canadians) who were customers in the student's bike shop, and the other instance involved a student's African American professor during class. The offending parties used the n-word but in two distinctly different ways. For the bicyclists, they were using it to denigrate a group of Caribbean bicyclists they perceived to be inferior and less qualified, despite the fact that they had top-of-the-line gear and were obviously competent athletes and worthy of participating in the race. The professor, however, used the word "jokingly" as a warning of how the class "may become offensive at times and that's how the class is. I may ask him why it's OK for African-Americans to use the N-word if they don't want other people using it, but that is the extent to which I will question him." In both instances, however, the students chose an avoidant approach, which may be attributed to fear of the consequences that may occur because of a confrontation. The female cyclist wrote that confronting the Canadians about their behavior would only result in problems on her job, since they frequent the bike shop where she worked. Similarly, the student with the African American professor may have feared retribution for questioning his remarks, thus resulting in her decision to do nothing. In both circumstances, the offending party had some form of power within the relationship that significantly impacted the rhetor's response to the offending behavior.

Casual Consciousness

Two students reported occasions where they employed a *casual conscious* response involving the use of a racial slur by another. In using this strategy, the rhetor-student uses the information they learn in class to inform their reactions to readily (and not so readily) identifiable racial encounters. One white female confronted her grandfather's reference to Brazilian nuts as "n-word toes." In her essay, the student describes how after her grandparents explained how innocuous the phrase was, she still felt a need to educate them about how inappropriate, antiquated, and offensive their language was. The second student, also a white female, used a unique yet somewhat subtle strategy to educate an associate who also used the n-word. Rather than directly confronting the offender, she made it her goal "to make her as uncomfortable as she did to me in the car." As a self-described "tough ass" that "will stand for what I believe in," she made a point to approach every African American friend she ran into that night, greet them with a hug, and invite them to join her, the offender, and their mutual friend. This student obviously recognized that any effort to confront the offender's behavior would be futile, which may have been due in part to the lack of true relationship or emotional connection she had with the associate. In contrast, the former student used a similar approach but in such a way that it clearly functioned to educate the offenders. Her grandparents appeared naïve about the offensiveness of their comments, and were receptive to what their granddaughter had to say. Both of these encounters reflect a student's direct application of their classroom knowledge to real world contexts and situations.

Aggressive Confrontation

A third strategy that emerged was *aggressive confrontation* and was employed by a white male student and a white female student. This strategy occurs when a rhetor feels compelled and obligated to directly confront racist behaviors, sometimes giving little thought to the consequences. The relationships in question were a parent/child (male) relationship and friendship, which suggests relational security that facilitates comfort with confronting the offensive behavior. The male student confronted his father when he referred to his tailor as "the China Lady." This student chose to confront the racist behavior he described as "latent, subconscious prejudice and racism" with the potential for creating more harm than "blatant, overt racism." The student shares that this confrontation is coming on the heels of an in-class role-play activity (the Crayola Activity; see Harris, Groscurth, and Trego, 2007) that made him attuned to racial indiscretions he otherwise would not be privy to because of his privileged status.

As this entry demonstrates, this student was prompted by his conscience and the class to confront his father's remarks with the hope that his father would recognize the racist dimensions of his rhetoric. The female who also used aggressive confrontation had a similar experience with a friend who was assisting her on a photo shoot. When asked to carry some of the student's equipment, the offender responded, "No way, we'll get you a n-word for that." After the shock wore off, the student "then jumped all over her about how ridiculously uncalled for that comment was." After reflecting on how the situation was handled, the student felt things could have been done differently and more effectively if she had defended the black community in addition to her own views about racism.

Active Confrontation

A type of racial microaggression that emerged from the data was the use of racist language, which includes a general discussion or comment that is perceived as "heavily loaded" in negative racial content. The response of active confrontation involves a concerted effort or attempt to engage the offender in dialogue about the offensive behavior. It is inferred from the data that this approach is different from the others in that the rhetor is purposely attempting to address the infraction without creating a defensive climate or posture. One instance of this active confrontation involves a time when a white female student was casually hanging out with her friends one evening playing the board game "Scruples." According to the website, the premise of the game is to "[make] players sweat as they ask each other what they would do in a moral predicament." Throughout the game, the student was making informal observations of the behaviors of her friends as they contemplated different scenarios where they were expected to use their moral compass. She finally concluded that many of their decisions were informed by their racial biases, thus resulting in the racist language that played out during the game.

What is most notable is that as she is confronting her friends about their behavior, this student acknowledges her own issues with race. She further notes that this game of "Scruples" was a catalyst for a substantive 30-minute discussion about race, which was in her recollection the first time such conversation had taken place amongst any of her friends. This student also attributes this opportunity for discourse to her enrollment in the interracial communication class. By being part of a community engaging in regular discourse about race, this student appears to have developed skills that allow her to extend those discussions into her interpersonal network.

This experience is quite possibly symptomatic of the kinds of informal discourses that occur in (everyday) life. Although the women were making life decisions about hypothetical situations, it is quite possible that they would engage in the same thinking process if in fact those situations presented themselves in real life.

Helpless Bystander

The fifth strategy or response participants had to a racial microaggression was that of the *helpless bystander*. While this strategy was used with other types of microaggressions, its use in response to a racial slur occurred with a white male student whose grandmother referred to his African American baseball teammate as "that little n-boy." In his journal entry, the student describes the thought process he experienced as his grandmother verbally attacked his friend who happened to be of a different race. He later shares that he felt helpless in the fight against racism with his grandmother because of her espousal of racist ideologies that are in clear opposition to his own way of thinking. In describing this awkward and obviously racist encounter, this student conveys to the reader his feeling of being a "helpless bystander." The implication is that he is placed in the unfortunate position of not being able to confront racially offensive behavior, thus rendering any such efforts futile. His response to this racial microaggression is to choose to do nothing, a choice that is forced upon him because of his grandmother's resistance to change. It may also be inferred that confronting his grandmother may adversely affect their relationship, and in order to preserve their relationship, his decision functions to keep their connection in tact. A more important byproduct of this experience is that the student engaged in a self-reflective process that allowed him to identify the factors deemed salient in determining whether or not to engage in discourse about race.

Self-Preservation

The sixth strategy is self-preservation which refers to a behavior that appears to be self-serving. The rhetor opts to respond to a racial microaggression by engaging in a form of impression management that minimizes the risk of being perceived by others as racist or perpetuating the cycle of racism. The one instance where this response was used involved a white male's reaction to the treatment of a white female friend by a group of African American women at a club. By the student's admission, the white female was dressed very provocatively, and several people in the group thought her outfit was inappropriate and contrary to her personality and identity as a female. As they waited in line to get in, the African American women were making inappropriate comments about the friend. While his instinct was to protect his friend, the student opted to say nothing because he "did not want to be perceived as the arrogant, aggressive, overly-dominant white male that is so often criticized for his insensitivity towards issues concerning race and gender differences." For this student, choosing to not directly address the verbal aggressiveness of the women was his way of not perpetuating a stereotype, which in turn took power away from the racial assault directed toward his friend.

Self-Censure

Self-censure, the seventh strategy, is also a form of impression management and challenges the rhetor to make a conscious effort to become actively involved in changing his/her language choices and ways of thinking about self, race, and/or racially different others. This was a recurring theme in many journal entries and most frequently referred to students' experiences as participant-observers in classroom discussions about a myriad of topics relative to race and interracial communication. For many, this is the first time they have ever engaged in formal discussions on this taboo topic and, as such, they are very careful in how they present themselves to others. Similarly, a student is giving more critical thought to the cognitive processes associated with their classroom experiences. Although these are not accounts in the "real world," per se, they provide students with the opportunity to exercise their interracial communication skills in a safe space.

One white female described how she actively engages in self-talk or intrapsychic conversations about race before sharing her thoughts with the class. This is an attempt "to ensure that [her ideas and feelings] are interpreted the way I intend for them to be," which she believes is a common practice for many of her classmates. Fear of being misinterpreted is the driving motivation behind this strategy, and in order to avoid being misunderstood or perceived as racist, rhetors who self-censure choose to give careful thought to message construction or opt not to say anything at all. According to this student's entry, self-censure is a positive communicative strategy in several ways; however, it is the discomfort many have about discussing race that prohibits honest and sincere discourse from occurring. Although she limited her focus to her in-class experiences, it is quite possible the same strategy would be used in contexts outside of the college classroom.

Mediation

The eighth strategy is *mediation* and only occurred once in the data set; nevertheless, this was a strategy deserving of our attention. As previously noted, mediation involves a very conciliatory approach by the rhetor-student, wherein s/he is attempting to reduce conflict that could potentially occur between the offender and the offended party. For this one female student, the offender was her friend. The friend–in an aborted attempt to relate to an African American couple attending a country and western concert–drew attention to the fact that they were the only non-white people attending. Recognizing this social blunder, the student offered an apology to the couple and qualified it by stating that "she is extremely drunk and has been making inappropriate comments all evening." The couple communicated that they were not offended, whereas the student was offended by the drunken woman's behavior. She followed up on the incident with the offender and advised her in the future to use a different approach, preferably one that was non-racial, if she wants to have casual conversation with someone of a different race. While the other parties did not perceive any behaviors to be offensive or racial, the student's defensive approach is worthy of inclusion because she demonstrated an ability to identify a communication behavior that, in other situations, could be highly problematic and conflictual.

It may also be inferred from this entry that the student felt a moral obligation or responsibility to assume the role of mediator and apologize to the strangers on her friend's behalf. To that extent, it may also be a form of face-saving but on behalf of another. So as not to be perceived as racist, the rhetor-student offered the apology on behalf of the offender in an attempt to acknowledge and then take responsibility for the offensive remark. The ideal outcome might be recognition of societal efforts to address social issues such as race within an interpersonal context, which is possibly more impactful than other macro-level efforts such as political correctness.

Concerted Self-Reflection

The ninth and final strategy of *concerted self-reflection* is distinctively different from the other strategies that emerged from the data. While the other journals include student-identified instances of racial microaggressions in various social contexts, several journal entries elicited concerted self-reflection for students. Students submitting such entries chose to isolate an incident that may not have specifically involved race and write about how it (the incident) served as a catalyst for self-reflection or critical thought about race. For example, one white female began to think about the racial composition of friends. She states in the entry that prior to being enrolled in this class, she had never given much thought about their racial group membership; "However, after taking this class I have come to [the] realization that all my friends are exactly like me … I do not have a single friend at Georgia who is of a different race or from a different culture." She continues to share that she is disappointed that she did not take advantage of the opportunities the university had to offer her in terms of developing relationships with other students from a racial group different from her own. Her entry concludes with a resolution to make more concerted efforts in the future to diversify her friendship.

In a similar vein, another white female describes her own awareness of race that crystallized during a church service. She and her parents were attending a Sunday service and were surprised to find that the minister preaching that day was an African American male. In fact, he was the only non-white congregant in attendance. They were initially apprehensive about the encounter but were, as she describes, "humbled, convicted, and yet encouraged by this man who walked in such purity with the Lord." She further notes that she "learned from this experience not only how much work needs to be done in my own heart, but more importantly, where to go for it to be done." As this entry demonstrates, the incident of interest did not have a racial connotation; however, it was the presence of the African American minister and the expectation that racial differences would frame the experience that prompted her to reflect on this experience.

Thus, it stands to reason that similar experiences occur in real-world contexts where one does not have the opportunity to journal and respond to racial encounters such as these. It is likely that being in the presence of the *proverbial Other* functions to bring to one's consciousness the relevance of race and the subconscious ideals associated with racial group membership. Although journaling in this context is specific to a course, this approach to self-reflection could reasonably be applied to life outside of the academy.

Discussion

As this cluster analysis demonstrates, narratives from those in positions of societal power and privilege are essential in the process of deconstructing rhetorics of race. Although our approach was different from the tradition of CRT in that our attention was not directed toward the marginalized, we introduced a new scholarly inquiry of social justice that explores the private and public discourses that perpetuate a system of oppression through discourse or communication. The students enrolled in IRC were required to engage in the self-reflective process of journaling during the course of the semester. The analysis revealed that students identified a myriad of racial microaggressions perceived as racially volatile and blatant barriers to effective interracial communication. Their responses ranged from aggressive confrontations to the helpless bystander, and were significantly impacted by their relationship with their interactant, the context within with the racial microaggression occurred, and/or their emotional response to the racial transgression.

In their narratives, the students were able to provide firsthand accounts of forms of systemic oppression that occurred as a result of the racist, prejudiced, and discriminatory behaviors employed by those within their interpersonal networks. Though not explicitly articulated, these narratives suggest that students were becoming more cognizant of the role that they and their family and friends were taking in social injustice. Many acknowledged that they felt a moral obligation to confront racial microaggressions as they occurred, giving little or no thought to the consequences. In contrast, there were others who felt that confronting one whose ideological beliefs are entrenched in a power imbalance was a moot point, resulting in the racial microaggression being ignored.

Overall, the narratives demonstrate that through the IRC course, students are exposed to a variety of pedagogical tools that challenge them to think more critically about communication processes and the influence that a racial hierarchy and societal power have on their thoughts and ideologies about race. In addition, they shared that their exposure to different theories and concepts also served to facilitate their increased awareness of race relations and, for many, prompted them to be more active, in varying degrees, in their responses to racial microaggressions that occurred primarily outside of the classroom context. For those who failed or chose not to confront, their relational connections with the perpetrator, a desire to self-protect, or the fear of using an ineffective communication strategy prevented them from addressing those transgressions. It must also be noted that there were occasions where the rhetor-student recognized her/himself as a perpetrator of the very social injustice they were "being trained" to recognize, and because of their shame and guilt, they opted for even more active engagement in self-reflection and change that would prevent the cycle of racism from being perpetuated.

Regardless of the outcome, the four-step process to address racial microaggression is a very effective tool for civic engagement and social justice. Students are challenged to make a connection between the academy and the real world. Through the journal assignment, students are afforded the opportunity to self-reflect and give serious thought to the reality of race as it affects us all. This provides a site within which they can gain increased knowledge and understanding of the power of communication as mechanism for dismantling racism.

Conclusion

It was the goal of this chapter to demonstrate how a college classroom, or the academy in general, is a fertile site to challenge rhetors-students of privilege to take an active role in promoting social justice in every area of their lives. While their performance is not measured by the success rate of their confrontations with microaggressions, it is an underlying assumption and expectation that students will in fact use this knowledge for a greater good beyond academic credit. Our cluster analysis of the narratives demonstrates that the vicious cycle of racism is definitely perpetuated in the informal, casual contexts involving interpersonal networks. These "innocuous" transgressions are symptomatic of a larger, societal inability (or failure) to hold those in positions of power and privilege accountable for the racial indiscretions that are committed on a daily basis. As demonstrated by CRT research, social justice can only occur when narratives are heard that speak to the realities that come from a society preoccupied with racial differences that result in societal oppression.

We have specifically identified the stages through which a student enrolled in an IRC may navigate as they engage in the process of moving theory into practice. Rather than ingesting course content and remaining relatively inactive in their educational experience, students are acquiring the tools necessary for critical thought and self-reflection about issues relative to social injustices borne from a racial hierarchy. Some may argue that these narratives are classroom artifacts that fail to reflect the reality of racism in the real world. We, however, argue the contrary. Students are instructed to reflect on experiences that occur in their lives outside the classroom, which most definitely include experiences with individuals (i.e., parents, siblings, friends, co-workers, customer service representatives) who are active participants in and members of larger society. As such, they are reflections of the larger ideological frameworks that perpetuate the institutional racism that has been in existence for decades. These racial microaggressions are occurring outside of the "safe space" of the college classroom, which leaves the rhetor-student in a very vulnerable state. They are forced to put into practice what they have been learning for four-and-a-half months, which is a very daunting task, to say the least. Their classmates or professor only "have their back" in spirit when they are faced with the possibility and potential reality of confronting the prejudiced comments made by an aunt at a Japanese steakhouse, or the friend who sends a "funny" e-joke at the expense of the *proverbial Other*. But what *really* happens when those situations do occur? Will they sit tight-lipped and say nothing, or will they strategically employ a strategy that breaks the cycle of racism, one relationship at a time? Based on their narratives, my students answer with a resounding "yes" to the latter.

This analysis demonstrates that directing our attention to communication behaviors in discourse about race in the real world is key to bringing about social justice in regards to race. Their narratives of privilege tell us that the consequences of such societal infractions are plenteous; however, it is our hope that by using the interracial communication classroom, we have prompted scholars to give consideration to the richness that belies our pedagogy and commitment to making a difference within and beyond our classrooms. By designing course assignments that challenge students to (a) identify microaggressions as they occur in their public and private spheres and (b) develop individualized strategies eradicating racism on an individual interpersonal level, we are creating a simulated boot camp where training in the fight against racism, discrimination, and prejudice has begun. By analyzing these artifacts as relics of our past, we can pave the way for understanding our future through our real world discourses about racial differences. IRC prepares students for their role as global citizens who will have more interracial encounters than generations that have gone before them. While they will be better prepared to confront those who are resistant to this inevitable change, they will be in a position to recognize and embrace their moral imperative and duty to use their experiential knowledge and learning experiences to move theory into practice. We anticipate their responses will serve as models for larger society and promote the enactment of the aforementioned communication strategies and behaviors that we believe will facilitate positive race relations on an individual and eventually institutional level, one relationship at a time.

DISCUSSION QUESTIONS

1. Reflecting on your own communication behaviors, how would you assess your responses to hearing (and being in the presence of) others who make inappropriate, racist, or prejudiced remarks about a racial/ethnic group other than your own? Are you typically satisfied with your behaviors? What would, or could you do differently?

2. What level of responsibility do you believe people should have for confronting racial microaggressions when they are happening? Why, or why not?

3. What other types of microaggressions (gender, class, etc.) do you believe serve as barriers to effective interracial communication?

4. What are some of the costs and rewards of personally confronting racial microaggressions?

References

Berthold, C. A. (1976). Kenneth burke's cluster-agon method: Its development and an application. *Central States Speech Journal, 27*, 302–309.

Delgado, R. (1995). *The Rodrigo chronicles: Conversations about race in America*. New York: New York University Press.

Delgado, R. (2005). *When Equality Ends: Stories about Race and Resistance*. Boulder, CO: Westview Press.

Delgado, R., & J. Stefancic (2005). *The Derrick Bell Reader*. New York: New York University Press.

Dixson, A. D., & C. K. Rousseau (2005). And we are still are not saved: critical race theory in education 10 years later. *Race Ethnicity and Education, 8*(1), 7–27.

Foss, S. (1989). Rhetorical criticism: Exploration and practice. Illinois: Waveland Press.

Gilborn, D. (2006). Critical race theory and education: Racism and anti-racism in educational and theory praxis. *Discourse: studies in the cultural politics of education, 27*(1), 11–32.

Harris, T. M., Groscurth, C., & Trego, A. (2007). Coloring Outside the Lines: Unmasking Performances of White Identity through Classroom Role-Play. In Leda M. Cooks and Jennifer S. Simpson (Ed.). *Whiteness, Performance, Pedagogy: Dis/Placing Race:* Lexington Books (a division of Rowman & Littlefield), 169–191.

Hasian, M., & Delgado, F. (1998).The trials and tribulations of racialized critical rhetorical theory: Understanding the rhetorical ambiguities of Proposition 187. *Communication Theory, 8*(3), 245–270.

Lynn, M. (1999). Toward a critical race pedagogy: A research note. *Urban Education 33*(5), 606–626.

Lynn, M. (2004). Inserting the 'race' into to critical pedagogy: An analysis of 'race-based epistemologies. *Educational Philosophy and Theory, 3*(6I2), 153–165.

Lynn, M., Benigno, G., Williams, A. D., Park, G., & C. Mitchell (2006). Critical theories of race, class, and gender in urban education. *Encounter: Education for Meaning and Social Justice, 19*(2), 17–25.

Orbe, M., & Harris, T. M. (2008, 2nd ed.). *Interracial Communication: Theory To Practice*. Thousand Oaks, CA: Sage Publications.

Parker, L., & D. O. Stovall (2004). Actions following words: Critical race theory connects to critical pedagogy. *Educational Philosophy and Theory, 26*(2), 167–182.

Solorzano, D., Ceja, M., & Yosso, T. (2000). Critical race theory, racial microaggressions, and campus racial climate: The experiences of African American college students. *Journal of Negro Education, 69*(1), 60–73.

Tate, W. (1997). Critical race theory and education: History, theory and implications. In M. W. Apple (ed.), *Review of Research in Education, vol. 22*, (pp. 195–247). Washington, DC: American Educational Research Association.

19

"America has a dominant language— Learn it!": An Analysis of Whiteness in the Construction of International Teaching Assistant Identity in the *Daily Egyptian*

Richie Neil Hao

Abstract

As international teaching assistants (ITAs) continue to increase their presence in U.S. classrooms, so do the numbers of complaints raised by undergraduate students that ITAs are incomprehensible. The so-called "ITA problem" has been a significant issue that faces the academy in recent years, which has generated attention and debate on college campuses across the U.S. In fact, the Southern Illinois University, Carbondale (SIUC) campus newspaper, *Daily Egyptian* published a featured article, guest columns, and letters in 2007 that discussed issues surrounding ITAs and students' perception of them. Based on the conversations in the *Daily Egyptian*, it is timely to address the "ITA problem" by critically analyzing how mediated texts make us understand the role of whiteness in the construction of ITA identity.

KEY TERMS: *Daily Egyptian*, international teaching assistants, "ITA problem," pedagogy, whiteness

Introduction

University faculty and graduate teaching assistants across the United States have become more culturally diverse than ever before. In fact, one-third of all graduate teaching assistants are considered to be non-native English speakers (Rubin, 2002). More importantly, it is not uncommon for U.S. American undergraduate students to have an international teaching assistant (ITA) as a teacher. Due to a growing number of ITAs in the U.S. who are foreign born and "non-native speakers of mainstream North American

Englishes" (Rubin, 2002, p. 129), universities turn to international graduate students to teach introductory courses in a wide range of subjects, including but not limited to math, engineering, English, and communication. Many studies suggest that undergraduate students across the U.S. have expressed frustration at being taught by ITAs (see, for example, Fitch & Morgan, 2003; Yook & Albert, 1999). More specifically, many undergraduate students think that ITAs are incomprehensible (Fitch and Morgan, 2003). Due to the students' negative perception of ITAs, it is estimated that "more than two out of every five students reported that they had withdrawn from a class or switched classes when they found that their teacher was a non-native speaker of English" (Rubin, 2002, p. 127).

Because of the perceived problem of ITAs' incomprehensibility, some states decided to take extreme measures to ensure that ITAs are prepared to teach. For example, North Dakota State Representative Bette Grande introduced legislation in which state universities are required to give refunds to students who complain in writing about their instructor's inability to "speak English clearly and with good pronunciation" (Gravois, 2005, p. A10). In addition, students who report their instructor's incomprehensibility are also entitled to withdraw from the class without grade penalty (Gravois, 2005). The proposed legislation did not stop there. In fact, if ten percent of students in a class complained about the teacher's incomprehensibility, the university can remove the instructor in question from his or her teaching responsibilities and be reassigned to a "non-teaching position" (Gravois, 2005).

While the legislation proposed above, and other ethnocentric education policies, practices, and discourses can be analyzed through Communication Accommodation Theory, I argue that whiteness theories allow us to unpack how both Whites and non-Whites can reenact, reproduce, and reconstitute White Eurocentric ideologies in the academy and other everyday contexts. Whiteness is "a system of domination" (Moon, 1999, p. 178), which is perpetuated through performances of white identity (Warren, 2001). Whiteness is also part of the everyday performance, and through these performances, it gets constituted, reproduced, and socially constructed (Hytten & Warren, 2003). Nakayama and Krizek (1995) add that whiteness has been constructed as universal, which places non white bodies as "the other" (p. 293). For those ITAs who do not fit the White American image or do not have a standard White American accent, many students tend to complain about their ITAs being incomprehensible; therefore, ITAs who do not speak English as their first language are often subjected to scrutiny of whether or not they are proficient in English and can teach effectively. In essence, whiteness "perpetuate[s] relations of domination and oppression against nonwhites while simultaneously securing whites with a disproportionate amount of power and privilege" (Giroux, 1997, p. 90).

Due to the influence of whiteness in the academy, the "ITA problem" continues to be debated today; it has been publicized in different news media, including college and university newspapers. The *Daily Egyptian*, a Southern Illinois University, Carbondale (SIUC) campus newspaper, published a 2007 article that featured the training program available to ITAs in the university (Rendleman, 2007). Even though the article provided some insights to how this program can aid ITAs, it was also problematic in how it constructed the ITA identity. As a former ITA, I was compelled to write a letter to the editor because the article seemed to suggest that the language barrier in the classroom exists because many ITAs are not proficient in English. The ITA body is always implicated by the politics of race, culture, and language in the classroom, which makes such a body vulnerable to how students interpret it as an unqualified teacher. When I was an ITA, I had to negotiate my body in the classroom in order to be perceived positively as the instructor of record. Due to stereotypes of Asians not being able to speak English fluently and properly, I faced difficulties in establishing my credibility to teach public speaking. Because of my own personal experiences as an ITA and how I resonated with the *Daily Egyptian's* construction of the ITA identity, I decided to write a letter to the editor to create sites for discussion on why ITAs should not be the scapegoat of the communication barriers in the classroom. Instead, both ITAs and students should work together to improve pedagogical interactions and experiences. After the publication of my letter, a total of four responses (two letters to the editor and two guest columns) followed within the next few days.

Based on the conversations that occurred in the *Daily Egyptian*, it is timely to address the "ITA problem" by analyzing how an article, letters, and guest columns make us understand the influences of whiteness (more specifically, ethnocentrism) to the ITA identity. Even though there is no way to tell if all respondents who have written a letter, column and/or were quoted in the *Daily Egyptian* were White U.S. Americans, whiteness can be performed discursively by non-whites as well where Eurocentric worldviews are privileged and sustained in the U.S. (Shome, 2002).

There is no doubt that whiteness can shape our attitudes and behaviors towards international faculty and ITAs, which is why I want to examine the constitutive effects of the discourses in the *Daily Egyptian*. Although there have been studies that talk about whiteness in the academy in general, very few scholars—if any—explore whiteness in analyzing the "ITA problem," specifically using student newspapers as a rhetorical medium to understand the phenomenon. My study not only contributes by exploring intercultural communication through how whiteness affects perceptions of ITAs in the academy, but it also provides a critical rhetorical lens in understanding how mediated texts, such as the *Daily Egyptian*, can perpetuate whiteness in society at large. In order to address how whiteness is valued in the *Daily Egyptian*, I will first provide an overview of all six published pieces that have generated discussion of the "ITA problem." Second, I will analyze how the featured article and two letters to the editor participated in whiteness discourses. Third, I will discuss how the two editorial columns responded to other published pieces' whiteness rhetoric. Finally, I will conclude with my reflections on what I have learned in such discourse.

Overview of the Conversations in the *Daily Egyptian*

The article, "Course helps TAs, students understand each other," was published on January 26, 2007 in the *Daily Egyptian*. The article featured the ITA training program at SIUC, which was created in the 1980s in response to a great number of ITAs coming to the United States. In addition to improving language proficiency, the ITA program recently added an American culture component to its curriculum. The ITA program, which is a three-hour a week course, is intended to be used for ITAs who did not pass the initial oral interview test.

Even though "Course helps TAs, students understand each other" legitimized why the ITA training is needed, what ultimately bothered me was when Arifin Angriawan, an ITA, was quoted: "I learned [from the training program] that I have to speak slowly and louder" (Rendleman, 2007, p. 3). My letter to the editor "Language barrier a two-way street" on February 20, 2007 was not a response against the ITA program (although I will address some of my concerns about it later), but rather it was my concern that ITAs like Angriawan are forced to perform whiteness in the classroom in order to accommodate

Language Barrier a Two-Way Street

Language barrier a two-way street

DEAR EDITOR:

After reading the article featured in the DE on Jan, 26, "Course helps TAs, students understand each other," I had a mixed reaction. Although I applaud SIUC for making an International Teacher Assistant Training Program available for International Teaching Assistants (ITAs) who need it, I feel that some kind of training program should also be available for our undergraduate students, If there is a language barrier, why are ITAs always blamed for it? I cannot help but write to the editor about this article because of Arifin Angriawan, an ITA from business administration, who was quoted, "I learned how to speak slowly and louder [from the training program]." I feel badly for Arifin for having to say that because he has to negotiate his ITA identity in order to sound "American" for students who are not willing to make the same effort to do whatever it takes to break communication barriers.

Don't you think our students should also learn how to listen more carefully so that they can understand their ITAs? We now live in a multicultural U.S. society, and unfortunately, many of us are too lazy to learn another language and/or try to learn ways to communicate more effectively with people who are from different cultural backgrounds. If we want student-teacher communication to work in the classroom, both parties—ITAs and their students alike—should make efforts to break the language and cultural barriers. Unfortunately, it has always been a one-way street where ITAs are the root of the problem in the classroom. Don't you think it's time to make a change?

Richie Neil Hao
doctoral student,
international teaching assistant
department of speech communication

Hao, R. N. (2007, February 20). Language barrier a two-way street [Letter to the editor]. *Daily Egyptian*, p. 7.

their U.S. American students who are not willing to make the same effort to break communication barriers that exist between ITAs and their students. Consequently, according to Giles and St. Clair (1979), individuals such as ITAs who engage in communication convergence must shift their speech patterns (language choice, accent, dialect, and/or paralinguistic cues) in order to closely resemble their interlocutors (in this case, students), which ultimately perpetuates the idea that ITAs have speech deficiencies that warrant the need to change how they speak.

A day after my letter to the editor was published, an undergraduate student who is majoring in health care management wrote a letter to the editor on February 21, 2007 entitled "America has a dominant language—learn it." In her letter, she misinterpreted my message by assuming that I expect undergraduate students to learn a language of their ITAs in order to communicate well with them. She ultimately complained about the inability of ITAs to teach well in the classroom because they lack English proficiency. Therefore, she suggested that ITAs should learn the "dominant language" in the U.S.

America has a Dominant Language—Learn it

America has a dominant language—learn it

Dear Editor:

I would like to comment on yesterday's letter, "Language barrier a two-way street" which ended with the question, "Don't you think it's time to make a change?"

No, I do not feel students who attend SIUC should have to learn another language just to be able to communicate with international teaching assistants. Yes, an attempt should be made to first try to understand, but when that fails, what else is there to do?

This is America and it is a multicultural society, but just like with most other countries, there is a primary language. If you choose to be here then you should make an attempt to learn the language. I would not go to Germany and expect everyone to cater to me and learn English. I would have to learn the language if I wanted to live and work there. That's just how it is.

It is an asset to know other languages. Sometimes employers even prefer it, but you should not have to worry about understanding your teacher's speech because of a language barrier.

A couple semesters ago I actually had to drop a math class because I just could not understand my teacher. I tried and I tried but still did not understand a word out of their mouth. I even went to tutoring where I encountered yet another person who was experiencing a language barrier.

Should my understanding of a subject be compromised because of these language barriers? If I can speak the dominant language of this country, why should I have to learn another to understand an ITA?

junior studying health care management

[Name Withheld]. (2007, February 21). America has a dominant language—learn it [Letter to the editor]. *Daily Egyptian*, p. 7.

On February 22, 2007, a day after a student's letter was published, another letter and a guest column followed. An SIUC alumnus and active military personnel wrote a letter entitled "What country are we in?" He resisted the idea of undergraduate students having to share the responsibility for communication problems in the classroom. Instead, he argued that ITAs should learn how to speak English and blamed them for communication barriers.

What Country Are We In?

[Name Withheld]. (2007, February 22). What country are we in? [Letter to the editor]. *Daily Egyptian*, p. 7.

On the same day that the SIUC alumnus' letter was published, ITA coordinator for the Center for English as a Second Language (CESL) Cheryl Ernst's (2007) column "International TAs and students should compromise" was also published. In this column, Ernst entered the debate as a mediator of both sides and advocated that both ITAs and undergraduate students need to work together to break communication barriers in the classroom. Ernst also pointed out in her column that ITAs are doing everything in their power to become better teachers; therefore, students must make an effort to listen carefully.

The last letter came from ITAs in the Psychology Department at SIUC. They wrote a guest column called "International TAs deserve respect, acceptance" on February 27, 2007. The ITAs expressed their concern of the recent letters to the editor that "seem to reveal there may be some resentment and prejudice from some U.S. students on campus towards ITAs" (p. 7). They wanted to address the fact that ITAs work very hard and spend a lot of time preparing for their class lectures. As a response against the assumption that ITAs are incomprehensible, the ITAs argued that every person or group speaks with an accent, a particular intonation, enunciation, and pronunciation. Therefore, they recommended students to train their ears in order to adjust to their ITAs' speech.

Whiteness Discourses in the *Daily Egyptian*

After reading the published article and letters to the editor in the *Daily Egyptian*, I argue that they reinforced whiteness as the educational norm. Citing Shome (1999) earlier, it is worth repeating that whiteness is not limited to the actions of white people; non-Whites can also perform whiteness discursively in everyday contexts. With that said, I acknowledge that writers of the article, letters, and columns could be non-White individuals, which is why it is appropriate to use whiteness as a theoretical framework in understanding how it impacts education rituals and discourses such as those published in the *Daily Egyptian*. While there are different ways to engage and reinforce whiteness, I will specifically focus on my analysis of how the authors' ethnocentric viewpoints toward ITAs demonstrated their whiteness. According to Martin and Nakayama (2005), ethnocentrism is understood as one's belief that his or her culture is superior to other cultural groups. Even though the authors of the article and letters to the editor do not perceive all ITAs negatively, I will demonstrate in my analysis how they communicated ethnocentrism, which could emphasize that all ITAs have a speech deficiency and construct ITAs as non-U.S. Americans.

ITAs have a Speech Deficiency

Communicating whiteness as a rhetorical strategy was evident in the article and the letters to the editor by marking ITAs as having a speech deficiency. The article, "Course helps TAs, students understand each other," introduced Arifin Angriawan as "an ITA from Indonesia who took the class twice" (Rendleman, 2007, p. 3). With the latter statement, Rendleman reinforced whiteness in the article by pointing out that Angriawan has taken "the [training] class twice" (Rendleman, 2007, p. 3), which shows his lack of proficiency in English. In a way, Rendleman invited his readers to see the otherness of Angriawan and other ITAs. Rendleman's construction of the ITA identity as Other reminded me of what Shome (2002) says about how her "accent" often led to her white students thinking that she is not a native English speaker because she is "a 'third-world' nonwhite female instructor speaking with what is perceived to be an 'accent' ..." (p. 125). Like Shome and many other Asian ITAs, I too struggled to legitimize my Asian body in the classroom because of my linguistic background. As a college instructor teaching public speaking it was difficult to maintain the authenticity of whiteness in the classroom, especially when I was negotiating and continue to negotiate the complexity of language translation from Tagalog to English and vice-versa. Although Filipinos speak English in general, the linguistic pronunciation and articulation are different from U.S. Americans. Hence, my Filipino accent is usually evident. As a performance of whiteness, I tried so hard to cover my slight Filipino accent, which sometimes resulted in utterance of certain words that did not sound the way they should be. In light of what Rendleman said in the article, I argue that his emphasis of Angriawan having to take the ITA training class twice is an example of how ITAs are not considered as typical teachers in the classroom for their perceived speech deficiency.

Ethnocentric messages can also be found in Rendleman's (2007) article when Marilyn Rivers, Director of the Center for English as a Second Language (CESL), suggested in the article that "students can help an ITA pronounce words or even reword a question the ITA doesn't understand" (p. 3). Rivers communicated her whiteness by suggesting that students should "help" their ITAs to pronounce words correctly. Rivers' suggestion not only demeans ITAs for supposedly not knowing how to speak English properly, but it also gives students the power to embarrass their ITAs in front of their peers. It is like what Said (1978) describes when the Orientalist has the power to speak for the Oriental; an Orientalist is anyone who researches, teaches, and writes about the Orient, and s/he can be an anthropologist, historian, sociologist, and so on. Therefore, the Orientalist commits the act of Orientalism, which is a form of Western-style domination that controls the Oriental. In this case, the Orientalist forces the Oriental to conform to his writing, vision, study, perspectives, and ideologies. Like the Oriental, ITAs' bodies in the classroom first and foremost have been constructed as Other due to their perceived speech deficiency, and then their bodies are specified and commodified as incomprehensible teachers that need to be taught how to speak properly.

Furthermore, Rivers appears not to realize that it can be embarrassing for ITAs to lose their face in front of students, which can lead to further assumptions that ITAs have a speech deficiency. While everyone can engage in face loss, employing face loss can be considered as a performance of whiteness, especially if the marginalized other is humiliated in public by locating his or her "difference" (in this case, difference in speech) (Shome, 1999, p. 119). According to Ting-Toomey (2004), "face loss occurs when we are being treated in such a way that our identity claims in a conflict situation are challenged or ignored" (p. 218). For example, most ITAs come from cultures that value power distance where teachers should have more power than their students; therefore, cultures that value high power distance emphasize hierarchical relationships and formalized decision-making processes (Martin & Nakayama, 2005). Rivers' suggestion does not take into consideration what problems could arise if students were allowed to correct their ITAs' speaking patterns.

The assumption that ITAs have a speech deficiency can also be traced in the undergraduate student's letter "American has a Dominant Language—learn It." She misinterpreted my message by assuming that I expect undergraduate students to learn a language of their ITAs in order to communicate well with them. As the student clearly objected, "No, I do not feel students who attend SIUC should have to learn another language just to be able to communicate with international teaching assistants." The student's expression, however, is not atypical for many U.S. Americans who tend to believe that English is the only and best way to communicate, which implies that those who are not proficient in English should be considered to have a speech deficiency. Although I acknowledge that English is the primary language of instruction in U.S. colleges and universities and all instructors must be proficient in English, the student's remark in regards to monolingualism is an example of ethnocentrism. The student adds in her letter: "Yes, an attempt should be made to first try to understand, but when that fails, what else is there to do?" The student's statement is a good example of downplaying her performance of whiteness, but at the same time promoting her privileged status by saying that it is an "all or nothing" approach. Her "all or nothing approach" is what Johnson (2006) calls getting "off the hook" (p. 124), which is an excuse that allows people with power and privilege to distance themselves from unprivileged people. As a result, the student reasoned that she was "helpless," and it was not her fault if she got frustrated with ITAs' speech. Due to this strategy, the student got off the hook, but at the same time she succeeded in establishing blame toward ITAs.

Another performance of whiteness is evident in "Course helps TAs, students understand each other" because of how ITAs have been classified as having limited English fluency and familiarity. For instance, toward the end of the article, I also found two statements problematic, which reinforced the power of whiteness in the classroom. First, Ernst recommended students to "avoid using slang because it would probably not be understood" (Rendleman, 2007, p. 3). Even though Ernst's recommendation sounded legitimate, it is also problematic because it implied that all ITAs have a speech deficiency by not understanding U.S. slang. Ernst's statement also suggested that all ITAs are alike; therefore, U.S. American students should not use slang in the classroom altogether. The "ITAs are all alike" mentality creates the notion that everyone who is a member of the group shares the same characteristics. It resembles Cushman and Kincaid's (1987) argument of how people from the "East" have been clumped together as those who come from China, Japan, and Korea, even though the "East" can cover a wide range of geographical locales.

While some ITAs are not familiar with U.S. slang, others have learned it while attending school in their home country. For example, ITAs who come from U.S. colonized countries such as the Philippines, are likely to be familiar with slang expressions spoken by U.S. American students. Like those who were born and raised in the Philippines, I grew up speaking American English slang as part of the daily talk when conversing in English. It is therefore important to not jump to conclusions that all ITAs will have difficulty understanding American English slang. Additionally, considering the globalization of the U.S. media in different parts of the world, many ITAs have also been exposed to American slang. In fact, Shome and Hegde (2002) argue that "events and developments in far-away distant places can have an impact on local happenings and events …" (p. 174). Because of globalization, it is possible for the U.S. media to have a great influence on others' communication patterns, such as the use of American slang.

ITAs as Non-U.S. Americans

The *Daily Egyptian's* featured article on ITA training and two letters to the editor also communicated ethnocentrism through the construction of the ITA identity as non-U.S. Americans. Unfortunately, the problem is that the U.S. American identity is often assumed as a White American. In fact, Nakayama and Krizek (1995) state that whiteness is often confused with nationality. Therefore, whiteness is recentered within the understanding of what U.S. American means. For instance, in Nakayama and Krizek's (1995) study, one white respondent they interviewed said, "A lot of times when people think of American, I bet you they probably think of white …" (p. 300). As in Nakayama and Krizek's (1995) study, many U.S. Americans consider people of color, such as those who are ITAs, as non-U.S. Americans. Consequently, I was not surprised to read the letters to the editor that emphasized ITAs as foreigners.

For instance, the SIUC alumnus who wrote a letter to the editor opposed a formal intercultural training program for undergraduate students: "You can't honestly expect the student population to add a seminar or course on communicating with international faculty and ITAs … in order to accommodate the 40 or so TA's/Professors who came to THIS country." Marking ITAs as non-U.S. Americans, the SIUC alumnus expected ITAs to assimilate to the U.S. American culture and not the other way around, in which students should learn how to communicate effectively with their ITAs. The latter statement also communicated the alumnus' nationalistic attitude by capitalizing the word "THIS" which preceded "country;" that linguistic act placed hierarchical importance to the U.S. as a nation-state that must be protected. In so many ways, the alumnus' letter was personal to me. Many years ago when I taught a public-speaking class, I had a student who seemed to be curious about my national identity. He asked me about my nationality and how long I have lived in the United States. Even though my student's question made me uncomfortable, I answered politely to him: "I'm ethnically Chinese, but I was born and raised in the Philippines, so my nationality is Filipino. And I have been living in U.S. for ten years now." He then quickly asked, "So, do you speak Tagalog fluently?" "Of course," I answered with a fake smile on my face. I felt that my student's questions were related to issues of authenticity, points of origin, longevity, and cultural performance which would further mark me as "the Other." I answered his questions, but I "was not … a free subject of thought or action" in the moment of the engagement (Cazden, 1988, p. 3).

To me, like the alumnus' letter, my student's public questioning of my national identity in the classroom served as evidence that I did not belong in the U.S. classroom—much less in the U.S. as a national locality—because of my foreignness as an ITA. As a former ITA, I could not sit still with the idea that many U.S. Americans continue to consider ITAs as non-Americans. For instance, in his letter to the editor, the alumnus said, "I do give credit to the people who come to the U.S., work hard, pay taxes, call themselves Americans, and try to make a better life for themselves and their families." He went on to say, "Without getting too wrapped up in the 'I'm proud to be American' mantra, I think that the responsibility lies with those who come to OUR country to better themselves in the English language." With such statements, the alumnus engaged in the "us vs. them" mentality in which "us" represents those who are "real" U.S. Americans and "them" as foreigners (in this case, ITAs). The alumnus' construction of who the real U.S. Americans are also emphasized that they must be able and willing to assimilate. He believed that ITAs, international faculty, and immigrants in general should assimilate and learn English in "OUR country." However, whose "country" are we talking about?

It seems to me, at least according to the alumnus, that the U.S. is a country that only speaks English. The alumnus' nationalistic mantra is like what Hytten and Warren (2003) talk about when white students engage in the discourse of connections, which is "premised on the belief that at the most fundamental level, we all share some core human experience" (p. 71). In a way, the alumnus advocated uniformity for those who want to be in the U.S., which ignores people's diverse experiences. Since the U.S. has often been dubbed as "the nation of immigrants," it is frightening that the alumnus advocated an English-only nation that ultimately privileges White and monolingual (English-speaking) Americans.

Like the alumnus, the undergraduate student also proposed the need for ITAs to assimilate by learning how to speak English with a standard U.S. American accent because this is the "dominant" language that is spoken and valued in the U.S. The undergraduate student stated the following: "This is America … If you choose to be here then you should make an attempt to learn the [English] language." She then compared Germany, a somewhat homogenous country, to the U.S.: "I would not go to Germany and expect everyone to cater to me and learn English." The undergraduate student did not realize her privilege knowing how to speak English fluently can certainly benefit her in many European countries such as Germany, where English is also spoken ("Languages of Germany," 2007). More importantly, considering that the U.S. is a culturally diverse and multilingual nation, the undergraduate student's point reinforced that ITAs' foreignness is to blame for the incomprehensibility that exists between ITAs and their students.

Moreover, the undergraduate student continued to construct the ITA identity as foreign because she believed that ITAs do not speak the "dominant language." She concluded her letter by asking the following question: "If I can speak the dominant language of this country, why should I have to learn another to understand an ITA?" The undergraduate student used the word "dominant language" as a form of rhetoric to emphasize a particular way of speaking that must be privileged over other languages and dialects. By saying that she speaks a "dominant language" and that there is no need for her to learn another language, the undergraduate student suggested that the "dominant language" spoken in the U.S., which is also spoken by ITAs, is superior to other languages that ITAs speak. In some ways, she marked ITAs as non-U.S. Americans for assuming that they do not speak English and pointing out that they do not belong in the U.S. for speaking another language. The undergraduate student's rhetorical strategy of imposing the "dominant language" to ITAs is like what Anzaldua (1999) talks about when her Anglo teacher told her to speak (American) English: "If you want to be American, speak 'American.' If you don't like it, go back to Mexico where you belong" (p. 75). Anzaldua's academic experience shows the similarity of what the undergraduate student proposes: a hegemonic discourse that requires and expects everyone to speak English as the "right way" of speaking.

Because the ITA identity is constructed as foreign for having a speech deficiency, many students blame ITAs for their poor grades. In fact, "nearly three out of five … attributed a poor grade in at least one class to the poor communication skills of an international instructor" (Rubin, 2002, pp. 127–128). For example, the undergraduate student blamed an ITA for dropping a math class because she could not understand her ITAs: "I tried and tried but still did not understand a word out of their mouth." In another part of her letter, the undergraduate student continued to perform whiteness by ridiculing another ITA she has encountered through tutoring, which emphasized the widespread nature of the problem. She certainly wanted to make a point that ITAs should not be around to teach, due to their inability to become comprehensible speakers.

The alumnus also blamed ITAs and international professors for his poor grade: "I received a 'C' grade in this class [Math 113]. Why? Because I couldn't understand the professors, not because I goofed off in the class." The problem with the alumnus' argument is that any "good" student who does not "goof off" should not be getting a "C" in a class. However, there are many factors that could have contributed to an "average" course grade: low grades on midterm and final exams, student's lack of material comprehension, student's inability to take good notes, and so on. Therefore, blaming the ITA solely for one's undesirable grade in a class is fallacious.

Response to Whiteness Discourses

As a response to whiteness discourses, Ernst and two ITAs from SIUC's Psychology Department wrote columns that appeared in the *Daily Egyptian*. Since many undergraduate students tend to complain that ITAs do not deserve to be in the classroom because of their perceived speech deficiency, Ernst (2007) made an effort to prove that ITAs do not get into the classroom to teach without prior screening. Ernst made the case that every ITA takes an oral proficiency test, and that ITAs do speak English. It is SIUC's practice to interview each potential international student TA to assure that they have oral proficiency in English before they are given a teaching appointment. The interview team consists of a three-person committee from the Center for English as a Second Language (CESL). This process should assure students that ITAs are screened before an appointment is made.

More importantly, Ernst (2007) made a point that "not all students of English will—or physically can—achieve native-like fluency … Language is fluid. Language is dynamic. Most significantly, language is difficult … Even in the U.S. there are differences in pronunciation. We learn to adjust to them" (p. 6). In essence, Ernst questioned the authenticity of the English language as if everyone should adhere to the standard White American speech. In fact, similar to speech, Akindes (2006) confirms Ernst's point about the instability of culture: "There was no static, monolithic, pure culture that … were expected to maintain, perpetuate, and/or reproduce … because culture is dynamic and constructed …" (p. 333). What Akindes said emphasizes that no culture (including its language) is pure in which there is only one way of doing and speaking; therefore, ITAs should not be expected to reach some unattainable standard in their oral communication.

The ITAs who wrote a column also expressed their concern for the recent ethnocentric letters that "seem to reveal there may be resentment and prejudice from some U.S. students on campus towards ITAs." Unfortunately, it is not unusual for some ITAs to become targets of inappropriate and/or disrespectful responses from students. For instance, student misbehavior, such as "derisive laughter, disrespectful gestures like throwing hands in the air, disrespectful comments …" are frequently performed in the classroom (Fitch & Morgan, 2003, p. 302). Fortunately, I have not had students in the classroom making racist or inappropriate comments to me. Perhaps I did not necessarily fit the typical international student identity, as my linguistic and cultural ways are somewhat Americanized. In other words, I performed the liminality of my international student identity in ways that I can mask my Asianness and show my Americanness in the classroom.

Because many ITAs continue to be perceived negatively in the classroom, the ITAs who wrote a column wanted to address the fact that ITAs work very hard and spend considerable time preparing for their class lectures. Despite ITAs' hard work and expertise in the subject areas they teach, many U.S. American students still perceive their ITAs as not fluent in English. Unfortunately, many U.S. Americans do not realize that many

ITAs come from nations that speak English with different variations from the one that is used in the U.S. In essence, these ITAs speak what has been known as "world Englishes" (Rubin, 2002, p. 129).

Moreover, in regards to accents, many U.S. American students cannot distinguish between accents from different nationalities, supporting the notion that everyone has a "threshold of foreignness" (Rubin, 2002, pp. 132–133). So, why do U.S. American undergraduate students continue to have distorted perceptions of ITAs? Rubin (2002) theorizes that many of them "have heard of college folklore conveying horror stories about 'foreign' teachers, and this creates high levels of anxiety," which prevents students from listening accurately to their ITAs' speech patterns (pp. 133–134). Many students perceive "foreign" teachers to be just that—"foreign." Teachers who are marked physically as "foreign"—nonwhite and those who speak with a non-U.S. American accent—are typically perceived to have difficulty communicating clearly with their students because the power of whiteness affects how non-white teachers' bodies are positioned in the classroom. Shome (1999) claims that U.S. anti-immigrant sentiments mark her body as a "nonwhite 'foreign' body, which is less desirable than a white body" (pp. 125–126). Shome's experience may therefore suggest that many students have already made up their mind not to listen to "foreign" teachers as soon as they walk into the classroom.

The point made in my letter to the editor that the language barrier is a "two-way street" is supported by Ernst (2007) where she states: "This is not a dichotomous situation. It is not about the undergraduates learning to listen, nor is it about ITAs learning to speak English. It is about both" (p. 6). Ernst pointed out that it should not be an "us against them" debate, but rather about reaching a compromise on the part of both parties. Unfortunately, it is too often the position of U.S. Americans and U.S. American students that the Other should do whatever it takes to assimilate, while U.S. Americans in general should not have to make any adjustments. According to Supriya (1999), "The construction of identity" of the Other can be understood in two interrelated practices (p. 131). First, Surpriya (1999) points out that the construction of identity reinforces the performance of patriarchal and colonial power. Therefore, it is not surprising that those who belong to the dominant group (i.e., White Americans) have the power to impose assimilation strategies to those who are marginalized. Second, Supriya (1999) states that the construction of identity is a trope for performances in which women and the colonized position themselves within the social order discursively and materially. With ITAs being subjected to speak and sound like White Americans, they are consequently expected to conform to U.S. American academic norms of what is "acceptable" and/or "appropriate" speech.

However, the ITAs who wrote a column that appeared in the *Daily Egyptian* argued that every person or group speaks with an accent, a particular intonation, enunciation, and pronunciation. No matter where we live—in the Midwest, California, or China—everyone grew up with accented speech. While some accents, such as Australian, British, and French, tend to be perceived favorably, Asian accents are often considered "foreign." In fact, students who were surveyed associated "foreign" accent to someone who has an Asian face after listening to an "accented" speech (Rubin, 2002). Because "accented" speech has typically been equated to an Asian face, many Asian teachers and ITAs have often been marked as incomprehensible, which leads to the assumption that they must assimilate in order to sound more "American"; therefore, the ITAs recommended that students train their ears in order to adjust to the ITAs' speech without dismissing their credibility altogether.

The ITAs who wrote a column continued to discuss why ethnocentric discourses that marked ITAs as non-U.S. Americans were evident in the conversations that emerged in the *Daily Egyptian*. For instance, they problematized the tendency to compare ITAs to U.S. TAs, which continues to categorize ITAs as Other. They stated that ITAs have "unique teaching challenges … on top of the challenges that are commonly shared by all teaching assistants." Therefore, they wanted to have a conversation in the *Daily Egyptian* by highlighting that ITAs should not be compared to U.S. TAs because their experiences are different and unique from their U.S. American colleagues. In some ways, their previous point mirrors Scheurich's (1993) recommendation of facilitating a white discourse on white racism within the academy, which is "to begin to understand and make conscious, especially within our intellectual work, the fact that in our society all people are racialized persons, that is, all people are socially influenced in significant ways by their membership in a racial group" (p. 9). Scheurich adds that Whites need to acknowledge their status and how that affects their thinking, behaviors, attitudes, and decisions from micro to macro level. By not acknowledging their privileges, White Americans and others who are in a privileged position cannot understand why ITAs should not be held accountable to the norms of the U.S. American classroom that values Eurocentric ideologies.

Due to ethnocentric discourses that marked ITAs as having a speech deficiency and non-U.S. Americans, the ITAs who wrote a column pointed out that it is "invalid for U.S. students to attribute failing a class, getting a bad grade in a class, or having to drop a class solely because of the English spoken by their ITA." After all, they explained that if ITAs have to get used to the speech of U.S. American professors and students, why shouldn't U.S. American students do the same? In the end, the ITA columnists proposed that "a mutual collaboration between ITAs and U.S. students" is needed to "bring a positive classroom learning experience from which both groups can benefit."

Conclusion

There is no doubt that ITAs play a major role in academia. It is safe to assume that without ITAs, colleges and universities in the United States would not have a diversified teaching staff and faculty. Students would also miss out on the type of meaningful intercultural educational experience that they need in order to successfully navigate a multicultural society. Unfortunately, whiteness plays a role that prevents us from having a classroom space where ITAs are valued for who they are and what they can offer to our students. As can be seen in this essay, whiteness is communicated through different pieces published in the *Daily Egyptian* by using ethnocentrism as a rhetorical strategy that mark ITAs as having a speech deficiency and as non-U.S. American.

When "Course helps TAs" was published, I decided to write a letter to the *Daily Egyptian* mainly to address the so-called "ITA problem" more so than the ITA training program at SIUC. In particular, I wanted to comment on how unfortunate it is for ITAs to always negotiate their ITA identity "in order to sound 'American' for students who are not willing to make the same effort to do whatever it takes to break communication barriers" (Hao, 2007, p. 7). In the end, I proposed that it should be a two-way street where both ITAs and students work to overcome or eliminate communication barriers that exist between them. If the ITA lacks English proficiency, s/he has the responsibility to use the resources of the training program in order to become proficient. On the other hand, many U.S. American students are monolingual; therefore, they also have the responsibility to "train" themselves to learn another culture and listen more carefully and effectively.

I knew that my letter would promote dialogue from many sides (pro-ITA, against ITA, and somewhere in between); however, I was surprised to see the magnitude of responses to my letter. At first, I did not know how to react to the undergraduate student's anti-ITA remarks. I was not sure whether or not I should write back to let her know that she had misinterpreted me. In the end, I decided not to respond to the student, which turned out to be a good decision since the dialogue continued with other participants within the SIUC community.

A day after the undergraduate student's letter was printed, another "angry letter" was directed toward me and other ITAs. After looking at the title of the letter ("What Country Are We in?"), I paused and then read it meticulously. I could not believe that I got through this "angry letter" without tearing it apart. I suppose it was because I found a column on the next page that finally understood what I was feeling as an ITA. Ernst (2007) wrote a beautiful and insightful letter that reminded U.S. American students that they are lucky to have met ITAs. In addition, I was happy to hear that Ernst agreed with me that both ITAs and students need to work together in order to alleviate communication problems that may exist in the classroom.

Several days later, I read another well-written column by ITAs from the Psychology Department at SIUC. Their letter captivated me in so many ways that words could not express. There were points they raised that I wished I could have said to U.S. American students who may have negative perceptions of ITAs. The ITAs who wrote the column expressed my sentiments precisely. The two ITAs' column spoke to me on a personal level, especially when they clearly pointed out that they and other ITAs deserve some respect. After reading their column, I smiled with joy. The joy was in part because two other ITAs joined me in this conversation. At the end of the day, I was glad that I made the decision to write a letter to the editor. I have no regrets, especially if it means that my actions helped to give two ITAs the courage to step forward to speak their mind and shed some insights as to why students and others should not be too quick to make negative assumptions and categorize ITAs as Other. Like other teachers, most ITAs are competent and skilled to teach.

I hope the dialogues that were generated in the *Daily Egyptian* will not stop; they should continue in other places that would foster an understanding of where ITAs and U.S. American students are coming from in terms of linguistic and cultural differences. My intention in writing about the conversations surrounding how ITAs are perceived in the academy was not to further create an "us vs. them" mentality, but rather to point out why the "ITA problem" existed in the first place and what must be done to break communication barriers between them. I support Rubin's (2002) recommendation that U.S. American students should look at the merits of ITAs rather than their expectations of what ITAs should be. As Rubin (2002) says, "We must all acknowledge and explore our stereotypes and then figure out how to deal with those stereotypes so that we can treat people in an equitable fashion, according to their merits rather than according to our expectations" (p. 134).

Perhaps successful intercultural communication can only occur when both parties make efforts to accommodate each other. To accomplish this, ITAs and other teachers may also need to take the initiative to invite their students to engage in dialogue on this issue. In my own classrooms, for example, I distributed all of the articles, letters, and columns published in the *Daily Egyptian* for students to read. These assigned readings were used as a way to supplement discussions on verbal, nonverbal, and/or intercultural communication, specifically exploring issues of racial, ethnic, cultural, and linguistic differences. Even though discussions became heated at times, my students and I had the opportunity to at least talk about their perceptions of ITAs and some ways to break communication barriers. As Giroux (1997) states, it is necessary to engage in "color-talk" by "naming culture, race, and racism as significant dimensions of social experience, [which] provides us with tools for understanding how race works in a racialized society" (p. 144). Engaging in "colortalk" allows white undergraduate students in particular to realize that ITAs should not be compared to U.S. TAs because their experiences are not alike. Giroux (1997) also states that it is important to position whiteness within a notion of cultural citizenship, which leads to the affirmation of difference politically, culturally, and socially; this way, white students can see their own whiteness as a racial identity and its relationship with their citizenship.

There are certainly many ways to dismantle whiteness and try to de-center it. I have only provided one example here. Performances of whiteness in the academy continue to exist, because both white and non-white individuals participate in a system that values whiteness as the norm. In order to counter this behavior, we must begin to question and challenge performances of whiteness in the classroom and beyond.

DISCUSSION QUESTIONS

1. Hao's analysis of *Daily Egyptian* articles and letters suggested that some writers identified two negative characteristics of international teaching assistants (ITAs). What are those two characteristics? How does Hao argue against the validity of these characteristics?

2. What is whiteness? Do you see examples of whiteness in your community or on your campus?

3. How often are intercultural or interracial issues covered in your campus or local media outlets? Do you see evidence of constructive dialogue in these media?

4. Can non-white persons possess a whiteness mentality? What would explain this situation, if it exists?

References

Akindes, F. Y. (2006). Braiding lives: Raising African Pacific Asian children in-between homes. In W. Leeds-Hurwitz (Ed.), *From generation to generation: Maintaining cultural identity over time* (pp. 319–334). Cresskill, NJ: Hampton Press.

Anzaldua, G. (1999). How to tame a wild tongue. In G. Anzaldua (Ed.), *Borderlands/La frontera: The new Mestiza* (2nd ed.) (pp. 75–86). San Francisco: Aunt Lute Books.

Cazden, C. B. (1988). *Classroom discourse: The language of teaching and learning.* Portsmouth: Heinemann Educational Books.

Cushman, D. P., & Kincaid, D. L. (1987). Introduction and initial insights. In D. L. Kincaid (Ed.), *Communication theory: Eastern and western perspectives* (pp. 1–9). San Diego: Academic Press.

Ernst, C. (2007, February 22). International TAs and students should compromise. *Daily Egyptian*, p. 6.

Fitch, F., & Morgan, S. E. (2003). Not a lick of English: Constructing the ITA identity through student narratives. *Communication Education, 52,* 297–310.

Giles, H., & St. Clair, R. N. (1979). *Language and Social Psychology.* Baltimore: University Park Press.

Giroux, H. A. (1997). *Channel surfing: Race talk and the destruction of today's youth.* New York: St. Martin's Press.

Gravois, J. (2005, April 8). Teach impediment: When the student can't understand the instructor, who is to blame? *The Chronicle of Higher Education*, pp. A10–A12.

Hao, R. N. (2007, February 20). Language barrier a two-way street [Letter to the editor]. *Daily Egyptian*, p. 7.

Hytten, K., & Warren, J. (2003). Engaging whiteness: How racial power gets reified in education. *Qualitative Studies in Education, 16,* 65–89.

Johnson, A. G. (2006). *Privilege, power, and difference* (2nd ed.). Boston: McGraw-Hill.

Languages of Germany. (n.d.). Retrieved April 16, 2007, from http://www.ethnologue.com/show_country.asp?name=Germany

Martin, J. N., & Nakayama, T. K. (2005). *Experiencing intercultural communication* (2nd ed.). Boston: McGraw-Hill.

Moon, D. (1999). White enculturation and bourgeois ideology: The discursive production of "good (white) girls." In T. K. Nakayama & J. N. Martin (Eds.), *Whiteness: The communication of social identity* (pp. 177–197). Thousand Oaks, CA: Sage.

Nakayama, T. K., & Krizek, R. L. (1995). Whiteness: A strategic rhetoric. *Quarterly Journal of Speech, 81,* 291–309.

Rendleman, R. (2007, January 26). Course helps TAs, students understand each other. *Daily Egyptian*, p. 3.

Rubin, D. L. (2002). Help! My professor (or doctor or boss) doesn't talk English. In J. N. Martin, T. K. Nakayama, & L. A. Flores (Eds.), *Readings in intercultural communication* (2nd ed.) (pp. 127–137). Boston: McGraw-Hill.

Said, E. W. (1978). *Orientalism*. New York: Pantheon.

Scheurich, J. J. (1993). Toward a white discourse on white racism. *Educational Researcher, 22*, 5–10.

Shome, R. (1999). Whiteness and the politics of location. In T. K. Nakayama & J. N. Martin (Eds.), *Whiteness: The communication of social identity* (pp. 107–128). Thousand Oaks, CA: Sage.

Shome, R., & Hegde, R. S. (2002). Culture, communication, and the challenge of globalization. *Critical Studies in Media Communication, 19*, 172–189.

Supriya, K. E. (1999). White difference: Cultural constructions of white identity. In T. K. Nakayama & J. N. Martin (Eds.), *Whiteness: The communication of social identity* (pp. 129–148). Thousand Oaks, CA: Sage.

Ting-Toomey, S. (2004). Translating conflict face-negotiation theory into practice. In D. Landis, et al. (Eds.), *Handbook of intercultural training* (3rd ed.) (pp. 217–248). Thousand Oaks, CA: Sage, 2004.

Warren, J. T. (2001). Doing whiteness: On the performative dimensions of race in the classroom. *Communication Education, 50*, 91–108.

Yook, E. L., & Albert, R. D. (1999). Perceptions of international teaching assistants: The interrelatedness of intercultural training, cognition, and emotion. *Communication Education, 48*, 1–17.

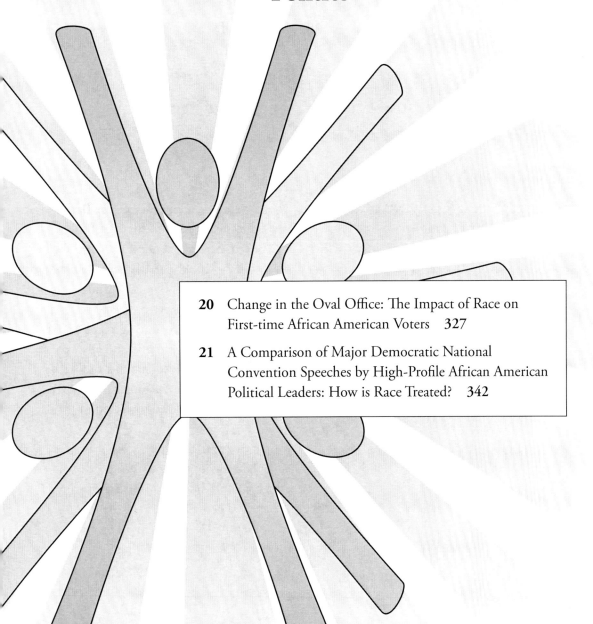

Context V

Politics

327

20

Change in the Oval Office: The Impact of Race on First-time African American Voters

Vanessa G. Cunningham-Engram

Abstract

Early CNN polls indicated that some voters were not going to vote for Barack Obama as president of the United States expressly because of his race (2008), despite his education and qualifications. But having been nominated by the Democratic Party at the National Convention in 2008, for the first time in American history an African American candidate, Senator Barack Obama, was on the ballot to become president of the United States of America. Many college and university students of all races joined Barack Obama's campaign and lined up to cast their vote for him as their choice presidential candidate. Students were able to take part in the presidential race because they had media access and freedom to communicate via various technological and print mediums. Founded on the access theory, which espouses Abbot Joseph (A. J.) Liebling's notion that "Freedom of the Press is guaranteed only to those who own one!" (1960, p. 109), this research discloses how access to information, particularly the use of mobile phones, the Internet, and cable television, had an impact on the race to the White House on first-time African American voters who are university students. This study also reveals the significance of Barack Obama's race as the first African American president of the United States. Students surveyed attend a prominent predominantly black university in a battleground state in the south.

KEY TERMS: African American, president, change, race, university, first-time voters, access theory

Introduction

Having been nominated by the Democratic Party at the National Convention in 2008, for the first time in American history an African American candidate, Senator Barack Obama, was on the ballot to become president of the United States of America. Early CNN polls (2008) showed that some voters were not going to vote for Barack Obama as president expressly because of his race, despite his education and qualifications. Many college students of all races throughout the United States, however, joined Barack Obama's campaign and lined up to cast their vote for him as their choice presidential candidate because they had media access, and freedom to communicate via various technological and print mediums, and he won.

Some attribute Barack Obama's victory to the need for "change" in the White House because the economy is in bad shape and we are in a recession. Author, pollster, and political consultant Frank Luntz (2008) said:

> Obama overcame incredible odds because he understood, long before John McCain, Hillary Clinton, and almost everyone else, that Americans wanted 'change' above all else and were fully prepared to accept inexperience and a lack of details in return for a genuine break with the past.

Others attribute the triumph to the media. For example, in *A Slobbering Love Affair*, bestselling author Bernard Goldberg said, "The media's crush on Barack Obama began even before his presidential campaign. There was just something about the guy—his personal charisma, his liberalism, and, of course, the fact that he is black—that made him irresistible to mainstream journalists" (Goldberg, 2009, p. 4).

Whether some believe Barack Obama won because change was needed or because they believe the media influenced voters, it is clear from this study that both played a significant role in the outcome, particularly based on the access theory. Hence, this study will show how technology overall, and specifically the "news media," have become a key messenger of our increasingly globalized world (Zhong, 2008, p. 111), providing access to information and influencing decision-making.

Access Theory

A. J. Liebling, a renowned American journalist for the *New Yorker*, wrote "freedom of the press belongs to the man who owns one" (Diamond, 1991, p. 203). As it relates to the access theory:

> What the iconoclast meant was that a constitutional guarantee of freedom of expression had little meaning if a citizen did not have the economic means to exercise this right. Owners of magazines, newspapers, and broadcasting stations could take advantage of the promises of the First Amendment, whereas the average person lacked this ability. Put differently, access to the metaphorical marketplace of ideas is not equal for all, but is skewed in favor of those with the most economic resources. What Liebling wrote is true today (Pember & Calvert, 2008, p. 46).

However, long before the occurrence of a booming technological transformation gave access to millions to exercise their speech freedoms, a United States patent was granted to Alexander Graham Bell on March 7, 1876, for new and useful improvements in telegraphy to transmit speech sounds over electric wires (*The Telephone Cases*, 1888). This patent is often called the most valuable patent ever issued because the telephone was thereby invented. Notwithstanding, for decades after the invention, the telephone remained an unobtainable and unaffordable instrument for some households, for economic or geographical reasons.

After the telephone, the radio became the next primary source of electronic communication. The first permanent public service radio stations in the United States were established by the Federal Telegraph Company, between San Francisco and Los Angeles in 1911 (Marriott, 1917, p. 179). Again, many did not have access to information disseminated by the airwaves in their homes, for the same reasons they did not have a telephone. According to the Federal Communications Commission (FCC, n.d.), it was not until April 9, 1927, that the first long-distance television broadcast ever took place [featuring then Secretary of Commerce Herbert Hoover (2009)].

People kept informed by word of mouth and newspapers before the telephone, radio, and television. Then computers, mobile phones, and wireless access arrived decades later; but many homes were not wired to carry electronic communications. Over time, however, electronic media became more affordable and accessible. Millions of people began to acquire computers and laptops in their homes; but numerous other households had neither a computer nor Internet access. In North Carolina, for example, a March 2009 report on the digital divide disclosed that nearly 5 million residents in rural areas still did not have high-speed Internet; and a July 2007 study of the same area showed that telephone and cable companies refused to provide service to people living in remote rural areas (See www.internetforeveryone.org). Despite the lack of Internet access in their homes to follow the 2008 presidential campaign, thousands of residents in the battleground state of North Carolina made their way to the polls to cast their ballot in a record turnout of registered voters (as seen in Table 1).

TABLE 1. Statistics for Presidential Election—North Carolina

Year	Voting Age Population	Turnout	Registered Voters	% Turnout Registered Voters
2000	6,085,266	3,015,964	5,122,123	59%
2004	6,483,010	3,551,675	5,526,981	64%
2008	7,148,000	4,354,052	6,262,566	70%

Source: North Carolina State Board of Elections (2009)

What made this race so significant is that North Carolina had what "Obama was looking for: an under-registered African-American population, a slew of new voters who were nonnative North Carolinians, and a fairly youthful population. … [which] went overboard in its attempt to register new voters" (Todd & Gawiser, 2009, p. 84). "The Obama coalition was made up of African-Americans, college-educated whites, and young voters" (p. 13) who worked hard for the campaign and made sure voters had access to information and to the polls.

The use of cell phones and the Internet has made it easy for millions of Americans to communicate with others around the world and that is exactly what happened during the Obama campaign. People were transmitting messages on Facebook.com and MySpace.com, blogging, tweeting, and viewing video messages on YouTube.com. They were watching local and cable television day and night, gathering information about their candidate, sending and receiving e-mail messages on their wireless networks, many from the Obama campaign (www.barackobama.com), and they were texting on their cell phones, occasionally receiving messages from the Obama campaign.

Today, despite a weak economy, not only do countless Americans have some means of access to television, most have cable television; not only do they have some mode of access to a telephone, many have cell phones. Most also have access to the Internet, whether personally, through their job, library, or school. According to the FCC, high-speed Internet connections were available to 83 percent of the households to whom local telephone service could be provided, and high-speed cable modem service was available to 96 percent of the households to whom cable system operators could provide cable TV service. High-speed Internet lines increased by 32 percent to 132.8 million from the prior year (79.1 million of the total primarily serves residential end users). According to the data, there are no Zip Codes where there is not at least one such connection. And "in just 26 years since its invention, half of the world's population—3.3 billion people—now have a cell phone," said FCC Commissioner Robert M. McDowell (2008).

The access theory emphasizes the power of the press to reach an intended audience and those who have a means to acquire and disseminate information. As stated by Thomas L. Tedford and Dale A. Herbeck (2005):

> As it turns out, most gates to the marketplace of ideas are privately owned and operated—and the gates are operated for a profit, so would-be communicators must often pay extremely high prices to the gatekeeper. Finally those who own the gates can deny entrance to whomever they wish, and, for a variety of reasons, do exactly that. (p. 391)

Access to information played an important role in the race to the White House because first-time African American voters who were in past times denied access to gates or did not have access to gatekeepers were now using technological resources available to them to pass along information to others who had never voted before or had access to information about voting. Yes, while in times past some American citizens may not have been as educated as others about candidates running for office because they lacked access to information, this time was different. This time voters were relatively knowledgeable about the contenders, because more information was readily available. As Justice William H. Brennan elucidated in *New York Times v. Sullivan* (1964, p. 270) "debate on public issues should be uninhibited, robust, and wide-open"—and so it was. Communication was widespread with grassroots word-of-mouth efforts playing a significant part in the dissemination of information, but technology playing an even greater role than ever before. For example, African American voters increased their percentage of the electorate from 11 percent in 2004 to 13 percent in 2008 (Todd & Gawiser, 2009, p. 29).

Race to the White House

In working to accurately report and disseminate information swiftly via technological means, for the viewers, it was the longest media circus ever staged. Notwithstanding, local and cable broadcast networks announced increased viewership and record ratings. "After a year of explosive audience growth, the cable news channels head into 2009 buoyed by record ratings, a rare bright spot in what has otherwise been a gloomy media season," says *Los Angeles Times* staff writer Matea Gold (2008). "This was an emotionally wrenching election, and an awful lot of viewers who are not normal news viewers tuned in to see who would win," said CNN/U.S. President Jon Klein (Gold, 2008).

Viewers tuned in particularly to learn more about candidate Barack Obama (Wenger & MacManus, 2009). The cameras loved him and everything was newsworthy as it related to him directly or indirectly—whether it concerned his former pastor, Reverend Jeremiah A. Wright, Jr., whether he played basketball that day, or had holes in the bottom of his shoes. According to Bernard Goldberg, the media gave Barack Obama favorable coverage and took "Hillary Clinton, into the back room and beat her with a rubber hose [because it] was more important … that America get its first black president than its first woman president" (p. 4). Some tended to turn a deaf ear to the race issue, denying it had any relevance at all on voters. Nevertheless, polls everywhere spoke to the contrary. "[S]omewhere between 10 and 30 percent of voters thought that race would be an important factor in the election. Some of these were black voters who were likely to vote for Obama, and some were white" (Thomas & *Newsweek*, 2009, p. 57). Obama and his team of advisers made a decision to curtail the race factor so that it would not negatively affect the outcome of his race to the Oval Office. "So Obama was to become the world's most famous black man not by denying his biracial identity but by embracing parts of it selectively" (Ifill, 2009, p. 54).

Racism, says Alana Lentin (2008), "has entered into culture and determined social interaction, thus having a direct effect on individuals' lives. ... There are those who argue that race is quite simply unimportant" (p. 88); but our actions speak otherwise, particularly in the race to the Oval Office. Gwen Ifill, long-time journalist, reports that along the campaign trail Obama walked a perilous tightrope attempting to reach out to some voters without alienating others by crafting his persona and his speeches to appeal to all listeners. It became clear early on, however, that this would be no color-blind campaign (2009, p. 55). So race did have a patent place in the race to the Oval Office— even to the point of some heated discussions among Democratic National Committee members such as Donna Brazile, who tried to remain neutral throughout the campaign. She discovered, however, that neutrality did not satisfy her old friends in the Clinton campaign—many who owed their success to the Clinton organization. As a result of not siding with Hillary Clinton, both Donna Brazile and South Carolina representative William Clyburn, Democrat, and the highest-ranking Black lawmaker in the House of Representatives, occasionally found themselves "on the receiving end of Bill Clinton tongue-lashings" (Ifill, 2009).

Still there was another high-ranking official many were waiting to hear from— former Secretary of State Colin Powell, a Republican. He had not announced whom he was backing until late in the race. Just two weeks before Election Day, on NBC's "Meet the Press" on October 19, 2008, retired four-star General Colin Powell announced his endorsement and support for Barack Obama, "declaring the senator from Illinois to be a 'transformational' figure who would 'electrify our country ... [and] the world'" (DeYoung, 2008). "At least one of his daughters was a supporter of Obama, while his son ... supported John McCain" (Ifill, 2009, p. 49).

While Colin Powell waited awhile to make up his mind or publicly announce his decision, the same was not true of Nobel Peace Prize winner Desmond Tutu. When Senator Obama was in South Africa to address the AIDS crisis in 2006, Desmond Tutu had already stated his position even prior to Obama casting his net and putting his hat in the race. In a professorial manner he said to Senator Obama, "You're going to be a very credible presidential candidate" (Mendell, 2007, p. 330).

Although Obama ran on the theme "Hope," CNN's Jack Cafferty (2009) said, "In the run-up to Barack Obama's inauguration, the expectations for this man went beyond hope and approached euphoria—a setup wired for major disappointment" (p. 253). With the votes now counted and Barack Obama the clear winner of the contest, it is clear that race was a factor in the presidential election, says Cafferty. "As the Obama administration gets into gear, after the celebration and euphoria about this nation's quantum leap forward in race relations, the racial repercussions of his win will become clearer" (p. 238).

Race, as difficult a subject as it is for some to discuss, had its place in the presidential campaign, and many voters said it influenced their vote. In fact, Todd and Gawiser (2009) said, "Twice as many African-American voters as white voters said the race of the candidate was important in their vote, just a little over one in five" (p. 41).

Survey Questions

Based on the numerous television, newspaper, magazine, telephone and Internet polls that were constructed, a high probability existed to evince race as a factor in the race to the White House, particularly among African Americans. To test this notion, the following questions were posed to participants:

1) Did the news media influence your decision to vote? Explain.

2) How did/do you feel about an African American running for president? Explain.

3) Did you believe it was possible for an African American to win the presidential race? Explain.

4) Should there be change in the Oval Office? Explain.

5) If any, what change do you recommend for the Oval Office and our country?

6) How does having President Barack Obama in the Oval Office influence, affect, impact, or change you?

7) How does having President Barack Obama in the Oval Office influence, affect, or impact our nation?

To answer these questions, 113 college students were surveyed. The sample consisted of students age 18 and over attending a predominantly black university in the south. Along with being college students, participants had to meet the following criteria: (1) they had to be a first-time voter in a presidential election; (2) they had to be at least 18 years of age but not more than 65 years of age; and (3) they had to be African American.

A survey containing 30 open and closed-ended questions was designed to gather information from college students voting for the first time in a presidential election. The goal was to discover their views concerning the impact of race as a social construct on the campaign and election of an African American president of the United States. The questions pertained to the demographics of the participant such as age, race, number of family members in household, and family income, as well as voting history (e.g. first time voters and family's tendency to vote, etc.). Participants were recruited by distributing surveys to students in a journalism department where students learn about mass media and its effects. Surveys were also made available campus-wide via a professional online resource. The survey could be accessed shortly after the presidential inauguration until early March 2009.

Participants were told that they were not required to answer every question. Of the students who filled out surveys, five students were not included in the study at all because they did not meet at least one of the four conditions stated in the methodology. Excluding the five unusable surveys, a total of 108 students started the survey and left some questions unanswered and 102 (94.4%) students completed the survey in its entirety. Of the 108 students meeting the criteria, 43 students filled out the survey online and 65 students filled out the paper version. All data were entered into the professional online service resource for analysis.

Findings

Major implications of this study evince that (1) the media played a major role in the outcome of the presidential race as students learned a lot about the candidates by viewing the debates and listening to the commentators report on the contenders; (2) students were eager to vote in this election because they were making history and voting for the first African American president; and (3) students felt it was time for a change in the Oval Office, and Barack Obama was the best change agent for the job. Following are summary responses to the survey questions posed.

1: Did the news media influence your decision to vote? Explain.

Of the students surveyed, 46 percent said the news media greatly influenced their decision to vote (and 30% of them said the media helped them to decide who to vote for) because of all the televised debates, commentary, and discussions about the candidates and their activities along the campaign trail. Fifty-two percent of the respondents said the decision was their own, while two percent (2%) said the question did not apply to them. One student journalist said, "Everything I knew about the candidates was information gathered from the media," while another student said, "I am aware of the media's power and am not affected. However, I do believe it affected numerous others." Still another student observed that "Without the news media I would not have known the different views of the different candidates."

2: How did/do you feel about an African American running for president? Explain.

In their responses, several participants felt it was an incredible dream that came true that many of their parents and older relatives never thought would happen in their life-time. They said they now feel optimistic, empowered, and inspired to accomplish their goals because of Barack Obama. One participant responded "It means so much to me that an African American was running for president. It also made me happy because it was an intelligent black man who had views that were fair." Another participant said, "I think it is liberating, especially for African Americans who were losing hope. For instance, people tell young, black urban boys that they can do anything, but I don't think they really believed that until now." Another participant commented that "It was a challenge at first, but he made people look pass the color of his skin and focus on the quality of his message"; and another remarked, "It's great to see how far black people have come from being slaves to being prominent leaders of the U.S."

3: Did you believe it was possible for an African American to win the presidential race? Explain.

Nearly every participant believed it was possible in their lifetime to have an African American president because they feel that America is a different America than it was; but many felt that he could win because of the economic condition of the country after the last eight years. One student said he believed Barack Obama could win the presidency after he saw "his journey and support from the media and public." Another student posited, "Honestly, I always thought in order for an African American to be president there must be a white woman president. I am glad I was wrong." One uncertain student said, "I truly can't say. I was once told as a child that there would never be a black president."

4: Should there be change in the Oval Office? Explain.

Nearly every participant said change was needed in the Oval Office and Barack Obama was the best change agent for the job. The participants viewed change as neces-sary, positive, and beneficial for the country. To the participants, change meant progress. One student said change was needed in the Oval Office "because some people in office haven't been exposed to the 'real' America where people struggle every day so they don't know the best changes to make."

Another student said, "Yes, there should be change, but people must come to the understanding that change does not occur overnight."

5: If any, what change do you recommend for the Oval Office and our country?

Here, students were given an opportunity to state the change(s) they felt were needed. In no particular order, their primary concerns and recommendations are: (1) lower college tuition; (2) lower health care and health care for all Americans; (4) economic equality; (5) focus on education; (6) transparency; (7) better capital management and lower taxes; (8) employment opportunities; (9) healthy environments; and (10) no war.

6: How does having President Barack Obama in the Oval Office influence, affect, impact, or change you?

One student said, "It makes me sad"; but the participant did not state a reason for the sadness. Other participants said they are now hopeful, proud, and inspired. Comments include the following statements: "It has changed me to be more positive and more active in my community and school work"; "It gives me hope for a better tomorrow"; "It makes me believe anything is possible with hard work and dedication"; "Having Obama as my president makes me feel like I'm finally a part of America. My voice is finally heard"; "I am more interested in politics. … Before I used to dread hearing about politics"; and "I finally feel like a true American."

7: How does having President Barack Obama in the Oval Office influence, affect, or impact our nation?

Participants had the following responses: (1) "It impacts our nation because he's bringing all colors, all genders, all political parties, and all types of people together 'under one nation and one God' as stated in the U.S. Pledge of Allegiance"; (2) "This will help our nation to do bigger and better things and hopefully make people see that it doesn't matter what race you are but what you can really do for the country"; (3) "It shows the nation that people should not be judged by the color of their skin, but by the content of their character"; (4) "People have been affected worldwide"; (5) "Every race sees that they can achieve greatness"; (6) "He's brought so many people together"; and (7) "He makes everyone believe in hope and change for the betterment of our country."

Discussion and Conclusion

"They said this day would never come!"
—Barack Obama's first words after winning the Iowa caucuses,
January 3, 2008.

This study shows how access to information, whether electronic or otherwise, makes a difference in behavior, as this was the case during the 2008 presidential campaign. Informed students literally knocked on the doors of neighbors, physically brought them a voter registration card to fill out (explained their rights to them) and then escorted them to their polling site. Prior to this motivation by the Obama campaign, college students were not involved at the grass roots level in voting and registering voters in droves. Until the Obama campaign integrated the use of technology, specifically cell phones and the Internet (including e-mail and social media such as Facebook and YouTube), as a major part of his political campaign strategy, students had little interest in participating in the process.

Access to information, however, brought about a change in motivation and organization of grass roots efforts. This was evident by the survey comments of previously non-registered voters who had reached the age of eligibility but had not bothered to register to vote until this race. Some reasons given were "because they didn't think their vote mattered" or "because they didn't think it would make a difference."

As this research shows, Barack Obama won the presidency largely due to an unprecedented level of support among young people and new voters—in this case, even in a battleground state in the south. "Obama was supported by those voters under 30 by an impressive 66 percent to 31 percent margin, much higher than in any previous election, as well as 68 percent of first-time voters" (Todd & Gawiser, 2009, p. 30). Clearly he was supported by student participants in this study. The Obama campaign did well among new voters, as one out of every ten were first-time voters. (p. 31). "Two-thirds of new voters were under 30, and one in five was black, almost twice the proportion of blacks among voters overall. ... Almost half were Democrats, and a third called themselves Independent" (p. 32). This research also reveals how Barack Obama's race had a major impact on how African American college students voted. It shows the significance of Barack Obama's race as the first African American president of the United States. Students seemed starved for a leader to look up to—someone who looked like them, someone they could identify with, who knew their history and their struggle. They seemed ready for something new—change in the Oval Office.

If Barack Obama did not have access to all of the media he did–in the way he did–we can assume he might not have achieved the victory. The power and ability to get information to voters made a big difference in the outcome of this race to the White House. In times past, only the privileged had access to the marketplace, venues and gates, but with the Internet, cell phones, and other technological resources currently available to the public, the 2008 presidential campaign was different. Voters who were previously denied or did not have access were informed and in turn informed others. Indeed, change has come.

DISCUSSION QUESTIONS

1. In your opinion, was this race to the Oval Office different from in past elections? If so, how?

2. Do you believe young people are now more politically astute as a result of the 2008 presidential campaign and election?

3. Do you believe media access in the 2008 presidential campaign has an impact on current student? political involvement?

4. Are young voters more empowered, inspired, and challenged to do greater exploits than they were prior to this race to the Oval Office? How so?

5. What else can young voters do to make sure there is access in their communities for people to have a voice and a say in democracy?

References

Cafferty, J. (2009). *Now or never: Getting down to the business of saving our American dream*. Hoboken, New Jersey: John Wiley & Sons.

CNN.com. (2008, September 22). Race could play big role in election, poll suggests. Retrieved June 14, 2009, from http://www.cnn.com/2008/POLITICS/09/22/race.politics/index.html

DeYoung, K. (2008, October 20). Obama endorsed by Colin Powell. *Washington Post*. Retrieved April 5, 2009, from http://www.washingtonpost.com/wp-dyn/content/article/2008/10/19/AR2008101900598_pf.html

Diamond, E. (1991). *The media show: The changing face of the news, 1985–1990*. Cambridge, MA: MIT Press.

Federal Communications Commission. (n.d.). *Visionary period, 1880's through 1920's*. Retrieved March 30, 2009, from http://www.fcc.gov/omd/history/tv/1880-1929.html

Federal Communications Commission. (2009). High-speed services for Internet access: Status as of June 30, 2008. Retrieved August 29, 2009 from http://www.fcc.gov/wcb/stats

Five days on the digital dirt road (n.d.). Retrieved August 29, 2009, from http://www.Internetforeveryone.org/americaoffline/nc/intro

Gold, M. (2008, December 31). Fox News, CNN and MSNBC see record ratings in 2008. *Los Angeles Times*. Retrieved April 5, 2009, from http://articles.latimes.com/2008/dec/31/entertainment/et-cable31

Goldberg, B. (2009). *A slobbering love affair: The true (and pathetic) story of the torrid romance between Barack Obama and the mainstream media*. Washington, D.C.: Regnery Publishing.

Ifill, G. (2009). *The Breakthrough: Politics and Race in the Age of Obama*. New York: Doubleday.

Lentin, A. (2008). *Racism: A beginner's guide*. Oxford, England: Oneworld Publications.

Liebling, A. J. (1960, May 14). *The wayward press: Do you belong in journalism? New Yorker*, 109.

Luntz, F. (2008, November 5). Barack Obama is president because he understood the need for change. *Telegraph*. Retrieved March 12, 2009, from http://www.telegraph.co.uk/news/worldnews/northamerica/usa/barackobama/3387373/Barack-Obama-is-president–because-he-understood-the-need-for-change-Frank-Luntz.html

Marriott, R. H. (1917). United States radio development. *Proceedings of the Institute of Radio Engineers*, 179–197. Retrieved March 30, 2009, from earlyradiohistory.us/1917 dev.htm

McDowell, R. M. (2008). *Quello communications law and policy symposium*. National Press Club. Washington, D.C. Retrieved August 29, 2009, from http://fjallfoss.fcc.gov/edocs_public/attachmatch/DOC-281772A1.txt

Mendell, D. (2007). *Obama: From promise to power.* New York: Amistad. *New York Times v. Sullivan,* 376 U.S. 254, 270 (1964).

North Carolina State Board of Elections. (2009). *Statistics for presidential election.* Raleigh: NC. Retrieved from http://www.sboe.state.nc.us/VoterLookup.aspx?Feature=voterinfo

Pember, D. R., & Calvert, C. (2008). *Mass media law* (16th ed.). New York: McGraw-Hill. *The Telephone Cases,* 126 U.S. 1, 6 (1888).

Tedford, T. L., & Herbert, D. A. (2005). *Freedom of speech in the United States.* State College, PA: Strata Publishing.

Thomas, E., & *Newsweek.* (2009). *A long time coming: The inspiring, combative 2008 campaign and the historic election of Barack Obama.* New York: Public Affairs.

Todd, C., & Gawiser, S. (2009). *How Barack Obama won: A state-by-state guide to the historic 2008 presidential election.* New York: Vintage Books.

Wenger, D., & MacManus, S. (2009, June). Watching history: TV coverage of the 2008 campaign. *Journalism Studies, 10*(3), 427–435.

Zhong, B. (2008). Thinking along the cultural line: A cross-cultural inquiry of ethical decision making among U.S. and Chinese journalism students. *Journalism & Mass Communication Educator, 63*(2), 111.

21

A Comparison of Major Democratic National Convention Speeches by High-Profile African American Political Leaders: How Is Race Treated?

Erin Brining Hammond

Abstract

This essay examines how race is treated by six African American speakers at Democratic National Conventions (DNC) over a 40-year span, and based on an analysis of the content of the speeches, whether or not the treatment of race has changed over time. The text of eight speeches delivered by six different speakers is explored: Fannie Lou Hamer, Barbara Jordan, Jesse Jackson, Al Sharpton, David Alston, and Barack Obama. Results indicated that both the historical context and individual priorities of the speaker proved to be important factors that influenced how these orators treated race overall, and the treatment of race in DNC speeches delivered by African American speakers has changed over time. For example, using race to describe a person or group of people was more prevalent in earlier speeches than it was in later presentations and mentions of race with regard to history increased after Hamer's 1964 address. Every address in this analysis that followed Hamer's, however, included mentions of race intended to unify.

KEY TERMS: Democratic National Convention speeches, African American speakers, content analysis, race

Introduction

As the first African American President of the United States, Barack Obama has been increasingly criticized by some members of the Black community for not identifying enough with African American experiences and concerns (Carter, 2007;

Longest race, 2007). Following in the footsteps of such dynamic and outspoken African American political leaders as Al Sharpton, Barbara Jordan, and Jesse Jackson, it is clear that Obama possesses their charisma. It is less apparent, however, whether he treats race in the same manner as African American political leaders who precede him.

In this study, I examine selected speeches delivered by African American political leaders across several meetings of the Democratic National Convention (DNC). Through content analysis, I analyze how the issue of race is treated by these speakers. I examine the treatment of race with regard to speaker, year, gender, and age. Also pertinent is the context in which the speeches were given.

African American Rhetoric

Understanding African American Rhetoric

Molefi Asante (1987) identifies four components of African rhetoric: frame of mind, context, linguistic code, and delivery. Frame of mind refers to the social, creative, and psychological influences of the speaker and audience, including rhythm and styling. Context deals with the social realities of the communication experience. Linguistic code involves lyrical quality, vocal artifact, and indirection, while delivery in African rhetoric generally involves audience participation (Borchers, 2006).

In addition to the ideas put forth by Asante, a model of Afrocentric rhetoric was proposed by Knowles-Borishade (1991). This model is based around enveloping an atmosphere of harmony and unity. The five components in the model are (1) nommo, (2) spiritual entities, (3) responders, (4) caller or chorus, and (5) spiritual harmony. The job of the first four components is to reach the fifth component, which is spiritual harmony.

First, nommo is defined as "the Word pregnant with value-meanings drawn from the African experience which, when uttered, give birth to unifying images that bind people together in an atmosphere of harmony and peace" (Knowles-Borishade, 1991, p. 495). Nommo refers to the vibrations caused by the words that are spoken, which relate spiritually to the audience and bring them closer to spiritual harmony. Next, in African rhetoric, invoking spiritual entities, whether God, angels, or even the dead, helps to create a more spiritual environment. Third, African rhetoric involves responders, or the audience. The audience is an integral part of the rhetorical event by either approving or rejecting the message. Knowles-Borishade (1991) notes, "call-and-response promotes levels of perfected social interaction through these verbal checks and balances as the event progresses" (p. 498).

The fourth component of African rhetoric includes the caller and the chorus. The caller is a speaker with high moral character and appropriate voice, movement, and articulation. The job of the chorus is to contribute to the caller's message. The final component of African rhetoric is spiritual harmony, which is the goal of the rhetorical event.

Research in African American Rhetoric

Prior research of African American rhetoric highlights the need for further research in this area (Goldzwig, 2006; Jackson, 2000; Kochman, 1981; McPhail, 2003; Sullivan, 1993). Some scholars note that African American rhetoric is misunderstood by many audiences. For instance, Jesse Jackson's 1988 DNC speech sparked extensive commentary. Sullivan (1993) notes, "Commentators questioned Jackson's ethical standards and charged that he was overly emotional, dishonest, and vague. ... Ultimately, negative responses to Jackson centered on his extraordinary powers as an oral communicator" (p. 4). Some of Jackson's powers as a communicator, however, are culture-specific. Many people and scholars equate aspects of culture-based signification with demagoguery, which is a speaking style that relies upon emotional, prejudicial, and irrational appeals in order to sway an audience (Goldzwig, 2006; Sullivan, 1993). Conducting more research in this area will help to challenge our frameworks for viewing what constitutes effective rhetoric. "Text, context, cultural contract, and norms for performance all play crucially interdependent roles in determining the quality, value, and ethicality of discursive practices" (Goldzwig, 2006, p. 472).

Previous Speech Analyses

A number of rhetorical analyses have been conducted on speeches by African American speakers at Democratic National Conventions. Analyses of Jesse Jackson's 1988 address to the DNC show that Jackson used rhythm, as well as patterns of African American signification, including set expressions or call response formulas, tall tales, and stories grounded in common sense throughout his speech (Sullivan, 1993; Wilson, 1996). Wilson (1996) also notes Jackson's use of "southern Baptist Black oratory" in the 1988 address. Hallmark (1992) compared Jackson's 1984 and 1988 addresses to the DNC, noting Jackson's use of analogy and imagery in both. The speeches were much different in approach, however. The 1984 speech was more epideictic; the 1988 speech was more deliberate. Epideictic or demonstrative speeches deal with the present and either praise or place blame, thus attempting to persuade the audience to accept certain values. Deliberative speeches, on the other hand, deal with the future and attempt to persuade the audience to accept or reject a certain policy (Borchers, 2006).

Atwater (2007) analyzed Obama's 2004 address, specifically focusing on Obama's "rhetoric of hope" (p. 121). In a fascinating analysis, Frank and McPhail (2005) separately examined Barack Obama's 2004 keynote address at the Democratic National Convention. While Frank, a White American, found Obama's speech to be one advancing racial unity and healing, McPhail, an African American, viewed the speech as being raceless. Frank saw unity, equality, and hope as the core values of the 2004 speech. At the same time, McPhail noted, "Obama's speech offers little hope for reconciling an America divided by racial difference and indifference" (p. 572).

Frank and McPhail (2005) also compared Obama's 2004 DNC speech with Al Sharpton's 2004 DNC speech. Frank believed Sharpton's speech failed to acknowledge that white audience members experienced suffering from their own personal traumas (p. 577). On the other hand, McPhail noted that "compared to Sharpton's speech, Obama's message ignored and obscured America's racial realities" (p. 572). Sharpton's speech cohered "more closely with the rhetorical practices and principles necessary for reconciliation" (p. 584). The authors note that the differences in their rhetorical criticism of the same speech are very telling examples that illustrate how persuasive both background and cultural influence are upon our perceptions of how a speaker treats race.

While speech analyses have been conducted on Democratic National Convention speeches, a content analysis on the treatment of race has yet to be conducted. In addition, the varying perspectives in the analyses presented illustrates the need for a broader look at the treatment of race in DNC speeches. The following research serves to provide that broader perspective.

Historical Relevance and Speaker Background

Because this analysis spans decades and includes speakers from differing perspectives and platforms, a knowledge of historical relevance is especially imperative. In the following section, I have included historical summaries of the years in which the speeches were delivered, as well as brief biographies of each speaker.

1964

With the height of the Vietnam War on the horizon and the Civil Rights Movement in full swing, 1964 was a turbulent year for the United States. The Civil Rights Bill was passed after a long filibuster in the Senate. President Lyndon B. Johnson signed the Economic Opportunity Act and the Medicare Act (World history timeline-1964, 2007). During the Democratic National Convention (DNC), delegates from the Mississippi Freedom Democratic Party, led by Vice-Chair Fannie Lou Hamer, brought their own delegation to the DNC in an attempt to protest Mississippi's all-White delegation. After negotiating with an intimidated President Johnson, the party was offered two seats, provided the DNC would select the delegates. The delegates rejected the offer and left the DNC, but not before drawing much publicity (Lee, 1999).

Fannie Lou Hamer. Fannie Lou Hamer, born in 1917 in Mississippi, worked on a cotton plantation alongside her parents, who were sharecroppers. Hamer, the granddaughter of slaves, was an influential civil rights leader, active in organizing the Student Nonviolent Coordinating Committee's Freedom Summer in Mississippi. As an advocate for civil rights, Hamer also served as Vice-Chair of the Mississippi Freedom Democratic Party. Hamer's emotion-filled speech given at the 1964 Democratic National Convention, which detailed her own personal struggles registering to vote, was both powerful and persuasive (Lee, 1999). Hamer died in 1977.

> The plantation owner was raising cain because I had tried to register. … "Fanny Lou, do you know … what I said?" And I said, "yes, sir." He said, "I mean that … if you don't go down and withdraw your registration, you will have to leave … because we are not ready for that in Mississippi." And I addressed him and told him and said, "I didn't try to register for you. I tried to register for myself." I had to leave that same night (Hamer, 1964).

1976

In 1976, "the United States vetoed a United Nations Security Council resolution that proposed total Israeli withdrawal from Arab areas" (World history timeline-1976, 2007). The Supreme Court ruled the death penalty constitutional. Gerald Ford and Jimmy Carter vied for the presidency.

Barbara Jordan. Barbara Jordan was born in Houston's Fifth Ward in 1936. Jordan began her career in politics by serving as the first African American woman in the Texas Senate from 1967 to 1972 (Burgchardt, 1996). She then served as the first African American woman from the South in the United States House of Representatives from 1973 to 1979 (Gill, 1997, p. 51; United States, n.d.). During her time in the United States Congress, Jordan was instrumental in renewing the Voting Rights Act and was well-known for delivering a famous and influential speech encouraging support of President Nixon's impeachment (McNair, 2000). Jordan's 1976 speech to the Democratic National Convention has been deemed one of the greatest speeches of all time. She also spoke at the 1992 DNC (Rediscovering Barbara, 2006). Jordan died of multiple sclerosis in 1996 (Rogers, 1998).

"But there is something different about tonight. There is something special about tonight. What is different? What is Special? I, Barbara Jordan, am a keynote speaker" (Jordan, 1976).

1984

In 1984, Los Angeles held the Olympic Games, while 14 countries in the Soviet bloc boycotted them (World history timeline-1984, 2007). Geraldine Ferraro became the first woman to run for vice-president. She and fellow Democrat Walter Mondale ran against Republicans Ronald Reagan and George H.W. Bush. Reagan and Bush won the election (Ferraro & Francke, 1985).

Jesse Jackson. Jesse Louis Jackson, Sr. was born in South Carolina in 1941. Jackson, a Baptist minister, is well-known for his work as a civil rights activist. It was in the sixties that Jackson participated in demonstrations with Dr. Martin Luther King, Jr. through the Southern Christian Leadership Conference. Jackson organized the National Rainbow Coalition in 1984, a non-profit organization dedicated to representing the interests of all minority groups (Keep hope, n.d.). This became the Rainbow PUSH organization in 1996. Jackson ran for president of the United States on a platform serving the interests of minorities in both 1984 and 1988 (Ifill, 2009, p. 7). He delivered speeches at the DNC both years (Jesse Louis, n.d.). Jackson is well-known for his oral delivery, specifically his use of alliteration, rhyme, and antithesis (Niles & Morrison, 1996, p. 197).

> There is the call of conscience, redemption, expansion, healing, and unity. Leadership must heed the call of conscience, redemption, expansion, heal-ing and unity, for they are the key to achieving our mission. Time is neutral and does not change things. With courage and initiative, leaders can change things. (Jackson, 1984)

1988

In 1988, the United States indicted Panamanian dictator Manuel Noriega for bribery in an attempt to remove him from power, but failed to oust him from Panama's admin-istration (World almanac 1989, 1988, p. 57). The Iran-Iraq war ended after eight years and a death toll of 1.5 million people (World history timeline-1988, 2007). Jordan's King Hussein renounced control of the West Bank, legitimizing power to the Palestinian Liberation Organization (World almanac 1989, 1988, p. 62–63). George H. W. Bush, then vice-president, defeated Michael Dukakis for the United States presidency.

Jesse Jackson. Candidate Jesse Jackson presents his second DNC address entitled "Keep Hope Alive" in Atlanta, Georgia, four years after delivering his first speech to the 1984 delegates in San Francisco.

1992

In 1992, the Internet began to change the way Americans lived. In addition, in 1992, about one-third of all American businesses were owned by women, four percent were owned by African Americans, and five percent were owned by Hispanics. United States forces left Subic Bay in the Philippines, but entered Somalia in an effort to provide aid to people starving due to the civil war. The North American Free Trade Agreement was established by the United States, Mexico, and Canada to become the world's largest trading bloc (World almanac 1993, 1992, p. 67). Bill Clinton defeated President George H. W. Bush for the presidency. Police officers in Los Angeles, California were acquitted in the 1991 beating of an African American man, Rodney King, resulting in riots throughout the city (World history timeline-1992, 2007).

Barbara Jordan. Barbara Jordan spoke at the 1992 DNC, 16 years after her famous keynote address in 1976. At the 1992 convention, the DNC nominated Bill Clinton for President and Al Gore for Vice President. Jordan, then a Texas Representative, delivered the keynote address.

2004

The year 2004 was eventful. The United States continued involvement in the war in Iraq (World almanac 2005, 2004, p. 41). Amidst the war, the Abu Ghraib prison scandal hit the media and caused outrage both in the United States and abroad (World almanac 2005, 2004, p. 32). A terrorist attack in Madrid killed almost 200 people and injured over 1,000 (World almanac 2005, 2004, p. 29). Genocide in Darfur sparked international attention. An earthquake in the Indian Ocean created a tsunami, causing one of the worst natural disasters ever and killing approximately 150,000 people. Former President Ronald Reagan died, as did Palestinian Liberation Organization leader Yasser Arafat (World almanac 2005, 2004). Afghanistan held its first presidential elections. Debate in the United States during 2004 centered largely around the war in Iraq and stem cell research. President George W. Bush defeated Democrat John Kerry for a second term as president (World history timeline- 2004, 2007).

Al Sharpton. Alfred "Al" Sharpton was born in Brooklyn, New York in 1954. After being licensed and ordained to preach at the age of nine, Rev. Sharpton began a career in activism. He is well-known for establishing or helping to establish a number of organizations for the purpose of advancing opportunities for minorities and other disadvantaged groups, including the National Youth Movement in 1971, the National Action Network in 1991, and Second Chance in 1999 (Rev. Al, n.d.). Sharpton ran for President of the United States in 2004 (Greenfield-Sanders & Mitchell, 2008).

> I'm also convinced that at a time when a vicious spirit in the body politic of this country that attempts to undermine America's freedoms–our civil rights, and civil liberties–we must leave this city and go forth and organize this nation for victory for our party and John Kerry and John Edwards in November. (Sharpton, 2004)

Barack Obama. Barack Obama was born in Hawaii in 1961. He graduated from Columbia University and Harvard Law School, and he worked as a civil rights attorney in Chicago. His career choice led him to politics, where he served in the Illinois Senate for eight years and the United States Senate for four years. He delivered the keynote address at the DNC as an Illinois State Senator in 2004. In 2007, Obama announced he would be running for president of the United States (Obama '08, n.d.), and on November 4, 2008, Obama was elected as the first African American President of the United States (Ifill, 2009; Thomas, 2009).

> Our pride is based on a very simple premise, summed up in a declaration made over two hundred years ago, 'We hold these truths to be self-evident, that all men are created equal' (Obama, 2004)

David Alston. Rev. David Alston served as a crewman with John Kerry in Vietnam. Alston, an ordained minister from South Carolina, was invited to deliver a speech during the 2004 DNC (Page, 2004). Walsh (2004), a delegate from Massachusetts, wrote that Alston was the best speaker at the convention.

> Friends, here in this city more than two centuries ago, patriots launched a revolution that changed history. Generations since have marched, fought, and died to defend the sacred ideals of life, liberty, and the pursuit of happiness. … It is now our turn to defend these ideals. (Alston, 2004)

The diversity of the speakers is apparent. Perhaps even more evident is the historical significance of each speech. Knowing the context of the speeches will prove important when examining the results of the analysis. Two research questions were developed to compare these speeches:

RQ1: How is the topic of race treated in Democratic National Convention speeches delivered by African American speakers?

RQ2: Has the treatment of race in Democratic National Convention speeches delivered by African American speakers changed over time?

To answer these questions, a content analysis was performed on eight major speeches delivered by African American political leaders at Democratic National Conventions.

The speech texts examined were those of Fannie Lou Hamer (1964), Barbara Jordan (1976, 1992), Jesse Jackson (1984, 1988), Al Sharpton (2004), David Alston (2004), and Barack Obama (2004).

Although the goal of the speeches was to rally support for the Democratic presidential candidate; however, the historical and situational contexts for some of the speeches differ greatly, at least in part because of the time the speeches were delivered: The first speech analyzed was from the 1964 Democratic National Convention (DNC), and the last speeches analyzed were from the 2004 DNC. This is especially true in consideration of the history of African Americans during this forty-year span.

Coding

Two coders, one male and one female, analyzed the eight speeches for every mention of race. In order to ensure intercoder reliability, two of the eight speeches were analyzed by both coders. Using Cohen's Kappa, an acceptable score of .97 was obtained for intercoder reliability. Each mention of race was counted as a unit of analysis and was coded for 14 variables. The variables and categories chosen are important and essential in answering the research questions. For each mention of race, coders examined the speaker, year of the speech, gender of the speaker, age of the speaker at the time the speech was delivered, the race mentioned, and the connotation, or meaning, of the mention of race. Coders also made note of how race was used in the speech, including whether or not race was used to describe a particular person, to describe something from history, to discriminate, to separate, to unify, to claim responsibility, or to hold responsible. Coders were also encouraged to list any additional uses or strategies for each mention of race.

In creating the coding variables for the ways race was used in the speeches, a number of related analyses were conducted in an effort to identify which issues continued surfacing. To elaborate, sometimes race is used merely to describe someone or to explain something from history (Frank & McPhail, 2005; Gregg, 1971). At times race is used to divide or separate persons of a specific race from other races, or to provide distance between groups (McPhail, 1998; Watkins, 2001). Oftentimes, however, race is used in speeches to unify races or other groups of people (Frank & McPhail, 2005; Gregg, 1971; Sullivan, 1993; Watkins, 2001). Race can also be used to claim responsibility or to identify where someone should take responsibility. This variable includes the discussion of "broken promises" (Crenshaw, 2004; see also Frank & McPhail, 2005) and blame. And, race can also be used to discriminate, defame, or abuse (Clegg, 1997; McPhail, 1998; West, 1993).

In addition to these variables, coders indicated whether or not the mention of race included implied racial code words instead of blatant mentions of race. Himelstein (1983) defines a *racial code word* as a "word or phrase that communicates a well understood but implicit meaning to a segment of an audience while preserving for the speaker a deniability of that meaning by reference to its explicit meaning" (p. 156). Racial code words are used to allow wiggle room for candidates and politicians so that they can save face when having to appeal to diverse audiences (Edsall & Edsall, 1991; Jeffries, 2002). Jeffries (2002) uses the example of the Willie Horton advertisements used during George Bush's 1988 presidential campaign. Jeffries argues that by showing images of an African American man committing a crime, the Bush campaign was actually attempting to draw on White prejudices. "The story was effective because the association of Blacks and violent crime resonated with Whites" (Jeffries, 2002, p. 682).

Data Analysis

Chi-Square analyses were run for each of the following variables: 1) race mentioned, 2) connotation of the mention of race, 3) use of racial code words, 4) race used to describe a person, 5) race used to describe an historical event, 6) racial reference used with regard to discrimination, 7) race mentioned to separate, 8) race mentioned to unify, and 9) race mentioned to address responsibility. These variables were compared with speaker, year of the speech, gender of the speaker, and age of the speaker at the time the speech was delivered.

Results

Race

The amount of times race was mentioned in DNC speeches greatly varied according to the speaker. The total number of coded responses was 341. Jesse Jackson, for example, mentioned race over a hundred times in his first speech, while David Alston had three mentions of race in his entire speech. Most frequently, all of the following races were mentioned at least once in the coded speeches: African American, Native American, Hispanic or Latin American, Asian American, Jewish, Middle Eastern or Arab, and Caucasian. The races mentioned were overwhelmingly African American or Caucasian, or were coded as *Not Applicable* or not specified. In fact, until Jackson's 1984 speech, the only races coded were African American or Caucasian, or were coded as *Not Applicable*. Significance was identified in the relationships between the race mentioned and speaker, $\chi^2(40, N = 341) = 77.56$, $p = .000$; year,

$\chi^2(40, N = 341) = 94.59, p = .000$; gender of the speaker, $\chi^2(8, N = 341) = 20.26, p = .009$; and age of the speaker, $\chi^2(24, N = 341) = 43.08, p = .010$ (See Table 1). "When I look out at this convention, I see the face of America: Red, Yellow, Brown, Black and White. We are all precious in God's sight–the real rainbow coalition" (Jackson, 1988).

Connotations/Meanings

Connotations of race varied with the speaker. In 2004, for example, Al Sharpton's comments on race were primarily negative, while in the same year, Barack Obama's were primarily positive. Significance was found in the relationships between connotation and speaker, $\chi^2(24, N = 341) = 43.08, p = .010$; year, $\chi^2(15, N = 341) = 83.66, p = .000$; gender of the speaker, $\chi^2(15, N = 341) = 108.31, p = .000$; and age of the speaker, $\chi^2(9, N = 341) = 21.66, p = .010$ (See Table 1). "It's that fundamental belief: 'I am my brother's keeper, I am my sister's keeper' that makes this country work. It's what allows us to pursue our individual dreams, yet still come together as a single American family" (Obama, 2004).

Racial Code Words

Most mentions of race were not coded. Fannie Lou Hamer's 1964 speech, for example, was very straightforward. Nothing she said regarding race seemed to be coded. Significance was identified in the relationships between racial code words and speaker, $\chi^2(10, N = 341) = 52.79, p = .000$; year, $\chi^2(10, N = 341) = 66.88, p = .000$; and age of

TABLE 1. *p*-values for Chi-Square Analyses

Variable	Speaker	Year	Gender	Age
Race Men.	**.000	**.000	**.009	*.010
Connotation	**.000	**.000	*.045	*.010
Code Words	**.000	**.000	.082	**.000
Description	**.000	**.000	.493	**.001
Hist. Desc.	**.000	**.000	**.000	**.004
Discrimination	**.000	**.000	**.002	.605
Separation	**.000	**.000	.248	.062
Unification	**.000	**.000	.925	**.001
Responsibility	**.000	**.000	.371	**.000

Note: Race Men. = Race Mentioned; Hist. Desc. = Historical Description.
*$p < .05$.
**$p < .01$.

the speaker, $\chi^2(6, N = 341) = 79.69$, $p = .000$ (See Table 1). "After the first Negro had beat until he was exhausted, the State Highway Patrolman ordered the second Negro to take the blackjack" (Hamer, 1964).

Race as Description

Using race to describe a person became less prevalent after Jackson's 1988 speech. To illustrate, the last four speeches coded had fewer combined mentions of race used to describe a person than either of Jackson's DNC speeches during the 1980s. Significance was identified in the relationship of using race as description and the speaker, $\chi^2(10, N = 341) = 35.98$, $p = .000$; year, $\chi^2(10, N = 341) = 47.27$, $p = .000$; and age of the speaker, $\chi^2(6, N = 341) = 22.63$, $p = .001$ (See Table 1). "We look from Virginia around to Texas, there's only one Black Congressperson out of 115" (Jackson, 1984).

History

Mentions of race with regard to history increased after Hamer's 1964 speech, as some speakers actually referred to Hamer in their own DNC speeches. References to history varied greatly with regard to the speaker. Significance was identified in the relationship of historical references and speaker, $\chi^2(10, N = 341) = 74.46$, $p = .000$; year, $\chi^2(10, N = 341) = 59.90$, $p = .000$; gender, $\chi^2(2, N = 341) = 28.25$, $p = .000$; and age of the speaker, $\chi^2(6, N = 341) = 18.99$, $p = .004$ (See Table 1). "Forty years ago, in 1964, Fannie Lou Hamer and the Mississippi Freedom Democratic Party stood at the Democratic convention in Atlantic City fighting to preserve voting rights for all America and all Democrats, regardless of race or gender" (Sharpton, 2004).

Discrimination

Mentions of race with regard to discrimination varied among speakers, but mentions of race that did not deal with discrimination were prevalent among mentions of race in two of the three speeches delivered during the 2004 Convention. Significance was found in the relationshsip of references to discrimination and speaker, $\chi^2(20, N = 341) = 127.46$, $p = .000$; year, $\chi^2(20, N = 341) = 79.61$, $p = .000$; and gender, $\chi^2(4, N = 341) = 16.45$, $p = .002$ (See Table 1). "It is frightening to think that the gains of civil and women's rights and those movements in the last century could be reversed if this administration is in the White House in these next four years" (Sharpton, 2004).

Separation and Unification

Mentions of race used to separate were identified in six of the eight speeches analyzed. Both speeches that did not use race to separate were delivered in 2004. Significance was identified in the relationship between mentions of race to separate and speaker, $\chi^2(10, N = 341) = 54.98$, $p = .000$, and year, $\chi^2(10, N = 341) = 37.69$, $p = .000$ (See Table 1). Mentions of race used to unify were identified in all of the speeches delivered after Hamer's 1964 speech. Significance was identified in the relationship between mentions of race used to unify and speaker, $\chi^2(10, N = 341) = 37.90$, $p = .000$; year, $\chi^2(10, N = 341) = 63.40$, $p = .000$; and age of the speaker, $\chi^2(6, N = 341) = 23.72$, $p = .001$ (See Table 1). "For alongside our famous individualism, there's another ingredient in the American saga: a belief that we are connected as one people" (Obama, 2004).

Responsibility

Mentions of race with regard to the variable dealing with responsibility varied among speakers. Mentions of race dealing with placing responsibility, or blame, were identified in all of the speeches before Jordan's 1992 speech. Significance was identified in the relationship between responsibility and speaker, $\chi^2(15, N = 341) = 71.87$, $p = .000$; year, $\chi^2(15, N = 341) = 59.40$, $p = .000$; and age of the speaker, $\chi^2(9, N = 341) = 33.19$, $p = .000$ (See Table 1). "We seek to unite people, not divide them. As we seek to unite people, we reject both White racism and Black racism. This party will not tolerate bigotry under any guise" (Jordan, 1992).

Discussion

RQ1: How is the topic of race treated in Democratic National Convention speeches delivered by African American speakers?

The topic of race has been treated in a number of different ways by African American speakers at Democratic National Conventions. The connotations of the mentions of race were split between positive and negative, with 40 percent and 36 percent respectively. Only 13 percent of the mentions of race included racial code words, which appears to indicate that the DNC speakers were not interested in beating around the bush with regard to race, but, rather, were more interested in getting to the heart of the issue. This was never more true than with Fannie Lou Hamer's 1964 speech to the DNC.

By raising and discussing matters dealing with race, a speaker gives power and legitimacy to those issues. Hamer did just that. She not only gave power and legitimacy to the issues, but also gave them publicity. Because the speech was widely broadcast, Hamer informed the public about issues and details about civil rights, voting registration, discrimination, the Democratic National Convention, and the Mississippi Freedom Democratic Party. These were all issues of which the general public may not have been aware. For example, Hamer told of her experiences being jailed and beaten as a result of being with other African Americans who attempted to use a washroom intended only for Whites.

The State Highway Patrolmen ordered the first Negro to take the blackjack. …
The first Negro began to beat, and I was beat by the first Negro until he
was exhausted. … After the first Negro had beat until he was exhausted, the
State Highway Patrolman ordered the second Negro to take the blackjack.
(Hamer, 1964)

Ms. Hamer's speech was very much a narrative, serving to inform the country of the
many injustices she had personally suffered.

Race was not used to describe a person or group of people the majority of the time.
Twenty-nine percent of the mentions of race were used to describe a person, and 61 percent
of those were from Jesse Jackson's two speeches. Jackson's idea of a diverse America is evident
throughout his speeches.

America is not like a blanket–one piece of unbroken cloth, the same color, the
same texture, the same size. America is more like a quilt–many patches, many
pieces, many colors, many sizes, all woven and held together by a common
thread. (Jackson, 1984)

In addition, only 25 percent of racial mentions were used to describe something
historical. Because of the context of a DNC speech, the present and future are likely
more pertinent than the past. More relevant, however, was the issue of discrimination.
Almost half of the mentions of race dealt with discrimination, and within these mentions,
83 percent of the persons of the race mentioned were portrayed as victims.

Surprisingly, 43 percent of the mentions of race were used to separate or distance
the speaker from another race. These results are interesting considering the purposes of
the conventions. Generally, a primary function of the convention is to unify the political party before a presidential election. At the same time, however, 31 percent of the
mentions of race were used to do the opposite–to unify the speaker with other races. For
example, Jackson (1984) noted, "we are bound by Dr. Martin Luther King, Jr. and Rabbi
Abraham Heschel, crying out from their graves for us to reach common ground. We are
bound by shared blood and shared sacrifices."

Just over half of the mentions of race pertained to responsibility. Thirty-five percent
were used to place responsibility or blame on someone, and 16 percent were used to take or
claim responsibility. For example, Al Sharpton (2004) brought up the topic of reparations.

You said the Republican Party was the party of Lincoln and Frederick
Douglass. It is true that Mr. Lincoln signed the Emancipation Proclamation,
after which there was a commitment to give 40 acres and a mule. That's where
the argument, to this day, of reparations starts. We never got the 40 acres.

Further, none of Obama's comments about race were used to separate, and none of Hamer's comments were used to unify. For example, Obama (2004) stated, "there's not a Black America and White America and Latino America and Asian America; there's the United States of America."

Sharpton had more than four times as many comments that separated races than comments that unified races in his speech. In both of her speeches, Jordan had more comments that unified than comments that separated. Overall, with the exception of Jordan's 1992 speech, when a speaker mentioned race in regards to responsibility, the speakers were more likely to indicate or imply blame than responsibility.

In general, the use of race by African American speakers in DNC speeches is unique to the particular speaker. Jesse Jackson, for example, had more mentions of race in each of his speeches than any other speaker. Jackson had an average of 80.5 mentions of race in each of his speeches, while Barbara Jordan had an average of 31.5 in each of her speeches. In total, the average number of mentions of race was 42.6.

Jackson mentioned race in his speeches more than any other speaker. In one of his speeches, he mentioned every race included in the code book, and in the other speech, he mentioned all but one. Jackson's considerable number of mentions of race, as well as his inclusiveness of races can be attributed to his affiliation with the Rainbow Coalition, which, by its nature, seeks to unite and find justice for people of all races.

The connotations of the mentions of race varied greatly among speakers, as well. Hamer's speech, for example, included only one positive comment with regard to race. Jackson's speeches contained more positive comments than negative, while Sharpton's speech contained more negative comments than positive. Over 71 percent of Obama's mentions of race were positive, while seven percent were negative.

The mentions of race dealing with discrimination also varied greatly according to the speaker. Seventy-six percent of Sharpton's comments about race and 3.5% of Obama's dealt with discrimination in which the persons of the race mentioned were portrayed as victims. Clearly, the most important factor in these speeches is the individual speaker.

RQ2: Has the treatment of race in Democratic National Convention speeches delivered by African American speakers changed over time?

Based on the results of this research, the treatment of race in DNC speeches delivered by African American speakers has changed *somewhat* over time. It appears that, for the most part, mentions of race have decreased. Obama and Alston, two of the 2004 speakers, as well as Jordan in 1992, had fewer than the average 42 mentions of race. With the exception of Al Sharpton in 2004, the number of mentions of race actually increased after Jordan's 1976 speech, and then decreased after Jackson's 1988 speech.

One possible explanation for these results is that a speaker can gain support from audience members that identify with the specific racial issues brought to the public's attention. If the issues appear to be pertinent, other people will respect the speaker for bringing up issues that other speakers may disregard, avoid, or ignore. Perhaps this was Al Sharpton's purpose in 2004 when he brought up issues that he felt were relevant, issues that other speakers did not address.

On the other hand, to people who do not have to deal with issues of race on a regular basis, race can become a non-issue. Therefore, when an African American speaker discusses race as an issue, some may have trouble identifying with the speaker, and the speaker may lose credibility and appeal with these audience members. "Even the indirect referencing of racism continues to traumatize many white Americans" (Frank & McPhail, 2005, p. 572).

With the exception of Sharpton's 2004 speech, a second trend was identified. The connotation of the mentions of race were predominately positive after Jackson's 1984 speech. The use of race to describe a person also changed dramatically over time. Over 42 percent of the mentions of race in Hamer's 1964 speech were used to describe a person, compared with just under 29 percent in Jackson's 1984 speech, 26 percent in Jordan's 1992 speech, and 11.7 percent in Sharpton's 2004 speech. Because it is no longer customary to indicate a person's race when discussing them publicly. It is no surprise that the percentage of mentions of race used to describe a person decreased over time.

Also interesting is to examine how treatment of race changed over time for both Barbara Jordan and Jesse Jackson. Each gave two speeches at Democratic National Conventions. Barbara Jordan had *more* mentions of race in her second DNC speech than she did in her first speech. Jackson, however, had over 40 percent *fewer* mentions of race in his second speech to the DNC than he did in his first speech. Because some people attribute Jackson's failed presidential bid in 1984 to his disproportionate use of race while campaigning, it is no surprise that his mentions of race decreased in his 1988 speech. Interestingly, however, Jackson had over three times more mentions of race appealing to unity in his first speech than he did in his second speech. His use of mentions of race appearing to separate, however, remained about the same. Both Jackson and Jordan had fewer mentions of race regarding history in their second speeches. So, while some general trends were identified over time, examining how one speaker changed over time is just as notable.

Implications and Conclusion

Some limitations emerged during this content analysis. First, the speeches selected for the analysis were drawn from a convenience sample. A suggestion for further research would be to obtain a comprehensive list of speakers and transcripts so as to offer a more complete analysis of African American speakers at DNC conventions. In addition, among the list of speakers that was accessible, transcripts of every speech were not readily available. A second limitation concerns the context of the specific speakers and speaking situations. While general historical summaries of the years in which the speeches were delivered is provided in this analysis, the specific circumstances surrounding each of the speakers and their purposes in delivering the speeches drastically affected the mentions of race in each speech. A future study might delve into a more thorough historical analysis.

The results of this study show that a number of factors contribute to how race is treated by African American speakers at Democratic National Conventions; Some speakers may highlight race more than others; The reasons for mentioning racial issues are numerous; and The ways in which discussions of race are used are many. Barack Obama (2004), the youngest of the speakers analyzed, born 44 years after Fannie Lou Hamer, 25 years after Barbara Jordan, 20 years after Jesse Jackson, and 7 years after Al Sharpton, tackled the race issue but also highlighted other issues he felt were salient. Perhaps Obama represents a new generation of speakers. In his speech, references to race were intentional, but at the same time, were used sparingly. Yet, just because race may not be the most vital issue to the speaker does not mean that the issue is not still significant to the speaker. In his own book, Obama (2006) notes that "to suggest that our racial attitudes play no part … is to turn a blind eye to both our history and our experience–and to relieve ourselves of the responsibility to make things right" (p. 81).

Perhaps those who spoke before Obama did their job–they informed and fought and changed the world to the point that an African American candidate or speaker no longer has to run or speak primarily on the platform of race, but can run or speak on whichever issues he or she deems most salient at the time. Americans want to hear a speaker who is not afraid to tread through the tough issues and one who is aware of and informed on many issues. What is clear from this study is that race is still an issue, whether we discuss it or not.

DISCUSSION QUESTIONS

1. What is African American rhetoric? Have you heard this form of speaking? Describe the occasion, and what impact the speech had upon you and other listeners.

2. Compare and contrast the historical context or setting during the speech of Fannie Lou Hamer and Barack Obama. Do you think the time period in which these speeches were delivered affected the types of key phrases regarding race that each speaker used?

3. How have previous writers described the Democratic National Convention (DNC) speeches of Jesse Jackson? Of Barack Obama? Do you agree or disagree with these interpretations?

4. How are speakers using African American rhetoric compared with other speakers? Should African American rhetoric be taught in schools?

References

Alston, D. (2004, July 26). *David Alston's speech to the Democratic National Convention*. Speech presented at the 2004 Democratic National Convention, Boston, MA.

Asante, M. K. (1987). *The Afrocentric idea*. Philadelphia: Temple University Press.

Atwater, D. F. (2007). Senator Barack Obama: The rhetoric of hope and the American dream. *Journal of Black Studies, 38*(2), 121–129.

Borchers, T. (2006). *Rhetorical theory: An introduction*. Thomson Wadsworth: Belmont, California.

Burgchardt, C. R. (1996). Barbara Charline Jordan. In R. W. Leeman (Ed.), *African American orators: A bio-critical sourcebook* (pp. 207–215). Santa Barbara, CA: Greenwood.

Carter, R. (2007, January 18). Barack Hussein Obama: Is he black enough for black Voters? *New York Amsterdam News, 98*(4), 10–32.

Clegg, C. A., III. (1997). *An original man: The life and times of Elijah Muhammad*. New York: St. Martin's Press.

The constitutional significance of the discriminatory effects of at-large elections (1993). *The Yale Law Journal, 91*(5), 974–999.

Crenshaw, K. W. (2004). Sharpton sharpens the challenge with an overtime victory. *Common Dreams Newscenter*. Retrieved July 5, 2007, from http://www.commondreams.org/views04/0730-12.htm

Edsall, T. B., & Edsall, M. D. (1991). *Chain reaction*. New York: Norton.

Ferraro, G., & Francke, L. B. (1985). *Ferraro: My story*. New York: Bantam.

Frank, D. A., & McPhail, M. L. (2005). Barack Obama's address to the 2004 Democratic National Convention: Trauma, compromise, consilience, and the (im)possibility of racial reconciliation. *Rhetoric & Public Affairs, 8*(4), 571–594.

Gill, L. M. (1997). *African American women in Congress: Forming and transforming history*. New Brunswick, NJ: Rutgers University Press.

Goldzwig, S. R. (2006). Demagoguery, democratic dissent, and "re-visioning" democracy. *Rhetoric & Public Affairs, 9*(3), 471–478.

Greenfield-Sanders, T., & Mitchell, E. (2008). *The black list*. New York: Atria.

Gregg, R. B. (1971). The ego-function of the rhetoric of protest. *Philosophy & Rhetoric, 4*, 71–91.

Hallmark, J. R. (1992). Jesse Jackson's argumentation as an explanation of political success: A comparison of Jackson's 1984 and 1988 addresses to the Democratic National Convention. *Howard Journal of Communications, 4*, 126–140.

Hamer, F. L. (1964, August). *Fannie Lou Hamer's Democratic National Convention speech*. Speech presented at the 1964 Democratic National Convention, Atlantic City, NJ.

Himelstein, J. (1983). Rhetorical continuities in the politics of race: The closed society revisited. *Southern Speech Communication Journal, 48,* 153–166.

Ifill, G. (2009). *The breakthrough: Politics and race in the age of Obama.* New York: Doubleday.

Jackson, J. (1984, July 18). *Jesse Jackson's Democratic National Convention address.* Speech presented at the 1984 Democratic National Convention, San Francisco.

Jackson, J. (1988, July 19). *Common ground and common sense.* Speech presented at the 1988 Democratic National Convention, Atlanta, GA.

Jackson, R. (2000). So real illusions of Black intellectualism: Exploring race, roles, and gender in the academy. *Communication Theory, 10,* 48–63.

Jeffries, J. L. (2002). Press coverage of Black statewide candidates: The case of L. Douglas Wilder of Virginia. *Journal of Black Studies, 32*(6), 673–697.

Jesse Louis Jackson Biography. (n.d.). *Biography.* Retrieved June 28, 2007, from http://www.biography.com/search/article.do?id=9351181

Jordan, B. (1976, July 12). *Who then will speak for the common good?* Speech presented at the 1976 Democratic National Convention, New York, NY.

Jordan, B. (1992, July). *Change: From what to what?* Speech presented at the Democratic National Convention, New York, NY.

Keep Hope Alive Radio. (n.d.) *History: Rev. Jesse L. Jackson, Sr.* Retrieved June 28, 2007, from http://www.keephopealiveradio.com/history.html

Knowles-Borishade, A. F. (1991). Paradigm for classical African orature: Instrument for a scientific revolution? *Journal of Black Studies, 21,* 488–500.

Kochman, T. (1981). *Black and white styles in conflict.* Chicago: University of Chicago Press.

Lee, C. K. (1999). *For Freedom's Sake: The Life of Fannie Lou Hamer.* Athens: University of Georgia Press.

The longest race: Presidential hopefuls hit the campaign trail early. (2007, February 26). *Current Events, 106*(19), 4–5.

McNair, J. D. (2000). Barbara Jordan: African American politician: Journey to freedom. Mankato, MN: Child's World.

McPhail, M. L. (1998). Passionate intensity: Louis Farrakhan and the fallacies of racial reasoning. *Quarterly Journal of Speech, 84,* 416–429.

McPhail, M. L. (2003). The politics of (in)visibility in African American rhetorical scholarship: A (re)quest for an African worldview. In R. L. Jackson and E. B. Richardson (Eds.), *Understanding African American rhetoric* (pp. 99–113). New York: Routledge.

Niles, L. A., & Morrison, C. (1996). Jesse Louis Jackson. In R. W. Leeman (Ed.), *African American orators: A bio-critical sourcebook* (pp. 192–200). Santa Barbara, CA: Greenwood.

Obama '08 (n.d.). *Meet Barack.* Retrieved June 28, 2007, from http://www.barackobama.com

Obama, B. (2004, July 27). *Keynote address at the 2004 Democratic National Convention.* Speech presented at the 2004 Democratic National Convention, Boston.

Obama, B. (2006). *The audacity of hope: Thoughts on reclaiming the American dream.* New York: Crown.

Page, S. (2004, July 27). Speakers offer few barbs, try to stay warm and fuzzy. *USA Today*. Retrieved June 28, 2007, from http://www.usatoday.com/educate/election04/article5.htm

Rediscovering Barbara Jordan. (2006, February). *Kut*. Retrieved June 27, 2007, from http://www.kut .org/items/show/5525

Rev. Al Sharpton biography. (n.d.). *The History Makers*. Retrieved June 28, 2007, from http://www .thehistorymakers.com/biography/biography.asp?bioindex=171&category=civicMakers

Rogers, M. B. (1998). *Barbara Jordan: American hero*. New York: Bantam.

Sharpton, A. (2004, July 27). *Al Sharpton's address Democratic National Convention speech*. Speech presented at the 2004 Democratic National Convention, Boston.

Sullivan, P. A. (1993). Signification and African American rhetoric: A case study of Jesse Jackson's "Common ground and common sense" speech. *Communication Quarterly, 41*(1), 1–15.

Thomas, E. (2009). *A long time coming: The inspiring, combative 2008 campaign and the historic election of Barack Obama*. New York: PublicAffairs.

United States Congress. (n.d.). *Biographical Directory of the United States Congress: Barbara Jordan*. Retrieved June 27, 2007, from http://bioguide.congress.gov/scripts/biodisplay .pl?index=J000266

Walsh, J. E. (2004, July 27). Delegate diaries: The view from the best seat in the house. *The Boston Globe*. Retrieved June 28, 2007, from http://www.boston.com/news/politics/conventions/ delegate_diary/072704_walsh?pg=2

Watkins, S. C. (2001). Framing protest: News media frames of the Million Man March. *Critical Studies in Media Communications, 18*(1), 83–101.

West, C. (1993). *Race matters*. Boston: Beacon Press.

Wilson, P. (1996). The rhythm of rhetoric: Jesse Jackson at the 1988 Democratic National Convention. *Southern Communication Journal, 61*, 253–264.

The world almanac and book of facts: 1989. (1988). Cleveland: Pharos.

The world almanac and book of facts: 1993. (1992). Cleveland: Pharos.

The world almanac and book of facts: 2005. (2004). Cleveland: Pharos.

World history timeline- 1964. (2007). *The History Channel website*. Retrieved June 29, 2007, from http://www.history.com/wt.do?year=1964

World history timeline- 1976. (2007). *The History Channel website*. Retrieved June 29, 2007, from http://www.history.com/wt.do?year=1976

World history timeline- 1984. (2007). *The History Channel website*. Retrieved June 29, 2007, from http://www.history.com/wt.do?year=1984

World history timeline- 1988. (2007). *The History Channel website*. Retrieved June 29, 2007, from http://www.history.com/wt.do?year=1988

World history timeline- 1992. (2007). *The History Channel website*. Retrieved June 29, 2007, from http://www.history.com/wt.do?year=1992

World history timeline- 2004. (2007). *The History Channel website*. Retrieved June 29, 2007, from http://www.history.com/wt.do?year=2004

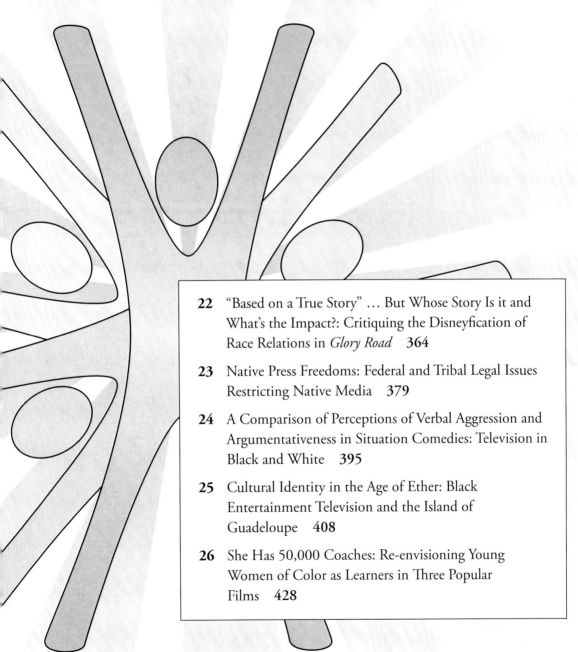

Context VI

Mass Media

22

"Based on a True Story" … But Whose Story Is it and What's the Impact?: Critiquing the Disneyfication of Race Relations in *Glory Road*

Joseph A. Ciccarelli and Mark P. Orbe

Abstract

This critical analysis compares and contrasts historical accounts of the 1966 Texas Western College NCAA championship team with that which was portrayed in the film, *Glory Road*. More specifically, we examine the Disneyfication process which strategically manipulated the story–through the addition of certain fictional events as well as the elimination and/or distortion of actual occurrences–in order to produce an attractive story for viewers. We conclude our analysis by explicating how the film–and others like it–hinder effective race relations in the present-day United States.

KEY TERMS: *Glory Road*, race relations, racism, collective memory, Disneyfication

Introduction

The 1966 NCAA championship game where Texas Western College defeated the University of Kentucky has been described as the "biggest upset in basketball history" (Sanchez, 1991). Yet, given the unwritten rule regarding race in college athletics,[1] the fact that Texas Western played seven Black athletes against the all-White Kentucky squad, the victory has been heralded as "the Emancipation Proclamation of 1966" and "Basketball's *Brown v. Board of Education*" (Haskins, 2006, p. 9). The significance of this event has resulted in several different written accounts, and in 2006, a Disney feature film–Glory Road–was created and distributed based on Don Haskins' (2006) book.[2]

Based on the premise of *Glory Road*, it was no coincidence that the film was released across the United States on the long holiday weekend celebrating the legacy of Rev. Dr. Martin Luther King, Jr. in January, 2006. Hailed as meticulous in its ability to "capture the look and feel of the '60s" (Lowry, 2006, p. 33), the film was applauded for avoiding "the Tarzan trap of exalting the white coach at the expense of his black players" (p. 34). In addition, several reviewers (e.g., Eagan, 2006) spoke to the important role that the film played in terms of exposing younger audience members to an event with so much historical significance. The success of the film was apparent from the first weekend when it was released in 2,222 theatres and grossed over 13.5 million dollars, claiming the number one slot in box office sales. Ultimately, *Glory Road* earned close to 43 million dollars in 17 weeks of distribution.

Glory Road, as both a Disney product and historical race film, is a mass-mediated text that begs for analysis. Disney films are worthy of study, given that the media texts "influence tens of millions of people for whom the Disney version of history becomes real history" (Bryman, 1995, p. 142). However, historically, the Disney phenomenon has largely been neglected by media and cultural studies scholars (Buckingham, 1997). While this has changed somewhat within the past 10 years or so, the focus of analysis has primarily been on children's entertainment (e.g., Cuomo, 1995; Haas, 1995; Ono & Buescher, 2001; Wickstrom, 2005). Within our analysis, we build upon this genre of studies by focusing on one particular contemporary Disney film that portrays race relations to a general audience. In particular, the two-fold objective of the study is to (1) analyze the Disneyfication[3] process in creating the film, *Glory Road*, and (2) critique the ways in which the film contributes to a collective memory, and current-day understanding, of race relations. Prior to our critical analysis, we review the literature on Disney films, race relations, and the generation of a public collective memory.

Review of Key Literature

The Global Hegemonic Power of Disney

Disney's longstanding domination within children's media culture is unparalleled, and has provided the foundation for a present-day media and entertainment conglomerate which has been described as a form of "global hegemony" (Buckingham, 1997, p. 285). Arguably the largest commercial producer of cultural symbols, Disney films have the power to subvert our understandings of our own lifeworlds, as well as those of others (Madison, 1995). While Disney is best known for the creation of children's entertainment, it has—on its own accord and through its subsidiaries Touchstone and Hollywood pictures—increasingly moved into the adult film market with such movies as

The Joy Luck Club, The Hand that Rocks the Cradle, Pretty Woman, and *Good Morning Vietnam* (Buckingham, 1997). Consistent with their other films, Disney works to provide "adults with opportunities for nostalgic fantasies about their own past" (p. 286).

According to Buckingham (1997), an increasing trend is for scholars to compare Disney movies with the texts/events/persons that they purport to represent. In this vein, Zipes (1995) describes Disney as a source of corruption, in terms of the ways in which films systematically domesticate and sanitize the more subversive or troubling elements contained in original stories. In his critical analysis of *Good Morning Vietnam*, Giroux (1995) supports Zipes' assertion by describing multiple examples of how the film suffers from an ideological false memory syndrome, where historical reality is replaced by cultural myth. In this regard, historical events undergo a transformation process whereby they are oversimplified, sanitized, and repressed (Buckingham, 1997) to match audience desires for an entertaining product. Multiple studies (e.g., Cuomo, 1995; Haas, 1995; Smoodin, 1994) have critiqued the problematic nature of the "Disneyfication" that occurs within film depictions of historical events. Yet, while scholars are quick to point out that "these writers are largely correct in their analyses," they also describe such insight as "ultimately rather obvious" (Buckingham, 1997, p. 290). Buckingham goes on to urge scholars to recognize "what the text might be attempting to achieve in its own right, and in relation to its actual target audience" (p. 290).

A small, but significant, body of research has analyzed the ways in which Disney films (such as *Song of the South* and *The Jungle Book*) represent issues of race, racism, and race relations (e.g., Cuomo, 1995; Miller & Rode, 1995). According to Miller and Rode (1995), such films appear to focus on interracial cooperation and de-emphasize social inequalities between different racial groups. In addition, these films introduce problematic racial tensions, only to have them "solved" in neatly packaged endings (Buckingham, 1997). This is largely the case given that the films are first and foremost created as entertainment. According to Patton (1995), entertainment films are "subject to taste but not to truth" (p. 68).

U.S. Collective Memory of Race

"Historical" films–even if they are not historically accurate–are important because they play a pivotal role in the construction of collective memory (Zelizer, 1995). By definition, collective memory "refers to the shared memories that are recollections of social groups" (Madison, 1999, p. 400). While historical films contribute to the collective memories of all people, they can serve as the primary source for those individuals who lack any real-time exposure to past events (Gabriel, 1998). In light of this, Zelizer (1995) argues that collective memories are constructed, nurtured, and used as tools in terms of socio-political agendas. Given the focus of our analysis, Madison's (1999) work on "anti-racist-white-hero" films is especially relevant.

Madison's (1999) analysis of "anti-racist-white-hero" films provides significant insight in terms of how a genre of film beginning in the late 1980s worked to establish collective memory. In particular, she critiques a number of films that depict civil rights struggles–in the U.S. and abroad–that privilege white heroes and marginalize black agency [*Cry Freedom* (1987), *Dry White Season* (1988), *Mississippi Burning* (1988), *A World Apart* (1988), *Heart of Dixie* (1989), *The Long Walk Home* (1990), *The Power of One* (1992), *A Time to Kill* (1996), *Ghosts of Mississippi* (1996), and *Amistad* (1998).] While other scholars (Gabriel, 1998; Shohat & Stam, 1994) have alluded to the ideological role that these films have played in terms of their portrayal of dramatic historical moments of resistance to racism, Madison (1999) critiques the general narrative structure that each film follows, and makes three assertions. First, the films work to distance the issue of racism from the viewers, often times both in terms of geography and time. Second, the films privilege white experiences over black experiences. This is accomplished through great character development of European American protagonists, including the dramatic ways in which they (as well as their families and friends) face racial discrimination. African Americans, in contrast, are signified as victims with no real agency. Third, Madison asserts that white supremacist ideologies are perpetuated through these films since African Americans are portrayed as lacking the abilities to enact social change on their own. Instead, they must rely on European American "heroes" to create complex plans of action.

Our analysis seeks to extend the work on collective memory and race relations by examining *Glory Road*. In doing so, we address a contemporary Disney text that reflects a recent genre in feature film–those that highlight interracial sports teams that overcome the odds in the journey toward greatness.[4] Through our analysis, we critique the ways in which the Disneyfication of the story of the 1966 NCAA champion Texas Western College helps to facilitate a collective memory of race relations that hinders present day understandings of racism.

Exposing the Disneyfication of *Glory Road*

Hollywood films that are "based on a true story," such as *Glory Road*, are grounded in an unwritten agreement with the viewer. The audience, creators, and even the historical figures involved have come to understand, that for dramatic purposes, every event that is portrayed on screen may not be an exact replication of reality. Even Harry Flourney, a player on the 1966 Championship team, admits "the movie [*Glory Road*] is probably 75–80% accurate" (as quoted in Robinson, 2006). This is seemingly accepted by everyone involved, due to the mere fact that most people are watching a movie for entertainment value, rather than an exact depiction of historical events. The words "based on" suggest room for creative interpretation; however, our focus is not on the interpretation itself. Instead, we critically examine the ways in which that interpretation affects how we view historical and contemporary realities.

According to promotional materials, the film *Glory Road* is an "exciting and inspirational true story of the team that changed college basketball and the nation forever" (Glory Road official DVD website, n.d.). "This inspiring, exhilarating film is the true story of legendary basketball coach Don Haskins and his 1966 NCAA championship team, the first all African-American squad to win the national title" (Glory Road DVD review, 2006). Haskins is situated as the main character throughout the film, and it is through his perspective that we come to understand the story. The primary reason for this limited point of view is that the film is adapted from Don Haskin's book (2006) depicting not only the championship story, but also his own life leading up to that point in time. This raises an interesting question when analyzing a film that is based on a true story. Whose story is the film based on, and what are the ramifications of this? If the film is based on a singular perspective of historical events, then there will be obvious discrepancy between how the events are viewed. These discrepancies arise out of the fact that we are not only dealing with the different cultural perspectives of a European American coach and his African American players, but also the positions of power that they find themselves in. For example, David Lattin brings attention to this issue:

> In order to pull this thing off [creating a movie about the team], though, they had to tell the coach's story to tell the movie. That's basically how it is. They had to do Don Haskin's life story in order to talk about the game, even though they didn't talk about any other season or any other players but the players who played on this team, even though this is supposedly his life story. You get the drift? That's just the way it is. That's still the world we live in (quoted in Robinson, 2006).

In choosing to recount this historical event through the interpretation of Don Haskins' book, Disney takes liberty with his character to fit him into the mold of the anti-racist-white-hero. In other words, the personal aspects of his life are manipulated to create a character that fits the traditional Disney mold. According to Madison (1999), there are four criteria for a character to assume the role of anti-racist-white-hero: (1) The white hero experiences some form of racism vicariously through some Black contact, (2) the white hero develops a radical anti-racist consciousness, (3) the white hero sacrifices a great deal at the hands of white racists to further the cause of the black people's struggle (usually in the form of leadership), and (4) finally the white hero suffers for his or her efforts but manages to somehow prevail in the end. At each step of the way, Haskins' character is orchestrated to fit the bill. From the onset of the film the coach steps into a role that is not well received by most. Haskin's character then witnesses instances of racism that his players faced. He begins to understand what they are going through, and in an act of sacrifice and civility, decides to start his five black players as a statement with explicit civil rights implications. Haskins and his family soon feel the ramifications of this controversial decision from the media, fans, and the racist contingent in his home state of Texas and across the country. Through Disney's (re)creation of Don Haskin's character, they have adequately produced an on-screen individual that is dramatically pleasing, connects effortlessly with the audience, and, above all else, reflects an extremely racially conscious human being. Unfortunately, this characterization does not reflect the reality as described in his autobiography and other sources.[5]

Considering the discrepancies between a film that is "based on a true story" and the actual records of historical events, we critically analyzed numerous accounts of the Texas Western Miners championship year, including the film *Glory Road*, player accounts, articles, original screenplay and other texts. Consistent with existing analysis, we organize our analysis around three areas that work to critique "the movie you see, the movie you don't" (Miller & Rode, 1995, p. 86). In particular, we focus on how: (1) key aspects of the story were excluded from the film; (2) creative license was used to add certain nonfactual events to the story, and (3) several aspects of the story were manipulated in order to enhance its intensity.

Eliminating Story Content through the Disneyfication Process

Due to the restrictive length of a feature film, every aspect of an adapted story cannot be brought to life during the movie. The decision is left up to the director and screenwriter to figure out what is important to the story that they are trying to convey. Many times this results in important pieces of the events that transpired being entirely left out.[6] The case of the film *Glory Road* is no different. While the movie features a couple of scenes that illustrate the blatant racism that the team faced, other examples of racism more subtle, ongoing, and institutionalized forms of prejudice, discrimination and racism—were noticeably eliminated from the film. As such, the film does not clearly illustrate the athletes' true struggles. This may be due to the fact that documentation of this championship run, like those written by El Paso sports writers, downplayed the racism that players experienced. For example, in talking about the "biggest upset in basketball history," no mention is made of the racism that the team faced—only that they were young, had to face homesickness, were subject to face a horrendous training regiment, and up against an established basketball powerhouse (Sanchez, 1991).

The film is set in 1965, a time period when the civil rights movement in the United States was coming into its own. However, besides a brief montage of African American heroes during the opening credits, there is no mention of the larger cultural subtext of the times—that is the civil rights movement, minority experiences, and student protests (Blackman, 2006). According to Blackman (2006), *Glory Road* would have us believe that, while the student and working class contemporaries across the globe organized in an effort to fundamentally alter society, all that the African American athletes at Texas Western wanted to do was play basketball. At a time in which racism was very prevalent in everyday society, the true nature of what the African American athletes faced during their time at Texas Western was eliminated from the film.

Through the absence of any substantial accounts in the film, we are led to believe that the black athletes are treated as equals to other students on campus. However, upon the critical analysis of accounts from others, including the players themselves, we have come to realize that this is patently false. Willie Cager, a player from the 1966 team, discusses the Texas Western institution: "They just don't understand. Prejudice is prejudice. Either you got it or you ain't. They got it" (Olsen, 1968, p. 52). The African American athletes were seemingly brought there for one purpose, and that was to win basketball games. "The coaches say that education is the important thing and sports come second," Willie Cager remembers, "but you soon learn better. They want you to win first" (Olsen, 1968, p. 54). This becomes abruptly apparent when we realize that even years after they won the championship and all of the players had completed their athletic eligibility, none of the African American players earned a college degree from Texas Western University (Blackman, 2006) and only 4 of the 7 black players eventually earned any type of college degree (Sanchez, 1991).

These players were not only discouraged in the academic endeavors, but they were also exposed to other forms of racism that were apparently deleted through the Disney-fication process. The players regularly faced institutional racism at their own university, where one may assume that they would be hailed as heroes for their accomplishments. According to Olsen (1968), the African American athletes lived in segregated housing units at home and on the road, were denied routine and extralegal assistance provided to white teammates, and were repeatedly referred to by their own athletic director George McCarty as "n****r" athletes." Interestingly, the film version of *Glory Road* does not portray McCarty as a blatant racist—something supported by other historical documents (Blackman, 2006; Olsen, 1968).

Throughout the film, racism is represented as something that was generated by competing teams, coaches, and the larger society as a whole. However, according to historical accounts, the treatment of African American athletes on campus was so oppressive that students staged different protests against the Texas Western administration. While there are no reports of collective protests involving the basketball players as a group, that was not the case for the black athletes on the track and football teams, whose demonstrations against racial inequality occurred on campus as well as at sporting venues in New York City and Salt Lake City (Olsen, 1968).

Creative License to Enhance Dramatic Effect: Adding Content to the Movie

Throughout the entire film, the underlining theme is how Coach Haskins and his team overcame societal racism, persevered to win the National Championship, and in doing so, broke down racial barriers in sports. Although the players did experience a great deal of racism throughout their tenure at Texas Western (Blackman, 2006; Olsen, 1968), the film does not portray their experiences accurately. Many instances throughout the film depict Don Haskins' character not only involved in, but also openly discussing the trials and tribulations that his African American athletes were experiencing, when in fact, it seems to be a blatant misrepresentation of reality. "On our team, as far as I knew then or have ever heard, there were no racial problems, no divisions," said Haskins (2006) in his account of the championship run. "While I am sure my players dealt with some racism outside of the team, I wasn't aware of it. Not in El Paso, not on the road. Race just wasn't a topic that was brought up by the team" (Haskins, 2006, p. 167). The entire film is based on a blatant fabrication, signifying that Haskin was a trailblazer for racial justice. Haskins himself negates this myth. He states that he agreed to write his own account of these events only "because he wants everyone to know the truth–that he wasn't a racial pioneer or a civil rights hero; he was just a simple coach seeking victory" (Haskins, 2006, p. 9).

Considering Haskins' descriptions in his autobiography, the two most dramatic scenes of the film dealing with racism appear to be a complete manifestation of the creators of *Glory Road*. In the final scene, before the film's climax, Don Haskins' character sits his team down the night before the championship game. He tells the team that he is going to start five African American players and then he will not play anyone else except for the seven black athletes on the team. In the film, Haskins asks his players: "Are you as sick of the same old tired line of b.s. as I am? I am so sick of it that tonight I made the decision that we are going to put a stop to it forever … I am only gonna play the black players in the final game tomorrow. Just you." In a riveting scene he lets his team know that this decision is to show all of the critics and racists out there that they are just as capable as their counterparts and are in no way mentally inferior. The scene was without a doubt the most powerful and moving moment in the film; unknown to viewers, however, is the fact that the conversation never took place. According to Haskins' (2006) account, the racial significance of the game was a moot point:

> When the game started there was no noticeable reaction from the players or the fans about the racial aspect of the game. None. It was just another game. It may have gone down in history, but at the time I don't think anyone even considered it. (p. 182)

In Haskins' own account of the story, he makes it explicitly clear that he was only there to win and admitted at one point that "I don't want to get into a situation where I am starting all black kids. I don't want to deal with what everyone is going to say" (Haskins, 2006, p. 115). Throughout his autobiography, Haskins works to avoid any other discussion of race at all. "I don't think it would have dawned on me at all what the race of my player was. Anyone who played for me can tell you that I treated everyone the same, that race was not a factor in how I coached the team" (Haskins, 2006, p. 117). The fact that he treated every person as an equal on his team may have been advancement toward some sort of civility during the time period; however, such equal treatment may be inappropriate given the blatant racism that African American athletes experienced. In any case, *Glory Road* revolves around the racial consciousness of the anti-racist-white-hero (Haskins), something that is a Disney creation. For instance, despite the hype that is contrived throughout the film, the championship game was not the first time that five African American starters were set out on the floor. Five African American players were on the floor together many times three years earlier during the 1962–63 season and they actually started together for the first time earlier in the 1965 championship season (Haskins, 2006). In fact, according to the account of one El Paso sports writer, "Haskins had been using mostly his black players as the season progressed. No white player had seen action against Cincinnati and only Armstrong had seen action against Kansas, and that only briefly" (Sanchez, 1991, pp. 118–119).

Throughout the film, two scenes most vividly represent the racism that the Texas Western team faced while playing on the road. In one scene, a Texas Western player is assaulted in the restroom by a group of white men. He helplessly stumbles out of the bathroom and, with a beaten and bloodied face, falls into the arms of his teammates and coach. While this seems to be the one of the only scenes dealing with a substantial representation of racism these players faced, it is not found in any other account of the season, including those of the players. David Lattin, the starting center, discusses this point. "There was one scene in the movie where one of our players is beaten up in a restaurant bathroom and his head gets shoved in the toilet, but that never happened. If anybody would've stuffed one of my guys heads in the toilet like that, they wouldn't have lived to tell about it" (quoted in Blackman, 2006). *Glory Road* suggests that, with the exception of unruly fans and the general public during away games, Texas Western's black players did not encounter much tangible racism (Blackman, 2006). The film itself attempts to represent the broad scope of racism in a few blatant scenes; interesting, these scenes were fabricated through the Disneyfication of *Glory Road*. The irony is that the creators of the film made this decision as opposed to including representations of multiple examples of everyday prejudice, discrimination, and racism that were documented through players' own accounts.

Manipulating the Facts for Heightened Audience Consumption

In the same way that films "based on a true story" omit and insert material, they are also subject to the distortion of reality. Disney has taken license on the film once again, by modifying major details to convey the story that they wish to portray to their audience. These changes begin to appear as soon as the opening credits come to a close. From the onset of the film, the viewer is led to believe that the 1965 championship run is Haskins' first year as the head coach of Texas Western, fresh off his last season coaching a high school girls' basketball team the year before. However, not only was this not his first year coaching at Texas Western, but also Haskins did not even win the title in his first season as the head coach (Blackman, 2006). According to Sanchez (1997), Haskins actually arrived during the 1961–62 season and led the team to a respectable 18–6 record (p. 71). The film also makes it appear that Coach Haskins' recruitment of black players was the first at Texas Western–when in fact black athletes had attended the school for several years (Haskins, 2006; Sanchez, 1997).

In a short description of the Glory Road DVD from UltimateDisney.com, they explain exactly how Haskins seemingly accumulated his championship team. "Through vigorous recruiting, Haskins assembles a line-up with many African-Americans, a novelty in college basketball" (UltimateDisney.Com, 2006). Haskins' character in the film further emphasizes this point when he states, "If we're going to win, we are going to have to change everything, including who we recruit. There are a bunch of guys that no other teams want … I see skill, I see quick, that's what I am putting out on the court." *Glory Road* will have us believe that Haskins was the sole reason for the black players' arrival at Texas Western, when in fact, Black players, including Nolan Richardson, were already on the team when Haskins arrived in 1961–1962 season (Ingram & Sanchez, 1997). Haskins actually dreaded the idea of having to recruit so much that he rarely left Texas to do so (Haskins, 2006). Contrary to the film, historical accounts demonstrate that Don Haskins was not responsible for the integration and recruitment of the African American athletes. When Haskins arrived at Texas Western they were already an integrated institution and had given out scholarships for football, basketball and track to African American athletes (Olsen, 1968). In fact, George McCarty is actually responsible for bringing the first black player to TWC when he was head basketball coach, nearly a decade before Haskins ever set foot in Texas Western University (Ingram & Sanchez, 1997).

Another manipulation that was perpetuated through the Disneyfication of *Glory Road* was related to the competitive nature of the championship season. In order to keep the audience on the edge of their seats, Disney portrayed each game during the season as a hard-fought, nail-biter decided at the sound of the horn. However, according to Harry Flourney, "they had to change a lot of the scores of the games in the movies to make them seem closer and heighten the drama" (quoted in Robinson, 2006). The Texas Western Miners actually produced one of the greatest seasons in college basketball and achieved a top national ranking for most of the season; with a 28–1 record; they were not involved in many close contests (Sanchez, 1997). Ignoring these facts, the film portrays each game as if they were almost lucky to come out with a victory. Even in the championship game the announcers refer to their team as the "little mining college from west Texas," that no one would have predicted would be in the national championship. The 1966 team, building off of the success of previous seasons, was rated number three overall in the national poll and had a 28-1 record (Haskins, 2006). These credentials would be impossible to ignore by anyone involved in the NCAA, and according to Sanchez (1991), Texas Western was favored in the semifinal game against Utah and, out of ten coaches, one picked them to win the National Championship against the University of Kentucky.

After the exciting win against the basketball powerhouse Kentucky, the Texas Western Miners return as heroes to their hometown of El Paso. At least that is what we understand based on the airport scene, during which the players are warmly greeted by thousands of fans at the airport. While that scene matches historical accounts, Willie Worsley talks about the reality after this initial celebration. He states that after the airport reception, a parade and a banquet, "that was about the end of it. We were never campus heroes. We were never invited to mixers or anything like that" (quoted in Blackman, 2006). Before and after that game, the predominately white university community, including the coaches and administration, made it clear to the black players that they were there to play basketball and garner little else. In fact, Worsley stated that he and the other black players continued to be treated like "animals by their white coaches, teammates, and others at the school" (quoted in Blackman, 2006). Even Ed Sullivan, who usually invited the national championship team on his show when they won the big game, never invited the team to attend the show (Haskins, 2006, pp. 187–188).

In summary, our critical analysis compared and contrasted historical accounts of the 1966 Texas Western College NCAA championship team with that which was portrayed in the film, *Glory Road*. More specifically, we examine the Disneyfication process, which strategically manipulated the story—through the addition of certain fictional events as well as the elimination and/or distortion of actual occurrences—in order to produce an attractive story for viewers. Within our final section, we explicate how this process in *Glory Road*, and other films like it, hinder effective race relations.

Conclusion: Collective Race Memory and Contemporary U.S. Society

According to Madison (1999), "films are not simply about how we remember the past; they affect how we interpret the present" (p. 414). As such "historical" films, like *Glory Road*, play a significant role in the creation—and maintenance—of the collective memory of race in the United States. While it is commonly understood that creative license will be used to maximize the film's attraction to potential viewers, we draw critical attention to the consequences of such strategies. In particular, we critique the Disneyfication that occurs when historical events are manipulated, sanitized, and co-opted with little or no concern to accuracy. Within this final section, we articulate how the film contributes to a collective memory that regards racism as a non-issue in 21st century U.S. race relations.

Glory Road, and other anti-racist-white-hero films, contributes to an understanding of racism that is reflective of the privileged racial locations of European Americans. In other words, the collective memory that is established is one that facilitates an understanding of racism as of marginal importance in a color-blind present-day society. In other words, viewers are led to believe that race is no longer important in a country that has moved beyond race problems of the past. The film promotes this ideal in three different ways. First, racism is constructed as something within a historical context and relieves the viewer from any responsibility to see it as a salient contemporary issue. The fact that "historical" films like *Glory Road* are made, while others that reflect current racialized events are not, is telling. Second, racism is defined in terms of the most explicitly blatant forms possible (e.g., use of racial epithets, death threats, violence). Accordingly, little or no attention is given to the everyday ways in which racism is institutionalized within U.S. society. Third, racism is situated as a threat from external sources, something that is removed from the community itself. In this regard, the problem of racism is never motivation for self-exploration; instead it is seen as an issue for others, and never self.

The result of a collective memory of racism—constructed in such a manner—leads to the premature acceptance that we are currently living in a color-blind society. In particular, *Glory Road* serves to demonstrate how racial inequality on and off the field is a thing of the past. The strides of African American athletes, and by extension African American coaches, are undeniable. However, the reality of collegiate sports is far from idyllic, especially when one critically examines the over-representation of African American athletes in select sports and the small number who assume post-collegiate positions of power (Mangan & Ritchie, 2004; Wiggins & Miller, 2005). When one contextualizes these numbers against the backdrop of national statistics that illustrate how African Americans are over-represented in every major social ill (crimes, disease, poverty, illiteracy, etc.), the legacy of racism becomes apparently clear (Hecht, Jackson, & Ribeau, 2003). However, given liberal sensibilities that desperately want to embrace the ideal of a color-blind society, the necessity of *Glory Road* becomes clear. We need this story, because if we didn't have it—and others like it—we would have to face the fact that racism is real and continues to plague all aspects of U.S. society.

DISCUSSION QUESTIONS

1. What are your reactions to the arguments made in this chapter? What aspects do you agree, and/or disagree, with?

2. Do you think that the arguments extend to other similar films, such as *Wildcats* (1986), *Sunset Park* (1996), and *Remember the Titans* (2003)? Why, or why not?

3. How do you think that other films—like those with an African American coach (e.g. *Coach Carter*, 2005 and *Pride*, 2007)—compare to *Glory Road*?

4. What, if any, feature films exist that reflect "realistic/honest" depictions of contemporary race relations?

---

[1] According to different accounts, college basketball in the 1950s and 1960s followed an unwritten rule: "You can play two blacks at home, three on the road, and four if you were losing. But never, ever five at once" (Haskins, 2006, p. 8). Interestingly, the rationale behind the rule remains unclear: Was the rule in place because playing five black players was (1) unfair given their athletic superiority, or (2) unwise given their intellectual inferiority? In either case, the problematic stereotype of the African American athlete is evident.

[2] The accolades for the 1966 championship team continue to present time: Coach Haskins accepted a lifetime award from the NCAA, and in 2007 the entire team was nominated for entry into the Basketball Hall of Fame.

[3] Disneyfication, in this context, refers to a process by which a factual event is transformed into a media product. As such, the process results in a version of the original story that is oversimplified and sanitized, and therefore, viewed as more marketable to a large viewing audience (see, for example, Buckingham, 1997).

[4] Other films that help to define this genre include *Wildcats* (1986), *Sunset Park* (1996), *Remember the Titans* (2003), and *Coach Carter* (2005).

[5] In order to transform Don Haskins into the anti-racist-white-hero, the Disneyfication of character involved eliminating any mention of his drinking and gambling and creating a racial consciousness that reportedly did not exist (Haskins, 2006).

[6] A review of the 117-page screenplay reveals that many scenes, which were included in the original adaptation of the Haskins' (2006) autobiography, were deleted from the ultimate project. This natural elimination of content, due to length restrictions, speaks to multiple locations through which the Disneyfication process was enacted.

References

Blackman, D. L. (2006). *Glory Road, a miscarriage of glory. The Black Commentator.* Retrieved on January 19, 2007 from http://www.blackcommentator.com/171/171_think_blackman_glory_road.html

Bryman, A. (1995). *Disney and his worlds.* New York: Routledge.

Buckingham, D. (1997). Dissin' Disney: Critical perspectives on children's media culture. *Media, Culture, & Society, 19,* 285–293.

Cuomo, C. (1995). Spinsters in sensible shoes: *Mary Poppins* and *Bedknobs and Broomsticks.* In E. Bell, L. Haas, & L. Sells (Eds.), *From mouse to mermaid: The politics of film, gender, and culture* (pp. 212–223). Bloomington: Indiana University Press.

Eagan, D. (2006, February). *Glory Road movie review,* pp. 27–28.

Gabriel, J. (1998). *Whitewash: Racialized politics and the media.* London: Routledge.

Glory Road DVD Review. (2006). Retrieved on March 17, 2007 from http://www.ultimatedisney.com/gloryroad-pressrelease.html

Glory Road Official DVD Website. (n. d.). Retrieved on March 17, 2007 from http://disney.go.com/dsineyvideos/livaction/gloryroad/

Giroux, H. (1995). Memory and pedagogy in the "Wonderful World of Disney:" Beyond the politics of innocence. In E. Bell, L. Haas, & L. Sells (Eds.), *From mouse to mermaid: The politics of film, gender, and culture* (pp. 43–61). Bloomington: Indiana University Press.

Haas, R. (1995). Disney does Dutch: *Billy Bathgate* and the disneyfication of the gangster genre. In E. Bell, L. Haas, & L. Sells (Eds.), *From mouse to mermaid: The politics of film, gender, and culture* (pp. 72–85). Bloomington: Indiana University Press.

Haskins D. (with D. Wetzel) (2006). *Glory road* New York: Hyperion.

Hecht, M. L., Jackson, R. L., & Ribeau, S. A. (2003). *African American communication: Exploring identity and culture.* Mahwah, NJ: Erlbaum.

Ingram, B., & Sanchez, R. (1997). *The Miners: The history of sports at University of Texas at El Paso.* El Paso, TX: MESA Publishing Corporation.

Lowery, B. (2006, January 16). Disney hoops it up. *Variety,* pp. 33–34.

Madison, D. S. (1995). *Pretty Woman* through the triple lens of black feminist spectatorship. In E. Bell, L. Haas, & L. Sells (Eds.), *From mouse to mermaid: The politics of film, gender, and culture* (pp. 224–235). Bloomington: Indiana University Press.

Madison, K. J. (1999). Legitimation crisis and containment: The "anti-racist-white-hero" film. *Critical Studies in Mass Communication, 16*(4), 399–416.

Mangan, J. A. & Ritchie, A. (2004). Ethnicity, Sport, Identity: Struggles for status. London: Frank Cass.

Miller, S., & Rode, G. (1995). The movie you see, the movie you don't: How Disney do's that old time derision. In E. Bell, L. Haas, & L. Sells (Eds.), *From mouse to mermaid: The politics of film, gender, and culture* (pp. 86–103). Bloomington: Indiana University Press.

Olsen, J. (1968). *The black athlete a shameful story: The myth of integration in American sport*. New York: Time-Life Books.

Ono, K., & Buescher, D. T. (2001). Deciphering Pocahontas: Unpackaging the commodification of a native American woman. *Critical Studies in Media Communication, 18*(1), 23–43.

Patton, C. (1995). White racism/black signs: Censorship and images of race relations. *Journal of Communication, 45*(2), 65–77.

Robinson, J. (2006). *Starting five: The true story behind Glory Road and the Texas Western Miners*. Retrieved on January 21, 2007 from http://ign.com/articles/679/679216pl.html

Sanchez, R. (1991). *Basketball's biggest upset*. New York: Authors Choice Press.

Shohat, E. & Stam, R. (1994). *Unthinking eurocentrism: Multi-culturalism and the media*. London: Routledge.

Smoodin, E. (Ed.) (1994). *Disney discourse: Producing the magic kingdom*. New York: Routledge.

Zelizer, B. (1995). Reading the past against the grain: The shape of memory studies. *Critical Studies in Mass Communication, 12*(2), 214–239.

Wickstrom, M. (2005). The Lion King, Mimesis, and Disney's Magical Capitalism. In M. Budd and M. H. Kirsch (Eds.), Rethinking Disney: Private control, public dimension (pp. 99–124). Middletown, CT: Wesleyan University Press.

Wiggins, D. K. & Miller, P. B. (2005). The Unlevel Playing Field: A documentary history of the African American experience in sport. Urbana: University of Illinois Press: Champaign, IL.

Zipes, J. (1995). Breaking the Disney spell. In E. Bell, L. Haas, & L. Sells (Eds.), *From mouse to mermaid: The politics of film, gender, and culture* (pp. 21–42). Bloomington: Indiana University Press.

23

Native Press Freedoms: Federal and Tribal Legal Issues Restricting Native Media

Rebecca J. Tallent and Rubell S. Dingman

Abstract

Native American tribes are separate, sovereign nations with their own governments and laws. These laws directly influence how media outlets may operate within their borders, by determining what gets reported, and by whom. Journalists who work for tribal outlets, therefore, do not have the same press freedoms granted under the First Amendment as their non-Native counterparts who work for mainstream media. Non-Native journalists may also encounter tribal resistance as they work on stories about Native issues. In this essay, we examine the history of Native press freedoms, how some Native nations cope within these laws, and how these legal statutes affect news reporting by both tribal and non-Native journalists.

KEY TERMS: Native American news media, mainstream U.S. media, Cherokee Nation, Independent Press Act of 2000, the First Amendment, Indian Civil Rights Act of 1968, *Santa Clara Pueblo v. Martinez*

Congress shall make no law respecting an establishment of religion, or prohibiting the free exercise thereof; or abridging the freedom of speech, or of the press; or the right of the people peaceably to assemble, and to petition the Government for a redress of grievances —(First Amendment to the U.S. Constitution).

Introduction

For generations, most journalists in the United States have been able to count on the 47 words of the First Amendment as the ultimate guarantor of a free press. Many Americans may take this constitutional declaration for granted because it has been in place for more than 220 years. But the rights the First Amendment guarantees may not be applicable for reporters writing for tribal newspapers, for non-Native journalists who work for tribal news organizations, or for mainstream journalists who try to report on Indian Country. How these Native and non-Native journalists write and report their stories depends upon how the tribal courts view freedom of the press.

Many Native Nations do have freedom of the press built into their separate constitutions, and many of these documents are modeled after the U.S. Constitution. However, as Mark Trahant, respected Native journalist and former editorial page editor of the *Seattle Post-Intelligencer* said, there is frequently no application of these measures, because the tribal government that grants the press freedom also oversees management of its media (M. Trahant, personal communication, March 12, 2008). Under the complexities of Native American laws, press freedom may not apply to all journalists in Indian Country. And Indian Country is found throughout the entire United States and its territories. The uneven separation between media and government has prompted many tribal reporters to say they are caught between two worlds: tribal and the rest of the country. This creates a paradox for Native journalists who choose to work for their tribal news organizations. Mainstream journalists who cover Native America are also challenged by tribal laws, because they additionally face cultural barriers, suspicion by tribal leaders, and general mistrust of their motives.

This essay explores restrictions placed on Native media by federal laws, and analyzes the specific Press Freedoms Amendments held by the three tribes with press freedom acts: The Oklahoma and Eastern Band of the Cherokee Nation (the same people but geographically divided as a Nation following the Trail of Tears journeys, which began in 1838) and the Navajo Nation. The actions of the Navajo Nation are important because it is the only Native Nation where the tribal newspaper has become an independent organization. We also explore the impact of these laws upon mainstream journalists and their efforts to report tribal news. Section One provides an overview of these Native Nations and the media-related laws that affect news reporting. Section Two offers insights about the conflicts and negotiations that occur between journalists and tribal governments as reported to us in interviews conducted with persons from both groups and by review of historical documents.

I. Native Nations and Media Laws

Native Media Tied to Federal Laws, Court Decisions

Native media have been expanding since 1980, primarily due to (1) economic growth in tribal communities, (2) increased professionalism among Native reporters and editors and (3) a heightened sense of tribal sovereignty (Loew & Mella, 2005). The 2007 *Reading Red Report* shows about 322 Native journalists work in both tribal and mainstream media outlets in the United States (Azocar, 2007). As Native Nations gain in political power, mainstream newspapers seem to be taking Native tribes more seriously, although not always for positive reasons (Azocar, 2007). These factors may all be contributing to more uncertainty or conflict between tribal media outlets and tribal councils.

Native press law is tied to many laws and court decisions involving Native Americans. *However, some of these laws and decisions do not seem to have any relationship to media law unless they are viewed within the context of how the U.S. government has perceived all American Indian issues.* It is important to note Native Americans and tribal governments have long been viewed as sovereign nations, a concept that stems from Thomas Jefferson as he articulated it in his 1793 letters to President George Washington (Johnson, 1982). This concept of sovereignty is core to Native media issues because, as sovereign nations, each individual tribe is separated from U.S. federal and state governments, meaning tribal media are therefore separated from laws on these levels governing media. In this essay, the federal rulings discussed relate only to reporters (both Native and non-Native) who work for tribal media. The first landmark change in the sovereignty issue came in 1831 when the *Cherokee Nation v. Georgia* case was decided by the U.S. Supreme Court. The Cherokees had petitioned the court to decide if the tribe was a sovereign nation, which would prevent the U.S. federal government from stripping their powers and forcing the tribe to move (Marshall, 1831). The court ruled the Cherokee Nation was neither a state of the union nor a foreign state but a "domestic dependent nation" (Marshall, 1831; Johnson, 1982). In the 1832 case of *Worcester v. Georgia*, the high court upheld the sovereignty of the Cherokee Nation and granted full governing power of tribal affairs to tribal government (Johnson, 1982). Johnson observed:

> *Cherokee Nation* and *Worcester* established the American Indian nations as unique political entities existing within the boundaries of the states. The tribes' independence from the states and their sovereignty over their own affairs were clearly affirmed in the *Worcester* decision. Furthermore, the concept of "domestic dependent nations" linked them to the federal government for guardianship and support. Federal protection of tribal sovereignty had been guaranteed (Johnson, 1982, p. 32).

In spite of the exemptions from federal protections to guarantee a free press, American Indians have successfully produced newspapers and other traditional forms of journalistic communications since 1828 when Elias Boudinot established the *Cherokee Phoenix* newspaper in New Echota, Georgia using the syllabi or "alphabet" developed by Sequoyah (Murphy, 1998). Despite many internal issues within the tribe, including arguments for and against removal from Georgia, this original bi-lingual (Cherokee and English) newspaper was published until May 31, 1843, when it was closed for lack of funds. The *Cherokee Phoenix* remained closed until 1954 when it was resurrected in Oklahoma (Murphy, 1998). George Frizzell of Western Carolina University said the *Phoenix* was founded contemporaneously with other well-known U.S. newspapers, such as the *Charleston Mercury* (1822), *New York Evening Post* (1829), and *New York Sun* (1833) (Worthy, 2007).

Many other Native newspapers were soon formed, including the *Navajo Times*, the *Seminole Tribune* and the *Shawnee Sun* (Trahant, 1995). Each of these publications was also run much as newspapers of that time period operated: giving the news of the day, usually in the language of the people the reporters and editors served. Frequently, these newspapers were perceived and understood as were other ethnic publications–that is, with little or no thought or consideration from the mainstream American media.

Native journalists, however, understood there was one major difference between them and the mainstream press: *In representing a sovereign nation, they were not subject to the First Amendment of the U.S. Constitution and therefore were lacking in the essential element of freedom of the press.* The difference stems from a combination of federal actions: The U.S. government declaring Native Nations sovereign (*Cherokee Nation v. Georgia*) in 1831, the federal government returning some rights to tribal members in the 1968 Indian Civil Rights Act, and the U.S. Supreme Court's decision in the landmark 1978 Santa Clara case that tribal courts or ruling councils could interpret which rights could be held by Native citizens. We believe, as do others who study Native issues, that this Supreme Court ruling served to make the nature and the extent of press freedoms in Native Nations unclear both to people who own and work in Native media, as well as outside forces.

As a direct result of the Santa Clara case, many Native publications, radio, and TV stations became little more than a public relations arm of the tribe's government, giving only "good" news or information dictated from the tribal government. Because tribal media outlets are owned and operated by the individual tribes, reporters and editors could be fired or transferred if they chose to cover a news story over the objections of the tribal government, which may ask tribal courts to remove any press freedoms.

Federal Law and Native American Press

A peculiar issue for the United States is that, although Native Nations are recognized as sovereign entities, they are also overseen by the U.S. government and somewhat controlled by existing federal laws, including both Congressional acts and U.S. Supreme Court decisions. A key element to understanding many of the issues involving Native news media restrictions lies in understanding the two primary laws that impact tribal media outlets, which are the Indian Civil Rights Act of 1968 and the Santa Clara Case. Each is discussed below.

Indian Civil Rights Act of 1968 and the Santa Clara Case

An attempt by Congress to clarify and correct the status of Native Americans was the Indian Civil Rights Act (ICRA) of 1968. Similar in overall tone to the Civil Rights Act of 1964, the 1968 act was specifically designed to address the issue of Native Americans who lived in the United States as citizens, but were also citizens of sovereign nations (*Harvard Law Review*, 1982). It gave Native Americans rights similar to, but not identical to, the rights enjoyed by mainstream U.S. journalists under the U.S. Constitution (*Harvard Law Review*, 1982). Of the 564 federally recognized Native nations located within the United States, the tribal members are not subject to either state or federal law within tribal lands (Saharko, 2006).

The ICRA provided that Native Americans, within their own sovereign nations, have rights similar to those in the U.S. Constitution, including:

> No Indian tribe in exercising powers of self-government shall make or enforce any law prohibiting the free exercise of religion, or abridging the freedom of speech, or of the press, or the right of people peaceably to assemble and to petition for a redress of grievances (ICRA, 1968).

Although worded similar to the First Amendment, this phrase has a negative twist. Although the IRCA would not allow the sovereign nations to create laws prohibiting free speech or free press, the measure left open the opportunity for tribal courts to intervene by providing for an appeal of any section through tribal and federal courts (Harvard Law Review, 1982).

One of the country's larger tribes, the Cherokee, has bills of rights in their own Constitutions–one for the Oklahoma and one for the Eastern Band–that expressly provide for press freedom. Other tribal governments still directly influence the majority of their news media by controlling the economic livelihood of the tribal media outlets. One exception to this condition is media operated by the Navajo Nation (Hamby, 2005). In 2002, the *Navajo Times* separated from the tribe's government for a five-year trial period as an independent newspaper. Currently, the newspaper remains separated as an independent press subsisting on advertising revenues and subscriptions.

Because Native nations are seen as separate, sovereign nations, *the U.S. Supreme Court has also given tribal members the right to exclude people from their lands and business dealings*–places most Americans would consider "public" (Saharko, 2006). This allows tribes to keep traditional mainstream reporters and journalists at bay because the U.S. Supreme Court has ruled the tribes have the power to exclude non-members from lands and organizations (*Atkinson Trading Co. v. Shirley*, 2001).

In recent years, the mainstream media have been successfully turned away from events on tribal lands, including the March 21, 2005 mass shootings at the Red Lake Band of the Chippewa High School in Minnesota (Saharko, 2006). Following the shootings by 16-year-old Jeffrey Weise, who killed seven people, the Minnesota and national news media descended on the reservation, but were stonewalled about information. What the frustrated non-Native reporters failed to realize is that as a sovereign nation, the leaders of the Red Lake Band felt they did not need to share what happened because they did not consider the event public information (Saharko, 2006).

Santa Clara Pueblo v. Martinez. Despite the freedoms guaranteed under the ICRA, the law ran into problems when the Martinez family sued the Santa Clara Pueblo of New Mexico. Martinez was a tribal member who was seeking recognition of her children by the Santa Clara government. As argued before the U.S. Supreme Court on Nov. 29, 1977, the case centered on the right of a female member of the Pueblo to have her children (who were fathered by a non-tribal member) recognized as tribal members. The case cited the ICRA as providing several civil rights, including the inability of a tribal government to create a law that would "deny to any person within its jurisdiction the equal protection of its laws or to deprive any person of liberty or property without the due process of law" (ICRA, 1968). The case brought all the rights, including press freedom, of the ICRA into the spotlight of Native law.

This was a very complex case that, on the surface, involved tribal membership and responsibilities. The Supreme Court ruled in a majority opinion written by Justice Thurgood Marshall that tribal sovereignty means tribal courts may interpret constitutional provisions incorporated under the ICRA in a different light from federal courts that may read and/or interpret them (*Santa Clara Pueblo v. Martinez*, 1978). This decision also affected press freedom and left Native journalists in the same dilemma they had prior to the ICRA: If tribal courts decided they did not want a free press, the Native courts could restrict press freedom by ignoring the specific provision under the ICRA as granted by the Santa Clara case.

In his dissent on this case, Justice Byron White argued the ICRA gave no indication that the constitutional rights extended to Native Americans must only be enforced by one line of legal justice. He noted specifically that "any Indian tribe in exercising its powers of local self-government shall be subject to the same limitations and restraints as those which are imposed on the Government of the United States by the United States Constitution" (Dissent of Justice White, *Santa Clara Pueblo v. Martinez*, 1978). In addition, White said:

> While I believe that the uniqueness of Indian culture must be taken into
> consideration in applying the constitutional rights granted in 1802 [the ICRA],

I do not think that it requires insulation of official tribal actions from federal court scrutiny. Nor do I find any indication that Congress so intended (Dissent of Justice White, *Santa Clara Pueblo v. Martinez*, 1978).

In his research for the Reporter's Committee for Freedom of the Press, Peter Saharko (2006) found this key decision demonstrates the deference the U.S. Supreme Court has given tribal courts, noting the Santa Clara case severely weakened the ICRA because there is little chance that tribal cases will be appealed to the federal court system; therefore, the tribal government is in complete control of the courts and tribal law (Saharko, 2006). As the *Harvard Law Review* said in a 1982 examination of tribal sovereignty, in *Santa Clara* the Supreme Court unambiguously reaffirmed the doctrine of tribal immunity, holding the ICRA was not a general waiver of tribal immunity (*Harvard Law Review*, 1982). *Because of this decision, one of the complications Native news organizations face is that the government is the owner of the media rather than the media operating under individual ownership.*

> Even if there is a Press Freedom Act in place, if the government oversees the press then that changes the outcome. If I try to argue, and we realize that argument is the trappings of dissent and discourse, to use that (Press Freedom Act) rather than the First Amendment changes things? Every adult, because they are people, have a right to speak (M. Trahant, personal communication, March 12, 2008).

II. Journalists and Tribal Governments: Conflicts and Negotiations

Journalists Tell Their Stories

How do the aforementioned laws and court cases play out in the actual news reporting by Native and non-Native journalists? Some tribes have put their own press laws in place, while others work quietly behind the scenes trying to make small changes. For this section, we conducted formal, journalistic-style interviews with Native reporters and editors who were selected because their tribe had a press freedom act or because they were known as individuals who are quietly trying to make changes to press law within their respective nations. The non-Native journalists interviewed for this essay were selected because of their recent experiences with a Native Nation in trying to cover an event on tribal lands. All of the reporters were interviewed by telephone. The Native journalists were asked specifically about their process of covering their tribes with or without an Independent Press Act. Non-Native journalists were specifically asked about their experience with local tribes. Here, we share their perspectives by first providing the backdrop of a specific case of the Cherokee Independent Press Act and then including other instances across several Native nations.

The Cherokee Independent Press Act

In 1997, the Cherokee Nation of Oklahoma found itself in a heated and, from a public relations viewpoint, disastrous political situation in which some members of the tribe physically took over the tribal courthouse in Tahlequah, Oklahoma. They held the courthouse building, with all the official documents of the nation, hostage as a reaction to what some said were unfair actions by the principal chief. As part of the election controversy, *Cherokee Advocate* (now the *Cherokee Phoenix and Advocate*) editor Dan Agent was removed by Principal Chief Joe Byrd for reporting on allegations of misconduct by Byrd (Hamby, 2005), although Agent said it was part of the tribe's reorganization move by Byrd (Agent, 1998). Interestingly, Agent was not the only journalist facing the same problem at that time. In 1998 *Navajo Times* editor Tom Arviso, Jr., survived two attempts to fire him for running allegations of misconduct by the Navajo President Albert Hale (Hamby, 2005).

Responding to the aftermath of the Cherokee crisis, the new Principal Chief Chad Smith called on his nation to allow for press freedom, and the Cherokee nation passed the Independent Press Act of 2000. The act codified both the Native nation's free press provision in the Constitution and the Nation's commitment to free press and free speech (Saharko, 2005; Hamby, 2006).

Specifically, the Independent Press Act for the Oklahoma Cherokees based in Tahlequah, states as policy:

> The Cherokee Nation's Press shall be independent from any undue influence and free of any particular political interest. It is the duty of the press to report without bias the activities of the government and the news of interest to have informed citizens (Independent Press Act of 2000).

The Act also provides that the editor must:

> … be free from the political influence from any department of the government of the Nation and may be removed only for cause. The Editor shall not directly or indirectly solicit, receive, or in any manner be concerned in soliciting or receiving any assessment or contribution for any political organization, candidacy or other political purpose. The Editor shall not participate in any political campaign or be involved in any tribal political activity, except to exercise his or her individual opinion and to exercise his or her right to vote (Independent Press Act of 2000).

In personal communication (January 15, 2008), Bryan Pollard, executive editor of the *Cherokee Phoenix and Advocate* (the newspaper for the Oklahoma Cherokees) said that for his paper, the Independent Press Act is strictly applied: "Separation of power is very strict. ... The branches honor the Free Press Act." He adds, "There is no prior restraint although I do get criticized for some things that are published, but (tribal) officials don't take action to punish the *Phoenix*." In his five years with the paper, Pollard goes on to say that he has never seen a time when he felt officials with the Oklahoma Cherokees were violating the Act. According to Pollard, "The story really illustrates how legislation is different from tribe to tribe." He argues that "In the Eastern Band, the act is identical but it is not honored by the Eastern Band" (2008).

In an apparent contradiction of the act, in 2007 the Eastern Band of the Cherokee Nation based in Cherokee, N.C. (which had passed an identical Independent Press Act in 2006), Joe Martin, editor of the *Cherokee One Feather* newspaper, was involuntarily reassigned by the tribal management (Good Voice, 2007). The Martin case is complicated because the North Carolina Tribal officials claim Martin was re-assigned for (a) violating the tribe's ethical principles, (b) specifically for speaking with the *Ashville (NC) Citizen-Times*, (c) expressing his own opinion of the administration and (d) identifying his position within the tribe. Martin has said his reassignment was due to "undue political pressure" on tribal government, especially pressure to remove the "Rants and Raves" (editorial comment) section of the tribal newspaper (Good Voice, 2007). Martin rejected the reassignment and is currently appealing the involuntary job transfer through federal channels.

Pollard said the Martin case is a good example of two tribes with identical legislation where one tribe supports its free press protections while the other doesn't. "For us, the Act works well and has [the] same freedoms than any other press. We do have occasional disagreements with Communications Department; but we have the freedom to find our stories," Pollard said (personal communication, Jan. 15, 2008).

Some tribal editors say, while their papers are owned by the tribe, their pages are not controlled by the tribe. For instance, Jennifer DeGraffenreid Fletcher, editor of the Coeur d'Alene *Council Fires* in Plummer, Idaho, explained that her paper is more like a small town newspaper than a public relations piece for the Coeur d'Alene Nation. "Our council doesn't interfere," she said. "The previous editor had a lot of interference, but since I've taken over I've only been asked not to run something once; they wanted to wait until a court case was final, and it was more of a suggestion. Like any journalist, there are some things they won't tell me such as legal settlements, but it's not really an issue. My goal is to provide information through our paper" (J. Fletcher, personal communication, March 12, 2008).

Like Fletcher, Dodie Manuel, editor of the Salt River Pima Maricopa Nation's Au-Authm Action News said her paper is not reviewed by council members prior to publication, but her staff is taking small steps in making the paper more hard news oriented. Manuel explained her newspaper staff began by publishing the council meeting minutes, and after some discussion by tribal members, the minutes are still printed. She said the staff does not do anything drastic, but continues to make small changes.

Native journalists including Bryan Pollard of the *Cherokee Phoenix* and Mark Trahant, formerly of the *Seattle Post-Intelligencer* have recently indicated that financial independence from tribal government may or may not be a future solution for many Native journalists. In December 1996, Reese Cleghorn predicted a situation similar to Martin's (Eastern Band) when he discussed the issue of Native press rights in his *American Journalism Review* column:

> It is natural enough for tribal politicians to think they deserve a pass from the media they pay for ... The dilemma for the journalists, whose overall number and stature have grown greatly in recent years, is how to stand up to the power and still publish or broadcast. (Cleghorn, 1996, p. 4).

So far, financial independence has only been achieved by the *Navajo Times*. In 2002, the tribe separated the newspaper as an independent organization serving a base circulation of 16,800 people in New Mexico, Arizona, Colorado and Utah.

Mainstream Journalists and Native Nations

There is also the question of how Native Nations treat and interact with mainstream journalists. Much of that treatment stems from the sovereignty issue. Trahant said that in addition to most mainstream journalists not understanding tribal issues, they also fail to recognize that Natives see themselves as being only a few decades away from termination or complete elimination as a people, and they are suspicious of outsiders (M. Trahant, personal communication, March 12, 2008). Loew & Mella (2005) stated that non-tribal journalists–and by implication their readers–misunderstand tribal sovereignty "and fail to understand how it informs public debate" of Native America in today's U.S. society (p. 102).

These sovereignty and cultural clashes can often place tribal reporters in an untenable position. For instance, during the 2005 mass shootings at the Red Lake Band of the Chippewa High School in Minnesota, tribal reporter Dalton Walker said he was caught between two worlds: trying to protect his tribe while also trying to help the non-Native journalists understand the tribal issues (Saharko, 2006). These tensions and competing interests jump to the foreground for Native journalists, particularly when there are news events that attract mainstream media. The 2007 *Reading Red Report* said that many newspapers, even those papers with high local Native populations, poorly reported on tribes, rarely getting beyond issues such as casinos and smoke shops (Azocar, 2007).

In their 2005 monograph, Loew & Mella clearly show the differences in understanding by explaining the case of *Time* magazine's critical 2002 series of tribal casinos by a pair of Pulitzer Prize-winning journalists, David Bartlett and James Steele. The reporters produced universal outrage in Indian Country with their lack of understanding about how tribes work as independent sovereign nations and by making accusations about unfair distribution of casino earnings (Loew & Mella, 2005). The articles promoted a response from Jodi Rave, a reporter for the *Lincoln Journal Star* in Nebraska and a former board member of the Native American Journalists Association. In the monograph, Rave said the *Time* series reduced all Native Nations into a single entity. She concluded it was written in a tone that would make the articles acceptable to White audiences without a shred of historical underpinning to explain the concept of tribal sovereignty as well as differences between tribes (Loew & Mella, 2005).

An opposite view was shared by Kevin Graman, a reporter with *The Spokesman-Review* newspaper in Spokane, Washington, who had a situation with the Spokane Tribe in the fall of 2006. Graman said he had been told by the tribe's communications director that tribal members were upset about stories he had written about allegations of corruption by tribal business leaders. The communications director said she would no longer speak with Graman or cooperate with the newspaper, despite the fact Graman was covering the tribe as he would another government and wanted to continue doing so (K. Graman, personal communication, March 28, 2008).

Graman said to help clarify the problems he arranged a meeting between his editors and tribal leaders. "When I arrived, I was told I would have to wait outside council chambers; that only tribal leaders and my editors would be allowed inside," he said. "It was later explained to me by a friend who is a Spokane tribal member that not being allowed 'inside the teepee' was a deliberate sign of disrespect. I had guessed as much" (K. Graman, personal communication, March 28, 2008). While waiting, the reporter said he noticed an oversized binder on a table which was the master plan and marketing study for an off-reservation casino, hotel, and shopping complex. After taking notes from the book, Graman enlisted the aid of a business reporter and wrote a front-page story about the venture (K. Graman, personal communication, March 28, 2008). As of March, 2008, Graman said he still has a strained relationship with some tribal leaders, but has a good working relationship with tribal members, including a few tribal activists (K. Graman, personal communication, March 28, 2008).

Trahant said that non-Native journalists frequently fail to establish a good working relationship with tribes prior to a crisis situation, so there is no trust between the tribal members and the news media. In addition, he said, non-Native journalists do not understand that as sovereign nations, tribes do not need to comply with federal laws concerning freedom of information (M. Trahant, personal communication, March 12, 2008). "Why would they (tribal members) give up information that would be dangerous to them?" he asked, referencing back to the idea that Native nations are disappearing (M. Trahant, personal communication, March 12, 2008).

> (Mainstream) Reporters have no right to go cover Indian Nation governments. Now, if the reporters have taken the time to be on the reservation before the crisis and have opened avenues of respect then they might be able to report, otherwise it isn't going to fly no matter what the law is. Look back at Red Lake, reporters went in there with satellite trucks and expected the rules to be the same. They're not (M. Trahant, personal communication, March 12, 2008).

Trahant was quoted in Loew & Mella's 2005 monograph as saying colleges and universities do not teach the basics of why tribes are sovereign governments, which results in a fractured view of Native Nations by journalists and journalism students. He said it leaves open the door for detractors or opponents to have their views understood more than the tribal perspective because they are accessible to the mainstream media. In a personal interview, Trahant also said that mainstream media do not understand the cultural differences between Native cultures and the cultural mainstream of the United States (M. Trahant, personal communication, March 12, 2008). For instance both cultures perceive time very differently; whereas most Americans would see 10 years as a long period, in the Native world 10 years is a very short amount of time. He said it is these types of cross-cultural differences in perspectives that mainstream media often do not understand, which creates problems in covering Tribal affairs (M. Trahant, personal communication, March 12, 2008).

Conclusion

Loew and Mella (2005) make the clear point that mainstream journalists fail to understand tribal sovereignty as a legal issue, which is compounded by an error made by many journalists of equating sovereignty with affirmative action, gaming (casinos), hunting, and other programs. The majority of mainstream journalists also fail to see that tribal sovereignty is a key issue for reporting in and on Native lands and issues. On the other hand, Native journalists are keenly aware of their limitations under tribal sovereignty, and work within their varying tribal systems. Most tribal news outlets do their jobs reporting information to their communities in spite of a lack of explicit press freedom. While the Oklahoma and Eastern Band of the Cherokee Nation have put Independent Press Acts into place, they have had varying responses to the letter and the spirit of the acts. This leaves open the question: how dedicated is the Eastern Band to its Press Freedom Act?

For Native journalists who operate without an Independent Press Act, there is not a large amount of freedom when they are reporting. They must instead operate under the rules of the tribal council and through whatever the tribal court has determined the extent of their press freedom might be. For Native media outlets, taking small steps may be one approach to expanding press freedom. While this method appears slow to the outside world, in tribal life, this is an acceptable method of movement. For non-Native media, there are multiple areas that need improvement, starting with the concept of covering the local Native Nations rather than ignoring them due to access and cultural issues. It is a slow process for a non-Native journalist to gain trust with a Native community; but once gained, it is an invaluable ally in obtaining correct information and providing information about an aspect of local communities that are often ignored by the mainstream press.

This review provides a limited focuses on the complex issue of Native news media's access to freedom of the press. Future study should include how tribal news organizations operate without an Independent Press Act or active free press rights from tribal constitutions. A future investigation could also examine tribes who are purchasing mainstream media, and how these acquisitions might impact mainstream reporting.

Native Americans are a minority group in America today and Mark Trahant in his 2008 interview made an observation that Native Americans understand, but seems startling to non-Natives: tribes may be only a generation removed from termination. But that should not stop both Native and non-Native journalists from fully covering Native America and its issues. Or, to fully flesh out the Society of Professional Journalists Code of Ethics (1996), journalists should strive to "… tell the story of the diversity and magnitude of the human experience boldly, even when it is unpopular to do so" (SPJ Code of Ethics, 1996).

DISCUSSION QUESTIONS

1. Why do some journalists feel they are torn between two worlds? What impact might this cross-cultural tension have upon their professional goals?

2. Tallent and Dingman describe a tenuous and sometimes tense relationship between the Native Nations and non-Native mainstream journalists. What could be done

by tribal leaders to improve this relationship? What could non-Native mainstream journalists do to improve the situation?

3. Documents such as the Independent Press Act (Western Band of the Cherokee Nation) often present an idealized view of the way society should operate. Can you think of documents in your school or in your community that express an idealized vision of what they are or what they wish to become? Are there such documents in mainstream U.S. society? What factors make it difficult to make these visions reality?

4. Mark Trahant, formerly of the *Seattle Post-Intelligencer,* states "… colleges and universities do not teach the basics of why tribes are sovereign governments, which results in a fractured view of Native Nations by journalists and journalism students." How would you respond to Trahant's position?

References

Agent, D. (1998, Spring). Cherokee chief attacks Cherokee Constitution and Press. *News Watch*.

Associated Press (2007, May 19). Tribe banishes blogger from reservation after critical column. Retrieved from the First Amendment Center on Jan. 24, 2008 at http://www.firstamendmentcenter.org/news.aspx?id=18577.

Associated Press (2006, July 30). American Indian journalists to discuss tribal press. Retrieved from the First Amendment Center on Jan. 24, 2008 at http://firstamendmentcenter.org/news/asp?id-17216.

Atkinson Trading Co. Inc. v. Shirley, et. al. (2001). Supreme Court of the United States, No. 00-454. Argued March 27, 2001—Decided May 29, 2001. Retrieved on Nov. 10, 2007 from Cornell University Law School Legal Information Institute at http://www.law.cornell.edu/supct/html/00-454.ZS.html.

Azocar, C. L. (2007). *The reading red report a content analysis of general-audience newspapers in circulation areas with high percentages of American Indians*. San Francisco. Center for Integration and Improvement in Journalism.

Cleghorn, R. (1996, December). A struggle: Will tribal journalists be free? *American Journalism Review*.

Good Voice, C. (2007, Nov. 9). Eastern Band editor removed from job. Retrieved Nov. 14, 2007 from *The Cherokee Phoenix* online, http://www.cherokeephoenix.org/News/News.aspx?StoryID=2656.

Hamby, C. (2005, August 8) American Indian press freedom: a developing story. The First Amendment Center. Retrieved from the First Amendment Center on-line on Jan. 24, 2008 at http://firstamendmentcenter.org//news.aspx?id=15639.

Harvard Law Review. (1977). Equal protection under the Indian Civil Rights Act: *Martinez v. Santa Clara Pueblo. Vol. 90:627*. pp. 627–636.

Independent Press Act of 2000, legislation passed by the Western Band of the Cherokee Nation (Legislative Act. 11-00) approved by the Tribal Council on July 17, 2000.

Indian Civil Rights Act of 1968 (25 USC SS 1301-03). Retrieved Jan. 24, 2008 from the Tribal Law and Policy Institute Website, http://tribal-institute.org/lists/icra1968.html.

Johnson, B. B. (1982, January). American Indian jurisdiction as a policy issue. *Social Work*, the National Association of Social Workers, Inc.

Loew, P., & Mella, K. (2005). Black ink and the real red power: American Indian newspapers and tribal sovereignty. Monograph for the Association for Education in Journalism and Mass Communications.

Marshall, J. (1831) Opinion of the Court, C. 30 US 1 Cherokee Nation v. Georgia. Retrieved March 25, 2008 from the Cornell University Law School Archives at http://www.law.cornell.edu/supct/html/historics/USSC_CR_0030_0001_ZO.html.

Murphy, S. M. (1998) Native American Media. History of the Mass Media in the United States: *An encyclopedia.* Pages 420–422. Abingdon, Oxfordshire, United Kingdom: Taylor & Francis, Ltd.

Odum, M. (1991, Oct. 4). Money shortage seen as hindering Indian justice. *The New York Times* Online retrieved March 5, 2008 from http://query.nytimes.com/gst/fullpage.html?res=9D0CE7DC113AF937A3573C1A967958.

Santa Clara Pueblo v. Martinez, 436 U.S. 49 (1978). U.S. Supreme Court decision found through Find Law, retrieved Jan. 24, 2008 from http://caselaw.lp.findlaw.com/scripts/printer_friendly.pl?=us/436/49.html.

Saharko, P. (2006, Fall). *A reporter's guide to American Indian law.* The Reporter's Committee for Freedom of the Press/Ethics & Excellence in Journalism Foundation.

Society of Professional Journalists (1996). Code of ethics. Indianapolis, IN.

Trahant, M. N. (1995). *Pictures of our nobler selves: A history of American Indian contributions to news media.* Nashville, TN; The Freedom Forum First Amendment Center.

Worthy, L. (2007). The Cherokee Phoenix (And Indian Advocate). About North Georgia. Retrieved Nov. 10, 2007 from http://ngeorgia.com/history/phoenix.html.

24

A Comparison of Perceptions of Verbal Aggression and Argumentativeness in Situation Comedies: Television in Black and White

Felecia F. Jordan-Jackson

Abstract

This investigation compares perceptions of verbal aggression (VA) and argumentativeness in television situation comedies. Participants viewed one of two popular situational comedies: one consisting of a predominantly white cast and one consisting of a predominantly black cast of characters. After viewing, participants completed a survey indicating their perceptions of the sitcom, including the number of verbally aggressive messages they observed and their overall perception of both argumentative and verbal aggressive conduct. Results showed significant differences in the actual and perceived number of VA messages within each episode, and differences in perceptions of verbal aggressive conduct between the two episodes. Implications for results, limitations, and suggestions for future research are provided.

KEY TERMS: verbal aggression, argumentativeness, cultural stereotypes

Introduction

"Sticks and stones may break my bones, but words...." We are all familiar with how the original saying goes. Most of us are also aware that words can and too often do hurt far more than sticks and stones and with far-reaching effects.

Infante (1987) defined aggressive interpersonal communication as that which:

> ... applies force physically or symbolically in order, minimally, to dominate and perhaps damage or, maximally, to defeat and perhaps destroy the locus of attack. The locus of attack in interpersonal communication can be a person's body, material possessions, self-concept, position on topics of communication, or behavior (p. 158).

Verbal aggression involves an attack on a person's self-concept, which indeed could be used as a weapon to hurt or harm. Argumentativeness, on the other hand, is defined as "a generally stable trait which predisposes the individual in communication situations to advocate positions on controversial issues, and to attack verbally the positions which other people take on these issues" (p. 72). Thus, verbal aggression is a destructive form of aggressive communication that attacks the person, while argumentativeness is a constructive form of aggressive communication that attacks one's position on an issue, rather than the person (Infante, 1987; Rancer & Avtgis, 2006).

Research on the construct of verbal aggression is pervasive; however, racial and cultural comparisons on these variables have been a focus of limited research studies. The purpose of this study is to examine perceptions of verbal aggression and argumentativeness of Blacks and Whites within the genre of television situational comedies. But first, a brief overview of the existing research focusing on race/ethnicity and communication is in order.

Comparing Black and White Communication

Communication of Blacks and Whites has been a focus of research over several decades. Much of the research forwarded by communication scholars on the subject has indicated some differences in communication styles, patterns, perceptions, and overall conversational interaction of Blacks and Whites (Booth-Butterfield & Jordan, 1989; Gudykunst & Hammer, 1987; Hecht, Ribeau, & Alberts, 1989; Hecht, Larkey, & Johnson, 1992; Kochman, 1981; Pennington, 1979; Popp et al., 2003).

Any examination of communication differences of racial and ethnic groups must consider the intolerance, at times, for behavior that is different from that of the larger cultural norm. Historically, integration of the races and ethnicities in school, business, and society has undoubtedly contributed to how people of different races interact with each other; however, as suggested by Hecht et al., (1989), increased contact does not necessarily equate to increased communication effectiveness. Communication problems may still arise partly because in these contexts "[o]ne cannot assume that all interactants share a similar definition of the situation, messages, [or] conversational rule" (Hecht et al., 1992, p. 210). It is reasonable to assume that tension, anxiety, and uncertainty associated with interracial/interethnic communication may continue to exist.

Cultural Stereotypes and Expectations

Some of the actual differences found in the communication of Blacks and Whites may be less significant than perceptions, stereotypes, and expectations each racial group has about the other. For example, in studies by Ogawa (1971), Leonard and Locke (1993) and Popp et al. (2003) both Blacks and Whites identified some traits in the other racial group that might be considered undesirable group discussion traits. For example, Whites described Blacks as argumentative, emotional, aggressive (Ogawa, 1971), as well as manipulative, noisy, demanding, and boastful (Leonard & Locke, 1993). Blacks have described Whites as ignorant, boastful, aggressive, critical, conservative, and concealing (Ogawa, 1971); also as rude, aggressive, noisy, critical, and manipulative (Leonard & Locke, 1993). Additionally, Hughes and Baldwin (2002) conducted research that suggests Blacks perceived Whites to be rude, ignorant (especially when speaking on trivial topics), phony, and manipulative. Corroborating previous studies, they posit that Whites would perceive Blacks as aggressive, argumentative, and noisy.

Racial/ethnic groups have been studied and compared on communication content, patterns, and styles. Collier (1988), for example, compared conversations among and between African Americans, European Americans, and Mexican Americans. Although some general rules of conversational expectations and appropriateness were shared among groups, marked differences occurred, including expectations regarding relational climate, individuality in politeness, and verbal content. For African Americans and European Americans generally, the "rules for conversing with members of one's own group were different from rules for intercultural conversations" (p. 122). Racial stereotypes in regard to aggression are perpetuated in the media. For example, Coltrane and Messineo (2000) indicated that when African American characters were compared to European American characters in television advertisements, African American characters were more likely to be portrayed as aggressive and active and less likely to be portrayed as passive. Further, African American men were reported to be nearly three times more likely to be shown as aggressive than European American men. Such portrayals may serve to reinforce negative perceptions that result in ineffective communication between the races.

Further evidence that perceptions and stereotypes might affect interracial communication effectiveness is that there appears to be an intergroup (race) bias when it comes to identifying similarities and differences. Doise, DeChamp, & Meyer (1978) found that Blacks tend to emphasize intergroup differences and intragroup similarities. Whites were found to attribute greater attitude similarity among their own racial group than to their out-group members (Brewer, 1993; Ashburn-Nardo, Knowles, & Monteith, 2003; Shelton, 2000). Given these findings it is apparent that there are at best some differing, and at worst, some negative perceptions that prevail between the two racial groups.

Byrnes and Kiger (1988) suggest that assessment of racial attitudes in modern society is difficult. One reason for this difficulty as it pertains to European Americans in particular is that many verbalize the importance of racial fairness, justice, and equality and believe that racial discrimination is a thing of the past (Schuman, Steeh, & Bobo, 1985; Dovidio et al., 2002). At the same time, their behaviors are characterized by avoidance of Hispanics, Blacks, and other ethnic groups, which supports the notion that negative racial stereotypes still exist (Dovidio & Gaertner, 1986). An insightful phenomenological study forwarded by Orbe (1994) revealed that black men characterized their communication with non-African Americans (including European American males) as involving "… unbelievable tension; … and fear" (p. 293). The African American males in the study reported that they felt compelled to maintain a certain distance from "non-Blacks", particularly with those in authority and/or white American males whom they described as "the most intimidated; and threatened by the presence of capable African American men" (p. 293). Further, based on Stephen and Stephen's (1996) Integrated Threat Theory (ITT) of Prejudice, among the four causal factors that lead us to stereotype and be prejudiced against outgroups is intergroup anxiety. As Orbe (1994) explains, "[b]ased on ethnic and gender stereotypes, African American men are often perceived as intimidating, and produce great anxiety and fear for most European Americans" (p. 296), which is likely to manifest itself during interethnic communication and interactions. Similarly, Blacks tend to approach interracial interactions with a heightened sense of anxiety, guardedness, and mistrust (Dovidio et al., 2002; Shelton, 2000; Shelton, 2003).

Strong biases associated with interracial communication prevail among black and white women as well. In a study by Houston (2004), when asked to describe their communication style and that of the "other" race, black women described their own style as "standing behind what you say, not being afraid to speak your mind, [and] speaking with a strong sense of self-esteem (p. 121). Black women described the style of white women as "friendly (with an air of phoniness), arrogant, [and] know-it-all" (p. 121). White women described their own talk as "all kinds of speech patterns, distinct pronunciation [and] using appropriate words for the appropriate situations" (p. 121). They described the talk of black women as "using black dialect [and] using jive terms" (p. 121). This study adds more evidence to support the notion that, whether or not significant differences exist in the communication of Blacks and Whites, intergroup biases remain and undoubtedly affect interracial relationships.

Verbal Aggression, Argumentativeness, Race, and Culture

The goal of this study is to compare two racial groups on perceived use of verbal aggression (VA) and argumentativeness. As discussed above, both forms of communication are considered to be aggressive, although verbal aggression is described as a destructive communication trait and argumentativeness as a constructive communication trait (Infante, 1987; Rancer & Avtgis, 2006).

The current study compares two television situation comedies on 13 components of verbal aggression originally identified by Rancer and Infante (1985). An impetus for the study is previous research that suggests that perceptions of verbal aggression differ based on the source of the message. For example in 1996 Infante, Rancer, and Jordan found that although men and women used an identical number of VA messages, observers perceived that women used significantly more VA messages than men. Similar findings were reported by Jordan-Jackson et al. (2008) when men and women were compared on perceptions of verbal aggression and argumentativeness. In another study, men and women reported significant differences in self-reports of verbal aggression (Jordan-Jackson, 2007). If perceptions of communication based on sex differences prevail, perceptions of racial differences based on this construct might also be evident.

European Americans and African Americans were chosen as participants in the present study. While European Americans represent the majority (mainstream) culture, African Americans are one of the largest ethnic groups in the U.S. and "play an increasingly visible role in American public life" (Hecht et al., 1992, p. 211). Consequently, conflict and tension between these racial groups has a long and tumultuous history in the U.S. Verbal aggression, or at least perceptions of the trait, may play a role in keeping these tensions prevalent. Infante, Chandler, and Rudd (1989) proposed a relational model that suggests that along with other factors, verbal aggression may contribute to physical violence. When this model was tested with couples, results indicated that "… where physical aggression is present … verbal aggression is almost always present" (Rancer & Avtgis, 2006, p. 96). While the model does not suggest that VA is a cause of physical violence, it does suggest that VA may promote physical aggression in couples. It is possible that this model may also explain some of the physical aggression that ensues between Blacks and Whites particularly when both real and perceived differences between the co-cultures are evident, when stereotypes prevail, and there is little motivation to reduce uncertainty about each other?

Although racial and cultural comparisons of communication have been a focus of many research studies, the number of investigations focusing specifically on verbal aggression, argumentativeness, and race is minimal. One study by Nicotera, Rancer, and Sullivan (1991) tested whether European Americans and African Americans perceived differences in their own and the other race's VA and argumentativeness. Results showed that African Americans were perceived as being higher in VA. There was a general tendency for European Americans, compared with African Americans, to stereotype others as being higher in VA regardless of the target person's race. On the other hand, African Americans self-reported and were perceived by others as being higher in argumentativeness than European Americans.

A study of interethnic communication which focuses upon verbal aggression could extend the scholarship in this area and "… yield insight not only into a specific culture but also promote understanding of ways to improve interethnic communication effectiveness" (Hecht et al., 1989, p. 385). In general, African Americans may be perceived as using more verbal aggressive messages than European Americans partly due to their general style (i.e. being louder, more expressive, etc.). A question that comes to mind is, do these perceptions prevail when the aggressive messages are imbedded in a scripted television show meant to engender humor? The first two research questions are posited to test perceptions of verbal aggression:

RQ1A: How will verbal aggression within the two situational comedies be perceived based on the number of verbally aggressive messages in the episode?

RQ1B: How will verbal aggression within the two situational comedies be perceived based on the overall perceptions of verbal aggressive conduct?

Additionally, this study attempts to test whether the two situational comedies will be perceived differently on characteristics associated with the constructive communication trait of argumentativeness. To this end, the following question was forwarded:

RQ2:   Will perceptions of argumentative conduct be perceived differently when the two episodes are compared?

Method

Participants and Procedures

The purpose of this study was to assess perceptions of verbal aggression of two television situational comedies that originally aired in primetime on U.S. network television. The shows include one episode each of *Living Single*, which aired on the Fox network from 1993 to 1998, and *Frasier*, which aired on NBC from 1993 to 2004. Both shows were aired in syndication in various media markets at the time of this study. The main cast of *Living Single* consists of a group of single African American professional men and women in their mid- to late twenties. Three of the women share an apartment in a Brooklyn Brownstone, and a fourth spends most of her time in their apartment. Two African American men, who are cast as roommates, share an apartment in the same brownstone with the women. The lives of the cast members are integrated through friendship, love, and antagonism.

The second show, *Frasier*, is composed of a middle-aged white man as the title character, and his father, who moved with his dog into the son's penthouse apartment in Seattle. The father is a retired police officer, and might be described as "rough around the edges" in terms of social style. A younger adult son in his mid- to late thirties lives in the same city and is an ever-present part of their lives. Both sons are psychiatrists who, much different than their father, are used to "the finer things in life." Most of the dialogue occurs in Frasier's penthouse or in a radio station where he gives psychological advice on a call-in talk show.

Participants in the study consisted of volunteers from communication courses at a large southern university. Participants were randomly assigned to view either *Living Single* (n = 83) or *Frasier* (n = 85). After viewing the episode, respondents completed a questionnaire consisting of three sections. In the first section, participants indicated their biological sex, age, and the name of the situational comedy viewed (i.e. *Living Single* or *Frasier*). The second section asked the participants to indicate the extent to which they perceived the television show to be verbally aggressive and argumentative. These perceptions were each assessed via six items previously used by Infante, Myers, and Buerkel (1994). Verbal aggressive conduct was assessed using a five-point Likert-type scale on which participants were to give their perceptions of the episode's level of verbal aggression (e.g. responses ranging from "almost none" to "a great deal"), self-concept attacks, level of emotion, pleasantness of communication, coolness of communication, and level of anxiety. The items were summed to assess perceptions of "verbally aggressive conduct." Alpha reliability for this scale was .67.

An additional six items developed by Infante et al. (1994) were used to obtain an "argumentative conduct" score. This five-point Likert-type scale asked participants to indicate their perceptions of how rational the plot/theme was (e.g. responses ranging from "not at all" to "very rational"), emphasis on factual information, flexibility of the characters' communication, agreeableness, and willingness to reach a compromise. Alpha reliability for the argumentative scale was .65.

The third section of the questionnaire asked participants to estimate the number of verbally aggressive messages they thought each episode contained. Thirteen categories of verbal aggression were listed including blame, competence attacks, character attacks, personality attacks, profanity/swearing, command, physical appearance attacks, global rejection or disconfirmation, negative comparison, threat, aggressive emblems, attacks on close others, and slurs. Based upon the operational definitions used in this study, a total of 44 and 17 verbally aggressive messages were exchanged in each episode of *Living Single* and *Frasier*, respectively. The misperception of verbal aggression was therefore computed by subtracting the respective totals from the number of verbally aggressive messages observed by the participant for each type of message.

Data Analysis

Research question 1A was tested using one sample t-test procedures. Research questions 1B and Research Question 2 were tested using independent t-test procedures. Version 15 of the SPSS statistical package was used for all analyses.

Results

Three research questions were posited to assess perceptions of verbal aggression (VA) and argumentativeness in two situational comedies. The first two research questions, 1A and 1B respectively, addressed perceptions of VA by asking participants to indicate the number of VA messages they could identify, and their overall (i.e. global) perception of VA in the episode they observed. For research question 1A the difference between the estimated/perceived and actual number of times 13 different types of verbal aggression occurred in each sitcom was compared via one-sample t-tests. Results indicated a significant difference between perceived VA and actual VA for *Living Single* (*M* = 29.74, *SD* = 22.9), t(–5.5) = –14.25, p = .000. Similarly, a test of the difference between perceived and actual VA for *Frasier* was significant (*M* = 26.16, *SD* = 18.0), t(4.44) = 9.16, p = .000.

To test research question 1B, verbal aggression was assessed globally by participants indicating their overall perceptions of verbal aggression conduct. An independent samples t-test compared the means of both episodes. Results showed a significant difference in the overall perceptions of levels of verbal aggressive conduct for *Living Single* (*M* = 16.09, s = 3.53) and *Frasier M* = 17.32, t(164) = 153.33, p = .013, α = .05.

In addition, to test research question two, the episodes were compared on perceptions of argumentative conduct. A *t*- test failed to reveal a statistically significant difference between perceptions of argumentative conduct for *Living Single* (*M* = 12.77, s = 3.18) and *Frasier*, (M = 12.67, s = 2.82), t(163) = .200. p= .094, α = .05.

Discussion and Conclusion

The results of this study revealed that perceptions and "reality" are not necessarily the same. The verbal aggression observed indeed differed from the actual number of messages used. Further, the overall perception of verbal aggression differed by episode. However, the limited number of studies that have examined race, verbal aggression, and argumentativeness makes it difficult to generalize these results. Further, we have to consider the part that social expectations may play in how these messages are responded to when used by certain groups. In a previous study when sex differences were observed, not only were women perceived to have used more verbally aggressive messages than men, but also they were the recipients of more negative perceptions overall, although "in reality" they used the same number and type of verbal aggressive messages as did men (Infante et al., 1996). The implication for such results is that women may be expected to limit the amount of verbal aggression they use and when they exceed that expectation it engenders perceptions of greater use of VA messages (a destructive aggressive trait) than are actually used. Additionally, in such cases women are seen as less argumentative (a constructive aggressive trait). Men in that study were perceived as using higher levels of argumentative skills than were women.

The results found in the current study are both interesting and informative. One point worth emphasizing is that VA messages were underestimated by participants for the episode featuring the all-black cast, and overestimated for the episode featuring the all-white cast. Although research questions were forwarded, and not hypotheses, these results on one level were contrary to what was expected. Given previous findings, for example where African Americans have been described by European Americans as having a style that is loud, direct, and forceful (see for example Ogawa, 1971; Leonard & Locke, 1993), we might expect that when estimation/perceived errors are made on verbal aggression, they would be made on the side of overestimating the number that actually appeared for African Americans. Consequently, we might also expect that perceptions of argumentativeness would be lower for Blacks than Whites. For this study, these expectations were not supported. A limitation for this study might explain these results. Indeed, the episode of *Living Single* featuring the black cast had a greater number of verbally aggressive messages than did *Frasier*, featuring a white cast. The number of VA messages in *Living Single* exceeded those in *Frasier* by more than two-to-one, 44 and 17, respectively. A clearer comparisons might have been made by choosing episodes with identical, or at least a similar number (and types) of VA messages. Given this fact, however, the finding that verbal aggression was underestimated for *Living Single*, while no significant differences were found between the two episodes on argumentative conduct, is intriguing. As stated above, we might expect that with a large number of VA messages, perceptions of argumentativeness would decrease particularly in comparison with an episode with significantly fewer VA messages. Oddly, social perception and expectation may still be the explanation here. It is possible that viewers expected "a great deal" of VA messages from the black cast and, even with 44 VA messages in a 30-minute episode, the participants expectations were not met, thus the cast of *Living Single* was judged to be no less argumentative than the white cast of characters. It is notable that the means of verbal aggressive messages perceived by participants for the two episodes were similar. Specifically for *Living Single* the mean for VA messages was 29.47; the mean for *Frasier* was 26.16. While the mean for *Living Single* was well below the actual number of VA messages found in the episode, the mean for *Frasier* was well above the actual number of VA messages found in the episode.

In considering these results, we should be mindful that the majority of the participants for this study were European American college students between the ages of 18 and 22. This demographic is in contrast to the viewership of both comedies. *Living Single* was ranked in the top five among African American viewers during its entire run (Wikepedia), winning two NAACP Image awards in that time (tv.com). During its 11 seasons, *Frasier's* audience was arguably predominantly European American. It was described as a "… situation comedy for adults," (Stevens, 2004) which one may assume refers to viewers who are considerably older than the college-age students who reviewed the episode for the current study.

This study may be viewed in keeping with the trend in the communication discipline toward conducting research that is insightful and informative, and that lends itself to more effective communication and relationships. Although the research on verbal aggression is prevalent and expands over several decades, the need for extending the research still exists, as evidenced by the current study. Additionally, a survey by Rancer and Avtgis (2006) determined other directions that research on aggressive communication could take including the biological basis for aggressive communication and the effects of verbal aggression on the user. The current study is an example of an other direction of study that could add to the rich body of empirical research on a fascinating topic.

DISCUSSION QUESTIONS

1. Compare and contrast the communication traits of verbal aggression and argumentativeness.

2. What do you think led to the situational comedy with the predominantly white cast being perceived as more verbally aggressive than the situational comedy with the predominantly black cast?

3. Discuss the implications of our perceptions of a person, group, or culture being different from reality. For example, what are some consequences of one racial/ethnic group being perceived as using more (or fewer) verbally aggressive messages when in reality, they used fewer (or more) verbally aggressive messages when compared with another racial/ethnic group?

4. What stereotypes do you have about a race or culture other than your own? After reading this chapter, consider whether those stereotypes are based primarily in fact (i.e. actual differences) or on perceptions.

References

Booth-Butterfield, M., & Jordan F. F. (1989). Communication adaptation among racially homogeneous and heterogeneous groups. *Southern Communication Journal, 54*, 253–272.

Ashburn-Nardo, L., Knowles, M. L., & Monteith, M. J. (2003). Black Americans' implicit racial associations and their implications for intergroup judgment. *Social Cognition, 21*(1), 61–87.

Brewer, M. B. (1993). Social identity, distinctiveness, and in-group homogeneity. *Social Cognition, 11*(1), 150–164.

Byrnes, D. A., & Kiger, G. (1988). Contemporary measures of attitudes toward Blacks. *Educational and Psychological Measurement, 48*, 107–118.

Collier, M. J. (1988). A comparison of conversations among and between domestic culture groups: How intra-and intercultural competencies vary. *Communication Quarterly, 35*(2), 122–144.

Coltrane, S., & Messineo, M. (2000). The perpetuation of subtle prejudice: Race and gender imagery in 1990's television advertising. *Sex Roles, 42*, 363–389.

Doise, W., Deschamps, J. C., & Meyer, G. (1978). The accentuation of intra-category similarities. In H. Tajfel (Ed.), *Differentiation Between Social Groups: Studies in the Social Psychology of Iintergroup Relations* (pp. 159–168). London: Academic Press. Sage.

Dovidio, J. F., & Gaertner, S. L. (1986). Prejudice, Discrimination, and Racism. New York: Academic Press.

Dovidio, J. F., Gaertner, S. L., Kawakami, K. & Hodson, G. (2002). Why can't we just get along? Interpersonal biases and interracial distrust. *Cultural Diversity and Ethnic Minority Psychology, 8*(2), 88–102.

Gudykunst, & Hammer, M. (1987). The influence of ethnicity, gender, and dyadic composition on uncertainty reduction in initial interaction. *Journal of Black Studies, 18*, 191–214.

Hecht, M. L., Larkey, L. K., & Johnson, J. N. (1992). African American and European American perceptions of problematic issues in interethnic communication effectiveness. *Human Communication Research, 19*(2), 209–236.

Hecht, M. L., Ribeau, S., & Alberts, J. (1989). An Afro-American perspective on interethnic communication. *Communication Monographs, 56*, 385–410.

Houston, M. (2004). When Black women talk with White women: Why dialogues are difficult. In Gonzalez, M. Houston, & V. Chen (Eds.) *Our voices: Essays in Culture, Ethnicity, and Communication* (pp. 119–125). Los Angeles, CA: Roxbury.

Hughes, P. C., & Baldwin, J. R. (2002). Communication and Stereotypical Impressions. *The Howard Journal of Communication, 13*(2), 113–128.

Infante, D. A. (1987). Aggressiveness. In J. C. McCroskey & J. A. Daly (Eds.), *Personality and Iinterpersonal Communication* (pp. 157–192). Newbury Park, CA: Sage.

Infante, D. A., Chandler, T. A., & Rudd, J. E. (1989). Test of an argumentative skill deficiency model of interspousal violence. *Communication Monographs, 56,* 163–177.

Infante, D. A., Myers, S. A., & Buerkel, R. A. (1994). Argument and verbal aggression in constructive and destructive family and organizational disagreements. *Western Journal of Communication, 58,* 1–7.

Infante, D. A., Rancer, A. S., & Jordan, F. F. (1996). Affirming and nonaffirming style, dyad sex, and the perception of argumentation and verbal aggression in an interpersonal dispute. *Human Communication Research, 22,* 315–334.

Jordan-Jackson, F. F. (2007). A Worldview on race and gender: An assessment of verbal aggression of black and white men and women. Paper presented at the annual meeting of the National Communication Association, Chicago.

Jordan-Jackson, F. F., Lin, Y. Y., Rancer, A. S., & Infante, D. A. (2008). Perceptions of males and females' use of aggressive affirming and nonaffirming messages in an interpersonal dispute: You've come a long way baby? *Western Journal of Communication, 72,* 239–258.

Kochman, T. (1981). *Black and white: Styles in conflict.* Chicago: University of Chicago Press.

Leonard, R., & Locke, D. C. (1993). Communication stereotypes: Is interracial communication possible? *Journal of Black Studies, 23*(3), 332–343.

Nicotera, A. M., Rancer, A. S., & Sullivan, R. G. (1991, November). Race as a factor in argumentativeness, verbal aggressiveness, and beliefs about arguing. Paper presented at the annual meeting of the Speech Communication Association, Atlanta, GA.

Ogawa, D. (1971). Small-group communication stereotypes of Black Americans. *Journal of Black Studies, 1,* 273–281.

Orbe, M. P. (1994). "Remember it's always White's ball: Descriptions of African American male communication. *Communication Quarterly, 42,* 287–300.

Pennington, D. (1979). Black white communication: An assessment of research. In M. Asante, E. Newmark, & C. Blake (Eds.), *Handbook of Intercultural Communication,* (pp. 383–401). Beverly Hills, California: Sage.

Popp, D., Donovan, R. A., Crawford, M., Marsh, K. L., & Peele, M. (2003). Gender, Race, and Speech Style Stereotypes. *Sex Roles, 48*(7), 317–325.

Rancer, A. S., & Avtgis, T. A. (2006). *Argumentative and Aggressive Communication.* Thousand Oaks, CA: Sage.

Rancer, A. S., & Infante, D. A. (1985). Relations between motivation to argue and the argumentativeness of adversaries. *Communication Quarterly, 33,* 209–218.

Shelton, J. N. (2000). A Reconceptualization of how we study issues of racial prejudice. *Personality and Social Psychology Review 4*(4), 374–390.

Shelton, J. N. (2003). Interpersonal concerns in social encounters between majority and minority group members. *Group Processes & Intergroup Relations 6*(2), 171–185.

Shuman, H., Steeh, C., & Bobo, L. (1985). *Racial Attitudes in America*. Cambridge, MA: Harvard University Press.

Stephen W. G., & Stephen, C. W. (1996). Predicting prejudice: The role of threat. *International Journal of Intercultural Relations, 20*, 409–426.

Stevens, D. (2004-05-12). "Where Have All the Grown-Ups Gone". *Slate Magazine*. Washington Post. http://www.slate.com/id/2100411/. Retrieved on 2009-05-31.

http://www.tv.com/living-single/show/473/summary.html?tag=blackout#, retrieved December 15, 2009.

http://en.wikipedia.org/wiki/Living_Single#cite_note-0, retrieved December 15, 2009.

25

Cultural Identity in the Age of Ether: Black Entertainment Television and the Island of Guadeloupe

David William Seitz

Abstract

This essay explores issues of cultural identity, communication in the age of globalization, and human rights implicit in both the exporting of the white-owned, American television network Black Entertainment Television (BET) to the black, Francophone, Caribbean island of Guadeloupe, and the subsequent consumption of the network by Guadeloupean youths. I begin by providing a brief glimpse of Guadeloupe's turbulent cultural and racial histories. Next, I discuss contemporary American public discourse regarding BET's programming, values, and influence. I then explain the origins of BET's presence in Guadeloupe, a process that speaks to Michael Hardt and Antonio Negri's (2000) concept "ether," those invasive modern systems of communication against which the means for resistance are increasingly hard to find. Finally, through an analysis of original informant responses, I examine the diverse opinions Guadeloupeans hold for BET's presence. In the conclusion, I suggest that human rights should be an integral part of discussions about cultural change in any community, specifically when the agent for cultural change is part of the "ether."

KEY TERMS: communication, culture, media, globalization, African American identity, Caribbean Studies, human rights

Introduction

Following my graduation from college in 2002, I taught English at two middle schools in the Francophone island of Guadeloupe, a population that is 90 percent Black. Nestled just south of Antigua between the Caribbean Sea and the North Atlantic Ocean, this French overseas territory boasts a diverse natural environment—lush rainforests, an active volcano, the tallest waterfall in the Caribbean, and rocky limestone cliffs that overlook swirling waves—and a vibrant local Creole culture comprised of African, Caribbean, and European traditions. I lived and worked in the island's largest city, Pointe-à-Pitre, for eight months: from September 2002 to May 2003. During that time I became intimately familiar with Guadeloupe's cultural history. My students, some of the most talented musicians I have ever met, introduced to me the rhythms of *gwo ka*, Guadeloupe's folklore drum music, which is played during celebratory gatherings (including community Christmas sing-alongs or *chanté noels*). Neighbors taught me how to cook local delicacies, such as *poulet columbo* (a curry chicken dish) and *poisson avec sauce chien* (fish in a spicy chili pepper sauce). And Veteran schoolteachers with whom I worked lent me books by Guadeloupe's greatest writers: Saint-John Perse, winner of the 1960 Nobel Prize for Literature; Guy Tirollen, famed poet and contributor to the theory of Négritude; and Maryse Condé, whose internationally-acclaimed works explore the immense struggles black Caribbean women have faced against racism, sexism, and colonialism. I quickly apprehended that Guadeloupe's culture is distinguished by high artistic achievement and a communal sense of self, both of which are rooted in a mixed soil of Afro-Caribbean and European customs and practices.

As a middle school teacher of English as a second language, my contact with Guadeloupean youths was immediate and intense. Thus, like middle school and high school level teachers anywhere, I was constantly exposed to the trends of local youth culture. After a few weeks of talking and interacting with my students in class and on the streets of our neighborhood, I became aware of a pervasive and, to me, intriguing phenomenon: many Guadeloupean youths were enthralled with Black Entertainment Television (BET). An American television network designed for consumers of African American popular culture, BET is transmitted "as is"—without translation or subtitles—from the U.S. into the homes of Guadeloupean cable subscribers.

In the classroom, I found that when a car blasting the latest American rap song from its windows passed by the school, many students who expressed little interest in learning English, or who had difficulties pronouncing even the simplest of English phrases, would perk up and sing along with the car's stereo, reproducing perfectly the lyrics and delivery style of the respective performer we heard. When they finished, if I asked where they had learned the song, more often than not they would tell me: "BET!" If I asked if they knew the meaning of the lyrics they had recited, they usually admitted that they did not. I discovered that many students, upon returning home from school, would discard their mandatory school uniforms in favor of the baggy jeans, "hoochie shorts," high-top sneakers, sports jerseys, sideways baseball caps, bandanas, and glistening jewelry found on BET's rap video programming. Each late afternoon, Pointe-à-Pitre neighborhoods metamorphosed into aesthetic simulations of P Diddy, Ja Rule, and Snoop Dogg videos.

When I shared my observations with teachers and neighbors, I was startled to find that most of them believed that BET was impacting the local youth culture. Some of these adults thought BET's influence was harmless, if not productive, for the network served as an accessible window to a different black culture and a different language. Others, however, were more troubled by the children's embrace of BET; some claimed that BET was part of an ongoing project of modernization that was eroding the island's Creole culture. One teacher went so far as to make a link between the introduction of the network to Guadeloupe in 1997 and the recent increase in homicide, rape, and violent theft rates on the island. Curious about these responses, I began to conduct informal research regarding BET's presence in Guadeloupe. In 2004, I revisited this phenomenon and conducted original fieldwork for my Master's thesis, which serves as the origin of this essay.

The purpose of this essay is twofold. First, it presents and analyzes complex cultural issues that can arise when an American media product (in this case, the racially charged network BET) is introduced to a non-American, non-English speaking community. Second, it urges communication scholars to consider the nature of modern systems of communication and the limited options that concerned members of a community have to resist undesired media products. This essay begins by offering a brief glimpse of Guadeloupe's turbulent cultural history, which is highly influenced by the legacy of the island's bygone African-slave system. It then examines Black Entertainment Television within a cultural and corporate context and discusses the immense criticism BET's controversial rap video programming has elicited from African American intellectuals. Next, it explains the origins of BET's presence in Guadeloupe, a process that speaks to Michael Hardt and Antonio Negri's (2000) concept "ether"—those invasive modern systems of communication against which the means for resistance are increasingly hard to find. Finally, through an analysis of original informant responses, I bring forth the diverse opinions that Guadeloupeans hold about BET's presence within their society. In the conclusion, I pose several open-ended questions that fall under one larger, overarching question: Given the nature of modern systems of communication, how might small communities resist unwanted media products? My goal is not to preach that BET is "bad" and should be blocked in Guadeloupe. Instead, I hope to present a case study that raises thought-provoking questions about mass communication, mediated portrayals of race, and cultural change in the twenty-first century.

Guadeloupe's Cultural History

For the purposes of our discussion, it is vital to have an understanding of Guadeloupe's history and local culture. Guadeloupe's timeline has followed the well-known historical evolution of a colonized territory in the Americas. Prior to Christopher Columbus' invasion in 1493, Carib and Arawak natives inhabited the island. Over the following century, rival explorers from Spain, France, and England exploited Guadeloupe's exotic natural resources, and murdered its indigenous populations (Abenon, 1992; Abraham & Maragnes, 2001).[1] These rival Western powers vied for control of Guadeloupe until it fell to French control in 1635. During the 1660s, French settlers established an African-slave-based colony in Guadeloupe. The island's black population suffered under the weight of the imposed, and particularly brutal, slavery system until the permanent French abolition of slavery in 1848. Whereas Haiti's slave population had successfully revolted against the French to secure their freedom in 1803, Guadeloupe's Blacks never completely severed themselves from their relationship with their white oppressors. Instead, after the demise of slavery, Guadeloupe's Blacks were gradually inducted into France's governmental and social structures.

In 1946, Guadeloupe became a department of France, and the island's Blacks became full French citizens.[2] Whereas Haiti's population formed a collective local identity out of a revolution, Guadeloupeans have remained closely tied to the culture of mainland France, from which they obtain their standard of living (very high when compared with their Caribbean neighbors—a fact that makes satellite cable television affordable to most Guadeloupeans); their defense, education, and health and welfare funding; their official language, and their Roman Catholicism (Brana-Shute, 1996). According to the last available figures, roughly 90 percent of the island's 440,000 inhabitants are of African descent (Central Intelligence Agency).

The complex black Guadeloupean identity is composed of a multiple set of post-colonial conditions, which have been explored by cultural critics such as Aimé Césaire and Frantz Fanon. To summarize one of Fanon's main theses in *Black Skin, White Masks* (1952), black Guadeloupeans are neither solely African, nor Caribbean, nor French; instead, they are all three in a context of uninterrupted conflict and negotiation. Attempts by Guadeloupeans to construct a delineated African or Caribbean identity have been hindered by the fact that they are citizens of France. However, while they are legal citizens of France, they have never been considered (by themselves nor by white French citizens) to be authentically "French" because they are Afro-Caribbean. This dilemma helps maintain a cultural bind in which Guadeloupeans are simultaneously socially accepted and rejected by their governing nation, France—which by and large has prolonged its colonial mind frame into the twenty-first century.[3]

At the same time, this dilemma has served as a source of pride in Guadeloupe's Creole culture. When Guadeloupe was under the yoke of slavery, the island's population retained its African ancestral heritage while accepting the cultural conditioning imposed by the French. The result of this process, or what cultural anthropologist Walter Mignolo (1989) calls "cultural semiosis"—that "conflictive domain of semiotic interactions among members of radically different cultures engaged in a struggle of imposition and appropriation, on the one hand, and of resistance, opposition, and adaptation on the other" (p. 93)—was Guadeloupe's Creole culture, a hybrid of African and French languages, customs, and symbols. As in other Afro-Caribbean communities, Guadeloupe's Creole culture was a representation of both defiance and submission, as well as an act of ancestral preservation. Orality was the matrix of interaction and remembrance for Caribbean slaves who could not read or write (Montiel, 2004). At its simplest, orality entails a social condition in which speaking and listening constitute the primary medium through which communication occurs and memory is maintained (Durant, 2005). For the slaves, the creation and maintenance of the oral arts became, in Montiel's words (2004), a "weapon used to combat the devastating effects of colonialism. The Africans employed it as a living means of preserving their traditional cultures." After the breakdown of slavery in Guadeloupe, the island's population, like many other former slave communities throughout the Caribbean, employed their shared Creole culture to shake off "the dead weight of Europe" and "reconstruct their ancestry" (p. 461).

Even as the freedoms, development, and material wealth of Guadeloupe increased during the second half of the twentieth century, the island's Creole culture continued to manifest itself in food and drink, music and dance, day-to-day greetings, and Christmas and "Carnaval" celebrations—all aspects of the oral, visual, and gastronomical cultural arts that the slaves developed under French rule. Carnaval, a massive festival that occurs during the week before Lent, is the strongest demonstration of Guadeloupe's Creole culture today. Businesses and schools shut down for eight straight days as people put on a series of parades through the streets of the island's bigger cities. It is a week of traditional music, dance, and food. Based on slave customs dating back to the seventeenth century, men and women of all ages wear vibrant costumes, beat on large drums, and sing and dance to reinforce their shared historical bonds. Tens of thousands of citizens sing and cheer as they eat *bokits* (a favorite local sandwich) and sip on glasses of *ti punch* (a potent rum-based aperitif).

While the festival's tone is one of collective happiness and exuberance, some Carnaval customs are meant to recall, and mock, the painful days of slavery. For example, each parade is led by a boisterous group of whip-cracking, tar-covered Guadeloupeans who effectively invoke both dreadful memories of slavery and jubilant emotions of freedom. By conjuring such images of misery, joy, and strength, Carnaval provides an annual opportunity for the island's population to recognize and celebrate their collective and conflicted Creole heritage.

BET in a Cultural and Corporate Context

Black Entertainment Television, the Black-founded but currently White-owned music television network,[4] was made available in Guadeloupe in 1997. Over the years, it has become a popular cultural space through which young, black Guadeloupeans can assemble a visual and perhaps virtual, if not entirely definable, identity. Piercing through the island's cultural contradictions, the cable network suggests to the youths the not-too-inchoate alternative of "being an African American." It seems many of the youths interpret BET's images to mean, "All you need to do is listen to this music, wear this clothing, and behave this way. …" The reality that black Guadeloupeans have historically been unable to be (as Fanon might put it) "what they are supposed to be" (because of the cultural bind mentioned above) seems to open the door for the race-based television network's simple and powerful visual seduction, despite the fact that Black identity portrayed in much of BET's rap programming has been criticized as being inauthentic, exploitative, and even false—a point that is arguably unknown to most Guadeloupeans.

In recent years, a number of American cultural critics and advocacy groups have attacked BET, as well as other "biased imperialist white-supremacist patriarchal" mass media outlets that promote and display a formulaic "gangsta" way of life, for making large profits through stereotypical, violent, hypersexual, and misogynistic portrayals of African Americans (hooks, 2004, p. 27; Smith-Shomade, 2008). Throughout the 1980s, corporations such as Anheuser-Busch, Time, Pepsi-Cola, Sears, and Kellogg had advertised on BET in order to reach a niche African American audience. But BET's embrace of gangsta rap in the 1990s—which propelled both BET and the gangsta rap industry—helped usher in a new marketing ideology in the corporate world that would negatively shape images of African Americans in mass media. American corporations began to see this new, "cool" black culture as a potential marketing device (Pulley 2004, pp. 106–115). In *No Logo* (1999, pp. 73–76), Naomi Klein argues that the legacy of this phenomenon has been the worldwide commodification (the act of turning something into an economic good to be bought and sold) of African Americanism. "The truth," she writes, "is that the 'got to be cool' rhetoric of the global brands is, more often than not, an indirect way of saying, 'got to be black.' For many of the corporations, 'cool hunting' has simply become 'black-culture hunting.'" Bakari Kitwana, in *The Hip Hop Generation* (2002), seconds the notion: "One can find the faces, bodies, attitudes, and language of Black youth attached to slick advertisements that sell what have become global products, whether it's Coca-Cola and Pepsi, Reebok and Nike sneakers, films such as *Love Jones* and *Set It Off*, or popular rap artists like Missy Elliot and Busta Rhymes" (p. 9). Although BET occasionally plays videos by what many consider to be progressive and socially conscious hip hop artists, the overabundance of corporate-sponsored, exploitative "blackness" on the network poses a difficult choice for concerned viewers. As Tricia Rose (2008, pp. 196–197) writes: "How can you turn off one video by, say, the Ying Yang Twins but turn it back on in time for one by Talib Kweli or Common? You'd have to be a psychic to know when the videos that take the art of hip hop and the importance of community seriously are going to be aired."

Cornel West, in his pivotal book *Race Matters* (1993, pp. 16–17), condemns corporations and media outlets such as BET for commodifying the African American identity:

> "Needless to say, the primary motivation of these institutions is to make profits, and their basic strategy is to convince the public to consume. These institutions have helped create a seductive way of life, a culture of consumption that capitalizes on every opportunity to make money. Market calculations and cost-benefit analyses hold sway in almost every sphere of U.S. society. … The common denominator of these calculations and analyses is usually the provision, expansion, and intensification of pleasure." West adds that the African American identity—as portrayed in television, radio, video, music—is associated with "sexual foreplay and orgiastic pleasure" (p. 17). These seductive images appeal to all consumers and contribute to "the predominance of the market-inspired way of life over all others." In hijacking the African American identity, corporations have been able to spread a contagious rhetoric of pleasure and consumerism to populations throughout the U.S. and abroad. Somewhere down this path, West writes, the noncommercial values of "love, care and service to others" have been lost (p. 17).

The cultural commodity of gangsta rap is far more complex than the "good/bad" dichotomy that seems most often to frame public discourse of gangsta rap in the United States. As Erik King Watts (1997) argues, "[H]ard-core rap artistry participates in a complex and fluid set of economic exchange relations among the lived experiences of artists, the operations of a consumer culture, and the dictates of rap music industry" (p. 42). Furthermore, Watts points out that gangsta rap speaks directly to real conditions shared by many African American communities. As George Lipsitz (1990) shows, Americans often draw upon popular culture texts such as those found in gangsta rap as repositories of cultural knowledge and identity-building; not because such texts reflect our lives directly, but rather because they reflect the core contradictions of our lives (denied in dominant narratives) indirectly enough to make discussion of them bearable. One possible explanation for Guadeloupean youths' affinity for BET and rap music is that, like many Americans, they draw upon popular texts to help make sense of the core contradictions of their "real world" experiences. However, it remains questionable whether the average Guadeloupean, when watching BET, possesses the prior cultural and contextual understandings and the linguistic tools necessary to move beyond the superficial—yet overt, powerful, and seductive—codes of the kind of gangsta rap that hooks, West, and others criticize.

BET's Introduction to Guadeloupe and the Concept "Ether"

How, exactly, does BET become available on an island like Guadeloupe? According to BET International—the division responsible for marketing and distributing the network to overseas markets—it varies. Sometimes a local cable provider will approach BET in an effort to become the first to air the network in the region. In such cases, it seems, the channel eventually appears on subscribers' cable boxes, entering domestic spaces with little prior note or fanfare. In other instances, BET will aggressively investigate and create possibilities for expansion in foreign countries. If internal market research recommends spreading to a place like Guadeloupe, BET will hire a local public relations firm in that region to conduct "ethnographic research" (focus group research, omnibus surveys, etc.) and execute a detailed advertising campaign.

To manufacture desire for the (theretofore-unknown) television network within the local, non-English speaking community, the public relations firm will publicize BET in a range of forums. This effort can include "street marketing" (mass street events, in-venue events and promotions, leafleting, and "brand ambassador programs"); web-based advertising; mainstream media advertising (television, radio, print, and billboards); and press releases. Conducted in the official language of the local community, this all-out advertising blitz serves the function of a town crier for BET's imminent presence.

In light of BET's recent expansion into Asian, Caribbean, European, and Sub-Saharan African nations, it seems that this approach is highly effective; it does not take long for word of the network to spread, especially in small, isolated places like Guadeloupe. BET is usually successful at quickly getting a cable provider to carry the network. As a representative of BET International claims, the network has not run into any major difficulties overcoming language and cultural barriers in its international marketing efforts.[5] Unfortunately, I argue, this kind of calculated corporate assault (facilitated by market and cultural analysis) quickly collapses space for communal discussion of, and perhaps resistance to, BET's placement of its product (and, thusly, messages and values) within the dynamics of local cultural milieus.

BET's tactics speak to Michael Hardt and Antonio Negri's (2000) concept "ether," one of the three major imperial forces—the other two being "the bomb" (military force) and "money" (global markets that benefit the needs of financial and commercial powers)—shaping contemporary geopolitics. "Ether" is composed of those invisible systems of communication that are not subordinated to the sovereignty of territory, nations, or culture. Hardt and Negri write, "The deterritorialization capacities of communication are unique: communication is not satisfied by limiting or weakening modern territorial sovereignty; rather it attacks the very possibility of linking an order to a space. It imposes a continuous and complete circulation of signs. Deterritorialization is the primary force and circulation the form through which social communication manifests itself" (pp. 346–347).

Hardt and Negri argue that communication is no longer confined to national borders (think: the Internet, Hollywood films, digital music, satellite radio and television, cellular phones, etc.). Because of its diffuse nature, ether can be conceived as an invisible, but ever-present fog that influences cultures in unexpected ways. While immense amounts of planning, negotiation, investment, and physical action occur behind the scenes to maintain this deterritorialized system of communication (as we saw in the previous paragraph), average people (or, as companies tend to think of us, *consumers*) remain largely unaware of how the system works. Thus we tend to access instantly, enjoy, and use things like the Internet, our cell phones, or Black Entertainment Television—sometimes for free, sometimes at a cost—without the tools or space necessary to contemplate how and why such things became available, or what effects they might have on our lives. Perhaps, then, we can also consider "ether" to be, at its worst, an invading force—not in the sense of armed forces that show up at a nation's border or shores—but rather as a subtle and surreptitious reach for people's imagination, sense of self, and feelings of belonging.

BET's Reception: Procedure and Findings

Consonant with the way ether deploys itself around the globe, a cable provider introduced BET to Guadeloupe in 1997. As of 2004, it was one of three English-speaking channels available to the island (the other two were BET Jazz and CNN International). While ninety percent of Guadeloupe's population is of African descent—seemingly the basis for BET's presence—very few people speak English. Although students begin taking English classes in grade school, few people are fluent. Yet even in the absence of linguistic comprehension, many of the island's youths visually interpret and reenact BET's messages.

To better comprehend the reception of BET in Guadeloupe, I designed an open-ended questionnaire, written in French, which gave Guadeloupeans the ability to openly express their opinions and thoughts on the network's presence and programming. Specifically, the questions I posed were:

1) How many hours per day do you watch BET?

2) When did you start watching BET?

3) How many hours per day do you watch French television?

4) Do your parents watch BET?

5) Do you watch CNN International regularly?

6) Have you ever heard of the company Viacom?

7) Have you ever been to the U.S.? Where?

8) If you have not been to the U.S., do you hope to go in the future? Where?

9) Have you ever visited www.BET.com?

10) Are you learning English? Why?

11) Is BET impacting the culture of Guadeloupe? If "yes," is the impact negative or positive?

12) In your opinion, how has Guadeloupe's culture changed during the last five to ten years?

I sent roughly one hundred copies of the questionnaire to various contacts throughout Guadeloupe. These contacts—middle school and high school level English teachers—distributed the questionnaires to students, friends, and relatives of all ages.[6] I received 81 completed questionnaires. Most participants responded in French, though some wrote in English. Notably, 54 of the total 81 respondents indicated that BET is having some kind of impact on the local youth culture. While judgments of this impact varied, respondents of all ages held valuable opinions regarding the matter.

Respondents who criticize BET's presence often drew upon two general, and often intertwined, themes. The *first theme* is: that by embracing and imitating BET's images, Guadeloupean youths are turning away from cultural traditions and values. The *second theme* focuses on the notion that modernization, which BET represents, is not good for the island. A 12-year-old girl states that boys who watch BET's videos are "changing their behavior" for the worse. A 12-year-old boy describes his distaste for the popular trend of "sagging one's pants like the Americans." Likewise, a 13-year-old girl says that watching BET is "making the boys lazy." One 15-year-old boy speaks of a definite change in "attitude and dress" among his peers, while another says that BET is causing young people to "neglect their culture and their traditions." A 15-year-old girl, who has visited the U.S., writes: "Guadeloupe's culture is changing in the worst ways under the constant influence of BET and American culture." Another 15-year-old girl expands upon this notion: "Due to globalization, Guadeloupe's culture has lost its identity. The positive attitudes and attributes of the island's youths are being lost to bad behaviors learned from television." A 17-year-old girl, who has been to the U.S., sees BET as a negative influence because the network tries to shape Guadeloupeans' perspectives on African Americans: "I think that BET has a definite influence on young Guadeloupeans—the way they dress, their opinions of the United States, etc … BET creates our opinions of African Americans."[7]

The comments of adults who consider BET's impact to be negative echo some of the youths' observations. A 25-year-old woman, who has visited the U.S., writes: "BET influences the youths enormously, but not in a good way; the youths are unable to understand that what they are watching is not reality. The behavior of certain rappers is not the example that youths should be following (violence, drugs, etc.)." A 20-year-old woman says, "The youths are identifying with rappers and adopting their styles too much." And a 29-year-old woman, who has traveled through the U.S., claims that BET is just another example of the Americanization of the island. "There is a general desire to override our Caribbean culture by making foreign, important cultures more important," she says.

TABLE 1

	People Who Believe BET Is having an Impact on Guadeloupe's Culture	People Who Believe BET's Impact on Guadeloupe's Culture Is Negative	People Who Believe BET's Impact on Guadeloupe's Culture Is Positive
Age: 11–12 16 participants	6	3	3
Age: 13–14 19 participants	14	4	10
Age: 15–16 21 participants	16	11	5
Age: 17–19 13 participants	12	4	8
Age: 20's 4 participants	4	3	1
Age: 30+ 8 participants	2	1	1

While a considerable proportion of the respondents find BET's presence in Guadeloupe to be negative, a greater number believe the opposite to be true (Table 1). Of the 28 respondents who find BET's presence to be positive, only three have ever visited the United States (thus, only a few of these respondents have had the opportunity to see some aspects of African American culture firsthand). Some of these respondents state that BET provides exciting and entertaining imagery and music. Others claim that BET allows Guadeloupeans to learn about African Americans and global Black issues. Still others say that modernization, which BET represents to them, is good for Guadeloupe. A 12-year-old enthusiast of BET says that she enjoys "the clothing, the accessories, and the dance moves" that she sees in the rap videos. Another 12-year-old girl says that she is "not obligated to listen to French music," and that she thinks "songs in English are very beautiful." For one 13-year-old boy, embracing American music is simply a good thing: "BET's impact is positive because it has allowed me to become interested in American music." A 16-year-old girl states that BET helps her improve her English. One 17-year-old girl identifies with BET's images of African Americans more than she does with images of Blacks on French television: "European television does not provide the same music that BET offers ... Guadeloupeans and African Americans are one in the same because we listen to the same music." This response indicates that, at least for some Guadeloupeans, BET has successfully introduced the notion that one can somehow be African African merely by watching the network's programming.

Finally, a 39-year-old female claims that exposure to foreign cultures, in any capacity, is good for Guadeloupeans: "I do not think that BET negatively influences the youths of Guadeloupe ... I think that the youths have become an 'audio-visual group,' and BET has become a good way for them to learn about other black populations."

This woman, who has been to Miami, New York City, Vermont, and Washington, D.C., continues: "BET allows the youths to explore their love of hip-hop music and dance ... Over the last five to ten years, Guadeloupe has opened its eyes to other cultures around the world." The fact that many Guadeloupeans found BET's impact to be positive was unsurprising and in large part explains BET's growing popularity. As several testimonies suggested, supporters of BET regarded the network as a window to foreign cultures and customs. However, these advocates for BET may have failed to realize that the network, owned and operated by media conglomerate Viacom, was marketing an impoverished, skewed, and formulaic representation of African American life. It was telling that participants of this study who have visited the United States tended to challenge BET's portrayals of African Americans.

Three emergent issues appear to arise from all of the responses discussed here. First, many Guadeloupeans associate BET with modernization. Second, for some

Guadeloupeans, BET is providing an alternative to French television, which does not tend to present nor represent black people. And third, some Guadeloupeans find BET's stereotypical portrayals of African Americans to be less than authentic, while others see the portrayals as authentic and representative of shared bonds between Blacks of all nations and cultures. In light of these issues, it is appropriate to consider a letter I received (written in English) from Claire Hanson, a veteran teacher at a middle school in the island's largest city, Pointe-à-Pitre, and a person of African descent. Her letter was written in response to my survey.

A respected local elder and social observer who has traveled throughout much of the United States, Hanson is critical of BET, which she identifies as "the trendsetter for most teenagers." Hanson claims that many of the island's youths "are interested in the video clips, music, and choreography, because they have difficulties understanding the lyrics— thank God for small miracles." She states that many youths, who "rely on BET to establish their dress code," "end up making heavy competition for scarecrows in the fields." The scarecrow comparison is somewhat apt, for, as we know, the typical scarecrow is dressed up, strikes a pose, simultaneously mimics and caricatures the human form, but ultimately lacks substance, and, to take from the *Wizard of Oz*, lacks the ability to think.

Hanson fears that "the girls are the ones that are the most seriously affected" by BET's programming, as many youths are "persuaded that American girls dress and behave like that." Ultimately, Hanson sees BET as a part of globalization and modernization, which Guadeloupeans in general are openly embracing (as represented by the appropriation of the American holiday Halloween—the meaning of which is misunderstood—and the increased consumption of cell phones and the Internet). "Guadeloupeans are becoming a purely colonized society—meaning no strongly-rooted identity—ready or even eager to adopt anything from anywhere as long as it is commercially interesting … My only hope is that they manage to remember where their roots are." It is important to note Hanson's perspective of BET. Seemingly, as a middle school English teacher, Hanson would welcome the English language channel as a potential learning aid for her students, much as a French language channel might be for students in the United States. But in her letter, Hanson echoes the tones of other concerned respondents—and social critics like Cornel West—who find little social, moral, aesthetic, and educational value in BET's depictions of African Americans.

Conclusion

What are these "roots" Hanson speaks of? Based on one reading of her letter, we might say that Hanson, a representative of an older generation of Guadeloupeans, defines her culture as the viable result of a long, brutal, turbulent colonial period. While we might question the price paid for this outcome, the fact remains that some people, like Hanson, hold on to those "roots" as a site of empowerment, action, memory, and resistance. Indeed it is the negotiated process of moving from slave to French citizen—the long process of overcoming horrid oppression—that, for Hanson, serves as the Guadeloupean cultural identity. Although black Guadeloupeans may remain simultaneously accepted and rejected by their governing nation, Hanson aligns herself with the results of the French colonial past that the descendents of slaves have been able to fashion into a functioning culture for themselves. These "roots," which to a large extent override any virtual, mediated, "authentic" racial identity that BET, or any other agent of the ether, claims to offer as a new source of pride.

Peter L. Berger in *The Sacred Canopy* (1967) writes: "Culture must be continuously produced and reproduced by man. Its structures are, therefore, inherently precarious and predestined to change. The cultural imperative of stability and the inherent character of culture as *un*stable together posit the fundamental problem of man's world-building activity" (p. 6). But despite this inherent tension between change and continuity, a given culture does in fact objectively exist in the lives and minds of its members, for "the institutions of the individual's society, however much he may dislike them, will be *real*. In other words, the cultural world is not only collectively produced, but it remains real by virtue of collective recognition. To be in culture means to share in a particular world of objectivities with others" (Berger, p. 10). Guadeloupeans, like Claire Hanson, wish to keep their culture identifiable and rooted in some measure of stability so that it can serve as both a guide for behavior within their community and a source of historical knowledge about their particular shared condition. But as part of the ether, BET invades and cuts through Guadeloupe's cultural, linguistic, and national barriers, dismissing real political, social, and economic questions as to what it means to be a contemporary black French citizen. For people like Ms. Hanson, BET represents new invading forces: globalization, modernization, "the ether," invading forces against which the means of resistance are increasingly difficult to find.

Given the nature of modern systems of communication, how might people like Hanson attempt to resist unwanted media products? Such a question might seem moot to those who believe that "the ether" is inevitable, or that the "invisible hand of the free market" determines all. But for those of us concerned with the insidious and overwhelming ability that faceless, transnational corporations possess to alter cultures and shape global perceptions of race, it should be a vital question. Many scholars—perhaps most notably Dick Hebdige, author of *Subculture: The Meaning of Style* (1979)—have shown that a relatively small group can be capable of appropriating and transforming the forms and styles of larger, more influential cultural agents to create a culture that is new, personal, life-sustaining, or subversive. But I am less interested in how, for example,

Guadeloupean youths might appropriate and transform the things they see and hear on BET as a way to confront the problems of their everyday lives, than I am interested in how concerned members of a community can resist the nearly instant cultural change that the ether so often seems to bring.

In closing, I would like to suggest that human rights, perhaps, could be an integral part of a discussion about cultural change in the age of ether. If we accept general definitions of culture laid out by scholars such as Berger and Clifford Geertz, we recognize that human beings are, by definition, *cultural beings*. That is, to be human is to depend on a culture that enables you to have historical knowledge about the community in which you live and provides you with the tools to navigate everyday life successfully.[8] If we accept that culture is *essential* to being *human*, then perhaps we should accept that culture is a human right that—like freedom, equality, and religious and national affiliations—should be defended. We might say that when Claire Hanson feels that nefarious, unidentifiable outside forces are threatening her sense of cultural identity for nothing more than profit, she feels and understands that *the very possibility of her being is under attack.*

What, then, might be the intersection between human rights and cultural change in the twenty-first century, when physical resistance has been all but nullified by the invisible, ever-present, unsolicited, and seductive power of ether? The phenomenon of Guadeloupe and BET, which pits a tiny postcolonial island with few broadcasting capabilities of its own against the strength of capital as expressed in a multinational broadcasting company, speaks of a power differential that communication scholars might well address within the framework of human rights in relation to cultural change. Such an approach might be applicable to the study of other communities, large and small, inside and outside the borders of powerful nations, which struggle to cope with the transformative power of ether.

DISCUSSION QUESTIONS

1. What is "ether?" Do you think this concept explains how BET has influenced ideas and behaviors on Guadeloupe? Does "ether" influence the culture and ethnic groups in your community or country?

2. Are Guadeloupean opinions about BET based solely upon the respondent's age? What other personal characteristics and experiences might explain respondents' opinions?

3. What would an accurate portrayal of African American culture entail? If you were able to introduce a different media product besides BET to Guadeloupe, what would it be? What impact do you think it would have upon the viewers?

4. Given the nature of "ether" and its deterritorializing effect, how can a community resist unwanted symbols or images that threaten to change its culture? Should the production, reproduction, and protection of local cultural identity fall under the umbrella of human rights?

---

[1] "Carib" and "Arawak" (or "non-Carib") are general terms that European invaders applied to Amerindians they encountered in the Caribbean. For more on the Caribs and Arawaks, as well as an excellent history of the destruction of indigenous civilizations throughout the Caribbean between the fifteenth and eighteenth centuries, see Hulme (1992).

[2] As a department of France, Guadeloupe's relationship with France is similar to Hawaii's relationship with the United States; each island is an integral, hemmed-in part of its governing nation, yet each is geographically situated outside of the governing nation's physical borders. Guadeloupeans have the rights to vote in French elections. The island's primary and secondary level students receive the same education as their counterparts in mainland France. Guadeloupeans can attain quality higher education only by moving to mainland France, a fact that further entrenches upwardly mobile Guadeloupeans in French culture.

[3] In February 2005 France's ruling party, the right-wing Union for a Popular Movement, passed a law that urged French historians, professors, and textbook authors to emphasize the "positive role" France played in the development and civilization of its colonial territories. Decried by intellectuals, immigrant organizations, and the governments of former colonies like Guadeloupe, this controversial law preceded the printing of the 2005 edition of *Le Petit Robert*, France's most popular dictionary, which defined colonialism as simply "valuing, enhancing, and exploiting the natural resources" of foreign territories (Godoy, 2005). In November 2005, Arab, Muslim, and African youths from "les banlieues," the lower-class suburbs of Paris, rose up to protest their government, which continues to marginalize its non-white citizens. Though the civil unrest began when two boys of African descent died accidentally while hiding from police, this event reflected the pent up anger of immigrant families who faced unbridled social and economic discrimination (Honicker, 2006; Smith, 2005).

[4] In 2000, African American Robert Johnson, the founder and majority owner of BET, sold the network and other holdings to Viacom's Sumner Redstone, a white man, for $3 billion. This event angered many within the African American community, who did not like the idea of BET's programming falling under the control of a white-owned company (Pulley 2004, pp. 186–205).

[5] This information comes from my personal communication with Marquida Webster of BET International (September 29, 2009); my personal communication with Glen Yearwood, Founder of the Glen Yearwood Group public relations firm (September 30, 2009); and, http://www.glenyearwoodgroup.com/.

[6] This questionnaire and its distribution were approved for my master's thesis at Johns Hopkins University. Handed out to participants in informal settings, the questionnaire included open-ended questions designed to elicit varied responses from Black Guadeloupeans of all ages. Respondents were not required to participate, and there was no penalty for not taking part. Furthermore, my contacts and participants were not offered, nor were given, any compensation for assisting my study.

[7] This statement is particularly startling when we consider the negative experiences many African Americans have when they travel outside the United States. On February 16, 2006, I attended the African American Cultural Center of Greater Pittsburgh's "An Evening with Spike Lee," a question-and-answer session with the acclaimed film director. At one point during the event, Lee described how a black female friend of his was constantly inappropriately and aggressively propositioned by strangers during a trip through Europe. Lee's friend claimed that her antagonistic suitors were surprised to discover that she was not like the promiscuous black women depicted in American rap videos.

[8] The most widely accepted definition of culture (from the *Random House Dictionary*) tells us that culture is "the sum total of ways of living built up by a group of human beings and transmitted from one generation to another." Along similar lines, Clifford Geertz (1973, p. 89) argues that culture is an "historically transmitted pattern of meanings embodied in symbols, a system of inherited conceptions expressed in symbolic forms by means of which men communicate, perpetuate and develop their knowledge about and attitudes towards life." It follows that cultural identity refers to an individual's or community's identification with a historically transmitted pattern of meanings—an individual's or community's relationship to that which supplies the tools for the navigation of everyday life.

Reference

Abenon, L. R. (1992). *Petite histoire de la Guadeloupe*. Paris: Editions L'Harmattan.

Abraham, M., & Maragnes, D. (2001). *Guadeloupe: Temps incertains*. Paris: Editions Atrement.

Berger, P. L. (1967). *The Sacred Canopy*. New York: Anchor.

Brana-Shute, R. (1996). Martinique and Guadeloupe. In B. A. Tenenbaum (Ed.), *Encyclopedia of Latin American History and Culture* (pp. 538–539). New York: Scribner's.

Central Intelligence Agency. (2003, August 1). *The World Factbook, Guadeloupe*. Retrieved 3 February, 2009, from http://www.umsl.edu/services/govdocs/wofact2003/geos/gp.html

Durant, A. (2005). Orality and literacy. In M. Groden, M. Kreiswirth & I. Szeman (Eds.), *The Johns Hopkins Guide to Lliterary Theory and Criticism* (pp. 714–716). Baltimore: The Johns Hopkins U P.

Geertz, C. (1973). *The Interpretation of Cultures*. New York: Basic.

Godoy, J. (2005, September 11). France: How Beautiful Was my Colony. *Inter Press Service*. Retrieved February 10, 2008, from http://ipsnews.net/africa/nota.asp?idnews=34672

Hardt, A., & Negri, M. (2000). *Empire*. Cambridge, MA: Harvard U P.

Hebdige, D. (1979). Subculture: The Meaning of Style. London: Routledge.

Honicker, N. (2006). On the outside looking in: Paris and its banlieues. *American Scholar, 75*(2), 31–40.

hooks, b. (2004). *We Real Cool: Black Men and Masculinity*. New York: Routledge.

Hulme, P. (1992). *Colonial Encounters: Europe and the Native Caribbean 1492–1797*. New York: Routledge.

Kitwana, B. (2002). *The Hip Hop Generation*. New York: Basic.

Klein, N. (1999). *No Logo*. New York: Picador.

Lipsitz, G. (1990). *TimePassages: Collective Memory and American Popular Culture*. Minneapolis: U of Minnesota P.

Mignolo, W. (1989). Colonial situations, geographical discourses, and territorial representations: Toward a diatopical understanding of colonial semiosis. *Dispositio: American Journal of Semiotic and Cultural Studies 14*(36–38), 93–140.

Montiel, L. M. M., (2004). African orality in the literary culture of the Caribbean. In M. J. Valdés & D. Kadir (Eds.), *Literary Cultures of Latin America: A Comparative History* (pp. 460–470). Oxford: Oxford U P.

Pulley, B. (2004). *The Billion Dollar BET: Robert Johnson and theIinside Story of Black Entertainment Television*. Hoboken, NJ: Wiley.

Rose, T. (2008). *The Hip Hop Wars: What We Talk About When We Talk About Hip Hop—and Why it Matters*. New York: Basic.

Smith, C. S. (2005, November 7). 10 officers shot as riots worsen in French cities. *The New York Times*. Retrieved February 3, 2009, from http://www.nytimes.com/2005/11/07/international/europe/07france.html

Smith-Shomade, B. E. (2008). *Pimpin' Ain't Easy: Selling Black Entertainment Television*. New York: Routledge.

Watts, E. K. (1997). An exploration of spectacular consumption: Gangsta rap as cultural commodity. *Communication Studies, 48*(1), 42–58.

West, C. (1993). *Race Matters*. New York: Vintage.

Acknowledgement

"The author wishes to thank the following professors, each of whom offered advice, support, or feedback during this project: Dr. Sara Castro-Klarén, Dr. Milad Doueihi, Dr. Brent Malin, Dr. Gordon R. Mitchell, Dr. Ronald J. Zboray, and Mary Saracino Zboray."

26

She has 50,000 Coaches: Re-envisioning Young Women of Color as Learners in Three Popular Films

Gordon Alley-Young

Abstract

Real Women Have Curves, *Akeelah and the Bee*, and *Half Nelson* challenge the stereotypes of young women of color seen in popular education films. Ana, Akeelah, and Drey contrast with their film counterparts who are often defiant, sexualized, downtrodden, and/or comical. Using Cartesian dualism and theories of the gaze and minority education, this chapter argues that these films re-envision the identity of young women of color within the popular education film genre. These films represent young women of color in more complex ways by referencing their social and cultural identities, connecting their minds and bodies, extending learning outside of school in meaningful ways, and subverting audience assumptions about race and educational authority.

KEY TERMS: code switching, linguistic convergence, dualism, null curriculum, educación, objectification, gaze, popular education film

Introduction

Ana in *Real Women Have Curves* (2002) dreams about going to college but, with family obligations, she tells her teacher Mr. Guzman to focus on mentoring others. In *Akeelah and the Bee* (2006) Akeelah watches a spelling bee on television. The camera alternately brings Akeelah and her television counterpart's faces into focus as she is uncertain of her possibilities for success. In *Half Nelson* (2006) Drey is torn between Frank, who wants a drug messenger and Dan Dunne, her teacher who tries to mentor her while he battles his own addiction. This chapter argues that these three films dramatize the educational struggles of three minority young women while avoiding, subverting, or complicating previously seen representations. In order to understand how these films are a departure, we must first consider what has come before.

Socio-Cultural Criticisms of Popular Education Films

Film critics level three main charges against popular education films. First, minority students are token characters presented as racist, classist, and sexist stereotypes (Boyd, 2004; Giroux, 1997; Grant, 2002; Trier, 2005). Second, teachers, who are often white males, are presented as minority students' saviors (Christensen, 1995; Farhi, 1999; Heilman, 1992; Wells & Serman, 1998). Finally, the school curriculum is reduced to the creative, pleasurable, and extracurricular (Ayers, 1994; Dalton, 1999). Female students in popular education films are shaped by racist and classist stereotypes, while their physicality/sexuality is often central to their characterizations.

Two key gender critiques emerge from education film criticism. First, young women's sexuality is overemphasized (Alley-Young, 2006; Weber & Mitchell, 1995). In films like *Dead Poets' Society* (1989) and *The Emperor's Club* (2002), young women are a means for young men from boys-only schools to express their sexuality, while in films like *Blackboard Jungle* (1955), *Dangerous Minds* (1995), and *187* (1997) women are sexually harassed. Second, there is a lack of awareness of how race and class position young women of color differently (Alley-Young, 2006; Hamdan, 2005; hooks, 2000). Critics point to films like *Clueless* (1995), *Legally Blonde* (2001), and *Mean Girls* (2004) where beautiful affluent young women move fluidly between socially privileged groups; this is in contrast to films like *Stand and Deliver* (1988), *Lean on Me* (1989), *Dangerous Minds* (1995) and *Save the Last Dance* (2001) where minority women struggle to stay in school in spite of poverty, absent or sexist families, and/or teen motherhood.

Some films have tried to equalize the playing field for young women, but in problematic ways. Hamdan (2005) argues that the film *Mona Lisa Smile* (2003), designed to focus on feminism and empowerment, overlooks the issues of color and class. Also, Alley-Young (2006) argues that while Elle, the protagonist of *Legally Blonde* (2001), does not discriminate on the basis of class or sexual orientation, she does not give these factors or her own privilege much consideration. Similarly hooks (2000) argues that Dionne, a black character in the film *Clueless* (1995), is indistinguishable from her affluent white peers and that this creates a false sense of cultural unity. She argues that Dionne allows audiences to forget that racial divisions still exist.

The point of creating new, positive representations is not to ignore social and cultural issues. The challenge is that representations should realistically balance the issues with young, diverse protagonists who are strong and savvy enough to manage the challenges of living in a sexist and racist society while their families may face financial or parenting issues. It is ironic that Weber & Mitchell (1995) argue that the school experience is more marketable to females because many more popular education films focus on male protagonists. They argue that producers know that young women will consume educational stories with a male protagonist, while males are less accommodating. The three films discussed in this chapter offer more thoughtful and complimentary representations of young women of color in education. These films are *Real Women Have Curves* (2002), *Akeelah and the Bee* (2006), and *Half Nelson* (2006).

Diversifying Representations of Young Women of Color

Real Women Have Curves (2002) centers on the story of Ana, a full-figured Latina from east L.A., and is based upon Josefina Lopez's play of the same name. The film opens with Ana daydreaming on the last day of high school in Beverly Hills. Despite her dreams Ana initially resists her teacher's offer of help with gaining admission to Columbia University. When Ana's sister, who runs a dress factory, loses workers, Ana is recruited to fill their place. Ana's summer teaches her about love, life, and acceptance. In the fall Ana ventures off to Columbia without her mother's blessing but more prepared, thanks to her mother's lessons and her summer experiences.

Akeelah, an eleven year old African American student from south central L.A., dreams of happier times before her father's death, in *Akeelah and the Bee* (2006). Akeelah's mother fights to keep her son out of a gang, and works hard to support him, Akeelah, and her other daughter. Akeelah honors her deceased father's memory by spelling difficult words, their favorite game. At school a reluctant Akeelah is placed into a school spelling bee, which she wins. To get to the national spelling bee and win, she must earn her mother's permission, study with the difficult Dr. Larabee, and overcome her own insecurities.

In *Half Nelson* (2006) thirteen-year-old Drey is an AfricanAmerican student living in Brooklyn with an overworked single mother and an imprisoned brother. She connects to her middle school teacher Dan Dunne whom she discovers smoking crack in the girl's bathroom after a basketball game. Mr. Dunne tries to keep young Drey engaged in school and away from Frank, a local drug dealer. Drey gravitates towards Frank as his drug messenger until she finds Mr. Dunne with crack addicts in a motel room. The experience leads Drey to leave Frank and help to bring her teacher back home.

These three films respond to earlier critiques. First, critics argue that education films create physically intimidating, unruly, and/or illogical minority characters (Boyd, 2004; Giroux, 1997; Grant, 2002; Trier, 2005). In contrast Ana, Akeelah, and Drey are in control of both their bodies and their minds. Second, critics argue that education films sexualize young women (Alley-Young, 2006; Weber & Mitchell, 1995). Conversely Ana,

Akeelah, and Drey are not represented in this way. Third, critics argue that no substantial learning takes place in education films (Ayers, 1994; Dalton, 1999). However, Ana, Akeelah, and Drey learn powerful lessons about civil rights, history, politics, language, and feminism, and they take their lessons outside of the classroom to learn meaningful life lessons. Finally, critics argue that education films establish teachers, often white and male, as the saviors of minorities (Christensen, 1995; Farhi, 1999; Heilman, 1992; Wells & Serman, 1998). Alternately Ana and Akeelah work with teacher-mentors from their own cultural communities. Drey's teacher is white but at the end of the film it is Drey who ends up rescuing her teacher. In short, these films constitute a critique of earlier popular representations of race and learning. This chapter will interpret the images and dialogue of these three films by considering what has come before, and by using three critical theories/perspectives: the gaze, dualism, and educación.

Critical Framework: The Gaze, Dualism, and Educación

The gaze, dualism, and educación are useful constructs both for highlighting the contrast between the three films studied here and previous films. The following section briefly outlines each of these perspectives and how they will structure a critical-interpretive film analysis. Scholes (1985) argues that interpretation is an active search for a less obvious or apparent level of meaning in a popular text. Scholes (1985) argues that the values of a group that is outside the dominant culture (e.g., women, Blacks, Latinos) are used to both read and critique this obscured level of meaning. Criticism in this chapter will contrast these three films with films that have come before, to explore how popular representations of minority women as students have changed, and to argue that this change is necessary and welcome.

Lacan (Sherridan, Trans., 1977) argued that the "gaze" exists beyond the surface of an image and represents the viewer's castration anxiety. Mulvey (1975) argues that Hollywood film is shot for men's pleasure as men's gaze controls the female image. That is, female images represent the male viewer's fear of castration, so these images must be controlled by being sexualized, objectified, infantilized, and/or pathologized in the male gaze. Fanon (1967) argues that Whites project their fear (e.g., as victimization fantasies) onto black bodies in society. Mulvey (1975) and Fanon (1967) argue that women and people of color, or their images, are simultaneously feared and desired, so the gaze tries to control their representation. In these three films the construct of the gaze is resisted by subjects who speak back, evade, and/or disrupt the gaze, which seeks to fragment and control non-white and female subjects on the screen.

Dualism, like the gaze, perceives the non-White other in a fragmented way as a physical object. Originally from Descartes (Sutcliffe, Trans., 1968) dualism was reinterpreted through colonialism. Mohanram (1999) argues that white Europeans saw themselves as the mind and thus above the colonized natives, who were perceived as mere physical bodies requiring the guidance of a white mind. Alley-Young (2008) argues that dualism characterizes films like *Dangerous Minds* (1995), where minority students are unpredictable physical bodies and white teachers are authoritarian minds. In the films studied in this chapter, the body focuses the mind of the young women protagonists (Ana, Akeelah, and Drey) and is a source of identity, strength, and restraint.

Educación views learning as socially and culturally situated. Valdéz (1996) argues that *educación* (a respectful way of being in the world) goes beyond *education* (book learning). Educación includes knowledge from all social spaces, home, and community. Having book knowledge but no ability to conduct healthy social relations would make one *maleducato* or ill-bred and thus not properly educated. Valenzuela (1999) argues that educación should be used by teachers to show immigrant students that they are in a caring learning relationship. Villenas & Moreno (2001) argue that cultural ways of being in the world are central to educación. Educación occurs across these three films. Caring educational relationships teach the young subjects to be respectful and strong women who can make their way in the world.

When we speak of gaze in a critical perspective we make connections to dualism. To fetishize, sexualize, or fear someone via the gaze requires fragmenting a person's image into their constitutive physical parts. Educación, as interpreted above, is in contrast to the gaze and dualism, which take away a subject's personhood, as educación calls for fostering personalized and caring relationships. Taken together these theories, gaze, dualism, and *educación*, will articulate how representation of young women of color as seen in popular education films has changed through the three films discussed in this chapter.

Turn the Lights On: Challenging the Gaze

The films examined in this chapter attempt to reclaim the gaze in some meaningful ways. In *Real Women Have Curves* (2002) Ana asserts control over her own body when coupling with her classmate Jimmy. The scene is not a spectacle for the viewer as love on screen is often depicted. As the couple prepares to spend the night together, Ana tells Jimmy to turn the lights on, that she wants him to see her. Ana looks thoughtfully at her image in the mirror. The viewer sees nothing; Ana controls what is seen. Holm & Daniels (2003, p. 97) agree arguing, "She was proud of her body rather than ashamed. The movie portrayed Ana as gaining her sexuality rather than losing her virginity." After lovemaking Jimmy starts saying how he will stay in touch from college but Ana rejects his clichéd script and leaves him calling after her. The next day Ana views herself the mirror. The camera angle obscures the viewer from seeing anything, which suggests that Ana, and not the viewer, is in charge of her physical image. Ana's mother Carmen tries to shame Ana for being fat and for losing her virginity. Ana resists this shame and in one scene she defiantly eats a piece of flan (a rich egg and cream custard covered in soft caramel) while her mother protests that Ana is fat and will not find a man. Holm & Daniels (2003) view this as a victory for women; the title of their article mimics a viewer talking back to the screen saying, "Eat the flan." This is a contrast to other previously mentioned films in the genre where women bodies are objectified.

Later at her sister's factory Ana disrobes to beat the heat and also to show her coworkers not to be ashamed. They compare cellulite, size, stretch marks, and sagginess. They explode the myth of the flawless film body and in so doing they become real women. The women deconstruct their flaws with humanity and humor. This scene is a contrast to how mainstream film often portrays female bodies on screen as objects for the benefit of male audience members' gaze. Ana's mother Carmen tells the story of Ana's birth through a large caesarian scar. The large scar reminds Carmen of a happy time and also makes her ashamed of her body. Carmen represents the negative impact of the gaze on real women's bodies and minds.

In *Akeelah and the Bee* (2006) the gaze is highlighted when Akeelah stands and watches the spelling bee on television. The focus shifts back and forth between Akeelah and her white television counterpart. The juxtaposed focus reminds viewers that achievement is frequently represented as white and middle class in film. As Akeelah and the girl's faces juxtapose in and out of focus we see Akeelah contemplating her possibilities to become the protagonist in her own story. As we see her coming into focus in the film, we see her coming into her sense of self.

In another scene Akeelah meets Dr. Larabee for the first time and she poses as a reluctant urban youth. Dr. Larabee is working in his back garden and he corrects Akeelah for being late. Akeelah pretends that she is not hurt by his correction and talking in an urban dialect she asks him why he is home during the day saying, "Ain't you gotta job?" Dr. Larabee mocks her dialect and suggests that she is using it as a pose to appear cool with her friends and noncommittal with him. Provoked by his critique Akeelah takes charge of how Dr. Larabee and the viewers see her by critiquing him in standard dialect as a "dictatorial, truculent, supercilious gardener." This scene demonstrates that Akeelah wants to be in charge of how she appears to others as intelligent and capable of adapting to different challenges. Akeelah does not want Dr. Larabee or the viewers to mistake her for a one-dimensional character that never changes as one might see in film representations of young black women produced from and for the perspective of the gaze.

In *Half Nelson* (2006) it is through Drey's perspective that we see key events unfold. Her long direct stares make it clear that she is the chief spectator in this film. In different scenes Drey watches her teacher intently, observing his behavior. Dan Dunne is the focus of the gaze, not Drey, as he represents audiences' fears of addiction and losing control. We often see him through Drey's eyes notably when she discovers him in a school washroom doing drugs.

All too often it is minority characters like Drey who are viewed as spectacle in popular education films. For instance, in the film *Save the Last Dance* (2000) Sara, a white student from the suburbs, relocates to an urban high school populated primarily by black students. The first day of school Sara is fixated on a black male student being frisked by officers and later she is both intrigued and intimidated by a young woman dancing suggestively. Friend Chenille disrupts Sara's view by saying, "It's just a little hip hop." Many popular education films depict whites as border crossers who view black bodies as physical spectacles to be watched cautiously from a distance. Another example is the first classroom scene in *Dangerous Minds* (1995) where teacher LouAnne Johnstone cannot get her unruly class to come to attention. LouAnne's eyes scan the class of singing, dancing, and conversing students who seem oblivious to her presence. Here the roles are reversed as Drey spends time watching her teacher who we see through Drey's eyes.

The bathroom scene is disturbing because of the inappropriate way in which Drey must see her teacher. Critics could charge that this film is not a departure from the degrading images of urban life seen in other popular education films. The film is certainly open to this reading but it also complicates the student-teacher film relationship. Mr. Dunne is not a naïve white border crosser and Drey is not a jaded black youth. They are able to forge a caring relationship because they reflect their environments in intricate ways while they also reach for greater accomplishments in their lives. Their contradictions complicate the gaze and keep viewers from falling back on patterned ways of viewing race and identity.

We get Drey's perspective as she enters the crack room in the motel and finds Dan. Her white teacher has become a spectacle of addiction, and his state of decline forces her to depart as her anxieties, through viewing Dan, overwhelm her. Back in Frank's SUV she is stoic and says nothing but her lack of response tells viewers she is affected. It leads Drey to break away from Frank, return to the motel, and retrieve Dan. In the end they are sitting on Dan's couch, Dan has cleaned up and they both look symbolically forward from the couch seemingly looking back at the viewers who would view them as doomed symbols of urban life. Drey resists attempts to portray her as someone who does not change or grow. When we see the inside of Dan's motel room through Drey's eyes the individuals getting high there show few if any signs of acknowledging her as she looks at them in their drug induced oblivion as if they were characters in a dream. Drey watches the motel dwellers in a way that suggests that, while she is physically participating in the world of drugs as a messenger, there is also a distance between her and them. We see Drey's agency, or her ability to make and follow through with her own choices, when she easily leaves Frank to help her teacher. It is a choice that her brother could not make but she does it effortlessly and it speaks to her ability to make her own choices and to change.

These films represent a different way of looking at young women of color and their surroundings. When sexuality is depicted it is conducted for and by Ana herself. For Akeelah and Drey, who are eleven and thirteen respectively, it is refreshing to see that their characters are not sexualized, even as their surroundings lure them to grow up early. These characters stand in contrast to outdated ways of viewing minority young women; in key scenes these films appear to speak directly to both the film viewer and to conventional ways of filming minority characters on screen. The films encourage a diversity of gazes that represent self-acceptance, ambition, and redemption, while they resist the stereotyped images of earlier education films.

An Embodied Mind: Subverting Dualism

In many U.S.-American education films, students of color are represented as physical threats to white educational authorities. The dualistic model of education wants students' minds but would rather that they check their bodies at the door. In the three films discussed in this chapter dualism is not portrayed. Instead we see each character's lived embodied experiences as Mexican American or African American and as young women connected to the significant lessons they are being taught in these three films.

In *Real Women Have Curves* (2002) Ana's factory experience extends her classroom lessons on oppression. When Ana first arrives at the factory she criticizes her mother and the other women for valuing a woman's virginity (her body) over her mind in the way they gossip about others. Ana also labels her sister Estella's factory as a sweatshop. Ana offers these tidbits of liberal education while at the same time she looks down at her coworkers for being manual laborers. When she first arrives, her disdain is evident as she meets the other women and tells then, "I'm just helping out my sister until I find a better job." Coworker Pancha mocks Ana's attitude by replying, "Me too, I'm just working here until I win the lottery." It is not until Ana endures physical exhaustion and indignities (Ana and her sister are dressed down by a buyer who refuses to extend a deadline) experienced by a factory worker that she mentally appreciates these women for the work that they do even while they yearn for better lives. Ana's experience teaches her a real lesson about real women that cannot be learned intellectually in class.

Ana's experience of living in her coworkers' skin tells her that these women need better treatment and more respect. In the scene previously discussed, where the factory women compare the flaws of their bodies, they are acknowledging the negative connection between their minds and their bodies. We see in this scene that the women come to the realization that their flaws are not physical but mental as they have bought into society's view that their bodies are insignificant and flawed and as such they must remain covered.

As previously discussed in *Akeelah and the Bee* (2006) Akeelah shows Dr. Larabee an urban pose the first time they meet. Dr. Larabee, who is also African American, challenges Akeelah's use of "ghetto talk" and tells her she does it to fit in. Stung by having her performance deconstructed, Akeelah immediately code-switches. Akeelah walks away a dejected little girl hiding her hurt behind a pose, which Dr. Larabee easily sees through. The scene underscores the message that we give the bodily performance that is expected of us, or in Akeelah's case she does it to hide her insecurity, even when it belies our internal reality.

The defiant urban youth pose that Akeelah attempts can be seen in films like *Dangerous Minds* (1995) when on the first day of class new teacher LouAnne Johnson asks a young black female student listening to music what happened to the last teacher. Incensed by having her music interrupted, the student stands on a desk chair, and then uses the teacher's question to lead the class in mocking her as "white bread." The class responds heartily that they fed the last teacher, Miss Sheppard, to a pack of dogs. The scene is meant to reinforce how the students actively oppose any attempts by the school to impose order or substantial learning, and to characterize the students as physically intimidating.

Intercultural communication scholars will know that when Dr. Larabee tells Akeelah that she speaks in an urban dialect to fit in with her friends that he is describing linguistic convergence (we will talk like those whom we want to affiliate with). Akeelah switches into Standard English when she is called out; this is called code-switching. She knows she has used the wrong codes by talking in urban dialect and quickly translates her speech into standard dialect. Akeelah assesses the situation and uses a dialect to mask her fears that she is not smart enough and will be rejected by this professor. However, to move fluidly between dialects Akeelah must know both fluently, which speaks to her linguistic and intellectual abilities. The lesson to audiences is to not confuse a bodily performance of identity with one's intellect.

Overcoming dualism is also achieved when Akeelah connects words to experiences. When Akeelah reads a speech by W.E.B. DuBois, she questions why she is reading speeches when she could be memorizing words. Dr. Larabee makes her read and understand the speeches to know the words in their context. Dr. Larabee is trying to teach her to experience the words rather than to memorize them. For Dr. Larabee, words are lived in the civil rights struggles that he and Akeelah have inherited. Dr. Larabee does not allow Akeelah to separate learning from experience for, as a potential role model to other black youth, she is situated in this same struggle.

In a more literal sense Akeelah overcomes mind-body dualism when she channels her body's rhythm into the learning process. To focus, Akeelah learns and thus remembers words according to their rhythm, which she beats using her fist on her thigh. Akeelah must keep a steady rhythm to beat and her mind works with her body. She later replaces her hand-tapping with skipping rope that she uses to keep time and focus. This is antithetical to how the mind is thought to work best in dualistic views of white education where the body must be stationary as physical involvement is subjugated to the activity of the mind. Alley-Young (2008) argues that, in popular films set in private schools, learners do not move, speak out of turn, or deviate from the uniform to make the point that formal education makes a place only for the mind. In the end this presence of both mind and body help Akeelah to focus when the physical symptoms of stage fright threaten to overwhelm her senses. In so doing she validates learning as both a physical and a mental activity.

Akeelah's friend, gangster Derrick T., is shown to have a mind and a conscience, which is in contrast to how gangsters are presented on film. For instance, Malakai from *Save the Last Dance* (2001) is driven by revenge, and settles his scores with a gun. Instead Derrick T. is impressed with Akeelah's achievement and shares with her that he once won an award for writing a poem. The viewer assumes that Derrick T. was not encouraged, and to ensure that Akeelah is encouraged Derrick T. bars her brother from his gang and makes him help her study for the bee. Derrick T. also joins the ranks of Akeelah's 50,000 coaches as she practices her vocabulary cards on the hood of his car. As a result we see Derrick T. not just as a foreboding physical presence, but also as a flawed but whole person with a mind and unfulfilled potential.

Drey from *Half Nelson* (2006) is similarly thoughtful, and her mind and body clearly work together. Mid-way through the film Dan Dunne tries to persuade Drey to go with him instead of Frank, but she cannot see how he is trying to help her. Drey learns experientially from her teacher's addiction. When she sees how her teacher has descended into a dark dream world of a drug motel, her lack of response and dreamy stare as she takes in the scene tells us that she has internalized the lesson. Drey sees the physical and emotional manifestation of her and Frank's work in Dan Dunne. When Drey breaks from Frank at the end of the film we are left to assume that she will not become a thug, a thug's girlfriend, or a prisoner like her brother.

We get a sense that Drey is reflective of her experiences when earlier in the film, while confronting a boy who has stolen her bike, she leaves him with a verbal rather than a physical lashing. When Frank asks why she held back Drey asserts that there was no need for violence. She confronts the difficult situations of her life with her words and her mind but not her fists. This instance shows that her body is clearly connected to and focused by her mind. She is not an unpredictable physical presence as some films represent black youth, but is shown as in control of her choices and of her body and she is shown being unsettled by some of these same choices.

Ana, Akeelah, and Drey reject a mind-body division. Instead they live whole authentic lives in which the lessons they learn are reinforced by their lived experiences of difference and discrimination. Many of the scenes in this theme also evoke learning outside of the classroom, which is a significant theme to be discussed in the next section.

Educación as an Augment to Education

Ayers (1994) argues that real lessons are not taught on the screen and that when education focuses on the pleasurable or the extracurricular, it is a null curriculum. This is valid in many senses. Think of the examples of teachers who give students candy or take them to a theme park but are not depicted teaching subjects of much depth. Two of these films spend much of the time away from school, and the third happens over summer vacation. This does not make them less about education, but it shows that learning takes place through educación or being socially connected in a caring relationship with responsibility to others (Valdéz, 1996; Valenzuela, 1999).

In *Real Women Have Curves* (2002) we see educación when Ana's mother tells her husband she is going to teach Ana. Ana is book smart but she is unschooled in the way that her mother wants her to be (e.g., as someone who is responsible for her family). Though viewers will see Ana's mother Carmen as misguided for trying to force Ana into a restrictive role as a wife and a mother, Carmen also wants to make Ana responsible to and for someone other than herself. For when we first see Ana at work, she expresses feminist and liberal ideals intellectually but shows little empathy or concern for the actual daily struggles of her mother, sister, or the other women she works with. What Ana learns outside of class is not contradictory to the curriculum but reinforces it. Ana learns that, by taking out her frustration on a dress that she burns deliberately, she burdens everyone in the factory. This shows Ana that she is interconnected to these other women from whom she initially struggles to distinguish herself.

In another scene Carmen teaches Ana to walk, and the lesson is seemingly lost on Ana about how to carry herself with dignity. However, when Ana decides to go and attend Columbia University to the disapproval of her mother, then the lesson finally registers. As Ana exits the 49th street subway into Times Square she uses the walk her mother taught her. It is a signal to the viewer that even though Ana seemed resistant to her mother's lessons that she learned them in the end. Also by carrying herself with dignity she is upholding her responsibility to her mother, sister, coworkers, community, and culture whose sacrifices have allowed her this opportunity.

A notable contributor to Ana's success is Mr. Guzman, who finds a position for Ana at Columbia University, prods her to finish her entrance essay, and then travels to her house to help Ana convince her family of her need to go to school. This goes above and beyond the classroom responsibilities of Mr. Guzman, and perhaps this is the point. Having the film take place over the summer, when many teachers are on vacation or working other jobs, shows that the true value of a teacher like Mr. Guzman is not in the classroom lessons that he teaches, but in the mentorship through which he fosters a caring educational relationship with students like Ana.

This film holds a special place in the realm of popular education films. A formal school setting appears once at the beginning of the film on the last day of high school and when Mr. Guzman is shown calling Ana to get her essay completed. Otherwise, the film occurs outside of school but it is about how Ana comes to educación by realizing that she is interconnected to her family and coworkers and that their struggles are her struggle. Perhaps it is more apt to call *Real Women Have Curves* (2002) a popular educación film based on what it aims to teach.

In *Akeelah and the Bee* (2006) educación emerges through the relationships. When we first see Akeelah she is content hiding her achievement and only enrolls in the spelling bee when she is forced to do so. Even when she is clearly enjoying herself she is non-committal with Dr. Larabee. She poses and struts as unaffected and he corrects her English, her behavior, and makes her read about the Civil Rights Movement. While Dr. Larabee is teaching Akeelah about spelling, he is also teaching her to care about learning by caring about her teacher and her community. The educación is effective because when Dr. Larabee steps back to let Akeelah take charge of her learning she is distraught. We realize that Akeelah hungers not just for an increased vocabulary but for the warmth of a mentoring relationship that is like what she had with her deceased father. Instead of stifling Akeelah's love of learning, Dr. Larabee's step back gives her community, friends, and family the impetus to step into this nurturing role.

By learning the educational value of nurturing relationships Akeelah is given the chance to succeed but learning this lesson almost costs her winning the bee. During the final stage of the bee Akeelah tries to throw the competition to allow her sole competitor Dylan to win. Dylan is harangued by his father's demands for success and Akeelah empathizes with his dilemma as this is his last year to compete. Dylan then throws his chance to benefit from Akeelah's intentional mistake because he realizes what she is doing and he does not want to win this way. In the end the two tie as winners. Akeelah reflects educación by seeing how she and Dylan are interconnected by fate. She realizes that he has more to lose in terms of his father's love and respect than she does. Previous to this she reaches out to him across the lines of competition to offer him a soda and friendship even when he was not as charitable to her.

While Dr. Larabee teaches Akeelah to respect herself and to talk with the powerful language of leaders, Akeelah also teaches Dr. Larabee about educación and being open to others. Dr. Larabee's young daughter Denise died, leading to his divorce and his withdrawal from the world. When we first see him, he teaches online courses and tends to his garden. Akeelah brings Dr. Larabee back to the world by reestablishing the father-daughter bond, just as he is reestablishing the same for her. As a result of his relationship with Akeelah Dr. Larabee is able to accept a job teaching at a brick and mortar university and emerge from his seclusion.

For Drey in *Half Nelson* it is her care for teacher Dan Dunne that allows her to walk away from drug dealer Frank. Drey weighs the effects of what is happening to her teacher against what Frank expects of her. She chooses her teacher in the end because Dan Dunne has cared about what happens to her while Frank allowed her brother to be sent to prison. Dan cares for Drey and wants the best for her. Earlier in the film we see an interesting interaction between Dan and his father (also a teacher) where he makes fun of Dan's teaching in a predominantly black school by asking, "Teach me how to speak in Ebonics." Dan clearly cares about his minority students because he rejects his father's generation of white border-crossing teachers with high ideals and unexamined racism. Dan's father represents that white teacher, identified by film critics in other education films, who believes he is a savior to minority students. Dan is not Drey's savior because his requests that she avoid Frank do not represent his own cultural superiority but rather his fallibility, as he is addicted to the drugs that Frank sells and he wants better for Drey.

This theme highlights how learning cannot end at the classroom door. Educación teaches that significant learning about social life is a necessary component of education. Thus, caring relationships between teachers and students, and learning the social impact of ideology, are key elements throughout these films. Even in the case of a film like *Half Nelson* (2006), which clearly steps over the line of an appropriate relationship between teacher and student, the effect of that relationship impacts its main characters' lives more than a classroom lesson ever could.

Implications and Future Directions

Ana, Akeelah, and Drey help to redeem the popular education film after critics have charged the genre with sexism and racism. At the same time, it is interesting to note that two of the three films examined in this chapter are independent ventures (*Real Women Have Curves* (2002) and *Half Nelson* (2006)). These films and their stars have garnered critical attention, which speaks to the thirst of the public for multifaceted and hopeful images. In contrast. I remember that when previously researching the film *Mona Lisa Smile* (2003) for another project I read Internet writings by women, and spoke to female fans of the education film genre who were critical of the lack of diversity in the film but also eagerly anticipated an education film focusing solely on women. So, while independent film may have promise to revitalize the genre, this chapter is being written in a time of economic recession and as belts tighten we have yet to see the impact of this on independent filmmakers/producers. Will companies seek to distribute such projects or will they seek out more of the same in the push to guarantee sales figures?

Mainstream film does not provide as many opportunities for thoughtful minority women characters and the actresses who play them to impact audiences. The most telling evidence of this fact is the career of Lupe Oltiveros, the college educated and critically praised Mexican American actress who plays Ana's mother Carmen in *Real Women Have Curves* (2002). In a 2002 *New York Times* article, Oltiveros estimated that she had portrayed Hispanic maids in film and television 150 times (Navarro, 2002). Even as the film was being distributed, some wondered publically if actress America Ferrera (Ana) would fall into that same trap (Kauffman, 2002). Luckily Ferrera has broken free from being typecast like previous generations of actresses to find mainstream success as a character, Ugly Betty, who emphasizes her intellect over looks, persistence over privilege, and her culture and family over being cutthroat and famous.

Mainstream popular culture often fails to diversify its films. For instance when we look at *Harry Potter and the Sorcerer's Stone* (2001), released the year before *Real Women Have Curves* (2002), Wolfgram (2002) notes that seven out of nine in the major cast are white and male. She wonders what children will think when they do not see themselves represented in a film franchise so monumental to the popular culture: "[H]ow it may impact their sense of self when they ask, 'Where am I in this movie?'; 'How do I fit in?'; and ultimately, 'Do I matter?'" (p. 131). Ana, Akeelah, and Drey tell youth, and especially young women, from underrepresented groups that they do matter as more than tokens that are placed in a scene for diversity's sake or worse as stereotypes used by Hollywood to make a comment about urban life.

Also significant to the discussion of educación is that in two of these three films young women are mentored by teachers from their own cultural groups (Mr. Guzman and Dr. Larabee). Mr. Guzman uses his connections to pursue a spot for Ana at Columbia University. Even as Ana dissuades him, Mr. Guzman is undaunted and even comes to Ana's home to try to convince her family. *Akeelah and the Bee* (2006) highlights the mentoring relationship in dramatic fashion when Dr. Larabee is supplemented with a hyperbolic 50,000 coaches from Akeelah's own community who push her towards her goal. Representing these nurturing relationships within ethnic communities ultimately affirms the dignity, intelligence, and problem-solving abilities of traditionally underrepresented groups. When we do see a white teacher, he is not a savior but is saved by a young woman who ultimately chooses to break free of the negative cycle of drugs and incarceration set by her older brother. Drey is her own and her teacher's savior, which is an admirable theme in an otherwise gritty film.

As film and television begin to reflect racially diverse school experiences, it is important to examine how these new images either advance us forward or recycle earlier images. Future studies should examine recent contributions by television to the education film genre in the update of the *90210* series and in *Gossip Girl*. These series are followed eagerly by young viewers and the Internet and iPods extend the reach of these images. These programs sexualize their young characters and depict sex and social status as powerful tools of upward advancement. More importantly, when minority characters are written into these privileged portrayals of education, how are issues of race and difference handled or not handled?

Identity is created and performed to meet the expectations of others. We lose this insight when we focus on race and gender as unchanging archetypes in the production of education films. Let's represent these characters for who they really are, which is minority youth who are facing social, cultural, and educational challenges in the midst of a society obsessed with whiteness, patriarchy, affluence, and sexuality. When education films thoughtlessly include racial diversity in a tokenistic way in the name of inclusion, they fail to convey culturally situated achievement and problem-solving, and this will leave young women of color in the audience asking: *Where is my place in this film? Am I important?* and *Where are my coaches?*

DISCUSSION QUESTIONS

1. Why is it problematic when popular education films depict white teachers solving the problems of inner city schools and inner city students?

2. How would Ana, Akeelah, and Drey's stories be told differently if they were White and middle-class or if they were male?

3. How does the way that we as viewers watch these popular education films reflect our own social positions including our race, class, gender, and sexual orientation?

4. Gaze, dualism, and educación are the three concepts the author uses to analyze *Real Women have Curves, Akeelah and the Bee,* and *Half Nelson*. Have you observed these concepts in other films? If so, how are these concepts addressed?

References

Abraham, M. (Producer), & Hoffman, M. (Director). (2002). *The Emperor's Club* [Motion picture]. United States: Universal Pictures.

Alley-Young, G. (2006). "Celebrate diversity even if that included the hopelessly superficial": Lessons on gender, race, class, and sexuality in *Legally Blonde. North Dakota Journal of Speech & Theatre, 19*, 14–25.

Alley-Young, G. (2008). "Try to see this movie as an educational movie about life will you": A critical cultural study of race and education in popular film. In Z. Bekerman, N. C. Burbules, H. A. Giroux, & D. Silberman-Keller (Eds.) (2008). *Mirror Images: Popular Culture and Education* (pp. 23–38). New York: Peter Lang.

Atchison, D. (Director/Writer). (2006). *Akeelah and the Bee* [Motion picture]. United States: Lions Gate Films.

Ayers, W. C. (1994). A teacher ain't nothing but a hero: Teachers and teaching in film. In P. B. Joseph & G.E. Burnaford (Eds.), *Images of schoolteachers in twentieth-century America: Paragons, polarities, complexities* (pp. 147–156). New York: St. Martin's Press.

Boyd, J. (2004). Dance, culture, and popular film: Considering representations in *Save the Last Dance. Feminist Media Studies, 4*, 67–83.

Brooks, R (Director/Writer). (1955). *Blackboard Jungle* [Motion picture]. United States: Warner Home Video.

Cantet, L. (Director), & Bégaudeau, F. (Writer). (2008). *The class/Entre les murs.* France: Sony Pictures Classics.

Cardoso, P. (Director), & LaVoo, G. (Producer/Writer). (2002). *Real Women Have Curves* [Motion picture]. United States: HBO Films.

Christensen, L. (1995). *Dangerous Minds*: Decoding a classroom. *Rethinking Schools, 10* (1), 22–26.

Cort, R. W. & Madden, D. (Producers), & Carter, T. (Director). (2000). *Save the Last Dance* [Motion picture]. United States: Paramount Pictures.

Dalton, M. M. (1999). *The Hollywood Curriculum: Teachers and Teaching in the Movies.* New York: Peter Lang.

Davey, B. (Producer), & Reynolds, K. (Director). (1997). *187* [Motion picture]. United States: Icon Productions.

Descartes, R. (1968). *Discourse on Method and the Meditations.* (F.E. Sutcliffe, Trans.). London: Penguin Books.

Fanon, F. (1967). *Black Skin, White Masks.* (C. L. Markmann, Trans.). New York: Grove.

Farhi, A. (1999). Recognizing the superteacher myth in film. *Clearing House, 72*, 157–159.

Fleck, R. (Director/Writer), & Boden, A. (Writer). (2006). *Half Nelson* [Motion picture]. United States: THINKFilm.

Giroux, H. A. (1997). Race, pedagogy, and whiteness in *Dangerous Minds. Cineaste, 22,* 46–49.

Grant, P. (2002). Using popular films to challenge preservice teachers' beliefs about teaching in urban schools. *Urban Education, 37*(1), 77–95.

Haft, S. & Witt, P. J. (Producers), & Wier, P. (Director). (1989). *Dead Poets Society* [Motion picture]. United States: Touchstone Pictures.

Hamdan, A. (2005). "Mona Lisa Smile": More than a smile. *International Education Journal,* 6, 417–420.

Heckerling, A. (Director). (1995). *Clueless* [Motion picture]. United States: Paramount Pictures.

Heilman, R. B. (1991). The great-teacher myth. *American Scholar, 60,* 417–423.

Holm, K. & Daniels, K. (2003). Eat the flan: Real Women Have Curves. *Journal of Feminist Family Therapy, 15*(4), 95–98.

hooks, b. (2000). *Where we stand: Class matters.* New York: Routledge.

Kauffmann, S. (2002). Real women, problematic men. *New Republic*, 227(20), 22–23.

Lacan, J. (1977). *The Four Fundamental Concepts of Psycho-Analysis.* (A. Sherridan, Trans.). London: Hogarth.

Luketic, R. (Director). (2001). *Legally Blonde* [Motion picture]. United States: MGM.

Mohanram, R. (1999). *Black Body: Women, Colonialism, and Space.* Minneapolis: University of Minnesota Press.

Mulvey, L. (1975). Visual pleasure and narrative cinema. In E. A. Kaplan (Ed.). (2000). *Feminism & Film: Oxford Readings in Feminism* (pp. 34–47). New York: Oxford Press.

Musca, T. (Producer). Menéndez, R. (Director). (1988). *Stand and Deliver* [Motion Picture]. United States: Warner Brothers.

Navarro, M. (2002, May 16). Trying to get beyond the role of maid. *The New York Times,* p. E1.

Newell, M. (Director). (2003). *Mona Lisa Smile* [Motion picture]. United States: Columbia Pictures.

Scholes, R. (1985). *Textual Power: Literary Theory and the Teaching of English.* Binghampton, NY: Vail-Ballou Press.

Simpson, D. & Bruckheimer, J. (Producers), & Smith, J. N. (Director). (1995). *Dangerous Minds* [Motion picture]. United States: Hollywood Pictures.

Trier, J. (2005). 'Sordid fantasies': Reading popular 'inner-city' school films as racialized texts with pre-service teachers. *Race Ethnicity and Education, 8*(2), 171–189.

Twain, N. (Producer), & Avildsen, J. G. (Director). (1989). *Lean on Me* [Motion picture]. United States: Warner Brothers.

Valdéz, G. (1996). *Con Respeto: Bridging the Distances Between Community, Diverse Families and Schools.* New York: Teachers College Press.

Valenzuela, A. (1999). *Subtractive Schooling: US-Mexican Youth and the Politics of Caring.* Albany: SUNY Press.

Villenas, S., & Moreno, M. (2001). To valorize por si misma between race, capitalism, and patriarchy: Latina mother-daughter pedagogies in North Carolina. *International Journal of Qualitative Studies in Education (QSE), 14*(5), 671–687.

Waters, M. (Director), & Rosalind, W. & Fey, T. (Writers). (2004). *Mean Girls* [Motion picture]. United States: Paramount Home Entertainment.

Weber, S. & Mitchell, C. (1995). *That's Funny, You Don't Look Like a Teacher*. Washington, DC: The Falmer Press.

Wells, A. & Serman, T. (1998). Education against all odds: What films teach us about schools. In G. Maeroff (Ed.). *Imaging Education: The Media and Schools in America* (pp. 181–194). New York: Columbia University Press.

Wolfgram, S. M. (2002). Gender-informed parenting: A review of the film *Harry Potter and the Sorcerer's Stone*: Why not Hermione Granger? *Journal of Feminist Family Therapy, 14* (3/4), 130–132.